THE
STORM
OF WAR

The Holy Fox: A Life of Lord Halifax

Eminent Churchillians

The Aachen Memorandum

Salisbury: Victorian Titan

*Napoleon and Wellington: The Battle of Waterloo—
and the Great Commanders Who Fought It*

Hitler and Churchill: Secrets of Leadership

*What Might Have Been: Imaginary History from
Twelve Leading Historians* (EDITOR)

Waterloo: June 18, 1815: The Battle for Modern Europe

*The Correspondence Between Mr Disraeli
and Mrs Brydges Willyams* (EDITOR)

A History of the English-Speaking Peoples Since 1900

*Masters and Commanders: How Four Titans Won
the War in the West, 1941–1945*

THE
STORM
OF WAR

A NEW HISTORY OF THE
SECOND WORLD WAR

ANDREW
ROBERTS

HARPER

An Imprint of HarperCollins*Publishers*
www.harpercollins.com

HarperCollins books may be purchased for educational, business, or sales promotional use. For information, please write: Special Markets Department, HarperCollins Publishers, 10 East 53rd Street, New York, NY 10022.

First published in Great Britain in 2009 by Allen Lane, an imprint of Penguin Group UK.

FIRST U.S. EDITION

Library of Congress Cataloging-in-Publication Data has been applied for.

ISBN: 978-0-06-122859-9

11   12   13   14   15   OFF/RRD   10   9   8   7   6   5   4   3   2   1

To the memory of Frank Johnson
(1943–2006)

I have, myself, full confidence that if all do their duty, if nothing is neglected, and if the best arrangements are made, as they are being made, we shall prove ourselves once again able to defend our Island home, to ride out the storm of war, and to outlive the menace of tyranny, if necessary for years, if necessary alone.

Winston Churchill, House of Commons, 4 June 1940

Contents

PART I

Onslaught

PART II

Climacteric

PART III

Retribution

List of Illustrations

List of Maps

Poland, 1939

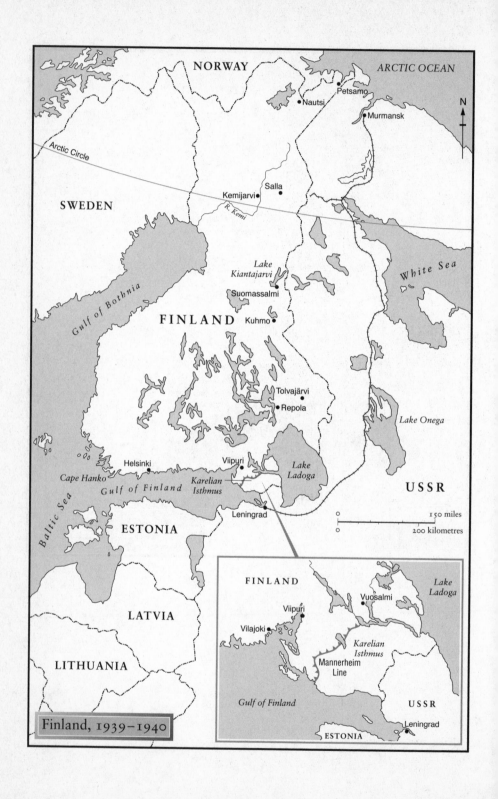

NORWAY

ARCTIC OCEAN

N

• Nautsi
Petsamo

• Murmansk

Arctic Circle

SWEDEN

Kemijarvi • Salla

R. Kemi

Lake Kiantajarvi

White Sea

Suomassalmi •

FINLAND   Kuhmo •

Gulf of Bothnia

Tolvajärvi •

• Repola

Lake Onega

Helsinki •

Viipuri •

Lake Ladoga

Cape Hanko

USSR

Gulf of Finland

Karelian Isthmus

Baltic Sea

Leningrad •

ESTONIA

0   150 miles

0   200 kilometres

LATVIA

LITHUANIA

Finland, 1939–1940

FINLAND

Lake Ladoga

Vuosalmi •

Viipuri •

Vilajoki •

Karelian Isthmus

Mannerheim Line

Gulf of Finland

USSR

Leningrad •

ESTONIA

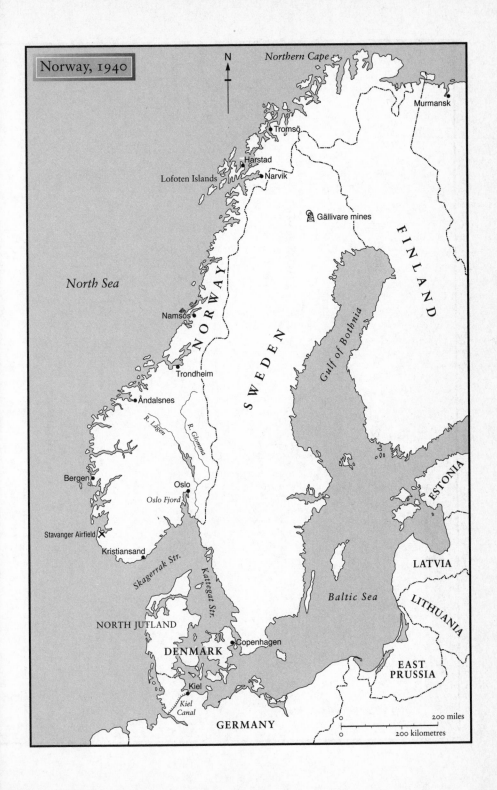

Norway, 1940

N

Northern Cape

Murmansk

Tromsö

Harstad

Lofoten Islands   Narvik

Gällivare mines

North Sea

NORWAY

Namsos

FINLAND

SWEDEN

Gulf of Bothnia

Trondheim

Åndalsnes

R. Lågen

R. Glomma

Bergen

Oslo

Oslo Fjord

ESTONIA

Stavanger Airfield

Kristiansand

Skagerrak Str.

Kattegat Str.

LATVIA

Baltic Sea

LITHUANIA

NORTH JUTLAND

DENMARK

Copenhagen

EAST
PRUSSIA

Kiel

Kiel
Canal

GERMANY

200 miles

200 kilometres

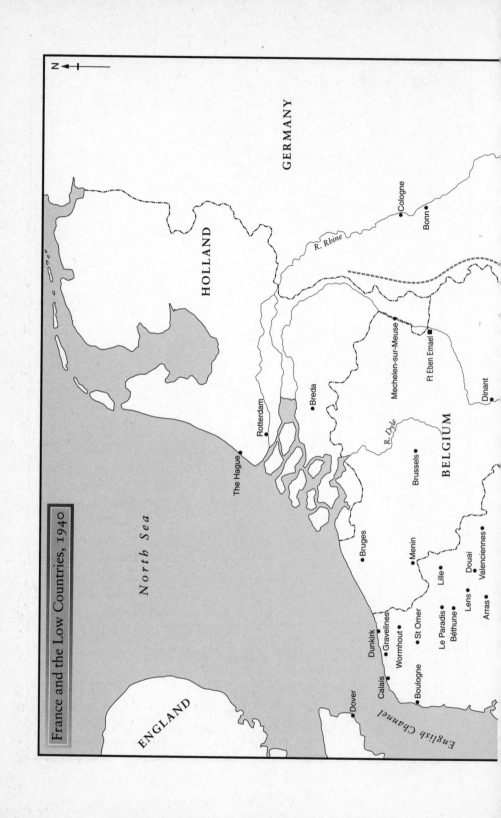

France and the Low Countries, 1940

N

GERMANY

HOLLAND

R. Rhine

Cologne

Bonn

Breda

Rotterdam

Mechelen-sur-Meuse

Ft Eben Emael

Dinant

The Hague

R. Dyle

BELGIUM

Brussels

North Sea

Bruges

Menin

Lille

Douai

Valenciennes

Lens

Arras

Dunkirk

Gravelines

St Omer

Le Paradis

Béthune

Calais

Wormhout

Boulogne

Dover

ENGLAND

English Channel

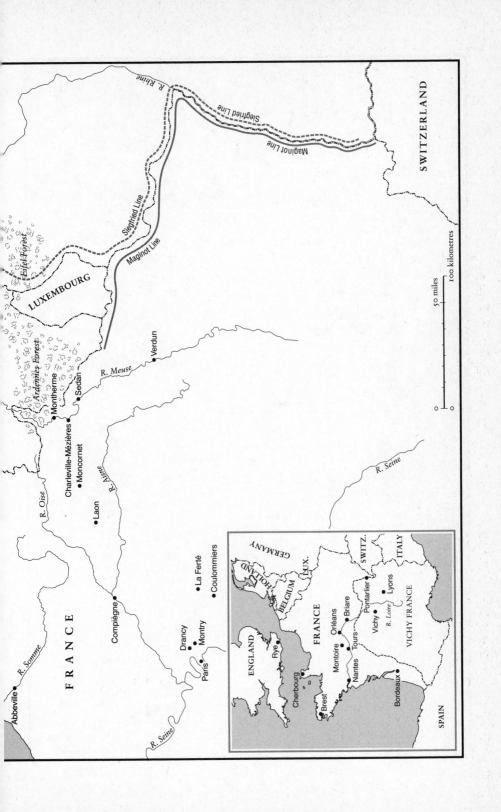

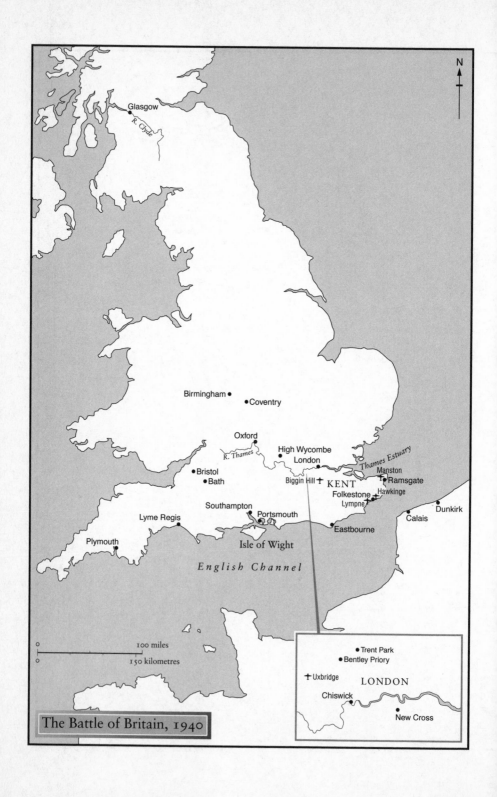

N

Glasgow
R. Clyde

Birmingham ● ● Coventry

Oxford
High Wycombe
R. Thames ● London
Bristol ● Biggin Hill ✝ KENT
● Bath Manston
Folkestone ● Ramsgate
Lympne ✝ ● Hawkinge
Southampton Eastbourne
Lyme Regis ● Portsmouth Calais ● Dunkirk
Plymouth Isle of Wight
Thames Estuary

English Channel

100 miles
150 kilometres

● Trent Park
● Bentley Priory
✝ Uxbridge LONDON
Chiswick
New Cross

The Battle of Britain, 1940

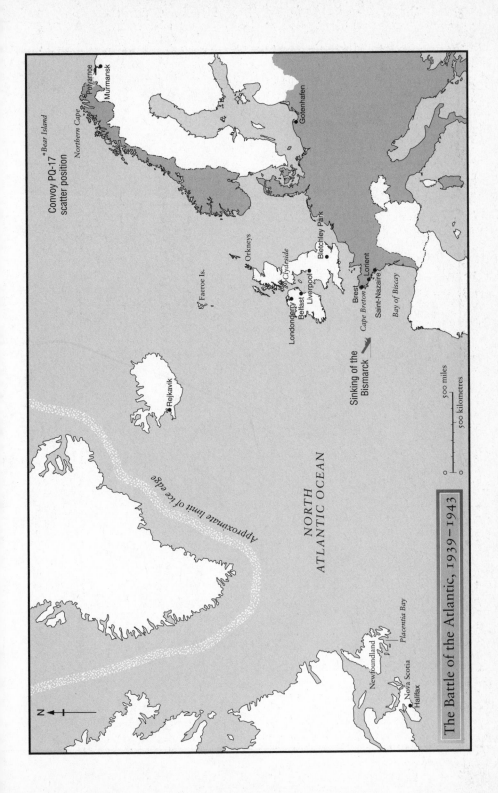

Convoy PQ-17
scatter position

Bear Island

Northern Cape

Polyarnoe
Murmansk

Gotenhafen

Orkneys

Faeroe Is.

Bletchley Park

Clydeside

Londonderry
Belfast
Liverpool

Brest
Lorient
Saint-Nazaire

Cape Breton
Bay of Biscay

Sinking of the
Bismarck

Rejkavik

Approximate limit of ice edge

NORTH
ATLANTIC OCEAN

500 miles
500 kilometres

Placentia Bay

Newfoundland

Nova Scotia
Halifax

N

The Battle of the Atlantic, 1939–1943

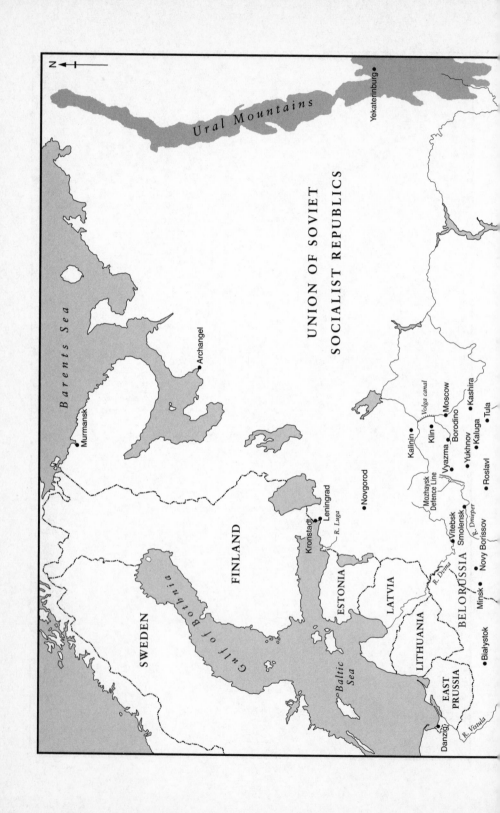

N

Ural Mountains

Yekaterinburg

UNION OF SOVIET

SOCIALIST REPUBLICS

Barents Sea

Archangel

Murmansk

Volga canal

Kashira

Moscow

Kalinin

Klin

Tula

Kaluga

Borodino

Yukhnov

Vyazma

Roslavl

Novgorod

Mozhaysk
Defence Line

Leningrad

Kronstadt

R. Luga

Vitebsk

Smolensk

R. Dnieper

Novy Borissov

R. Dvina

FINLAND

ESTONIA

LATVIA

BELORUSSIA

Minsk

Gulf of Bothnia

LITHUANIA

SWEDEN

Baltic
Sea

Białystok

EAST
PRUSSIA

R. Vistula

Danzig

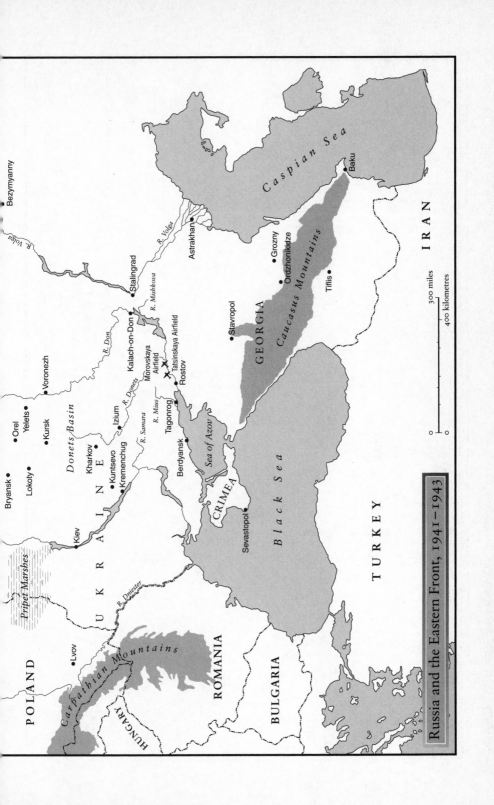

Russia and the Eastern Front, 1941–1943

POLAND

Lvov

Bryansk
Orel
Lokoty
Yelets
Kursk
Voronezh

Kiev

UKRAINE

Pripet Marshes

Donets Basin

Kharkov
Kuntsevo
Kremenchug
Izium

R. Don
R. Donets
R. Samara
R. Mius

Carpathian Mountains

HUNGARY

ROMANIA

R. Dniester

BULGARIA

Berdyansk

Tagonrog

CRIMEA

Sea of Azov

Sevastopol

Black Sea

TURKEY

Morovskaya Airfield
Tatsinskaya Airfield
Rostov

Kalach-on-Don

R. Mishkova

Stalingrad

R. Volga

R. Volga

Bezymyanny

Astrakhan

Stavropol

GEORGIA

Grozny
Ordzhonikidze
Caucasus Mountains
Tiflis

Caspian Sea

R. Ural

Baku

IRAN

300 miles
400 kilometres

0   0

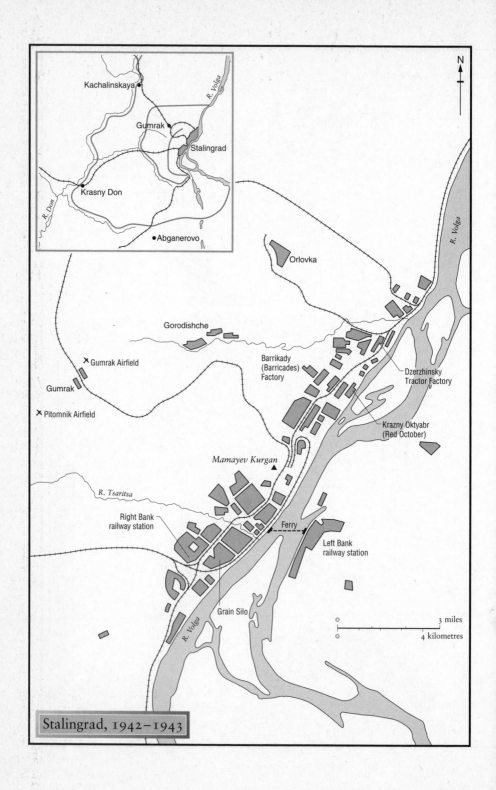

N

Kachalinskaya

R. Volga

Gumrak

Stalingrad

R. Don

Krasny Don

•Abganerovo

Orlovka

R. Volga

Gorodishche

✕ Gumrak Airfield

Gumrak

✕ Pitomnik Airfield

Barrikady
(Barricades)
Factory

Dzerzhinsky
Tractor Factory

Krazny Oktyabr
(Red October)

Mamayev Kurgan ▲

R. Tsaritsa

Right Bank
railway station

Ferry

Left Bank
railway station

3 miles

4 kilometres

R. Volga

Grain Silo

Stalingrad, 1942–1943

N

NORWAY

SWEDEN

ESTONIA

Novgorod

North Sea

LATVIA

Rumbula

USSR

DENMARK

Baltic Sea

LITHUANIA

Kovno

Ponary

EAST
PRUSSIA

Belsen

Berlin

Wannsee

Jedwabne

Białystok

R. Vistula

Treblinka

Pripet Marshes

Chelmo

Warsaw

G E R M A N Y

Łódź

Sobibor

Józefów

Lublin

Babi Yar
Ravine

POLAND

Lidice

Prague

Auschwitz-Birkenau

Lvov

Baranowice

Krakow

R. Sola

CZECHOSLOVAKIA

Türkheim

Dachau

Mauthausen

AUSTRIA

Budapest

HUNGARY

ROMANIA

The Holocaust

200 miles

300 kilometres

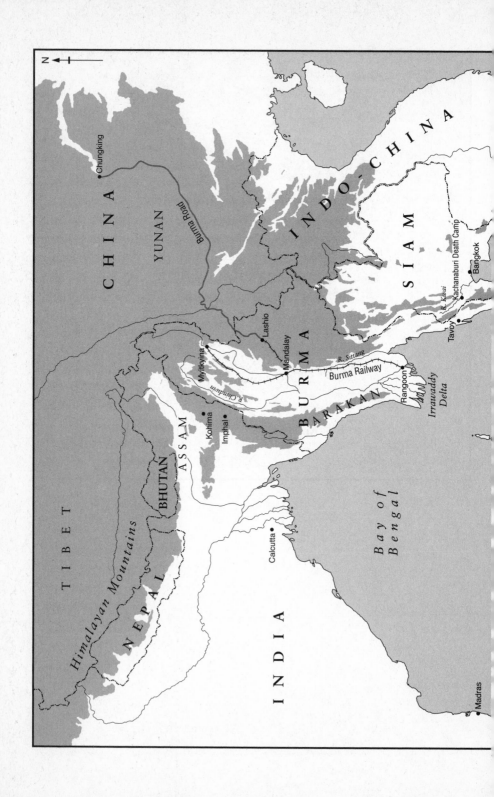

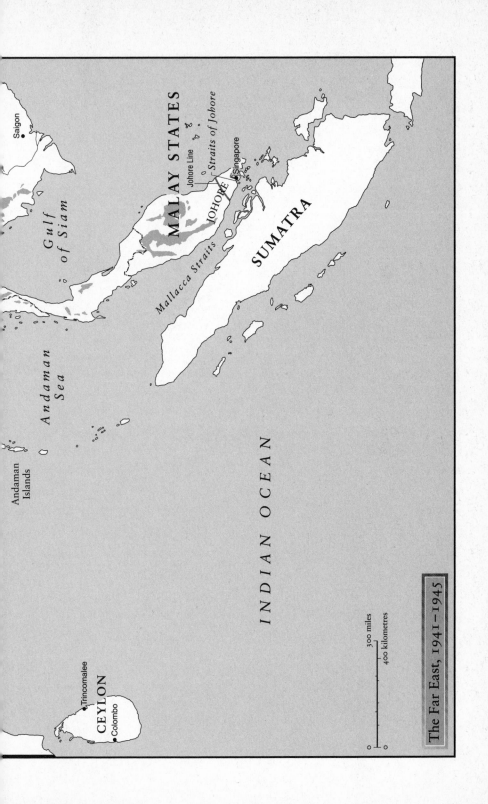

Saigon

MALAY STATES

Johore Line

Straits of Johore

Singapore

JOHORE

Gulf of Siam

Mallacca Straits

SUMATRA

Andaman Sea

Andaman
Islands

INDIAN OCEAN

300 miles

400 kilometres

Trincomalee

CEYLON

Colombo

The Far East, 1941–1945

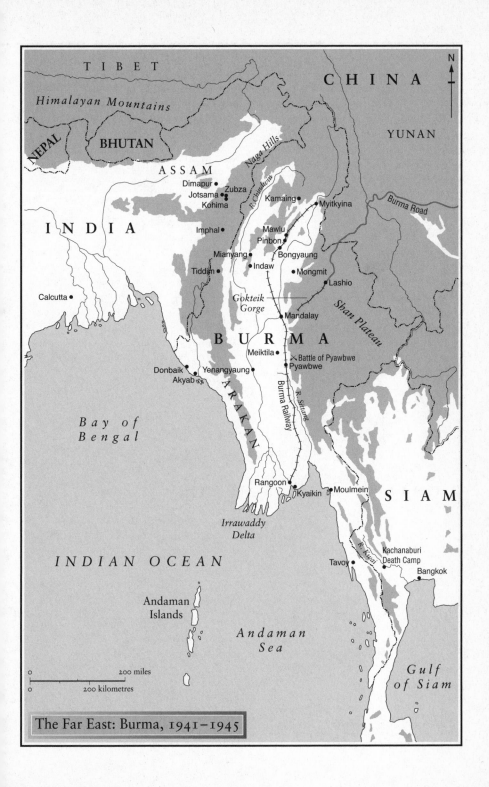

N

TIBET

CHINA

Himalayan Mountains

YUNAN

NEPAL

BHUTAN

ASSAM

Naga Hills

Dimapur
Zubza
Jotsama
Kohima

R. Chindwin

Kamaing
Myitkyina

Burma Road

INDIA

Imphal

Mawlu
Pinbon

Mianyang
Bongyaung

Tiddim
Indaw
Mongmit

Lashio

Calcutta

Gokteik
Gorge

Mandalay

Shan Plateau

BURMA

Meiktila

Battle of Pyawbwe
Pyawbwe

Donbaik
Yenangyaung

Akyab

ARAKAN

Burma Railway

R. Sitang

Bay of
Bengal

Rangoon

Kyaikin
Moulmein

SIAM

Irrawaddy
Delta

INDIAN OCEAN

R. Kwai

Kachanaburi
Death Camp

Tavoy

Bangkok

Andaman
Islands

Andaman
Sea

Gulf
of Siam

200 miles

200 kilometres

The Far East: Burma, 1941–1945

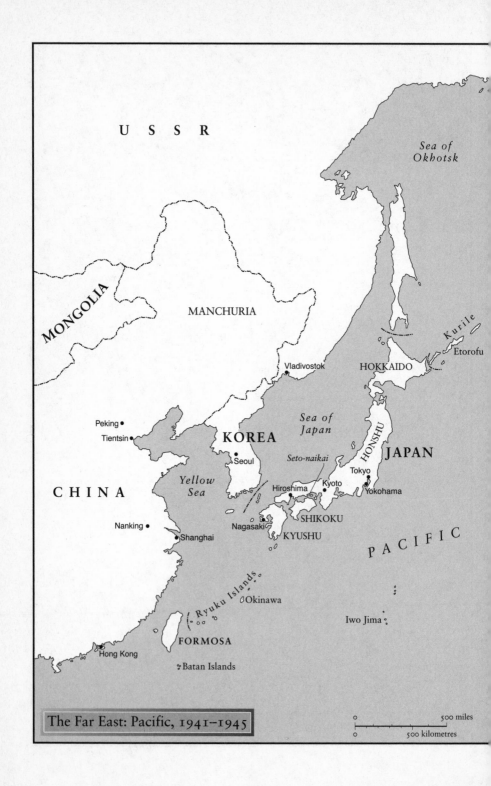

U S S R

Sea of
Okhotsk

MONGOLIA

MANCHURIA

Kurile

Etorofu

Vladivostok

HOKKAIDO

Peking

*Sea of
Japan*

Tientsin

KOREA

Seoul

Seto-naikai

HONSHU

JAPAN

CHINA

*Yellow
Sea*

Hiroshima

Tokyo

Kyoto

Yokohama

Nanking

Shanghai

Nagasaki

SHIKOKU

KYUSHU

PACIFIC

Ryuku Islands

Okinawa

Iwo Jima

FORMOSA

Hong Kong

Batan Islands

The Far East: Pacific, 1941–1945

500 miles

500 kilometres

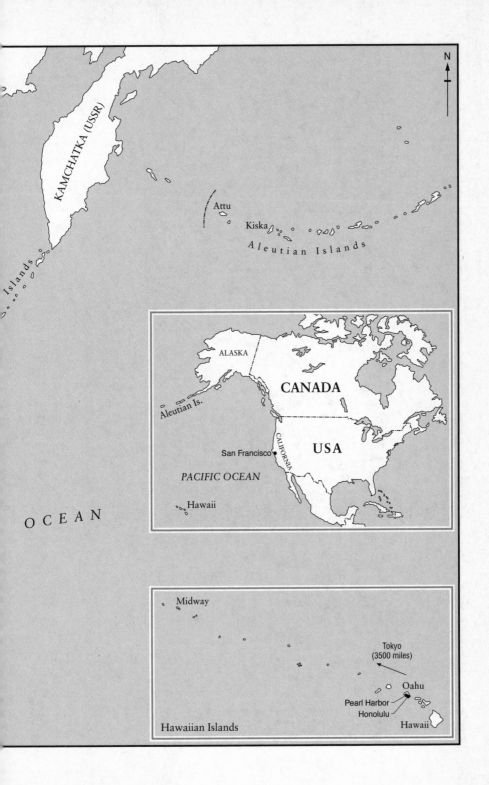

N

KAMCHATKA (USSR)

Attu

Kiska

Aleutian Islands

Islands

OCEAN

ALASKA

CANADA

Aleutian Is.

CALIFORNIA

San Francisco

USA

PACIFIC OCEAN

Hawaii

Midway

Tokyo
(3500 miles)

Oahu

Pearl Harbor
Honolulu

Hawaii

Hawaiian Islands

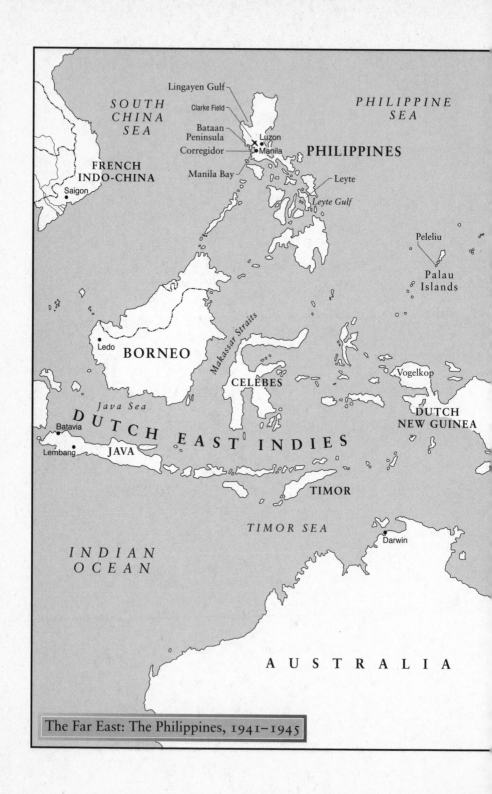

SOUTH
CHINA
SEA

PHILIPPINE
SEA

Lingayen Gulf

Clarke Field

Bataan
Peninsula

Corregidor

Luzon
Manila

FRENCH
INDO-CHINA

PHILIPPINES

Saigon

Manila Bay

Leyte

Leyte Gulf

Peleliu

Palau
Islands

Makassar Straits

Ledo

BORNEO

CELEBES

Vogelkop

Java Sea

DUTCH
NEW GUINEA

Batavia

DUTCH EAST INDIES

Lembang

JAVA

TIMOR

INDIAN
OCEAN

TIMOR SEA

Darwin

AUSTRALIA

The Far East: The Philippines, 1941–1945

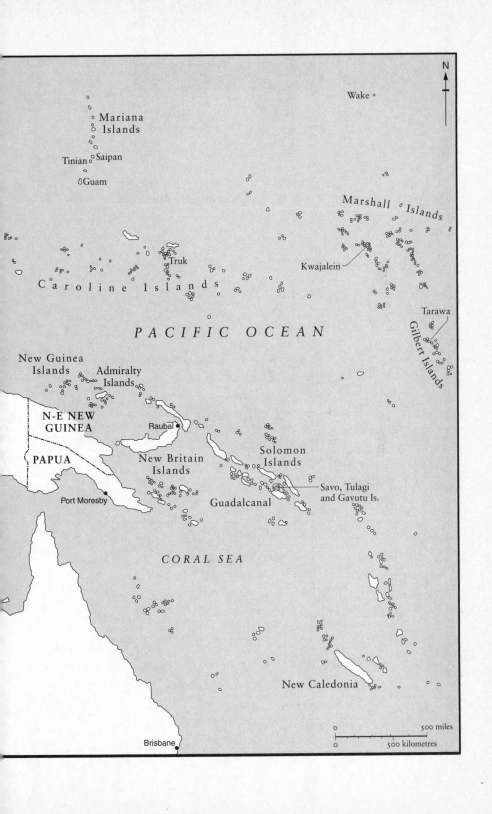

N

Wake ○

Mariana
Islands

Tinian ○ Saipan

ᗕGuam

Marshall ○ Islands

Kwajalein

Truk

C a r o l i n e   I s l a n d s

PACIFIC OCEAN

Tarawa

Gilbert Islands

New Guinea
Islands   Admiralty
             Islands

N-E NEW
GUINEA

Raubal ●

PAPUA

New Britain
Islands

Solomon
Islands

Savo, Tulagi
and Gavutu Is.

Port Moresby ●

Guadalcanal

CORAL SEA

New Caledonia

500 miles

500 kilometres

Brisbane ●

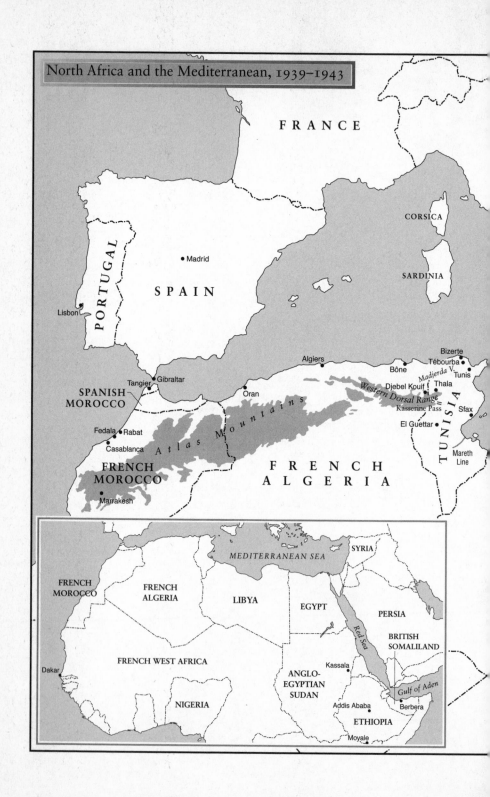

North Africa and the Mediterranean, 1939–1943

FRANCE

CORSICA

PORTUGAL

• Madrid

SPAIN

SARDINIA

Lisbon

Algiers

Bizerte
Bône
Tébourba •
Madjerda V.
Tunis
SPANISH
MOROCCO
Tangier Gibraltar
Oran
Western Dorsal Range
Djebel Kouif
Thala
Kasserine Pass
Sfax

Fedala • Rabat
Casablanca
Atlas Mountains
El Guettar
TUNISIA

FRENCH
MOROCCO
FRENCH
ALGERIA
Mareth
Line

• Marrakesh

MEDITERRANEAN SEA
SYRIA

FRENCH
MOROCCO
FRENCH
ALGERIA
LIBYA
EGYPT
PERSIA

BRITISH
SOMALILAND

Red Sea

FRENCH WEST AFRICA
Kassala

Dakar
ANGLO-
EGYPTIAN
SUDAN
Gulf of Aden
Berbera

NIGERIA
Addis Ababa

ETHIOPIA

Moyale

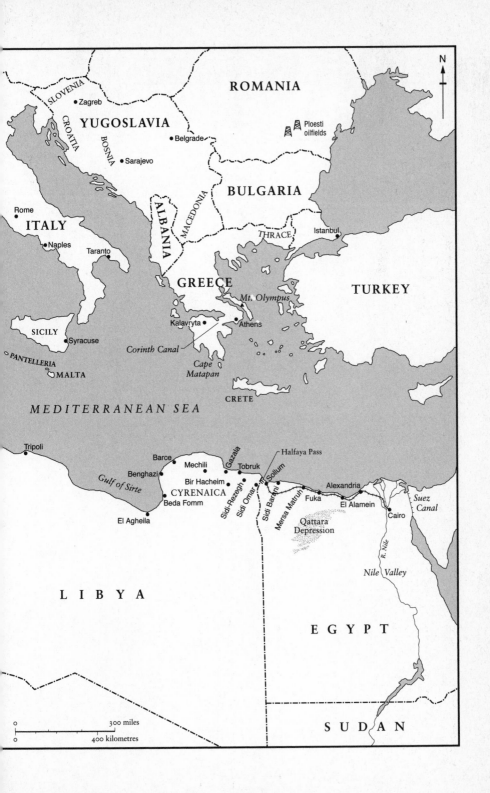

N

Zagreb
SLOVENIA
CROATIA
YUGOSLAVIA
Belgrade
BOSNIA
Sarajevo

ROMANIA

Ploesti
oilfields

BULGARIA

Rome
ITALY
Naples
Taranto

ALBANIA
MACEDONIA

THRACE
Istanbul

GREECE

TURKEY

Mt. Olympus

SICILY
Syracuse

Kalavryta
Athens

PANTELLERIA
MALTA

Corinth Canal

Cape
Matapan

CRETE

MEDITERRANEAN SEA

Tripoli

Barce
Benghazi
Gulf of Sirte

Mechili
Gazala
Tobruk

Halfaya Pass

Bir Hacheim
CYRENAICA
Beda Fomm

Sidi-Rezegh
Sidi Omar
Sidi Barani
Sollum
Mersa Matruh
Fuka

Alexandria
El Alamein

Suez
Canal

El Agheila

Qattara
Depression

Cairo

R. Nile

Nile Valley

L I B Y A

E G Y P T

S U D A N

0   300 miles
0   400 kilometres

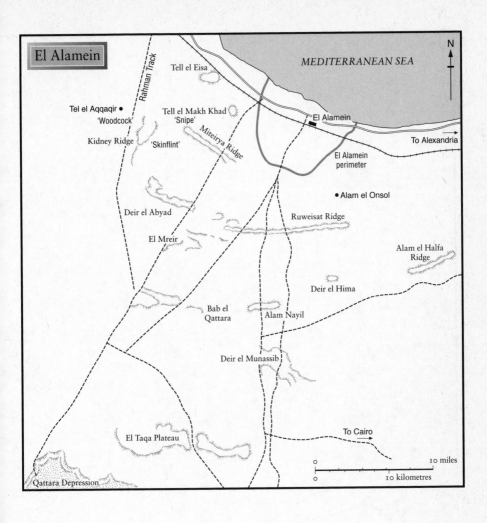

El Alamein

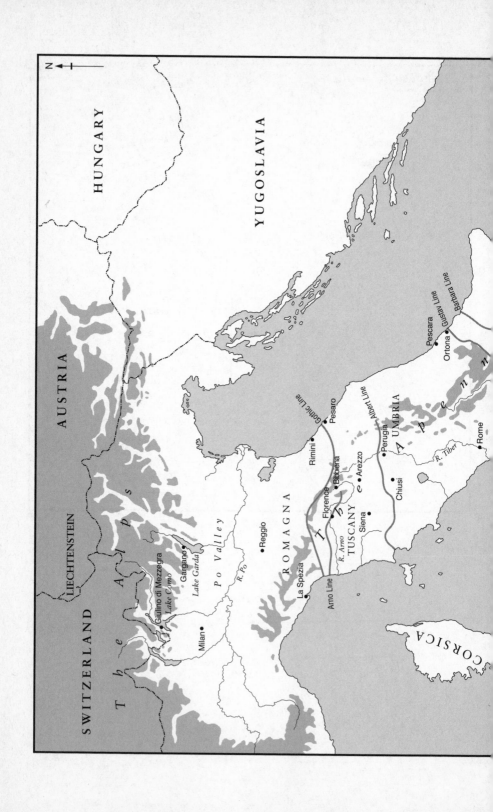

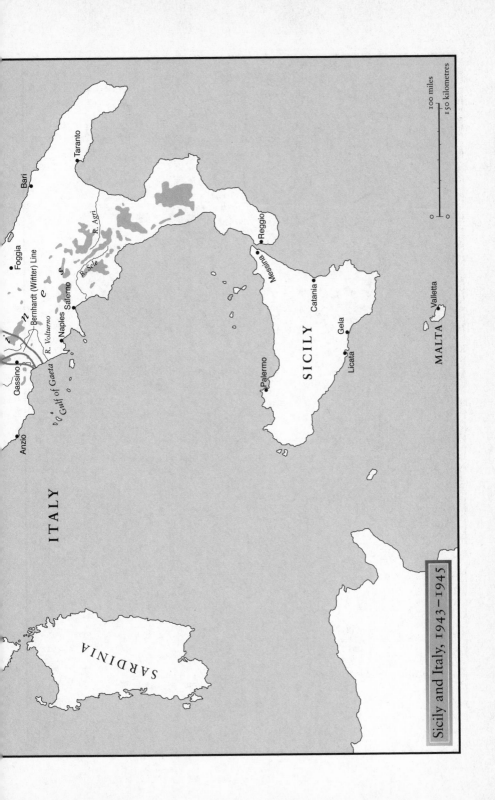

ITALY

Anzio

Cassino

Gulf of Gaeta

R. Volturno

Bernhardt (Winter) Line

Naples

Salerno

R. Sele

Foggia

Bari

R. Agri

Taranto

Reggio

Messina

Palermo

SICILY

Catania

Gela

Licata

MALTA   Valletta

SARDINIA

Sicily and Italy, 1943–1945

100 miles

150 kilometres

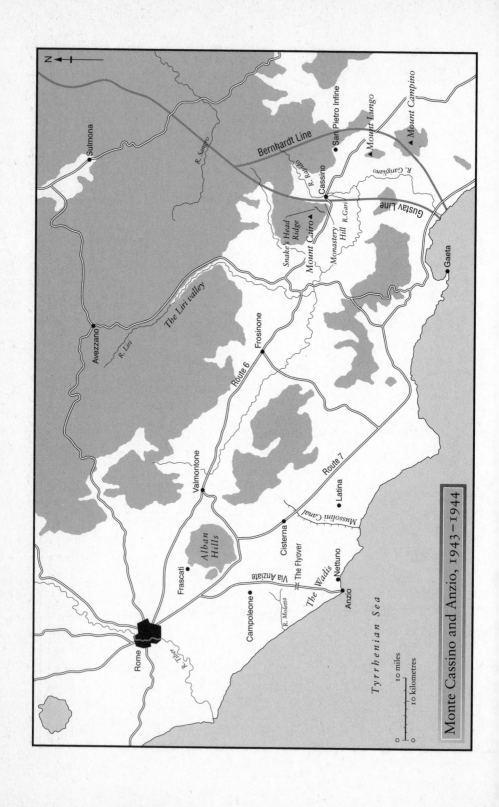

Monte Cassino and Anzio, 1943–1944

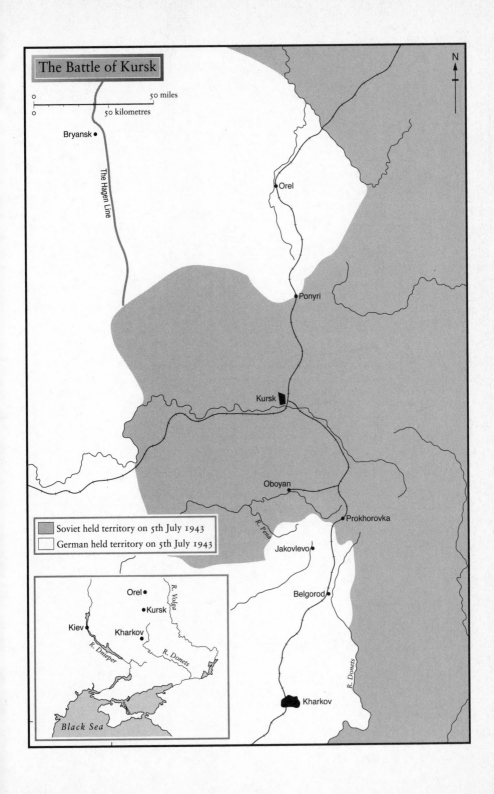

The Battle of Kursk

0 ———————————————— 50 miles
0 ———————————————— 50 kilometres

Bryansk •

The Hagen Line

• Orel

• Ponyri

Kursk ■

Oboyan •

• Prokhorovka

■ Soviet held territory on 5th July 1943
☐ German held territory on 5th July 1943

Jakovlevo •

R. Pena

Belgorod •

R. Donets

N

Orel •
• Kursk

R. Volga

Kiev •
Kharkov •

R. Dnieper

R. Donets

Kharkov

Black Sea

The Allied Combined Bombing Offensive

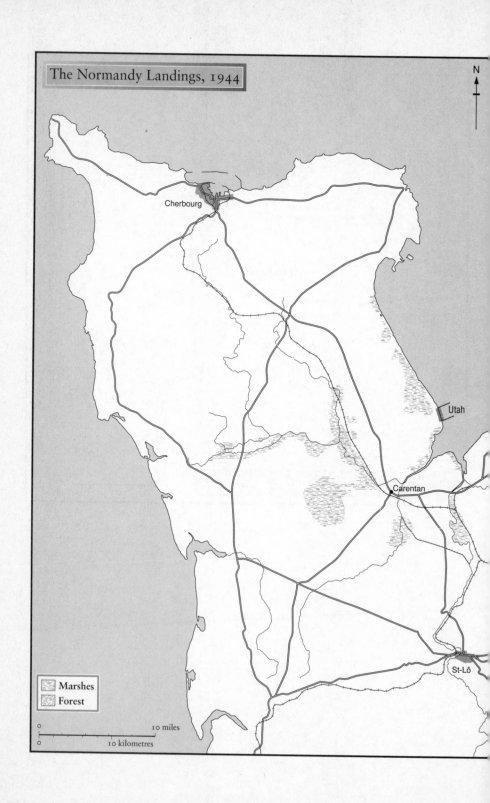

The Normandy Landings, 1944

N

Cherbourg

Utah

Carentan

St-Lô

Marshes
Forest

10 miles

10 kilometres

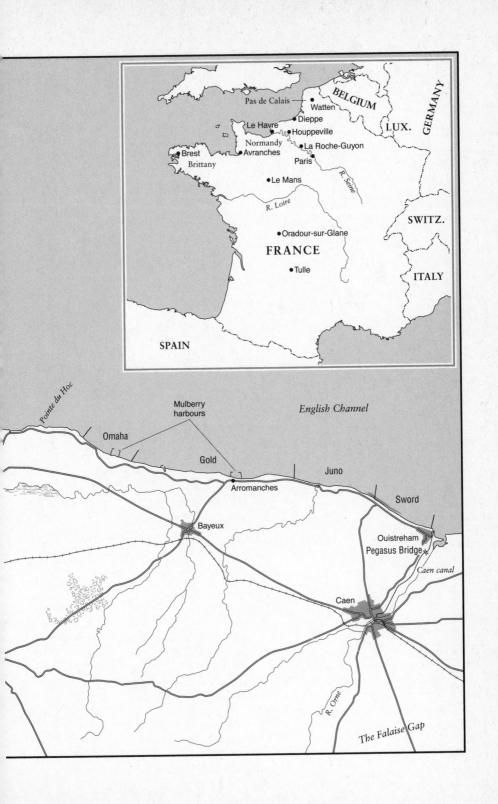

BELGIUM

GERMANY

LUX.

Pas de Calais

Watten

Dieppe

Le Havre

Houppeville

Normandy

La Roche-Guyon

Avranches

Brest

Paris

Brittany

Le Mans

SWITZ.

R. Seine

R. Loire

Oradour-sur-Glane

FRANCE

Tulle

ITALY

SPAIN

Pointe du Hoc

Mulberry
harbours

English Channel

Omaha

Gold

Juno

Arromanches

Sword

Bayeux

Ouistreham

Pegasus Bridge

Caen canal

Caen

R. Orme

The Falaise Gap

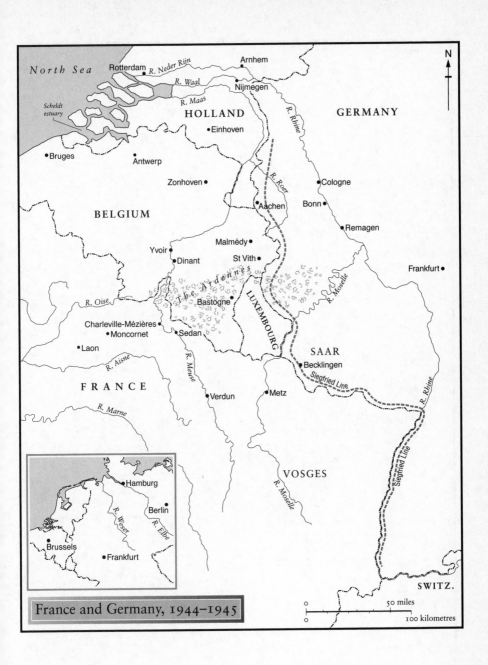

France and Germany, 1944–1945

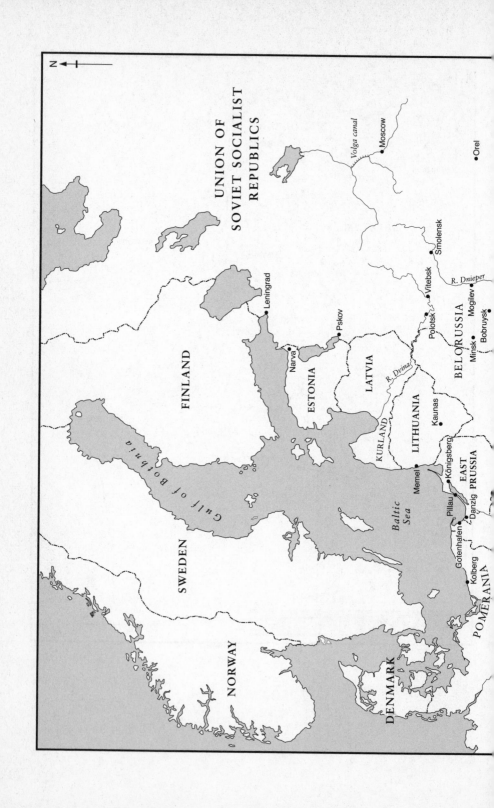

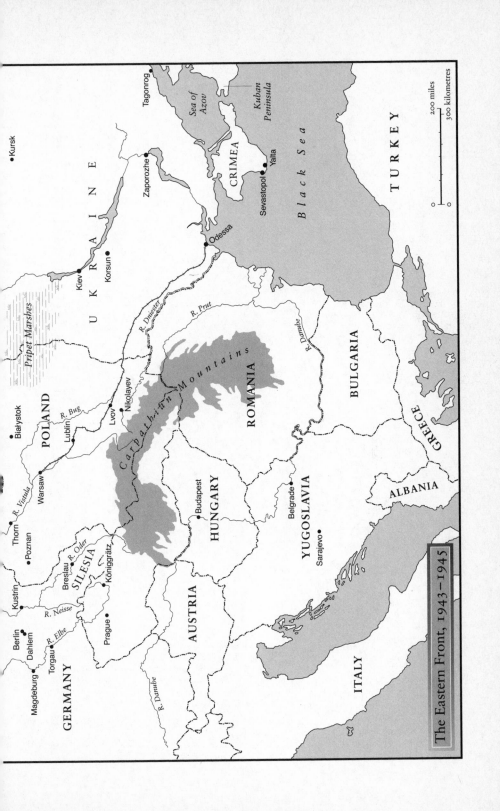

The Eastern Front, 1943–1945

Kursk

GERMANY
Magdeburg
Berlin
Dahlem
Torgau
R. Elbe
Kustrin
Prague
Königgrätz
SILESIA
R. Oder
Breslau
R. Neisse
Poznan
Thorn
R. Vistula
AUSTRIA
R. Danube
HUNGARY
Budapest
Warsaw
Lublin
R. Bug
POLAND
Białystok
Kiev
Korsun
U K R A I N E
Pripet Marshes
Lvov
Nikolayev
R. Dniester
Carpathian Mountains
ROMANIA
R. Prut
R. Danube
Belgrade
YUGOSLAVIA
Sarajevo
BULGARIA
GREECE
ALBANIA
ITALY
Zaporozhe
Odessa
CRIMEA
Sevastopol
Yalta
Sea of Azov
Kuban Peninsula
Tagonrog
Black Sea
TURKEY

200 miles
300 kilometres

Preface

Writing history, A. J. P. Taylor used to say, was like W. C. Fields juggling: it looks easy until you try to do it yourself. The writing of this book has been made much easier for me through the enthusiastic support of friends and fellow historians.

The historian Ian Sayer owns Britain's largest private archive of hitherto unpublished Second World War material, and he has been fabulously generous with his time, advice and extensive knowledge of the period. It has been a great pleasure getting to know him in the course of researching this book, which I wrote at the same time as *Masters and Commanders*, since many of the sources and actors overlap.

Visiting the actual sites and scenes of many of the climactic moments of the war has been invaluable, and I would like to thank all those who have made my visits to the following places so enjoyable: the Wehrmacht headquarters at Zossen-Wunsdorf; the Maginot Line; Göring's former Air Ministry and Goebbels' former Propaganda Ministry in Berlin; RAF Uxbridge; the estate Hitler gave Guderian in Poland; the Cabinet War Rooms; the U-boat 534 in Birkenhead; the Lancaster bomber *Just Jane* at East Kirkby, Lincolnshire; the site of Hitler's Reich Chancellery on the Wilhelmstrasse in Berlin; the Sevastopol diorama and U-boat pens in the Crimea; the Siemens Dynamo Works in Berlin; RAF Coltishall; Colombey-les-Deux-Eglises; the Old Admiralty Building in Whitehall; the Maison Blairon in Charleville-Mézières; the former German air-raid shelters on Guernsey; the Bundesarchiv Lichterfelde outside Berlin; the Obersalzberg Documentation Centre at Berchtesgaden; the Wolfschanze at

Rastenburg; the Livadia Palace at Yalta; and Stalin's dacha at Sochi in the Crimea.

I should particularly like to thank Oleg Germanovich Alexandrov of the excellent Three Whales Tours (www.threewhales.ru) for taking me around the Moscow Defence Museum, the Kremlin, the Armed Forces Museum in Moscow and the Museum of the Great Patriotic War; also Svetlana Mishatkina for showing my wife Susan and me around Volgograd (formerly Stalingrad) and in particular the Grain Elevator, the Mamayev Kurgan, the Red October, Barrikady and Dzerzhinsky Tractor factories, Crossing 62, Field Marshal Paulus' headquarters, the Rossoschka Russo-German Cemetery and the Panoramic Museum; also Lieutenant-Colonel Alexandr Anatolyevich Kulikov for taking me round the Museum of Tank Construction at Kubinka, and Colonel Vyacheslav Nikolaevich Budjony for showing us the museum of the Officers' Club in Kursk and the battlefields of Jakovlevo and Prokhorovka.

I should like to thank the indefatigable Colonel Patrick Mercer MP for taking me on a fascinating tour of the 1944 battlefields south of Rome, and in particular to the Alban Hills, the Allied Landing Museum at Nettuno, the former 'Factory' (Aprilia), Campoleone, the Commonwealth Beach Head Cemetery at Anzio, the crossing over the Moletta river where Viscount De L'Isle won his Victoria Cross, the 'Boot' wadi off the via Anziate, Monte Lungo, San Pietro Infine, the Gari river crossings, Sant'Angelo in Theodice, the Commonwealth, Polish and German War Cemeteries in and around Cassino, the Rapido river, the Monte Cassino Monastery Museum and the Monte Cassino History Museum. I should also like to thank Ernesto Rosi at the American War Cemetery at Nettuno for showing me where to find the grave of General George C. Marshall's stepson, Lieutenant Allen Tupper Brown.

I should once again like to thank Paul Woodadge of Battlebus Tours (www.battlebus.fr) for conducting me on battlefield tours of Omaha Beach, Beuzeville-au-Plain, La Fière, Utah Beach, Les Mézières, Sainte-Marie-du-Mont, Bréville, Angoville-au-Plain, Merville Battery, Strongpoint Hillman, Sword Beach, Pegasus Bridge, Juno Beach, Sainte-Mère-Eglise, Lion-sur-Mer, Gold Beach and Crépon, as well as taking me to the Ryes Commonwealth War Cemetery at Bazenville and the Normandy American Cemetery at Colleville-sur-Mer.

It was kind of SPC Trent Cryer of Fort Myer, Virginia, to show me around the Pentagon, and in particular for tracking down the pen used by Douglas MacArthur, Admiral Nimitz and the Japanese delegation aboard USS *Missouri* on 2 September 1945 to sign the surrender document that ended the war. I would also like to thank Magdalena Rzasa-Michalec for Susan's and my visit to Auschwitz–Birkenau, which she guided us around with great expertise, and David and Gail Webster for giving us a tour around de Gaulle's wartime country residence of Rodinghead in Ashridge Park. Richard Zeitlin of the Veterans' Museum in Madison, Wisconsin has also been most helpful.

The historian Paddy Griffith very kindly organized an advanced wargame of Barbarossa, which lasted almost as long as the operation itself, the lessons of which have greatly helped to inform my views as set out in Chapters 5 and 10. For giving so much of their time, I would like to thank Ned Zuparko (who played Brauchitsch); Max Michael (Hitler); Simon Bracegirdle (Stalin); Tim Cockitt (Timoshenko). Thanks too to Martin James, General John Drewienkiewicz and Colonel John Hughes-Wilson for their views and thoughts on that occasion.

I also owe debts of thanks to the late Mrs Joan Bright Astley; Allan Mallinson; Mrs Elizabeth Ward; Bernard Besserglik; Ion Trewin; the late Professor R. V. Jones; St John Brown; John Hughes-Wilson, RUSI; the Guild of Battlefield Guides; Hubert Picarda; Colonel Carlo D'Este; Professor Donald Cameron Watt; Major Jim Turner; Rory Macleod; Miriam Owen; Air Chief Marshal Sir Jock Stirrup; Daniel Johnson; and Robert Mages, Richard Sommers and David Keough at the USA Military History Institute, Carlisle, Pennsylvania.

A number of friends have read various chapters for me, and in some cases the entire book, including Johnnie Ogden, Conrad Black, my father Simon Roberts, Oleg Alexandrov, John Curtis, Antony Selwyn, Ian Sayer, Hugh Lunghi, Eric Petersen, Paul Courtenay and David Denman. Although the errors that have doubtless survived are all my own, I would very much like to thank them, as well as the genius Penguin proofreaders Stephen Ryan and Michael Page.

Without the superb, good-natured professionalism of my publisher Stuart Proffitt, agent Georgina Capel and copy-editor Peter James this book would never have happened.

I would like to thank my wife Susan for accompanying me to many of the places that appear in this book, including Mussolini's execution spot above the village of Giulino di Mezzegra (the day after we got engaged), Auschwitz–Birkenau, the Kachanaburi death camp on the River Kwai, the battlefields of Kursk and Stalingrad, and other war-time sites in Budapest, Vienna, Cairo, Libya and Morocco.

This book is dedicated to Frank Johnson, in memory of our long walks discussing the issues raised by the war, and especially our visit to the Wolfschanze, Hitler's headquarters in Poland. I will always regret that we never made the trip to Charles de Gaulle's grave at Colombey-les-Deux-Eglises together. He is hugely missed by all those who knew and loved him.

Whether I use imperial or metric measurements generally depends on my sources: no one, for example, wants to convert into inches well-known German calibres measured in millimetres. And where I quote from the verbatim notes taken at War Cabinet meetings by Lawrence Burgis, assistant secretary to the Cabinet Office, I have expanded their original abbreviated form for the sake of readability.

Andrew Roberts
April 2009
www.andrew-roberts.net

Prelude
The Pact

On Thursday, 12 April 1934, General Werner von Blomberg, Germany's Reichswehrminister (Minister of Defence), and thus the political master of the German armed forces, met the Chancellor of Germany, Adolf Hitler, aboard the *Deutschland*, an 11,700-ton pocket battleship. There they entered into a secret pact by which the Army would support the Nazi leader in taking the presidency of Germany upon the death of Paul von Hindenburg, on condition that the Reichswehr would retain complete control over all matters military. The chief of the Sturmabteilung (SA, or Brownshirts), Ernst Röhm, had been pressing for a new ministry comprising all the armed forces of Germany, with himself at its head, a situation that augured ill for both Blomberg and ultimately possibly also for Hitler. Showing his readiness to put the *Deutschland* Pact into immediate effect, on 1 May Blomberg ordered the incorporation of the swastika motif on to the uniforms of the armed forces.

On 21 June, with Röhm forcefully continuing to press his case, Blomberg warned Hitler that unless measures were taken to secure internal peace, Hindenburg would declare martial law and ask the Army to restore order, a situation that would leave the Chancellor sidelined and weakened. Hitler took the hint. Nine days later, his personal Schutzstaffel (SS) bodyguard acted with sudden ferocity against Röhm on what became known as the Blood Purge or the Night of the Long Knives, in a series of summary kidnappings and executions that left 200 people dead. Not only did the Army not act during the Purge, but the very next day, 1 July, Blomberg issued an Order of the Day commending 'the Führer's soldierly decision and exemplary courage' in liquidating the 'mutineers and traitors' of the SA.

A month later, on Thursday, 2 August 1934, Hindenburg died, and – with the complete support of the Army – Hitler assumed the presidency and with it the supreme command of the armed forces under a law agreed by the Cabinet during Hindenburg's lifetime.[1] Blomberg ordered that a new oath of allegiance be sworn to Hitler personally, rather than to the office of the presidency or to the state. 'I swear by God this sacred oath,' its unambiguous wording went, 'that I will render unconditional obedience to Adolf Hitler, the Führer of the German Reich and *Volk*, Supreme Commander of the Armed Forces, and will be ready as a brave soldier to risk my life at any time for this oath.' At Hindenburg's funeral on 7 August, Blomberg suggested to the new President that all soldiers should henceforth address him as 'Mein Führer', a proposal which was graciously accepted.

Hitler had won ultimate power, but only at the sufferance of the German Army, and just two days after Hindenburg's funeral, on Thursday, 9 August 1934, Blomberg wrote a terse, one-sentence (and hitherto unpublished) letter to Hitler, stating: 'Mein Führer! Ich bitte an die in Aussicht gestellte Verfügung an die Wehrmacht erinnern zu dürfen. Blomberg' (My Leader, I would like to remind you of your statement to the Wehrmacht. Blomberg').[2] The tone was somewhat peremptory, reminding Hitler of his side of the *Deutschland* Pact, a pledge without which he would not have been able to gain the military and political supremacy that was to allow him, only five years later, to plunge the world into the most catastrophic war mankind has ever known. Blomberg was in a position to insist on proper observation of the Pact, for as the British historian of the German High Command, Sir John Wheeler-Bennett, wrote:

Till August 1934 the Army could have overthrown the Nazi regime at a nod from their commanders, for they owed no allegiance to the Chancellor; but, with the acceptance of Hitler's succession, the Generals had added one more fetter, perhaps the strongest of all, to those psychological bonds which chained them ever more inescapably to a regime which they had thought to exploit and dominate.[3]

A week after receiving Blomberg's letter, Hitler published the full text of Hindenburg's Last Will and Testament in the Nazi Party newspaper, *Völkischer Beobachter*. This document stressed that in the Third German Reich:

The guardian of the state, the Reichswehr, must be the symbol of and firm support for this superstructure. On the Reichswehr as a firm foundation must rest the old Prussian virtues of self-realized dutifulness, of simplicity, and of comradeship ... Always and at all times, the Reichswehr must remain the pattern of state conduct, so that, unbiased by any internal political development, its lofty mission for the defence of the country may be maintained ... The thanks of the Field Marshal of the World War and its Commander-in-Chief are due to all the men who have accomplished the construction and organization of the Reichswehr.[4]

The next day, 19 August, the German people voted in a plebiscite on whether Hitler should hold the combined offices of president and Reich chancellor, with more than thirty-eight million people, or 89.9 per cent, voting yes.

On 20 August, Hitler continued to repay his *Deutschland* debt, writing to Blomberg and in effect confirming that the secret Pact was still operative. He thanked the general for the Army's oath of loyalty, and added, 'I shall always regard it as my highest duty to intercede for the existence and inviolability of the Wehrmacht, in fulfilment of the testament of the late Field Marshal, and in accord with my own will to establish the Army firmly as the sole bearer of the arms of the nation.'

Nothing so consolidated the Führer's standing with his generals as the series of politico-diplomatic coups that he pulled off around the borders of Germany between March 1936 and August 1939, which turned the humiliated power of the Versailles Treaty – under which she had lost 13.5 per cent of her territory – into the potentially glorious Third Reich. Hitler's regular protestations of pacific intentions worked well in lulling foreigners' suspicions, but were correctly seen as utterly bogus by the senior commanders of the Wehrmacht, Kriegsmarine and Luftwaffe whom he was simultaneously ordering to prepare for a general European conflict sooner rather than later. 'Germany will of its own accord never break the peace,' he told the journalist G. Ward Price of London's *Daily Mail* in February 1935, for example, but a few days later he decided that the Wehrmacht needed to be increased from twenty-one to thirty-six divisions as soon as possible. His intention was to have a sixty-three-division army – almost the same size as in 1914 – by the year 1939.[5]

The tempo of Hitlerian aggression increased exponentially during the second half of the 1930s, as the German dictator gained in confidence and the generals absented themselves from political decision-making. Hermann Göring's official announcement of the existence of the Luftwaffe took place in March 1935, the same month that Germany publicly repudiated the disarmament clauses of the Versailles Treaty, clauses that she had been secretly ignoring ever since Hitler had come to power. That September the Nuremberg laws effectively outlawed German Jews, and made the Swastika the official flag of Germany.

It was on 7 March 1936 that Hitler comprehensively violated the Versailles Treaty by sending troops into the industrial region of the Rhineland, which under Article 180 had been specifically designated a demilitarized zone. Had the German Army been opposed by the French and British forces stationed near by, it had orders to retire back to base and such a reverse would almost certainly have cost Hitler the chancellorship. Yet the Western powers, riven with guilt about having imposed what was described as a 'Carthaginian peace' on Germany in 1919, allowed the Germans to enter the Rhineland unopposed. 'After all,' said the influential Liberal politician and newspaper director the Marquis of Lothian, who had been Chancellor of the Duchy of Lancaster in Ramsay MacDonald's National Government, 'they are only going into their own back garden.' When Hitler assured the Western powers in March 1936 that Germany wished only for peace, Arthur Greenwood, the deputy leader of the Labour Party, told the House of Commons: 'Herr Hitler has made a statement . . . holding out the olive branch . . . which ought to be taken at face value . . . It is idle to say that those statements are insincere.' That August Germany adopted compulsory two-year military service.

November 1936 saw active German intervention in the Spanish Civil War, when Hitler sent the Condor Legion, a unit composed of over 12,000 'volunteers' as well as Luftwaffe warplanes, to support his fellow Fascist General Francisco Franco. Benito Mussolini's Fascist Italy, meanwhile, sent forces that were eventually to number 75,000

men. It was in Spain that the technique of carpet bombing was perfected by the Legion, which dropped nearly 2.7 million pounds of
bombs, and fired more than 4 million machine-gun bullets. Britain and
France held a conference in London attended by twenty-six countries,
which set up a committee to police the principle of non-intervention
in Spanish affairs. Both Germany and Italy took seats on it, which
they kept until June 1937, by which time the farce could not be played
out any longer.

November 1936 also saw Germany, Japan and subsequently Italy
sign the Anti-Comintern Pact, aimed at opposing the USSR's Third
Communist International, but also creating what became known as
the Axis. The *mise-en-scène* for the Second World War was almost in
place, except for one sensational twist in the plot still to come.

For the moment, however, Hitler cranked up his sabre-rattling
policy towards his neighbours, and particularly those with large German populations contiguous with the borders of the Reich. That it
was all part of a wider master-plan – albeit one that was to be moved
forward as opportunities presented themselves – was conclusively
proven by the minutes of a meeting he called in the Reich Chancellery
for 4.15 p.m. on Friday, 5 November 1937. This lasted nearly four
hours and was intended to leave the senior executive officers of the
Reich under no illusions about where his plans were leading. Speaking
to Blomberg (who had been made the first field marshal of the Third
Reich in 1936), General Werner von Fritsch, commander-in-chief of
the Wehrmacht, Admiral Erich Raeder, commander-in-chief of the
German Navy, Göring, commander-in-chief of the Luftwaffe, and the
Foreign Minister, Baron Konstantin von Neurath, with the minutes
taken carefully by his adjutant Colonel Friedrich Hossbach, the Führer
began by stating that the purpose of the meeting could not be discussed
before the Reich Cabinet 'just because of the importance of the
matter'.[6]

He then explained how the histories of the Roman and British
Empires 'had proved that expansion could be carried out only by
breaking down resistance and taking risks'. These risks – by which he
meant short wars against Britain and France – would have to be taken
before the period 1943–5, which he regarded as 'the turning point of
the regime' because after that time 'The world would be expecting

our attack and would be increasing its counter-measures from year to year. It would be while the world was still preparing its defences that we would be obliged to take the offensive.' Before then, in order to protect Germany's flanks, Hitler intended 'to overthrow Czechoslovakia and Austria' simultaneously and 'with lightning speed' in an *Angriffskrieg* (offensive war). He believed that the British and French had 'already tacitly written off the Czechs' and that 'Without British support, offensive action by France against Germany was not to be expected.'[7] Only after the speedy destruction of first Austria and Czechoslovakia and then Britain and France could he concentrate on the creation of a vast colonial empire in Europe.

The seeming immediacy of these plans deeply alarmed Blomberg and Fritsch – Fritsch even proposed postponing his holiday which was due to start the following Wednesday – and both men 'repeatedly emphasized the necessity that Britain and France must not become our enemies'. Together, Blomberg and Fritsch might have been able to prevent Hitler carrying out the last part of the Hossbach plans. Yet on 27 January 1938 Blomberg was forced to resign his powerful post when it emerged that his new bride Margarethe Gruhn, who was thirty-five years his junior, had in 1931 posed for pornographic photographs taken by a Czech Jew with whom she had been cohabiting, and that she had also graced a register of known prostitutes kept by the Berlin police force. To make matters worse, both Hitler and Hermann Göring had stood witness for the couple at their wedding in the War Ministry on 12 January. Within a week, Fritsch was also forced to resign on suspicion of being blackmailed by a Berlin rentboy called Otto Schmidt, a charge of which he was innocent and later exonerated in court on the grounds of mistaken identity.[8] It is likely that he had been framed by Heinrich Himmler, head of the SS, but any collective opposition to his sacking by the German generals was undermined by General Wilhelm Keitel, a devotee of Hitler.[9]

Although Hitler had sought neither outcome, he was swift in exploiting the potentially embarrassing situation, and used it massively to extend his personal control over Germany's armed forces. By appointing no formal successor to Blomberg, he effectively took over the role of war minister himself, appointing Keitel to be his adviser on all Wehrmacht matters, a man who was selected on the basis of his sycophancy and his solid lack of personality and intellect. 'From then on Hitler gave orders directly to the army, navy and air force,' Keitel explained to an interviewer at the Nuremberg Trials after the war. 'No one issued orders independently of Hitler. Of course I signed them . . . but they originated with Hitler. It was the wish and desire of Hitler to have all the power and command reside in him. It was something he could not do with Blomberg.'[10]

In replacing Blomberg and Fritsch with himself and Keitel, *de facto* if not immediately *de jure*, Hitler had finally sealed his control of the German armed forces. Within days he carried out a massive reorganiz-ation of the top echelons of the military machine: twelve generals (not including Blomberg and Fritsch) were dismissed and the occupants of no fewer than fifty-one other posts were reshuffled.[11] The way was now clear for Hitler to establish complete domination of Germany's armed forces. Over the coming years, he would become more and more closely involved in every aspect of strategic decision-making, both through Keitel and through his equally obedient deputy, Colonel – later Major-General – Alfred Jodl. The German High Command – proud, often Prussian, much of it aristocratic, and just as resentful of the humiliations of 1918–19 as anyone else in the Reich – allowed its traditional role of creating grand strategy to be usurped by a man whom many of them admired as a statesman, but whose talent as a military strategist none of them knew anything about. And all because of a former prostitute and a mendacious Berlin rentboy.

As it turned out, Austria did not need to be fought in order to be absorbed into the Reich. On 11 March 1938 German troops entered the country and encountered enough genuine popular support for Hitler to declare *Anschluss* (political union) two days later, before being driven in triumph through the streets of Vienna. Although the union of the two countries had been expressly forbidden by the Versailles Treaty, Hitler presented the West with a fait accompli. The only shots fired in anger during *Anschluss* were by the many Jews who committed suicide as the Wehrmacht crossed the border.

The next crisis – over the German-speaking Sudeten areas of Czechoslovakia awarded to Prague at Versailles – was handled as deftly by Hitler as the earlier ones. The Sudeten Germans had been agitating to join the Reich in carefully orchestrated demonstrations, which had occasionally, as in October 1937, descended into violence. In November the Sudeten Nazis in the Czech parliament had staged a walk-out, following a ban on political meetings. Hitler stoked the crisis adroitly throughout 1938, mobilizing the Wehrmacht on 12 August and demanding the annexation of the Sudeten areas to Germany the following month. As before, he stated that this would be his last territorial acquisition in Europe.

On 15 September the British Prime Minister Neville Chamberlain flew to Hitler's Alpine home at Berchtesgaden to try to negotiate a resolution of the crisis. On his return he wrote to his sister Ida, 'In short I had established a certain confidence which was my aim and on my side in spite of the hardness and ruthlessness I thought I saw in his face I got the impression that here was a man who could be relied upon when he had given his word.'[12] It required a second meeting with Hitler, at Bad Godesberg a week later, before Chamberlain was able to come to specific terms that Britain and France could urge the Czechs to accept, in order to avoid a war for which the Western powers were still (unforgivably) unprepared. Reporting to the Cabinet after his return from Godesberg, Chamberlain said that he believed that Hitler 'would not deliberately deceive a man whom he respected with whom he had been in negotiation'.[13]

It took a third meeting, at Munich at the end of September, before agreement could be reached between the Germans, Italian, British and French over the geographical extent and the timetable for the Sudetenland's absorption into the Reich. Recommending the Munich Agreement to the House of Commons, Chamberlain said on 3 October: 'It is my hope, and my belief, that under the new system of guarantees the new Czechoslovakia will find a greater security than she has ever enjoyed in the past.'[14] For all the gross naivety of that statement, at least we can be sure that Chamberlain believed it.

During the Munich period the British Government received a number of indications from anti-Nazi German generals that they would overthrow Hitler if the Western powers refused his blandishments over the Sudetenland. Yet these promises could not be relied upon, not least because they were not representative of the Wehrmacht officer class as a whole. The reasons why the German generals never overthrew their Führer, even once the war was certainly lost, are many. They include the vital fact that they could not necessarily count on the loyalty of their own men against Hitler, they were still isolated from public affairs, they felt bound by the oath of obedience to the Führer which they had sworn, they stood for a conservative order which did not appeal to German youth, and they found it impossible as a group to put their duty to Germany over their personal interests and ambitions.[15] They were far too weak a reed for Chamberlain (and later Churchill) to base British foreign policy upon.

A month after Munich, on 2 November 1938, Hitler and Mussolini supported Hungary's annexation of southern Slovakia, which took place suddenly and without consultation with Britain and France. This reduced Chamberlain to stating in the House of Commons that 'We never guaranteed the frontiers as they existed. What we did was to guarantee against unprovoked aggression – quite a different thing.' A week later the Nazis unleashed the vicious six-day pogrom against German Jews known to history as Kristallnacht, leaving few under any illusions about the vile nature of Hitler's regime.

When on 15 March 1939 German troops occupied the Bohemian and Moravian rump of Czechoslovakia and dragged non-Germans into the Reich for the first time – and Hitler was driven through a sullen Prague in further triumph – the Chamberlain ministry ran out of explanations and excuses, especially when later that month Hitler denounced the non-aggression pact that he had signed with Poland five years before.

On 1 April Britain and France therefore guaranteed Poland, promising to go to war against Germany if she invaded. The guarantee was intended as a trip-wire to deter any future adventures by Hitler, and similar promises were made to Romania and Greece a fortnight later. On 27 April Britain introduced conscription for men aged twenty and twenty-one, on the same day that Hitler denounced the 1935 Anglo-German Naval Agreement that had set limits to the size of both countries' fleets. The next month Mussolini and Hitler signed a ten-year alliance, known as the Pact of Steel.

'War is not only not inevitable,' Sir Thomas Inskip, the Minister for Defence Co-ordination nonetheless reassured the British public in August 1939, 'but it is unlikely.' He had not counted on Hitler pulling off perhaps the greatest coup of his entire career so far. With the

German generals insisting that Poland should not be invaded unless Russia's neutrality had first been secured, Hitler decided upon the most astonishing political volte-face of the twentieth century.[16] In total contravention to everything he had always said about his loathing of Bolshevism, he sent his new Foreign Minister, Joachim von Ribbentrop, to Moscow to negotiate with Josef Stalin's new Foreign Minister, Vyacheslav Molotov. Placed beside the imperative for Stalin to encourage a war between Germany and the West, and the equal imperative for Hitler to fight a war on only one front rather than two as in the Great War, their Communist and Fascist ideologies subsided in relative importance, and in the early hours of 24 August 1939 a comprehensive Nazi–Soviet non-aggression pact was signed. 'All the isms have become wasms,' quipped a British official.

Up until that point Hitler's treatment of the Austrian President Kurt von Schuschnigg, the Czech President Emil Hácha and the British and French leaders had been characterized by hucksterism, bullying and constant piling on of pressure, to which they had responded with a combination of gullibility, appeasement and weary resignation. Yet with his lifelong enemies the Bolsheviks, Hitler was attentive and respectful, though of course no less duplicitous. Their time would come.

The Molotov–Ribbentrop Pact safely signed, Hitler wasted no time. One week later, on the evening of Thursday, 31 August 1939, an unnamed inmate of a German concentration camp was taken by the Gestapo to a radio transmitting station outside the frontier town of Gleiwitz. He was then dressed up in a Polish Army uniform and shot. A propaganda story was quickly concocted alleging that the Poles had attacked Germany, thus enabling Hitler to invade Poland 'in self-defence', without needing to declare war first. Operation Himmler, as this farcically transparent pantomime was codenamed, thus encompassed the very first death of the Second World War. Considering the horrific ways in which fifty million people were to die over the next six years, the hapless prisoner was one of the lucky ones.

The *Deutschland* itself – launched in 1931 – was renamed the *Lützow* in 1940, because Hitler was concerned about the demoralizing effect if a ship of that name was sunk. (For the same reason he never allowed a ship to be named the *Adolf Hitler*, despite plenty of prompting from obsequious admirals.) The *Lützow* saw action off Norway in 1940, fought Allied convoy escorts in 1942, was heavily damaged in air raids and was finally scuttled in May 1945, along with National Socialism itself. Yet had Hitler stuck to the terms of the Pact that he agreed with Blomberg on board the battleship in April 1934, allowing the professional strategists of the Reichswehr to set the timing, course and pace of the coming war while he confined himself to boosting morale and making exhortations to self-sacrifice, might the outcome of the Second World War have been different? Might the Pact that was made aboard the *Deutschland* have left *Deutschland über alles*? This is one of the questions which this book will seek to answer.

PART I

Onslaught

It is recorded of the great Moltke, that when he was being praised for his generalship in the Franco-Prussian War, and was told by an admirer that his reputation would rank with such great captains as Napoleon, Frederick or Turenne, he answered 'No, for I have never conducted a retreat.'

Frederick von Mellenthin, *Panzer Battles* (1955), p. 236

I

Four Invasions

September 1939–April 1940

If we lose this war, then God have mercy on us.
Hermann Göring to Hitler's interpreter,
Paul Schmidt, 3 September 1939[1]

Although the international situation, and his months of sabre-rattling against Poland, meant that his invasion of that country could not be a surprise attack, Hitler hoped, with good reason, that the Wehrmacht's new Blitzkrieg (lightning war) tactics would deliver a tactical shock to the Poles. Blitzkrieg tactics, which relied on very close, radio-controlled contact between fast-moving tank columns, motorized artillery, Luftwaffe bombers and fighters and truck-borne infantry, swept all before them. Hitler's dislike of static, attritional warfare was a natural response to his years in the 16th Bavarian Infantry Regiment between 1914 and 1918. His job as a *Meldegänger* (battalion runner) in that conflict involved waiting for a gap in artillery salvoes and then springing forward in a semi-crouched stance, sprinting from trench to shell-hole taking messages. He was thus brave and conscientious, probably never killed anyone himself, and always refused promotions that would take him away from his comrades because, as his regimental adjutant Fritz Wiedemann later stated, 'For Gefreiter [Corporal] Hitler, the Regiment was home.'[2] He even won two Iron Crosses, Second Class and First Class.

Having survived four years of stalemate and attrition, Hitler had learnt by the age of twenty-nine, when the war ended, that tactical surprise was of inestimable advantage in warfare, and as he was later to write in *Mein Kampf*: 'Even a man of thirty will have much to learn in the course of his life, but this will only be a supplement.' Through-out his political career as a revolutionary, he constantly attempted to employ surprise, usually with great success. The attempted coup of 1923 known as the Beerhall Putsch had surprised even its titular leader, General Ludendorff, and Röhm had had no inkling of the Night of the Long Knives. Yet the Poles were expecting Hitler's sudden attack, because exactly one week beforehand their country had been invaded by a tiny detachment of Germans who had not been informed of the postponement of the invasion originally planned for dawn on Saturday, 26 August.

Part of Germany's plan to invade Poland, Fall Weiss (Plan White), involved small groups of Germans dressed in *Räuberzivil* (robbers' civvies) crossing the border the night before and seizing key strategic points before dawn on the day of the invasion. The secret Abwehr (German intelligence) battalion detailed to undertake these operations was given the euphemistic title of Construction Training Company 800 for Special Duties. A twenty-four-man group under the command of Leutnant Dr Hans-Albrecht Herzner was instructed to prepare the way for the assault of the 7th Infantry Division by infiltrating the border and capturing a railway station at Mosty in the Jablunka Pass running through the Carpathian mountains, to prevent the destruction of the single-track railway tunnel which was the shortest connection between Warsaw and Vienna.[3] Crossing the border into the forests at 00.30 on 26 August, Herzner's group got lost and was split up in the dark, but Herzner managed to capture the railway station at Mosty with thirteen men at 03.30 and cut the telephone and telegraph lines, only to discover that the Polish detonators had already been removed from the tunnel by the defenders. Polish tunnel guards then attacked his unit, wounding one of his men. Out of contact with the Abwehr, Herzner could not know that, with only a few hours to go, the previous evening Hitler had postponed Plan White until the following week, and that every other commando unit had been informed of this except his. It was not until 09.35 that the Abwehr finally managed to get through and order Herzner, who by then had lost another man wounded and had killed a Pole in the firefight, to release his prisoners and return to base immediately.

After a further series of incidents Herzner's group recrossed the border at 13.30. The German Government explained to the Poles that the whole affair had been a mistake due to the lack of a defined border line in the forest. As the operation had not been an official military one, therefore, and had taken place in peacetime, Herzner very Teutonically put in for overnight expenses of 55 Reichsmarks and 86 pfennigs.[4] Equally Teutonically, the authorities did not initially want to award him the Iron Cross (Second Class) for exploits that technically took place in peacetime. (They eventually did, but it did him little good: after breaking his back in a motor accident in 1942 Herzner drowned during his swimming therapy.)

On 28 August Hitler had abrogated the 1934 German–Polish non-aggression treaty – a curious and unusual act of legalism from him – so the Poles could hardly have had a clearer indication that Germany was on the verge of invading their country, but they could have had little intimation of Blitzkrieg tactics, hitherto the preserve of certain German and British theoretical tacticians. They could estimate accurately where and roughly when the attack would come, but crucially not how. The Poles therefore chose to place the bulk of their troops close to the German border. The Munich crisis the previous autumn, and Hitler's seizure of the rump of Czechoslovakia the following spring, meant that Poland's border with the Reich had been extended from 1,250 to a full 1,750 miles, much further than the Polish Army could adequately defend. Its commander-in-chief, Marshal Edward Śmigły-Rydz, therefore had to decide whether to keep the majority of his forces back behind the natural defensive line formed by the Vistula, San and Narev rivers, or to try to protect Poland's industrial heartlands and best agricultural land in the west of the country.

Śmigły-Rydz decided to commit his troops to defending every inch of Polish soil, which left them perilously exposed. He attempted to deploy across the whole front from Lithuania to the Carpathians, and even kept a special assault group for invading East Prussia, retaining one-third of his force in Poznia and the Polish Corridor. As so often in the history of poor, martyred Poland, the dispositions were brave: otherwise Śmigły-Rydz would simply have had to abandon cities as important as Kraków, Poznań, Bydgoszcz and Łódź, which all lay to the west of the three rivers. Nonetheless, it is hard not to agree with Major-General Frederick von Mellenthin, then the intelligence officer of the German III Corps, that Polish 'plans were lacking a sense of reality'.[5]

At 17.30 hours on Thursday, 31 August 1939, Hitler ordered hostilities to start the next morning, and this time there would be no postponement. So at 04.45 on Friday, 1 September German forces activated Plan White, which had been formulated that June by the German Army High Command, the Oberkommando des Heeres (OKH). The OKH was composed of the commander-in-chief of the Field Army (Feldheer), the Army General Staff, the Army Personnel Office and the commander-in-chief of the Reserve Army (Ersatzheer). Above the OKH in terms of creating grand strategy was the Oberkommando der Wehrmacht (Armed Forces High Command, or OKW). Soon after assuming personal command of the German armed forces in February 1938, Hitler had created the OKW to function as his military staff under his direct command, with Keitel as its chief. Whereas Blomberg had been strenuously opposed by the Navy and Army in his efforts to set up a unified high command, Hitler was not to be baulked. In August 1939, when general mobilization went ahead, OKW consisted of the office of the Chief of Staff (Keitel), a central administrative division, the armed forces administration office (under Jodl) which kept Hitler informed of the military situation, an intelligence office under Admiral Wilhelm Canaris, a war production office and various smaller units concerned with military justice and finance.

According to Plan White, on either side of a relatively weak and stationary centre, two powerful wings of the Wehrmacht would envelop Poland, crush its armed forces and capture Warsaw. Army Group North, under Colonel-General Fedor von Bock, would smash through the Polish Corridor, take Danzig (present-day Gdańsk), unite with the German Third Army in East Prussia, and move swiftly to attack the Polish capital from the north. Meanwhile an even stronger Army Group South, under Colonel-General Gerd von Rundstedt, would punch between the larger Polish forces facing it, push east all the way to Lvov, but also assault Warsaw from the west and north. (At the Jablunka Pass, the Poles did at least destroy the railway tunnel, which was not reopened until 1948.)

The Polish Corridor, which had been intended by the framers of the Versailles Treaty of 1919 to cut off East Prussia from the rest of

Germany, had long been presented as a *casus belli* by the Nazis, as had the ethnically German Baltic port of Danzig, but as Hitler had told a conference of generals in May 1939, 'Danzig is not the real issue; the real point is for us to open up our *Lebensraum* to the east and ensure our supplies of foodstuffs.'[6] Yet much more than mere practicalities drove Hitler. This was to be an existential conflict, fulfilling the prophecies he had made fourteen years before in his political testimony *Mein Kampf*. The German master race would subjugate the Slavs – *Untermenschen* (subhumans) according to Nazi precepts of racial hierarchy – and use their territory to nurture a new Aryan civilization. This was to be the world's first wholly politically ideological war, and it is a contention of this book that that was the primary reason why the Nazis eventually lost it.

The strategy of having a weak centre and two powerful flanks was a brilliant one, and was believed to have derived from Field Marshal Count Alfred von Schlieffen's celebrated pre-Great War study of Hannibal's tactics at the battle of Cannae. Whatever the provenance it worked well, slipping German armies neatly between Polish ones and enabling them to converge on Warsaw from different angles almost simultaneously. Yet what made it irresistible was not German preponderance in men and arms, but above all the new military doctrine of Blitzkrieg. Poland was a fine testing ground for Blitzkrieg tactics: although it had lakes, forests and bad roads, it was nonetheless flat, with immensely wide fronts and firm, late-summer ground ideal for tanks.

Because the British and French Governments, fearful that Germany was about to invade at any moment, had given their guarantee to Poland on 1 April 1939, with the British Prime Minister Neville Chamberlain formally promising her 'all support in the power' of the Allies should she be attacked, Hitler was forced to leave a large proportion of his hundred-division Army in the west, guarding the Siegfried Line, or 'West Wall' – a 3-mile-deep series of still-incomplete fortifications along Germany's western frontier. The fear of a war on two fronts led the Führer to detail no fewer than forty divisions to protect his back. However, three-quarters of these were only second-rate units and they had been left with only three days' ammunition.[7] His best troops, along with all his armoured and mobile divisions and almost all his aircraft, Hitler devoted to the attack on Poland.

Plan White was drawn up by the OKH planners, with Hitler merely putting his imprimatur on the final document. At this early stage of the war there was a good deal of genuine mutual respect between Hitler and his generals, aided by the fact that he had not so far interfered too closely in their troop dispositions and planning; his two Iron Crosses gave him some standing with his generals. Hitler's own self-confidence in military affairs was singular. This may have come in part from the sense of superiority of many veteran infantrymen that it was they who had borne the brunt of the fighting in the Great War. Both the OKW Chief of Staff Wilhelm Keitel, and his lieutenant the Chief of the Wehrmacht Operations Staff, Alfred Jodl, had been artillerymen and Staff officers in the Great War: their battle had been an indirect one, although Keitel had been wounded. General Walther von Reichenau, Colonel-General Walther von Brauchitsch and General Hans von Kluge were also artillerymen, and General Paul von Kleist and Lieutenant-General Erich Manstein had been in the cavalry (although Manstein too had been wounded). Some generals, such as Heinz Guderian, had been in Signals, and others such as Maximilian von Weichs had spent most of the war on the General Staff. Whatever the reason, Hitler was not as cowed as an ex-corporal would usually have been among generals. Although he had been a mere *Meldegänger*, he would also have learnt something about tactics. It is possible that had Hitler been a German citizen he would have been commissioned; knowing this himself, he might well have emerged from the war with a sense of being capable of commanding a battalion, which only a technicality had prevented.[8] Many of the generals of 1939 had spent the 1920s in the paramilitary militia known as the Freikorps and the tiny 'Treaty' Army that was permitted under Versailles. Before Hitler came to power, this had involved little more than Staff work, training and studying. That would not have overly impressed Hitler, whatever titular rank those serving in it had achieved. For all that former Lieutenant-Colonel Winston Churchill was to mock 'Corporal' Hitler for his lowly Great War rank in the trenches, the Führer seems to have been under no inferiority complex when dealing directly with soldiers who had wildly outranked him in the previous conflict.

*

Plan White devoted sixty divisions to the conquest of Poland, including five Panzer divisions of 300 tanks each, four light divisions (of fewer tanks and some horses) and four fully motorized divisions (with lorry-borne infantry), as well as 3,600 operational aircraft and much of the powerful Kriegsmarine (German Navy). Poland meanwhile had only thirty infantry divisions, eleven cavalry brigades, two mechanized brigades, 300 medium and light tanks, 1,154 field guns and 400 aircraft ready for combat (of which only 36 Łoś aircraft were not obsolete), as well as a fleet of only four modern destroyers and five submarines. Although these forces comprised fewer than one million men, Poland tried to mobilize her reservists, but that was far from complete when the devastating blow fell from 630,000 German troops under Bock and 886,000 under Rundstedt.

As dawn broke on 1 September, Heinkel He-111 bombers, with top speeds of 350kph carrying 2,000-kilogram loads, as well as Dorniers and Junkers Ju-87 (Stuka) dive-bombers, began pounding Polish roads, airfields, railway junctions, munition dumps, mobilization centres and cities, including Warsaw. Meanwhile, the training ship *Schleswig Holstein* in Danzig harbour started shelling the Polish garrison at Westerplatte. The Stukas had special sirens attached whose screams hugely intensified the terror of those below. Much of the Polish Air Force was destroyed on the ground, and air superiority – which was to be a vital factor in this six-year conflict – was quickly won by the Luftwaffe. The Messerschmitt Me-109 had a top speed of 470kph, and the far slower Polish planes stood little chance, however brave their pilots. Furthermore, Polish anti-aircraft defences – where there were any – were inadequate.

In charge of the two armoured divisions and two light divisions of Army Group North was General Heinz Guderian, a long-time exponent of – indeed passionate proselytizer for – the tactics of Blitzkrieg. Wielding his force as an homogeneous entity, by contrast with Army Group South where tanks were split up among different units, Guderian scored amazing successes as he raced ahead of the main body of the infantry. Polish retaliation was further hampered by vast numbers of refugees taking to the roads. Once they were bombed and machine-gunned from the air in further pursuance of Blitzkrieg tactics, chaos ensued.

Hitler needed the Polish campaign to be over quickly in case of an attack in the west, but it was not until 11 a.m. on Sunday, 3 September that Neville Chamberlain's Government finally declared war on Germany, with the French Government reluctantly following six hours later. It soon became clear to everyone – except the ever hopeful Poles – that the Western Allies were not about to assault the Siegfried Line, even though the French had eighty-five divisions there facing forty German. A fear of massive German air attacks devastating London and Paris partly explained Allied inaction, but even if Britain and France had attacked in the west Poland could probably not have been saved in time. As it was, although the RAF Advanced Air Striking Force reached France by 9 September, the main British Expeditionary Force (BEF) under Lord Gort VC did not start to arrive on the Continent until the next day.

What was not appreciated by the Allies at the time was the ever present fear that Hitler had of an attack from the west while he was dealing with matters in the east. In a letter to the Deputy Prison Governor at Nuremberg in 1946, Wilhelm Keitel averred that 'What the Führer most feared and repeatedly brought up' was firstly the possibility of a 'Secret agreement between the French and Belgian general staffs for a surprise thrust by the French high-speed (motorized) forces through Belgium, and over the German frontier, so as to burst into the German industrial zone in the Ruhr', and secondly the possibility of a 'Secret agreement between the British Admiralty and the Dutch general staff for a surprise landing of British troops in Holland, for an attack on the German north flank'.[9] In the event, Hitler needn't have worried about either development, as neither France nor Britain, let alone neutral Belgium and Holland, was so much as contemplating anything so imaginative and vigorous. It was true that Chamberlain brought the long-term anti-Nazi prophet Winston Churchill into his government as first lord of the Admiralty, with political responsibility for the Royal Navy, but that was going to be Britain's most bellicose act for the moment, except for one unsuccessful bombing raid on the Wilhelmshaven naval base and the dropping of twelve million leaflets on Germany, urging her people to overthrow their warmongering Führer. It was unlikely that this would happen just as he was about to pull off one of Germany's greatest victories.

German propaganda, controlled by Dr Joseph Goebbels, a man who fully deserves the cliché 'evil genius', had long claimed that the Reich had a fifth column of supporters inside Poland, further adding to the atmosphere of terror and mistrust there. It was to be a tactic used often in the future, although on this occasion it was to lead to around 7,000 ethnic Germans being massacred by their Polish neighbours and retreating Polish troops.[10] This baleful aspect of racial Total War was to be acted out on a monstrous scale across the Continent, but while on this occasion the Poles did it from terror of betrayal, soon the Nazis were to respond in cold blood, and on a far, far larger scale.

By 5 September the Polish Corridor was cut off entirely. The Polish Pomorze Army was encircled in the north by 8 September and the German Tenth Army under General Walther von Reichenau and the Eighth Army under General Johannes Blaskowitz had soon broken over and around the Polish Kraków and Łódź armies by the 17th. The Polish Government fled first to Lublin and thence to Romania, where they were initially welcomed, but then, under pressure from Hitler, interned.

On the night of 6 September, France invaded Germany, at least technically. Hoping to give the Poles some respite, the French Commander-in-Chief, General Maurice Gamelin, ordered an advance 5 miles into the Saarland along a 15-mile-wide front, capturing a dozen abandoned German villages. The Germans retreated behind the defences of the Siegfried Line and waited. As France was still mobilizing, no further action was taken, and five days later the French returned to their original positions with orders simply to undertake reconnaissance work. It was hardly 'all support in the power' of the Allies, and there is no evidence that Hitler removed a single man from the east to counter it.

On 8 September, Reichenau's Tenth Army reached the outskirts of Warsaw, but was initially repulsed by fierce Polish resistance. Despite years of threats by Hitler, the Poles had not built extensive fixed defences, preferring to rely on counter-attacks. This all changed in early September when the city centre of Warsaw witnessed makeshift barricades being thrown up, anti-tank ditches dug and turpentine barrels made ready for ignition. Hitler's plan was to seize Warsaw before the US Congress met on 21 September, so as to present it and the world with a fait accompli, but that was not quite to happen.

'The Polish Army will never emerge again from the German embrace,' predicted Hermann Göring on 9 September. Until then, the Germans had operated a textbook attack, but that night General Tadeusz Kutrzeba of the Poznań Army took over the Pomorze Army and crossed the Bzura river in a brilliant attack against the flank of the German Eighth Army, launching the three-day battle of Kutno which incapacitated an entire German division. Only when the Panzers of the Tenth Army returned from besieging Warsaw were the Poles forced back. According to German and Italian propaganda, some Polish cavalry charged German tanks armed only with lances and sabres, but this did not in fact happen at all. Nonetheless, as Mellenthin observed, 'All the dash and bravery which the Poles frequently displayed could not compensate for a lack of modern arms and serious tactical training.'[11] By contrast, the Wehrmacht training was completely modern and impressively flexible: some troops could even perform in tanks, as infantry and as artillerymen, while all German NCOs were trained to serve as officers if the occasion demanded. Of course it helped enormously that the Germans were the aggressors, and so knew when the war was going to start.

In 1944 the Guards officer and future military historian Michael Howard went on a course 'learning everything that was to be known about the German army: its organisation, uniforms, doctrine, personnel, tactics, weapons – everything except why it was so *bloody good*'.[12] Part of the answer goes back to the way that the Junker state of Prussia in the seventeenth century had allowed bright middle-class youths to win advancement in the Prussian Army: Voltaire said, 'Where some states have an army, the Prussian army has a state!' and his contemporary the Comte de Mirabeau agreed, quipping that 'War is the national industry of Prussia.' Status, respect and prestige attached to officers in uniform. The lesson of the great national revival of 1813 was discipline, and it was not forgotten even in the defeat of 1918. Hindenburg, even though a defeated general, was elected president. The Germans were fighting their fifth war of aggression in seventy-five years, and, as Howard also records, when it came to digging deep slit-trenches or aiming howitzers they were simply better than the Allies. Blitzkrieg required extraordinarily close co-operation between the services, and the Germans achieved it triumphantly. It took the Allies half a war to catch up.

With only three Polish divisions covering the 800-mile-long eastern border, it came as a complete surprise when at dawn on 17 September the USSR invaded Poland, in accordance with secret clauses of the Nazi–Soviet Pact that had been agreed on 24 August. The Russians wanted revenge for their defeats at Poland's hands in 1920, access to the Baltic States and a buffer zone against Germany, and they opportunistically grasped all three, without any significant resistance. Their total losses amounted to only 734 killed.[13] Stalin used Polish 'colonialism' in the Ukraine and Belorussia as his (gossamer-thin) *casus belli*, arguing that the Red Army had invaded Poland 'in order to restore peace and order'. The Poles were thus doubly martyred, smashed between the Nazi hammer and the Soviet anvil, and were not to regain their independence and freedom until November 1989, half a century later. In one of the most despicable acts of naked viciousness of the war, in the spring of 1940 the Red Army transported 4,100 Polish officers, who had surrendered to them under the terms of the Geneva Convention, to a forest near Smolensk called Katyń, where they were each shot in the back of the head. Vasily Blokhin, chief executioner of the Russian secret service, the NKVD, led the squad responsible, wearing leather overalls and an apron and long leather gloves to protect his uniform from the blood and brains, and using a German Walther pistol because it did not jam when it got hot from repeated use.[14] (Nonetheless he complained he got blisters on his trigger finger by the end of the third day of continuous executions.) In all, 21,857 Polish soldiers were executed by the Soviets at Katyń and elsewhere – an operation which, after the Germans had invaded Russia, Stalin's police chief Lavrenti Beria admitted had been 'a mistake'. When the Germans uncovered the mass graves on 17 April 1943, Goebbels broadcast the Katyń Massacre to the world, but Soviet propaganda made out that it had been undertaken by the Nazis themselves, a lie that was knowingly colluded in by the British Foreign Office until as late as 1972, even though charges against the Germans over Katyń were dropped at the Nuremberg Trials.

Because by mid-September the Germans had already moved into several areas behind Warsaw, and had indeed taken Brest-Litovsk and Lvov, some fighting inadvertently broke out between Russians and Germans, with two Cossacks killed in one incident and fifteen Germans in another. Ribbentrop, the German Foreign Minister, flew to Moscow in order to agree the lines of demarcation, and after an evening at the Bolshoi watching *Swan Lake*, and tough negotiations with his Russian counterpart, Molotov, lasting until 5 o'clock the next morning, it was agreed that the Germans would get Warsaw and Lublin, and the Russians the rest of eastern Poland and a free hand in the Baltic. The Germans withdrew from towns such as Brest-Litovsk and Białystok in the new Russian sector, and the fourth partition in Poland's history was effectively complete. Molotov would have done well, however, to take note of Hitler's statement made many years before in *Mein Kampf*: 'Let no one argue that in concluding an alliance with Russia we need not immediately think of war, or, if we did, that we could thoroughly prepare for it. An alliance whose aim does not embrace a plan for war is senseless and worthless. Alliances are concluded only for struggle.'[15]

After a full day of bombing on 25 September, with no prospect of meaningful help from the Western Allies, a full-scale assault from the Russians in the east, communications cut between Śmigły-Rydz and much of his Army, and with food and medical supplies running dangerously low, Warsaw capitulated on the 27th. It was then three days before the Germans agreed to help the wounded in the city, by which time for many it was too late. Field kitchens were set up only for as long as the newsreel cameras were there. By 5 October all resistance had ended; 217,000 Polish soldiers passed into Russian captivity and 693,000 into German. Fortunately between 90,000 and 100,000 managed to escape the country via Lithuania, Hungary and Romania, to make their way westwards and join the Free Polish forces under General Władysław Sikorski, the Prime Minister in exile, who was in Paris when the war broke out and who set up a government in exile in Angers in France. About 100,000 Poles in the Russian sector – aristocrats, intellectuals, trade unionists, churchmen, politicians, veterans of the 1920–21 Russo-Polish War, indeed anyone who might form the nucleus of a new national leadership – were arrested by the

NKVD, and sent to concentration camps from which virtually none emerged.

In the four-week campaign the Germans had lost 8,082 killed and 27,278 wounded, whereas 70,000 Polish soldiers and 25,000 civilians had been killed, and 130,000 soldiers wounded. 'The operations were of considerable value in "blooding" our troops,' concluded Mellenthin, 'and teaching them the difference between real war with live ammunition and peacetime manoeuvres.' It had indeed been 'lightning war', and on 5 October a triumphant Adolf Hitler travelled to Warsaw in his special train, for some reason named *Amerika*, to visit his victorious troops. 'Take a good look around Warsaw,' he told the war correspondents there. 'That is how I can deal with any European city.'[16] It was true.

What was to be called the policy of *Schrecklichkeit* (frightfulness) had begun as soon as the Germans had entered Poland. For the master race to have their living space, large numbers of Slavic and Jewish *Untermenschen* had to disappear, and during the war Poland lost a staggering 17.2 per cent of her population. The commander of three Totenkopf (Death's Head) SS regiments, Theodor Eicke, ordered his men to 'incarcerate or annihilate' every enemy of National Socialism that they found as they followed the troops into Poland.[17] Since Nazism was a racial and political ideology, that meant that huge swathes of the Polish people were automatically classed as enemies, to whom no mercy could be shown. The Wehrmacht took active part in the violence: the country was handed over to civilian administration on 26 October, only eight weeks after war broke out, but by then the German Army had, without special orders needing to be given, burnt 531 towns and villages and killed thousands of Polish POWs.[18] The claim made by many German soldiers to Allied re-education officers, and to each other, that they had been simple soldiers who had known nothing of the genocide against the Slavs and the Jews – or at best had heard only rumours – was a lie.

The Schutzstaffel (defence unit, or SS) was originally the protective guard of the National Socialist Party. It was formally described as an independent *Gliederung* (formation) of the Party, led by its Reichsführer-SS (Chief of the SS), Heinrich Himmler. Yet by the time of the outbreak of war it had grown, and by 1944 could be described accurately by an Allied briefing book as 'a state within a state, superior both to the Party and the government'. Officially described after Hitler came to power as 'protecting the internal security of the Reich', the SS revelled in the terror its ruthlessness and cruelty inspired. 'I know that there are millions in Germany who sicken at the sight of the black uniforms of our SS,' wrote Himmler in a brochure for his organization entitled *Die Schutzstaffeln*, in 1936. 'We understand that well, and we do not expect to be loved by too many.'[19]

From the early days when it provided the bodyguards for Nazi street and beerhall speakers, the SS grew – especially after it wiped out the leadership of its rival the SA – into an organization that was intimately involved in many aspects of the state. As well as providing 'the Führer's most personal, selected guard', the SS promoted the doctrine of 'Race and Blood'; dominated the police force; set up a military section – the Waffen-SS – numbering 830,000 by 1945, which fought in every campaign except Norway and Africa, and the Toten-kopf Verbände, a self-contained entity which ran the concentration and extermination camps; ruled the state security service, the Sicher-heitsdienst (SD); and had its own depots and notoriously tough training establishments, as well as having departments covering economics, supply, works and buildings, finance, legal affairs, industrial and agricultural undertakings, medical matters, personnel, racial quality, the family, resettlement, discipline, camp construction, the regions, liaison, pardons and reprieves, the strengthening of Germanism, signals and communications, education, folk schools and the repatriation of racial Germans. These SS entities were quite separate from the rest of the German state.[20] Hitler devised their motto: *Meine Ehre heisst Treue* (My honour is loyalty) in 1931, neatly encapsulating his need to have a force that he could trust to put allegiance to him before any system of morality.

The nature of their operations became immediately apparent. On 5 September 1939, a thousand civilians were shot by the SS at Bydgoszcz, and at Piotrków the Jewish district was torched. The next day nineteen Polish officers who had surrendered were shot at Mrocza. Meanwhile, the entire Jewish population began to be herded into ghettos across Poland. This happened even to Jewish farmers, despite the pressing need for efficient food production in the new eastern satrapy of the Third Reich – early evidence that the Nazis would be willing to put their war against the Jews even before their war against the Allies. On the Day of Atonement, the holiest day in their calendar, thousands of Jews were locked into the synagogue in Bydgoszcz and refused access to lavatories, forcing them to use their prayer shawls to clean themselves. Worse was to come.

Both the Nazi–Soviet Pact of 24 August 1939 and its coda in Moscow the following month gave Stalin a completely free hand in the north, and he moved swiftly to capitalize on it. Hoping to protect Leningrad against any future German attack, he tried to turn the Gulf of Finland into a Soviet seaway, even though its northern shore was Finnish and most of its southern shore Estonian. Latvia, Lithuania and Estonia were bullied into agreements that allowed the Red Army to be stationed at key points on their territory, and in June 1940 their sovereignty was extinguished altogether by effective annexation. Surrounded on three sides by mighty Russia, they had no real choice but to acquiesce. Finland was another matter, even though she had a tiny fraction of Russia's population and an 800-mile border with her.

In October Stalin summoned the Finns to Moscow to be presented with Soviet demands. They sent the leader of the Social Democrat Party, Väinö Tanner, who has been described as 'tough, tactless, stubborn and frequently bloody-minded', a curious choice of representative when the survival of one's nation was at stake. Meanwhile, they mobilized. Stalin and Molotov wanted a thirty-year lease on the naval base of Cape Hanko, the cession of the Arctic port of Petsamo and three small islands in the Gulf, as well as the moving back of the frontier on the Karelian Isthmus, which was presently only 15 miles from Leningrad. In return for these 1,066 square miles of territory, the Russians were willing to give Finland 2,134 square miles of Russian Karelia around Repola and Porajorpi.

On the face of it, the deal did not look unreasonable, but when considered strategically the key nodal points the Bolshevik leaders were demanding made it clear that Finnish sovereignty would be hopelessly compromised, and the Finns decided to fight rather than submit. Matters were not helped when Tanner mentioned his and Stalin's supposedly shared Menshevik past, a libel on the Bolshevik leader. On 28 November the USSR abrogated its 1932 non-aggression treaty with Finland and two days later, without declaring war, the Russians bombed Helsinki and invaded Finland with 1.2 million men, opening a bitter 105-day struggle that some have likened to the Spartans' stand at Thermopylae.

The world prepared to watch another small nation being crushed by a totalitarian monolith. The Finnish Army comprised ten divisions, with only thirty-six artillery pieces per division, all of pre-1918 vintage, and inadequate small arms (although they did have the excellent 9mm Suomi machine pistol), supported by few modern aircraft. 'They lacked everything,' one historian has noted, 'except courage and discipline.'[21] The Russians, by contrast, came across the border with 1,500 tanks, 3,000 aircraft and a complete assumption of a quick victory, as in Poland.[22] The Red Army divided its attack into four parts: the Seventh and Thirteenth Armies would smash through the Finnish defences on the Karelian Isthmus known as the Mannerheim Line and capture Viipuri (Viborg), the second city of Finland. Meanwhile the Eighth Army would march round the northern shore of Lake Lagoda to fall on Viipuri from the north. The Ninth Army would attack the waist of Finland, slicing it in two, and in the far north the Fourteenth Army would capture Petsamo and Nautsi, cutting the country off from the Arctic Sea. The comprehensiveness of the plan has been described by one military historian as 'imaginative, flexible and totally unrealistic'.[23]

Although the Fourteenth Army took its objectives in the first ten days, nothing else went right for the Russians for the next two months. The Seventh Army, comprising twelve divisions, three tank brigades and a mechanized corps, could not break through the wilderness of barbed wire, gun emplacements, anti-tank 'dragons' teeth' and well-camouflaged pillboxes of the Mannerheim Line, which was fiercely defended. The frozen ground was so hard that the Red Army occasionally had to use dynamite to move enough earth to build makeshift trenches. Even though the Finns had never faced tanks before, and were woefully under-equipped with anti-tank weapons – at least until they captured them from the Russians – they devised makeshift ways of stopping their advance, including, ironically enough, 'Molotov cocktails' (bottles of petrol lit with rags).[24] This proved easier in the early stages when Russian tanks were not supported closely enough by Russian infantry, and in the dark that descended early in the Arctic winter and stayed till late.

The seventy-two-year-old 'Defender of Finland' after whom the Line was named, Field Marshal Baron Carl von Mannerheim, proved an inspired leader throughout the campaign, keeping his reserves in the south and correctly predicting the Russians' next moves, possibly because he had been an officer in the Tsarist Army throughout the Great War. Told by Moscow that the Finnish proletariat would welcome them as liberators, the Russian soldiers were shocked when the entire nation united behind 'the Defender of Finland' instead.

It was the five divisions of the Russian Ninth Army in the centre of the country that suffered the most. Although on the map the vast wastes might seem to favour an invader, the many forests and lakes channelled the Russian forces, unfamiliar with the terrain, into a series of ambushes as temperatures dipped in that unusually cold winter to as low as −50 Celsius. The Leningrad–Murmansk railway line had only one siding going off towards the Finnish border, and although the Russians took Salla in central Finland, they were flung back before they reached Kemijärvi. The Finns burnt their own farms and villages, booby-trapped farm animals, destroyed anything that could provide the Russians with food and shelter, and, equipped with skis and local knowledge, laid mines on tracks through the forests that were soon covered in snow. Wearing white camouflage uniforms, which inexplicably the Russians were not given, the Finns were nicknamed Bielaja Smert (White Death) by their bewildered enemy.

Further south, the Russian 163rd and 44th Divisions were annihilated around the ashes of the village of Suomussalmi, in a ferociously brilliant Finnish operation that ranks with any of the Second World War. A logging, fishing and hunting community of 4,000 people before the war, it was captured by the 163rd (Tula) Motorized Rifle Division on 9 December, but was then cut off by the Finnish 9th Brigade under Colonel Hjalmar Siilasvuo. Because their leaders had assumed an easy victory, many of the Russians had been sent into sub-Arctic Finland in December lacking winter clothes and felt boots, as the Finns discovered by listening to their radio transmissions, which were equally astonishingly sent *en clair* rather than in code. Freezing, starving and cut off from retreat by the Finnish 9th Brigade for a fortnight, the morale of the 163rd Division broke on Christmas Eve and they fled eastwards across the frozen Lake Kiantajärvi. The Finns then sent up two Bristol Blenheim medium bombers to smash the ice, sending tanks, horses, men and vehicles tumbling into the freezing water below. As the historian of the Russo-Finnish Winter War laconically records: 'They are still there.'[25] The Russian 44th Division that had come to rescue the 163rd were within earshot of the débâcle, and could hear their comrades dying, but they were not given orders to move. On the night of New Year's Day they became the next victims of the White Death, as the barometer dipped again to –30 Celsius. By constantly mortar-bombing their sixty field kitchens at mealtimes, the Finns kept the Russians short of hot food, and when the Russians lit fires the Finns machine-gunned them from the treetops, 'easily picking out the dark silhouettes of the men against the snow'.[26] The standard Red Army rifle, the single-shot bolt-action 7.62mm 1902 Moisin-Nagant, became inoperable when its gun-oil lubricant froze in conditions below –15 Celsius, and armoured vehicles either had to be kept running, at ruinous expense in fuel, or they would seize up and block the narrow passageways through the forest.

'We don't let them rest,' said General Kurt Wallenius of the Finnish Northern Army; 'we don't let them sleep. This is a war of numbers against brains.' Sleep for the 44th was next to impossible because of the vehicle engines, terrified horses, Finnish professional trackers and hunters who made excellent snipers, and even 'the sharp reports of the trees as their very sap froze'. Those who resorted to vodka found that, despite the initial sense of warmth, body heat was ultimately lost. The slightest wounds exposed to the air froze and went gangrenous. Frozen corpses were piled up, one on top of the other, as the Finns methodically moved from sector to sector, wiping out Russian resistance. By 5 January, a thousand Russian prisoners had been taken, a further 700 soldiers had escaped back to the Russian lines, and over 27,000 had been killed, all for the loss of 900 Finns. As one of his officers remarked to Colonel Siilasvuo, 'The wolves will eat well this winter.' The Finns captured 42 tanks, 102 field guns and 300 vehicles at Suomussalmi, as well as thousands of the conical-shaped Red Army hats (*budenovka*) that they later used in deception operations. Indeed, they captured more military hardware than they received from outside sources, however much the League of Nations supported Finland's struggle (expelling the USSR from its ranks on 14 December) and however much the Western Allies' Supreme War Council debated sending aid (they agreed to it only on 5 February, by which time it was too late).

The loss of the two divisions at Suomussalmi, when compounded with the reversals at the Mannerheim Line and the victory of Colonel Paavo Talvela, who destroyed the 139th and 75th Red Army Divisions at Tolvajärvi on Christmas Eve, sent a humiliating message around the globe for the USSR, even though the Finns could not follow up these successes for lack of troops (they were conscripting fifteen-year-olds as it was). Hitler in particular believed he learnt lessons about the performance of the Red Army that were to affect his decision to invade Russia the following year. Yet they were substantially the wrong ones.

Stalin's purging of the officer corps in 1937 had seriously weakened the Red Army. The former Chief of Staff Marshal Tukhachevsky was shot, and with him died new thinking about the development of mass armoured formations operating deep inside enemy territory. General Konstantin Rokossovsky, one of those who were tortured during that time – though not shot despite his Polish origins – later said that purges were even worse for morale than when artillery fired on one's own troops because it would have to have been very accurate artillery fire to achieve such damage. Three out of the five Soviet marshals were purged in 1937–8, thirteen of the fifteen army commanders, fifty-seven of the eighty-five corps commanders, 110 of the 195 divisional commanders and 220 of the 406 brigade commanders.[27] In total, around 43,000 officers were killed or imprisoned, although 20,000 were later released. Yet no fewer than seventy-one out of the original eighty-five senior members of the USSR's Military Council were dead by 1941.[28] When Rokossovsky, who had been beaten so badly in prison that he lost eight teeth and had three ribs broken, reported to Stalin for duty after being reinstated, Stalin asked him where he had been. Rokossovsky told him, whereupon Stalin laughed and said, 'A fine time you chose to go to prison!' before getting down to business.[29]

Although the Soviet forces were staggeringly badly led at the outset of the Winter War, they learnt quickly. A trusted member of the Supreme Soviet from its creation in 1937, General Semyon Timoshenko was sent to take over on 8 January, and after four or five attacks a day he broke through the Mannerheim Line on 13 February. In Finland the Soviets came to understand the importance of co-ordinating armour, infantry and artillery. However heavy the Russian losses, there were always fresh troops to fling into the struggle. As one Finn put it after the battle of Kuhmo, 'There were more Russians than we had bullets.' When the fighting became purely attritional on the Isthmus, the Finns simply could not carry on bleeding like the Russians could. Furthermore, the Winter War showed that men fought harder when patriotically defending the Soviet Motherland than when in attack. (That was eventually to apply to the German Fatherland too.) Instead of these lessons, Hitler learnt the almost banal one that Stalin had shot a lot of good generals in the late 1930s. He was not the only one, however; on 20 January 1940 Churchill said that Finland 'had exposed for all to see the incapacity of the Red Army'.

On 11 February the Russian 123rd Division broke through the Mannerheim Line close to Summa, leading much of the Seventh Army through two days later. They then moved on to Viipuri. With neutral Norway and Sweden denying access across their territory to the Allies, Petsamo in Russian hands and Hitler closing off the eastern Baltic, no significant help was likely from the West. Since by March as much as one-fifth of his army had become casualties, and there were only 100 Finnish planes left to fight 800 Russian, Mannerheim urged the Government to negotiate, and the Treaty of Moscow was signed on 13 March, while Russian and Finnish troops were still engaged in hand-to-hand combat in central Viipuri. Except for the loss of the whole Karelian Isthmus, the terms were not very much worse from those demanded by Stalin and Molotov in November, before around 200,000 Russians and 25,000 Finns had died, and 680 Russian aircraft and 67 Finnish had been destroyed.[30] Yet Russian military prestige had been severely damaged, and Stalin had created a situation on his north-western border that would require fifteen divisions to police. The moment that Finland sniffed her opportunity for revenge, at the time of Operation Barbarossa in June 1941, she seized it.

*

The six-month hiatus on land between the end of the Polish campaign in October 1939 and Hitler's sudden invasion of Denmark and Norway on 9 April 1940 is known as the Phoney War. With little going on in the West on land and in the skies, the British and French publics were lulled into thinking that the war was not truly a matter of life and death for them in the way that it obviously was for the Poles, and their daily existence was carried on substantially as usual, in all its bureaucracy, inefficiency and occasional absurdity. The National Labour MP Harold Nicolson recorded in his war diaries that the Ministry of Information censors had refused to publish the wording of a leaflet, of which two million copies had been dropped over Germany, on the grounds that 'We are not allowed to disclose information that might be of value to the enemy.'[31]

There was nothing phoney about the war at sea, however. It was perfectly true that the British Air Minister Sir Kingsley Wood made the asinine remark that the RAF should not bomb munitions dumps in the Black Forest, because so much of it was private property, but at sea no such absurdities pertained.[32] As early as 19 August, U-boat captains were sent a seemingly anodyne signal about the scheduling of a submarine officers' reunion, which was the coded order to take up their positions around the British Isles in readiness for imminent action. Within nine hours of the declaration of war, the 1,400 passengers aboard a blacked-out British liner SS *Athenia* were torpedoed on their way from Glasgow to Montreal by *U-30*, whose captain mistook the ship for an armed merchant cruiser. 'There was a column of water near the ship,' recalled a Czech survivor, 'and a black thing like a cigar shot over the sea towards us. There was a bang, and then I saw men on the submarine turn a gun and fire it.' Had they hit the radio mast, and the SOS signal not been transmitted, many more than 112 passengers would have perished.

The first of hundreds of Atlantic convoys left Halifax, Nova Scotia, on 15 September 1939. Learning the doleful lessons of the Great War, the convoy system was adopted, if slowly, by the British between 1939 and 1945, even for ships moving along the coastline between Glasgow and the Thames. Destroyers, frigates and corvettes used an echo-sounding device called Asdic (named after the Allied Submarine Detection Investigation Committee) to try to track U-boats, while the convoys' merchantmen sailed together within a protective cordon. They also adopted a zig-zagging route, the better to outfox their submerged foes. Overall the system was a success, but when a waiting U-boat 'wolf-pack' broke through, the losses among the huddled merchantmen could be correspondingly high, and on occasion as many as half of the vessels were sent to the bottom.

The Royal Navy started the war with only five aircraft carriers, and on 17 September the veteran HMS *Courageous* was sunk in the Western Approaches by two torpedoes from *U-29*, which had already despatched three tankers. She slipped beneath the Hebridean waves in less than fifteen minutes, with only half of her thousand-strong crew being saved, some after an hour in the North Atlantic, where they kept up morale by singing popular songs of the day such as 'Roll Out the Barrel' and 'Show Me the Way to Go Home'. The sea, recalled a survivor, 'was so thick with oil we might have been swimming in treacle'. The following month the Kriegsmarine scored an almost equally spectacular success near by when Lieutenant-Commander Günther Prien's *U-47* got through a 50-foot gap in the defences of Scapa Flow and fired seven torpedoes at the 29,000-ton battleship HMS *Royal Oak*. Three hit, capsizing the ship and killing 810 of her 1,224 crew in only thirteen minutes.

One task of the U-boats was to place magnetic mines in the sea-lanes around the British Isles; this could also be done by parachute by low-flying Heinkel He-111s and by E-boats (motor torpedo boats) and destroyers. By the end of November these had sunk twenty-nine British ships, including the destroyer HMS *Gipsy*, and had also put the brand-new cruiser HMS *Belfast* out of action for three years. Through the immense bravery of bomb-disposal experts Lieutenant-Commanders R. C. Lewis and J. G. D. Ouvry, who removed the two detonators, one of which was ticking audibly, from a mine spotted in the Thames Estuary, the secrets of the steel-hull-activated device were discovered. Within a month, Admiralty scientists had discovered a way of counteracting the mines by fitting electric cables around ships' hulls, to create a negative magnetic, or 'degaussed', field. Soon afterwards a means of blowing up the mines, using wooden-hulled trawlers towing buoyant electrical cables, was also invented.

It was the spotting, disabling and eventual forced scuttling of the

German pocket battleship the *Admiral Graf Spee* that was the Royal Navy's greatest victory during the so-called Phoney War. Operating off South America, Captain Hans Langsdorff had sunk ten ships totalling more than 50,000 tons. The term 'pocket' battleship is somewhat misleading; although a limit of 10,000 tons had been imposed on German warships by the Versailles Treaty, once the *Graf Spee* was loaded up with her six 11-inch, eight 5.9-inch and six 4.1-inch guns, as well as ammunition and stores, she weighed more than half as much again. In the battle of the River Plate on 13 December she took on the 8-inch guns of the cruiser HMS *Exeter*, along with the 6-inch guns of the light cruisers HMS *Ajax* and the New Zealander-crewed HMS *Achilles*, badly damaging the first two ships.

When the *Graf Spee* was forced into the harbour of Montevideo, capital of neutral Uruguay, on 15 December by the pounding she had received, Langsdorff magnanimously released the Allied sailors he had captured from the ships he had sunk, who reported that they had been well treated. Trusting to BBC radio broadcasts about the imminent arrival of the aircraft carrier HMS *Ark Royal* and the battle cruiser HMS *Renown*, and unable to hire a small plane to see whether this was in fact so, Langsdorff sailed the *Graf Spee* to the entrance of Montevideo harbour just before dusk on Sunday, 17 December and scuttled her. The explosions were watched by over 20,000 spectators on the shore, and heard on the radio by millions around the world. In fact only the cruiser HMS *Cumberland* had managed to reach Montevideo; the BBC had patriotically taken part in a giant bluff. Five days later, Langsdorff shot himself.

By the end of 1939, Britain had lost 422,000 tons of shipping (260,000 by mines) against Germany's 224,000, but as a proportion of their total tonnages Germany at 5 per cent had lost more than Britain at 2 per cent. In the naval war of attrition that this was going to be, the relative proportions were more important than the sheer overall tonnages. Had Hitler given first priority in terms of funding to his U-boat fleet on coming to power in 1933, rather than to the Wehrmacht and Luftwaffe, he might have built a force that would have strangled and starved Britain into surrender. Perhaps realizing this, on 15 February 1940 the Führer issued a directive to all U-boat captains stating that any ship, neutral or otherwise, sailing towards a

British-controlled war zone, such as the English Channel, must be sunk without warning. For all the protests this new policy engendered from the neutral ship-owning countries such as Denmark, Sweden and Norway, it was if anything surprising that such orders had not been issued earlier. Besides, the level of respect that Germany felt for Scandinavian neutrality was to be spectacularly demonstrated only three weeks later.

If Poland and Finland had merely demonstrated the impotence of Britain and France – with many Britons and Frenchmen concluding that the appeasing spirit of the 1930s had not been entirely expunged from their Governments' souls – the Norway campaign represented a definite defeat for the Western powers. Grand Admiral Erich Raeder urged Hitler as early as 10 October 1939 to consider invading Norway as a way of protecting the transportation of iron ore from the Gällivare mines in northern Sweden to Germany, and establishing U-boat bases along the fjords, especially at Trondheim. Hitler ordered the OKW to start planning for an invasion in late January 1940. At that point Hitler did not want to divert troops from the attack he was planning in the west, and was persuaded to do so only by signs that the Allies were planning to invade Norway themselves, possibly using aid for Finland as a cloak for their actions.

An incident on 16 February, in which the neutral Norwegians seemed to have taken the Royal Navy's side when HMS *Cossack* daringly rescued 299 British prisoners from a German vessel, the *Altmark*, also persuaded the Führer of Norway's iniquity. Telling General Nikolaus von Falkenhorst, the commander of the corps which was to lead the expedition, that a British invasion of Norway 'would lead them into the Baltic, where we have no troops nor coastal fortifications' and eventually to Berlin itself, Hitler decided to strike.[33] In order to simplify lines of communication, and prevent the Royal Navy operating in the Skagerrak and Kattegat Straits, Denmark would be invaded also.

Although the Allies had lost any Finnish excuse for intervention in mid-March after the Treaty of Moscow was signed between Finland and the USSR, they did indeed plan to invade neutral Norway in order to deny the Gällivare ore fields to Germany, and had actually boarded troops at Scapa Flow, the Royal Navy's base in the Orkney Isles, in order to do so, when the German attack began only twenty-four hours beforehand. (The British military historian Captain Basil Liddell Hart later called the race to invade Norway a 'photo-finish'.) Starting on 8 April, Allied planes dropped mines into the Norwegian Leads, the deep, sheltered waterways between the fjords and the islands along the coast from Stavanger to the Northern Cape, hoping to force German ore ships out into the Norwegian Sea where the Royal Navy could sink them. Operation Wilfred was a blatant incursion into Norwegian territorial waters that preceded Germany's own, and was to lead to the sinking of twenty Norwegian vessels as well as twelve German ones, and when at the end of the Nuremberg Trials Admiral Raeder was given a life sentence for, in part, violating Norway's neutrality, the hypocrisy led to accusations of 'victors' justice'.

The British Admiralty believed that with Britain's naval superiority in the Norwegian Sea it was impossible for the Germans to effect an amphibious invasion of Norway, and so were caught utterly by surprise when at dawn on Tuesday, 9 April Operation Weserübung (Weser Crossing) successfully landed troops – initially no more than 2,000 in each location – and soon secured Oslo, Kristiansand, Bergen, Trondheim and Narvik (the railway terminus for the Gällivare iron-fields). It was one of the great coups of the Second World War. Paratroopers also captured Oslo and Stavanger airfields by daybreak. The British simply could not believe the news that a place as far north as Narvik – 1,200 miles from Germany – had fallen, thinking it must be a mistransmission of the name Larvik, a town near the mouth of the Oslo fjord. The Norwegians, who at the time were concentrating more on the threat to their sovereignty from the Allies than on that from the Axis, were caught by surprise as much as anyone and had no time to mobilize. The Norwegian defence budget of the early 1930s was 35 million kroner, which had increased to only 50 million (£2.5 million) by the time she was invaded. Her Navy was entirely for coastal defence and the Army was small too.[34] Employing only three divisions – although one of those was General Eduard Dietl's crack 3rd Mountain Division – but supported by 800 warplanes and 250 transport planes, the Germans had achieved every objective by the end of their first day. The hazy weather, intricate coastline and German inter-service co-ordination and efficiency, as well as the considerable distances involved, meant that the Allies were unable to interdict the German operation.

Bergen was taken by the light cruiser *Köln* tricking its way into the harbour by using British radio signals. Two brave Norwegian coastal vessels fought back at Narvik, but were sunk. At Trondheim, the *Admiral Hipper* blinded coastal batteries with searchlights, and destroyed one that managed to open fire. Off Bergen, the Luftwaffe's X Air Corps sank the destroyer HMS *Gurkha* and damaged the cruisers HMS *Southampton* and HMS *Glasgow* and the battleship HMS *Rodney*. Allied strategists took this, and the further battering the Royal Navy was to receive from the Luftwaffe during this campaign, as the foremost lesson of Norway: that power had tilted towards the air and away from the sea. With only one of its four active aircraft carriers, HMS *Furious*, in the region – and for reasons of time she had sailed with her torpedo bombers on board but without her fighter squadron – the British could not match the Luftwaffe. Although HMS *Ark Royal* and HMS *Glorious* were sent post-haste from Alexandria to assist the Allied counter-attack, they didn't arrive until 24 April.

The RAF never managed to deploy more than a hundred planes during the campaign, against more than a thousand German, flying from aerodromes as close as Oslo and Stavanger. When the RAF did set up makeshift airfields in Norway its planes had to be kept running around the clock, and 'had to be refuelled with jugs and buckets'.[35] The news that the two battle cruisers *Scharnhorst* and *Gneisenau* were supporting the operation in the Norwegian Sea also distracted Admiralty minds from the possibility of sinking smaller troop-carrying warships.[36] The Allied response to Germany's invasion was swift enough, but haphazard and badly disorganized, and the plans changed more than once as they were being put into practice, with confusion and occasionally chaos resulting. The British troops who were embarked for the invasion of Norway had to be disembarked in Scotland so that the battle cruisers could be chased, leading one military historian to argue that 'the Admiralty saw the whole operation through blinkers'.[37] When they were later re-embarked for the counter-invasion, but without the correct equipment, a sense of incompetence began to attach itself to the campaign which was only to get worse, and which was eventually to help bring down the Chamberlain Government.

Although on 9 April artillery from the Oscarburg fortress near Oslo sank the cruiser *Blücher* – one of the very few victims of coastal guns during the Second World War – the Norwegian capital fell. It nonetheless gave King Haakon VII and his Government time to escape and make a long, brave fighting retreat northwards, with the impressive Otto Ruge being appointed the new Army chief of staff in the process. By contrast, King Christian X of Denmark had no opportunity to flee. As he woke up at 5.15 a.m. that day, he was handed a list of thirteen ultimata by the German Minister (soon to be Plenipotentiary) Cecil von Renthe-Fink. After the deaths of twelve Danes, and appreciating that his country was encircled and unable to resist in any meaningful way, he and the Cabinet prevented a massacre by ordering a general surrender. A fiction was concocted by which it was announced that Denmark had agreed 'to place her neutrality under the protection of the Reich', a somewhat tautological construction but one that allowed the country to retain her non-Nazi government. When the Führer's appeal to Denmark was about to be read over Danish radio, it was discovered that the appeal to Norway had been provided instead, one of the only inefficient aspects of the whole operation, so the announcer had to rewrite it hurriedly just before going on air.[38] With Denmark's collapse in under four hours, the vital Aalborg airfield in North Jutland could now be used by the Luftwaffe to pour supplies and troops into Norway. It also meant that the Royal Navy could not enter the Skagerrak with anything other than submarines.

The Royal Navy could punish the Kriegsmarine once it had landed the invasion force, and in two battles in the fjord off Narvik, on 11 and 13 April, no fewer than nine German destroyers were sunk or put out of action, most of them by the battleship HMS *Warspite*. But the fear that *Scharnhorst* and *Gneisenau* were at Bergen or Trondheim meant that the chance of recapturing the ports early on was lost, even though, as it transpired, the German battle cruisers were not there. Instead the Allies landed 125 miles north of Trondheim at Namsos on the night of 18 April, and 190 miles south of it at Åndalsnes the same day, hoping to cross the snowy wastes in between and take it from the land. After being briefed on this operation at the Admiralty, its designated commander, Major-General Frederick Hotblack, had a heart attack on the Duke of York's Steps on the Mall, on his way back to his club. His successor's plane then crashed on its way to Scotland.

After the Allied force landed at Namsos, under Major-General Sir Adrian Carton de Wiart vc, ceaseless heavy pounding from Heinkel bombers ended hopes that it might take Trondheim. 'The town was destroyed, the timber houses burned, the railhead and everything on it obliterated. Electricity and water supplies were cut off, even the wharves were wrecked,' records one who was there. 'Namsos had ceased to exist.'[39] The bombing in 'the land of the midnight sun' seemed to be round the clock, and was demoralizing for the Allied troops, as was the fact that a French ship carrying skis, snow-shoes, guns and tanks proved too large to get into the harbour.[40] The one-handed, one-eyed, sixty-year-old de Wiart was one of the bravest British officers of the twentieth century. Wounded during earlier wars in the ankle, hip, ear and leg, his body was a virtual scrap-metal yard. He even had shrapnel lodged in his head that he said tickled every time his hair was cut. Yet even he saw no possibility of moving southwards without any RAF support. Namsos was evacuated on 2 May, by which time the British force had already evacuated Åndalsnes.

Up at Narvik the Allied force, which had landed at Harstad in the Lofoten Islands on 14 April, soon numbered 20,000 to the Germans' 4,000. Although inter-Allied co-operation worked well, relations between the British Army and Navy collapsed at Narvik because they were, incredibly enough, acting under contradictory instructions. Admiral of the Fleet the Earl of Cork and Orrery had been ordered to take Narvik whatever happened, whereas the commander of the land forces, Major-General Pierse Mackesy, had been authorized to wait for the thaw before taking the town. While the admiral and the general argued, and Mackesy tried to pull Cork out of the battle, German supplies reached the town, gun emplacements were built and enemy morale soared. Mackesy, whose troops had inexplicably had their snow-shoes offloaded in Scotland, had a point, however, as Cork discovered for himself when he went out to reconnoitre the position and slipped up to his waist in snow.[41] These inter-service problems were soon dealt with, but reflected badly on the Chamberlain Government at the time.

Some fine Polish mountain troops, two battalions of the French Foreign Legion and General Béthouart's Chasseurs Alpins, as well as the British and the Norwegians, were finally to take Narvik on 27 May, prior to attempting to start pushing the German forces eastward towards the Swedish border. However, after Hitler's victories in France and the Low Countries, such a tiny Scandinavian foothold was untenable, and the Narvik force was evacuated between 2 and 7 June, along with the Norwegian royal family and Government, but not Otto Ruge, who decided to stay with his men and was imprisoned. The Germans ran Norway directly until February 1942 when the Norwegian Nazi Vidkun Quisling was appointed minister-president and was permitted to run the most autonomous of all the Reich's puppet governments, because the Germans knew they could trust him ideologically. He had made his name as a humanitarian during the Russian famines and Armenian refugee crises of the 1920s, although his dreams of world federation under Nordic leadership never appealed to the Norwegian electorate, and his small Nasjonal Samling party was only ever a marginal force in the 1930s.[42] The Norwegians despised him throughout his period of rule, and had the court trying him for high treason somehow not imposed the death penalty upon him in 1945, his prison guards had agreed among themselves to murder him anyhow.

On 8 June, *Scharnhorst* and *Gneisenau* intercepted the British aircraft carrier *Glorious* (carrying two squadrons of aircraft, including Hurricanes) and her escort destroyers *Acasta* and *Ardent*, and sank all three, although not before the skipper of *Acasta*, Commander C. E. Glasfurd, had sailed his ship straight at the enemy and managed to launch a torpedo that damaged *Scharnhorst* moments before she was herself sunk by a salvo from the cruiser's 11-inch guns. The only man in *Acasta* to survive the sinking, after three days on a raft in the North Sea, Leading Seaman C. G. 'Nick' Carter, recalled: 'When I was in the water I saw the captain leaning over the bridge, take a cigarette from a case and light it. We shouted to him to come on our raft, he waved "Goodbye and good luck" – the end of a gallant man.'[43]

A number of factors had coalesced to make the Norway campaign a disaster for the Allies, including frequent changes of plan, radio sets that General Sir Claude Auchinleck thought worse than the ones used on India's North-West Frontier, and 1919-era Arctic boots that were several sizes too large, meaning that 'days were devoted to doctoring'.[44] Although the Allies were humiliated in Norway, and the myth of the invincibility of the Führer and his master race that had been sedulously promoted since the remilitarization of the Rhineland was further boosted, the German victory came at a high cost. Compared to the 6,700 British, Norwegians, French and Polish killed (1,500 on *Glorious*) and the 112 aircraft destroyed, the Germans lost 5,660 killed and 240 aircraft in the Norwegian campaign. While the Royal Navy lost one aircraft carrier, one cruiser (with three more damaged), eight destroyers and four submarines, and the Poles and French one destroyer and one submarine each, the Germans lost three cruisers, ten destroyers, four U-boats and several months in which *Scharnhorst* and *Gneisenau* were out of action. These figures may seem almost even, but the much smaller Kriegsmarine could ill afford such losses compared to the Allies, especially when General Franz Halder's plans to invade southern England on a wide initial front, codenamed Operation Seelöwe (Sealion), required much naval support.

Once France fell in June 1940, the Germans had the Alsace-Lorraine iron-ore fields and the Atlantic ports that took the place of Gällivare and Trondheim. But 125,000 square miles of Norway still needed to be garrisoned for much of the rest of the war by at least twelve German divisions, totalling around 350,000 men. Hitler expected an attack on Norway for several years after 1940, and kept an inordinate number of troops idle there who could have been far better employed on the Eastern Front; it was not until after D-Day in June 1944 that they were brought south. He was right to fear an attack there, however, as Churchill always wanted to secure northern Norway for the Allies and prevent its use by the Kriegsmarine and Luftwaffe in their interdicting of the convoys that were sent to Murmansk after Hitler had invaded Russia. The ice-free ports of the Northern Cape were certainly useful to Germany in that respect.

The German invasion of Denmark legitimized the Allies' capture of Reykjavik and the Faroe Isles the following month, which were to yield air bases vital to the anti-submarine campaigns of the battle of the Atlantic. Furthermore, no fewer than 4.6 million tons of shipping – Norway had the fourth-largest merchant navy in the world in 1939 – were added to Allied resources, and used from Murmansk to the Pacific.[45] Since the entire aggregate of all Allied losses by submarines did not exceed that figure until December 1941, the Germans had to pay a high price for violating Norwegian sovereignty twenty-four hours before the Allies did.

Speaking of Adolf Hitler in the Central Hall, Westminster on 4 April, only five days before the German invasion of Norway, Neville Chamberlain said: 'One thing is certain – he missed the bus.' Along with his prophecy of 'Peace in our time' after meeting Hitler at Munich, it was one of his less impressive predictions, but he was not the only person to have spoken too soon. Churchill also told the House of Commons on 11 April that 'We are greatly advantaged by ... the strategic blunder into which our mortal enemy has been provoked.' The Norway campaign was a serious setback for the Allies, but if it achieved nothing else, the two-day House of Commons debate on the subject on 7 and 8 May 1940 did at least destroy the Chamberlain Government, and bring to power an energetic coalition under the premiership of Churchill, ironically enough the Briton most directly responsible for the Norway expedition and the Admiralty's unimpressive part in it.

Winston Churchill's most important, most dangerous but ultimately his most constructive characteristic had always been his impatience. He had exhibited impatience throughout his life, both with himself and with the world around him, especially during the imperial and world wars in which he had risen to prominence in British public life. By May 1940 he was sixty-five years old, yet still at the height of his very considerable intellectual and oratorical powers. His long years of largely unheeded warnings about the rise of Nazism had given him an unassailable moral right to the premiership during the parliamentary crisis that month, and he grasped it as soon as it became clear that Chamberlain could not carry on without the support of the Labour and Liberal parties and a small but growing band of Conservative rebels. Churchill was impatient for the premiership, and he took it, bluntly telling his rival for the post, the Foreign Secretary Lord Halifax, that he could not be prime minister from the House of Lords.[46] (He later invented a story in which Halifax almost offered him the premiership out of embarrassment after a long period of silence.)

Churchill had a certain idea of heroism – both his own and that of the British people – and in 1940 the two came together in what in retrospect was a sublime way, but which struck many in the British Establishment at the time as dangerously romantic. For over the past forty years there had hardly been a major subject of domestic or international politics in which Churchill had not been intimately involved, very often on the losing side. His judgement had been called into question over such important issues as votes for women, the Gallipoli disaster, sterling rejoining the Gold Standard, the General Strike, Indian self-government, the Abdication crisis and very many more. He had crossed the floor of the House of Commons not once, but twice. Yet now his monumental impatience, especially once he had invented for himself the post of minister of defence immediately after King George VI had appointed him prime minister, was precisely what the nation needed. He demanded, in the wording of the red labels that he was to attach to urgent documents, 'Action This Day', and he got it.

Churchill's preternatural eloquence and world-historical sense, as well as a self-belief that bordered on the messianic, had brought to the fore in Britain a leader who could frame the global struggle in profoundly moving, almost metaphysical terms. In his unpublished essay of 1897 entitled 'The Scaffolding of Rhetoric', Churchill had written:

Of all the talents bestowed upon men, none is so precious as the gift of oratory. He who enjoys it wields a power more durable than that of a great king. He is an independent force on the world. Abandoned by his party, betrayed by his friends, stripped of his offices, whoever can command this power is still formidable.[47]

Almost throughout the 1930s – what he called his Wilderness Years – Churchill's opposition to Indian self-rule and latterly his warnings about Hitler's revanchism had left him abandoned by his party, let down by his friends and out of office. Now, however, he was about to wield 'a power more durable than that of a great king', but would it be enough? For, on the very same day that Churchill became prime minister, Friday, 10 May 1940, Hitler unleashed Blitzkrieg on the West.

2

Führer Imperator

May–June 1940

*I asked you to go without sleep for forty-eight hours. You
have gone for seventeen days. I compelled you to take risks
... You never faltered.*
General Heinz Guderian to XIX Panzer Corps, May 1940

For a quarter of a century it had been the collective assumption that
the plan to destroy France in 1914 had failed only because, between
the plan's inception by Count Alfred von Schlieffen in 1905 and
its being put into operation nine years later, too many troops had
been drawn off its powerful right flanking movement and instead
assigned to the weak left flank. So when in October 1939 the Oberkommando der Wehrmacht (German General Staff, or OKW) planners were instructed by Hitler to create a new blueprint to destroy
France, they produced Fall Gelb (Plan Yellow) which comprised a far
stronger right-flank attack, by Army Group B spearheaded by all ten
of Germany's Panzer divisions, and an even weaker left, stationed
behind the Siegfried Line. Yet everyone knew that such a mass assault
through Belgium and northern France was precisely what the Allies
– given their identical experience of the autumn of 1914 – would
expect.

Nevertheless when on 10 January 1940 a German courier aircraft
flying from Münster to Cologne got lost in fog and was forced to
crash-land at Mechelen-sur-Meuse in Belgium, and Major Helmuth
Reinberger, a Staff officer of the German 7th Airborne Division, was
unable to destroy his copy of Plan Yellow, either behind a hedge
before he was captured or by attempting to fling it into a stove

afterwards, Hitler was forced to consider entirely altering the OKW plans.[1] In fact, because the neutral Belgians passed on only a two-page synopsis to the British and French military attachés the next day, refusing to say how they came by it, leading the Allied High Command initially to suspect a German deception operation, the alteration was probably unnecessary. The Belgians knew the plans to be genuine, however, since they had placed microphones in the room where the German air attaché subsequently met Reinberger, and his first question had been whether he had destroyed the documents. Yet still they and the Dutch did not revoke their neutrality and join the Allies, fearing it might 'provoke' the Führer.

'If the enemy is in possession of all the files,' Major-General Alfred Jodl, Chief of Operations of OKW, wrote in his diary on 12 January, 'situation catastrophic!'[2] Fearing Plan Yellow to be compromised, Hitler approved an alternative entitled Operation Sichelschnitt (Sickle Cut), the brainchild of Erich von Manstein, chief of staff to Gerd von Rundstedt, who was to command Army Group A in the centre. This comprised taking seven Panzer divisions from the right flank and positioning them in the centre, while keeping the left (Army Group C) as weak as before. After Army Group B in the north had attacked Holland and Belgium, it was hoped that the Allies would move into those countries to meet it, and then at the key moment Army Group A in the centre would burst out of the Ardennes Forest, strike at the *Schwerpunkt* (point of maximum effort), the fulcrum in the Allied line, pierce it, and race forward to the English Channel, thus cutting off one-third of the Allied armies from the other two-thirds.

Hitler, who from the early hours of 10 May was based at his Felsennest (cliff nest) command post in the Eifel forest 20 miles south-west of Bonn, was later given personal credit for Manstein's new plan. Keitel described the Führer as 'the greatest field marshal of all time', and even six years later he admitted to his Nuremberg psychiatrist: 'I thought he was a genius. Many times he displayed brilliance . . . He changed plans – and correctly for the Holland–Belgium campaign. He had a remarkable memory – knew the ships of every fleet in the world.'[3] Keitel also regularly told the Führer he was a genius. Dr Goebbels' propaganda was at that period putting out the message that Hitler was 'the greatest warlord of all time', but at least Hitler knew that was state propaganda. To be told by one's chief of staff the same thing could not but induce hubris.

Hitler's sheer knowledge of matters military was undoubtedly impressive, and has certainly bowled over modern apologists such as Alan Clark and David Irving, with the former stating that 'His capacity for mastering detail, his sense of history, his retentive memory, his strategic vision – all these had flaws, but considered in the cold light of objective military history, they were brilliant nonetheless.'[4] It was true that Hitler had a phenomenal recall for the technical details of weaponry of all kinds. Of his original 16,300-book library, 1,200 volumes can be found in the Library of Congress in Washington and they include nearly a dozen almanacs on naval vessels, aircraft and armoured vehicles, such as the 1920 edition of *The Conquest of the Air: A Handbook of Air Transport and Flying Techniques*, a 1935 copy of *Hiegl's Handbook of Tanks*, a 1935 edition of *The Navies of the World and their Fighting Power*, and a well-thumbed 1940 edition of *Weyer's Handbook of War Fleets*.[5] 'There are exhaustive works on uniforms, weapons, supply, mobilization, the building-up of armies in peacetime, morale and ballistics,' wrote the Berlin correspondent of United Press International who was allowed into the Führer's libraries in Berlin and Berchtesgaden before the war, 'and quite obviously Hitler has read many of them from cover to cover.'[6] Hitler's press secretary, Otto Dietrich, was deeply impressed with his boss:

He had an exceptional knowledge of weaponry. For example, he knew all the warships in the world insofar as they were listed in . . . reference works. He could give in detail from memory their age, their displacement and speed, their armour strength, their towers and weaponry. He was thoroughly informed about the most modern artillery and tank construction from every country.[7]

Instances when Hitler displayed his technical interest in weaponry during the war are legion. When not asking pointed questions at his Führer-conferences with senior OKW figures and military commanders, he liked nothing better than showing off his detailed knowledge. Subjects upon which he would dilate included the horsepower needed for wheeled tractors to pull heavy field howitzers (85hp); gearshift problems in the Tiger tank; the ricochet hazards associated with the 15cm anti-tank gun; hollow-charge projectile technology for anti-tank weaponry; the night-flying capabilities of the Heinkel He-177; the lowest altitudes at which elite paratroopers can jump; the percentages of ferries in Italy and Germany that were fully operational; altitudes at which Mosquito fighters could fly; the top speed of electric submarines (18 knots); the size of underwater bombs necessary to blow up submarine-base sluice gates (3,000 kilograms); the advantages of flame-throwers over grenades over 30 yards, and so on.[8] Yet knowing the calibre of a weapon or the tonnage of a ship is far removed from being a strategic genius, and Keitel confused the two, unforgivably for someone with his role and responsibilities. Because a train-spotter can take down the number of a train in his notebook, it doesn't mean he can drive one.

Of course Churchill also took a close interest in the minutiae of war-making, especially in tactics, but not so much in the technical side of weaponry unless there were problems associated with it. Whereas Hitler paid little or no heed to his troops' material comforts, Churchill was constantly interesting himself in such matters. Would there be brass bands playing when they returned home? Were they getting their post on time? On 17 July 1944, he referred the Secretary of State for War, P. J. Grigg, to a *Daily Mail* article about the way the troops were 'tired of compo [rations]' and lacked bread. Grigg answered that six out of the Army's twelve bakery units were in France. 'Should not put up with it,' replied Churchill. 'Ought to get decent cooked bread and meat.' He instructed the War Office to accelerate the movement of mobile bakeries to France.[9] Such an exchange would have been unthinkable at a Führer-conference, not least because the German equivalent of the *Daily Mail* would not have dared to criticize the Wehrmacht over its rations.

Manstein correctly identified the *Schwerpunkt* as the 50-mile-wide sector of the Meuse river between Danant and Sedan. Once that was crossed, the Channel reached and forty Allied divisions in the north surrounded and captured, the rest of France to the south could be attacked from across the Somme and Aisne in a separate operation, entitled Fall Rot (Plan Red). Speed was vital, and this would be gained by close co-operation between the Luftwaffe and advanced Panzer units, as had worked so well in Poland. The Panzer divisions would be grouped closely together to hit the *Schwerpunkt* simultaneously, taking advantage of the fact that despite the lessons of the Polish campaign the Allies had spread out their armour widely across the whole front. Though the Germans were actually outnumbered by the Allies in terms of men and tanks, and used not significantly better equipment, their superior training, generalship, surprise and especially Manstein's strategy would deliver the defeat of France. That strategy had come about as the result of a chance crash-landing of a nondescript courier plane caught in fog.

Manstein's plan, which Hitler approved in early February, contained significant risks. The Ardennes is a heavily wooded, mountainous region of narrow roads which was considered virtually impassable to heavily armoured vehicles; the left flank of Army Group A would be wide open to Allied counter-attack from the south as it raced across northern France towards Abbeville on the Somme river and then northwards to Boulogne, Calais and eventually Dunkirk; there was a limited number of bridges over the River Meuse, which had to be captured quickly; the weak left flank guarded by the unarmoured twenty divisions of Army Group C on the Siegfried Line would be vulnerable to the forty French divisions facing it behind the Maginot Line. Over the last issue the Germans need not have worried unduly. The Maginot Line was as much a state of mind as a line of fortifications, and there was no likelihood of the French surging forward from it to engage Army Group C. Named after a French defence minister of the 1930s, André Maginot, the Line had been built between 1929 and 1934. Stretching from Pontarlier on the Swiss frontier all the way along the Franco-German frontier to Luxembourg, it was 280 miles long, comprised 55,000 tons of steel and 1.5 million cubic metres of concrete, and was connected by an underground railway, which still works today.

After Belgium short-sightedly re-established her neutrality after the Great War, the Line should have been continued all the way along the Belgian border to the Channel coast, and some extra fortification did take place; however, there were several difficulties. The technical ones – a higher water table in the east, and the heavily industrialized areas of Lille and Valenciennes through which the Line needed to pass –

might have been dealt with, but the huge financial cost threatened to break the French military budget.[10] Moreover the Belgians somewhat hypocritically complained that an extension of the Line to the coast would effectively sacrifice them to Germany, a factor that the French might understandably have taken in their stride considering Brussels' repudiation of the defensive treaty on the basis of which the Line had been built in the first place.

As it turned out, although the majority of the Wehrmacht skirted round to the west of the Line, the German First Army breached it south of Saarbrücken on 14 June despite its lack of tanks, finding its shallowness meant that it was relatively easy to attack with grenades and flame-throwers.[11] What had been originally intended merely to slow the Germans down and deny them the element of surprise had instead engendered a defensive mentality in the French that had – along with their 1870 defeat and the terrible bloodletting of 1914–18 – robbed them of offensive spirit. An all-out attack on the Siegfried Line in September 1939 was the French High Command's best hope, as officers such as General André Beaufre readily admitted, after it was too late.[12] At the outset of war, neither France nor Britain was politically prepared for such action.

What the Allied plans, drawn up during the Phoney War, did propose was a swift movement into Holland and Belgium as soon as Germany invaded those countries, just as Manstein had predicted. Under Plan D, three French armies under Generals Giraud (Seventh Army), Blanchard (First Army) and Corap (Ninth Army), as well as most of the British Expeditionary Force (BEF) under Lord Gort, would move from their entrenched positions along the Franco-Belgian border up to a line between Breda and the Dyle river, in order to cover Antwerp and Rotterdam. To allow these vital Channel ports – invaluable for U-boats to threaten shipping – to fall into German hands was unthinkable. Yet, as the Panzer strategist and historian Major-General Frederick von Mellenthin acutely observed, 'The more they committed themselves to this sector, the more certain would be their ruin.'[13]

The Wehrmacht comprised 154 divisions in May 1940 and the western attack employed no fewer than 136 of them.[14] The Allies, once Belgium's twenty-two and Holland's ten divisions were belatedly added to the total, numbered 144 divisions in the theatre. Both sides had around 4,000 armoured vehicles, with the German forces heavily concentrated in ten Panzer divisions of 2,700 tanks, supported by mechanized infantry. The 3,000 French tanks were hopelessly disseminated in a linear manner, as they had been in attack during the Great War, while the British had only around 200 tanks in all. 'By dispersing their armour along the whole front,' argued Mellenthin, 'the French High Command played into our hands, and have only themselves to blame for the catastrophe that was to follow.' It was true: the Allies had ignored the lessons of Poland.

In the all-important sphere of air superiority, whereas the Allies had 1,100 fighters and 400 bombers in the region, the Luftwaffe had 1,100 fighters, 1,100 horizontal bombers and also 325 dive-bombers, of which the Allies had no equivalent.[15] Allied planes were committed to aerial reconnaissance and defence, but not to close support of troops on the ground, a tactic which the Germans had perfected in pre-war manoeuvres and in the Polish and Norwegian campaigns, and which was greatly aided by the sophistication of ground-to-air communications. Much French heavy, field and anti-tank artillery was actually better than the Germans' – except for the Wehrmacht's superb 88mm anti-aircraft gun, which could double as an anti-tank weapon – and the British Matilda tank's 2-pounder gun was also a match for the German Mark III Panzer's 37mm gun. Yet this campaign was to prove once again how much more important psychology, morale, surprise, leadership, movement, concentration of effort and retention of the initiative are in warfare than mere numbers of men and machines and quality of equipment. The German concept of *Auftragstaktik* (mission-orientated leadership), developed over the previous decade, was to deliver victory just as surely as any piece of weaponry they deployed.

Early on the morning of Friday, 10 May 1940, Captain David Strangeways of the BEF, whose regiment was stationed near Lille in northern France, was woken by the battalion's orderly room clerk shouting, 'David, sir, David!' It was only as he was about to rebuke the man for addressing an officer by his Christian name that Strangeways remembered that 'David' was the codeword for the event that the

Allies had been waiting for since September.[16] Hitler's assault on the West had begun.

Considering that the Allies had been at war with Nazi Germany for over eight months it is astonishing that the Wehrmacht achieved such surprise as it unleashed Blitzkrieg on the West, especially as only one month earlier it had equally suddenly invaded Denmark and Norway. The day before the quadruple invasion of France, Holland, Belgium and Luxembourg, the Belgian Army had increased the amount of leave from two to five days per month, and in one strategically vital Belgian fort on the Albert Canal the warning gun was discovered to be out of order. As many as 15 per cent of France's front-line troops were on leave and General René Prioux, commander of her Cavalry Corps, was 50 miles behind the lines engaged in target practice.

Army Group B under General Fedor von Bock made what Mellenthin called its 'formidable, noisy and spectacular' attack on Belgium and Holland at 05.35 hours. Many Dutch and Belgian aircraft were destroyed in their hangars, for very light losses by the Luftwaffe. Paratroopers captured strategic points near Rotterdam and The Hague, including airfields, although fierce resistance the next day allowed Queen Wilhelmina and the Dutch Government to escape capture. In Belgium eleven gliders, towed by Ju-52 transport planes, landed on the roof of the great fortress of Eben Emael, which covered the advance of Reichenau's Sixth Army into the country. A mere eighty-five German paratroopers debouched from them and destroyed the fortress's massive gun emplacements from above with specially designed hollow charges, while its 1,100 defenders withdrew to defensive positions beneath the fortress. Later that day, Hitler told the German people that a battle had begun that 'will decide the fate of the German people for the next thousand years'.[17]

The French Commander-in-Chief, General Maurice Gamelin, ordered the French and British armies to the Dyle–Breda Line, where they advanced largely unhampered by 12 May, for, as Mellenthin recorded, the OKW 'was delighted to see the enemy responding to our offensive in the exact manner which we desired and predicted'. When Giraud advanced too far into Holland, however, he was flung back at Tilburg. Some Allied generals, such as Alan Brooke commanding the British II Corps, Alphonse Georges of the French North-West

Army, and Gaston Billotte of the 1st Army Group, deeply disapproved of Plan D, but Gamelin's mind was made up.

The lack of preparation by the Belgians for an eventuality they had known was probable ever since the Mechelen crash-landing in January, was illustrated by their not having removed the roadblocks into Belgium from France, which took an hour to demolish. Nor were there any trains on hand to transport French troops and equipment to the Dyle, as King Leopold III of the Belgians complained to Major-General Bernard Montgomery when British troops went through Brussels.[18] 'All the Belgians seem to be in a panic from the higher command downwards,' noted Gort's chief of staff, Lieutenant-General Henry Pownall, on 13 May. 'What an ally!' Bad communications, mutual suspicion and, later on, mutual recriminations characterized the relationships between the Allies during this disastrous campaign.

Matters were made worse by the way in which the physical organization of Allied command was ridiculously decentralized: Gamelin's headquarters were as far back as Vincennes, virtually in the Paris suburbs, because the Commander-in-Chief felt he needed to be closer to the Government than to his own Army. His field commander, Alphonse Georges – who had never truly recovered from being wounded during the assassination of King Alexander of Yugoslavia in Marseilles six years earlier – was based at La Ferté, 35 miles east of Paris, but spent much of his time at his residence 12 miles from the capital. Meanwhile, the French General Headquarters was at Montry, between La Ferté and Vincennes, except for the Air Force which was at Coulommiers, 10 miles from La Ferté. Even in the land of châteaux this was taking château-generalship ludicrously far.

The attack of General Wilhelm List's Twelfth Army, part of Army Group A, through the Ardennes was a masterpiece of OKW Staff work. Panzer Group Kleist, under General Paul von Kleist, comprising Heinz Guderian's XIX Panzer Corps and Georg-Hans Reinhardt's XLI Panzer Corps, arrived at Sedan and Montherme on the Meuse on 13 May, at the perfect time and place to effect the *Schwerpunkt* against General André Corap's Ninth Army. After fierce fighting along the Meuse, especially at Sedan, the far heavier concentration of

German armour, closely supported by the Luftwaffe, broke the French force. Kleist ordered the crossing of the Meuse on 13 May without waiting for artillery support, because surprise and momentum were key to the success of Blitzkrieg. 'Time and again the rapid movements and flexible handling of our Panzers bewildered the enemy,' recalled a triumphant Panzer commander years later.[19] Colonel Baron Hasso-Eccard von Manteuffel agreed: 'The French had more, better, heavier tanks than we had but . . . as General von Kleist said, "Don't tap them – strike as a whole and don't disperse." '[20] The battle of Sedan had a moral and historical as well as a strategic significance for Frenchmen: it had been there in 1870 that Napoleon III had been crushed by Bismarck in the decisive battle of the Franco-Prussian War. When General Georges heard about Corap's defeat at Sedan, he burst into tears. 'Alas, there were to be others,' wrote Beaufre of the generally lachrymose French High Command. 'It made a terrible effect on me.'[21]

Guderian was at Montcornet by 15 May, Saint-Quentin by the 18th, and his 2nd Panzer Division reached Abbeville on the 20th. 'Fahrkarte bis zur Endstation!' (Ticket to the last station!) he called to his Panzer troops, telling them to go as far as possible.[22] At one point Guderian was temporarily relieved of his command for going too fast, leaving his superiors fearful of a co-ordinated counter-attack from the north and south, one that he intuitively guessed would never come. Liddell Hart, an admirer of Guderian, described how the German tank commander had long been a proponent of 'the idea of deep strategic penetration by independent armoured forces – a long-range tank-drive to cut the main arteries of the opposing army far back behind its front'.[23] This was Guderian's moment to prove his pre-war theorizing right and his detractors correspondingly wrong. By stretching the meaning of 'using his initiative' to its limits – ignoring orders he disliked and taking the wording of others far beyond their normal meaning – Guderian effected the sickle cut faster than anyone could have imagined possible.

'I was conscious of a profound sense of relief,' Churchill later wrote of his feelings when he finally got to bed at 3 a.m. on Saturday, 11 May 1940. 'At last I had the authority to give directions over the whole scene. I felt as if I were walking with destiny, and that all my past life had been but a preparation for this hour and for this trial.' On 13 May, he gave his first speech as prime minister in the House of Commons, conscious that Neville Chamberlain received a greater cheer than he when the two men entered the chamber separately. 'I have nothing to offer but blood, toil, tears and sweat,' he told parliament and soon afterwards the nation. To the question 'What is our policy?' Churchill answered that it was 'to wage war against a monstrous tyranny, never surpassed in the dark, lamentable catalogue of human crime'. Morale was a vital factor in the Second World War, and Churchill's oratory was invaluable in focusing British pride and patriotism. Stalin once cynically asked how many divisions had the Pope: Churchill's larynx was worth the equivalent of an army corps to Britain, as radios were switched on in the nation's homes at 9 p.m. to hear the Prime Minister's words of inspiration. Drawing on English history, mentioning figures such as Drake and Nelson, he pointed out that the British had been in dire peril before, but had prevailed.

'The hammer-blows . . . in May began to descend upon us almost daily,' the military historian Michael Howard recalled, 'like a demolition contractor's iron ball striking the walls of a still-inhabited house.'[24] On 15 May the Dutch capitulated, even though the Dyle–Breda front had not yet been broken by Army Group B. The bombing of Rotterdam had destroyed a large part of the city and left 80,000 people homeless, so the Dutch Commander-in-Chief, Henri Winkelmann, broadcast the Dutch surrender on Hilversum Radio before any other cities were subjected to a similar fate. Although only 980 people died in the raid, it became a stark symbol of Nazi terror-tactics. The fear of such bombing caused an exodus of between six and ten million terrified French refugees from Paris and the areas behind Allied lines, who clogged the roads southwards and westwards. Ninety thousand children were separated from their parents in the process, and the ability of the Allies to respond to the German invaders was severely hampered.

On 18 May the French Prime Minister, Paul Reynaud, reshuffled his Government and High Command. He appointed the eighty-four-year-old Marshal Philippe Pétain, the symbol of resistance during the battle of Verdun in 1916, as vice-premier, and himself took over as minister of war from the ex-premier who had signed the Munich agreement, Edouard Daladier, who became foreign minister. Two days later Reynaud sacked Gamelin and replaced him with the seventy-three-year-old Maxime Weygand, who had never commanded troops in battle and who arrived from Syria too late to affect the struggle that was developing around the Channel port of Dunkirk.

Charles de Gaulle, at forty-nine the youngest general in the French Army, commanded a spirited counter-attack at Laon on 18 May, but was forced back, and a brave attempt was made by the British 50th Division and 1st Tank Brigade south of Arras on 21 May to break through the sickle cut and reconnect with the French forces to the south. If successful this would have isolated Guderian and Reinhardt, but in the event it came to nothing in the face of Major-General Erwin Rommel's 7th Panzer Division and 88mm anti-aircraft guns being used as artillery. Rommel had won fame at the battle of Caporetto in 1917 when, not even a captain, he captured 9,000 Italians and eighty-one guns. An instructor at the Infantry School at Dresden from 1929, he wrote textbooks on infantry tactics and was commandant of the War Academy in 1938, before going on to command Hitler's body-guard. A believer in remorselessly taking the offensive, Rommel under-stood Blitzkrieg and had a superlative sense of military timing.

With the French armour divided between three armoured cavalry divisions, three heavy armoured divisions (initially all held in reserve) and more than forty independent tank battalions supporting infantry units, other than General René Prioux's Cavalry Corps no French motorized formations acted in concert during the campaign.[25] Having failed to break through southwards, the BEF and French First Army fell back towards Dunkirk. Gaston Billotte died in a car crash on 21 May, an accident that led to a 'feeling of inexorable Fate' over-coming the French High Command, whose morale, in Beaufre's view, was never to recover from Corap's defeat at Sedan.[26] The next day, 22 May, the RAF lost Merville, its last airfield in France, so that henceforth every British plane that flew over the Allied armies had to come from across the Channel, severely limiting the amount of time they could spend engaging the Luftwaffe.

A full week before the evacuation from Dunkirk began on 26 May, no fewer than 27,936 men who were not central to the functioning of the BEF were evacuated, in an operation organized by Lieutenant-Colonel Lord Bridgeman of the Rifle Brigade on the Continent and Vice-Admiral Bertram Ramsay, the Flag Officer in Dover.[27] Cartographers, bakers, railwaymen and other 'useless mouths to feed', as they were accurately if rather uncharitably described by Bridgeman, were shipped back, a clear indication that things were not expected to go well. Nor did they: on 24 May Army Group A and Army Group B joined forces to push the Allies into a rapidly diminishing corner of France and Belgium, by then stretching only from Gravelines to Bruges and inland as far as Douai.

Then something astonishing happened. With Kleist's Panzers only 18 miles from Dunkirk, indeed closer to it than the bulk of the Allied forces in the Belgian pocket, they were given an order to halt by Hitler that countermanded the Wehrmacht Commander-in-Chief Brauchitsch's order to take the town. This specified that the line of Lens–Béthune–Saint-Omer–Gravelines 'will not be passed'.[28] For reasons that are still debated by historians, Hitler's so-called Halt Order of 11.42 hours supported Rundstedt's request to halt Kleist's Panzers at the front line on 24 May and not move into the pocket.[29] To the amazement and immense frustration of commanders like Kleist and Guderian, the *coup de grâce* that might have scooped up the entire northern Allied force was not put into operation, giving the Allies a vital forty-eight-hour breathing space which they used to strengthen the perimeter and begin the exodus from the beaches of Dunkirk. General Wilhelm von Thoma, chief of the tank section of OKH, was right up forward with the leading tanks near Bergues, from where he could look down into Dunkirk itself. He sent wireless messages to OKH insisting that the tanks push on, but was rebuffed. 'You can never talk to a fool,' he said bitterly of Hitler (after the Führer was safely dead). 'Hitler spoilt the chance of victory.'[30] When Churchill later spoke of a 'miracle of deliverance', it was one performed by the grace of Rundstedt and Hitler, as well as by Gort and Ramsay. It was the first example of very many cardinal errors that were to cost Germany the Second World War.

'I must say that the English managed to escape that trap in Dunkirk which I had so carefully laid', recalled Kleist afterwards, only with the personal help of Hitler. There was a channel from Arras to Dunkirk. I had already crossed this channel and my troops occupied the heights which jutted out over Flanders. Therefore, my panzer group had complete control of Dunkirk and the area in which the British were trapped. The fact of the matter is that the English would have been unable to get into Dunkirk because I had them covered. Then Hitler personally ordered that I should withdraw my troops from these heights.[31]

Kleist was underestimating Rundstedt's important role in the initial decision-making, but with Hitler willing to take the ultimate glory for the campaign, he must also take the ultimate blame for not allowing Kleist to scoop up the BEF outside Dunkirk. When Kleist met Hitler on the airfield at Cambrai a few days later he had the courage to remark that a great opportunity had been lost at Dunkirk. Hitler replied: 'That may be so. But I did not want to send the tanks into the Flanders marshes – and the British won't come back in this war.'[32] Another excuse Hitler gave elsewhere was that mechanical failures, and the subsequent offensive against the rest of the French Army, had meant that he wanted to build up strength before passing on.

Flying over Dunkirk in September 1944, Churchill told André de Staerke, private secretary to the Prince Regent of Belgium, 'I shall never understand why the German Army did not finish the British Army at Dunkirk.'[33] The answer might be that by the morning of 24 May the troops had fought continuously for nearly a fortnight, and from his own time in the trenches in the Great War Hitler knew how exhausting that could be. Moreover the ground around the Dunkirk pocket was not ideal for tanks. The infantry needed time to catch up, considering the startling amount of ground the tanks had crossed since Sedan, and as Franz Halder wrote in his diary: 'The Führer is terribly nervous. Afraid to take any chances.' Too much had been achieved already to take the risk of falling into an Allied trap at that late stage, and there were still large French forces and reserves to deal with south of the Somme and Aisne rivers. Street fighting in Warsaw had also shown the vulnerability of tanks in built-up areas, such as Dunkirk was. Furthermore, Hermann Göring was confidently promising that the Luftwaffe could destroy the pocket without any need for the Wehrmacht to do much more than conduct mopping-up operations afterwards.

'He was mistrusting of his generals,' Jodl's deputy General Walter Warlimont recalled years later of Hitler:

thus at Dunkirk he delayed the main aim of the whole campaign, which was reaching and closing the Channel coast before any other considerations. This time he was frightened that the clay plains of Flanders with their many streams and channels ... according to his memories of World War One would endanger and possibly inflict heavy losses on the Panzer divisions. Hitler failed to follow up the overwhelming success of the first part of the campaign, and instead initiated the steps for the second part before the first had been accomplished.[34]

Rundstedt himself, who was credited with issuing the Halt Order that the Führer later rubber-stamped, vehemently denied having done so. 'If I had had my way the English would not have got off so lightly at Dunkirk,' he later recalled with bitterness:

But my hands were tied by direct orders from Hitler himself. While the English were clambering into the ships off the beaches, I was kept uselessly outside the port unable to move. I recommended to the Supreme Command that my five Panzer Divisions be immediately sent into the town and thereby completely destroy the retreating English. But I received definite orders from the Führer that under no circumstances was I to attack, and I was expressly forbidden to send any of my troops closer than ten kilometres from Dunkirk ... This incredible blunder was due to Hitler's idea of generalship.[35]

This claim can be safely disregarded, since the order was given by Hitler at a meeting at Army Group A's headquarters in the Maison Blairon, a small château at Charleville-Mézières only after Rundstedt himself had said he wanted to conserve the armour for a push to the south, to Bordeaux, where he feared the British would open another front soon, and anyway the numerous canals in Flanders made it bad country for tanks. Hitler merely concurred, but as his Luftwaffe adjutant Nicolaus von Below recorded: 'The British Army had no relevance for him.'[36]

One theory that must also now be safely discarded was that Hitler did not expect or want to capture the BEF because he hoped for peace with Britain. Not only is it illogical – his chances of forcing peace on Britain would have been immensely strengthened by eliminating the BEF – but there is a piece of hitherto overlooked evidence that proves that the OKW assumed the Allied force would be destroyed despite the Halt Order. A handwritten note from Alfred Jodl, written at Führer-Headquarters and now in private hands, to the Reich Labour Minister Robert Ley and dated 28 May 1940, states:

Most esteemed Labour Führer of the Reich!

Everything that has happened since 10 May seems even to us, who had indestructible faith in our success, like a dream. In a few days ⅕ of the English Expeditionary Army and a great part of the best mobile French troops will be destroyed or captured. The next blow is ready to strike, and we can execute it at a ratio of 2:1, which has hitherto never been granted to a German field commander ... You, too, Herr Labour Führer of the Reich, have contributed significantly to this greatest victory in history. Heil Hitler.[37]

The hubris of the letter is undeniable, especially since the BEF had started to embark from Dunkirk on 26 May, but equally there is not the slightest sense that the OKW were holding back from attempting to 'destroy or capture' as much of the Allied force as possible; evidently they believed total victory to be in their grasp.

Although it was Rundstedt's initial decision to halt Kleist's Panzers outside Dunkirk on 24 May, it took the Führer's influence to silence the opposition from Brauchitsch, Halder, Guderian and Rommel. 'We could have wiped out the British army completely if it weren't for the stupid order of Hitler,' Kleist later recalled.[38] Certainly, if the BEF had been captured wholesale – more than a quarter of a million POWs in German hands – there is no telling what concessions must have been wrung out of the British Government, or whether Churchill could have survived as prime minister if he had demanded a continuation of the war. Hitler knew how to use POWs as a bargaining tool, as he was soon to prove with his 1.5 million French captives. Kleist's belief that after the capture of the BEF 'an invasion of England would have been a simple affair' is harder to accept, as the RAF and Royal Navy were still undefeated, and the Germans had no advanced plans for getting men across the Channel.

Although the Allied forces were overwhelmed at Boulogne and

Menin on 25 May and at Calais on the 27th, Dunkirk was to hold out until the day on which all the Allied troops in the pocket who could embark to Britain had done so. Ramsay and the British Government initially assumed that no more than 45,000 troops could be saved, but over the nine days between dawn on Sunday, 26 May and 03.30 on Tuesday, 4 June, no fewer than 338,226 Allied soldiers were rescued from death or capture, 118,000 of whom were French, Belgian and Dutch. Operation Dynamo – so named because Ramsay's bunker at Dover had housed electrical equipment during the Great War – was the largest military evacuation in history so far, and a fine logistical achievement, especially as daylight sailings had to be suspended on 1 June due to heavy Luftwaffe attacks.

The Halt Order was finally rescinded by dawn on 27 May and heavy fighting took place along the shrinking perimeter, as the Allied rearguard – especially the French First Army near Lille – bought precious time for the rest of the troops to embark on several hundred ships and boats. That same day ninety-seven British prisoners of war from the 2nd Battalion, the Royal Norfolk Regiment were massacred in cold blood by the 1st Battalion of the SS Totenkopf Division's 2nd Infantry Regiment, machine-gunned in a paddock in the inappropriately named hamlet of Le Paradis in the Pas-de-Calais. The next day, ninety POWs from the 2nd Battalion, the Royal Warwickshire Regiment were executed by grenade and rifle-fire by the Liebstandarte Adolf Hitler Regiment in a crowded barn at Wormhout, near the Franco-Belgian border.[39] On seeing two grenades tossed into the crowded barn, Sergeant Stanley Moore and Sergeant-Major Augustus Jennings leapt on top of them to shield their men from the blasts. These despicable, cold-blooded massacres give lie to the myth that it was desperation and fear of defeat towards the end of the war that led the SS to kill Allied POWs who had surrendered; in fact such inhumanity was there all along, even when Germany was on the eve of her greatest victory. Although the officer responsible for Le Paradis, Hauptsturmführer (Captain) Fritz Knochlein, was executed in 1949, Hauptsturmführer Wilhelm Mohnke, who commanded the unit that carried out the Wormhout atrocity, was never punished for this war crime and died in 2001 in a Hamburg retirement home.[40] Already perilous as the Dunkirk perimeter came under full-scale assault, the

Allies' situation worsened at 11.00 on 28 May when, with minimum warning, King Leopold III of the Belgians agreed his country's unconditional surrender. This suddenly opened up a 30-mile gap in the Allied line which was swiftly, but necessarily only partially, filled by Alan Brooke's II Corps.

As well as 222 Royal Navy vessels, some 800 civilian craft of every type were called upon by Ramsay to sail across the Channel to bring the troops home. Some refused to heed the call – including some lifeboatmen and much of Rye's fishing fleet – but an armada of 860 vessels did take part, including pleasure steamers, liners, troopships, trawlers, barges, ferries and forty Dunkirk coasters. Larger ships sometimes towed smaller ones across, and many went back and forth several times. In this they were hugely helped by the weather in the Channel. 'For days it suddenly remained calmer than a millpond,' recalled Signalman Payne. 'During the entire lift-off of that multitude not a ripple was seen. This allowed men to stand up to their shoulders in water and boats to operate within a few inches of freeboard, loaded to double and treble their safe carrying capacity. The calm sea was the miracle of Dunkirk.'[41] Pausing only to cut his many medal ribbons off a jacket he had to leave behind – he'd won the VC and DSO and was mentioned in despatches nine times in the Great War – 'for of course he would take home nothing more than any private soldier', Gort boarded with his troops.[42]

Of the fifty-six Allied destroyers that played a part in the operation, nine were sunk and nineteen damaged; of the thirty-eight minesweepers, five were sunk and seven damaged; of the 230 trawlers, twenty-three were sunk and two damaged; of the forty-five ferries, nine were sunk and eight damaged. Of the eight hospital ships – each of which was emblazoned with large Red Cross markings easily visible to the Luftwaffe – one was sunk and five damaged.[43] It was quite untrue, as the BBC was to allege in 2004, that the British civilians who sailed to Dunkirk to save the BEF did it 'because they were paid'. They were indeed paid for their service, as was the entire BEF for theirs, but there were far easier ways of earning a living during those nine days in May 1940.

For all the inspiring, Victoria Cross-worthy stories of men like Sergeant-Major Augustus Jennings or Lieutenant Dickie Furness of the Welsh Guards, who led a suicidal attack on a German machine-gun post, there were others who tried to rush the embarkation stations at Dunkirk in order to get home safely. 'While a mixed party of men was forming up to embark,' recalled Sam Lombard-Hobson, First Lieutenant of the destroyer HMS *Whitshed*, 'a single soldier, unable to take any more, broke ranks and made a dash for the gangway. Without a moment's hesitation, the subaltern in charge took out his revolver and shot the man through the heart, who lay motionless on the jetty. The young officer then turned to his section, and calmly told them that he wanted only fighting men with him. The effect was electric, and undoubtedly prevented a stampede by other troops awaiting evacuation.'[44] Although there were occasional scenes of panic and drunkenness – 'I saw chaps run into the water screaming because mentally it was too much for them,' recalled Sergeant Leonard Howard – overall the long queues that snaked over the sand dunes, especially those officered by Regular Army regiments, were patient and orderly, despite the exhausted, defeated men occasionally coming under fire from German fighters and dive-bombers that broke through the RAF cordon. Captain E. A. R. Lang, a Royal Engineer who came off on 29 May, recalled that when the Navy – nicknamed 'blue jobs' – came to the rescue, 'As soon as our Cockney boys met the sailors, a verbal battle started and the jokes were cracked in good taste and bad language ... "Blimey, chum, what about a trip round the lighthouse?", "Bye, bye china, where's yer little boat?"'

The RAF was less popular with the Army than the omnipresent Navy, because it was not so visible and was incapable of protecting the beaches from attack by the Luftwaffe round the clock, although it shot down 150 German planes during the operation, at the cost of 106 of its own. The RAF assigned sixteen squadrons to cover the Dunkirk evacuation; however, because of the distance from England, very few airfields could be used, allowing a maximum of only four squadrons to be engaged at any one time, and often only two. It did not help that the Royal Navy continually fired at RAF fighters, shooting down three, and the paramount need for home defence had anyway to be considered. Many of the dogfights took place far from the beaches, where the Army was unable to witness what the Air Force was doing for it, but when the German fighters and especially Stuka dive-bombers did get through to the embarkation points, massacres resulted. 'I hated Dunkirk,' recalled an unusually sensitive *Flugzeug-führer* (pilot officer) called Paul Temme, who flew an Me-109. 'It was just unadulterated killing. The beaches were jammed full of soldiers. I went up and down at three hundred feet hose-piping.'[45]

The experience of being dive-bombed by Stukas was never forgotten by a BEF lorry-driver, Tom Bristow: 'They looked like filthy vultures, their undercarriage not being retractable so that their landing gear reminded one of the cruel talons in which they held their victims. What was held between the wheels, however, was not a victim but a big fat bomb. My eyes became riveted on that bomb . . . it held a strange fascination for me, it was my executioner. And I could do nothing about it.'[46] The bomb missed Bristow, but Lance-Corporal John Wells of the South Staffordshire Regiment was not so lucky: 'I was up on the prow of the ship when we were dive-bombed,' he recalled years afterwards.

A Stuka dropped its bomb straight down the aft funnel. Direct hit. The ship literally folded in about three seconds. I was fortunate because being up in the front end, I just fell off. The fuel tanks had been ruptured, so the sea was a mass of diesel oil. I took an involuntary swim and managed to get ashore but I still twinge a bit with pain nowadays because I swallowed a lot of that diesel oil and most of the lining of my stomach's gone west.[47]

Yet, for all the Luftwaffe's successes, Göring could not make good his boast to destroy the BEF from the air, as Hitler discovered too late. 'Even if the waters had parted, like the Red Sea before Moses, to allow the soldiers to walk home,' one military historian has noted, continuing the miracle analogy, 'the watching world could hardly have been more surprised.'[48] Nonetheless the BEF lost 68,111 men in the campaign, of whom 40,000 were marched into five years of captivity.

As importantly for the Army in the short term, the British were also forced to leave behind 65,000 vehicles, 20,000 motorcycles, 416,000 tons of stores, 2,472 guns, 75,000 tons of ammunition and 162,000 tons of petrol. They destroyed as much as possible with petrol poured over food and grenades thrown down the barrels of artillery pieces, but essentially the soldiers of the BEF returned with little more than their rifles – indeed some officers said they would not be allowed to embark without them – and what they stood up in. The British Tommy of that period wore or carried a steel helmet of 2½ pounds in weight, a haversack of 5 pounds, an anti-gas cape of 3½ pounds, a respirator of the same weight, straps and belts ditto, two pouches containing sixty rounds each, weighing 10 pounds each, a bayonet and its scabbard of 1¾ pounds and boots of 4¾ pounds, and a rifle of nearly 9 pounds. Together these added up to 53½ pounds, or nearly 4 stone. The last man off the beaches at Dunkirk was Major-General Harold Alexander, commander of the 1st Division, who showed superb sangfroid throughout the evacuation. 'Our position is catastrophic,' a Staff officer told him there. 'I'm sorry,' he replied. 'I don't understand long words.'[49]

On 4 June, the day the operation ended, Winston Churchill told the House of Commons and the nation that they 'must be very careful not to assign to this deliverance the attributes of a victory. Wars are not won by evacuations.' He did not deny that being expelled from the Continent was 'a colossal military disaster', but he did produce the most sublime passage of all his magnificent wartime oratory when he said:

We shall not flag or fail. We shall go on to the end. We shall fight in France, we shall fight on the seas and oceans, we shall fight with growing confidence and growing strength in the air, we shall defend our island, whatever the cost may be. We shall fight on the beaches, we shall fight on the landing grounds, we shall fight in the fields and in the streets, we shall fight in the hills; we shall never surrender.

The words that Churchill used in these short, punchy sentences were all but two derived from Old English. 'Confidence' derives from Latin and 'surrender' comes from the French. In November 1942, the Conservative minister Walter Elliot told Major-General John Kennedy that after Churchill had sat down he whispered to him: 'I don't know what we'll fight them with – we shall have to slosh them on the head with bottles – *empty* ones of course.'[50]

Churchill's public insistence on continuing the struggle represented a victory for him inside the five-man British War Cabinet, which for five days between 24 and 28 May discussed the possibility of opening peace negotiations with Hitler, initially via Mussolini.[51] The proponent of this course, the Foreign Secretary Lord Halifax, nonetheless always made it clear that he would not countenance any peace that involved sacrificing the Royal Navy or essential national sovereignty, but Churchill – eventually supported by the other three members, Neville Chamberlain and Labour's Clement Attlee and Arthur Greenwood – opposed holding any discussions, at least until it was seen how many troops could be evacuated from Dunkirk. Churchill was right; any public accommodation with Germany would have destroyed British morale, legitimized Hitler's conquests, alienated American sympathy and allowed the Germans later to concentrate their entire might – rather than just the great bulk of it – against the USSR. Although the initial terms might have been favourable, in the long term a disunited Britain would have had to maintain an onerous level of defence spending for decades, or until such time as Germany was victorious in the east and turned to settle her scores against British bourgeois democracy. 'The belief in the possibility of a short decisive war', wrote the Irish literary essayist Robert Wilson Lynd, 'appears to be one of the most ancient and dangerous of human illusions.'

Instead the Ministry of Information, in co-operation with the War Office and the Ministry of Home Security, put out a leaflet entitled 'If the Invader Comes: What to Do – and How to Do It'. This began confidently enough, stating that if the Germans arrived 'They will be driven out by our Navy, our Army and our Air Force,' but because the civilian populations of Poland, Holland and Belgium had been 'taken by surprise' and 'did not know what to do when the moment came', certain instructions were laid down. (Of course the Ministries also meant French civilians too, but since France was still nominally in the war they could not be mentioned by name.) The first instruction was: 'If the Germans come, by parachute, aeroplane or ship, you must remain where you are. The order is "Stay Put".' The High Command wanted to avoid the scenes of millions of refugees clogging the roads, as had happened on the Continent. 'Do Not Believe Rumours and Do Not Spread Them' was the next invocation, although identifying a rumour was left to the individual: 'Use your common sense.' Some of the other instructions amounted to just that – common sense – such as 'Do Not Give Any German Anything.'

*

Dunkirk fell on 4 June to General Günther von Kluge, who marched in under a massive pall of acrid smoke from burning ships and oil installations, and the next day the Germans put Fall Rot (Plan Red) into operation, with Army Group A swinging south to try to break Weygand's line of forty-nine divisions along the Somme and Aisne rivers. Despite their still healthy numbers, the French were in a hopeless situation. The BEF had disappeared, leaving only one infantry division and two armoured brigades on the Continent; the Belgians had surrendered; the French had lost twenty-two of their seventy-one field divisions, six of their seven motorized divisions, two of their five fortress divisions and eight of twenty armoured battalions.[52] Furthermore, Air Chief Marshal Sir Hugh Dowding of RAF Fighter Command adamantly refused to send over any more Hurricanes or Spitfires to the battle of France, correctly assuming that the forthcoming battle of Britain would require every plane he could deploy. He had already committed the Advanced Air Striking Force squadrons at the start of the battle of France, but with Hurricanes being lost at the rate of sometimes twenty-five per day – when the factories were producing only four or five – he was right to threaten to resign rather than sacrifice any more.[53]

On Monday, 10 June, Mussolini declared war on the Allies, which seemed more serious at the time than in retrospect, coming at a bad moment psychologically. The Italian armed forces comprised 1.5 million men, 1,700 aircraft and a navy of six capital ships, nineteen cruisers, fifty-nine destroyers and 116 submarines.[54] It was nonetheless an opportunistic and short-sighted move that was to cost Italy dear. That same night the French Government quitted Paris, with Weygand declaring it a demilitarized 'open city'. Three million of the city's five million inhabitants also fled, amid terrible scenes. Nurses gave lethal injections to patients who could not be moved; babies were abandoned; a tank commander preparing to defend a bridge across the Loire was killed by local inhabitants who wanted no bloodshed.[55] Mayors were particularly desperate that the French Army should not make stands in their towns.

Churchill made the fourth of five trips across the Channel during the battle of France for a meeting of the senior Allied decision-making body, the Supreme War Council, on 11 June at the Château du Muguet near Briare, south-east of Orléans. Reynaud, Pétain, Weygand, the British War Minister Anthony Eden and General Charles de Gaulle were all present, as was Churchill's personal representative to Reynaud, Major-General Louis Spears. Spears recorded in his auto-biography *Assignment to Catastrophe* that 'The Frenchmen sat with set white faces, their eyes upon the table. They looked for all the world like prisoners hauled up from some deep dungeon to hear an inevitable verdict.' (By the end of the war, Reynaud, Weygand and Pétain had indeed all been imprisoned by one side or the other.) For relief from the woeful sense of defeatism emanating from Pétain and Weygand, the British turned to de Gaulle, whom Spears described as:

A strange-looking man, enormously tall; sitting at the table he dominated everyone else by his height, as he had done when walking into the room. No chin, a long, dropping, elephantine nose over a closely cut moustache, a shadow over a small mouth whose thick lips tended to protrude as if in a pout before speaking, a high, receding forehead and pointed head surmounted by sparse black hair lying flat and neatly parted.[56]

To this weirdly angular giraffe of a man was to be entrusted the honour of *la France éternelle*.

Churchill and de Gaulle tried to breathe fire into the Council, with the Prime Minister promising a second BEF that would fight in Normandy, reinforced by troops from Narvik, and hoping that France might survive until the spring of 1941 when a reconstituted British Army of twenty-five divisions would come to her aid. Yet it was patently clear that the fight had gone out of the French High Command, several of whose members saw the Dunkirk evacuation as a betrayal worse than that of Belgium. At Tours on 13 June – his final visit – Churchill refused to release France from her promise not to make a separate peace with Germany, and three days later he even proposed a scheme by which France and Britain would be fused into a single political entity, becoming one indivisible country. Pétain dismissed the idea, asking why France should wish to 'fuse with a corpse'. Later in the war Churchill admitted that France's refusal of the offer was 'the narrowest escape we'd had', because such a union 'would have impeded us in our methods completely'.[57] It nonetheless showed how desperate he had been for France to stay in the war.

Charles de Gaulle, who escaped from France with Spears on Sunday, 16 June, issued a proclamation to the French people two days later in which he said: 'France has lost a battle. But France has not lost the war!' Although few people heard this historic appeal, and even fewer had ever heard of him beforehand, once the inspiring words of the then obscure tank expert and now junior War Minister were disseminated widely, they formed the rallying cry for the Free French movement. 'I ask you to believe me when I say that the cause of France is not lost,' he said. 'Whatever happens, the flame of French resistance must not and shall not die.' A fortnight's experience in a relatively junior government post, and a fortuitous surname that sounded more like a *nom de guerre* than a baptismal reality, were slim enough justifications for the proclamation that 'I, General de Gaulle, a French soldier and military leader, realize that I now speak for France.' For this magnificent act of treason, he was condemned to death *in absentia* by a Vichy court.

The speed with which France fell shocked everyone, even the Germans. On 14 June, General Bogislav von Studnitz led the German 87th Infantry Division through the streets of a largely deserted Paris. The next day, as Verdun fell, Panzer Group Guderian and Colonel-General Friedrich Dollmann's Seventh Army surrounded near the Swiss border 400,000 Frenchmen of the Third, Fifth and Eighth Armies, who surrendered en masse. On 18 June – Waterloo Day – the Second British Expeditionary Force, commanded by Sir Alan Brooke, re-embarked for Britain. Brooke himself boarded the trawler *Cambridgeshire* at Saint-Nazaire, and he twice had physically to restrain the ship's stoker, who was having a mental breakdown. In all 192,000 Allied troops arrived back in British ports from this second evacuation, so that, between mid-May and 18 June 1940, a total of 558,032 troops came to Britain from different ports of the Continent, 368,491 of whom – two-thirds – were British.[58] The 110,000 French troops landing in Britain from Dunkirk were disarmed on arrival. 'As we disembarked,' reported an outraged Lieutenant Scalabre, 'my revolver was taken from me and not returned despite my protests.' Of these soldiers, who were sent back to Cherbourg and Brest only a few days later, fewer than half saw any active service before the armistice.[59] They were the lucky ones; on 17 June the Cunard White Star liner

Lancastria was sunk by five German planes, killing around 3,500 people. Survivors said that they continued to be strafed in the water as they tried to swim to safety. It remains the largest single maritime disaster in British history, and Churchill ensured that the story was not made public until after the war.

Once the Germans had broken through the French line at Reims, they covered vast areas of territory in astonishingly short periods of time. General Hermann Hoth's XV Panzer Corps took Brest on 19 June, the same day that General Otto von Stülpnagel's Second Army reached Nantes. The Second BEF had clearly re-embarked not a day too soon. Lyon fell to General Erich Hoepner's XVI Panzer Corps on 20 June, the same day that a general ceasefire was declared. Immense numbers of French troops, more than 1.5 million, fell into German captivity. Frederick von Mellenthin crowed that the scale of his Führer's victory had not been seen since the days of Napoleon, which can hardly be gainsaid. It was not bloodless for the Germans, however. They had lost 27,000 killed and 111,000 wounded, compared to France's 92,000 killed and 200,000 wounded. Great Britain lost 11,000 men killed and 14,000 wounded – who were given the first spaces on the evacuation boats – as well as the 40,000 captured.

Before the armistice, General Weygand advised Reynaud against trying to fight on from France's empire in Africa, the Middle East and Asia, and no efforts were made to sail the powerful French fleet away from Toulon and other southern ports. Had the French Navy decided to fight on from outside metropolitan France, it could have been a major addition to the anti-Nazi forces that otherwise had to struggle on in the west without them. Instead, on 17 June Reynaud resigned in favour of Pétain, who asked the Germans for an armistice the following day. 'People in all occupied countries were forced to co-operate but their governments were destroyed or fled,' an historian has written of the French experience in 1940, 'and in none – not even in tiny Luxembourg – did such a significant part of the political class agree to do the bidding of what they thought would be the winning side.'[60] In response to de Gaulle's call for continued resistance, Weygand said: 'Nonsense. In three weeks England will have her neck wrung like a chicken.'

The formal surrender took place shortly after 18.30 hours on

Saturday, 22 June 1940, signed by the French General Charles Huntzinger in the same railway carriage at Compiègne, 50 miles north-east of Paris, where the Germans had themselves surrendered in 1918. Under its terms, all Free French fighters were subject to the death penalty; anti-Nazi refugees were to be handed over to the Germans; captured Luftwaffe pilots were to be returned; the French Army was to remain in captivity and three-fifths of France, roughly the northern and western parts including the whole Atlantic seaboard, were to remain under an occupation whose costs, set at 400 million francs per day, were to be borne by France. It was thus forcibly brought home to the French that this was not simply going to be a repeat of the 1870 defeat, when the Prussians had left France after three years. The disaster of 1918, which Keitel described at Compiègne as 'the greatest German humiliation of all time', had to be, in his words, 'blotted out once and for all'.

After Hitler had viewed the granite memorial to the 1918 Armistice near the railway carriage, he ordered it to be destroyed. Spears was right to think that the French initially had 'a conception of the old days of royalty when you just exchanged a couple of provinces, paid a certain amount of millions and then called it a day and started off the next time hoping you would be more lucky', but they were soon to be vigorously disabused.[61] There would be plenty of Nazi propaganda about France taking her honoured place in the 'New Europe', which would be 'guided' by Germany, but in fact she was only ever intended to be another satrapy of the thousand-year Reich, and a rich source of foodstuffs and slave labour.

Reynaud having resigned and been imprisoned in Germany, Marshal Pétain became the president of the rump of France, ruling from a hotel in Vichy, a spa town in the Auvergne that the Germans had captured on 20 June. Meeting in the main auditorium of the opera house there on 10 July, the Assemblée Nationale voted – by 569 to 80, with seventeen abstentions – to dissolve the Third Republic, which would be replaced with an *Etat Français* under *le Maréchal*. As his foreign minister Pétain initially chose the slippery former premier Pierre Laval. As one historian has put it: 'The pre-war Third Republic had simply been turned inside-out like an old coat, and the New Order fitted straight into it.'[62]

On 19 July 1940, Hitler created no fewer than twelve field marshals – namely Walther von Brauchitsch, Albert Kesselring, Wilhem Keitel, Günther von Kluge, Wilhelm Ritter von Leeb, Fedor von Bock, Wilhelm List, Erwin von Witzleben, Walther von Reichenau, Erhard Milch, Hugo Sperrle and Gerd von Rundstedt – in order to celebrate his victory over France.[63] These represent almost half of the twenty-six field marshals created under the entire Nazi regime. Another sixteen generals were promoted in rank on that day, including four who subsequently became field marshals, namely Georg von Küchler, Paul von Kleist, Maximilian von Weichs and Ernst Busch. Hitherto the field marshal's jewel-encrusted baton had been a rare sight in Germany; there were only four living field marshals, and of those only Göring was on the active list, Blomberg having been forcibly retired and the other two – Prince Rupprecht of Bavaria and August von Mackensen – were of Great War vintage. (Only five had been created during the whole of the 1914–18 war.)

Of course the victory over France in a mere six weeks was the greatest in Germany's history, and thus deserved marking, but the sudden multiplication of active field marshals from one to thirteen in one day had the effect of heavily diluting the status of field marshals in the Wehrmacht, thus reducing their authority vis-à-vis the Führer. One of those honoured, Wilhelm Keitel, was conscious of this, telling his Nuremberg psychiatrist: 'I had no authority. I was field marshal in name only. I had no troops, no authority – only to carry out Hitler's orders. I was bound to him by oath.'[64] It is hard not to suspect that Hitler knew that his position as supreme commander would only be enhanced by having so many field marshals below him. The more the glory was shared, the more it really reflected on to him, for as Liddell Hart wrote of Hitler's generals: 'Their great contribution to history resulted, ironically, in a further weakening of their own position. It was Hitler who filled the world's eye after the triumph, and the laurels crowned his brow, not theirs.'[65]

Explanations for the fall of France are many, with some reaching back to the national disunity of the late nineteenth-century Dreyfus Affair. 'It was a period of decay, of very deep decay,' considered General Beaufre, 'caused by the excess of the effort during World War One. I think we suffered from an illness, which is not peculiar to France, that of having been victorious and believing that we were right and very clever.'[66] The illness was not restricted to the French – though their strain of it was particularly chronic – because the British also failed to put the new military theories regarding tank warfare into effective operation early enough. As late as 1936, Alfred Duff Cooper, then Secretary of State for War, apologized to the eight cavalry regiments that were about to be mechanized by saying that it was 'like asking a great musical performer to throw away his violin and devote himself in future to the gramophone'.

The tragedy of the Great War, in which France had lost proportionately more men than any other country, largely explained her fate in 1940. One of the reasons why Gamelin was so keen to march up to the Dyle–Breda Line, against the advice of several of his senior generals, was so that the next war would not be fought on French soil once again. The fact that in 1914–18 no fewer than 1.36 million French soldiers had been killed and 4.27 million wounded, out of a total force mobilized of 8.41 million, meant that, in Beaufre's words, 'Patriotism . . . had lost much of its magic.'[67] The extreme polarization of French politics in the 1930s, with Fascist groups such as Action Française fighting street battles against their mirror-image opponents on the left, led to a badly fractured nation going to war in 1939. Spears, who knew the country very well indeed, believed that 'The whole of the French upper and middle classes . . . preferred the idea of the Germans to their own Communists, and I think you can call that a powerful fifth column, and it was worked to death by the Germans.'[68] Pétain, Weygand and Laval certainly felt that way. Yet it was the short-term factor of failing to learn the lessons of modern mechanized warfare, as exemplified by Guderian's defeat of Corap at Sedan, that led directly to the fall of France.

The Nazis of course saw the fall of France in racial terms, as a Mediterranean and Latin race succumbing to the superiority of the Aryan master race, although where that left the racially Anglo-Saxon Britons was never satisfactorily explained. Hitler's growing suspicion that he, rather than Manstein, had thought of the *Sichelschnitt* – 'Manstein is the only general who understands my own ideas,' he would say at military conferences – certainly helped induce the hubris that was ultimately to cost him the war.[69] Unfortunately, the Allies also tended to see the fall of France in national, if not also racial, terms. Much unnecessary animosity was subsequently caused by British personal criticism of General Corap, and by French criticism of the Dunkirk and Normandy evacuations. The French perceived – not altogether wrongly – that the British adopted a superior attitude towards them over the scale of their later collaboration with the German conquerors. Nonetheless, there could hardly have been very good Anglo-French relations after 3 July 1940, when Churchill permitted the Royal Navy to bombard the Vichy fleet at Oran in Algeria, in order to try to prevent it sailing for French ports and thence possible incorporation into the Kriegsmarine.

Churchill himself, a lifelong Francophile, stayed aloof from such anti-French sentiment. In June 1942 he complained to Sir Alan Brooke about the Foreign Office's attitude. He pointed out that Britain had not supported French rearmament in the 1930s, had not rearmed herself, 'and finally dragged France into the war in bad conditions'. The Director of Military Operations at the War Office, Major-General John Kennedy, reflected that 'There is much truth in this. It should be remembered when we feel inclined to blame the French for their collapse.'[70] All too often, however, Britons ignored such considerations.

The fate of France between her surrender on 22 June 1940 and the start of her liberation on 6 June 1944 – D-Day – was harsh and humiliating, but at least the country escaped what was called *polonisation*, the ghastly ethnic depopulation carried out by Hans Frank's Government-General in Poland. France was the only country which was accorded the formality of an armistice, and until the Germans invaded the unoccupied part of France in November 1942 Pétain's Government retained a good deal of autonomy. Their counter-espionage agencies even executed as many as forty Abwehr spies and detained hundreds more, four-fifths of them French.[71] Of course in all essentials, France was run first by the Nazi Party ideologue and Ambassador to France, Otto Abetz, and then by the German Military Governor of France, General Karl von Stülpnagel (whose cousin Otto commanded the Second Army), from the Hôtel Majestic in Paris, but the appearance of independence was accorded to the Vichy client state of the Massif Central and Midi. This brought little solace to those whom the authoritarian Government there blamed for the catastrophe of 1940, principally socialists, intellectuals, Protestants, trade unionists, schoolteachers and, especially, Jews.

Vichy implemented anti-Jewish measures before it was even requested to do so by Berlin, partly in order 'to keep the advantages of property confiscation and refugee control for itself'.[72] Although it refused the German demand that Jews be forced to wear yellow stars, Vichy participated enthusiastically in sending non-French Jews to the death camps – principally Auschwitz – in a way that the Germans simply did not have the manpower or local knowledge to achieve.[73] It did not deport French Jews, at least at first, especially if they had fought in the Great War. In the Occupied Zone, the story was worse, with the gendarmerie rounding up French and non-French Jews alike, taking them via Bordeaux to the notorious transit camp of Drancy outside Paris, and to the Vélodrome d'Hiver inside the city, then to almost certain death in the east, with the trains driven by Frenchmen and the logistics managed by French policemen and *fonctionnaires* such as René Bosquet and Maurice Papon. (When there were too few Jews to justify hiring a coach, Papon signed for the taxi fares.) The deportation to Auschwitz in 1942 of 4,000 Jewish children aged twelve and younger, after being forcibly separated from their parents at the Vélodrome and starved for a week, was done not by the Gestapo or the SS but by ordinary Parisian gendarmes acting under orders from French officials.

Although around 77,000 French Jews died in the Holocaust, this represented 20 per cent of the total number of French Jews, a lower percentage than for other countries such as Belgium's 24,000 (40 per cent), quite apart from the Netherlands' 102,000 (75 per cent).[74] This had less to do with the authorities than with the ability of Jews to hide in a largely rural country; newcomers to inaccessible villages were often not denounced to the authorities. Many individual acts of heroism took place, such as teachers forging papers for Jews, or Gentile students of Paris wearing the yellow star in protest, or Catholic priests who protected Jews despite the intimate connections between the Church and the Vichy state.

There were also those French who collaborated willingly with the Germans – dining with them at restaurants such as Maxim's and La Tour d'Argent – just as there were others who joined the Resistance. Some 30,000 people were shot as hostages and *résistants*, and 60,000 non-Jewish French were deported to concentration camps. Yet the vast majority of Frenchmen simply tried to get on with their lives. Between 300,000 and 400,000 French enrolled in various German military organizations and Fascist movements, a significant number but still only 1 per cent of the overall French population of forty million in 1945. 'Long live the shameful peace,' was Jean Cocteau's pithy summation of the views of many. It was due to this that France could initially be held down by as few as 30,000 German troops in 1941.[75] During the first eighteen months of the Occupation, no Germans were deliberately killed by any French in Paris, and only one French patriotic demonstration was held, during which all of the one hundred people involved were arrested. Everything reopened, except of course the Assemblée Nationale, whose building had been converted into German administrative offices with a huge banner hanging from it proclaiming Germany's victories 'on all fronts'.

'I have been receiving politicians, town councillors, *préfets*, magistrates,' reported Abetz back to Berlin in June 1940. 'Out of fifty of these dignitaries, forty-nine have asked for special permissions of one sort or another, or for petrol coupons – and the fiftieth spoke of France.'[76] When French intellectuals discussed the Occupation, they were all too often merely flip. 'How do you respond to a young German soldier who politely asks you for directions?' asked Jean-Paul Sartre, for example. There were tiny acts of resistance, it was true, such as painting a dog's tail the colour of the tricolour, and in December 1940 a bookseller was arrested for placing portraits of Pétain and Laval in his shop window, between copies of *Les Misérables*.[77] Overall, however, most of the French retreated into pursuit of their immediate material interests, hating the Occupation of course, but doing next to nothing to hasten its end. This was precisely what the Germans needed.

It was Philippe Pétain himself who made Vichy respectable. The most controversial Frenchman of the twentieth century, he always despised politicians and it was his tragedy – and that of France –

that he decided to become one himself in 1940, thus mortgaging the reputation of the indomitable 'victor of Verdun' to a political situation that constantly moved faster than his failing powers were able to comprehend, let alone control. Born a peasant and rising through the ranks of the French Army through genuine ability, Pétain was about to retire as a colonel aged fifty-eight, but the Great War intervened and by the age of sixty-two he was commander-in-chief and a marshal of France. Despite having commanded the defence of Verdun for only the first two of its ten months of struggle from February to December 1916, his name was synonymous with the greatest French victory – albeit largely pyrrhic – of the war.

Even if the octogenarian Pétain were not simply too old for the job of protecting France – he was forgetful, going deaf and inclined to fall asleep – he did not have the basic political skills necessary for the job. On 17 June 1940, for example, the day before France surrendered, he managed to make no fewer than three cardinal errors. He illegally arrested the patriotic politician Georges Mandel (who was then released), appointed the collaborationist Pierre Laval as foreign minister (who was later demoted) and made a radio broadcast ordering French troops to lay down their arms in the middle of a major offensive, thereby weakening his negotiating position over peace terms.

Pétain evinced the absurdly vain belief that he was the modern-day Joan of Arc, even reading speeches about the saint to his British liaison officer in June 1940. Even on the rare occasions when he did manage to get a reasonable deal for France, as when he met Adolf Hitler at Montoire in October 1940 and refused to declare war on Britain, he was unable to prevent photographs of himself shaking Hitler's hand from being telegraphed around the world. It is true that he did keep lines of communication open to the Allies – including an offer to quit metropolitan France in 1943 – but he tended to agree with the last person who visited him, all too often an arch-collaborationist in his own Government such as Laval and Admiral Jean-François Darlan. He had few genuine friends, and for all his many gorgeous and besotted mistresses there were few people around him who gave unbiased advice. Although it was always going to be difficult keeping Vichy neutral between the Axis and Allied powers, Pétain deferred to the Nazis much more than he needed to, writing grovelling letters to Hitler about the 'new hope' that the Wehrmacht's victories offered for the New Europe. Had he fled to North Africa with the powerful French fleet, he could soon have made the Axis position in Libya untenable, and the Germans would in 1940 have had to expend the divisions necessary to annex unoccupied France, as they were forced to do after the Allied invasion of North Africa in November 1942.

While it was always unlikely that an elderly soldier was going to lead a genuine movement for national revival, what was called *la Révolution Nationale* ended in mere reactionary authoritarianism. Pétain's Government guillotined Marie-Louise Giraud for performing an abortion, the last woman to be so punished in France. Yet the marshal was personally very popular – more French took to the streets of Paris to cheer him when he visited Notre-Dame in April 1944 than when de Gaulle arrived at the same spot four months later – although his standing was damaged by staying on in office after the Germans had taken over Vichy in 1942.

What undermined the Vichy Government – it was not a 'regime', but the legally constituted Government of unoccupied France – and conversely helped de Gaulle in London more than anything else before D-Day, however, was the compulsory drafting of 650,000 French workers into German factories in 1943. The loathed *Service de Travail Obligatoire* was enforced by press-gangs, and many of those who escaped it were forced into the Resistance (known in rural areas as the Maquis) and the Free French almost out of a paucity of alternatives. 'In general most French workers did not mind working for Germany,' one historian has concluded, 'as long as they did not have to go to Germany.'[78] Before they were rounded up, many fled. It was often not the Germans who dealt the Resistance its heaviest blows, but Joseph Darnand's Vichy paramilitary police, the Milice.[79] As head of state, Pétain must take ultimate responsibility for the tortures and massacres perpetrated by the Milice death-squads in their vicious civil war against the Resistance. One of their commanders, Joseph Lecussan, carried a Star of David in his wallet made from the skin of a Jew, and in July 1944 he rounded up eighty Jews and had the men pushed into a well and buried alive under bags of cement. Pétain made regular bleating complaints to Laval about such horrors, but these were largely just for the record, and he certainly did nothing to end the atrocities.

The Vichy Government interned 70,000 suspected 'enemies of the state' (mainly refugees from the Nazis), dismissed 35,000 civil servants on political grounds and put 135,000 French on trial. 'There was no other occupied country during the second world war which contributed more to the initial efficiency of Nazi rule in Europe than France,' is the estimation of one distinguished historian.[80] There were millions of Frenchmen who made their private accommodations with Hitler's New European Order, in circumstances varying between sullen co-operation, compromise and outright collaboration, but as a British writer has put it: 'We who have not known hunger have no idea how empty bellies debilitate and dominate.'[81] We cannot know how the British would have behaved under the same circumstances, and tragically it seems that human nature is such that every society has enough misfits, fanatics, sadists and murderers to run concentration camps. Those few Jews who were living in the Channel Islands, the only British Crown territory to be occupied by the Germans during the war, were sent to the gas chambers, and the Channel Islands co-operated with the authorities, although their behaviour, with its lack of realistic alternative and orders from London not to resist, cannot in any way be treated as analogous with what the rest of the millions-strong British population might have done after an invasion. 'Certain people behaved well, others badly,' wrote Simone Weil, who survived Auschwitz, aged sixteen, 'many [were] both good and bad at the same time.' And many neither. For every saint and every sinner there were a dozen trimmers. A code of behaviour developed in France whereby it was considered widely acceptable to drink with Germans in a bar, for example, but not at home, and to cheat them financially, but not so badly that one's community suffered later.

One who behaved well was Jean Moulin, the *préfet* of Chartres in 1940, who went on to create the Conseil National de la Résistance, an umbrella organization for the otherwise disparate anti-Nazi groups in France which covered almost the whole political spectrum. Growing up on the anti-clerical left, Moulin, at one point the youngest *préfet* in France, nonetheless embraced Gaullism by 1943. In circumstances that are still unclear, a CNR meeting in a doctor's house in the Lyon suburb of Caluire was betrayed on 21 June 1943, and the handsome, brave, charismatic young Moulin was captured and afterwards tortured to death by Klaus Barbie of the Gestapo.[82] He died without revealing any information, and although his body was never found, ashes that were thought to be his were in 1964 buried in the Panthéon in Paris among the greatest heroes of France.

The Communist Party – which might well have betrayed Moulin, for his apostasy – began to resist the Germans only after Hitler had invaded Russia in June 1941, but its members proved effective *résistants* due to their commitment and the already existing cell structure of their organization. They always had their own political agenda, of which expelling the Nazis was only the first part. After the fall of Paris they concentrated their efforts on plans to seize power, and even assassinated other, anti-Communist *résistants* whose local popularity they believed might threaten their success. When in 1945 the French Army pursued the Wehrmacht through Alsace all the way to Bavaria, the French Communist Party awaited Stalin's call to rise up, which, for various strategic reasons to do with Soviet penetration of eastern Europe, never came.

A large number of French betrayed their country for what appear to be simply financial reasons. When 600 boxes of files captured from the Abwehr were finally released by the French authorities in 1999, it became clear that several thousand French had been willing to spy not only on foreigners but also on their countrymen, for relatively small amounts of money (although some could earn up to 10,000 francs per month).[83] Among their number were a hairdresser, actor, brothel manager, Air France pilot and magician; even more minor figures included a woman who for a small monthly stipend simply allowed the Abwehr to use her mailbox. Furthermore, tens of thousands of anonymous denunciations were sent to the Gestapo, often to settle old scores or in the hope of wiping out financial debts, or very often out of sheer, inexplicable malice, alleging Resistance connections with little or no evidence. This period has been referred to as the Franco-French War, and found no parallel in other countries, except perhaps politically riven Yugoslavia. 'While others united to fight against Hitler,' Vichy's foremost historian has written of the Dutch, Poles and Norwegians, 'the French fought each other.'[84]

In Vichy, Anglophobia also reached its highest levels since the Napoleonic Wars. The Vichy Air Force actually bombed Gibraltar in July and September 1940, and its Navy Minister, Admiral Jean-François Darlan, regularly expressed his personal desire to go to war with Britain. There were no fewer than fourteen military engagements that saw Frenchmen and Britons fighting against each other during the Second World War, as far apart as Dakar and Madagascar, Syria and of course Oran. There was some justification for this hatred; at 150,000, almost as many French civilians died in the Second World War as soldiers, two-thirds of them as a result of Allied military action. The air raids 'softening up' Normandy for invasion in 1944 alone killed tens of thousands of civilians.

'Less sugar in their coffee and less coffee in their cup,' opined André Gide of his countrymen, 'that's what they'll notice.' It was true that food and the threat of starvation played a central role during France's 'dark years' of occupation. Germany requisitioned half of all the food produced by France between 1940 and 1944, and in some areas of production – especially meat and wine – even more. Around 80 per cent of the meat that came into Paris was effectively confiscated, and incidents are recorded of 2,000 people queuing up from 3 a.m. onwards in order to buy only 300 portions of rabbit. Parisian criminal gangs would pose as the Gestapo to extort food and fuel from their compatriots, and a judge's daughter even married a peasant from the Loire, 'lured by his pork chops and rillettes'.[85] *La France éternelle.*

With 1.5 million French POWs working for years abroad (mostly in German factories), Wehrmacht soldiers, who seemed likely to be *in situ* for ever, charmed the impressionable shopgirls, waitresses and chambermaids they met, and there was a good deal of *collaboration horizontale* between 1940 and 1944, with as many as 200,000 babies being born as a result. (Considering the shame endured by the mothers in many communities, this must represent a tiny fraction of the sex that took place without such visible issue.) In the post-Liberation spate of purges and vengeance against collaborators, known as *l'épuration*, women who were accused of having slept with Germans were humiliated in public – enduring head-shaving, mud-pelting and even on occasion lynching – at the hands of crowds of self-righteous hypocrites who had almost all themselves made their own personal compromises with the enemy over the previous four years.

In Belgium, 'the powerful forces of Belgian politics and society – the political leaders, the major industrialists, the Catholic Church, the legal and administrative elites and even the trade union bureaucracies – shunned both collaboration and resistance.'[86] Only a small minority of Belgians – led by Léon Degrelle of the Rexist movement – worked as quislings for the Nazis. But neither did the terrain lend itself to active resistance, as the forests and hills of south-east France aided the Maquis. Although there were a few very brave Belgian *résistants*, overall 'The lives of most Belgians were less clear-cut and less heroic.'[87] The majority were in favour of their king making an accommodation in 1940, and of Allied liberation in 1944.

Denmark had brave resisters too, and between 28 September and 9 October 1943 more than 7,000 Danish Jews were ferried over to neutral Sweden, thus escaping the Holocaust. (The reason there were not more of them was that the Danes had restricted German Jewish immigration in the 1930s and actually closed the border to them in 1938.) There was a light touch to the German occupation of Denmark not only as a result of perceived shared ethnicity, but 'also because the Germans did not want to disrupt the vital flow of food from Danish farms to German stomachs'.[88] Denmark produced 15 per cent of the Reich's food supply, and the entire system needed to be policed by only 215 German officials.

When Weygand predicted that Britain would have her neck wrung like a chicken, it certainly seemed that Germany had, to all intents and purposes, won the war. Yet on 18 June, in order to counter panic over the coming news of the French armistice, Churchill made one of the most stirring of all his wartime speeches. 'Let us therefore brace ourselves to our duties,' he told the House of Commons, 'and so bear ourselves that, if the British Empire and its Commonwealth last for a thousand years, men will still say, "This was their finest hour."' In fact the term 'British Empire and Commonwealth' officially lasted only another twenty-six years, but Churchill's words will resonate down the ages for as long as the English tongue is spoken. With France's fate now sealed, the eyes of the world turned to Britain to see whether the same 21-mile stretch of water that had saved her from invasion by Philip II, Louis XIV, Napoleon and the Kaiser might now save her once again.

3

Last Hope Island

June 1940–June 1941

History is now and England.

T. S. Eliot, *Little Gidding*, July 1941

'The British between June 1940 and June 1941', writes an historian, 'stood completely alone.'[1] Of course they did not, having the vast resources of the British Commonwealth and Empire behind them, as well as their alliance with Greece. Nonetheless, on the ground in Britain itself, as distinct from in the air and on the waters, there was very little to oppose a German landing if one had come in 1940.

Despite having to fight the November 1940 election on a semi-isolationist platform, promising American parents in Boston on 30 October, 'I have said this before, but I shall say it again and again and again: Your boys are not going to be sent into any foreign wars,' President Roosevelt largely rearmed the British Army after Dunkirk, sent very encouraging messages to Churchill via his confidant Harry Hopkins, made fifty destroyers available to the Royal Navy during the election and pushed for the Lend-Lease Act until it was finally and only very narrowly approved on 11 March 1941. In a speech at Charlottesville, Virginia on 10 June 1941 Roosevelt made it clear he would provide the democracies with arms, and the Lend-Lease programme enabled America to supply Britain and later other Allied countries with war materials. Congress appropriated $7 billion for it in 1941, followed by $26 billion in 1942, and in all during the war $50 billion was given under the programme to thirty-eight countries, more than $31 billion of it to Britain. All this allowed the United States massively to extend her involvement in the war without direct military intervention.

87

It has been revealed that soon after Dunkirk Anthony Eden and the new Chief of the Imperial General Staff, Sir John Dill, convened a secret meeting in a hotel room in York which was attended by the senior officers of formations based in the north of England. The War Secretary asked whether the troops under their command 'could be counted on to continue to fight in all circumstances'. Brigadier Charles Hudson VC recalled that 'There was an almost audible gasp all around the table. To us it seemed incredible, almost an impertinence, that such a question should be asked of us.' Eden explained that in the circumstances the Government were envisaging, 'it would be definitely unwise to throw in, in a futile effort to save a hopeless situation, badly armed men against an enemy firmly lodged in England.'[2] They would have fought on the beaches, it seems, but not so far north as York.

The subsidiary question that Eden and Dill put to the officers was 'Whether our troops would, if called on, embark at a northern port, say Liverpool, while it was still in our hands, in order to be withdrawn to, say, Canada? Without such a nucleus of trained troops from the Home Country, the Prime Minister's declared policy of carrying on the fight from overseas would be infinitely more difficult.' Hudson related that it soon became very apparent that the officers were all of much the same opinion. While the proportion who would respond to the call among Regular officers would be high, and of Regular NCOs and men who were unmarried nearly as high, 'No one dared, however, to estimate any exact proportion amongst those officers and men who had only come forward for the war; a smaller proportion of unmarried men might respond but the very great majority of these would insist on either fighting it out in England, as they would want to do, or on taking their chances whatever the consequences might be.' The upper reaches of the British Army were therefore of the view that the majority of its troops would refuse to embark for Canada to continue the struggle from abroad, just as many French had not embarked for Britain for the same reason earlier that month. It was all the more vital, therefore, to prevent the Germans from landing in the first place.

Although Britain's gold reserves were transferred to Canada, and plans were made for the royal family, the Cabinet and ultimately whatever was left of the Royal Navy to follow them, it was not even certain that the British Establishment would be universally welcomed by the North Americans. Ever loyal Canada was sound, of course, but on 27 May 1940 Churchill's private secretary, John 'Jock' Colville, noted in his diary that the British Ambassador to Washington, Lord Lothian, had telegraphed that afternoon to say that President Roosevelt had told him that 'provided the Navy remains intact, we could carry on the war from Canada; but he makes the curious suggestion that the seat of Government should be Bermuda and not Ottawa, as the American republics would dislike the idea of monarchy functioning on the American Continent!'[3] (Churchill and Roosevelt were to clash over the concept of monarchy later on in the war with regard to Italy, when Churchill showed himself to be as instinctively monarchist as FDR was knee-jerk republican.)

Despite that discouraging message, however, a fortnight later, on 11 June 1940, the United States transferred to Britain – for legal and political reasons it was done via the US Steel Corporation – 500,000 Enfield rifles with 129 million rounds of ammunition, 895 guns of 75 mm calibre with 1 million rounds of ammunition, more than 80,000 machine guns, 316 mortars, 25,000 Browning automatic rifles and 20,000 revolvers plus ammunition. This helped arm the Home Guard and those members of the Regular Army who had returned from Dunkirk without their weaponry. Furthermore, ninety-three Northrop light bombers and fifty Curtiss-Wright dive-bombers came over, which were soon used to attack German ships and barges assembling for invasion. By February 1941 the US had shipped over 1.35 million Enfield rifles, and, as the US Army historians point out, this 'resulted in a serious shortage of rifles for training the vastly larger [American] forces mobilized after Pearl Harbor'.[4]

In the complicated maelstrom of fury and resentment that made up Adolf Hitler's political philosophy, hatred against Britain was hardly present, at least until the British behaved so illogically as to refuse his peace offer, dropped over Britain in mid-July 1940 in leaflet form and entitled 'A Last Appeal to Reason'. Nothing in the National Socialist canon prescribed war against the Reich's fellow Anglo-Saxon empire, and references in *Mein Kampf* to the British were in general highly complimentary. 'How hard it is to best England', Hitler wrote, 'we Germans have sufficiently learned ... I, as a man of Germanic blood, would, in spite of everything, rather see India under British rule than any other.'[5] In direct contrast to perceptions of national stereotype, when it came to the projected invasion it was the British who were ruthlessly efficient and the Germans who attempted to muddle through haphazardly. Because Nazi ideology did not call for the invasion of Britain – in the way that it called for that of Poland for racial reasons, France for revanchism and eventually Russia for *Lebensraum* – the Nazis and the OKW had failed to plan coherently for Operation Sealion.

Even during the campaign against France, Hitler had spoken of his 'admiration of the British Empire, of the necessity for its existence, and of the civilization that Britain had brought into the world', saying of the 'harsh' measures that Britain had employed in creating it: 'Where there is planing, there are shavings flying.'[6] He went on to tell his Staff officers General Rundstedt, General Georg von Sodenstern and Colonel Günther Blumentritt that the English were an essential element of stability in the world – along with the Catholic Church – and that he would offer troops to Britain to help her keep her colonies. Small wonder, therefore, that he did not exert himself to make Sealion a reality. 'He showed little interest in the plans,' recalled Blumentritt after the war, 'and made no effort to speed up the preparations. That was utterly different to his usual behaviour.'[7] His love-hate relationship with Britain, curiously reminiscent of Kaiser Wilhelm II's, is also clear from *Mein Kampf* and must partly explain his lack of energy in attempting invasion in 1940.

An indication of how slapdash the Nazi plans for the subjugation of Britain were is provided in the *Sonderfahndungsliste G.B.* (Special Search List for Great Britain) drawn up by Walter Schellenberg, head of the counter-espionage unit of the Directorate of Reich Security, the Reichssicherheitshauptamt (Head Office of Reich Security, or RSHA). This document, known as the 'Black Book', listed the 2,820 Britons and European exiles who were to be 'taken into protective custody' after the invasion. Of course it included Churchill – whose address was given as Westerham in Kent, as if he would be quietly waiting there for the Germans to call – but also writers such as H. G. Wells, E. M. Forster, Vera Brittain and Stephen Spender. (When the list was published after the war, one of those featured on it, the writer Rebecca West, telegraphed another, Noël Coward, to say, 'My dear, the *people* we should have been seen dead with!') Yet the Black Book was out of date before it was even printed: Sigmund Freud and Lytton Strachey had both died, the latter a full eight years earlier, and it featured others who were no longer living in Britain such as Aldous Huxley, who had been in America since 1936; Colonel Kenneth Strong, the former military attaché in Berlin, was shown as being in the Navy. The Germans' attitude to neutrality can be seen from the inclusion of several American journalists working in London. To their shame, George Bernard Shaw and David Lloyd George were absent from the list, because of the public statements they had made in favour of peace after the war had started. They would have escaped an unpleasant fate: the man who would have been responsible for commanding the six *Einsatzkommandos* (action groups), to be based in London, Birmingham, Bristol, Liverpool, Manchester and Edinburgh, SS Colonel Professor Dr Frank Six, went on to be indicted for war crimes in the USSR.

If, on coming to power in 1933, Hitler had developed long-range heavy bombers, built more fighters than he did and trained the Wehrmacht for amphibious operations; if he had not dissipated his naval forces by invading Norway; and if he had attacked much earlier to give himself months of better weather in the Channel, then the always risky Sealion would have stood far greater chances of success. If he had landed large numbers of well-supplied paratroopers on the major British airfields of southern England during the opening stages of the battle of Britain, though such an operation would undoubtedly have been risky, it might also have paid off. Yet as Eden sagely observed after the war: 'If you think, it took us four years of tremendous effort with all the resources of the United States behind us to prepare for the invasion of France, it's hard to see how Hitler ... could find the resources to switch quickly to attack Britain.'[8]

As it was, surprised by his successes in France in May and June 1940, Hitler wasted precious time going sightseeing to the Great War battlefields and Paris – he and the Eiffel Tower shared an 1889 birth year – and then he retired to the Berghof, his Alpine retreat at Berchtesgaden, a clear indication that his heart was not truly in the next necessary step. 'The British have lost the war, but they don't know it,' he told Jodl at Compiègne on 22 June; 'one must give them time, and they will come around.' Clearly he could not have been reading their prime minister's speeches. The British meanwhile used those precious weeks to bring their squadrons up to strength and prepare airfield defences.[9] Lord Beaverbrook, as minister of aircraft production, managed to treble the rate of aircraft production during 1940, when the Germans only doubled theirs.[10]

That Hitler was wrong about the Churchill ministry and the condition of the British psyche should have been revealed to him by the sinking of part of the French fleet by the Royal Navy at Oran (or Mers-el-Kébir) in Algeria on 3 July, and even more surely on 22 July when Lord Halifax rejected the peace offer that Hitler had made at the Kroll Opera House in Berlin three days earlier. The fratricidal nature of the action at Oran was underlined by the fact that the commander of the Vichy fleet, Admiral Marcel Gensoul, had commanded a force at the outbreak of war that had included HMS *Hood*, one of the ships that fired upon his fleet at Oran six months later and helped kill 1,297 French sailors, disabling three of the four French capital ships there.

Of course the OKW was already drawing up plans for Sealion, but these served only to show how differently the Wehrmacht, Luftwaffe and Kriegsmarine viewed the operation. Whereas Franz Halder and the German Army wanted to cross the Channel 'in the form of a river crossing on a broad front', with thirteen divisions assaulting the 190 miles between Ramsgate and Lyme Regis, Admiral Raeder's losses in Norway persuaded him that only a far narrower front – between Folkestone and Eastbourne – would be possible, which Halder thought 'complete suicide'. Meanwhile Göring boasted that the RAF could be smashed with relative ease, allowing an altogether less dangerous crossing. What none contested was that, before any invasion could be launched, total air superiority needed to be established over southern England, which could then be translated into naval supremacy once the British Home Fleet was driven from the south coast by unfettered German dive-bombing, as Norway had shown might be possible.

Despite the Luftwaffe's undeniable successes in Poland, Norway, France and the Benelux countries, these had been won fighting as merely the air arm of Blitzkrieg, with surprise on their side, close to their own bases and over areas that were shortly to be occupied by the Wehrmacht. In the battle of Britain, however, the Luftwaffe was acting on its own, with Stuka dive-bombers flying horizontally at speeds much slower than when diving, over hostile territory far from their bases, and where surprise was on the side of the RAF owing to the fortuitous invention only half a decade earlier of Radio Detection and Ranging (RDF or 'radar').

The first phase of the battle opened on 10 July, with the systematic bombing of British naval and merchant shipping and port installations. Even this shows how uncoordinated German plans were, because the Luftwaffe was often bombing harbours and airfields that would have been needed by the Wehrmacht if it had landed.[11] On 16 July, Hitler issued his Directive No. 16, which ordered that 'The British Air Force must be eliminated to such an extent that it will be incapable of putting up any substantial opposition to the invading troops.' Twenty divisions would be landed following the Jodl plan between Ramsgate and Lyme Regis, although issues such as how to transport across the Channel the vast number of horses needed to pull the majority of the Wehrmacht's artillery were not directly addressed.

Hitler's failure to grasp the fundamental principles of air warfare were in large part responsible for his defeat in the battle of Britain. 'The Führer had little understanding of a strategic plan by which Britain could be forced to sue for peace by the employment of air power,' concludes an historian of the battle. 'He never demonstrated wide awareness of the value of either air fleets or navies; subsequently the waters of the Channel proved too great an obstacle for his land-based military thinking. The crossing of a boisterous and unpredictable sea was too much for his vision, which therefore travelled elsewhere across the map table, allowing the impetus of the attack on Britain to be lost.'[12] Just as bad a strategist, though with far less excuse, was Göring, who not only spent much of the coming battle 735 miles away from Calais at his country house, Karinhall near Brandenburg in Prussia, but also regularly displayed an ignorance of the detail of logistics, strategy, technology and the capabilities of aircraft which was all the more reprehensible because he had been a First World War flying ace. For the coming assault, the Luftwaffe was split into three *Luftflotten* (air fleets), altogether totalling 1,800

bombers and 900 fighters and consisting of Marshal Albert Kesselring's Luftflotte II based in northern France, Marshal Hugo Sperrle's
Dutch- and Belgian-based Luftflotte III and General Hans-Jürgen
Stumpff's Norway- and Denmark-based Luftflotte V. A further two,
Luftflotten I and IV, were kept in defensive reserve. There were over
fifty air bases in northern France and Holland available to the Luftwaffe, but their wide distribution afforded them none of the tight,
centralized, interior defensive lines enjoyed by the RAF waiting for
them in England. Nor did Kesselring and Sperrle properly co-ordinate
their attacks.

The Commander-in-Chief of Fighter Command, Air Chief Marshal
Sir Hugh Dowding, had an initial total force of fewer than 700
fighters, divided between fifty-two squadrons.[13] He admitted to Lord
Halifax that when he heard of the fall of France he 'went on my knees
and thanked God' that no more RAF squadrons would be sucked into
that losing battle.[14] A calm, resolute, highly intelligent and somewhat
unemotional man, 'Stuffy' Dowding, based at Bentley Priory in
Middlesex, kept as many squadrons as he possibly could in reserve
throughout the battle. As Churchill had said of Admiral Jellicoe at
the time of the battle of Jutland in 1916, Dowding was 'the only man
on either side who could lose the war in an afternoon'.

Führer Directive No. 17, issued on 1 August, stated that very soon
the *verschärfter Luftkrieg* (intensified air war) would begin, in which
'The Luftwaffe is to overcome the English Air Force with all means at
its disposal and in the shortest possible time. The attacks are to be
primarily directed against the planes themselves, the ground organization, and their supply installations, also against the aircraft industry,
including plants producing anti-aircraft material.'[15] This would have
been devastating had it been adhered to. The second phase of the
battle of Britain began at 09.00 on Thursday, 8 August, with a series
of vast, virtually continuous German raids against British targets over
a 500-mile-wide front. The 1,485 sorties undertaken that day had
risen to 1,786 by the 15th. Owing to the invention of radar in the
mid-1930s by Professor Robert Watson-Watt of the radio department
of the National Physical Laboratory, and its enthusiastic endorsement
by the Chamberlain ministry – which also produced the majority of
the fighters that won the battle – the country was ringed by a network

of radar stations that transmitted generally accurate information about the position, numbers, height and direction of Luftwaffe planes to the RAF sector control stations. Dowding secured funding for Watson-Watt's research and encouraged Air Ministry officials to attend trials. Sophisticated ground-to-air communications meant that once RAF squadrons had been scrambled, usually only minutes after receiving warning of a raid, they could be constantly updated by radio-telephone with virtually real-time intelligence as they flew off to intercept. In what was known as the Dowding System, radar operators, Women's Auxiliary Air Force (WAAF) plotters, sector controllers, ground crew and of course pilots each had their interactive roles efficiently allotted, and although there was some tension between Dowding and the Air Staff in Whitehall, the System ran remarkably smoothly during the battle. The life-or-death stakes generally surmounted the usual pleasures of departmental infighting and blame-gaming.

By contrast, as the German flying ace Colonel Adolf Galland of Jagdgruppe (hunting group) 26 was to complain, 'When we made contact with the enemy our briefings were already three hours old; the British only as many seconds old.'[16] Since, as Galland also pointed out, 'The first rule of all air combat is to see the opponent first,' the RAF started off with an edge over its opponents. Of their radar and ground-to-air control, Galland wrote that 'The British had an extraordinary advantage which we could never overcome throughout the entire war.' Wing Commander Max Aitken, Lord Beaverbrook's fighter-pilot son, thought that 'Radar really won the Battle of Britain . . . We wasted no petrol, no energy, no time.'[17]

The standard German plane, the Messerschmitt 109E (Me-109), was a shade faster than the Supermarine Spitfire fighter and the Hawker Hurricane, and better in diving and climbing, although crucially not at turning.[18] 'The bastards make such infernally tight turns,' reported one German pilot. 'There seems no way of nailing them.' The Me-109 had three 20mm cannon and two 7.9mm machine guns, a top speed of 350mph and a ceiling of 35,000 feet, but it could only carry enough fuel to keep it airborne for a very little over an hour, which meant that, with twenty minutes spent flying across the Channel and back, it had very little time for fighting. The twin-engined Me-110 had greater range but much less manoeuvrability, a distinct disadvantage when pitched against the highly mobile Hurricanes and Spitfires.

The Me-109's effective range of only 125 miles was likened by Galland to 'a dog on a chain who wants to harm his foe, but cannot'. As a result, much of the dogfighting took place in 1940's glorious summer weather above 'Hellfire Corner', the region of southern Kent around Folkestone, Dover and Lympne that is closest to France: more fighter pilots on both sides died over Hellfire Corner than over the whole of the rest of the UK during the battle.[19] The contrails their exhaust fumes made in the stratosphere that summer – as caught so perfectly in Paul Nash's 1941 painting *The Battle of Britain* – might have been thought beautiful had they not depicted murderous gladiatorial struggles to the death. These were watched by the civilian population below, and when a German plane was shot down there would be, in the words of one spectator, 'cheering as if it had been a goal in the Cup Final'.[20]

The Hurricane, designed by Sydney Camm in 1934, shot down many more German planes during the battle than all the other RAF planes combined, could fly at 324mph at 16,200 feet and was the first British fighter to exceed 300mph in level flight.[21] The Germans badly underestimated the Hurricane, thinking it inferior to the Me-110, which it turned out not to be. It was also a sturdier plane than the Spitfire, could take more damage and was easier to repair. Its four .303-inch Browning machine guns in each wing produced a heavy concentration of fire outside the propeller arc. Yet pilots who flew the Spitfire, which was designed by R. J. Mitchell, tended forever afterwards to employ the language of love to describe 'her' (never 'it'). 'She was a perfect lady,' enthused the South African ace Adolf 'Sailor' Malan. 'She had no vices. She was beautifully positive. You could dive till your eyes were popping out of your head . . . She could still answer to a touch.' Another pilot agreed, writing: 'Nothing is perfect in this world, I suppose, but the Spitfire came close to perfection.' Alternative names considered for it were the Shrew and the Snipe, but in the event the word Spitfire proved sublime. An Elizabethan term for a fiery personality, it was also a popular name for warships and racehorses, and combined the best qualities of all three. Mitchell died in 1937 aged only forty-two, so he never saw what his brainchild would achieve. With its 1,030-horsepower Rolls-Royce Merlin liquid-cooled engine, two-bladed wooden propeller, bulletproof windscreen, raised canopy for increased visibility, elliptical wing shape and twenty-one variants of design by the time the last of more than 20,000 of them saw service in 1955, it fully deserved the encomia of its pilots, such as 'my personal swallow' and 'the fabulous Spitfire'.[22] Had the war started when Hitler originally intended, during the Munich Crisis, it would have had to have been fought largely without the Spitfire, because although the Air Ministry had ordered 310 of them in 1936, not a single one had been delivered by mid-1938.

It was Dowding who persuaded the Air Ministry to fit Hurricanes and Spitfires with bullet-proof Perspex hoods. 'If Chicago gangsters can have bullet-proof glass in their cars,' he told the Air Ministry, 'I can't see any reason why my pilots cannot have the same.' They also had armour-plated backs to the pilots' seats, but pilots still sat only a few feet away from 85 gallons of high-octane fuel.[23] 'In the mounting frenzy of battle,' recalled one RAF fighter ace, Group Captain Peter Townsend, 'our hearts beat faster and our efforts became more frantic. But within, fatigue was deadening feeling, numbing the spirit. Both life and death had lost their importance. Desire sharpened to a single, savage purpose – to grab the enemy and claw him down from the sky.'[24]

On Tuesday, 13 August 1940, *Adlertag* (Eagle Day), the Luftwaffe launched a formidable 1,485 sorties over Britain, but forty-six German planes were shot down for thirteen of the RAF (of which six pilots survived); the next day saw twenty-seven Luftwaffe planes lost for eleven RAF. Those figures fail to take into account the number of German bombers that returned too damaged for repair, and with dead and wounded aircrew. An obvious advantage for the RAF was that those pilots who survived being shot down were often back up in the air that same day, whereas German pilots wound up in British captivity, or worse still in the English Channel. It was thought marginally better to land on water than to parachute into the sea, because the pilot had around forty seconds to exit the cockpit before the plane sank. *Kanalkampf* (Channel War), as it was known, for all its heroism and seeming chivalry on occasion, was overall a ghastly engagement for both sides, with devastatingly high casualty rates.

A major problem for the Luftwaffe was that its intelligence division wildly exaggerated the RAF's casualty rates, with ultimately disastrous results. It took its information from no fewer than ten different agencies, several of which were politically hostile to one another.[25] Between 1 July and 15 August, the Luftwaffe's intelligence unit under Colonel 'Beppo' Schmid estimated that 574 RAF planes had been destroyed by fighter action, anti-aircraft fire or on the ground, with a further 196 put beyond repair by crash-landings and accidents, a total of 770. As Schmid believed that the RAF had had 900 planes on 1 July, and that the British were building new fighter aircraft at the rate of between 270 and 300 per month, he estimated that there could be only 430 left, which meant 300 operational if one assumed 70 per cent serviceability.[26] He was hopelessly wrong on almost every count.

In fact the RAF had lost only 318 planes in that period. Furthermore, Beaverbrook's factories spurred on by his encouragement, and subjected on occasion to his ire, had produced 720 planes in those six weeks, far more than Schmid reckoned. 'I must have more planes,' said Beaverbrook, who was appointed to the War Cabinet in August. 'I don't care whose heart is broken or pride hurt.' Whereas Fighter Command started out on 1 July with 791 modern single-engined fighters, which was over a hundred fewer than the Germans thought, by 15 August it had 1,065 Hurricanes, Spitfires and low-wing, 1,030-horsepower Defiants, and the serviceability rate was 80 per cent. Nor did that include 289 in storage and 84 stationed at training units. So when Schmid estimated that the RAF was down to its last 430, in fact there were 1,438, over thrice the number.[27]

Schmid's problem derived not so much from German pilots boasting or exaggerating their 'kills' when reporting to Luftwaffe intelligence officers on their return as from the fact that very often they simply did not have time to witness the demise of an opponent, because as soon as one fighter had been disposed of the next dogfight commenced. Smoke or even flames emanating from an opponent's plane over southern England did not always mean that it and its occupant had been destroyed. However the figures were arrived at, Schmid's massive miscalculations were to result in a demoralization of the Luftwaffe pilots, who were told to expect little resistance as they escorted bombers later in the battle, but in fact were regularly met with wave after wave of RAF fighters. Because of radar, the aircraft-spotters of the Observer Corps, the decryption of codes by the Government Code and Cypher School (GCCS) at Bletchley Park in Buckinghamshire, and Y Department of Bomber Command listening to German telegraph traffic, almost every single bombing raid during the battle was intercepted.

The third phase of the battle opened on Saturday, 24 August when the Luftwaffe began concentrating on bombing the RAF's major air bases further inland. This was the most perilous period for Britain, because had the Luftwaffe managed to put the airfields out of action even for a short period, and had it been able to redirect its attacks against the British Home Fleet, an invasion attempt might have been possible, especially if accompanied by large-scale parachute landings on airfields. The raids were often conducted by eighty to a hundred bombers accompanied by a hundred fighters, and within a week the RAF bases at Biggin Hill, Manston, Lympne, Hawkinge and elsewhere were either heavily damaged or effectively put out of action.

The Luftwaffe flew 1,345 sorties over Britain on 30 August and even more than that the following day. Fighter Command lost thirty-nine fighters on 31 August alone. During that calendar month, 260 RAF pilots finished their training, whereas 304 had been killed or wounded.[28] This rate of attrition and replacement was clearly unsustainable if the Luftwaffe were able to keep up its punishing attacks on British airfields, and some RAF pilots were being sent up with only twenty hours' training. By the end of the month eleven of the forty-six squadron leaders and thirty-nine of the ninety-seven wing commanders had also been killed or wounded. There were some extraordinary tales of heroism and devotion to duty. An historian of the Spitfire records that, in the course of destroying no fewer than seventeen enemy aircraft in the period up to August 1940, the New Zealand ace Al Deere 'was shot down seven times, bailed out three times, collided with an Me-109, had one Spitfire of his [at an aerodrome] blown up 150 yards away by a bomb, and had another explode just seconds after he had scrambled from its wreckage'.[29]

As well as victory or defeat in the struggle with the RAF hanging in the balance, Saturday, 31 August found Adolf Hitler having trouble with his domestic staff. On that day his adjutant at the Berghof, SS-Hauptsturmführer Max Wünsche, wrote to Himmler in Berlin to say that two of the Führer's personal servants there, Hauptscharführer Wiebiczeck and Oberscharführer Sander, had been dismissed for theft, and sent to Dachau. The Führer had not yet made up his mind about 'the duration of their imprisonment in the concentration camp'.[30] History does not record their ultimate fate, but we can safely assume that Adolf Hitler was an unsympathetic person from whom to thieve.

Just as Fighter Command was stretched to its outer limit, with two months still to go before the autumn weather made the Channel impassable to the flat-bottomed boats and barges that the Kriegsmarine was collecting across the Channel, the Germans made a cardinal strategic error. They changed the *Schwerpunkt* in the middle of the campaign, from Britain's airfields to her cities. This vital shift in emphasis gave Fighter Command a desperately needed breathing space in which to repair its heavily damaged bases. The reason that Hitler and Göring altered the campaign objective was primarily political. They fell for a trap of Churchill's making, which played on Nazi psychology. Inherent in National Socialism was utter intolerance of contradiction. Pluralism and debate were anathema to a political creed based entirely on the Führer's supposed omniscience and infallibility. Thus when on 25, 28 and 29 August the RAF attacked Berlin – with eighty-one bombers in the first instance – in response to a single Heinkel He-111 bombing the City of London on 24 August (possibly by mistake when lost), Hitler's promises to the German people to protect the capital were exposed as worthless, and in the most blatant possible way. It was inevitable that he would react with irrational fury, promising the German people on 4 September: 'When they declare that they will attack our cities in great strength, then we will eradicate their cities.'[31] Yet by switching from bombing airfields to bombing cities three days later, Hitler made as fundamental an error as he had when he ordered his Panzers to halt outside Dunkirk on 24 May.

The fourth phase of the battle thus began on the late afternoon of Saturday, 7 September, with a massive raid on London's docklands. Three hundred tons of bombs were dropped by 350 bombers, protected by 350 fighters. 'Send all the pumps you've got,' one fireman told his central command station. 'The whole bloody world's on fire.' Because it was at low tide, the Thames was low and water correspondingly hard to pump, and burning petrol, sugar and rum from destroyed warehouses set the river alight. It was both the first and the worst attack of the eight-month Blitz, the German bombing campaign against Britain (which should not be confused with 'Blitzkrieg'); and it has been estimated that the inferno of that single day caused more damage than the Great Fire of London of 1666.[32] That night – from about 8.30 pm to 4 am – the Luftwaffe returned with a further 247 aircraft, to drop 352 tons of high explosive (HE) and 440 incendiary canisters. 'Each of the participants realized the importance of the hour,' recalled Adolf Galland of that first raid, as the vast docks of what was then the world's greatest maritime trading nation began to burn. The valour of the firemen was ably recaptured by the Humphrey Jennings movie *Fires Were Started* (1943), and the heroism of the bomb-disposal units also inspires awe. Indeed, the raid was so heavy that the Home Guard convinced itself that the invasion was under way, and sent the codeword 'Cromwell' to mobilize all troops and ring the church bells as a warning tocsin. 'If ever there was a time when one should wear life like a loose garment,' wrote the American military attaché in London, General Raymond Lee, 'this is it.'

Dowding's personal assistant, Flight Lieutenant Robert Wright, later recalled: 'The Germans launched the heaviest raid we had ever known, but the attack didn't go to the airfields, it went to London. So we were able to pull ourselves together, repair things, and, most important of the lot, it gave the pilots more of a chance for a little rest.'[33] Bomb craters were filled in on runways, planes were repaired in hangars not now under immediate threat of bombing, and control and communication lines that had been damaged over the previous fortnight were put back into operation. In a short period, the hitherto heavily pressed RAF was fully restored on almost all its most important bases, and receiving more planes from the factories than it could fill with pilots. The RAF had more fighters operational at the end of the battle of Britain – despite the high attrition rates – than at the beginning.

Mid-September 1940 saw bombs fall on the West End of London,

Downing Street, Buckingham Palace, the House of Lords, the Law Courts and eight Wren churches. Whereas Hitler never visited an air base or bomb-site throughout the war, probably fearful of being publicly connected to failure, Churchill, King George VI and Queen Elizabeth regularly did so, and were often cheered there (although on at least one occasion Churchill was booed by those whom the local authorities had failed to re-house quickly enough). General Lee recorded in his diary on 11 September that there was not one unbroken pane of glass in the Air Raid Precautions (ARP) and Civil Commissioner Headquarters in London, but the working area deep underground, which was gas-proof and air-conditioned, continued to function 'quite undisturbed'. In Ovington Square in Knightsbridge he noted that two houses 'had had their fronts blown out and pictures and carpets hung forlornly out in the open.' The City had suffered heavily, and Threadneedle Street was roped off because of 'a giant crater' in front of the Bank of England. More severe was the damage to Whitechapel and Docklands. 'When a bomb hits one of those dismal brick houses,' Lee observed, 'it goes on into the ground, blows a big hole and all the dreary fragments of the house fall into it.' He noted that although people were 'grubbing about in the wreckage to salvage what they could', nonetheless 'no one was complaining,' and one workman told him: 'All we want to know is whether we are bombing Berlin. If they are getting all or more than we are, we can stick it.'[34]

'Successful landing followed by occupation would end war in short order,' Hitler told a Führer-conference on 14 September 1940. 'Britain would starve to death.'[35] That day the bombing moved to the industrial area of the River Clyde. In all, between 7 September 1940 and the end of the first period of the Blitz on 16 May 1941, there were seventy-one major attacks on London – that is, attacks dropping more than 100 tons of HE – eight each on Liverpool, Birmingham and Plymouth, six on Bristol, five on Glasgow, four on Southampton, three on Portsmouth and at least one on a further eight cities. The Blitz is thus different from, but related to, the battle of Britain. The initiation of the London Blitz during the battle of Britain allowed the RAF to achieve victory in the air battle, although the Blitz continued long after that victory was won. In total 18,291 tons of HE were dropped on London during these months and more than 1,000 tons on each of Liverpool, Birmingham, Plymouth and Glasgow, as well as between 919 and 578 tons on other British cities.[36] Despite this, ARP were so well advanced that it was very rare for the daily death toll to exceed 250 (in contrast with German cities that later were to see very many times that incinerated on a single night).[37]

Although Britain had 1,200 heavy anti-aircraft guns and 3,932 searchlights in July 1940, and 1,691 and 4,532 eleven months later, they were of limited use except for forcing German planes to higher altitudes than were ideal for accurate bombing. Overall during the night-time Blitz, more German bombers were lost to flying accidents than to anti-aircraft fire or night-fighters.[38] Ack-Ack, as it was known, nonetheless gave the civilians, sheltering below in converted cellars, London Underground stations, public shelters and private Anderson shelters in gardens, the morale-boosting sense that Britain was fighting back. (Surprisingly enough, although two million people left London during the Blitz, 60 per cent of those who remained slept in their beds rather than going to shelters.)[39]

Hitler's intentions were clear from a monologue he gave to his architect-in-chief (and later armaments minister) Albert Speer at a supper in the Reich Chancellery in the summer of 1940, in which he said:

Have you ever looked at a map of London? It is so closely built up that one source of fire alone would suffice to destroy the whole city, as happened once before, two hundred [sic] years ago. Göring wants to use innumerable incendiary bombs of an altogether new type to create sources of fire in all parts of London. Fires everywhere. Thousands of them. Then they'll unite in one gigantic area conflagration. Göring has the right idea. Explosive bombs don't work but it can be done with incendiary bombs – total destruction of London. What use will their fire department be once that really starts![40]

Although it sounds like the ranting of a pathological pyromaniac, the concentration on incendiary rather than high-explosive bombs did have logic behind it, as Hitler was to discover at the time of the bombing of Hamburg in July 1943.

The state of morale was obviously going to be vital if Britain was not going to buckle under the stress, pain and horror of the nightly bombing. Lieutenant-Commander John McBeath, who commanded the destroyer HMS *Venomous* that brought BEF troops back from Dunkirk, recalled that the attitude of their officers was 'that although they were naturally defeated and had been kicked out of Europe, there was no sort of idea that they'd been beaten. It was just, "Well, we'll get them next time." '[41] Yet how could there possibly be a next time, considering that Hitler was now the unquestioned master of Continental Europe from Saint-Jean-de-Luz on the Franco-Spanish border in the south to Narvik in the north, and from Cherbourg in the west to Lublin in the east? For all its lack of logic, the feeling did nonetheless exist in Britain that fighting on without Continental allies was almost a relief. The playwright J. B. Priestley remembered a mood of 'We're by ourselves now and really we can get on with this war.'[42] The King felt the same, telling his mother on 27 June 1940, 'Personally I feel happier now that we have no allies to be polite to and to pamper.'[43]

British agencies attempted to boost national morale through the subtle use of public information, certainly far less blatant than the vainglorious untruths told nightly by Dr Goebbels' vast propaganda machine in Germany. These British themes accepted vulnerability, something that was foreign to the Nazi self-perception. Thus the songs weren't uniformly jingoistic: Anne Shelton's haunting ballad 'I'll Be Seeing You' could refer as much to a dead lover as to an absent one; Flanagan and Allen's gentle 'Run, Rabbit, Run' expresses the hope that the rabbit will escape the British farmer's pot; Vera Lynn didn't know where or when she would see her man again, except 'some sunny day'. The movie *Waterloo Bridge* (1940), starring Vivien Leigh and Robert Taylor, was a stern defence of British decency and values. Set almost entirely as a flashback to the Great War, the beautiful ballerina Myra falls in love with the dashing aristocrat Captain Roy Cronin, but is forced into prostitution after he is listed as killed in action. When he reappears and replights his troth, she commits suicide sooner than sully the honour of her fiancé's family and regiment. The three Rendellshire Fusiliers officers who appear in the movie are all models of decency, affability and courage (the hero had won a Military Cross at the battle of Cambrai).

The movie *Mrs Miniver*, covering the events of 1940, was made in

1942. The eponymous heroine, played by Greer Garson, is married to an architect played by Walter Pidgeon. The scenes of stoical devotion to duty – Mr Miniver sailing to Dunkirk in his small boat, his wife disarming a wounded German pilot, their son joining the RAF and their house being bombed – do not underestimate the bereavement of war, especially with the death through strafing of the Minivers' beautiful young daughter-in-law, just returned from honeymoon. In the closing scene, where RAF planes can be seen through the bombed-out roof of the village church during Sunday service, the vicar concludes: 'This is not only a war of soldiers in uniform, it is a war of the people, of all the people . . . This is our war. Fight it then.' Civilian morale responded superbly during the Blitz, and when the Mass Observation polling organization asked Londoners in early 1941 what had made them most depressed that winter, more people cited the weather than the bombing.[44]

No propaganda was necessary to highlight the destruction of the city of Coventry, which became emblematic of the Blitz for many Britons after it was attacked by 500 German bombers on the night of 14 November 1940. Although the numbers killed and injured (380 and 865 respectively) were small in terms of the suffering of German, Russian and Japanese cities later in the war – and more RAF men died in raids on Germany than civilians died in the Blitz – the fact that it came early on in the conflict made it a powerful symbol of Hitler's ruthlessness.

The battle of Britain reached its zenith on 15 September 1940, which Churchill noted fell, like the battle of Waterloo, on a Sunday. It started off with a large raid on London of 100 bombers and 400 fighters, but ended with fifty-six German planes shot down at the cost of twenty-six RAF (some accounts have sixty-one to twenty-nine, according to different criteria, but the all-important ratio is similar).[45] 'How many reserves have we?' the Prime Minister asked the New Zealander Air Vice-Marshal Keith Park at the height of the battle. 'There are none,' came the reply. Although the numbers were minute by later standards – 400 Japanese planes were downed in the one-day battle in the Marianas in 1945 for example – in 1940 they were unsustainably large for the Germans.

After 15 September – today celebrated as Battle of Britain Day –

morale in the Luftwaffe plummeted. 'Failure to achieve any noticeable success,' recorded Galland,

constantly changing orders betraying lack of purpose and obvious misman-agement of the situation by the Command, and unjustified accusations, had a most demoralizing effect on us fighter pilots, who were already overtaxed by physical and mental strain. We complained of the leadership, the bombers, the Stukas and were dissatisfied with ourselves. We saw one comrade after the other, old and tested brothers in combat, vanish from our ranks.[46]

At one meeting at Karinhall, Göring asked Galland what he most needed for the battle. When the much decorated ace, who was to have an oak-leaf cluster added to his Knight's Cross after he shot down his fortieth Allied plane, over the Thames estuary on 24 September, answered, 'An outfit of Spitfires for my group,' the Reichsmarschall 'stamped off, growling as he went'.

Although the Stuka Ju-87 unleashed bombing power equal to a 5-ton lorry hitting a brick wall at 6omph, this was nothing like enough to force a vast city like London, the capital of the British Empire, to its knees. The Stuka's lack of speed and manoeuvrability in anything other than Blitzkrieg-style attack supporting ground troops made the plane a relatively easy target for Hurricanes and Spitfires. The complaints of Galland's colleagues about 'the bombers, the Stukas' referred to the fact that Germany had no efficient long-range bomber, and was not to deploy the Heinkel He-177 until early 1944. The largest twin-engined German bomber of the battle of Britain, the He-111, had bomb-loads of 4,000 pounds, a great deal at the time but puny in comparison with the Allied bombs dropped on Germany later on in the war – those could weigh up to 10 tons. The heavy raids on London after 7 September were largely undertaken by bomber wings of fifty to eighty planes, protected by fighters which could remain over London for a maximum of fifteen minutes. Further, as Galland readily admitted, the bravery of the RAF pilots 'undoubtedly saved their country at this crucial hour'. Nevertheless the rule that acts of extreme bravery have to be witnessed before a Victoria Cross can be given meant that only one was awarded during the battle of Britain. As the *London Gazette* recorded of the exploits of Flight Lieutenant J. B. Nicholson:

During an engagement with the enemy near Southampton on August 16, 1940, Flight Lieutenant Nicholson's aircraft was hit by four cannon shells, two of which wounded him whilst another set fire to the gravity tank. When about to abandon his aircraft owing to flames in the cockpit, he sighted an enemy fighter. This he attacked and shot down although as a result of staying in his burning aircraft, he sustained serious burns to his hands, face, neck and legs. Flight Lieutenant Nicholson has always displayed enthusiasm for air fighting and this incident shows that he possesses courage and determination of a high order by continuing to engage the enemy after he had been wounded and his aircraft set on fire. He displayed exceptional gallantry and disregard for the safety of his own life.[47]

The citation did not mention that Nicholson also survived gunshot pellet wounds when the Home Guard opened fire at what they assumed was an enemy parachutist. Tragically he went missing while flying as a passenger in a Liberator over the Bay of Bengal on 2 May 1945.

Another aspect in which Britain did not stand alone in 1940–41 was in the vital help afforded her by foreign pilots. Of the 2,917 pilots who fought with Fighter Command during the battle of Britain, no fewer than 578 – one-fifth – were not British. On that roll of honour there were 145 Poles, 126 New Zealanders, 97 Canadians, 88 Czechs, 33 Australians, 29 Belgians, 25 South Africans, 13 French, 10 Irish, 8 Americans, 3 Rhodesians and a Jamaican.[48] Indeed, statistically the most successful unit of the battle was 303 Squadron, composed of Poles. They and the Czechs were particularly ruthless pilots, their fanaticism fuelled by what their countries were suffering under German occupation and by what faced them if they were to be defeated in Britain, which Polish RAF officers dubbed *Wyspa ostatniej nadziei* (the island of last hope). Such were the strictures of American neutrality at the time that the Americans who volunteered were liable to lose their US citizenship under the 1907 Citizenship Act, and faced several years' imprisonment and a $10,000 fine. Eight joined up anyhow, but only one – John Haviland of 151 Squadron, who had learnt to fly while at Nottingham University and went into battle after less than twenty hours' flying fighters – survived the war.[49]

*

Two days after the Luftwaffe's mauling on 15 September, Hitler, who had already postponed Sealion until 27 September, this time put it off 'until further notice'. The last daylight raid on London took place on 30 September, although there were some heavy night-time raids thereafter. The first day that no planes were lost on either side was 31 October, by which time the battle of Britain could be safely described as over. Four nights later, on Monday, 4 November, no sirens sounded, for the first time since July. Britain was safe. By then, however, a quarter of a million people had been rendered temporarily homeless, with 16,000 houses destroyed, a further 60,000 uninhabitable and 130,000 damaged. Nonetheless the morale of the British people, though much further strained than the censored and self-censored press could admit, did not break, as Britain attempted to continue, in the phrase of the day, 'Business as usual'. A government poster summed it up perfectly with the words: 'Keep Calm and Carry On'.

The Blitz cost 43,000 British civilians killed and a further 51,000 seriously injured, but after September 1940 the country was out of mortal danger, for the moment at least.[50] Of course only the tiny number of those in receipt of German cipher decrypts in Britain could know this, and since the British Government wished to keep the people in a state of readiness, ordinary Britons remained on high alert until Hitler ended the bombing campaign a month prior to his invasion of Russia. Overall, since May 1940 the Germans had lost 1,733 planes to the RAF's 915. These were very modest numbers of planes compared to some of the losses that would be incurred in Russia and the Far East a few years hence, but at the time they were enough to decide the battle in Britain's favour, especially once added to the 147 Me-109s and 82 Me-110s lost in the battle of France. It was the first engagement that the Allies had won against the Germans. Hitler's demand in Directive No. 16, 'to eliminate the English mother country as a base from which the war against Germany can be continued', had been successfully resisted, and Britain was indeed to become just such a base.

Colonel Schmid's belief that the RAF was small compared to the Luftwaffe was taken on by the British too. Naturally, the Prime Minister idolized the brave young pilots, and rewarded them with his most precious gift: an immortal phrase. Returning from the Operations Room at RAF Uxbridge, west London, on 15 August where he had been watching No. 11 Group's battle in progress, he had told his chief Staff officer Major-General Hastings 'Pug' Ismay, 'Never in the field of human conflict was so much owed by so many to so few.' He repeated the phrase in the House of Commons five days later. On that occasion he added, 'All hearts go out to the fighter pilots, whose brilliant actions we see with our own eyes day after day.'[51] His words have helped to fix the battle and the heroism of 'the Few' in the collective consciousness of the British people ever since.

Churchill knew that, if Britain was to survive, what was called the Home Front needed to be made far more efficient, and so his ministry imposed radical changes on British society which were generally accepted in the mood of national emergency. The Chamberlain ministry had set in place the necessary legislative framework: compulsory military conscription had been introduced in April 1939 and the Emergency Powers (Defence) Act of August had given the Government sweeping powers. In May 1940 Churchill introduced a new subsection of the Act, numbered 18B(1A), which allowed him to intern Fascists without trial for the duration of the war, effectively an introduction of martial law in Britain. He disliked having to do this, describing the suspension of habeas corpus as 'in the highest degree odious', but he nonetheless took on powers that left him the closest Britain has come to a dictator since Oliver Cromwell.

Britain still imported 70 per cent of her food in 1939, so the invocation to 'Dig for Victory' meant the difference between life and death for the men of the Merchant Navy, 30,589 of whom lost their lives in the war. The amount of arable land was increased by 43 per cent, with 7 million acres of grassland going under the plough. The introduction of rationing and the virtual abolition of food wastage, as well as the swelling of the number of allotments to 1.7 million, meant that Britain could reduce food imports to the bare minimum. By the end of the war Britain grew about half her sugar consumption, enough for the entire domestic sugar ration.[52]

The Chamberlain ministry had achieved little in organizing the British economy for war. By May 1940 there were still more than a million Britons out of work and the labour force had increased by only 11 per cent, largely through the introduction of women into almost all areas of non-heavy industry. With men away serving in the forces, 80,000 women of the Women's Land Army took their places in agriculture and horticulture, while 160,000 women replaced men in the various transport services. 'Throughout the period of heavy German air-raids on this country, the arteries of the nation, the railways, with their extensive dock undertakings, were subjected to intensive attacks,' Churchill told the House of Commons in December 1943. 'In spite of every enemy effort the traffic has been kept moving and the great flow of munitions proceeds. Results such as the railways have achieved are only won by blood and sweat.'[53] As often as not, this was the blood and sweat of women.

Such a revolution in the mobilization of manpower would have been unimaginable in any other circumstance than total war, and it changed British society for ever. By June 1944, of the total of 16 million women aged between fourteen and fifty-nine in Britain, 7.1 million had been mobilized for war work in some form, including the auxiliary services, Civil Defence and the munitions industries, and 1.644 million were engaged in 'essential war work' which freed up men for the forces or heavy industry. The figure for male employment in various aspects of national service was even higher by late 1944, at 93.6 per cent of the total of 15.9 million between the ages of fourteen and sixty-four.[54] Yet despite this there were still enough men for 1.75 million to serve in the Home Guard and 1.75 million in Civil Defence, while many others took on Fire Guard duties. Despite general enthusiasm for the measures necessary for national defence, this was not all voluntary: for example, compulsory enlistment of women in the auxiliary services was introduced in December 1941, so all women between eighteen and sixty, married or single, could be ordered into factories, into the services or on to the land. Nor did they receive equal pay for equal work.

The state also played the major role in the enormous programme of evacuation that took place in Britain in the early months of the war, then again during the Blitz, and later on during the attacks from the V-1 'doodlebug' flying bombs and V-2 rockets. In all between 1939 and 1944 more than a million children were removed from the danger of the cities to the relative safety of the countryside, where in many cases they stayed with complete strangers for years far from home. Although there are many tales of happy evacuees, homesickness, lice, boredom, anxiety bed-wetting and a childhood separated from their parents were the sad experiences of many British children during Hitler's War.

The compulsory carrying of gas masks, the evening black-out – 'Put out that light!' was the habitual shout of ARP wardens – and nightly recourse to shelters in back gardens, Underground stations and cellars form the staple part of civilians' memories from the war. As does rationing. Butter, sugar, bacon and ham were rationed from January 1940, but the following year this had to be extended to almost all foodstuffs except bread. It was an indictment of British society of the 1930s that some people actually ate better under wartime rationing than they had during the Great Depression six years earlier.[55] Clothes and petrol were rationed, soap and water for washing were limited, and scrap metal was collected for aircraft. For those of a naturally economical – even miserly – nature, the Second World War was a godsend; for those who enjoyed life's indulgences, such as cosmetics and silk stockings, it was a series of tribulations.

If truth is traditionally 'the first casualty of war', then sound finance is the second. The British economy was driven into near-bankruptcy by the colossal expense of the struggle. Churchill was adamant that whatever needed to be spent on national defence would be, despite the repeated warnings of his chancellors of the exchequer Sir Kingsley Wood (up to his death in office in September 1943) and Sir John Anderson thereafter. Income tax rose from 7 shillings and 6 pence in the pound to 10 shillings, that is from 37.5 per cent to 50 per cent, and many people bought National Saving Certificates at patriotically low rates of return. Total employment in all the productive sectors of the British economy (that is, other than the armed services, health, education and so on) fell by 1.6 million during the war.[56] With more than half of Britain's industrial production devoted to arms, exports collapsed to the point where there was a negative balance of trade of £1.04 billion in 1945, against one of a manageable £387 million before the war. Although some in Whitehall recognized that a strong British economy was a powerful war weapon in itself, the sheer expense of keeping so much of the population out of productive employment and in uniform, as well as the cost of buying or producing war matériel, at a time of falling personal and corporate tax revenue, meant that Britain had to liquidate most of her financial reserves and sell almost all her foreign assets between 1939 and 1945.

By the end of the war Britain's foreign debt had quintupled to £3.35 billion, making her the world's most indebted nation, and had the economist John Maynard Keynes – who had predicted 'a financial Dunkirk' – not negotiated a $3.75 billion loan from the United States in December 1945, there was a real chance that Britain would have become technically insolvent. 'Without the loan,' considered the then financial editor of the *Guardian* Richard Fry, 'there could have been real starvation and long delays in reconstruction (housing, power stations, railways, etc) and the political considerations might have been revolutionary.'[57] Yet the Churchill ministry was willing to risk all that in order to keep Britain fighting the war to the best of her abilities. Though largely unsung compared to his other great acts of reckless courage, Churchill's largesse with the British Treasury was nothing short of heroic.

If Britain had preserved her independence through her own efforts, other countries that had also not been invaded by Germany tried to preserve theirs by declaring their neutrality. These included Turkey (which both the Allies and Axis tried to coax into their camps), Switzerland (which had a large citizen army and easily defensible terrain), Portugal (which was generally, if not always dependably, pro-Allied), the Vatican (which was anti-Nazi, though not undiplomatically so), Eire (which had the English Channel, the RAF and the Royal Navy for protection) and Sweden (which in July 1940 gave Germany the right to move troops over her borders and guaranteed sales of her iron-ore deposits to the German armaments industry). Another was Spain, whose dictator General Francisco Franco owed Hitler much for the military support so recently given in the Spanish Civil War, but who trod a carefully neutral path, waiting to see who would win. Hitler, having met the Caudillo in nine hours of discussions at Hendaye on the Spanish border with France in October 1940 to try to persuade him to declare war against the Allies, later remarked, 'Rather than go through that again, I would prefer to have three or four teeth taken out.'[58]

Churchill summed up the neutrals' position in a radio broadcast of 20 January 1940: 'Each one hopes that if he feeds the crocodile enough, the crocodile will eat him last. All of them hope that the storm will pass before their time comes to be devoured.' Several neutrals complained about the characterization, but it was essentially accurate. Switzerland, despite having 450,000 men under arms and a virtually impregnable 'national redoubt', had declared her neutrality in March 1938. Yet the Swiss also allowed German and Italian military supply trains to pass through their country, baulking only at the passage of actual troops. They charged well for these facilities. Before the war, the Swiss state-subsidized timber company had built the concentration camp of Dachau, with the contract for 13 million Swiss francs being negotiated by the son of the later Swiss Commander-in-Chief Henri Guisan.

It is impossible to calculate how many innocent lives were lost by the Swiss refusal to accept Jewish refugees escaping from the Vichy militia roundups of 1942–3. Pressure mounted for the Swiss to review their draconian immigration laws, by which only 7,000 immigrants had been allowed into the country since the outbreak of war. Nevertheless Dr Heinrich Rothmund, the chief of the police department of the federal Ministry of Justice and Police, instructed his men to repel Jews attempting to cross the frontier in the wooded area around Pontarlier–Besançon, and those found on Swiss soil were escorted back to France. 'Incredible scenes developed,' records the Swiss historian of his country's neutrality. 'Some committed suicide in front of the Swiss border guards.'[59] The argument the Swiss Government gave for refusing entry to persecuted Jews was that subversive agents might enter the country too, that Swiss people might lose jobs to the immigrants, and that many immigrants would not move on to third countries. A ban was thus imposed upon any refugee or immigrant 'engaging in any professional activity, paid or unpaid'. By May 1945, there were 115,000 refugees in camps, however, with more staying in hotels, in hostels and with friends or family. During the war a total of 400,000 people moved to or through Switzerland, including, of course, towards its end German and Italian Fascists.[60]

Swedish accommodation of the Nazis started early. Although they resolutely refused to allow the British and French expeditionary forces to cross their territory to aid Finland in her struggle against Russia in early 1940, the Stockholm Government allowed the Germans to cross it to reinforce their army of occupation in Norway later that same year. Between July 1940 and August 1943, no fewer than 140,000 German troops and countless thousand tons of military equipment and supplies had used the Swedish rail network, thus protecting the Kriegsmarine from the Royal Navy.

Just before the German invasion of Russia, the Swedes allowed an entire German division to traverse the country in order to take part in the assault. The next year, Swedish ships were carrying 53 per cent of Germany's iron-ore imports – the raw material most needed for her armaments industry – to German ports, thereby saving the German Navy further trouble and danger. It was only after the battle of Stalingrad in February 1943, when she saw which side would probably win, that Sweden gave in to Allied pressure and forced the Germans to carry the ore in their own ships; not until April 1944 did Sweden stop selling Germany ball-bearings, and after the war crucial components for the V-2 rockets were found to have 'Made in Sweden' stamped on them. Albert Speer records that Hitler intended his vast new capital at Berlin – named Germania – to be very largely built from Swedish granite, which was being obligingly shipped to him throughout the war along with the iron ore and ball-bearings. Had Hitler won the war, of course, the sovereignty of Switzerland, Sweden, Eire and several other neutrals would have been swatted overnight. In late January 1942, after saying that the Swedes and Swiss were merely 'playing at soldiers', the Führer told cronies at the Berghof that 'the Jews must pack up, disappear from Europe . . . they'll have to clear out of Switzerland and Sweden. We cannot allow them to retain bases of withdrawal at our doors.'[61]

The most notable absentee from civilization's line of battle, however, was Eire, whose actions cannot be explained, like Sweden's and Switzerland's, by a close physical proximity to Germany. Neither was it a case of malingering, for even when in the latter stages of the war there was no chance of a German invasion the Taoiseach, Eamon de Valera, still refrained from publicly denouncing the Nazis or Hitler himself. (When he criticized the invasion of the neutral Low Countries in 1940 he did not even specify who had been responsible.) Of his infamous gesture in visiting the German Legation in Dublin to express his condolences on the death of Hitler in April 1945, de Valera later said: 'I acted correctly and, I feel certain, wisely.' Since the concentration camp of Buchenwald had already been liberated by then, and the genocidal nature of the Nazi regime revealed, the British and Americans reacted with rage to this action, but it went largely unreported in Eire's heavily censored press.

Eire's neutrality aroused great resentment in the rest of the British Isles, and it was not just Churchill who considered the country to be 'legally at war, but skulking'. In 1938, the Chamberlain Government had turned over to Irish sovereignty the three strategically valuable Atlantic ports that Britain had retained under the terms of the 1922 Anglo-Irish Treaty, and Dublin's denial of their use to the Royal Navy on the outbreak of war the next year exposed this as having been a disastrous error by the British. As Churchill put it to the War Cabinet: 'Eire was strangling England quite pleasantly.'[62] For him the Irish joke of the day – 'So who are we neutral *against*?' – was not funny. The only explanation for Eire's neutrality was a lingering hostility to Britain after centuries of mutual antagonism, which blinded the de Valera Government to the greater issues that were at stake by 1939.

The loss through diplomacy of the Atlantic naval bases in southern and western Ireland meant that escorts could not sail as far out into the Atlantic as in the Great War; destroyers and corvettes took longer to be refuelled; tugs could not be sent out to ships in distress, but instead escorts had to go 'the long way round' from Scottish ports. 'To compute how many men and how many ships this denial was costing, month after month', wrote Nicholas Monsarrat, the novelist who commanded a frigate during the battle of the Atlantic, 'was hardly possible; but the total was substantial and tragic.' Although Monsarrat's classic tale *The Cruel Sea* was of course fictional, its hero, who also commanded a frigate on the transatlantic convoys during the battle, states:

it was difficult to withhold one's contempt for a country such as Ireland, whose battle this was and whose chances of freedom and independence in the event of a German victory were nil. The fact that Ireland was standing aside from the conflict ... posed, from the naval angle, special problems which affected, sometimes mortally, all sailors engaged in the Atlantic, and earned their particular loathing ... In the list of people you were prepared to like when the war was over, the man who stood by and watched while you were getting your throat cut could not figure very high.[63]

If the neutrals could not be prevailed upon to help, it was necessary to stir up those former Continental allies that had been subdued by the Germans, and on 19 July 1940 Churchill set up the Special Operations Executive (SOE), 'to co-ordinate all action by way of subversion and sabotage against the enemy overseas'.[64] This was to be the romantic world of moonlit parachutists, arms caches, cyanide pills, forged papers, weapons-drops, gold sovereigns and guerrilla units that occupied so much literature and film, a concentration of attention out of all proportion to SOE's actual operational importance.

'Regular soldiers are not the men to stir up revolution,' wrote the Labour politician Hugh Dalton of his new role in control of the newly founded SOE, 'to create social chaos, or to use all those ungentlemanly means of winning the war which come so easily to the Nazis.' Churchill had always been interested in irregular warfare, and SOE was his brainchild; on 16 July 1940 he appointed Dalton to the post with the inspiring invocation: 'And now set Europe ablaze.'[65] The intention was later to use resistance movements to hold down a large number of German divisions far away from the Eastern, and later the Italian and Western Fronts, but there was an horrific price to pay when this was put into operation. Targeted (and often untargeted) assassinations and the blowing up of communication lines behind enemy lines were sometimes strategically helpful before D-Day, but they tended to alienate the local populations upon whom the German wrath fell once the SOE operatives had got away. The Germans did not jib at mass shootings of hostages in reprisal against attacks on them in Occupied Europe, with entire villages occasionally paying the price for SOE operations that were strategically not worth the butcher's bill. Where SOE did succeed was in the intangible sense of helping to return a sense of self-esteem to European peoples after crushing defeats that had been measured in mere weeks. This was especially true of France, which had always seen herself as – indeed had always been – *la grande nation*.[66]

SOE also played an important part in holding back Stalin's ambitions. It was partly the arms provided by SOE that allowed the Yugoslav partisan leader Marshal Josip Broz Tito to stand up to the Russians in 1945–6 and the anti-Communists to triumph in Greece; the French Communists might have tried to stage a coup in the autumn of 1944 had not SOE distributed half a million small arms to *résistants* across France. SOE helped Queen Wilhelmina back on to the throne in Holland in March 1945; in Burma it persuaded U Aung San's militia to turn their coats and join the Allied side in the spring of 1945. It also carried out important operations against German 'heavy water' nuclear research facilities at Telemark and Vermork, the success of which may have retarded the German capacity for developing an atomic bomb. Furthermore, operations undertaken on the ground could sometimes achieve accuracy denied to precision bombing. For example, the Peugeot factory at Sochaux near Montbéliard, which manufactured tank turrets, had its key installation wrecked by a satchel-bomb delivered by SOE on 5 November 1943, four months after an RAF attack had missed the target and resulted in heavy civilian casualties near by.[67]

A severe problem for SOE was that European resistance movements were often torn by internal animosities. In Greece and Yugoslavia monarchists hated Communists, whereas the French *résistants* covered the whole political spectrum between right-wing Gaullists and Communist *francs-tireurs*. Then there were the central internal contradictions of all operations: how to create secret armies while not attracting attention but simultaneously carrying out high-profile sabotage, and how not to lose the support of the local populace while your actions inevitably bring down the murderous wrath of the Germans. Furthermore, SOE repeatedly clashed with the RAF over plane allocations, with the Foreign Office over neutrals' sovereignty, with local commanders-in-chief over strategy, and with the War Office (where SOE was nicknamed 'the Racket') over resources, and none of this was helped by the fact that Dalton was a naturally very combative politician.[68]

If Britons were willing to bring down the wrath of the Germans on innocent civilians, they were also prepared to do the same to themselves. The auxiliary units that were set up by Colonel (later Major-General) Colin Gubbins in 1940 in order to continue the resistance after a German invasion of Britain took great care not to allow their (sometimes quite elaborate) hide-outs to be noticed by the local population, in case they were betrayed as a result of the threat of reprisals. As for the Regular Army, 'We prepared road-blocks and cleared fields of fire; not that we had anything to fire except a few shot-guns,' recalled Michael Howard of his service in the Coldstream Guards in the summer of 1940.

I scoured the neighbourhood for hollow lanes across which we could stretch wires and decapitate German motor-cyclists. The thought that if we did anything of the kind the Germans would probably shoot the entire population of the village did not enter our heads, or at least my head. Nor did the realization that if we lost the war I would be deported, along with all fit young men over the age of seventeen, as slave-labour to Germany, and that for my mother, 100 per cent Jewish, an even worse fate might lie in store.[69]

The death of Hitler's Sealion meant that none of that happened in Britain as it did on the Continent. The British were thus saved from having to make the terrible choices and compromises which the populations of Occupied Europe were forced to make. The spirit of 1940 – the undoubted *annus mirabilis* of British history – was often to be called upon by Churchill in the remaining years of the war, and by many other politicians since.

For British strategists a vast void had opened up. Where were they to strike the Axis next, now that Europe was completely closed off? More out of a lack of any viable alternative than anything else, as well as to protect British interests further afield, the war was transferred to the North African littoral and the Mediterranean. Soon the victory of the battle of Britain was to seem like an all too isolated incident in a dangerously unpredictable struggle.

4

Contesting the Littoral

September 1939–June 1942

You seem to be the only enemy I can be sure of defeating these days.   Lord Wavell, playing backgammon with the
Countess of Ranfurly, 3 May 1941[1]

'Before Alamein, we never had a victory,' Churchill wrote in his war memoirs. 'After Alamein we never had a defeat.' Like so many generalizations, the remark had a kernel of truth, even if one ignores the huge exception of the battle of Britain. But Churchill should have qualified his words with 'over the Germans', because Britain won spectacular victories over the Italians in Africa. Indeed these were so significant that they encouraged Hitler to contest the Mediterranean with resources that would have been far better employed in Russia. Faced with the defeat of Fascism in Africa, Hitler decided to try to save his ideological soulmate, Benito Mussolini, in Africa (and later in Greece), even though his strategy dictated that neither place would be the key to the victory he sought, which was always going to be in Russia.

The first of several British commanders in the long Western Desert campaign was Archibald Wavell, a fine example of the British Army officer of the old school. Wavell's family came to Britain with William the Conqueror, both his father and grandfather had been generals, he had had a brilliant school career and was personally brave in action. A natural sportsman (especially golf and polo), captain of the regimental hockey team, a fine shot, an excellent linguist (Urdu, Pashtu and Russian), he served in the Boer War and on the North-West Frontier and entered Camberley Staff College in 1909 with an 85 per cent exam pass. He married a colonel's daughter called Queenie, of whom he wrote admiringly to a friend: 'She rides well to hounds.' Much to his chagrin, Wavell was stuck at the War Office when the rest of the Army decamped to France and Flanders in August 1914, but although he did later see action it was as a liaison officer with the Grand Duke Nicholas' army in Turkey, and later serving under General Allenby in Palestine, that Wavell spent most of the Great War. He not only distinguished himself, but got to know the Middle East and was sent out to command in Palestine in 1937–8. He was also the most literary and reflective of Britain's Second World War generals.

Yet there were always severe personality differences between Wavell and Churchill, amounting at times to mutual detestation. Even though Wavell had supported the creation of Ralph Bagnold's Long Range Desert Group in North Africa and later encouraged Orde Wingate in his unorthodox fighting practices in the Burmese jungle, Churchill thought him too cautious and conventional a commander, and longed to replace him. When in August 1940 Wavell returned to London to brief the War Cabinet's Middle East Committee, Anthony Eden thought his account of operations 'masterly', but Churchill's curt cross-questioning left him feeling bruised and insulted.[2] Nonetheless, great risks were run in Africa that month, virtually denuding Britain of tanks while the country was still under threat of invasion, in one of the toughest decisions of the war.

In mid-September Mussolini, fancying himself a second Caesar, sent Marshal Rodolfo Graziani's Tenth Army to invade Egypt with five divisions along the coast, taking Sidi Barrani. He stopped 75 miles short of the British, in Mersa Matruh, while both sides were reinforced. It was a nerve-wracking time for the British in Egypt. 'We actually made dummy tanks, dummy guns, and from the air when reconnaissance planes came across it looked as though we had a really good, strong army,' recalled Private Bob Mash, an engineer with the Nile Army. 'We've blown up rubber tanks, put them in position, taken them down in the evening, taken them three or four miles further away, blown them up again and laid them there, and from the air it looks as if we had plenty of tanks. Just the same as on the Canal Zone . . . every other anti-aircraft gun was a wooden one.'[3]

On 8 December 1940, Wavell's friend, Lieutenant-General Richard

O'Connor, commander of the Western Desert Force (numbering only 31,000 men, 120 guns and 275 tanks), counter-attacked fiercely against a force four times his size, concentrating on each fortified area in turn.[4] Operation Compass had close support from the Navy and RAF, and, aided by a collapse in Italian morale, by mid-December O'Connor had cleared Egypt of Italians and 38,000 prisoners were taken. Bardia fell on 5 January and on the 22nd the 7th Armoured Division (the 'Desert Rats') captured the key port of Tobruk, which was to loom large in the fortunes of both sides over the next two years. As so often, air superiority was vital, especially as there was less possibility of concealment in the desert than in other terrains. The RAF quickly established dominance over the Italian Air Force, the Regia Aeronautica.[5] British naval control of the North African littoral also helped O'Connor, because much of the coastal road was within the range of the large-calibre guns of the Royal Navy.

Encouraged by his success in the north, Wavell then moved to cover his southern flank. When Italy had declared war the Duke of Aosta, Viceroy of Ethiopia (Abyssinia), had crossed into the Sudan with 110,000 troops and taken Kassala, then into Kenya to capture Moyale, and also into British Somaliland, seizing Berbera. Wavell had bided his time before responding, but in late January 1941 he sent two British Commonwealth forces totalling 70,000 men – mainly South Africans – to exercise a massive pincer movement utterly to rout Aosta. Lieutenant-General Sir Alan Cunningham occupied Addis Ababa on 4 April, having averaged 35 miles a day for over a thousand miles, taking 50,000 prisoners and gaining 360,000 square miles of territory at the cost of 135 men killed and four captured.[6] The Emperor Haile Selassie of Ethiopia returned to his capital on 5 May, five years to the day since it had fallen to the Italians. Aosta and his enormous but demoralized army surrendered on 17 May, leaving the Red Sea and Gulf of Aden open to Allied shipping once more.

Meanwhile, in the north, very great victories greeted O'Connor, who saved the Suez Canal and drove the Italians back along the coast road to Benghazi. As the 6th Division forced Graziani into headlong retreat, O'Connor sent the 7th Division through the desert via Mechili to slice through the Cyrenaican bulge and cut off the Italians. At the battle of Beda Fomm on the Gulf of Sirte between 5 and 7 February

1941 the British Empire and Commonwealth won its first really significant land victory of the Second World War. In two months from 7 December 1940, the Western Desert Force had achieved successes that utterly belied Churchill's statement quoted above; they had destroyed nine Italian divisions and part of a tenth, advanced 500 miles and captured 130,000 prisoners, 380 tanks and 1,290 guns, all at the cost of only 500 killed and 1,373 wounded. In the whole course of the campaign, Wavell never enjoyed a force larger than two divisions, only one of them armoured. It was the Austerlitz of Africa, and prompted his prep school to note in the Old Boys' section of the *Summer Fields* magazine: 'Wavell has done well in Africa.'

Armoured mobility had been a key factor, yet as Michael Carver – later a field marshal but then GSO2 (Operations) at the headquarters of Lieutenant-General C. W. M. Norrie – recalled, up until then 'Nobody, senior or junior, whatever their arm of service, had any experience of highly mobile operations, ranging over wide areas, in which tanks fought each other . . . Everyone was learning on the job, even the Royal Tank Regiment had to rely on theory or . . . pragmatic common sense or even happy-go-lucky intuition.'[7] There was also the low morale of the Italians, which Lieutenant-Colonel Ronald Belchem of 7th Armoured Division described as 'a synthetic morale inspired by repetitive propaganda and one was very conscious that if they suffered a defeat this would probably peel off like a plastic wrapper, which in fact was the case'.[8] It is not true that the Italians lacked courage, William 'Strafer' Gott told Anthony Eden, but they were simply not properly trained for the realities of desert warfare.[9]

Yet after Beda Fomm Wavell decided not to allow O'Connor to press on to try to capture the Axis stronghold of Tripoli, instead ordering him to halt at El Agheila. For Mussolini's invasion of Greece in October 1940 led to the British War Cabinet's decision to support the Greeks militarily, as desirable and understandable a decision politically as it was disastrous militarily. Already very badly short of men in his Middle East Command, Wavell had to find extra troops to send across the Mediterranean as an expeditionary force, weakening him everywhere else in a command that stretched from the Persian Gulf to Malta to East Africa. Lieutenant-General Henry 'Jumbo' Maitland Wilson took a large number of troops off to Greece under orders from

Churchill. This was an error when the Mediterranean theatre was still far from safe. As an assistant secretary to the War Cabinet, Lawrence Burgis, noted in April 1941, when 'a terribly important convoy of tanks destined for Egypt was about to risk the perilous Mediterranean route, the PM informed the Cabinet of the timetable, adding: "If anyone's good at praying, now is the time" '.[10]

It was O'Connor's victory over the Italians in Libya that persuaded Hitler that Mussolini needed immediate support there. Five hundred planes were flown from Norway to Sicily, and their subsequent bombing of Benghazi meant that O'Connor could not use the port. Denuded of troops by the Greek and Crete campaigns, the Western Desert Force was anyway reduced to only one armoured division, part of an infantry division and one motorized brigade. In March 1941 Hitler sent Lieutenant-General Erwin Rommel to Tripoli to command the 5th Light and 15th Panzer Divisions, which had begun debouching on 12 February 1941. In August the force was raised to the status of Panzer group, and the 5th was renamed the 21st Panzer Division. Although technically only the 15th and 21st Panzer Divisions made up the Afrika Korps, the name came to encompass all of the German forces under Rommel's command in the desert, including the 90th Light Division. Although Rommel was formally under the command of the more senior Italian generals in Africa – but not Graziani, who had resigned after Beda Fomm – he actually took orders solely from Hitler. His success in the 1940 campaign against France had only added to his already high reputation in the Wehrmacht – he had been awarded the Pour le Mérite medal in the Great War, Germany's highest decoration for valour – and he was now ready to become the iconic 'Desert Fox'.

Back on 4 October 1940, when Hitler and Mussolini had met on the Brenner Pass, the Führer did not warn the Duce that he intended to occupy Romania only three days later.[11] What has been called 'the brutal friendship' was not based on much mutual trust and understanding. Similarly, Mussolini's invasion of Greece on 28 October, under General Sebastiano Visconti Prasca, was undertaken from occupied Albania with ten divisions without Hitler's prior knowledge. With temperatures of –20 Celsius, difficult territory and stiff Greek resistance under General Alexander Papagos, the Italians were soon forced back into Albania. 'Raging rivers, bottomless mud and bitter cold', wrote a contemporary commentator, 'completed the destruction of an Italian offensive that was politically inept and militarily under-prepared.'[12] Helped by units of the RAF sent by Wavell – who was keen to have bases from which to bomb Romania's highly productive Ploesti oilfields – the Greeks had marched so far into Albania by Christmas Eve that the Italian Chief of Staff, Marshal Pietro Badoglio, was forced to resign. Hitler, who had already decided to shore up the Italians in North Africa, was now faced with having to protect them from the Greeks and British as well.

To make matters worse for the Germans, Prince Regent Paul of Yugoslavia chose this moment to join the Axis and sign the Germany–Italy–Japan Tripartite Pact on 25 March 1941, causing outrage in Belgrade. Allied successes in Greece, Albania and Libya encouraged the eighteen-year-old Prince Peter II of Yugoslavia to declare himself of age and overthrow Paul the following night, assisted by SOE. Hitler was rendered incandescent with rage by this coup. Ever since 29 July 1940, he had been instructing the OKH to draw up plans for the invasion of the Soviet Union. Suddenly, his right flank in south-east Europe looked as if it might house a hostile Graeco-Yugoslav-British bloc. He ordered that Yugoslavia be subjected, 'with merciless bru-tality', to 'a lightning invasion'.[13] The brutality can be gauged by the fact that 17,000 Yugoslavs were killed by the Luftwaffe on a single day, almost as many certified deaths as the RAF were to cause in Dresden in February 1945.[14]

On 6 April 1941, just ten days into their new-found freedom, with only two-thirds of their thirty-three divisions mobilized, with no armour, little modern equipment and 300 planes, the Yugoslavs were subjected to a massive invasion from the north, east and south-east by over half a million Germans, Hungarians, Romanians and Bul-garians. It was a miracle of German Staff work and efficiency.[15] Zagreb fell on the fourth day, Belgrade on the sixth, Sarajevo on the ninth and Yugoslavia formally surrendered after eleven days, on 17 April, with King Peter and the Government escaping with only hours to spare. Total German losses amounted to 558 men, against 100,000 Yugoslav casualties and a further 300,000 taken prisoner. Mellenthin observed that 'Only the Serbs were really hostile to us,' otherwise the Germans pacified Croatia – which was given its independence – Slovenia and Bosnia very quickly.[16] Later on, Colonel Draža Mihailović led the pro-monarchist Chetniks and Marshal Tito led the pro-Communist partisans against the Germans (and each other), but for the moment Hitler had scored yet another lightning victory to follow those over Poland, Denmark, Norway, France, Belgium and Holland.

Nor did he lose a moment before also attacking Greece, which had been reinforced by Wavell on the command of the War Cabinet. In retrospect, the Commonwealth expedition to Greece was one of the worst British blunders of the war, stretching Wavell's forces far too thin, which did not allow him to fight effectively in either Greece or Libya. The Greeks and British – who did not co-ordinate their responses effectively, as the Greeks wanted (patriotically but wildly over-optimistically) to fight for Thrace, Macedonia and Albania – were outmanoeuvred by swift Panzer thrusts around Mount Olympus, forcing the surrounded Greek Army to capitulate on 23 April.[17] The swastika was hoisted over the Acropolis four days later. After gallant Australian and New Zealand defence at Thermopylae, full of historical echoes of an earlier defence of Western civilization, some 43,000 British Commonwealth forces were evacuated from eastern Peloponnesian ports to the island of Crete and elsewhere, although little heavy equipment could be saved. For German losses of only 4,500, Britain suffered 11,840 killed, wounded or captured and Greek casualties topped 70,000.[18] Nor would the Germans stop there.

Major-General Bernard Freyberg VC, nicknamed by Churchill 'the Salamander' because he had been through fire so often – wounded twelve times and winning four DSOs – was in command of the defence of Crete. He had 15,500 troops who had been evacuated (defeated and exhausted) from Greece, 12,000 troops from Egypt, 14,000 Greeks, little artillery and only twenty-four serviceable fighter aircraft to face the first wave of General Karl Student's XI Fliegerkorps (airborne corps) of 11,000 fresh, crack paratroopers. With control of Crete the Germans could threaten the eastern Mediterranean, bomb Egypt and Libya and protect the Corinth Canal, through which much of Italy's oil was transported. On the morning of 20 May, Operation Merkur (Mercury) was launched against three airfields on the north coast of the island composed of 716 aircraft (including 480 bombers and 72 gliders) which dropped General Alexander Löhr's 7th Airborne Division and, the next day, the 5th Mountain Division. One of the airfields, Maleme, was taken from the New Zealand 5th Brigade on 21 May, albeit with heavy German losses. It was then hugely re-inforced; between 20,000 and 30,000 German paratroopers had landed on Crete by 27 May. Engagements between the Luftwaffe and the Royal Navy, as Norway had already proved, were an unequal contest: three cruisers and six destroyers were sunk, and two battle-ships and one aircraft carrier, HMS *Formidable*, which lost all her fighters, were badly damaged.[19] Although Freyberg was forewarned by the GCCS cipher decrypts codenamed Ultra to expect the attack on the northern airfields, he was prevented from acting on the infor-mation too obviously, for fear of compromising its all-important source.

When Wavell met the Commander-in-Chief of the Mediterranean Fleet, Sir Andrew Browne Cunningham (elder brother of Lieutenant-General Sir Alan Cunningham), on board HMS *Warspite* in Alexandria on the morning of 26 May, the unanimous advice of the Staff was that Freyberg's entire force would have to surrender, because if the Royal Navy suffered any further losses in evacuating them the Allies could lose control of the eastern Mediterranean. The Germans would then take Syria and the Persian and Iraqi oilfields and cut off Britain's oil supply. Wavell added that it would also take three years to build a new fleet. In this gloomy analysis Wavell was supported by the Commander-in-Chief of Australian forces in the Middle East, General Sir Thomas Blamey, the Prime Minister of New Zealand, Peter Fraser, and the commander of the RAF in the Middle East, Air Marshal Arthur Tedder. This prompted one of the great ripostes of the war, when Cunningham, who spoke last, said:

It has always been the duty of the Navy to take the Army overseas to battle and, if the Army fail, to bring them back again. If we now break with that tradition, ever afterwards when soldiers go overseas they will tend to look over their shoulders instead of relying on the Navy. You have said, General, that it will take three years to build a new fleet. I will tell you that it will take three hundred years to build a new tradition. If, gentlemen, you now order the Army in Crete to surrender, the Fleet will still go there to bring off the Marines.[20]

Churchill meanwhile telegraphed from London: 'Victory in Crete essential at this turning point of the war. Keep hurling in all aid you can.' Wavell nonetheless ordered Freyberg to evacuate Crete without equipment from 28 May, and over the following four nights, coincidentally the first anniversary of the Dunkirk evacuation, 16,500 men were embarked. The British had lost 2,011 Royal Navy killed and wounded, 3,489 Army killed and 11,835 captured, for the German casualty figure of 5,670.[21] However, the Germans had lost 220 planes destroyed and 150 damaged, and were never to employ another airborne assault again. This was extremely fortunate in the case of Malta the following year, which was vulnerable to such an attack.

Greece was to suffer fearfully under German occupation. In the first eighteen months, no fewer than 40,000 Greeks starved to death, and the population was reduced by some 300,000 in the course of the war.[22] Olive oil became a major currency as inflation meant that a single loaf of bread could cost 2 million drachmae. The German Army resorted to methods of barbarism to keep control, as when all the male inhabitants of Kalavryta in the northern Peloponnese – 696 people in twenty-five villages – were shot by the 117th Jäger Division in December 1943 in reprisal for guerrilla actions.

Rommel on 24 March 1941 unleashed his Libyan offensive. Spread far too thinly because of political imperatives – in Greece, Crete, East Africa, Syria, Iraq, Palestine, Ethiopia and Egypt – Wavell's forces could not hold back the Afrika Korps in Cyrenaica. O'Connor was ordered to fall back to the high ground east of Benghazi if necessary, and not to expect reinforcement until May.[23] El Agheila fell on the first day and Rommel sent the 21st Panzers off through the desert via Mechili to Tobruk, which they tried unsuccessfully to capture from the 7th Australian Division between 10 and 13 April. Rommel flew from place to place in his Fieseler Storch plane – in which he at one point was in peril of being shot down by the Italians – but finally settled down to besiege Major-General J. D. Lavarack's 7th Australian Division in Tobruk on 14 April, a siege that was to last a gruelling seven and a half months. Although 238 tanks and 43 Hurricanes got through the Mediterranean on 12 May, the pressure was on.

O'Connor, one of the most talented British commanders of the war so far, was seized on 17 April and held in Italy. 'It was a great shock to be captured,' he said later. 'I never thought it would ever happen to me – very conceited, perhaps – but it was miles behind our own front and by a sheer bit of bad luck we drove into the one bit of desert in which the Germans had sent a reconnaissance group and went bang into the middle of them.'[24] He managed to escape in December 1943, after which he fought in Normandy, but he was *hors de combat* when desperately needed to face Rommel in the desert.

'The Axis decision to open a Mediterranean front', a leading historian considers, 'was a critical strategic mistake that the Allies would have been foolish not to exploit.'[25] In the long term, Germany's explosion into the Mediterranean theatre weakened the war effort against Russia in ways that could not have been predicted in the spring of 1941. It drew off German strength from the war's main *Schwerpunkt*, and in 1943 the invasion of Sicily meant that Luftwaffe units had to be brought down from Norway where they had been threatening the Murmansk route. In the short run, however, Germany won significant victories, and expected more.

Halfaya Pass, 65 miles east of Tobruk, nicknamed Hellfire Pass, was one of the few places where vehicles could negotiate the 500-foot escarpment from the coastal plain to the desert plateau, and was thus an important strategic point. Wavell's counter-offensive designed to relieve Tobruk – Operation Battleaxe – failed there between 15 and 17 June, with no fewer than fifteen of the eighteen Matilda tanks involved in one attack being lost to mines and anti-tank fire from a battalion of German tanks and four powerful 88mm guns.[26] During this battle Churchill decided to relieve Wavell, who, he told the new Foreign Secretary Anthony Eden, lacked 'that sense of mental vigour and resolve to overcome obstacles which is indispensable to a successful war'. Other similarly negative assessments from Churchill were that Wavell was like a golf-club chairman, 'a good average colonel' and – intended as equally damning – 'a good chairman of a Tory association'.[27] It was bad enough to scapegoat Wavell for errors of the War Cabinet and Chiefs of Staff without having to insult him too, but Wavell's victories over the Italians in late 1940 and early 1941, including Sidi Barrani, Bardia, Tobruk and Benghazi, had come to a crashing end after mid-February 1941 when the German Army landed in Tripolitania. 'I had certainly not budgeted for Rommel after my experience with the Italians,' Wavell said ruefully years afterwards.

Churchill had been furious when Wavell drew up a 'Worst Possible Case' Plan for withdrawing the British Army from Egypt altogether. 'Wavell has 400,000 men,' the Prime Minister blustered. 'If they lose Egypt, blood will flow. I will have firing parties to shoot the generals.'[28] Wavell never tried to shift the blame on to other shoulders; when finally he was packed off to be commander-in-chief in India on 22 June 1941 he bore the humiliation stoically, perhaps even welcoming it, and agreed with Churchill's telegram that said 'a new hand and a new eye', in the shape of General Sir Claude Auchinleck, were required.

The story was not entirely woeful for Britain throughout the Middle East in the spring and summer of 1941. Between April and August, the British had acted decisively in three important areas – Iraq, Syria and Iran – to protect and guarantee her all-important oil supplies for what turned out to be the rest of the war. 'The campaigns were not large,' writes their historian, 'they were conducted without much fanfare and each with laughably limited resources . . . but they were crucial for Britain's survival.'[29] Although the (still neutral) United States produced 83 per cent of the world's oil in 1941, and the Middle East only 5 per cent, American oil had to be shipped over the submarine-infested Atlantic and had to be paid for in Britain's rapidly diminishing hard currency. The 8.6 million tons of Iranian and 4.3 million tons of Iraqi oil that fuelled Britain's ships and tanks each year did not.

Worth more than hard currency, however, were the agreements that Churchill and Roosevelt came to at their momentous meeting, code-named Riviera, at Placentia Bay, off the village of Argentia in south-east Newfoundland from 9 to 12 August 1941. Churchill arrived in the 35,000-ton battleship HMS *Prince of Wales* and Roosevelt in the heavy cruiser USS *Augusta* and their conversations set the (very wide) parameters for Anglo-American co-operation for the next three years of the conflict. Before the United States entered the war, the Roosevelt Administration had afforded Britain invaluable help, and Placentia Bay was to see this greatly increased. As well as allowing Britain to buy much-needed arms and other vital supplies under the Lend-Lease system, the United States Navy had given the Royal Navy fifty destroyers in return for long leases on various British military bases in September 1940, and had also begun patrolling areas of the Western Atlantic against U-boats in such a way that had led to several clashes, usually to the Germans' cost. Yet at Placentia Bay this spirit of help and co-operation was massively extended, aided by an instantly good personal rapport that sprang up between Roosevelt and Churchill, who had not seen one another since an inauspicious meeting in 1918 (an occasion that Churchill had forgotten all about anyway).[30]

As well as agreeing that, in the event of having to fight against Germany and Japan simultaneously, Britain and the United States would concentrate on defeating Germany first, a crucial consideration for the hard-pressed British, on 12 August Roosevelt and Churchill signed what was soon afterwards dubbed the Atlantic Charter by the *Daily Herald* of London. This succeeded in putting eight Anglo-American war aims into a single, stirring declaration, one that emphasized the democratic, progressive values for which so many people were fighting and dying. By the following January it had been signed by twenty-four more countries.

The preamble announced that the two leaders, 'being met together, deem it right to make known certain common principles in the national policies of their respective countries on which they base their hopes for a better future for the world'. It then stated that Britain and America 'seek no aggrandisement, territorial or other', 'desire to see no territorial changes that do not accord with the freely expressed wishes of the peoples concerned', 'respect the rights of all people to choose the form of government under which they will live; and they wish to see sovereign rights and self-government restored to those who have been forcibly deprived of them.' There were five other such principles, covering economic collaboration, political liberty, 'freedom from fear and want', access to the world's oceans and 'the abandonment of the use of force'. Several of these were frankly utopian, and were to be flagrantly ignored as the nations of eastern Europe fell into the Soviet maw in 1945, but in 1941 they provided an idealistic basis that set the Second World War apart from the dynastic, commercial and territorial conflicts of the past.

In April 1941 a military coup in Iraq brought to power the Anglophobic General Rashid Ali, whose 'government of national defence' declared independence and besieged the British garrison in the Habbaniya air base on the Euphrates on 2 May. The commander of the flying school there, Air Vice-Marshal Harry Smart, fought off the attack after three days, and a column from Transjordan captured Baghdad at the end of the month. Rashid Ali escaped to Iran and was replaced by a pro-British regent. Next it was Vichy-controlled Syria's turn, which had agreed to supply Rashid Ali with German arms during the uprising. Along with the Free French, British forces attacked on 8 June, and by an armistice agreed only weeks later on 5 July established the right to occupy Syria for the rest of the war. The balance of power in the region had shifted dramatically on 22 June 1941 when Hitler invaded Russia and Churchill automatically declared Britain to be in alliance with the USSR. After the Iranian Government had refused an Anglo-Soviet demand to expel German agents from the country, the two powers invaded on 25 August, after which nationalist resistance collapsed in less than a week. The Shah was forced to abdicate in favour of his son, and British and Russian troops occupied Teheran on 17 September. Although Iraq, Syria and Iran thenceforth stayed firmly in the Allied camp for the rest of the war, with all that that implied for British oil supplies, there is no doubt that had Egypt fallen to Rommel there was very little that Britain could have done to protect her gains there.

With Tobruk still holding out behind him, and being resupplied by sea and air, Rommel could not push on further east until it fell, so the Afrika Korps sat out a long hot summer besieging it, until campaigning could be resumed when the weather cooled in November 1941. Meanwhile Churchill directed on to Auchinleck the ceaseless telegrams calling for the relief of Tobruk that Wavell had so long endured. The Prime Minister also wanted airfields established that could protect the air route between Alexandria and Malta. Auchinleck, by contrast, was more interested in protecting the Nile Valley and securing the vital oil sources of the Persian Gulf. Only once the Iraqi, Syrian and Iranian operations were finished successfully would he contemplate action, telegraphing Churchill on 4 July: 'No further offensive [in the] Western Desert should be contemplated until base is secure.'[31] It was not what Churchill wanted to hear.

Campaigning did not therefore start again until the night of Monday, 17 November, with the opening of Operation Crusader, the largest armoured offensive the British had launched to date. There was a serious risk involved; Michael Carver recalled that some of Auchinleck's tanks were so infirm that they had to be carried to the battle on transporters.[32] Nonetheless, in the intervening four months the Commonwealth's Eighth Army, which had been constituted in September 1941 from the Western Desert Force and reinforcements, had been enlarged to two corps and the attack took Rommel by surprise. Debouching from Mersa Matruh, the British were checked in the desert tank battle of Sidi-Rezegh from 19 to 22 November, and a sortie from Tobruk was also repulsed. German tanks were simply better than British ones at that stage of the war, something the Chiefs of Staff privately and reluctantly accepted. The man who took over as chief of the Imperial General Staff on 1 December, General Sir Alan Brooke, wrote to 'My dear Auk' – the nickname was apposite considering Auchinleck's beaky appearance – admitting that 'One of the fundamental defects that requires remedying is the lack of gun-power of our tanks. We are doing all we can to get the six-pounder in as quickly as possible . . . I can promise you we shall do all we can to press on with the 6-pounders.'[33] In March Churchill called for a special War Office inquiry to investigate why he had not received a report on how to counter the 4½-pound projectiles that German tanks could fire. In the course of a War Cabinet Defence Committee discussion, Brooke said that two defects had developed in the Cruiser tank, in the fan-belt drive and the lubrication system, although the necessary spares and equipment were being flown out.[34]

Although Rommel counter-attacked, even sending part of his force on a wide flanking movement towards Egypt, Auchinleck's nerve held, and by Sunday, 7 December the Afrika Korps was forced west of

Tobruk, which was relieved that day. It was a significant moment, but entirely overshadowed in history by the attack on Pearl Harbor on the same date. The Eighth Army, by then commanded by General Ritchie, forced Rommel all the way across Cyrenaica back to El Agheila by the end of the year. Just as events in Yugoslavia had forced Wavell to denude the Western Desert of troops, so the spectacular entry of Japan into the war cost Auchinleck his two excellent Australian Divisions, the 7th and 9th, which the Australian Government demanded be sent back to defend their homeland.

January 1942 saw the Afrika Korps and Eighth Army facing each other at El Agheila. The Axis had lost 24,500 killed and wounded since the launch of Crusader and 36,500 captured (mainly Italians), to British Commonwealth losses of 18,000. Rommel attacked on 21 January, capturing Benghazi and large quantities of stores, before the two lines settled down between 4 February and 28 May at Gazala. The British mined the 40-mile Gazala–Bir Hacheim Line, their 125,000 men, 740 tanks and 700 aircraft outnumbering Rommel's 113,000 men, 570 tanks and 500 aircraft – but being Rommel it was always likely he would attack next.[35]

The fighting in the desert, partly because there were fewer opportunities for German atrocities against civilians, has been considered more 'gentlemanly' than that in Europe, especially on the Eastern Front. An aspect of this was witnessed in February 1942 when the former commander of the Afrika Korps' 21st Panzer Division, Lieutenant-General Johann von Ravenstein, who had been captured by New Zealanders the previous November, wrote to Major-General Jock Campbell to express 'the greatest admiration' for his 7th Armoured Division and to avow that 'The German comrades congratulate you with warm heart on the award of the Victoria Cross. During the war your enemy, but with high respect, Von Ravenstein'.[36]

Rommel's offensive against the Gazala Line on 28 May inaugurated three weeks of heavy fighting. Carver later calculated that between 27 May and 1 July he averaged two and a half hours of sleep in every twenty-four.[37] On 31 May the Italians broke through the minefield and, despite coming under heavy attack from the RAF, on 13 June Panzers took a strategic crossroads nicknamed Knightsbridge. 'Messervy's unfortunate experiences in the Gazala battles illustrate the typical difficulties of a desert commander,' recalled Carver of the commander of the 7th Armoured Division, Major-General Frank Messervy. 'When he stayed with his headquarters, it was overrun; when he left it, he was ignominiously forced to seek refuge down a well.'[38] Rommel now threatened the Eighth Army's rear and, after the Free French had evacuated Bir Hacheim on the night of 10 June, Ritchie had no choice but to withdraw to Halfaya on the Egyptian border, once more leaving Tobruk behind to be besieged. This time, however, the day after the British reached Halfaya on 20 June, Tobruk fell to the Afrika Korps' concerted ground and air attacks, in one of the greatest blows to befall British arms in the Second World War. Churchill was in Washington at the time conferring with President Roosevelt (who actually handed him the note containing the news of Tobruk) and General Marshall, and on his return had to face a restive House of Commons. He won the vote, but was under no illusions about how long he would last if the string of defeats continued. It is sometimes forgotten that, despite Churchill's inspiring leadership in the Second World War, defeats such as Greece, Crete, Singapore and now Tobruk caused him serious political worries even as late as mid-1942.

Although the RAF had established local air superiority, helped as in the battle of Britain by the fact that its bases were far closer to the front line than the over-extended German ones, Rommel's Staff officers were soon planning which hotels in Cairo they would stay in, and which they would take over as their headquarters. Before they could relax, visit the Pyramids and bask in the Cairo sunshine, all they had to do was get past a small railway station about 60 miles west of Alexandria, set in hundreds of miles of absolutely nothing, called El Alamein. It lay in the shortest line of defence between the sea and the Qattara Depression only 40 miles inland from the Mediterranean, which closed off to Rommel any southern flanking movement. It was also the last line of British defence before the Suez Canal.

With the Alamein Line between the sea and the Depression forming the perfect defensive position for Auchinleck, Rommel should not have attacked on 1 July, but he did so because of the recent British defeat and perceived British demoralization, and because he succumbed to the lure of Cairo. The Afrika Korps was exhausted as well as over-extended, and after a counter-attack by Auchinleck on 2 July the rest of the month was spent in an inconclusive slogging match with neither side giving ground. At the beginning of August, the two sides settled down for the summer. Rommel constructed a massive minefield – a sure sign of the onset of defensive-mindedness – while the British brought up proportionately much greater quantities of supplies. In early August Auchinleck, who Churchill and Brooke had concluded was insufficiently offensive-minded, was replaced by General Sir Harold Alexander as commander-in-chief and Lieutenant-General Bernard Montgomery as commander of Eighth Army. The scene was thus set for the second battle of El Alamein in the autumn. Rommel could not have known it, but the capture of Tobruk was to be the greatest, but almost the last, victory of his career.

'If we speak of soil in Europe today,' Hitler had written in *Mein Kampf* of land that he believed Germany needed for *Lebensraum*, 'we can primarily have in mind only Russia and her vassal border states.'[39] He had been drawn into Yugoslavia and Greece in April and May 1941, which were not Russian border states, and had bailed out his militarily bankrupt junior partner and ally Mussolini in North Africa, while leaving the British unconquered in the west. So far the cost to him had been trifling in south-east Europe and the Mediterranean, and the propaganda effect of further effortless victories was welcome, but that did not alter the fact that he had departed from the important strategic principle of concentration. This did not matter so much in 1941, but it certainly did when events started to go awry in his next great campaign. This adventure was to dwarf everything that had taken place in the war so far, indeed in any war in the history of mankind, before or since.

5

Kicking in the Door

June–December 1941

*I've always hated snow, Bormann, you know, I've always
hated it. Now I know why. It was a presentiment.*
Adolf Hitler to Martin Bormann, 19 February 1942[1]

On 19 May 1940, just as victory in Belgium and Holland seemed
assured, Hitler was given a ninety-two-page study of the life and
thought of General Alfred Count von Schlieffen, written by Hugo
Rochs in 1921. The donor was Hitler's jovial factotum, hospitality
manager and court jester at the Reich Chancellery, Arthur 'Willy'
Kannenberg.[2] If Hitler had been capable of something as unFührerlike
as personal friendship, Kannenberg would have been one of his
friends. The choice of gift could not have been more apposite, nor
better timed. It had been Schlieffen who, as chief of the German
General Staff between 1891 and 1906, had devised the eponymous
plan for Germany to win a two-front war by a sweeping movement
through Belgium, principally featuring a strong right-flanking enveloping movement that would capture Paris. He had died in 1913, a
year before his plan was put into operation, and his last words are
said to have been 'Keep the right flank strong!' Despite that, it was
fatally weakened by his successor Helmuth von Moltke the Younger.
The result was the four years of trench warfare of the Western Front
in which Hitler had fought, and the two-front war that Germany was
to lose.

Hugo Rochs wanted his book to be both a work of strategy and a
'character study for the German people', believing the Prussian aristocrat to have embodied the virtues of hard work, self-effacement and

decency – Schlieffen had opposed the bombardment of innocent civilians during the Franco-Prussian War, for example – though it was not those lessons that Kannenberg hoped the Führer would glean from his victory gift.[3] From the extensive marginalia in the book, it is clear that Hitler read and thought deeply about what Schlieffen and Germany's past could teach the present. Thirty-two of his pencil marks cover the twenty pages of Chapter 4, entitled 'The Schlieffen Battle Plan for the Two-Front War', which warned of the dangers to Germany of fighting two wars simultaneously in east and west. Yet the professionally sycophantic Kannenberg had highlighted a passage which read:

But then again: as long as Schlieffen stood at the head of the general staff, the defence of the Reich lay in good hands. Schlieffen believed that he and his army were equal to any coalition. Rightfully so! . . . Schlieffen possessed the rare faith in victory that derived from the irresistible, invincible force that is shaped by the effect of a true leader – Führer – who, like a force of nature, crushes all resistance.[4]

This passage seems to make little sense: why 'Rightfully so!', when Germany lost because of the two-front war, and was therefore obviously not 'equal to any coalition'? But if its ultra-nationalist message, complete with its reference to a 'Führer', was the message Hitler took from Rochs' book, it goes some way towards explaining why he made precisely the same mistake as the Kaiser and Hindenburg in fighting a two-front war, at exactly the same time that he was also emulating King Charles xii of Sweden and Napoleon by invading Russia. For a man who prided himself on his historical knowledge, Hitler learnt little from the past.

The pencil marks the Führer made in the margin of Chapter 4 of the Schlieffen book also highlighted Rochs' view that 'Once the situation in France has been decided, the French–English army destroyed, and Germany stands victorious on the Seine, everything else will – according to Schlieffen – follow on its own accord.' Rochs noted that Schlieffen knew he must 'reckon with the entire Russian army as an additional enemy' and fight 'in the face of a Russian deluge'.[5] Since Hitler most probably annotated this before ordering Keitel on 29 July 1940 to draw up plans for the invasion of Russia, these pencil marks, in the opinion of the historian of his bibliophilia, 'represent the earliest recorded evidence of Hitler's plan to invade the Soviet Union', at least since the pretty heavy hints he had made sixteen years earlier in *Mein Kampf*. So the plans to attack the USSR seem to have been formed in Hitler's mind in 1940 while he was influenced by the idea that an unnamed Führer could 'crush all resistance' largely by the effort of his will to victory, 'like a force of nature', making this Führer and his army 'equal to any coalition'. However unlikely it might sound, that is what happened.

To have attacked the Soviet Union without having first defeated Great Britain was Hitler's next major blunder of the war. Besides underestimating the ordinary Russian's capacity for absorbing punishment, one of the reasons why Hitler acted as he did was from a deep consciousness of his own mortality. 'I know I shall never reach the ripe old age of the ordinary citizen,' he confided to his coterie one evening, explaining why he did not spend his life 'smoking and drinking my time away'.[6] On the night of 17 October 1941, speaking to Reich Minister Fritz Todt and Gauleiter Fritz Sauckel about the Europeanization of the steppes, he said: 'I shall no longer be there to see all that, but in twenty years' time the Ukraine will already be a home for twenty million inhabitants besides the natives.'[7] He believed that no one else could achieve the task of delivering *Lebensraum*, but he had no trust in his own longevity, so the sooner it was undertaken the better. 'It's lucky I went into politics at 30,' he told other cronies at the end of 1941,

became Chancellor of the Reich at 43, and am only 52 today ... With age, optimism gets weaker. The spring relaxes. When I suffered my [Beerhall Putsch and subsequent imprisonment at Landsberg] setback in 1923, I had only one idea, to get back into the saddle. Today I'd no longer be capable of the effort which that implies. The awareness that one is no longer capable of that has something demoralising about it.[8]

It was partly this consciousness of his declining energy levels that impelled Hitler into world war so soon after his fiftieth birthday in April 1939, and the invasion of the USSR was similarly driven.

Hitler was also impelled to invade Russia by each of the three major strands in his political credo. As Ian Kershaw points out, the Führer had 'a small number of basic, unchanging ideas that provided his inner driving-force'.[9] Hitler's self-reinforcing *Weltanschauung* (world-view) was based on the need for Germany to dominate Europe, win *Lebensraum* for herself and come to a final reckoning with the Jews. These views never altered or moderated, and stayed central to his thinking from the 1920s to his death two decades later. All three could be achieved by an invasion of Russia, and none could be achieved without one.

There were other reasons too. On 1 February 1941, Fedor von Bock – who had been raised to field marshal in the mass creation of 19 July 1940 – was ordered to report to the Führer, 'who received me very warmly'. According to Bock's extensive war diary, Hitler said, 'The gentlemen in England are not stupid; they just act that way,' adding that 'they will come to realize that a continuation of the war will be pointless for them if Russia too is now beaten and humiliated.' After Bock had raised the question of 'whether it would be possible to force [the Russians] to make peace', Hitler replied, 'If the occupation of the Ukraine and the fall of Leningrad and Moscow did not bring about peace, then we would just have to carry on, at least with mobile forces, and advance to Yekaterinburg.'[10] Since Yekaterinburg (which had in fact been called Sverdlovsk since the 1920s) is 880 miles east of Moscow in the Ural mountains, Hitler's certainty in total victory was palpable. He then used a curious simile: 'I am convinced that our attack will sweep over them like a hailstorm.' In a sense he was right; it was hard and nasty but did not last, and once the worst was over its residue evaporated.

Hitler believed that the huge labour shortage in Germany – the number of men in industry fell from 25.4 million to 13.5 million between 1939 and 1944 – could be ended by a combination of slave labour (7.5 million workers from conquered lands by September 1944) and demobilizing soldiers after victory over Russia.[11] Control of the Baku oilfields would furthermore feed Germany's insatiable need for fuel for her tanks, lorries, warplanes and ships, just as the Ukraine's agriculture would help feed the Reich.

In 1941 the USSR had more soldiers and more tanks than, and the same number of aircraft as, the whole of the rest of the world's armed forces combined. Hitler knew this perfectly well, of course; when

Halder remarked that the Russians boasted 10,000 tanks, the statement 'unleashed a more than quarter-hour retort from Hitler, in which he cited from memory the Russians' annual production for the last twenty years'.[12] Inherent in Hitler's concept of the Aryan master race, however, was the idea that Germans were so superior to Slavs as human beings that mere numerical inferiority meant nothing. This may also explain why when the Japanese Foreign Minister, Yosuke Matsuoka, visited Berlin in April 1941 Hitler threw away a perfect opportunity to force the USSR herself to fight a war on two fronts. Instead of confiding his plans to Tokyo, and offering the Japanese whatever they wanted territorially in the east in exchange for attacking Russia simultaneously with him, he made absolutely no mention of his plan, and made no attempt to recruit the Japanese into what he knew would be the greatest enterprise of his life. Yet drawing off scores of Russian divisions from the Leningrad, Moscow and Stalingrad fronts in order to protect Siberia and other eastern assets from a Japanese attack would have been invaluable to Germany in 1942 and 1943. If Japan had captured Siberia – which was by no means strategically unthinkable – Russia would have been forced to fight a war on two fronts. Japan was a member of the Axis, after all, and one for whom Hitler was willing to go to war with America eight months later. 'His failure to secure the collaboration of the Japanese against the Soviet Union', writes Roosevelt's biographer Conrad Black, 'must rank as one of Hitler's most serious errors.'[13]

Another major handicap was to have invaded as late as 22 June, by which time the days were already starting to shorten, in a campaign where time was going to be of the essence in covering the vast distances before Russia's autumn mud and winter snow forced an end to movement. The invasion was originally scheduled to be ready for 15 May, although that was not settled upon as the date for the attack. Once Halder had assured him that transport would be ready, Hitler chose 22 June for the attack, since any date much earlier than that would have run up against weather problems in that unusually wet spring. The invasion of Greece had always been planned to take place in conjunction with that of Russia and did not therefore lead to the postponement of Barbarossa. Re-equipping tanks that had driven too fast down bad Balkan roads took time, so in a sense the very speed of the defeat of Greece led to the late date for Barbarossa. Although Hitler was to blame the pushing back of the 15 May date to 22 June as a reason for his defeat, claiming that he could have won before the onset of winter, his biographer Ian Kershaw has rightly described that as 'simplistic in the extreme'.[14] It was too wet to invade very much earlier, with heavy tanks and trucks going down rutted, basic roads. The weather of 1941 was not kind to Adolf Hitler. It is often assumed that he should not have indulged in his Balkan, Greek and Crete campaigns in April and May because they delayed his assault on Russia. In fact it was because he could not invade Russia before June that he was able to indulge himself in south-west Europe and the Mediterranean at all.

At least Hitler cannot be accused of being alone in his desire to 'settle scores with the Bolsheviks'. When he held his last major military conference before the invasion, at the Reich Chancellery on 14 June – with the generals arriving at different times to allay suspicions – not one of them complained that it would open up a potentially disastrous two-front war along the lines of the one they had all, without exception, fought in and lost less than a quarter of a century before. Perhaps they thought that by then it was too late to alter the Führer's mind; maybe for career reasons they did not want to seem unenthusiastic; perhaps for each other's morale they did not want to point out the giant pitfalls; but the fact remains that no doubts or criticisms were expressed, and the Wehrmacht leaders, Brauchitsch and Halder, said not a word.[15] 'All the men of the OKW and the OKH to whom I spoke', recalled Heinz Guderian, 'evinced an unshakeable optimism and were quite impervious to criticism or objections.'[16] Guderian himself however, especially after the 14 June briefing, claimed to think that a potentially disastrous war on two fronts loomed, and 'Adolf Hitler's Germany was even less capable of fighting such a war than had been the Germany of 1914.'[17] General Günther Blumentritt, in a hitherto unpublished letter, wrote in 1965: 'Militarily and politically the war was lost when Hitler attacked Russia in 1941, without having peace in the West.'[18] He did not say so at the time, however, even if he thought it.

'I tried to dissuade Hitler from a two-front war,' claimed the Luft-waffe armaments chief Erhard Milch at Nuremberg. 'I believe Göring did, too. But I failed.'[19] In fact Göring believed, as he told his psychiatrist in May 1946, 'The Führer himself was a genius. The plans against Poland and France were also his plans. The plan against Russia was also that of a genius. But its execution was poor. The Russian campaign could have ended in 1941 – successfully.'[20] When Göring was told that Rundstedt had been calling the Russian invasion plans 'stupid', he frowned and said: 'The army generals are all suddenly smarter than Hitler. But when he was running things they listened to what he said and were glad of his advice.'[21] It was a valid criticism.

The other person who ought to have brought Hitler to confront the realities of invading the world's largest country – with 193 million inhabitants against Germany's 79 million pre-war – was the OKW Chief of Staff Wilhelm Keitel, but there was never any danger of that. When asked at Nuremberg why he had gone along with the plans, Keitel explained that the Führer had feared that the USSR might cut off the 150,000 tons of oil that Germany received from Romania every month, almost half of the 350,000 tons that the Reich required for the war, 100,000 of which went to the Luftwaffe alone. 'The attack on Russia was an act of recklessness,' he accepted with hindsight, but 'I believed in Hitler and knew little of the facts myself. I'm not a tactician, nor did I know Russian military and economic strength. How could I?'[22] The answer might be that it was Keitel's most important duty to have known the facts of Russian military and economic strength before invading, and as OKW chief of staff he was one of Germany's three most senior strategists. He claimed to have told Hitler often that he should have a better tactician than him in that post, 'but he said it was his responsibility as commander-in-chief'.[23]

Hitler was perfectly content to have someone as chief of staff with so little belief in his own strategic skills. In stark contrast with Roosevelt, who appointed George Marshall as Army chief of staff, and Churchill, who appointed Sir Alan Brooke as chief of the Imperial General Staff, Hitler did not want an adviser who knew more about grand strategy than he, and might therefore oppose his ideas. 'I always wanted to be a country gentleman, a forester,' Keitel said after the war, 'and look what a muddle I got into merely because I was weak and let myself be talked into things. I am not cut out for a field marshal.' He also complained that when invited to take over from

Blomberg, 'I was not prepared for this position. I was suddenly called on to take over without having had time to think things over. Developments followed too quickly. That was the way things proceeded.'[24]

Far from a 'muddle', Keitel faced the noose, which he deserved for the brutal orders he signed before the invasion of Russia. A human nullity, Keitel always obeyed his Führer unquestioningly. 'I had been in many adjutant and junior staff positions,' he explained, 'but of course always with professional soldiers, whose education was also my own. Therefore all the things which Hitler told me were, to my viewpoint, the orders of an officer . . . One had a superior officer who was a politician and not an officer – a man who had quite different basic viewpoints from mine.'[25] Yet instead of this encouraging Keitel to stand up for himself and the Army, his thirty-six years in the officer corps had bred an instinct for obedience, which Hitler's successive coups in the Rhineland, Austria, Sudetenland, Prague, Poland and France turned into slavish devotion. The fact that Keitel was a pathetic excuse for a senior officer is important in establishing how Hitler established such dominance over an officer corps that was, despite the débâcle of 1918, still proud of its long-term heritage and pre-eminent place in German society. Another explanation for the lack of criticism of Operation Barbarossa from the German generals was that, as Liddell Hart wrote having interviewed several of them after the war, 'like so many specialists, they were rather naive outside their own sphere, and Hitler was able to overcome their own doubts about his Russian adventure with the aid of political "information" designed to convince them of its necessity, and that Russia's internal weaknesses would affect her military strength.'[26] Hitler had long been a master of disinformation, and this time he used it against his own generals.

Hitler needed someone – anyone – in his close circle to remind him of the perils of invading Russia. Yet he believed, as he told Rundstedt, 'You have only to kick in the door, and the whole rotten structure will come crashing down.' The hubris was tangible; in the Armed Forces Museum in Moscow one can see the two tons of Iron Crosses that were struck to be awarded to those who captured that city. Hitler believed that, on the evidence of Stalin's Army purges of the 1930s, the inherent inefficiencies and cruelties of Communism and the Red Army's early defeats in Finland, the USSR would collapse. Yet he had not counted on the sheer bloody-mindedness of the ordinary Russian soldier – the *frontovik* – who, although 'abominably led, inadequately trained, poorly equipped, changed the course of history by his courage and tenacity in the first year of fighting'.[27] The Red Army soldier was fatalistic about the necessity of sacrifice for Mother Russia, and the political commissars attached to every unit were expert in exploiting the culture of subservience that was a traditionally distinctive feature of Russian life. Their forefathers had suffered horribly in the past for the Romanovs, now they would suffer no less horribly for their Bolshevik successors: 'Stalinism was indeed Tsarism with a proletarian face.'[28]

Yet even if Hitler had been surrounded by outspoken opponents, the plan to attack Russia was buried so deep within the Nazi DNA that it could not be stopped. The Führer invaded Russia because he believed that that was what he had been put on earth to do. 'We National Socialists must hold unflinchingly to our aim in foreign policy,' he had avowed in *Mein Kampf*, 'namely, to secure for the German people the land and soil to which they are entitled on this earth.'[29] It was clear where the lion's share was to be found, when he wrote a few pages later of 'an eastern policy in the sense of acquiring the necessary soil for our German people'. Nor did this mean just Poland. Elsewhere in the book he wrote of Germany 'swimming in plenty' if she controlled Ukrainian grain, the raw materials of the Urals and even Siberian timber. The fourteen countries that Germany occupied or controlled by 1941 would not be enough, for as he also wrote in his political credo: 'Much as all of us today recognize the necessity of a reckoning with France ... it can and will achieve meaning only if it offers the rear cover for an enlargement of our people's living space in Europe.'[30]

With France as the rear cover, Hitler believed Russia could be attacked – or 'kicked in' – with relative ease. At a Berghof conference on 22 August 1939, Hitler said: 'We will crush the Soviet Union.' On 29 July 1940 at Bad Reichenhall, OKW Staff were told by Jodl of the Führer's 'express wishes' that they plan for the invasion forthwith. On 12 November 1940, Führer Directive No. 18 made it clear that the discussions then going on with Molotov in Berlin that same day were a mere smokescreen and that 'Irrespective of the results of these discussions, all preparations for the East which have been verbally ordered will be continued.' The objectives were laid out on 18 December in Führer Directive No. 21, the first sentence of which read: 'The armed forces of Germany must be prepared, even before the conclusion of the war with England, to defeat Soviet Russia in one rapid campaign ("Operation Barbarossa").'[31]

One incident that might have discouraged Hitler from invading Russia, for fear that Operation Barbarossa had been compromised, was the bizarre flight of his Deputy Führer, Rudolf Hess, to the United Kingdom at 6.00 on the evening of Saturday, 10 May 1941. Hess, who had been Hitler's closest confidant and lieutenant through much of the 1920s and 1930s, had been gradually overtaken by several rivals in the Nazi hierarchy in recent years, especially since the start of the war. An ideological Nazi from the earliest days, he did not believe that Britain and Germany should be at war and so, unbeknown to Hitler, he conceived a daring – if unhinged – plan to make peace between the Anglo-Saxon races. The five-hour flight itself, in a Messerschmitt Me-110 with a detachable extra fuel tank, was a remarkable feat of flying and navigation, but once Hess had parachuted near the village of Eaglesham in Renfrewshire in Scotland, his plan started to unravel. His first problem was to find someone in authority with whom to conduct peace negotiations, and his choice of Scotland was actuated by the quaint if utterly misguided notion that the Duke of Hamilton – whom he wrongly believed he had met at the Berlin Olympics in 1936 – held significant political power in Britain, owing to his title. Once captured (he had broken his ankle on landing), Hess was interviewed by Lord Beaverbrook and the Lord Chancellor, Lord Simon, among others, and it quickly became clear to him that the Churchill Government had no intention of listening to any kind of peace terms.

Real or feigned amnesia, as well as the onset of other psychological disorders – including paranoia – seem to have descended upon Hess from that point onwards, and stayed with him to a greater or lesser degree for the rest of his life. Although Hitler was furious with him for his 'treachery', and German propaganda explained the embarrassment in terms of mental illness, Hess did not betray the secret of Barbarossa. He was interned in the Tower of London for some of the war, after which he was found guilty at Nuremberg of conspiring against peace, but crucially not of war crimes, and was thus given life imprisonment rather than the death penalty that he would assuredly have received had he not flown to Scotland. Owing to Soviet intransigence – Moscow had wanted him hanged in 1945 – Hess stayed in Spandau Prison in Berlin until his suicide aged ninety-three in 1987.

Barbarossa (Redbeard) was the nickname of the cruel, brave and ambitious twelfth-century Hohenstaufen conqueror Frederick I, perhaps the greatest Holy Roman Emperor of the Dark Ages. Yet Hitler failed to spot the paradox in his choice of codename, because after his defeat by the Lombard League at the battle of Legnano in 1176 Frederick altered his policy to one of conciliation and clemency. And while it was true that Frederick undertook the Third Crusade against Saladin and Islam in 1188, just as Hitler proposed to do against Stalin and Bolshevism, during the campaign he had been found drowned, possibly by his own men. Another explanation for Hitler's choice of the codename Barbarossa, indeed for the very mindset that led him to order the invasion of Russia, might stem from the extraordinary geographical and topographical position of his country house, the Berghof in the village of Obersalzberg, near Berchtesgaden in the Bavarian Alps. There was a local legend that under one of the highest peaks of the Berchtesgadener mountain range, the Untersberg, Emperor Barbarossa lay sleeping, ready to be called upon to rise again to save Germany. Hitler was proud of his long connection with the region, which began when he went on an incognito visit – calling himself 'Herr Wolf' – to a fellow Fascist politician Dietrich Eckart before the 1923 Beerhall Putsch. He stayed in several inns in the area over the following years and in 1927 bought a house which became the centre of a huge compound for the Nazi hierarchy. The Nazi Party Secretary Martin Bormann, Hermann Göring and Albert Speer had houses built on the hillside, in order to protect their all-important personal access to the Führer. During the war itself, once 400 villagers had been expelled from their homes, 9,000 feet of concrete bunkers were built for the Nazi hierarchy underneath the hillside.

'Yes, there are many links between Obersalzberg and me,' Hitler reminisced to his cronies in January 1942. 'So many things were born there, and brought to fruition there. I've spent up there the finest hours of my life. It's there that all my great projects were conceived and ripened. I had hours of leisure, in those days, and how many charming friends!' The Berghof itself was not the architectural master-piece Hitler believed it to be; the historian Norman Stone describes it as 'a building fit for an Ian Fleming villain. Huge slabs of red marble adorned it; looted pictures hung on the walls; there was a vast, thick carpet; a huge fire burning in the grate; oversized armchairs were placed an uncomfortable distance apart, in such a way that the guests would have to half shout their platitudes at each other as the sparks leapt from the fire in the gathering twilight.'[32]

From the Berghof, Hitler could see his beloved Salzburg and all the surrounding countryside. For his fiftieth birthday in April 1939 the Nazi Party presented him with the civil engineering miracle of the Eagle's Nest, a stone building 6,000 feet up, reached through the interior of a mountain, from which one can view the entire region. Yet the breathtaking scenery did not calm what passed for his soul. Paradoxically, these panoramic views seemed only to have helped him come to his most drastic decisions. It was while he was staying at Obersalzberg that he plotted his most daring coups, including the plan to dismember Czechoslovakia. Joseph Goebbels, a regular visitor, often complained to his diary about the amount of time the Führer spent at Obersalzberg, but was also gratified by the way 'the solitude of the mountains' always tended to spur his Führer on to more fanatical efforts. It was in late March 1933, while staying there, that Hitler decided upon a national boycott of all Jewish businesses, services, lawyers and doctors across the whole Reich. Staggeringly beautiful scenery clearly had an effect on Hitler that was opposite to how most other people reacted: rather than softening and humanizing him it hardened his heart and filled him with power-lust.

One of Hitler's major purposes in attacking Russia was to denude Britain of any hope of allies, thus forcing her to make peace. Franz Halder had noted in his diary for 13 July 1940 that 'The Führer is greatly puzzled by Britain's persisting unwillingness to make peace. He sees the answer (as we do) in Britain's hopes for Russia, and therefore counts on having to compel her by main force to agree.'[33] A fortnight later at the Berghof, Hitler himself told his generals: 'With Russia smashed, Britain's last hope would be shattered. Germany would be the master of Europe and the Balkans. Decision: Russia's destruction must therefore be made part of this struggle.'[34] He wanted, in one historian's phrase, to conquer 'London via Moscow', however geographically absurd that might sound.[35] The idea that Hitler invaded vast Russia partly in order further to isolate tiny Britain might seem astonishing until one recalls Hitler's racial beliefs and mind-set. He had fought and lost to the British on the Western Front, and he admired their imperial successes, especially in India. He considered their racially Anglo-Saxon background as essentially Aryan, which made them worthy opponents and logical allies; far more worthy, for example, than the swarthy, Mediterranean, racially weak French. (France's defeat of Prussia in 1806 he somewhat pedantically put down as a Corsican victory.) The Russian Slavs would last only six weeks, he told his generals on 14 June 1941, despite their superior numbers and the likelihood that they would try to put up stiff resistance. Although Hitler's decision to attack Russia as a means of defeating Britain is history's supreme example of inverting the cart and the horse, it is explicable in terms of his own racial theories, as well as in the light of the Luftwaffe's defeat in the battle of Britain the previous summer. In 1812 Napoleon had invaded Russia partly in order to force the protectionist Continental System on to a recalcitrant Russia, and thereby to strangle Britain; now Hitler was making the same mistake.

It was not the first time the Germans had unleashed *Drang nach Osten* (storm to the east): in the Great War it had resulted in the March 1918 Treaty of Brest-Litovsk with the Bolsheviks that had been very advantageous to Berlin, and which gave her control over Poland, Belorussia, the Ukraine and the Baltic. Hitler would also be marching through areas with a higher concentration of Jews than the Holy Land itself and his attack on the Soviet Union was intended to 'destroy the power of the Jews, embodied in his world-view by the Bolshevik regime'.[36] He had fought Communists since his days as a street orator and political agitator in Munich in the early 1920s and he believed implicitly in the Zionist–Bolshevik conspiracy, so here was his chance to destroy both enemy elements in a single blow. Nor would it take long to achieve: Directive No. 21 envisaged that 'a quick completion of the ground operations can be counted on.'[37]

Germany's armed forces – the best in Europe – were under no threat from the Red Army, which were among the worst. Although Keitel claimed that Hitler feared an attack from Stalin, and Russian troops did seem stationed too close to Germany's borders for effective defence, none was pending, and it is doubtful that Hitler genuinely believed one was. Certainly nothing was further from Stalin's mind at the time. Furthermore, vast quantities of oil and wheat were being transferred from the USSR to Germany every month under the terms of the Nazi–Soviet Pact, indeed trains full of both were in the process of crossing the German border westwards on the night of 21 June just as German troops crossed it in the opposite direction. From October 1939 the Russians had given a naval base, at Jokanga Bay (or 'Base North'), for U-boats to refit and resupply on Soviet sovereign territory, and in the summer of 1940 they had even allowed free passage to a German auxiliary cruiser, the *Komet*, to sail the Arctic route along the north Russian coast and the Siberian Sea all the way to the Pacific Ocean, where it used the element of surprise to sink seven Allied vessels.[38]

Furthermore there was an admirable alternative strategy beckoning, the one which in retrospect Hitler ought to have adopted. Supported by Halder, Brauchitsch and Raeder, this involved attacking British outposts in the Mediterranean, North Africa and the Middle East. Despite the losses in Greece and on Crete, Malta should have been attacked by Karl Student's paratroopers and invaded, and the Mediterranean then turned into an Axis lake by an invasion of North Africa with far larger forces than the four divisions Rommel was to be given for the Afrika Korps in 1942. With a mere fraction of the numbers unleashed in Barbarossa, Germany could easily have obliterated the British presence in Libya, Egypt, Gibraltar, Iraq, Palestine and Iran, cutting off Britain's oil supply and her direct sea route via Suez to India. Supplying a campaign in the Middle East would have been far easier for the Axis, via Italy and Sicily, than it would have been for the defenders via the Cape of Good Hope. Instead, Hitler decided in July 1940 to invade Russia the following spring, and while he was willing to entertain the Mediterranean strategy intellectually – principally out of respect for Admiral Raeder – he never wavered from the plan. He spurned the Mediterranean option

and an attack on his supposed racial cousins for the instant gratification of attacking those he vociferously believed to be his racial and
political enemies.

On 16 June 1941, in a long conversation with Goebbels at the
Reich Chancellery – the Propaganda Minister had to enter by the back
door to avoid being noticed – Hitler said that there must be no
repeat of Napoleon's experience in Russia.[39] During this in-depth,
heart-to-heart discussion they declared that the Greek campaign had
'cost us dear'; that the Wehrmacht and the Red Army had between
180 and 200 divisions each, although there was 'no comparison' in
terms of personnel and equipment; that Barbarossa would take only
four months – Goebbels thought fewer – and that Bolshevism 'will
collapse like a house of cards'. No geographical limits were set for the
operation: 'We shall fight until Russia's military power no longer
exists.' The Japanese, although they had not been forewarned, would
be supportive because they could not attack America 'with Russia
intact to her rear'. His pre-emptive strike would avoid a two-front
war, Hitler believed, and after victory Britain could be dealt with, as
'the U-boat war will start in earnest. England will sink to the bottom.'
The Luftwaffe would also be used against Britain 'on a massive scale'
because invasion was 'a very difficult prospect, whatever the circumstances. And so we must try to win victory by other means.' Together
the two men looked into the smallest details of the operation – the
printers and packers of the leaflets to be dropped over Russia would
live in total isolation until it had begun, for example – and, as a result
of its success, 'Bolshevism must be destroyed. And with it England
will lose her last possible ally on the European mainland.' Hitler told
Goebbels that this was the struggle they had been waiting for all their
lives: 'And once we have won, who is going to question our methods?
In any case, we have so much to answer for already that we must win,
because otherwise our entire nation – with us at its head – and all we
hold dear, will be eradicated. And so to work!'[40] They even evolved a
plan at that meeting to try to involve Christian bishops in supporting
the attack on atheist Bolshevism, something enthusiastically entered
into by Alfred-Henri-Marie Baudrillart, the Cardinal-Archbishop of
Paris, who sermonized on 30 July 1941 that 'Hitler's war is a noble
undertaking in defence of European culture.'

If anyone besides Hitler can be blamed for Germany's ultimately disastrous decision to invade Russia it was his economics minister, Walther Funk, who argued that, under the British naval blockade of the Continent, Germany's European *Großraumwirtschaft* (sphere of economic domination) ultimately depended on the supplies of food and raw materials that she presently received from the Soviet Union under the terms of the Nazi–Soviet Pact, which could not be counted upon for ever but which needed to be hugely increased. Economic imperatives thus neatly dovetailed with ideological, strategic, racial and opportunistic ones; indeed every factor pointed to an invasion, save one: logistical reality. Although in Directive No. 21 Hitler had made a passing reference to 'the vastness of Russian territory', he initially envisaged only swallowing European Russia 'from the general line Volga–Archangel', with Russian industry in the Urals being 'eliminated by the Luftwaffe'.[41] The sheer size of the steppes should have given him and his Staff pause for thought, but it does not seem to have done so.

Retaining the initiative had always been the key to Hitler's many spectacular successes up to June 1941, and he was to keep it for another four months, until he was checked at the gates of Moscow that October. For years he had gambled on his enemies' indecision and weakness, and again and again he had been proved right. The stakes might have increased exponentially over the years, but his gambler's instinct never left him. The magnitude of the adventure intoxicated this teetotaller, for as he told Fedor von Bock at their meeting on 1 February: 'When Barbarossa begins, the world will hold its breath.'[42] With four million troops, many of them battle-hardened and with the victories in Poland, Scandinavia, France and the Balkans behind them, the odds did not seem as bad as they did later.

By the summer of 1940, the genius of the Führer as 'history's supreme warlord' was an essential part of Nazi ideology, and part of that genius seemed to have lain in his ability to take decisions without needing to spend large periods of time poring over maps, reading reports and conferring with his Staff. Yet it is not even certain that if he had devoted more study to the issue he would have acted differently. He feared – probably too much, considering the Roosevelt Administration's isolationist domestic opposition – that the United

THE STORM OF WAR

States was likely to enter the war on Britain's side in 1942, and deduced from this that he needed to act swiftly. Fortress Europe had to be established, and its full productive capacity harnessed, before the resources of America could be brought to bear against Germany.

In choosing how to invade Russia, it is worth quoting from Führer Directive No. 21 of 16 December 1940, which had been sent to all the most important figures in the Reich and which was adhered to remarkably closely six months later:

The mass of the Russian Army in western Russia is to be destroyed in daring operations, by driving forward deep armoured wedges, and the retreat of units capable of combat into the vastness of Russian territory is to be prevented ... Effective intervention by the Russian Air Force is to be prevented by powerful blows at the very beginning of the operation ... On the wings of our operation, the active participation of Romania and Finland in the war against the Soviet Union is to be expected ... In the zone of operations divided by the Pripet Marshes into a southern and northern sector, the main effort will be made north of this area. Two Army Groups will be provided here. The southern group of these two Army Groups [that is Army Group Centre] will be given the task of annihilating the forces of the enemy in White Russia by advancing from the region around and north of Warsaw with especially strong armoured and motorized units. The possibility of switching strong mobile units to the north must thereby be created in order, in cooperation with Army Group North operating from East Prussia in the general direction of Leningrad, to annihilate the enemy forces in the Baltic area. Only after having accomplished this most important task, which must be followed by the occupation of Leningrad and Kronstadt, are the offensive operations aimed at the occupation of the important traffic and armament centre of Moscow to be pursued. Only a surprisingly fast collapse of Russian resistance could justify aiming at both objectives simultaneously ... By converging operations with strong wings, the Army Group south of the Pripet Marshes is to aim at the complete destruction west of the Dnieper of the Russian forces standing in the Ukraine ... Once the battles north and south of the Pripet Marshes have been fought, we should aim to achieve as part of the pursuit operation: in the south, the prompt seizure of the economically important Donets Basin; in the north, rapid arrival at

Moscow. The capture of this city means a decisive success politically and economically and, beyond that, the elimination of this most important railway centre.[43]

Führer Directive No. 21 therefore very much envisaged another Blitzkrieg operation, with deep armoured thrusts enveloping and cutting off enormous numbers of Soviet troops, who would then have no choice but to surrender to what they could not know was going to be a genocidal captivity. But instead of a two-month operation over a maximum front of 300 miles, which was what all Hitler's earlier wars had involved, Barbarossa envisaged a five-month assault over an 1,800-mile front, and against an enemy whose population more than doubled Germany's, and which was also more than the population of all the Reich's vassal states combined.

It is noticeable from Directive No. 21 that Hitler did not envisage a race straight to Moscow, that the capture of Leningrad was regarded as key to the operation, that economic and industrial considerations were very high on his agenda and that the city of Stalingrad was not even mentioned. Hitler even told Halder at this time that the capture of Moscow itself 'was not so very important', as the Directive itself indicates.[44] This needs to be taken into account when Hitler is criticized by his own generals for not concentrating enough on seizing the Russian capital.

Russian geography splits any western invader's route into going north and south of the Pripet Marshes, a 200-mile-wide impassable bog of reeds and trees. The rail networks servicing the north, leading to Moscow and Leningrad, are separate from those servicing the southern route which passes through the Ukraine into Russia's rich agricultural, manufacturing and arms-producing centres. The invasion force was therefore split into Army Group North under Field Marshal Ritter von Leeb, which was to enter the Baltic States, link up with the Finns and capture Leningrad, and Army Group Centre under Field Marshal von Bock – this was the strongest, with fifty divisions, including nine Panzer and six motorized – which would take Minsk, Smolensk and ultimately Moscow. Meanwhile, Army Group South, under Field Marshal Gerd von Rundstedt, would capture Kiev and the Ukrainian bread-basket, and then push on to take the huge oilfields of the Caucasus from where the USSR derived much of the fuel that powered her military–industrial complex.

Even though the invasion of Poland by Blitzkrieg had taken place twenty-one months earlier, and France only thirteen months earlier, the Red Army still failed to group its thirty-nine armoured divisions together in independent corps and armies, but rather distributed them evenly among infantry divisions, proving they had learnt nothing whatever about the mechanics of the new German methods of warfare. Yet since the Great War Russian generals had had far more experience than their foreign counterparts, having fought the Whites in the Russian Civil War, the Poles in 1920–21, the Japanese in 1938–9 and the Finns in the Winter War. The Red Army had mobilized 6.7 million men between 1918 and 1920, for example.[45] Generals such as Zhukov, Rokossovsky, Budenny, Konev, Voroshilov and Timoshenko certainly did not lack military experience, but they understandably did fear Stalin's anger if they took bold decisions that later met with failure. Individually they were hard men – Zhukov would strike his officers and personally attended the execution of those accused of cowardice or desertion – but they had their own lives to consider.[46] For Hitler to have been able thrice to employ substantially the same tactics over a twenty-month period was an indictment of the Red Army planners and senior commanders.

Stalin's scavenging acquisition of eastern Poland up to the River Bug, and his occupations of Bessarabia and the Baltic States in June 1940, also meant that the Red Army was positioned much too far forward by the time of Barbarossa, conveniently for Hitler's plans as outlined in Directive No. 21. In mid-May 1941, 170 divisions, that is more than 70 per cent of the total strength of the Red Army, were stationed beyond the 1939 borders of the USSR.[47] If Hitler had personally ordained the Russian dispositions he could scarcely have done a better job. Moreover the Red Army had spent its time in these advanced positions not in training, but in building fortifications that proved worthless and roads and railways that were soon being used by the Germans. The defensive Stalin Line was if anything more impressive even than the Maginot Line, but it did not connect all the way along its 90-mile length.[48] Soviet dispositions are all the more inexplicable considering that Barbarossa was the worst-kept secret of the Second World War, and Stalin received no fewer than eighty warnings of Hitler's intentions over the previous eight months.[49] These came from his own spies such as Richard Sorge in the German Embassy in Tokyo – who had the distinction of predicting 22 June as the actual date of attack – and also from counter-intelligence agents in Berlin, Washington and eastern Europe, and latterly from the British Ambassador Sir Stafford Cripps. Even the anti-Nazi German Ambassador to Moscow, Count Friedrich Werner von der Schulenburg, told the Russians what was about to happen. Yet Stalin still believed that the Germans were merely racheting up pressure, and that Churchill was a double-crossing warmonger spreading misinformation – *Angliyskaya provokatsiya* – in order to provoke a clash in the east, thus saving Britain from isolation and eventual defeat. Churchill's problem of how to get information from Enigma wireless interception decrypts to Stalin without the Russians guessing their source was solved by Claude Dansey, deputy head of the Secret Intelligence Service (SIS, or MI6), who infiltrated the Swiss-based Soviet spy ring codenamed Lucy, which in turn also warned Moscow Centre that the attack should be expected around 22 June.[50]

The day before the invasion, the NKVD reported no fewer than thirty-nine 'aircraft incursions' – that is, German reconnaissance flights in Soviet airspace. At last the Russian High Command put out a warning, but many units did not receive it until too late. It is impossible to escape the conclusion that the supposed arch-realist Stalin did not believe the warnings simply because he did not wish to, and the chief of military intelligence, General Filip Golikov, did not want to tell the brutal, unpredictable despot news that he did not want to hear. Never has 'group-think' worked more powerfully. 'We are being fired on,' reported one Russian unit in the early hours of 22 June. 'What are we to do?' The reply from GHQ illustrates perfectly the combination of ill-preparedness and bureaucracy that characterized the Red Army at that time: 'You must be insane. And why isn't your signal in code?'[51]

It was also extraordinary that Hitler managed to retain the advantage of surprise for Operation Barbarossa, given the colossal numbers of troops involved: 3.05 million German troops and almost 1 million in foreign contingents adds up to over 4 million men, stretching along the entire western border of the Soviet Union from Finland to the Black Sea. With 3,350 tanks in twenty armoured divisions, 7,000 field guns and 3,200 aircraft, as well as immense quantities of vehicles and stores captured undamaged from the French, Germany also had 600,000 horses taking part.[52] Against Hitler's 180 divisions, the Red Army had 158 immediately available, along with 6,000 combat planes and more than 10,000 tanks. Much of the Soviet Air Force was obsolete by 1941, and most tanks had no radios.

Attacking at 03.15 hours on Sunday, 22 June 1941, an hour before dawn, the Wehrmacht achieved almost total tactical surprise and virtually raced through Soviet territory. Around 1,200 Soviet aircraft were destroyed on the first morning, drawn up on the ground wing-tip to wing-tip; indeed, the Luftwaffe knocked out more Russian warplanes on the first day of Barbarossa than it did British planes in the entire battle of Britain. Lieutenant-General Ivan Kopets, the chief of Russia's Bomber Command, shot himself on the second day of the invasion, which under the circumstances in Stalin's regime counted as a smart career move. By the end of the first week of fighting, nine-tenths of the Red Army's new Mechanized Corps had also been destroyed.[53] Stalin's total failure to anticipate the invasion is evident from his disbelieving reaction once it had begun. Zhukov telephoned him at 03.30 to tell him of the attacks, but all the general could hear was heavy breathing down the line, so he had to repeat himself and ask, 'Did you understand me?' only to be treated to more silence. When the Politburo met at 04.30, Stalin's face was white and he was unable to grasp the fact that there had been a declaration of war by Germany.[54] His initial orders to the Army were ludicrous: to attack along the whole front, but not to infringe German territorial integrity without specific orders.[55] More rational, indeed vital, was the command to mobilize every Russian male born between 1905 and 1918 – and 800,000 women – under the *narodnoe opolchenie* (popular levy) system. In all, five million people were called up immediately, and by December almost 200 new divisions – averaging 11,000 soldiers each – were considered ready for battle. Citizens in their fifties and sixties also formed militia divisions. These reserve divisions would later prove decisive.

Despite a dearth of uniforms and weapons, let alone vehicles, at least at the beginning, these volunteers and levied troops were able to dig defences and were set to work throwing up anti-tank ditches, pillboxes and machine-gun posts, usually working twelve hours a day, often while being bombed. Even those units that were provided with weapons were often badly under-equipped: the 18th Leningrad Volunteer Division of 7,000 men, for example, had a grand total of only 21 machine guns, 300 rifles and 100 revolvers between them (that is, only 6 per cent were armed, not counting grenades and Molotov cocktails).[56]

Stalin seems to have suffered something akin to a mental breakdown one week into the invasion in the early hours of Sunday, 29 June, unless he was just testing the loyalty of his Politburo colleagues rather as his hero Ivan the Terrible had once withdrawn to a monastery to test the loyalty of his boyars. Stalin's 'prostration', as Molotov put it, during which he could neither undress nor sleep but simply wandered around his dacha at Kuntsevo outside Moscow, did not last long, which was just as well because the whole government machinery seized up in his absence, fearful of initiating anything without his personal imprimatur.[57] When a Politburo delegation finally went to visit, he initially suspected they had come to arrest him, whereas in fact they had arrived to ask him to head a new State Committee of Defence (the Stavka) that would supplant the authority of both the Party and the Government, which he agreed to do on 1 July. Two days later he broadcast to the Russian people for the first time, promising that 'Our arrogant foe will soon discover that our forces are beyond number,' and concluding: 'Forward to Victory!' He became supreme commander on 10 July, by which time the Germans had traversed 400 miles in eighteen days, and the Soviet Union had already lost 4,800 tanks, 9,480 guns and 1,777 planes.[58]

In the north, German bridgeheads across the River Dvina had been established by 26 June, and the Luga river was crossed on 14 July. Army Group Centre meanwhile snapped shut a giant Panzer pincer movement around Minsk on 29 June, capturing 290,000 Red Army troops in pockets at Białystok and Gorodishche, as well as seizing 2,500 tanks and 1,400 field guns. By destroying Soviet food and ammunition supply lines from the air, disrupting communications and racing around the rear to cut off huge numbers of unmotorized infantry, the Germans induced panic, surrender, self-mutilation and suicide among significant sections of the Russian officer corps.[59] Reports of German parachutists in Red Army uniforms – some true, others false – led to many deaths through what is now known as friendly fire. When General Dmitri Pavlov, commander of the Western Front, was unable to communicate with the Tenth Army, he parachuted into the army's territory two of his aides-de-camp, who were shot as spies because they had not been told of the change of codeword of the previous day.[60] Pavlov did not long outlive them, as Stalin soon had him court-martialled and shot for the defeats in his sector.

Almost as quickly as Poland and France, Russia seemed to have been comprehensively defeated by late August 1941, with over half her European territory and nearly half her total population and industrial and agricultural production soon in enemy hands. Fortunately, no one told the ordinary Russian soldier that Russia had apparently lost the war, and he never learnt a truth that otherwise seemed self-evident to the General Staffs of Britain, America, Japan and Germany, and privately to some in the Stavka itself. By the end of July, Smolensk, after initially fierce resistance, had yielded up a further 100,000 prisoners, 2,000 tanks and 1,900 guns. There was now no great conurbation between the Germans and Moscow, which began to be bombed on 21 July. The mass panic that seized the capital was dealt with by the Stavka's security director, Lavrenti Beria, who set up roadblocks on the exit routes and simply shot those attempting to flee (although Lenin's embalmed body and the red stars on the turrets of the Kremlin were secretly removed to Siberia for safe keeping).[61]

In Moscow the bread ration started out at 800 grams per day for manual workers, 600 for non-manual workers and 400 for everyone else (although blood donors got extra). Meat rations were 2.2 kilograms, 1.2 kilograms and 600 grams per month. Anyone whose ration card was lost or stolen faced starvation. The Nomenklatura, the notable and powerful people of the workers' paradise, and their families, got lavishly preferential treatment, as they had ever since

1917. At a time of siege this often meant the difference between life and death, and the entire Soviet rationing system – despite the inefficiencies and corruption – effectively became a means by which the authorities decided who lived and who died.

Fighting around Smolensk did not end with its fall to Guderian on 15 July, however. As late as the first week in September, the Soviets launched massive counter-attacks under Timoshenko and Zhukov, which the latter with some justification claimed as 'a great victory' because it held the Germans back from further advances, at least for the time being. In slowing the German advance towards Moscow as the weather was about to turn, some historians cite Smolensk as the first indication that the war might be approaching a turning point. The Smolensk battle had been fought for sixty-three days over 390 miles of front, and the Soviets had retreated 150 miles, with 309,959 'irrecoverable losses' out of 579,400 taking part. Once the 159,625 sick and wounded are added, this amounted to a staggering 80 per cent casualty rate.[62] At the Moscow Defence Museum it is possible to see the records of schools in which only 3 per cent of the male students who graduated in 1941 survived the war. In a sense the scale of Russian losses simply did not matter, since there were always more to fill the gaps, whereas Germans could not be replaced fast enough. As an historian of the Eastern Front writes, 'the three German Army Groups . . . had suffered 213,301 casualties, prisoners and missing in the first six weeks, until 31 July, and only received 47,000 new troops. The Soviets had suffered almost ten times as many irrecoverable losses – 2,129,677 – by 30 September, but, unlike the Germans', the losses seemed not to count.'[63]

Although Rundstedt's 1st Panzer Group broke through the Soviet Fifth Army and got to within 10 miles of Kiev by 11 July, it could not take the city. The very successes of the Germans, in hugely extending their lines of communication, caused grave logistical problems for the Wehrmacht, especially once partisans began disrupting supplies in the rear. Originally disorganized and often leaderless, the Soviet partisans became much better equipped and more centrally directed as the war progressed. Their most famous martyr was Zoya Kosmodemyanskaya, an eighteen-year-old girl whom the Germans executed for setting fire to stables in the village of Petrishchevo. She revealed nothing under torture, and cried: 'You can't hang all 190 million of us!' before she died.[64]

Hitler likened the war against the partisans to fighting lice in the trenches. 'A lice-covered soldier', he opined, 'has to start the fight against the lice.' He believed that gendarmeries stationed in every town should 'take it by the root . . . The bands can't keep forming – even in the towns the bandits have to be fished out individually . . . But if the British could cope with the nomads in the north-western provinces of India, we can manage this here, too.'[65] On 22 July 1941, Hitler had told the Croatian Defence Minister, Marshal Slavko Kvaternik, that Stalin rather than he would meet Napoleon's fate.[66] Clearly, Hitler was well aware of the shade of the Emperor on the steppes. Goebbels had spotted the Bonaparte problem earlier, writing about Barbarossa in late March 1941 that 'The project as a whole presents some problems from the psychological point of view. Parallels with Napoleon, etc. But we shall quickly overcome these by anti-Bolshevism.'[67] Jodl believed that Hitler had chosen his route into Russia specifically because he 'had an instinctive aversion to treading the same path as Napoleon. Moscow gives him an *etwas Unheimliches* [weird feeling].'

The size of Operation Barbarossa dwarfs everything else in the history of warfare. As one historian records:

Within a day, German attacks had demolished one-quarter of the Soviet air force. Within four months, the Germans had occupied 600,000 square miles of Russian soil, captured 3 million Red Army troops, butchered countless Jews and other civilians, and closed to within 65 miles of Moscow. But four months after that, more than 200,000 Wehrmacht troops had been killed, 726,000 wounded, 400,000 captured and another 113,000 had been incapacitated by frostbite.[68]

An astonishing number of Soviet aircraft losses – 43,100 out of a wartime total of 88,300 – came not as a result of combat but through accidents due to insufficient training, the hasty introduction of new plane types, air-crew indiscipline, lax flight procedures during training, structural failings and manufacturing defects.[69] Half of all Russian planes during the war, therefore, were not destroyed by bombing or shot down by the Germans, but were rather lost due to avoidable mistakes by the Soviets themselves.

The Russians were also unfortunate with their tanks, at least until they concentrated production on the excellent T-34. The 75–95mm armour of the KV-1 (designed in 1941 and named after Klementi Voroshilov) made them impervious to the attacks of most German tanks, but they were highly vulnerable from the air – as were almost all tanks throughout the Second World War – and were often outmanoeuvred in the early stages of Barbarossa and had to be destroyed by their own crews. They had only 76mm cannon and moved at no more than 35kph, but had crews of five and three 7.62mm machine guns. Equally slow at 34kph was its 1940 predecessor, confusingly called the KV-2, which was a 52-tonne, six-crew monster, with 75mm armour, three machine guns and a vast 152mm howitzer gun. Unfortunately, there were only a thousand ever made. Lighter and thus slightly faster was the 46-tonne IS-2 (named after Josef Stalin), despite its 90–120mm armour and 122mm cannon. Self-propelled cannon were similar to tanks except they were much cheaper to build because they did not have movable turrets. The SU-152 fired a 49-kilogram shell which, with its 20-kilogram case, was so heavy that it could blow the turret off a Tiger or Panther tank and have it land 15 yards away, thus earning its soubriquet Beast-killer. It was designed in less than a month in January 1943, when Stalin emphasized to the tank designer Josef Kotin – in the threatening way he knew best – how desperately it was needed. (The Panther was a specific marque of German tank and should not be confused with Panzer, which is the generic term for all German tanks.)

The most dire threats were also employed to try to prevent Red Army soldiers surrendering to the Germans. On 28 July 1941, Stalin's 'Not One Step Back' Order No. 227 ordained that anyone who retreated without specific orders or who surrendered was to be treated as a 'traitor to the Motherland', and his family therefore liable to imprisonment. Even Stalin's own son, First Lieutenant Yakov Dzhugashvili, battery commander of the 14th Howitzer Artillery Regiment of the 14th Armoured Division, who was captured near Vitebsk in mid-July, was not excluded; his wife spent two years in a labour camp.[70] (Yakov was shot in 1943, when he entered the perimeter zone of his POW camp, either in an escape attempt or, just as likely, as suicide-by-escape.)

As though the citizens of Occupied Poland, the Ukraine and the Baltic States did not have enough to be terrified of during the German advance, the NKVD also unleashed on them an orgy of sadistic violence quite unlike its normal murder sprees. After Stalin had ordered Beria to purge the Army, wipe out defeatism and rumour-mongering and investigate with maximum distrust anyone who had escaped from the Germans, horrific scenes took place in Russian-held areas just before the Wehrmacht's arrival. 'When the prisons were opened up after the Soviet retreat there were scenes of indescribable horror,' records Richard Overy. 'Bodies had been savagely mutilated; hundreds of prisoners had been tortured to death rather than dispatched with the usual bullet in the back of the head. In one incident in the Ukraine the NKVD dynamited two cells filled with women prisoners. In another prison the floor was strewn with the tongues, ears and eyes of the dead prisoners.'[71] Overy concludes that the NKVD guards had been 'convulsed by a spasm of retributive violence induced by fear, desperation and rage'. In Lvov alone, 4,000 people were shot, including almost everyone in the city's prison, which was then burnt down.

Small wonder, therefore, that when the Germans arrived in many parts of western Russia, the Ukraine and the Baltics, the village elders came out to greet the invaders with their traditional welcoming offers of bread and salt.[72] Briefing Hitler on 4 August 1941, Bock was able to 'plead the cause of the helpful and friendly population'.[73] After the Germans had allowed the churches to be reconverted from cinemas and atheist exhibition centres back into places of Orthodox worship, Bock noted in his diary that:

The population had come, often from far away, cleaned the churches and decorated them with flowers. Many pictures of Christ and icons which had been hidden for decades were brought out. When the military services were over, the people – not just the old, but many young as well – streamed into the churches and kissed the holy objects – including the crosses around the necks of the [German] armed forces chaplains – and often remained there praying till evening. This people will not be difficult to lead![74]

If the German Army had been instructed to embrace this anti-Bolshevik behaviour, and do all in its power to encourage anti-Soviet nationalism, the story of Barbarossa might have been very different. Yet that was not the Nazi way; these regions were earmarked for *Lebensraum*, so wholesale ethnic cleansing followed, and naturally forced the local populations into outright opposition and partisan activity.

The *Einsatzgruppen* that followed the Wehrmacht sacked and burnt villages, enslaving the inhabitants as Slavic *Untermenschen*, creating implacable enemies among those they did not shoot. Here was yet another crucial instance of Nazi ideology interfering with Germany's military best interests. 'One reason why Hitler's brutal "realism" in fact served him poorly', observes the historian of the Nazi empire in Europe, 'was that it deprived the Germans of the chance of exploiting nationalism as a tool of political warfare.'[75] When in September 1941 the Abwehr suggested to OKW that a Ukrainian army be raised to fight against the Red Army, the idea was turned down with contempt. It was brought up again in June 1943, but the Führer told Keitel that there was no use 'claiming that now we just need to establish a Ukrainian state and everything will be all right, and then we'll get one million soldiers. We won't get anything – not even one man. That's a figment of the imagination, just as it was in the past. But we would totally give up our war objective' – by that he meant *Lebensraum* and the enslavement of the Slavs.[76] Far from nurturing Slavic nationalism, therefore, Hitler merely crushed it.

Yet such were the cruelties and inefficiencies of the Bolshevik regime that there were many Russians who would have embraced non-Communist, nationalist puppet states if Hitler had set them up, rather than his relying on the same system of direct rule as the Government-General in Poland or the Occupied region of France. Leninism, collect-ivization, state atheism, the Civil War, repression and the Gulag system of prisons and penal colonies had left a bitter hatred against the Bolsheviks that the Germans ought to have used to their advantage. The nationality question had been decided in favour of the Russians over the 119 other nationalities of the Soviet Union, leaving the proud Ukrainians – several million of whom had been deliberately starved to death in the early 1930s – almost powerless. Many of these nationalities had been part of Greater Russia for less than a century anyway, and had cultures, languages and identities that had somehow survived vicious Bolshevik persecution.

Although the Germans did initially attempt to pose as liberators to some of these peoples, especially those in the Baltics, the Ukraine, Armenia and Georgia and the Crimean Tatars, this was merely for propaganda purposes and their behaviour on the ground soon made it clear that they simply regarded themselves as conquerors. Yet wherever the Germans did allow a measure of local autonomy – such as to Bronislav Kaminski's brutal RONA (the Russian National Liberation Army) in the so-called Lokoty Self-Governing District, and to the Cossacks – they tended to fight well. The Cossacks even had autonomous ministries for education, agriculture and healthcare.[77] In the Ukraine, for example, the German IL Mountain Corps asked local city leaders to guard their own communities, something that freed up troops for the front line. It worked for a while. The Nazis ought also to have promised the peasants of southern Russia massive agrarian decollectivization, reawakening the hopes of 1917 that they would be allowed their own land and the freedom to cultivate it and to sell their produce for their own profit.

Good, or at least reasonable, treatment of the immense numbers of Soviet POWs captured in the early stages – over 2 million by November 1941 and 3.6 million by the following March – was also a necessary prerequisite for mass collaboration. Yet here the Nazis, whose plans were for large-scale liquidation, proved themselves incapable of even pretending to act out the role of liberators rather than genocidal conquerors. Lebensraum required annexations, mass executions and the utter enslavement of all Slavic peoples, and this was deemed irreconcilable with a policy of liberation from Stalinism, whatever military advantages beckoned. A more cynical plan would have been to offer Stalin's subject peoples autonomy until the Bolsheviks were defeated, and only then to put the extermination and Lebensraum plans into operation. Yet the sheer numbers of POWs being captured, the overconfidence inspired by the initial crushing victories, and the food shortages that were already developing in the east made that impractical. With four million soldiers to feed in Russia, almost all of whom were expected under OKW rules to live off the land – despite

its being subjected to a scorched-earth policy by the Russians themselves – mass starvation of civilians in western Russia and the Ukraine
was probably the only likely outcome, even if the Reich had tried to
adopt a conciliatory policy towards Russia's subject peoples.

In all, 3.3 million Red Army prisoners were to die in German
captivity, or 58 per cent of the total of 5.7 million that were taken.
This had even been anticipated in the original German war plans. The
Wehrmacht's Central Economic Agency stated on 2 May 1941 that
all German forces involved in Barbarossa would have to 'be fed at the
expense of Russia . . . thereby tens of millions will undoubtedly starve
to death if we take away all we need from the country'.[78] This was
underlined by the Nazi ideologist Alfred Rosenberg, who on 20 June
1941, on the very eve of the invasion, told the bureaucrats who would
soon staff the Ministry for the Occupied Eastern Territories (Ukraine
and Ostland): 'The southern territories and northern Caucasia will
have to make up the deficit in food supplies for the German people.
We do not accept that we have any responsibility for feeding the
Russian population . . . from these surplus-producing regions.'[79] In
fact it was crueller even than that. 'The purpose of the Russian campaign is to decimate the Slavic population by thirty millions,' Himmler
told colleagues at a weekend party just before Barbarossa.[80] With the
final Russian death toll at twenty-seven million, he almost reached his
target. Hitler's concept of the *Völkerkrieg* (clash of peoples) was always
intended to end in genocide in the east, or at least in enough ethnic
cleansing (as it would later be called) to clear the necessary areas for the
Aryan farmer–soldiers who were going to colonize the rich agricultural
areas. In this as in so much else, the Nazi way of fighting the war
triumphed over the most efficient way of finding victory.

The march on Kiev in July 1941 provided the occasion for one of
Hitler's most controversial decisions of the war, when he opted to
take the Ukrainian rather than the Russian capital, although of course
he did not see it in those terms at the time. The Soviet Fifth Army had
pulled back, but was still capable of threatening the north flank of the
German advance into the Ukraine, so OKW determined that as soon
as the Red Army near Smolensk had been destroyed, Guderian's 2nd
Panzer Group and the Second Army from Army Group Centre should

break off their march on Moscow and swing due south behind the Pripet Marshes to destroy the Soviet Fifth Army and take Kiev in conjunction with the 1st Panzer Group already engaged there. Bock and Guderian opposed this change to the original plan, fearing – rightly as it turned out – that critical momentum would be lost in the drive on the Russian capital, but they were overruled by Hitler. By 11 August 1941 the truth had already dawned upon Franz Halder, as he recorded in his diary:

The whole situation makes it increasingly plain that we have underestimated the Russian colossus ... At the outset of war, we reckoned with about 200 enemy divisions. Now we have already counted 360. These divisions indeed are not armed and equipped according to our standards, and their tactical leadership is often poor. But there they are, and if we smash a dozen of them, the Russians simply put up another dozen. The time factor favours them, as they are near their own resources, while we are moving farther and farther away from ours.[81]

In fact the Russians were to field many more divisions than merely 360; some historians have enumerated as many as 600.[82]

The war diary of Fedor von Bock, the commander of Army Group Centre, shows how crucial Hitler was to the fateful decision not to push on to Moscow at full strength and speed in August and September 1941. A hint of the Führer's thoughts came after Generals von Kluge and von Bock had dinner together on 28 July, and Hitler's chief Army adjutant Rudolf Schmundt arrived at Bock's headquarters at Novy Borissov late that evening to say of the Führer's plans that 'the main thing is to eliminate the area of Leningrad, then the raw materials region of the Donets Basin. The Führer cares nothing about Moscow itself. The enemy at Gomel is to be wiped out to clear the way for future operations.' Bock's understandable reaction was: 'That differs somewhat from what is said in the Army Command's directive!'[83] Directive No. 21 had in fact been ambiguous, giving as equal priorities 'the prompt seizure of the economically important Donets Basin' and a 'rapid arrival at Moscow'.

A week later, on 4 August, Hitler arrived at Novy Borissov himself, and said that he saw the Crimea as a primary objective, otherwise it might become 'a Soviet aircraft carrier operating against the Rumanian oil-fields'. He congratulated Bock on his 'unprecedented success' so far, but Bock gleaned from the discussion after his briefing that 'it appears that he is not yet clear on how the operations should now proceed.'[84] Heinz Guderian (2nd Panzer Group) and Hermann Hoth (3rd Panzer Group) explained that relief and repairs necessitated by their rapid advance would take time, which Hitler accepted. The Führer then spoke of 'an attack to the east', with which Bock 'happily agreed and said that in this way we should surely meet the Russian strength and decision against what was probably his last forces to be hoped for there'. In fact of course the Russians had plenty more forces, but a massive assault on Moscow seems therefore still to have been contemplated in early August. This was thought of as the great *Entscheidungsschlacht* (decisive battle) as prescribed by Clausewitz.

The early nineteenth-century Prussian military theorist Carl von Clausewitz was the acknowledged guru of the German High Command, but was he actually read by them? Kleist thought not. 'Clausewitz's teachings had fallen into neglect by this generation,' he told Liddell Hart after the war. 'His phrases were quoted but his books were not closely studied. He was regarded as a military philosopher, rather than as a practical teacher.' Kleist believed that Schlieffen's writings 'received much greater attention', which was undoubtedly true in Hitler's case. As for Clausewitz's maxim that 'War is nothing but the continuation of politics by other means,' Kleist believed that 'Under the Nazis we tended to reverse Clausewitz's dictum, and to regard peace as a continuation of war.'[85] Certainly, Clausewitz's many Cassandrine warnings about the dangers of invading Russia – he had personally witnessed Napoleon's nemesis in the retreat from Moscow from the Russian side – went unheeded. In his chapter on the 'Interdependence of the Elements of War' in his magnum opus *On War*, he had written:

Within the concept of absolute war, then, war is indivisible, and its component parts (the individual victories) are of value only in relation to the whole. Conquering Moscow and half of Russia in 1812 was of no avail to Bonaparte unless it brought him the peace he had in view. But these successes were only a part of his plan of campaign: what was still missing was the destruction of the Russian army. If that achievement had been added to the rest, peace would have been as sure as things of that sort ever can be. But it was too late to achieve the second part of his plan; his chance had gone. Thus the successful stage was not only wasted but led to disaster.[86]

It was a vital part of Clausewitz's message, but not one quoted by many generals – including Kleist – in 1941–42 when it needed to be.

Hitler was having severe doubts about the wisdom of prioritizing the drive on Moscow over what were – for him – some even more important targets. 'Modern warfare is all economic warfare,' he stated, 'and the demands of economic warfare must be given priority.'[87] His desire to take the cereal crops of the Ukraine, the oil of the Caucasus and the coal of the Donets region – and thus simultaneously deny them to Stalin – led him to make the key error of not pushing on to Moscow, but instead driving south to take Kiev. The Clausewitzians on his General Staff wanted to defeat the enemy's main force, and take Moscow as soon as possible, but Hitler's more economics-based grand strategy prevailed. By dispersing his forces for these various tasks, he threw away his chance of taking Moscow, but he did not suspect so at the time, believing that that too was attainable before the onset of winter. Yet Moscow was the nodal point of Russia's north–south transport hub, was the administrative and political capital, was vital for Russian morale and was an important industrial centre in its own right.

On 21 August, Hitler sent Bock a new directive stating that:

The army's proposal for the continuation of the operations .... does not correspond with my plans. I order the following ... The most important objective to be achieved before the onset of winter is not the occupation of Moscow, but the taking of the Crimea, the industrial and coal region of the Donets Basin and the severing of Russian oil deliveries from the Caucasus area, in the north the encirclement of Leningrad and link-up with the Finns.[88]

This Directive was, in Halder's view, 'decisive to the outcome of this campaign'. The next day, on 22 August, OKW telephoned Bock with the details, informing him that 'on orders from the Führer, strong elements of the 2nd Army and the Guderian Group were to be diverted south, in order to intercept the enemy retreating east in front of the inner wings of Army Groups South and Centre and ease the crossing of the Dnieper by Army Group South.' Bock immediately telephoned

Brauchitsch 'and made clear to him the questionable wisdom of such an operation'. Yet he does not appear to have made himself clear at all, because when that afternoon someone else attempted to talk him out of the operation, Brauchitsch had said: 'Bock isn't at all unhappy about the affair.' Bock then called Halder, telling him that he considered the new plan:

unfortunate, above all because it placed the attack to the east in question. All the directives say that taking Moscow isn't important!! I want to smash the enemy army and the bulk of this army is opposite my front! Turning south is a secondary operation – even if just as big – which will jeopardize the execution of the main operation, namely the destruction of the Russian armed forces before winter.

That evening the Directive came through unaltered, however, and Bock concluded of his protest to Halder: 'It did no good!'[89]

Guderian flew off to see Hitler personally, but was greeted by Brauchitsch with the words: 'It is all decided and there's no point in griping!' Guderian nonetheless described the seriousness of the situation to Hitler, but when he was told 'how decisive to the war the advance to the south was', he buckled and told the Führer, in Bock's astonished words, 'that an immediate advance by XXIV Panzer Corps and other armoured forces was possible!' Bock, who wanted to be the general who captured Moscow, and despaired of having such large forces removed from his army group, can be forgiven his overuse of the exclamation mark considering the circumstances, noting of OKW on 24 August: 'They apparently do not wish to exploit under any circumstances the opportunity decisively to defeat the Russians before winter!'[90] He later added that 'the objective to which I devoted all my thought, the destruction of the main strength of the enemy army, has been dropped.'

Clausewitz would not have approved, but in Hitler's defence neither Halder nor Brauchitsch – who supported Bock – seems to have put up much resistance to the diversion southwards of Guderian's crack units, and thus almost the emasculation of Army Group Centre's forward thrusting power at such a critical stage. 'In our private circles,' Keitel recalled, 'the Führer had often cracked jokes at Halder's expense and labelled him a "little fellow".'[91] Bock contented himself with

writing a pre-emptive I-told-you-so in his diary: 'If, after all the successes, the campaign in the east now trickles away in dismal defensive
fighting for my Army Group, it is not my fault.'[92] Sacked in December
1941, recalled in March 1942 and then sacked again that July, Bock
died with his family in an air raid only three days before the end of
the war in Europe.

Subsequent events show that Hitler ought to have ordered Army
Group Centre to continue its attack on Moscow in August 1941.
Almost all the senior Wehrmacht officers outside OKW supported
this, as did almost all within OKW, except Keitel and Jodl. 'Hitler
made the most important decision of his life', writes one historian,
'against the professional judgment of virtually every German soldier
who had an opportunity to comment.'[93] The Allied committee system,
for all its time-consuming debates and profound disagreements, was
a far superior way of arriving at grand strategy than the method by
which each general scrambled for the ear of a dictator who was not
always listening anyway.

The Smolensk pocket had been eliminated by 5 August, and when
the German Second Army and 2nd Panzer Group came south, behind
Kiev, and linked up with the 1st Panzer Group coming north from
Kremenchug, they annihilated the Russian Fifth and Thirty-seventh
Armies of around half a million men at Gomel by 17 September. This
operation has been described as 'arguably the greatest single German
victory in the Eastern war', opening the way for the conquest of the
Donets industrial basin.[94] These Blitzkrieg victories had been huge,
well supported by the Luftwaffe, conducted at great speed over dry
ground against bewildered opposition, but nonetheless with serious
losses, owing to the fortitude of the ordinary Russian soldier.

The fall of Kiev, which cost the Soviets 665,000 prisoners, made it
possible for the OKW to concentrate once again on the capture of
Moscow, which it was hoped would force the Soviet Government and
the Red Army behind the Ural mountains, and knock the USSR out
of the war as an effective power. The Luftwaffe could then be given
the task of confining the Russians to a deindustrialized Siberian outpost that could only at best conduct minor border resistance operations against a German *Volk* in complete control of the whole
European land mass. Britain would then have no hope and would

have to come to terms, as the Reich geared itself up for the coming world-historical struggle against the United States, a war it could not fail to win because – as Hitler regularly averred at the Berghof – that country was internally rotten from the influence of so many Jews and blacks. In retrospect, it is possible to see how just such a nightmare world might have indeed come about had Moscow fallen in October 1941, and we now know that on the 16th Stalin even had his personal train made ready to evacuate him from the city.

The assault on Moscow was formidable. From the south came the Panzer Group Guderian via Orel, Bryansk and Tula. Army Group Centre provided the major thrust with the Second Army going via Kaluga and Hoepner's 4th Panzer Group from Roslavl via Yukhnov. Army Group North meanwhile contributed Hoth's 3rd Panzer Group which went via Vyazma and Borodino (another place with powerful Napoleonic connotations). Up in the very north of the sector, the Ninth Army made its way towards Kalinin. In all the Wehrmacht devoted no fewer than forty-four infantry divisions, eight motorized divisions and fourteen Panzer divisions to the assault, starting out on 30 September in Guderian's case, 2 October in the others'.[95] 'Today', declared Hitler, 'begins the last great offensive of the year!' As they converged on their target, the Wehrmacht worked closely together in cutting off vast Russian formations, so that by 7 October Hoth and Hoepner had surrounded the Russian Thirty-second Army at Vyazma, and Guderian and the Second Army had sliced off the Russian Third Army at Bryansk, destroying these trapped armies on 14 and 20 October respectively. In time, the Russians learnt to retreat and not get cut off, but they could not retreat beyond Moscow without losing the capital, so they threw up three huge defensive lines west of the city, and tried everything in their power to slow down the onslaught.

Meanwhile, in the north of Russia, Army Group North reached Novgorod by 16 August, and on 1 September was close enough to begin bombarding Leningrad. The Finns had joined the German invasion enthusiastically, hoping to avenge their defeat in the Winter War, and they managed to recapture Viipuri and much of the rest of the Karelian Isthmus, besieging Leningrad from the north-west. By 15 September, the second city in the Soviet Union was cut off, and the German decision to try to starve it into surrender, rather than simply to storm it, turned out in retrospect to have been crucial. It was a rational stance to take – 11,000 civilians starved to death in Leningrad in the month of November 1941 alone, for example, as opposed to 12,500 killed by shelling and bombing in the first three months of the siege – yet somehow Leningrad survived its gruelling 900-day ordeal, despite suffering over one million deaths, or an average of more than 1,100 people a day for nearly three years. It was by far the bloodiest siege in history, and more Russians died in Leningrad alone than British and American soldiers and civilians during the whole of the Second World War.

On 12 September the food commissar of Leningrad, D. V. Pavlov, set the ration for non-workers and children at one-third of a pound of (25 per cent edible cellulose) bread a day, plus a pound of meat and 1.5 pounds of cereals and three-quarters of a pound of sunflower-seed oil per month. It was a meagre figure that was nonetheless destined to be cut several times before the end of the war. On 20 November, front-line troops got 500 grams of bread per day, factory workers received 250, and everyone else 125 (that is, two slices). 'Twigs were collected and stewed,' records an historian of the siege. 'Peat shavings, cottonseed cake, bonemeal was pressed into use. Pine sawdust was processed and added to the bread. Mouldy grain was dredged from sunken barges and scraped out of the holds of ships. Soon Leningrad bread was containing 10% cottonseed cake that had been processed to remove poisons.'[96] Household pets, shoe leather, fir bark and insects were consumed, as was wallpaper paste which was reputed to be made with potato flour. Guinea pigs, white mice and rabbits were saved from vivisection in the city's laboratories for a more immediately practical fate. 'Today it is so simple to die,' wrote one resident, Yelena Skryabina, in her diary. 'You just begin to lose interest, then you lie on your bed and you never get up again.'[97] Yet some people were willing to go to any lengths in order to survive: 226 people were arrested for cannibalism during the siege. 'Human meat is being sold in the markets,' concluded one secret NKVD report, 'while in the cemeteries bodies pile up like carcasses, without coffins.'[98]

Even on those brief occasions when Soviet counter-offensives allowed small quantities of food to get into the city and the bread ration could be temporarily increased, the situation was never better than completely desperate. In October 7,500 shells, 991 explosive bombs and 31,398 incendiaries fell on Leningrad; in November 11,230 shells and 7,500 bombs; in December 6,000 shells and 2,000 bombs. On Christmas Day 1941, when supplies were being brought along an ice road over Lake Ladoga, 3,700 people still died of starvation. (The drivers of trucks crossing the frozen lake kept their doors open, despite the sub-zero temperatures, in order to jump out if their vehicle was hit or plunged through the ice.) The Russian Baltic Fleet was ice-bound at Leningrad and so took part in its anti-aircraft defence. They could hardly leave in any case, since the Baltic Sea was dominated by the German Navy. As the snow thawed in Leningrad in the spring of 1942, thousands of frozen bodies were dug up from the streets before the putrefaction could start epidemics.

The heavy rains that fell on Wednesday, 8 October 1941 were the first in a series of climatic changes that were ultimately to wreck Hitler's ambitions in Russia. The Russians called it *rasputitsa* (the time when roads dissolve). Thick mud slowed the pushes towards Kalinin, Kaluga and Tula, the key staging posts on the way to Moscow. Although the Vyazma Defence Line failed to hold back the Wehrmacht, the Mozhaysk Defence Line fared much better, so that by 30 October the Germans had stalled between 45 and 75 miles from the capital. Years later Rundstedt looked back at the likelihood of victory in Barbarossa:

Long before winter came the chances had been diminished owing to the repeated delays in the advance that were caused by bad roads and mud. The 'black earth' of the Ukraine could be turned into mud by ten minutes' rain, stopping all movement until it dried. That was a heavy handicap in a race with time. It was increased by a lack of railways in Russia for bringing up supplies to our advancing troops. Another adverse factor was the way the Russians received continual reinforcements from their rear areas, as they fell back. It seemed to us that as soon as one force was wiped out, the path was blocked by the arrival of a fresh force.[99]

As the weather worsened and barometers fell, however, the ground hardened, which for a short period gave the Germans another opportunity to encircle the city. By then, however, their original two-to-one superiority on the ground and three-to-one in the air had evaporated as the Soviet state threw everything into the defence, with Stalin making an uplifting address from the Kremlin on the anniversary of the Bolshevik Revolution, 7 November, in which he mentioned Alexander Nevsky, Michael Kutuzov and Lenin, as well as the help promised by the British and Americans. (When the speech had to be refilmed later on for propaganda purposes, it was noticed by observant Russians that no condensation came from Stalin's mouth, as would have been the case if it had been filmed in Red Square in freezing November.)

Relatively few buildings were destroyed in Moscow by German bombing during the war – only about 3 per cent of the total. This was because of the size and accuracy of Russian anti-aircraft units, as well as good anti-bomber cover provided by Ilyushin and Airacobra fighters and the barrage balloons over the capital. Until 1943 it even served the Red Air Force deliberately to ram into enemy planes. The AZP-39 anti-aircraft guns of 37mm calibre that ringed Moscow weighed 2,100 kilos, fired 730-gram shells at a speed of more than 908 yards per second at 180 rounds a minute to a maximum height of 19,500 feet, and were accurate up to 9,000 feet. The Katyusha (Little Kate) BM-13 mobile rocket was first used in the defence of Moscow, launched from the back of a truck (often an American-donated Studebaker). With their 132mm calibre, 1.41-metre length, 42.5-kilogram weight (and 4.9-kilogram weight of explosive) and 8.5-mile range, they were a terrifying weapon, despite their affectionate nickname, especially when up to sixteen were fired at once. The Germans had great trouble in capturing one for research, as they were rigged up to enable their commanders to destroy them easily. The Soviets had drastic plans in readiness for a German seizure of Moscow. In 2001, some 270 pounds of explosives were found during renovation work under the Hotel Moscow, next to the Kremlin, which had been placed there in 1941 by the NKVD in case Moscow had to be destroyed, and subsequently forgotten about.[100]

The next direct assault on Moscow began on 15 November, with elements of the 3rd Panzer Group coming within 19 miles of the city, on the Volga Canal, by the 27th. Meanwhile, Guderian reached Kashira on the 25th, but could not get any further. The Germans were unlucky with the weather, it is true, but they did not devote enough troops to this great assault on Moscow, and they had already lost 750,000 casualties, including 8,000 officers and nearly 200,000 men killed, since the launch of Barbarossa. It is no exaggeration to state that the outcome of the Second World War hung in the balance during this massive attack, but by 5 December the 3rd and 2nd Panzer Groups had to be withdrawn to the Istria–Klin and Don–Ulla Lines respectively and put on to the defensive. Could the Germans have taken Moscow if Hitler had not drawn Guderian's Second Panzer Army and the Second Army more than 250 miles south between 23 August and 30 September? We cannot know for certain, but must suspect so.

On the same day that Guderian had finally moved northwards towards Moscow – 30 September 1941 – General Paul von Kleist's 1st Panzer Group in Army Group South crossed the Dnieper and Samara rivers in the direction of Rostov-on-Don. Part of the force cut south to capture Berdyansk on the Sea of Azov on 6 October, thus trapping a large Russian pocket of 100,000 troops of the Soviet Eighteenth Army, despite much the same onset of rain and snow that had affected the German advance on Moscow further north. The momentum was somehow kept up with the capture of Kharkov on 24 October and then Rostov itself on 20 November. Nonetheless, it had all but run out. When on 29 November the hastily reconstructed Soviet Thirty-seventh Army threatened to cut the Germans off in Rostov, Rundstedt ordered Army Group South to withdraw to the Mius and Donets rivers. Hitler attempted – too late – to countermand the order, and Rundstedt wired a message on 30 November to say: 'It is madness to attempt to hold. In the first place the troops cannot do it and in the second place if they do not retreat they will be destroyed. I repeat that this order be rescinded or that you find someone else.'[101] The next day Hitler dismissed Rundstedt, who had suffered a mild heart attack, but quickly forgave him once apprised of the facts on the ground and gave him a large sum of money as a golden handshake. Embarrassed, Rundstedt accepted but never touched it.[102]

By Saturday, 6 December, the Germans were on the defensive along a vast front that began outside Rostov on the Sea of Azov in the south (with most of the Crimea in German hands) and wound up through Izium, Yelets (in German hands), Tula and Moscow (in Russian hands), Kalinin (in German hands) and up to Leningrad (in Russian hands). On that day, Zhukov – who had brought up forty Siberian divisions – began his winter offensive. This great counter-attack resulted in a spectacle that the world had not yet witnessed in more than two years of war: German soldiers surrendering en masse.

Keitel later narrowed the date of Germany's reversal of fortune down to 11 December 1941, explaining that 'the weather had drastically changed from the period of mud and slime to that infernal cold, with all the attendant and catastrophic results for our troops, clad as they were only in improvised winter clothing.'[103] The railway system had broken down as 'German locomotives and their water towers had just frozen solid.' Keitel thought Hitler's blanket refusal to countenance any withdrawals was nonetheless the right one, 'because he had correctly realized that to withdraw even by only a few miles was synonymous with writing off all our heavy armaments'. Tanks, artillery, anti-tank weapons and vehicles 'were irreplaceable. In fact there was no other solution than to stand fast and fight'. When a general asked Hitler for permission to retreat 30 miles, he was asked whether he thought it would be any warmer there, and whether, if the Wehrmacht carried on retreating, the Russians would stop at the borders of the Reich. For all his sarcasm, these were legitimate questions. As the year came to an end, Keitel recorded, 'We spent a cheerless Christmas at the Führer's headquarters.'[104]

The same day that Keitel chose as the turning point in Russia – Thursday, 11 December 1941 – also saw Hitler declare war on the United States, an insane decision that will be examined in the next chapter. Its effect on the Eastern Front was hugely to increase the quantity of arms and other supplies of all kinds that the Americans donated to the Soviet war effort, which included, on top of a vast amount of tanks, planes, trucks, ammunition and military supplies, no fewer than 15,000 saws and 20,000 knives for use in amputations.[105]

*

Contrary to the old adage, Napoleon had not been beaten in Russia by Generals Janvier and Février, because his Grande Armée had in fact been comprehensively defeated by the first week in December; however, those two old soldiers were indeed pressed into service against Hitler 130 years later. Although the Luftwaffe and Waffen-SS had provided winter greatcoats for their men, much of the Wehrmacht had not. So much for the celebrated Teutonic efficiency and General Staff foresight. Furthermore, although Russian Mosin rifles and PPSh sub-machine guns did not freeze up, the oil used to grease German Schmeisser sub-machine guns sometimes did. 'It is a delusion to imagine that a plan of campaign can be laid down far ahead and fulfilled with exactitude,' said Helmuth von Moltke the Elder. 'The first collision with the enemy creates a new situation in accordance with the result.' This is true of military campaigns in general and of Operation Barbarossa in particular, but one thing the OKH could have laid down with some exactitude was the certainty of a very cold winter in Russia, a matter of common sense and logistical foresight of the kind at which the High Command was supposed to excel. The Russians have a saying that there is no such thing as cold weather, only the wrong kind of clothing. The German commissariat had hubristically not transported anything like enough woollen hats, gloves, long-johns and greatcoats to Russia, and suddenly there was a desperate need for millions of such items, over and above what could be looted from the Russians and Poles. On 20 December 1941, Goebbels broadcast an appeal for warm clothing to send to the troops: 'Those at home will not deserve a single peaceful hour if even one soldier is exposed to the rigours of winter without adequate clothing.' Yet two years of clothes rationing meant that there was little to give.

In his table-talk at Berchtesgaden, Hitler let drop a number of remarks that might provide a clue to why he had not sufficiently concerned himself with his men's welfare when it came to the great Russian freeze. 'One can't put any trust in the meteorological forecasts,' he told Bormann and others on the night of 14 October 1941, arguing that the weathermen 'ought to be separated from the Army'. Although he considered that Lufthansa had a first-class meteorological service, the military organization was 'not nearly as good'. Believing himself to be an expert in meteorology as much as he was in everything else, this world-class know-all went on to state:

Weather prediction is not a science that can be learnt mechanically. What we need are men gifted with a sixth sense, who live in nature and with nature – whether or not they know anything about isotherms and isobars. As a rule, obviously, these men are not particularly suited to the wearing of uniforms. One of them will have a humped back, another will be bandy-legged, a third paralytic. Similarly, one doesn't expect them to live like bureaucrats.[106]

These 'human barometers', as Hitler dubbed them – who don't much sound like exemplars of the master race – would have telephones installed in their homes free of charge and would predict the weather for the Reich and 'be flattered to have people relying on [their] know-ledge'. They would be people 'who understand the flights of midges and swallows, who can read the signs, who feel the wind, to whom the movements of the sky are familiar. Elements are involved in that kind of thing that are beyond mathematics,' said Hitler. Or indeed parody.

Hitler was certainly proud of his own hardiness in the cold, boasting on 12 August 1942:

Having to change into long trousers was always a misery to me. Even with a temperature of 10 below zero I used to go about in lederhosen. The feeling of freedom they give you is wonderful. Abandoning my shorts was one of the biggest sacrifices I had to make . . . Anything up to five degrees below zero I don't even notice. Quite a number of young people of today already wear shorts all the year round; it is just a question of habit. In the future I shall have an SS Highland Brigade in lederhosen![107]

If Hitler was under the impression that the Wehrmacht could with-stand sub-zero temperatures in sub-standard winter clothing, he was soon proved wrong. In some areas the Germans were well prepared for Barbarossa; they had printed a German–Russian phrasebook, for example, with questions such as 'Where is the collective farm chairman?' and 'Are you a Communist?' (It was inadvisable to answer the latter in the affirmative.) Yet when it came to something as basic as proper clothing in a winter campaign in one of the world's coldest countries, there was simply not enough, and what they did provide was often not warm enough either. All this springs directly from Hitler's belief that the campaign would be over in three months, by late September 1941, before the weather turned.

The consequences of this lack of warm clothing were often horrific. The Italian journalist Curzio Malaparte recalled in his novel *Kaputt* how he had been in the Europeiski Café in Warsaw when he watched German troops returning from the Eastern Front:

Suddenly I was struck with horror and realized that they had no eyelids. I had already seen soldiers with lidless eyes, on the platform of the Minsk station a few days previously on my way from Smolensk. The ghastly cold of that winter had the strangest consequences. Thousands and thousands of soldiers had lost their limbs; thousands and thousands had their ears, their noses, their fingers and their sexual organs ripped off by the frost. Many had lost their hair ... Many had lost their eyelids. Singed by the cold, the eyelid drops off like a piece of dead skin ... Their future was only lunacy.[108]

This was the pass to which its ludicrous failure to prepare had brought the Wehrmacht. The title of the autobiography of Ribbentrop's private secretary, Reinhard Spitzy, was *How We Squandered the Reich*. For the Germans to be defeated in the field of battle was one thing – and it took another year for it to happen on any significant scale – but for them to have been improperly provided for by their own leadership and General Staff was quite another.

Churchill used the opportunity of the second anniversary of his taking the premiership to mock Hitler over his 'first blunder' of invading Russia, for 'There is a winter, you know, in Russia. For a good many months the temperature is apt to fall very low. There is snow, there is frost, and all that. Hitler forgot about this Russian winter. He must have been very loosely educated. We all heard about it at school; but he forgot it. I have never made such a bad mistake as that.'[109] As well as hearing of it at school, Hitler owned a library with many books on Napoleon and his campaigns, which were covered in extensive marginalia in his own handwriting, as well as several biographies of generals of the Napoleonic era.[110] Although the only time that Hitler ever mentioned Napoleon at his Führer-conferences was when he complained of the Wehrmacht's slow promotion policy – 'If a Napoleon could become a First Consul at the age of 27 [*sic*], I don't see why a 30-year-old man here can't be a general or lieutenant-general: that's ridiculous' – there is plenty of evidence that he thought a great deal about the man who had preceded him as Russia's scourge.[111]

When he captured Paris in 1940, Hitler hastened to pay his respects at Napoleon's tomb at Les Invalides, and ordered the remains of the King of Rome to be disinterred from Vienna and laid to rest with those of his father. 'A gesture that will arouse a grateful response,' thought Goebbels, though without much evidence for it.[112] At the Berghof, Hitler often spoke of 'that unique military genius, the Corsican Napoleon', and discussed Napoleon's supposed lack of threat to Britain, his error in assuming the imperial purple, his leadership qualities, and so on. Yet after his remark to the Croatian Defence Minister of July 1941, Hitler tended to stay off the subject of the glaring parallels between his own and the earlier invasion of Russia by Napoleon (and incidentally also that of Charles XII of Sweden which had ended in a similar disaster at Poltava in 1709).[113] On 19 July 1942, at the Berghof, Hitler complained that 'Just when our difficulties of the eastern winter campaign had reached their height, some imbecile pointed out that Napoleon, like ourselves, had started his Russian campaign on 22nd June. Thank God, I was able to counter that drivel with the authoritative statement of historians of repute that Napoleon's campaign did not, in fact, begin until 23rd June.'[114] Hitler's historians were correct; it was at 22.00 hours on 23 June 1812 that Napoleon's army began crossing the River Niemen.[115] Yet the unnamed imbecile's point was made, and he might also have mentioned that, unlike Hitler, the Corsican Ogre won a battle outside Moscow and captured the city – in the era before motorization too.

Hitler took over personal command of the Wehrmacht from Brauchitsch on 19 December 1941, in addition to his role as supreme commander of the armed forces. Although Brauchitsch had opposed the weakening of Army Group Centre and had been overruled by Hitler, he was made to accept responsibility for the resulting failure to seize Moscow. Yet from the moment Hitler assumed the commandership-in-chief of the Wehrmacht, all errors made could be directly blamed on him rather than on his myrmidons. 'Anyone can do the little job of directing operations in war,' he stated. 'The task of the Commander-in-Chief is to educate the Army to be National Socialist. I do not know any Army general who can do this in the way that I want it done. I have therefore decided to take over command of the Army.'[116] Eastern operations were now to be directed exclusively through OKH, the Army High Command based at Zossen outside Berlin, while the responsibilities for other theatres were devolved entirely upon OKW, Hitler's planning staff in overall control of the German armed forces. This had the (wholly foreseeable) effect of making the two organizations compete for resources for their respective theatres, rather than acting in relative tandem as hitherto. Hitler had long used this method of playing off Reich institutions and individuals against one another in peacetime – the Four Year Plan Office versus the Economics Ministry, for example, and Göring versus Himmler. This led sometimes to creative tension and useful competition, and sometimes to inefficiency and difficulties, but never to disaster. In wartime, however, the policy was far more dangerous. The very next day, 20 December, Hitler issued a 'Stand or die' order to Army Group Centre, admitting that 'Talk of Napoleon's retreat is threatening to become reality.'[117] Like Napoleon, he had managed to wound and anger the Russian bear, but not to kill it.

For ordinary German soldiers, the sheer scale of Russia was hard to comprehend. There were rivers so wide that the average German artillery piece could only just fire across them. The weather alternated from blistering heat to wind-chilled blizzards rolling off the endless steppes. The vast distance from home demoralized all but the most fanatical German stormtroopers, many of whom had to march on foot for thousands of miles. They had been victorious so far, it was true, but as one German tank commander commented as they drove further and further into that enormous country: 'If this goes on, we will win ourselves to death.'[118]

The Russians also had some technical advantages. The excellent Katyusha mortar had come into service on 15 July 1940, the same month as their standard battle tank, the T-34, which Guderian thought 'the best battle tank in any army up to 1943'. The T-34 was just about capable of taking on the Panzer Mark IV, and there were to be a much greater number of them made. Otherwise the obsolete Russian tanks were no match for the German (and captured French) tanks, even though the German Army Ordnance Office had ignored the Führer's direct order to provide the Panzer III with a 50mm cannon. Sometimes Soviet tank crews had only had a few hours' training before being flung into battle. (At the time of Barbarossa, three-quarters of Russian officers had been with their units for less than a year.)[119] The Russian cavalry horse, described as the 'shaggy little Kirkhil ponies from Siberia', could withstand temperatures of –30 Celsius. Moreover, Russian field artillery was generally superior to German. The Soviets also had a tactical doctrine that trusted to the steady application of heavy pressure by infantry and tanks working in conjunction. This is what had broken the Mannerheim Line, and what had won General Zhukov the battle of Khalkin Gol against the Japanese in 1939. The Russians had not had the opportunity to practise it against the Germans so far, having been in retreat for so long, but in December 1941 all that was about to change.

The Russians also had the inestimable advantage of Stalin's sheer ruthlessness. In the first six months after Barbarossa, the Soviet Government moved 2,593 industrial concerns eastwards in 1.5 million railway wagons and trucks, at the same time that 2.5 million troops were being moved in the opposite direction. The operation has been described as an 'economic Stalingrad' in its sheer size and importance. Industrial centres were being founded so fast that the Russians ran out of things to call them, and a town actually entitled Bezymyanny (Nameless) was built outside Kuybyshev, 500 miles east of Moscow. To shift a large part of Russia's industrial base, along with food, tools, equipment and prisoners, as well as twenty-five million Russians, so far eastwards, and then impose an eighteen-hour working day with one day's rest per month, probably required completely totalitarian power. Factory production began behind the Urals even before builders had constructed the roofs and walls of the factories. Managers were given targets, and were made to appreciate that meeting them was a life-and-death matter, for them personally as much as for the nation. Of course conditions were often unspeakable; at one factory 8,000 female workers lived in holes bored into the ground. Every industrial concern that could be turned over to war production was turned over. A factory producing champagne bottles, for example, was appropriately enough reassigned to the production of Molotov cocktails.[120] (There were two basic types of Molotov cocktail: the K-I that had a fuse and the K-S whose chemicals exploded on impact. Both could produce flames of 1,500 Celsius.)

At the heart of the Second World War lies a giant and abiding paradox: although the western war was fought in defence of civilization and democracy, and although it needed to be fought and had to be won, the chief victor was a dictator who was as psychologically warped and capable of evil as Adolf Hitler himself. Nor did the Red Terror end with the German invasion. Between June and October 1941, the NKVD arrested 26,000 people, of whom 10,000 were shot.[121] There were four million prisoners languishing in the Gulag, even in the year 1942. No fewer than 135,000 Red Army soldiers – the equivalent of twelve divisions – were shot by their own side during the war, including many who had surrendered to the Germans and been recaptured. The death penalty was imposed for panic-mongering, falling asleep on duty, cowardice, drunkenness, desertion, loss of equipment, refusing to charge through a minefield, destroying a Party membership card on capture (even though carrying one meant a death sentence from the Germans), striking an officer, 'anti-Soviet agitation', and so on and so on.

Under Stalin's 'Not One Step Back' order several generals were sentenced to death *in absentia*, and on one occasion the sentence was not carried out until 1950, when the soldier in question, General Pavel Ponedelin, foolhardily reminded Stalin of his existence by writing to him to protest his innocence. Marshal Zhukov ordered retreating Soviet troops to be machine-gunned, and even wanted to shoot the families of those who surrendered, but that was one act of brutality too far, even for the Stavka. Some 400,000 Russians served in the various punishment battalions that were set up to impose absolute obedience on the Red Army. Yet had the slightest backsliding been permitted, the Soviets could never have persuaded rational human beings to undergo the hell of the Great Patriotic War, especially for a regime that was widely (if necessarily privately) detested. 'Probably only a dictatorship as savage as Stalin's, and a people as inured to barbarism as the Russians, could have broken Hitler's power,' is Max Hastings' verdict. 'The story of how they did so has never been one for weak stomachs.' At one point in 1941 Stalin ordained that the entire ethnic German populations of the Volga, Rostov and Moscow regions of Russia, numbering over half a million people, simply be relocated to collective farms far to the east – Kazakhstan and beyond – in order to prevent them from welcoming their distant cousins to Russia. At the very same period in Britain, there were strikes over pay and conditions even in the aircraft-production factories, something that in Russia would have been inconceivable (although instantly resolvable).[122]

Although Britain could hardly have 'broken Hitler's power' on her own, if the Germans had been able to invade Britain or the United States, there is every indication that the inhabitants would have defended themselves just as bravely – even on occasion suicidally – as did the Russians. Churchill's plan was to broadcast an invocation on the radio when the Germans landed on the theme 'You Can Always Take One with You', whose peroration was to be simply: 'The hour has come; kill the Hun.'[123] The 1.75 million men of the Home Guard would then have attempted to do just that, whatever the cost.

6

Tokyo Typhoon

December 1941–May 1942

Across the sea, corpses in the water,
Across the mountain, corpses heaped upon the field,
I shall die only for the Emperor,
I shall never look back.
  'Umi Yukuba', the Japanese Army marching song[1]

At 06.45 hours on Sunday, 7 December 1941, the eagle-eyed Lieutenant William Outerbridge of the destroyer USS *Ward* spotted what he thought was the tiny conning tower of a midget submarine making its way at about 8 knots towards the mouth of Pearl Harbor, the huge naval base for the US Pacific Fleet on the island of Oahu in Hawaii. *Ward* immediately fired her 4-inch guns at the submarine, laid a pattern of depth charges and then reported the incident to shore headquarters. The news ought to have put the base on to full alert, but nothing happened. Soon afterwards, Privates Joseph Lockard and George Elliott, the operators of a mobile radar unit stationed at Kahuku Point on the northern tip of Oahu, reported to their officer at headquarters, Lieutenant Kermit Tyler, that a large number of aircraft had appeared on their screens, headed straight for Pearl Harbor. 'Don't worry about it,' replied Tyler, assuming them to be a squadron of B-17 Flying Fortress bombers due in from California later that morning.

In fact Lockard and Elliott had seen a force of forty-nine Japanese bombers, forty torpedo-bombers, fifty-one dive-bombers and forty-three fighters flying at 10,000 feet through thick cloud, led by Lieutenant-Commander Mitsuo Fuchida, a pilot who could already boast more than 3,000 hours' combat flying time. Fuchida had been personally chosen by Vice-Admiral Chuichi Nagumo, the commander of Japan's First Air Fleet, to lead this attack. As his squadron of 183 warplanes reached the northern coast of Oahu, the clouds parted, which both men were to take as an unmistakable sign of divine approval for what was about to happen.[2] With virtually no enemy aircraft in the sky to oppose them, next to no anti-aircraft fire directed against them, and a clear view of the eighty-two unprotected enemy vessels in the harbour – including eight battleships, two heavy cruisers, six light cruisers and thirty destroyers – as well as hundreds of planes parked wing-tip to wing-tip on the ground, Fuchida sent Nagumo the prearranged victory signal almost as soon as he had attacked: 'Tora! Tora! Tora!' (Tiger! Tiger! Tiger!)

Japan's journey to Pearl Harbor had been set as early as 13 April 1941 when she signed a non-aggression pact with the Soviet Union, thereby protecting both countries from a war on two fronts. Japan had been fighting a vicious war of aggression against China ever since September 1931, and the Roosevelt Administration were understandably concerned that she was attempting to dominate the Far East by force. So on 24 July 1941 America and Britain froze Japanese assets in protest at the extension southwards of the occupation of French Indo-China which Japan had begun in September 1940. Roosevelt assumed that Japan would respond rationally to such external stimuli, both positive and negative, whereas in fact her military-dominated, extreme nationalist Establishment and Government were fiercely proud and sensitive and far from logical, and ignored FDR. Days after freezing the assets, therefore, the Administration revoked US export licences for petroleum products, effectively placing an oil embargo on Japan, which at that time bought 75 per cent of her oil from the United States. Far from modifying her behaviour, this had the effect of making Japan seek alternative energy supplies, and look to the colonial empires of South-East Asia, especially the oil-rich Burma and Netherlands East Indies. America was under no legal or moral obligation to sell high-octane aviation fuel and other petroleum products to an empire that she knew would use them for imperialist oppression, any more than the embargo on those sales gave Japan the right to attack the United States. (In fact, the oil embargo was imposed without the President's knowledge, although he did nothing to revoke the decision once it had been taken.)[3]

The United States then adopted a classic carrot-and-stick approach towards Japan: the US Secretary of State, Cordell Hull, spent more than a hundred hours negotiating with Ambassador Kichisaburo Nomura at the State Department, while Roosevelt himself warned publicly on 17 August that further Japanese attempts at Asian hegemony would lead America to take active measures to safeguard her interests in the region.[4] To support these warnings, the US Pacific Fleet was transferred from California to Pearl Harbor, aid to the Chinese Kuomintang Nationalists fighting against Japan under the leadership of Generalissimo Chiang Kai-shek was increased, and thirty-five B-17 bombers were transferred to the Philippines – which had been an American protectorate since the close of the nineteenth century – from where they could bomb the Japanese home islands.

Tragically, the Roosevelt Administration – and Assistant Secretary for Economic Affairs Dean Acheson in particular – dangerously underestimated the pride of Showa Dynasty Japan, which mistook these attempted acts of deterrence as unacceptable provocations. Despite the example of over ten years' campaigning in China, Japan was not taken seriously enough by American policy-makers. It did not help that many senior politicians and soldiers genuinely believed that the slanted eyes of Japanese pilots meant they could not undertake long flights; as one historian has put it, 'American leaders, harboring all sorts of racist stereotypes about the Japanese, did not think that they were capable of such a feat' as the bombing of Pearl Harbor, which was 3,400 miles from the Japanese homeland.[5] 'Nobody now fears that a Japanese fleet could deal an unexpected blow on our Pacific possessions,' declared Josephus Daniels, a former secretary of the US Navy, in 1922. 'Radio makes surprise impossible.' Nor was this absurd overconfidence confined to Americans: in April 1941 the Chief of the British Air Staff, Sir Charles Portal, told the Foreign Secretary Anthony Eden that he rated the Japanese Air Force as 'below the Italian one'.[6]

Hopes for peace faded perceptibly on 17 October when Lieutenant-General Hideki Tojo, nicknamed Razor, came to power in Tokyo, heading a militarist government supported by the Chiefs of the Army and Naval Staffs. Within three weeks the Imperial General Headquarters had finalized plans to attack Pearl Harbor and to invade the Philippines, Malaya, the Dutch East Indies, Thailand, Burma and the Western Pacific, setting up a perimeter around what it privately called its Southern Resources Area and which was to be publicly dubbed the Greater East Asia Co-Prosperity Sphere. The second phase of operations would be to protect this area from Allied counter-attack, by making such assaults too costly. The third phase would involve attacking the Allies' long lines of communication until they were forced to accept the concept of a Japanese-dominated Far East in perpetuity.[7] There were also advocates of a strategy that involved invading and subjugating Australia, and another to assault India and link up with Germany in the Middle East. The creation of the Southern Resources Area was part of a plan to seize raw materials that was no less ambitious than Hitler's plan for *Lebensraum*, and it similarly depended upon a quick, Blitzkrieg-style victory, starting with a surprise attack that would neutralize the US Pacific Fleet. It was risky, of course, and was nearly ditched by the Naval Staff in August 1941, but in heated arguments Admiral Isoroku Yamamoto, the Commander-in-Chief of the Combined Fleet – who was against going to war – threatened to resign unless Pearl Harbor were attacked, insisting that the plan was Japan's best chance for glory. Three days after Tojo came to power in October, it was formally adopted in its entirety.

Yet the plan had severe flaws. The shallow harbour on Oahu meant that the American ships would be grounded rather than sunk, as they would have been in open water, and therefore might eventually be refloated. It was clear from the reports of spies on Oahu that Pearl Harbor did not have the tankers and supply ships necessary for a westward attack on Japan, so this was not an act of self-defence. Nor would a surprise attack allow for an eventual American acceptance of Japanese conquests elsewhere; as one of the planners, Rear-Admiral Onishi Takijiro, pointed out, American pride was such that there could never be a compromise settlement if Japan attacked without a declaration of war.[8] The precedents of the sinking of the *Maine* in 1898 and *Lusitania* in 1915 should have been enough to underline that. Fearing the loss of Japan's most prestigious field commander just before war broke out, however, the Naval Staff and Tojo Government embraced Yamamoto's demands.

The opposing naval forces in the Pacific theatre in December 1941 were so closely balanced except in one area – aircraft carriers – that if the Japanese had succeeded totally at Pearl Harbor they might indeed have bought enough time to consolidate the Southern Resources Area and make it vastly more difficult for America to bring her much larger resources to bear. The Japanese had eleven battleships and battle cruisers against the Allies' eleven; eighteen heavy (that is, 8-inch-gun) cruisers against the Allies' thirteen; twenty-three light (6-inch-gun) cruisers against twenty-one; 129 destroyers against 100; and sixty-seven submarines against sixty-nine. American naval planners had therefore balanced everything perfectly in the Pacific, with the vital exception that Japan had eleven aircraft carriers against the Americans' three.[9] (There were four other US carriers – *Ranger*, *Hornet*, *Wasp* and *Yorktown* – in the Atlantic.) If the *Lexington*, *Enterprise* and *Saratoga*, and their supporting heavy cruisers, had been in port at Pearl Harbor on the morning of 7 December 1941, the history of the Second World War might have been very different indeed. Fortunately, Admiral Husband Kimmel, the commander of the US Pacific Fleet, had sent the carriers westwards, with additional fighters on board, to support Midway and Wake Islands in the event of hostilities breaking out. It was one of the only correct decisions he had made in the whole sorry affair, but it was the crucial one.

Kimmel had every reason to suppose that war was indeed about to break out, though few reasons to suppose that Pearl Harbor would be the first target. On 24 November, Washington warned him that the 'chances of [a] favorable outcome of negotiations with Japan [are] very doubtful' and that 'a surprise aggressive movement in any direction including attack on Philippines or Guam is a possibility'. Three days later, he received an even more unequivocal cable, stating, 'This dispatch is to be considered a war warning. An aggressive move by Japan is expected within the next few days,' and ordering him to 'Execute appropriate defensive deployment.'[10] There are still those who consider Admiral Husband Kimmel and the Army commander in Hawaii, Lieutenant-General Walter C. Short, who were both dismissed soon after the attack, to have been made political scapegoats to protect the Administration, but in fact they were both culpably negligent and complacent. That said, the attack on Pearl Harbor was minutely and brilliantly planned. Vice-Admiral Chuichi Nagumo sailed east from the Kurile island of Etorofu on board his flagship *Akagi* on 26 November 1941 (or 25 November Washington dateline). His First Air Fleet consisted of six aircraft carriers, two cruisers, two battleships and a destroyer screen and eight support vessels.[11] It sailed inside a moving weather front, which served to disguise it, and maintained strict radio silence throughout the voyage. Refuelling was achieved despite heavy seas, and sailing north of the normal trade routes ensured that the large flotilla was not spotted.

Meanwhile, an intricate deception operation lulled Allied suspicions, insofar as there were any, about the Fleet's whereabouts. On 15 November, Special Ambassador Saburo Kurusu arrived in Washington to discuss American demands for a Japanese withdrawal from French Indo-China and official recognition of Chiang Kai-shek. Radio messages were sent to the 'phantom' fleet as if it was stationed in Japanese home waters in the Inland Sea between Honshu and Shikoku islands, knowing that Allied transmitters would be monitoring the frequency of signal. The luxury liner *Tatsuta Maru* set out on a twelve-day journey to San Francisco, albeit with orders to turn around and return to Yokohama at midnight on the night before the attack. Although the American Army Signal Corps had broken the Japanese Government cipher – codenamed Purple – in the 1930s, by a process codenamed Magic (the equivalent of the British Ultra), it was no help. Nagumo's fleet sent out no messages, so there was no indication of where it was. Even before Ambassadors Nomura and Kurusu requested a special audience with Hull timed for the exact moment of the attack on Pearl Harbor, the Americans knew from intercepts that they were going to break off negotiations, but since the message from Tokyo mentioned neither war nor Pearl Harbor, Washington was none the wiser.[12] The Administration's expectation was that the blow would initially fall on British and Dutch possessions in South-East Asia, and possibly the American-controlled Philippines, and nothing from the cryptologists could have prepared them for what was about to happen.

When Nagumo's fleet reached a point 275 miles north of Oahu, the detailed operation masterminded by Commander Minoru Genda, the planner on board *Akagi*, was put into action. Genda had studied the British use of aircraft carriers as offensive weapons during the raid on the Italian fleet at Taranto in 1940, and Japanese spies on Oahu had provided him with a detailed grid-referenced map of the principal American military assets on the island. Torpedoes with specially adapted fins were developed which could be dropped by bombers into shallow water, as well as newly invented armour-piercing shells dropped as bombs.[13] (Because Pearl Harbor was not deep, no torpedo nets had been placed in front of the ships for protection.) The plan provided for a first wave of aircraft to attack the ships and planes at Pearl Harbor from the west at 07.55 hours, a second wave from the east at 08.45 with the same targets, and then, as the Americans were reeling from the destruction of their fleet and air force, a third wave would destroy the massive oil installations and ship-repairing facilities on the island, effectively wiping Pearl Harbor off the map as a functioning naval base and forcing the fleet back to California for the foreseeable future.

At 06.00 (Hawaiian time) on 7 December, the first wave set off and Fuchida guided them unerringly to their target. They reached Oahu undetected because Kimmel had chosen to concentrate aerial reconnaissance on the 2,000 miles of the south-western sector, facing the Japanese Marshall Islands, rather than on the northern approaches. There were only three American patrol aircraft aloft that morning, and none covering the north. The Japanese Kate bombers and their Mitsubishi A6M2 Zero-Sen fighters (Zeros) therefore found seven American battleships moored in a row alongside Ford Island in the harbour and an eighth – the *Pennsylvania* – in dry dock. For fear of sabotage, the USAAF planes had been packed close together, which made them easier to guard. It also made it hard for the well-trained, veteran Japanese bomber pilots to miss. The anti-aircraft batteries had no ready ammunition, and the keys to the boxes were held by the duty officer. Only one-quarter of the Navy's machine guns were manned, and none of the main 5-inch batteries was. One-third of the ships' captains were ashore.[14] It was a Sunday morning, after all.

By 10.00 it was all over. Of the eight American battleships in port, three were sunk (that is, grounded), one – *Oklahoma* – capsized, and the others were more or less seriously damaged. Three light cruisers, three destroyers and other vessels were also sunk or seriously damaged, but vitally no submarine was affected.[15] Only 54 Navy and Marine planes out of 250 either survived intact or were reparable, but 166 out of the 231 USAAF planes also survived. The American death toll amounted to 2,403 servicemen and civilians killed and 1,178 wounded.[16] The Japanese lost only twenty-nine planes and a hundred lives, but all five midget submarines, only one of which made it inside the harbour, were sunk. Yet what was an undoubted disaster for America could easily have been a catastrophe. Fearing a counter-attack because the American aircraft carriers were not in harbour, Nagumo did not send in the third wave of bombers to destroy the very installations – oil depots and repair yards – that the Pacific Fleet would need to reconstitute itself. It was one thing for Pearl Harbor to be effectively neutralized for six months, but complete destruction would have been quite another. Even as their men celebrated, Nagumo, Genda (who was to command the Japanese Air Force from 1959 to 1962) and Fuchida (who was to become a Protestant pastor and in 1966 an American citizen) knew they had not achieved what they needed to. As it was, all the ships except two destroyers would be repaired and rejoin the Pacific Fleet. (The *Arizona* remains a tomb to this day.) Once Yamamoto had realized that the attack on Pearl Harbor had fallen far short of his original plans he dolefully wrote in a letter: 'A military man can scarcely pride himself on having "smitten a sleeping enemy"; it is more a matter of shame, simply, for the one smitten. I would rather you made your appraisal after seeing what the enemy does, since it is certain that, angered and outraged, he will soon launch a determined counterattack . . .'[17]

The very completeness of the surprise attack has spawned many conspiracy theories and accusations of cover-ups regarding Pearl Harbor, which allege that the Roosevelt Administration (and some-times also the Churchill Government) had prior warning of the attack but deliberately failed to warn Kimmel and Short in order to bring the United States into the war. This is nonsense: Roosevelt was keen to provoke Germany into conflict, it is true, but he did not want a war on two fronts, and indeed he would have liked to transfer part of the Pacific Fleet to the Atlantic.[18] Moreover, FDR loved the US Navy, had been its under-secretary during the Great War, and any such conspiracy would have needed the co-operation of, at the very least, the War Secretary Henry L. Stimson, Navy Secretary Frank Knox, Army Chief of Staff George C. Marshall and Navy Chief of Staff Admiral Harold Stark, all of them honourable and patriotic men. 'Nor was anything to be gained by allowing the great ships to be destroyed at their moorings if they could have been alerted and at sea,' states Roosevelt's biographer, Conrad Black. 'An ineffective Japanese attack would have been just as good a *casus belli.*'[19] Kimmel's culpability was all the worse because Churchill had sent Roosevelt the official summary of how the Taranto raid had been carried out; Roosevelt sent it to Stark, who sent it on to Kimmel, who ignored it.

Pearl Harbor certainly was the perfect *casus belli*, however. Recruitment offices had to stay open throughout the night as Americans volunteered for service; trade union leaders cancelled strikes, and on Monday, 8 December Congress voted 470 to 1 (the pacifist Jeannette Rankin of Montana) for war. This was the opportunity for Roosevelt to rally the nation with the words: 'Yesterday, December 7, 1941 – a date that will live in infamy – the United States of America was suddenly and deliberately attacked by naval and air forces of the Empire of Japan.' As well as the fact that 'very many American lives have been lost,' he reported attacks on Malaya, Hong Kong, Guam, the Philippines and Wake and Midway Islands. 'No matter how long it may take us to overcome this premeditated invasion, the American people, in their righteous might, will win through to absolute victory.'[20] The speech to Congress was only twenty-five sentences long, but so often was he interrupted by applause that it took him ten minutes to deliver.

Three days later, in a speech to the Reichstag on the afternoon of 11 December 1941, Hitler declared war on the United States, even though Germany was not obliged to come to Japan's aid under the terms of the Tripartite Pact of 27 September 1940 if Japan were the aggressor. It seems an unimaginably stupid thing to have done in retrospect, a suicidally hubristic act less than six months after attacking the Soviet Union. America was an uninvadable land mass of gigantic productive capacity and her intervention in 1917–18 had sealed Germany's fate in the Great War. 'The Navy and I had no idea that an attack by Japan on Pearl Harbor was planned,' Admiral Raeder stated at Nuremberg; 'we learned of this only after the attack had been carried out.'[21] This was true, and hardly the way allies should treat each other, giving Hitler the perfect let-out if he had wanted one, but he did not. Instead he exulted in Japan's ruthlessness, taking it almost as a compliment to himself on the basis of imitation being the sincerest form of flattery.

By 1943 the number of aircraft lost at Pearl Harbor represented only two days of American production, and in the calendar year 1944, while the Germans were building 40,000 warplanes, the United States turned out 98,000, underlining Hitler's catastrophic blunder.[22] In his 8 December 1941 speech to Congress, Roosevelt had not mentioned Germany or Italy because he did not have the political support necessary for including Japan's allies in the request for a declaration of war, especially when faced with the powerful America First movement and other isolationist organizations in the United States. Now, the Führer had solved Roosevelt's problem at a stroke. Hitler believed he was simply normalizing a state of affairs that had already been in *de facto* existence for many months, and in such a way that gave German U-boats the right to torpedo American warships that had been attacking them for over a year. Direct American support for Britain and the USSR could now be countered actively, even while the United States had her hands full in the Pacific. Hitler had long considered war with America to be inevitable: he thought it better to have the prestige of instigating it and to help the Japanese by forcing on America a war on two fronts.[23] Coming within a week of the checking of his offensive against Moscow, when Russians started taking German prisoners for the first time, it is now easy to see precisely when the seeds of Germany's defeat were sown.

Frederick Oechsner, the Berlin correspondent of United Press International, noted in the late 1930s that, when he was war minister, Blomberg had 'presented Hitler with 400 books, pamphlets and monographs on the United States armed forces and he has read many of these'.[24] It was the very worst time to have mugged up on the American war machine, as it scarcely existed then, with the United States still in the grip of isolationism. If Hitler divined from these monographs a sense of America's military weakness – the US Army numbered only 100,000 men in 1939 – he was soon to be sorely disabused: by 1945 General George C. Marshall and Admiral Ernest J. King had managed to put 14.9 million Americans into uniform and the Army Hitler had so despised from his reading of soon-to-be-out-of-date pamphlets would in 1952 – while it was still occupying Germany – blow up his beloved Berghof.[25] 'The entry of the United States into the war is of no consequence at all for Germany,' Hitler had told Molotov in Berlin on 12 November 1940, 'the United States will not be a threat to us in decades – not in 1945 but at the earliest in 1970 or 1980.' It was one of the greatest miscalculations of history.

Hitler also won nothing substantial from the Japanese for his declaration of war on America. The Axis consistently failed to act as close allies during the Second World War, with dire consequences for them all. Had Japan attacked the USSR in the east simultaneously with Barbarossa, it could have forced Stalin into a potentially disastrous two-front war, and taken the rich mineral and oil reserves of Siberia. Similarly, if Japan's attacks on eastern India and Ceylon had been co-ordinated with a German advance through Egypt, Iran and Iraq – prior to Operation Barbarossa – the British Empire could have been severely threatened in northern India. Hitler 'kept the foreign office out of the military', the Reich's Foreign Minister Joachim von Ribbentrop told his Nuremberg psychiatrist, when complaining that he had not had more than a day's warning of the invasion of Norway. 'The same with the Russian war. I never knew about it until 24 hours before it happened.'[26] Their utter inability to trust each other and co-ordinate their efforts left the Axis fighting two entirely separate wars, while the Allies fought on two flanks of the same war.

Hitler's great error – perhaps the second worst of his many blunders of the war next to invading Russia prematurely – was not to appreciate the potential capacity of American industrial production. This is all the more surprising given the chapters on American capitalism that he had written in his then unpublished sequel to *Mein Kampf* known as 'The Second Book'. 'The size of the internal American market and its wealth of buying power and also raw materials', he wrote in 1928, 'guarantee the American automobile industry internal sales figures that alone permit production methods that would simply be impossible in Europe. The result of that is the enormous export capacity of the American automobile industry. At issue is the general motorization of the world – a matter of immeasurable significance.'[27] Plenty more along those lines made it plain that Hitler had at least understood the power of American production in 1928, and although the Great Depression had thrown this off course, by 1941 it was far stronger than ever before.

Certainly Hitler's senior advisers were well aware of the economic dangers posed by the military productive capacity of the United States even before the Führer had declared war. Ernst Udet, the head of the Luftwaffe procurement organization at the Air Ministry, shot himself on 17 November 1941 after his warnings about the Anglo-American air programme had been consistently ignored; General Friedrich Fromm, head of the central administrative office of the Wehrmacht, was talking about the need to make peace in November 1941; General Georg Thomas of the supply side of OKW was deeply defeatist by January 1942; Fritz Todt, the Reich Armaments Minister, told Hitler as early as November 1941 that the war in Russia could not be won; Admiral Wilhelm Canaris, head of the Abwehr, was equally pessimistic, though more diplomatic; the great steel producer Walter 'Panzer' Rohland believed, as he told Todt, that 'the war against Russia cannot be won!'; the Economics Minister Walther Funk spoke at Göring's birthday party of the 'misfortune that had broken over the nation'. In the view of the historian of the Nazi economy, 'the vast majority' of the Nazi leaders understood 'the pivotal importance of the United States economy'.[28] Yet they did not apprise Hitler of their feelings, or at least not strongly enough to force him to see sense, except Todt, who (probably coincidentally) died in a plane crash less than two months later, and Udet, who at least emphasized his point in an unmistakable manner. The claims of many at Nuremberg to have tried to dissuade Hitler from declaring war on the United States are highly suspect, not least because he seems to have taken few soundings before making the announcement.

The Reich Foreign Minister Ribbentrop claimed in his memoirs that 'war was declared on the USA despite my advice to the contrary', but the evidence in fact points the other way. When the Italian Foreign Minister, Mussolini's son-in-law Count Galeazzo Ciano, rang him up in the middle of the night to tell him about Pearl Harbor, Ribbentrop was 'joyful . . . He was so happy, in fact, that I congratulated him,' even though Ciano wasn't sure quite what for. At his trial, Ribbentrop claimed that Pearl Harbor had come as an unpleasant shock, because 'We never considered a Japanese attack on the United States to be to our advantage.'[29] He had been regularly deriding the power of America, telling Japan's Foreign Minister Yosuke Matsuoka that American munitions were 'junk', Ciano that Roosevelt's foreign policy was 'the biggest bluff in world history', Japan's Ambassador Hiroshi Oshima that Germany was 'more than prepared to deal with any American intervention' and Admiral Darlan that the United States would be deluding herself if she thought she 'would be able to wage war in Europe'.[30] Fancying himself an expert on America because he had lived there for four years in his youth, Ribbentrop assured a delegation of Italians in 1942, 'I know them; I know their country. A country devoid of culture, devoid of music – above all, a country without soldiers, a people who will never be able to decide the war from the air. When has a Jewified nation like that ever become a race of fighters and flying aces?'[31] Ribbentrop had assured Hitler that Britain would not go to war in 1939 – indeed his entire career was built around telling Hitler what he wanted to hear; it is likely that his advice was to declare war on the United States.[32] Not that it mattered much: Hitler would not have followed Ribbentrop's – or anyone's – advice over an issue as important as that.

The speed with which Roosevelt put the United States economy on a war footing rivalled that with which he had installed his New Deal programme after his inauguration in 1933. Authoritarian planning of the mighty American economy was policed by a sea of regulatory authorities known by their acronyms, which managed almost every area of what effectively became a state-capitalist system. If Germans and Japanese doubted the American commitment to defeat them come what may, they needed only to look at the measures adopted by the previously free-market United States. Taxation was used to hold maximum after-tax salaries to $25,000; a freeze was introduced on commercial, farm and commodity prices, which under the Emergency Price Control Act would be fixed by the Office of Price Administration; wages and rents were similarly controlled; widespread rationing was imposed; consumer credit was mercilessly squeezed; war profiteering was aggressively combated; synthetic-rubber production was so increased that by 1945 the United States was making more of it than the entire global pre-1939 production of natural rubber.[33]

In January 1942, Roosevelt presented a $59 billion budget to Congress, $52 billion of which was devoted to military expenditure, in the same month that the sale of new cars and passenger trucks was banned by the Office of Production Management (which is why there is no such thing as a 1942-model American motor car). The Office of Economic Stabilization, chaired by James F. Byrnes, had immense powers which it had no hesitation in using. A flat 5 per cent 'Victory' tax was imposed on all incomes over $12 per week, exemptions were slashed and the number of Americans required to fill in tax returns rose six-fold in one year, from seven million in 1941 to forty-two million in 1942, something that would have been politically impossible to impose under any other circumstances.[34] Roosevelt sent the American economy into battle, with results that the German and Japanese production figures could not hope to match. By the end of the war, the USA had provided for her allies 37,000 tanks, 800,000 trucks, two million rifles. With 43,000 planes going abroad to allies, US pilot training had to be curtailed because of aircraft shortages.[35]

This is not to argue that American armaments were necessarily superior to German and Japanese. The American military historian Victor Davis Hanson has argued eloquently that this was not the case:

Our Wildcat front-line fighters were inferior to the Japanese Zero; obsolete Brewster F2A Buffalos were rightly known as 'flying coffins'. The Douglas TBD Devastator bomber was a death-trap, its pilots essentially wiped out at the Battle of Midway trying to drop often unreliable torpedoes. American-designed Lee, Grant, and Stuart tanks – and even the much-heralded Shermans ('Ronson Lighters') – were intrinsically inferior to most contemporary German models, which had a far better armor and armament. With the exception of the superb M-1 rifle, it is hard to rank any American weapons system as comparable to those used by the Wehrmacht, at least until 1944–45. We never developed guns quite comparable to the fast-firing, lethal German .88 artillery platform. Our anti-tank weapons of all calibers remained substandard. Most of our machine guns and mortars were reliable – but of World War I vintage.[36]

Yet the sheer quantity of weaponry being produced by America out-stripped anything the Axis could match.

Although it was Japan's attack on Pearl Harbor that brought an Anglo-American military alliance into being for the first time since 1918, with Churchill making good his promise at the Lord Mayor's luncheon on 10 November to declare war on Japan 'within the hour' of a Japanese attack, Hitler's declaration of war meant that the Western alliance would have teeth. A great deal had already been agreed in secret Staff conversations in Washington about the eventuality of war, and the scene was now set for closer and more direct conversations between Roosevelt and Churchill in that city before the year was out. There was nothing inevitable about the wartime alliance between America and Britain; the Axis brought it into being. There had been much rivalry between Britain and the United States in the 1920s and 1930s, exacerbated by ignorant stereotyping on both sides. According to the wartime journals of the aviator Charles A. Lindbergh, a Captain Smith asked the former US military attaché to London, Lieutenant-Colonel Howard C. Davidson, how the English really felt about the Americans. 'Well, I'll tell you,' Davidson replied. 'The English feel about us just the way we feel about a prosperous nigger.'[37]

Yet the Anglo-American alliance after 1941 was to be by far the closest of any of the collaborations between the major powers in the war, at sea where they immediately divided up the world's oceans into patrolling districts, in the air when the USAAF and RAF took it in turns to bomb Germany by day and night respectively, and on the ground where joint operations were undertaken in North Africa by November 1942, and subsequently in Italy, Normandy and finally Germany itself, all under supreme commanders who controlled the forces of both powers. Smarter diplomacy by Hitler might have pre-vented the creation of an alliance that was to fling his armies out of Africa, the Mediterranean and France over the coming three years.

In his memoirs published in 1950, Churchill was forthright about his emotions when he heard about the attack on Pearl Harbor. 'No American will think it wrong of me', he wrote in *The Grand Alliance*,

if I proclaim that to have the United States at our side was to me the greatest joy. I could not foretell the course of events. I do not pretend to have measured accurately the martial might of Japan, but now at this very moment I knew the United States was in the war, up to the neck and in to the death. So we had won after all! . . . Hitler's fate was sealed. Mussolini's fate was sealed. As for the Japanese, they would be ground to powder.[38]

*

Meanwhile, the Roosevelt Administration began to intern virtually the entire Japanese-American community of the United States, a panic measure for which subsequent Administrations have apologized and paid compensation. Nonetheless, this tough act needs to be seen in its proper historical context. Although 69 per cent of the 100,500 Japanese who were interned under Roosevelt's Executive Order 9066 were US citizens, that still leaves 31 per cent, or 30,500 people, who were not. With the level of danger posed by Imperial Japan in the spring of 1942, when their forces were spreading over vast areas of the Pacific and Far East, no country at that time would have allowed so many non-citizens of the same ethnic background as the prospective invader to reside in the precise areas – Hawaii and California – where the next blows were (rightly or wrongly) expected to fall. The British Government had taken similar measures against the German and Italian minorities, with similar speed and disregard of rights. The simple fact that Japanese-born citizens of Oahu had provided Tokyo, via the Japanese Consulate in Honolulu, with detailed information about the US Pacific Fleet, something that was known to American and British intelligence, was enough to put the loyalty of many thousands of innocent people under a cloud. When released from their barbed-wire desert camps, they were sent off with $25 each, the sum given to prisoners at the end of their sentences. It was not the Roosevelt Administration's finest hour.

Although in the long term Japan had committed a terrible blunder in provoking the 'righteous might' of the American people, in the short term her forces were able to sweep through Asia, capturing one-sixth of the surface of the planet in only six months and dealing the two-centuries-old British Empire what was effectively a lingering death blow. An analogy with Barbarossa is apt, because a massive surprise attack yielded huge ground initially, before other factors – in Russia the weather, size of population and spirit of the ordinary Red

Army soldier; in the Far East superior Allied technology and military production – could operate to reverse the early successes. Whereas Stalin had been remiss in not reading his fellow dictator's mind properly before Barbarossa, the Roosevelt Administration dangerously miscalculated Japanese psychology, intentions and capabilities.

In order to defend their lines of communication, the Japanese formulated a two-phase strategy for their conquest of South-East Asia. Hong Kong, Guam and Wake Island were to be captured immediately while troops were landing on the American Philippines and in British Malaya. Then, once the capacity of the Philippines and Malaya to interdict further operations had been neutralized, the Dutch East Indies and Burma would be occupied. Between 7 December 1941 and April 1942, the six aircraft carriers of the First Air Fleet that attacked Pearl Harbor went on to attack Rabaul, Darwin, Colombo and Trincomalee, covering one-third of the circumference of the globe and without losing a single ship.[39]

Simultaneously with the attack on Pearl Harbor, but dated 8 December because it was west of the international dateline, the Japanese attacked Wake Island, an atoll without natural food or water. Their initial assault was flung back heroically by the American defenders but a second, larger one on 11 December could not be and the island was overwhelmed by 23 December, by which time the Gilbert Islands and Guam had also fallen. Hours after Pearl Harbor, the British Crown colony of Hong Kong was invaded by the Japanese 38th Division. Forced back to Hong Kong Island on 17 December, the 15,000 Australian, Indian, Canadian and British defenders held out until Christmas Day.

Japanese forces violated Thailand's neutrality and occupied Bangkok on 8 December, prior to using that country as a springboard to assaulting Burma in phase two. The Japanese Twenty-fifth Army, comprising three divisions and a tank group under Lieutenant-General Tomoyuki Yamashita, also landed at the northern tip of Malaya and the Kra Isthmus of southern Thailand on 8 December. Yamashita's target was nothing less than the island fortress of Singapore, known as the Gibraltar of the East. Almost twice the size of the Isle of Wight, Singapore was a Royal Navy dockyard, barracks and communications centre, and, because more than £60 million had been spent on fortifying it in the 1920s, it 'seemed to double-lock the gateway of the British Empire so that it was useless for an unfriendly rival power, such as Japan, to dream of forcing an entrance'.[40] This was certainly true of the seaward approaches, which were guarded by huge naval guns set in deep bunkers, but what was needed were enough high-quality jungle warfare-trained forces to guard the landward side, from where it soon became clear that the Japanese attack was going to come. It was not only the French who had adopted a Maginot Line mentality.

Conventional British military thinking held that Singapore was safe from a northern attack because the 500 miles of dense jungle and rubber plantations of central Malaya were impassable by tanks. 'Well,' the British Governor of Singapore is alleged to have told the British commander in Malaya, Lieutenant-General Arthur Percival, 'I suppose you'll see the little men off.'[41] Percival also had more artillery and shells and many more troops than Yamashita, and on 2 December Admiral Sir Tom Phillips' Force Z, the battleship HMS *Prince of Wales* and battle cruiser HMS *Repulse*, with destroyer escorts, had arrived in Singapore harbour. Although aircraft had sunk ships in Norway and Crete, this had not yet happened to a battleship (the *Prince of Wales* had no fewer than forty automatic anti-aircraft weapons).[42] The RAF in Singapore, it was true, had only 180 aircraft, some of them outdated, but on paper Percival ought to have been able to withstand the coming onslaught, at least for a considerable length of time. But almost everything that could go wrong went wrong. 'Defeat', as one historian of the campaign has put it, 'was a team effort.'[43] The Japanese seized the initiative from the moment they landed amphibiously at Kota Bharu near the north-west tip of Malaya on 8 December 1941 and marched south, and Percival was never able to wrest it back from them. The invaders flung themselves into jungle warfare with gusto, and also proved enthusiastic and adept at hand-to-hand fighting. There was no particular reason why the Japanese should have excelled at jungle warfare in the early days; the fighting in China had not taken place in jungles, nor are there any in Japan. Yet they were trained for fighting there in a way the Commonwealth troops were not. 'The jungle betrayed the British,' recorded an historian; 'the jungle had been their possession for eighty years, whose possibilities for war they had never learned.'[44] Because the jungle impeded lateral movement and visibility along a defended front, it made it easy for front-line units to be cut off, and thus favoured the offensive over the defensive. All too often the Commonwealth units found themselves outmanoeuvred and surrounded, almost before they knew it. It turned out that tanks – of which Percival had almost none – could indeed move through the jungle and rubber plantations, and the British found themselves woefully short of anti-tank weaponry.[45] Only six weeks after landing, the Japanese had got to within sight of Singapore island.

Vast numbers of Japanese planes operating at first from southern Indo-China but subsequently from captured airfields in northern Malaya won the all-important air superiority. British intelligence reports proved inaccurate, and the two Indian divisions, one Australian division and smaller British units were ineffectually led. 'Defence arrangements were fully in British hands, but affected by a series of contradictions and complications which, but for their tragic implications, could have been considered too far-fetched for a Gilbert and Sullivan operetta.'[46] In a detailed War Office examination of what went wrong, compiled later that same year, and in subsequent historical estimations, Singapore fell because the Commonwealth leaders had underestimated the enemy, displayed lacklustre leadership, trained their troops badly, split divisions in battle, used reinforcements in a piecemeal manner, had a divided command structure, shown poor strategic grasp, had heavy commitments in the Mediterranean and Atlantic, and had insufficient air cover. It was this last that caused the greatest maritime disaster of the war for the Royal Navy, when both the 35,000-ton HMS *Prince of Wales* and the 26,500-ton HMS *Repulse* were sunk on Wednesday, 10 December 1941, with the loss of 840 lives.

Sailing southwards along the Malayan coast in the South China Sea without air cover, or even aerial reconnaissance, Z Force came under attack from eighty-eight Japanese planes from southern Indo-China. Less than two hours later the only two effective Allied battleships left in the Pacific were at the bottom. 'The *Prince of Wales* is barely distinguishable in smoke and flame,' recalled a survivor, 'I can see one plane release a torpedo . . . It explodes against her bows. A couple of

seconds later another explodes amidships and astern.'[47] In his memoirs
Churchill described his feelings when the First Sea Lord, Admiral Sir
Dudley Pound, reported the news to him over the telephone:

In all the war I never received a more direct shock. The reader of these pages
will realize how many efforts, hopes, and plans foundered with these two
ships. As I turned over and twisted in bed the full horror of the news sank in
upon me. There were no British or American capital ships in the Indian Ocean
or the Pacific except the survivors of Pearl Harbor, who were hastening back
to California. Over all this vast expanse of waters Japan was supreme, and
we everywhere were weak and naked.[48]

The collapse of morale among the defenders ashore was also shattering. Through January, the Commonwealth forces retreated steadily,
with the Johore Line 25 miles from Singapore breached on the 15th.
The Straits of Johore were only a mile wide, and the north coast of
Singapore island was poorly defended. On 31 January, the remaining
Commonwealth troops on the mainland, outfought and exhausted,
crossed over to the island and destroyed as much of the causeway link
as they could. It was another sign of poor British planning that no
preparations had been made for a siege of the island itself.

Without a pause, the Japanese assaulted the north of the island in
armour-plated barges on the night of 8 February – a further indication
of their excellent Staff work – rebuilt the causeway and sent tanks
across it. Counter-attacks were broken up by Japanese dive-bombing.
Accusations have been made that troops of the Australian 8th Division
deserted in significant numbers, drank and looted before returning to
try to find boats in the harbour on which to escape. 'There were
individual examples of cowardice,' concludes an authoritative study,
'but for the most part this is slander.'[49] It was a slander repeated by a
large number of British officers, despite the fact that the Japanese lost
half their battle dead in the campaign on Singapore island in the final
week, when the Australians provided most of the resistance. The
official war diary of the 8th Australian Division Provost Company
does use the word 'panic' to describe the confusion of 9 February and
'stragglers' two days later, 'sullen' on the 12th, troops 'very reluctant
to return to the line' on the 13th, 'All imaginable excuses being made
to avoid returning to the line' on the 14th, and on the 15th 'Morale

shocking. A lot of men hid themselves to prevent and avoid return to the line,' although this was also true of British and Indian soldiers.[50] 'In some units the troops have not shown the fighting spirit which is to be expected of men of the British Empire,' read Percival's covering note to senior officers attached to the Order of the Day for 11 February. 'It will be a lasting disgrace if we are defeated by an army of clever gangsters many times inferior in numbers to our own.'[51] The Japanese were not gangsters for using little conventional transport, attacking without large-scale artillery support, and pushing as far and fast ahead as possible, but they were clever. They had learnt the central lesson of the war so far, that Blitzkrieg and boldness worked. Churchill meanwhile on 10 February cabled Wavell, who had been appointed commander-in-chief of all Allied forces in the region, to say that since the Singapore garrison outnumbered the Japanese:

in a well-contested battle they should destroy them. There must at this stage be no thought of saving the troops or sparing the population. The battle must be fought to the bitter end at all costs. The 18th Division has a chance to make its name in history. Commanders and senior officers should die with their troops. The honour of the British Empire and of the British Army is at stake. I rely on you to show no mercy to weakness in any form. With the Russians fighting as they are and the Americans so stubborn at Luzon [in the Philippines], the whole reputation of our country and our race is involved. It is expected that every unit will be brought into close contact with the enemy and fight it out.[52]

Racial honour was one thing, the facts on the ground in Singapore quite another, but it is clear that Hitler was not the only leader of a great power to issue 'Stand or die' orders during the Second World War, although this was easily the harshest Churchill ever gave.

Tragically, large numbers of reinforcements continued to be landed in Singapore harbour, almost up to the surrender. They went straight into captivity, instead of being deployed where they were desperately needed to defend India, Burma and Australia. Most of their stores and equipment was also captured before it could be destroyed.[53] The 130,000 men who surrendered on 15 February included many local recruits, and refugees from the north who had lost the will to fight.

The Malays meanwhile swiftly made their peace with the Japanese, who promised them independence and freedom within the Greater East Asia Co-Prosperity Sphere. Yet it was not long before the Japanese military police, the notorious Kempeitai, began executing on the beaches Malay Chinese they considered untrustworthy. A sign of how disillusioned the Indians were with the British can be seen in the fact that, of the 55,000 Indians taken prisoner by the Japanese in Singapore, 40,000 volunteered to fight for the India National Army, the pro-Japanese force commanded by Subhas Chandra Bose.[54]

'This retreat seems fantastic,' wrote the commander of the Australian troops, General Gordon Bennett, on his way back to Singapore. 'Fancy 550 miles in 55 days – chased by a Jap army on stolen bikes, without artillery. It was a war of patrols. All that happened was that they patrolled outside our resistance [capabilities] and sat on a road behind us. Thinking we were cut off, we retreated . . . Never felt so sad and upset. Words fail me.'[55] The Japanese suffered only 9,824 casualties during the whole campaign. A photograph was beamed around the world of Percival and other senior British officers in their shorts and long socks, flat tin hats and rolled-up sleeves walking beside two Japanese officers to surrender to Yamashita, one Briton with a flagpole over his shoulder from which hung a white flag, another with a limp Union Jack. Indeed everything about the defence had been limp. Percival had been bluffed by Yamashita, who had outrun his supplies and might have buckled before a determined counter-attack from forces twice his size, but such was the demoralization that that was never going to happen. (Had they known the fate that awaited them, however, they would doubtless have tried.) It was not solely the British who had underperformed. 'Bennett and [Brigadier D. S.] Maxwell were unequivocal failures,' records an Australian historian. 'Although Australia and other Dominions were critical of British generalship in the world wars, they themselves had no mechanism for producing an obviously better type of senior commander.'[56]

Percival had lost only 7,500 casualties in the campaign, but when he surrendered to the much smaller force led by Yamashita he also lost the respect of the Japanese, who thought his soldiers cowards for having given up so easily. They would probably have been just as viciously ill-treated if they had held out for longer, but the lives of one million civilians were in jeopardy on the island, especially with water supplies in a critical state after the Japanese captured the reservoirs. A campaign that the Japanese General Staff had started planning for only in January 1941 had laid low an island fortress that had for decades and at immense cost been readied to withstand attack and siege. The German Staff had estimated that the capture of Singapore would take five and a half divisions and eighteen months; Yamashita had achieved it with two divisions in less than two months. In London on 10 February, accepting the likelihood of defeat in Singapore, Churchill had told the War Cabinet that Britain was 'In for a rough time – Smashing blows – [but we shall] not come out bust – No gloom or disheartenment . . . Screw down rations – Eat into reserves of food – Army at home [must] brace themselves.'[57] Yet Singapore was not about to become another Leningrad.

From being a bandy-kneed, myopic, oriental midget in Western eyes, the Japanese soldier was suddenly transformed into an invincible, courageous superman. Of course neither racial stereotype was accurate, but events in the Philippines, Malaya and elsewhere did nothing to damage the new myth, even though General Douglas MacArthur's 130,000-strong force in the Philippines fought much better and for much longer than Percival's had. The colonial powers – American, British, Dutch, Portuguese and Australian – were woefully underequipped to fight a modern war against a nearby major industrial power like Japan, which had already had ten years' combat experience. Run for years on prestige, minimal military commitment, small budgets and an element of bluster, the colonial territories of South-East Asia also suffered from poor infrastructure, long lines of communication with the metropolitan centres, plenty of invadable beaches, and nationalist local independence movements. A powerfully aggressive militarist nation of seventy-three million, with bases in Formosa (present-day Taiwan) and Indo-China, was eager to wrest power from them. Nonetheless, the various sections of the new Japanese Empire had very little in common with one another, as was displayed with sublime irony in November 1943 when General Tojo presided over a conference in Tokyo of the prime ministers of all the puppet governments in the Greater East Asia Co-Prosperity Sphere. The leaders took it in turns to praise the freedom that Japan had promised their countries from the evil Western imperialists, but as there was only one language common to all of them, the proceedings had to be conducted in English.[58]

Douglas MacArthur, a charismatic leader and former US Chief of Staff, had only ninety fighter aircraft, thirty-five Flying Fortress B-17 bombers and a hundred tanks to protect the Philippines on 8 December, and his army, though large on paper, was primarily made up of under-trained and under-equipped Filipinos, some of whom disappeared back to their *barrios* (villages) as soon as the Japanese invaded.[59] In trying to pursue his original policy of meeting the invasion on the beaches of northern Luzon and the Lingayen Gulf, MacArthur was stymied by the successful bombing of the Clark Field air base north of Manila. Even though news of Pearl Harbor had been received at Clark at 02.30 hours on 8 December, and other bases in the Philippines had been attacked, and the head of the USAAF General H. H. 'Hap' Arnold had telephoned a warning to Major-General Lewis H. Brereton, the commander of US Far East Air Forces, American planes were still stationed unprotected on the ground at 12.15 when 108 twin-engined Japanese bombers and 34 fighters arrived from Formosa. American pilots were queuing for lunch in the mess when they struck. No fewer than eighteen of the B-17s were destroyed, as were fifty-six fighters and other aircraft, at a total cost of seven Japanese planes.[60] Inter-service confusion at headquarters was blamed for the disaster, but, whatever caused it, by the eighth day of the campaign MacArthur had only fifty planes left and had therefore lost air superiority, a recurring feature in explaining defeats in the Second World War. The 22,400 US regular troops and many Filipino regulars, however, put up a sturdy resistance, especially once MacArthur had accepted on 23 December that he could not hold Manila, retreating into the jungles, mountains and swamps of the Bataan peninsula and eventually on to the island of Corregidor, fortified in the seventeenth century, which dominated the entrance to Manila Bay. There he faced a Japanese force of around 200,000.

Lacking enough air cover, Admiral Thomas C. Hart therefore withdrew the US Asiatic Fleet to the Java Sea, where it joined powerful units of other allies. The original American plan had been for

MacArthur to try to hold out on the Philippines for long enough to be relieved by the US Pacific Fleet. With the battleship part of that force now crippled at Pearl Harbor, the plan was moribund, but no alternative commended itself. Using captured air bases, the Japanese reinforced the initial invasion forces that had landed on 10 and 22 December. Soon outnumbered four to one and now completely blockaded in Bataan and Corregidor by the Japanese Navy, Mac-Arthur was personally ordered by President Roosevelt to leave the Philippines, which he managed to do by a hair's breadth – at one point his motor torpedo boat came 'in the shadow of a Japanese battleship' – on 11 March.[61] 'I have come through,' he said on reaching Australia, 'and I shall return.'

Bataan surrendered on 9 April, whereupon the Japanese victors took 78,000 starving members of the US and Filipino forces on the notorious 65-mile 'Bataan Death March' to prison. Somehow the 2,000 who had made it to Corregidor managed to hold out for a further twenty-seven days, even though only its headquarters and hospital, located in caves, survived the fifty-three air raids directed against it. 'The last regular US Army cavalry regiment would slaughter its mounts to feed the starving garrison, ending the cavalry era not with a bang but with a dinner bell.'[62] With malaria rife, and only three days' supply of water left, the garrison finally surrendered on 6 May. The defence of the Philippines had been an American epic – costing 2,000 US servicemen killed and wounded and 11,500 captured, against 4,000 Japanese casualties. Japanese brutality against the Filipinos, who unlike some other peoples had shown loyalty to their colonial masters, was horrific. 'The use of military and civilian prisoners for bayonet practice and assorted other cruelties', an historian wrote, 'provided the people of Southeast Asia with a dramatic lesson on the new meaning of *Bushido*, the code of the Japanese warrior.'[63]

With Malaya and the Philippines now closed down as bases for Allied counter-attack, the Japanese could embark on the second phase of their strategy. Sumatra and oil-rich Borneo were captured by mid-February, and Timor fell by the end of the month. Java was protected by a large Allied flotilla under the overall command of the Dutch Admiral Karel Doorman in his flagship RNNS *De Ruyter*. His force of five cruisers and ten destroyers had not worked in tandem and had no tactical doctrine or common communications system, but it nonetheless attacked Rear-Admiral Takeo Takagi's faster, larger, more modern force of four cruisers and thirteen destroyers.[64] In the seven-hour battle of the Java Sea on the afternoon and evening of 27 February – the largest surface naval battle since Jutland in 1916 – and then in subsequent running fights over the next two days, the Allies were comprehensively defeated, with all their cruisers sunk and the enemy landings postponed by only one day. It was to be the last significant Japanese naval victory of the Second World War, but since no one knew that at the time the Dutch, British, Americans and Australians on Java surrendered on 8 March, the same day that the Japanese landed on the north-east coast of New Guinea, and Rangoon in Burma fell. Two days earlier Batavia, the capital of the Dutch East Indies (present-day Indonesia) fell without much resistance and nearly 100,000 Dutch were marched off into a vicious captivity.[65] Further easy Japanese victories in the Admiralty Islands and Northern Solomons and the capture of the superb Rabaul naval base in the Bismarck Archipelago on 23 January 1942 gave Japan the chance to consolidate her Southern Defence Perimeter and possibly to threaten Australia herself.

The strategic imperative that led to serious disagreements between London and Canberra can be summed up in the pre-war phrase of the Australian Prime Minister Sir Robert Menzies, who pointed out that 'What Great Britain calls the Far East is to us the near north.' Although not a single Australian politician spoke against the declaration of war on Germany in September 1939, an increasing number came to resent what looked like Britain's prioritizing of herself over Australia. New Zealand, which was not attacked by Japan as Australia was, nonetheless had a proportionately higher level of enlistment than any other Allied country except Russia and Britain.

The Japanese, who had been fighting against China since 1937, had been planning the invasion of Burma for four years, and it was forced through with the same speed and resolve as elsewhere. As a springboard for the possible invasion of India, a means of keeping long-range enemy aircraft away from Malaya and especially of closing off the Allies' Burma Road land route to China, thereby finally breaking the

Chinese generalissimo Chiang Kai-shek's land communications with the outside world, the conquest of Burma was a vital military objective for the Staff planners in Tokyo. Part of the British Empire since Winston Churchill's father Lord Randolph had annexed it when he was secretary for India in 1886, Burma was also rich in oil and minerals, and would be an important staging post for the Allies in any attempted counter-attack.

A two-division detachment of Lieutenant-General Shojiro Iida's Fifteenth Army landed in Burma in the very south, Victoria Point, on 11 December 1941, and advanced northwards. It was not until after their Malayan and Philippines victories that the Japanese poured two more divisions, as well as tank, anti-aircraft, artillery and air units into Burma, overcoming Lieutenant-General Thomas Hutton's 17th (Black Cat) Indian Division, some British units and the local Burma Defence Force. The Japanese were supported by Burmese nationalists under the command of U Aung San (the father of Aung San Suu Kyi), who sabotaged British lines of communication in the vain and naive expectation that Burma would receive genuine independence from Tokyo. By the end of January 1942, Iida had driven Hutton's forces out of Tavoy and Moulmein, and between 18 and 23 February had comprehensively defeated him at the battle of Sittang River, where Hutton lost all his heavy equipment. As in Malaya, the British tended to concentrate on defending roads and cleared areas, and as a result were repeatedly outflanked by the Japanese.

During the battle of Sittang River, Hutton was replaced by General Sir Harold Alexander, one of whose corps commanders was Major-General William Slim. (This was six months before Alexander's appointment to the Middle East Command.) From a modest background, Slim had fought at Gallipoli, had been wounded fighting with the Gurkhas, had won the MC and had been wounded again in Mesopotamia, ending the Great War as an Indian Army major. A soldier's soldier, he had none of the vanity and ego of commanders like MacArthur, Montgomery and Patton, yet tactically and strategically he was certainly their equal. Burmese terrain included mountains, plains, jungles, coastal waters and wide rivers; Slim showed the highest qualities of generalship over all of them. Together he and Alexander co-ordinated the long retreat northwards out of Burma. The difficult decision was taken to abandon Rangoon on 6 March, where 100,000 tons of stores were captured by the Japanese two days later. In mid-March the Fifth and Sixth Chinese Armies entered Burma to cover the British retreat and try to protect the Burma Road. Chiang Kai-shek's chief of staff, the tough-minded but rebarbative and Anglo-phobic General Joseph 'Vinegar Joe' Stilwell, fought the battle of Yenangyaung between 10 and 19 April, but could not make significant headway, and soon afterwards the Japanese broke into the Shan plateau and forced the Chinese to flee northwards. Of the 95,000 Chinese, only one division managed to escape intact.[66] Mandalay fell on 1 May at the same time as Lashio, the southern terminus of the Burma Road.

Of the 42,000 British, Indian and Burmese troops involved in the campaign, no fewer than 29,000 were casualties by the end of May. Nonetheless, Alexander and Slim had managed to get 13,000 un-wounded men back to Imphal in Assam province in India, after a 600-mile retreat from Sittang, the longest in British history. 'They looked like scarecrows,' Slim said of his troops. 'But they looked like soldiers, too.' He also recalled the heart-rending sight of a four-year-old child in Imphal trying to spoon-feed her dead mother from a tin of evaporated milk.

It had been a momentous series of rearguard actions and last-minute escapes, but four-fifths of Burma had fallen to the Japanese, whose casualties numbered only 4,597. This had the effect of further isolating China, which could now be supplied only by the USAAF pilots under-taking most of the 550-mile flights over 16,000-foot Himalayan mountain ranges to Yunnan province, nicknamed the Hump. It was a gruelling mission also known as the Aluminium Trail because of all the planes that had crashed along the way. Nonetheless, by 1945 no fewer than 650,000 tons of supplies had been delivered by that route.

Service in Burma, believed George MacDonald Fraser, who fought in the 17th (Black Cat) Indian Division during the siege of Meiktila and the battle of Pyawbwe, was, with the sole exception of Bomber Command, 'generally believed to be the worst ticket you could draw in the lottery of active service'.[67] Nor was this just because of the nature of the enemy; there were also 15-inch poisonous centipedes, malaria, spiders the size of plates, typhus, jungle sores on wrists and ankles, dysentery and leeches with which to contend. And of course the weather; the 1941–2 Burma Campaign only ended with the monsoon breaking in May. Fraser described a Burmese monsoon in his war memoirs *Quartered Safe Out Here*:

There are the first huge drops, growing heavier and heavier, and then God opens the sluices and the jets of a million high-pressure hoses are being directed straight down, and the deluge comes with a great roar . . . after that the earth is under a skin of water which looks as though it's being churned up by buckshot. Before you know it you are sodden and streaming, the fire's out, the level in the brew tin is rising visibly, and the whole clearing is a welter of blaspheming men trying to snatch arms and equipment from the streams coursing underfoot.[68]

Just as the Russians had been saved by the weather outside Moscow in autumn 1941, so were the British by the weather on the Indian–Burmese border the following spring.

'It's a horrible World at present,' Clementine Churchill wrote to her husband on 19 December 1941. 'Europe over-run by the Nazi hogs, and the Far East by yellow Japanese lice.'[69] Once one has discounted the terminology that was typical of her generation, it was true that the Germans and Japanese seemed totally in the ascendant. The Japanese had captured a vast area of approximately 32 million square miles. In six months Japan had acquired 70 per cent of the world's tin supply and almost all its natural rubber, forcing the Americans to develop synthetic rubber for their vehicles' tyres.[70] Conquest had delivered to the Japanese a higher annual oil production from the Dutch East Indies (7.9 million tonnes) than California and Iran combined; they also took 1.4 million tonnes of coal per annum from · Sumatra and Borneo; 1.1 million troy ounces of gold from the Philippines – more than Alaska or any other state except California – as well as manganese and chromium and iron estimated at half a billion tonnes; tin from Thailand, and oil, silver, lead, nickel and copper from Burma, all of which they started exploiting without delay, using slave labour for its extraction. Less tangibly but just as importantly, Japanese morale had soared. The military triumphs since Pearl Harbor had been, in the words of a biographer of MacArthur, 'as spectacular as

213

any in the history of warfare'.[71] But if the Japanese believed, as some in their planning Staff did, that because America had anyway been due to give the Philippines her independence in 1946 she would not strain every nerve to retake them in the meantime, then they had misread the American national character as fundamentally as had Hitler.

Meeting in Washington in December 1941 and January 1942, Roosevelt and Churchill agreed that the policy of Germany First sketched out by them in Newfoundland the previous August would be adhered to. Japan would be allowed breathing-space, but her time would undoubtedly come. The Japanese people were given a taste of what that would involve when on 18 April 1942 sixteen B-25 bombers took off from the aircraft carrier USS *Hornet* and flew 800 miles to hit Tokyo, Yokohama, Yokosuka, Kobe and Nagoya, earning their commander, Lieutenant-Colonel Jimmy Doolittle, the Congressional Medal of Honor and promotion to brigadier-general. The amount of damage, at least in comparison to later bombing raids on those cities, was admittedly minimal and two captured American pilots were beheaded by the Japanese, but it was a potent augury of what was to come.

When the United States entered the war, she had the world's seventeenth largest army, numbering 269,023, smaller than that of Romania. She could put only five properly armed, full-strength divisions into the field, at a time when Germany wielded 180.[72] The Great Depression had taken a physical toll on American manhood; even though the Army would accept just about anyone sane over 5 feet tall, 105 pounds in weight, possessing twelve or more of his own teeth, and free of flat feet, venereal disease and hernias, no fewer than 40 per cent of citizens failed these basic criteria.[73] The Roosevelt Administration had begun rearming in 1940 as far as Congress would allow, passing a $9 billion defence budget for the fiscal year. Yet the attack on Pearl Harbor led to a massive extension of all types of military production, and the long-term results were nothing less than war-winning, especially considering the amount shipped to Britain, Russia, China and elsewhere.

By the end of the war, the USA had built 296,000 aircraft at a cost of $44 billion, 351 million metric tons of aircraft bombs, 88,000 landing craft, 12.5 million rifles and 86,333 tanks. Meanwhile, American shipyards had launched 147 aircraft carriers, 952 warships displacing 14 million tons, and no fewer than 5,200 merchant ships totalling 39 million tons. The total munitions budget from May 1940 to July 1945 alone amounted to $180 billion, or twenty times the entire 1940 defence budget.[74] Such was the United States' financial and economic commitment to victory, quite apart from the 14.9 million people she mobilized in her Army, Army Air Force and Navy. Grossly to oversimplify the contributions made by the three leading members of the Grand Alliance in the Second World War, if Britain had provided the time and Russia the blood necessary to defeat the Axis, it was America that produced the weapons.

PART II

Climacteric

The people will more readily forgive the mistakes made by a Government – which, as often as not, by the way, escape their notice – than any evidence of hesitancy or lack of assurance . . . However one lives, whatever one does or undertakes, one is invariably exposed to the danger of making mistakes. And so, what, indeed, would become of the individual and of the community, if those in whom authority was vested were paralysed by fear of a possible error, and refused to take the decisions that were called for?

Adolf Hitler, 15 May 1942 (ed. Trevor-Roper,
Hitler's Table Talk, p. 483)

7

The Everlasting Shame of Mankind

1939–1945

Dawn came on like a betrayer; it seemed as though the new
sun rose as an ally of our enemies to assist in our destruction.
Primo Levi, *If This Is a Man*, written in 1946[1]

Although hotly debated by historians, the exact date when Hitler ordered Heinrich Himmler to destroy the Jewish race in Europe through the industrialized use of the *Vernichtungslager* (extermination camp) is really almost immaterial. Hitler had always been, in the historian Ian Kershaw's phrase, 'the supreme and radical spokesman of an ideological imperative' to destroy the Jews. An unmistakable threat had been made even before the outbreak of war, on 30 January 1939, when he told the Reichstag:

In the course of my life I have very often been a prophet, and have usually been ridiculed for it. Today I will once more be a prophet; if the international Jewish financiers in and outside Europe should succeed in plunging the nations once more into a world war, then the result will not be the Bolshevization of the earth, and thus the victory of Jewry, but the annihilation of the Jewish race in Europe![2]

Of course it had been Hitler himself with his invasion of Poland, rather than the mythical Jewish–Bolshevik conspiracy, that had plunged the world into war, but that did not make his warning any the less menacing. He repeated it on several further occasions in public speeches during the war, and was more specific about exterminating the Jews in dozens of private speeches to his Gauleiters and Reichskommissars too. The use of poison gas on Jews had even been mentioned in *Mein Kampf* in which he had written that in the First World War 'the sacrifice of millions at the front' would have been unnecessary if 'twelve or fifteen thousand of these Hebrew corrupters of the people had been held under poison gas'.[3]

Hitler and Himmler had no difficulty in recruiting enough anti-Semites to do the work of extermination for them. Anti-Semitism was by no means confined to Germany, but it was particularly virulent there. Although the organized working-class left were not particularly anti-Semitic in Bismarckian and later Weimar Germany, the roots of the phenomenon went deep into much of the rest of German society. The foundation of the League of Anti-Semites in 1879, and the career of the thieving, blackmailing forger (and headmaster) Hermann Ahlwardt, who was elected to the Reichstag in the 1880s on a platform of spewing hatred against Germany's Jews – who only ever made up 1 per cent of the country's population – were potent signs of this.[4] What an historian has termed 'the domestication of anti-Semitism' took place in the 1880s and early 1890s, with novelists such as Julius Langbehn writing about the Jews in terms of 'poison', 'plague' and 'vermin'. Richard Wagner's widow Cosima, who lived until 1930, drew together a group of anti-Semites at Bayreuth, and the writings of the Englishman Houston Stewart Chamberlain at the turn of the century also contributed to the concept of German history as an Aryan-versus-Jewish struggle. If anything it is surprising that it took a full half-century of such propaganda and hatred before Hitler incorporated violence against the Jews into a political platform.

The milieu in which the young Hitler lived in Vienna, as well as the political tracts he read while scraping a living as a hack painter, seems to have drawn him towards a loathing of Jews. 'Hitler could scarcely ignore the everyday antisemitism of the kind of newspapers that were available in the reading-room of the Men's Home [the hostel where he lived], and the cheap antisemitic pamphlets he later described reading at this time,' writes an expert in this field. 'And his enthusiasm for Wagner, whose operas he went to hundreds of times in this period, can only have strengthened his political views.'[5] Yet it was not until Germany's defeat in 1918 that this anti-Semitism became murderous. The way that Hitler harnessed German anti-Semitism, which was common among small businessmen, shopkeepers, artisans and peasant farmers, was as deft as it was malevolent.

Yet the genocidal killing of *lebensunwertes Leben* (those unworthy of existence) in Nazi Germany began not with the Jews but with the euthanasia meted out to the mentally and physically disabled, in total around 212,000 Germans and 80,000 others. The mentally ill were also killed in converted shower rooms, which provided the inspiration for what would eventually take place in Auschwitz. It is true that as many as a thousand Jews were murdered in German concentration camps in the six months after the Jewish pogroms of *Kristallnacht* on the night of 9 November 1938, but it was not until 1939 that the true extent of the Nazis' plans for the Jewish race in Europe began to become apparent. Fortunately by then over half of the Jewish population of Germany had already emigrated, with 102,200 going to the USA, 63,500 to Argentina, 52,000 to Britain, 33,400 to Palestine, 26,000 to South Africa and 8,600 to Australia.[6] Tragically, many also left for places such as Poland, France and the Netherlands that were to afford no long-term safety at all.

With the outbreak of war in September 1939, and especially after their victory over Poland, the Germans adopted a policy of forcing enormous numbers of Jews into ghettos, small urban areas where it was hoped that disease, malnutrition and eventually starvation would destroy them. Over one-third of the population of Warsaw, for example, comprising some 338,000 people, was forced into a ghetto comprising only 2.5 per cent of the area of the city. The penalty for leaving the 300 ghettos and 437 labour camps of the Reich was death, and *Judenräte* (Jewish elders' councils) administered them on behalf of the Nazis, on the (often false) basis that they would ameliorate conditions more than the Germans. By August 1941, 5,500 Jews were dying in the Warsaw ghetto every month.[7]

Another, vaster ghetto – the Vichy-run island of Madagascar – was briefly considered by Hitler in the summer of 1940 as an eventual destination for Europe's Jews, as was British-owned Uganda and a massive death march into Siberia once the war in the east was won. The unhealthiness of these places – especially given Madagascar's yellow fever – constituted their principal attraction. When in February 1941 Martin Bormann discussed the practicalities of how to get the

Jews to Madagascar, Hitler suggested Robert Ley's 'Strength Through Joy' cruise line, but then expressed concern for the fate of the German crews at the hands of Allied submarines, though of course none for the fate of the passengers.[8] Even if they had got through the Royal Navy cordon unscathed, the Madagascar plan, as an historian has pointed out, 'would still have been another kind of genocide'.[9]

Instead, by early 1941, when, under Special Action Order 14f13, SS murder squads were sent by Himmler into concentration camps to kill Jews and others whom the Reich considered unworthy of life, an altogether more direct approach was adopted that borrowed the term *Sonderbehandlung* (special treatment) from the Gestapo, which had used it for extra-judicial killings.[10] This policy was applied on a Continental basis at the time of Operation Barbarossa, when four SS *Einsatzgruppen* (action groups) followed the Wehrmacht into Russia in order to liquidate those considered 'undesirable', primarily Jews, Red Army commissars and anyone thought likely to become partisans behind the German lines. They killed out of all proportion to their numbers; together the four comprised only 3,000 people, including clerks, interpreters, teletype and radio operators, and female secretaries.[11] By the end of July 1941, Himmler had reinforced this number ten-fold when SS *Kommandostab* brigades, German police battalions and Baltic and Ukrainian pro-Nazi auxiliary units totalling some 40,000 men complemented the role of the *Einsatzgruppen* in an orgy of killing that accounted for nearly one million deaths in six months, by many and various methods.[12] Far from feeling guilt and shame about this behaviour towards innocents, photographs of shootings were sometimes displayed on walls in SS barracks' messes, from which copies could be ordered.[13]

In 1964, a former SS member explained how Einsatzkommando No. 8 had gone about its grisly business in Russia twenty-three years previously: 'At these executions undertaken by shooting squads,' he told a German regional court,

it would occasionally be arranged for the victims to lie down along the trench so that they could be pushed in easily afterwards. For the later operations, the victims had to lie face down inside the trench and were then shot in the side of the head. During the shootings at Bialystok, Novgorod and Baranowice, the corpses were well covered over, more or less, with sand and chalk before the next batch was brought up. In the later shooting operations, this was only rarely done so that the next batch of victims always had to lie down on the corpses of those who had just been killed before. But even in those cases where the corpses had been covered with sand and chalk, the next victims often saw them, because body parts would frequently be jutting out of the thin layer of sand or earth.

Some time between mid-July and mid-October 1941, just as the mass murder of Russian Jews was being escalated after Operation Barbarossa, Hitler decided to kill every Jew that his Reich could reach, regardless of the help they could have afforded Germany's war effort. The exact date is impossible to determine, since the Nazis attempted to obliterate evidence of the Holocaust itself, quite apart from its organizational genesis. On 4 October 1943, for example, Himmler told senior SS officers that the murder of the Jews was 'a glorious page in our history that has never been written and cannot be written'. It is therefore vain to try to seek a piece of paper from Hitler actually authorizing the Holocaust, despite the wealth of circumstantial evidence that he and Himmler were its architects.

In October 1941 all Jewish emigration from Europe was banned, and deportations of German Jews from the Reich began. The next month, mobile gas vans were used to kill Jews in Łódź in Poland and soon afterwards in Chełmno. The SS had been using gas vans to kill more than 70,000 lunatic-asylum patients since 1939; it was an idea borrowed from Stalin's purges of the 1930s, during which people had been gassed in specially converted trucks and vans parked outside Moscow, into which the carbon monoxide from the vehicles' engines was introduced.[14] Reinhard Heydrich pioneered the use of these mobile gas chambers for the SS, sometimes disguised as furniture-removal vans. In 1959 one of the chemists involved, Dr Theodor Leidig, explained what happened after victims had been packed into them:

I was told that the people who would be getting into the lorry were Russians who would have been shot anyway. The higher-ups wanted to know if there was a better way of killing them ... I still remember that you could look inside the lorry through a peephole or window. The interior was lit. Then they opened the lorry. Some of the bodies fell out, others were unloaded by prisoners. As we technicians confirmed, the bodies had that pinkish-red hue which is typical of people who have died [of carbon-monoxide poisoning].

The process of these local massacres was still very haphazard, but before the end of 1941 the SS were starting to kill Russian POWs and the disabled with Zyklon B gas. In October 1941 the German Army in Serbia also began to shoot Jews under the pretext of 'reprisals' against partisan activity.

On 12 December 1941, the day after his declaration of war on America, Hitler spoke to senior Nazi Party functionaries. 'As far as the Jewish question is concerned,' recorded Goebbels afterwards, 'the Führer is determined to make a clean sweep.' Hitler had referred to his January 1939 Reichstag speech, saying, 'The world war is here, the extermination of the Jews must be the necessary consequence.' Six days later Himmler made a note of a meeting he had held with Hitler, which read: 'Jewish Question. To be extirpated as partisans.'[15] The policy was to be changed from killing Jews wherever they happened to be, while moving them eastwards and keeping them living in conditions also likely to kill them, to carrying out the Final Solution in specially adapted camps dedicated to the purpose. Sobibór camp was opened near Lublin in Occupied Poland in May 1942, and work was begun on Treblinka in north-east Poland the next month.

In order for the Nazis to exterminate almost two million Polish Jews in less than two years between early 1942 and late 1943, they needed to use units such as the Reserve Police Battalion 101, which was alone responsible for shooting, or deporting to their deaths, 83,000 people.[16] The battalion was mainly made up of middle-aged, respectable working- and middle-class citizens of Hamburg, rather than Nazi ideologues. Peer pressure and a natural propensity for obedience and comradeship, rather than political fervour, seem to have turned these people into mass murderers. Since no fewer than 210 members of the battalion were interviewed in depth in the 1960s, it was possible to ascertain that the recruits of Battalion 101 were not selected for their ideological ardour – only one-quarter were even Nazi Party members – and many joined up largely to avoid active service abroad. They represented a cross-section of German society and no one was coerced into killing Jews or ever punished for refusing to do so. Only a relatively small number of Germans approved of what was happening 'out east', yet the rest did not actively disapprove in any way. The vast majority were simply indifferent, and did not want to know. Yet when called upon specifically to help in the genocide, between 80 and 90 per cent of Battalion 101 acquiesced without undue complaint. After some initial squeamishness, recounts the historian Christopher Browning, they 'became increasingly efficient and callous executioners'.[17]

Only twelve of the battalion's 500 members – that is, 2.4 per cent – actually refused to take part in shooting 1,500 Jews in groups of forty in the woods outside the Polish village of Józefów 50 miles south-east of Lublin on 13 July 1942. During the remainder of that seventeen-hour day – interspersed with cigarette breaks and a midday meal – perhaps another forty-five or so members absented themselves for various reasons. The remaining 90 per cent simply got on with the job of shooting Jewish women and children at point-blank range, even though they knew that there would have been no retribution had they refused. Some reasoned that their non-participation would not alter the Jews' ultimate fate. Although they said they disliked shooting infants and small children, they did it, just as they shot decorated Great War veterans who begged for mercy on account of shared comradeship in the trenches. They found it 'disturbing' that none of the mothers would leave their children, and so had to be shot together with them, although 'It was soothing to my conscience to release [that is, kill] children unable to live without their mothers,' said a thirty-five-year-old metalworker from Bremerhaven.

Some physical revulsion was shown by the members of the battalion, but not ethical. 'At first we shot freehand,' one recalled. 'When one aimed too high the entire skull exploded. As a consequence, brains and bones flew everywhere. Thus, we were instructed to place the bayonet point on the neck.' They recalled how the Jews themselves showed an 'unbelievable' and 'astonishing' composure in the face of death, although the sound of shooting made it perfectly clear what was about to happen to them.[18] There was a large number of quite complex psychological reasons why normal people allowed themselves to become mass murderers, and of course fanatical anti-Semitism was present in some people. Most of these reasons – wartime brutalization, societal segmentation, careerism, sheer routine, the desire for conformity, a macho ethos, and so on – do not end at the physical or historical borders of Nazi Germany.

It is untrue that, as has often been suggested, the industrialized mass extermination of the Jews took place as a result of German frustrations on the Eastern Front, or even as a result of the entry of the United States into the war after Pearl Harbor, events which coincided with it but did not trigger it. In fact the Germans were constantly devising new ways to kill more Jews more efficiently, and the use of Zyklon B gas was merely the end of that process of improvisation. In a *Führerstaat* (dictatorship), career advancement depended on pleasing the Führer, and Hitler – though careful not to append his signature to any documents concerning extermination, and to use only word of mouth in giving directions – was known within the regime to favour whichever policy was harshest towards the Jews. Although he attached his name to any number of Führer directives and *Führerbefehlen* (orders), such was the criminal magnitude of the Holocaust that he distanced himself as far as possible from personal blame, to the extent that his apologists even attempt to argue that he wasn't responsible. No German official's career ever suffered from being over-enthusiastic for genocide and many – such as Obergruppenführer (Lieutenant-General) Reinhard Heydrich – prospered because of their anti-Semitic fanaticism. When in mid-August 1941 SS-Reichsführer Heinrich Himmler and Heydrich gave written instructions to escalate the killing of Jewish women and children as well as men in ever larger pogroms in eastern Europe, it happened, starting in Lithuania.[19]

Massacres of Jews – often through shooting at the edge of pits that had been dug by the victims themselves or by Russian POWs – took place at Ponary near Vilnius (55,000 killed), Fort IX near Kovno (10,000), Babi Yar ravine outside Kiev (33,771), Rumbula near Riga (38,000), Kaunas (30,000) and many other places. In all, around 1.3 million people died at the hands of the *Einsatzgruppen* before the more industrialized processes were adopted. We know the numbers because they sent back detailed reports of their massacres, which Hitler certainly saw and occasionally made tangential reference to in his discussions with lieutenants. On 25 October 1941, for example, at dinner with Himmler and Heydrich, Hitler said: 'Let no one say to me, we cannot send them into the swamp . . . It is good if our advance is preceded by fear that we will exterminate Jewry.' This was probably a reference to the SS reports of drowning Jewish women and children by their thousands in the Pripet Marshes.

The Wehrmacht both knew about and actively co-operated in the work of the *Einsatzgruppen*, despite its post-war protestations of innocence that fooled a number of prominent Western historians, including Basil Liddell Hart. After Babi Yar, Field Marshal Walther von Reichenau issued an order celebrating the 'hard but just punishment for the Jewish sub-humans' and Rundstedt signed a directive to senior officers along much the same lines. Equal complicity in genocide was exhibited by Field Marshal von Leeb, Field Marshal von Manstein – who wrote, 'The Jewish–Bolshevist system must now and forever be exterminated' – and General Hoepner, who ordered 'the total annihilation of the enemy', whom he identified as the Jews and Bolsheviks. The Germans had a long history of dealing viciously and arbitrarily with 'undesirable' elements among the domestic population of occupied territories, including suspected *francs-tireurs* in the Franco-Prussian War, Herero tribesmen in 1904–8 and Belgian civilians in the Great War. In 1940, some 3,000 black African soldiers were massacred after they had surrendered in the fall of France.[20]

The somewhat haphazard, semi-public mass killings by the *Einsatzgruppen* had their drawbacks, principally the sheer amount of ammunition expended, the odd escapee and the very occasional distaste felt by the SS men themselves, all of which Himmler wished to minimize. This meant that by the late summer and autumn of 1941 the Nazi High Command were keen to adopt a far more efficient method of conducting genocide. Therefore on 3 September 1941, in the cellars of Block 11 at the Oświęcim barracks to the west of Kraków in Poland – known to history by its German name of Auschwitz – 250 prisoners, mostly Poles, were poisoned using Zyklon B crystallized cyanide gas, hitherto used for anti-lice fumigation of clothes and buildings. Although gas vans, mass shootings and various other methods continued to be employed in the east, the use of Zyklon B in gas chambers became the primary way that the Nazis attempted, in the words of Heydrich, to provide 'the final solution to the Jewish question in Europe'. In Hitler's library there was a 1931 handbook on poison gas, which featured a chapter on the prussic-acid asphyxiant marketed commercially as Zyklon B.[21]

Zyklon (meaning Cyclone) and B for *Blausäure* (prussic acid) was originally intended by Auschwitz's camp commandant Rudolf Höss to 'spare' a 'bloodbath', by which he meant the SS having to kill Jews and others individually. Höss himself was a very early Party member, joining in November 1922; the number on his membership card was 3240.[22] In the words of one historian of Auschwitz, 'the use of Zyklon B alleviated the process of murder'.[23] In all, around 1.1 million people were killed at Auschwitz–Birkenau, more than 90 per cent of whom were Jews. Auschwitz was the camp headquarters where 30,000 prisoners were kept, and nearby Birkenau was a 425-acre camp – larger than London's Hyde Park – where around 100,000 lived, worked and died. The slogan *Arbeit Macht Frei* (work makes you free) fashioned in metal above the front gate at Auschwitz was of course another cynical Nazi lie, as work there was intended to make the inmates die, and no inmate was ever freed by the Germans in the history of the camp.

After they were rounded up in their local communities from all across German-occupied Europe, Jews were transported by train to Auschwitz or one of the other five extermination camps in eastern Europe. Typically they were allowed to take between 15 and 25 kilograms of personal belongings on the journey. This was intended to lull them into thinking that they would be resettled in communities 'out east'. Such lies were needed in order to keep them docile, and to trick them into entering the gas chambers without panicking, fighting back or trying to escape. On the long journeys, often by cattle truck – those from Greece could take up to eleven days – they were given little or nothing to eat and drink, and were provided with no lavatories.

Once the transports arrived at the siding at Birkenau, there would be the first *Selektion* (selection), where SS officials would choose the able-bodied men and women – numbering roughly 15 per cent – who would be taken to the camp barracks to join work details, leaving the old, the weak, the infirm, the children and the mothers of children, who would be immediately walked to the gas chambers and exterminated. No fewer than 230,000 children died at Birkenau, almost all within an hour of arriving there, whereas average life expectancy for men who survived the initial selection was six months to one year, and for women four months. Death came in many forms besides gassing and executions, including starvation, punishment beatings, suicide, torture, exhaustion, medical experimentation, typhoid, exposure, scarlet fever, diphtheria, petechial typhus and tuberculosis. Oswald 'Papa' Kaduk – his nickname came from his 'love for children' – gave Jewish children balloons just before they were squirted (*abspritzen*) in the heart with phenol injections at the rate of ten per minute.[24]

Those who were selected to be gassed were walked straight to the underground chambers, and were told that they were going to be given a shower. The word 'showers' was written in all the major European languages, and there were even false shower heads in the ceiling of the gas chambers. The victims were also told that if they did not hurry up the coffee that was waiting for them in the camp afterwards would get cold.[25] Once in the undressing room, they were told to hang their clothes on the hooks provided, and then they were herded into the chambers and the heavy metal doors were suddenly locked behind them. Green Zyklon B pellets were then dropped through holes in the roof, and within fifteen to thirty minutes – accounts differ – everyone inside was dead.

Much of the physically arduous task of running the gas chambers fell to the *Sonderkommandos* (special units), prisoners who also had to undertake the work of cleaning and preparing the chambers and crematoria. 'The only exit is by way of the chimney,' the Italian chemist Primo Levi was told on entering Auschwitz. 'What did it mean?' he wondered. 'Soon we were all to learn what it meant.'[26] Although only SS *Sanitäter* (medical orderlies) actually introduced the Zyklon B gas pellets into the chamber, the *Sonderkommandos* did almost everything else except locking the hermetically sealed gas-chamber doors. They calmed the prisoners on the way into the undressing room, often speaking in Yiddish, telling them they were going to be given a shower before joining work details and being reunited with their families; they led nervous, agitated or suspicious 'trouble-makers' out of sight and earshot and held them by each ear as an SS man shot them with a silencer-fitted handgun behind the crematoria; they helped the elderly undress, and led them towards the gas chambers, sometimes pushing them on with heavy rubber truncheons; while the gassing was taking place they sorted through the belongings, valuables, food and clothes left in the undressing room, looking for jewellery stitched into the lining of clothing; they burnt whatever the Nazis considered worthless, including photograph albums, books, documents, Torah scrolls, prayer shawls and toys; they cleaned out the remnants of the corpses and human excretion from the gas chambers, so the new transport would see no traces of what had happened to the previous one – women's scent taken from the victims was often used to hide the smell of gas and bodily discharges; they checked the victims' mouths for gold coins; they shaved the hair off the corpses, ripped off rings and earrings and extracted gold teeth and tight rings with pliers; they detached prosthetic limbs, then they threw the corpses into the metal freight lift 'like rags', piling them in fifteen to twenty at a time. Upstairs, using specially adapted pitchforks, *Sonderkommandos* pushed the corpses into the crematoria furnaces, which they had to keep well stoked (the smoke went up the 50-foot chimneys); afterwards they used large wooden stakes to crush any skulls, bones and body parts that had not been consumed; they removed the vast piles of human ash in wheelbarrows to a pond between two of the crematoria, or by truck to throw into the Sola river, a tributary of the Vistula.[27] Typically, in one gas chamber alone – and Auschwitz–Birkenau had six working round the clock – 2,000 Jews could be killed in ninety minutes by a team of ten SS men and twenty *Sonderkommando* members.[28] Many SS men volunteered for overtime in order to obtain rewards such as extra meat and alcohol rations. There were some twenty-four-hour periods when as many as 20,000 human beings were selected, gassed, cremated and their ashes disposed of in Auschwitz alone.

'Many of them knew they were going to their death,' recalled the former *Sonderkommando* prisoner Josef Sackar of the Jews he had escorted into the gas chambers: 'They had an intuition. They were afraid, pure and simple. They were terrified. Mothers held their children tight . . . They were embarrassed . . . Some of them cried out of shame and fear. They were very, very afraid. The children behaved like children. They looked for their parents' hands, hugged their parents. What did they know? They didn't know a thing.'[29] Victims were told to remember the number of the hook on which they had hung their clothes in the undressing room, a passageway 50 by 80 feet long with a concrete floor and wooden benches on each side. This too was intended to lull them into the belief that they were only going to be washed and deloused before getting dressed.

Once inside the gas chamber, the victims had no hope of survival. Rudolf Höss was adamant in the memoirs he wrote between his arrest in March 1946 and his hanging on his own gallows at Auschwitz that April that, compared with carbon monoxide,

Experience has shown that the preparation of prussic acid called Zyklon B caused death with far greater speed and certainty, especially if the rooms were kept dry and gas-tight and closely packed with people, and provided they were fitted with as large intake vents as possible. As far as Auschwitz is concerned, I have never heard of a single person being found alive when the gas chambers were opened half an hour after the gas had been inducted.[30]

Those thirty minutes were as horrific as it is possible to contemplate. In the state-of-the-art gas chambers of Crematoria II and III at Auschwitz, the pellets were lowered in containers down *Drahtnetzeinschieb-vorrichtungen* (wire-mesh introduction columns) and the gas was distributed relatively evenly, but in other gas chambers it collected on the floor and rose upwards, forcing the stronger people to climb on top of the weaker ones in a vain bid to avoid asphyxiation. 'The people there knew that the end was approaching and tried to climb as high as they could to avoid the gas,' recalled Sackar. 'Sometimes all the skin on the bodies peeled due to the effect of the gas.'[31] The victims clawed at the doors and walls, and their screaming and weeping could be heard even through the thick metal airtight doors. When the *Sonderkommandos* entered the chambers they encountered a dreadful sight. As their historian records: 'The purple, fissured flesh; the faces distorted with pain; and the eyes, bulging and agape, attest to the terrible agonies that these people experienced in their last moments.'[32]

Speaking at Nuremberg, the Auschwitz guard Otto Moll spoke of the fate of the babies whose mothers had left them hidden in discarded clothing in the undressing room: 'The prisoners had to clean up the room after it had been cleared of people, they would then take the babies and throw them into the gas chamber.' Elsewhere he was asked to estimate how quickly the Zyklon B gas took effect: 'The gas was poured in through an opening. About one half minute after the gas was poured in, of course I am merely estimating this time as we never had a stop-watch to clock it and we were not interested, at any rate, after one half minute there were no more heavy sounds, and no sounds at all that could be heard from the gas chamber.' Q: 'What kind of sounds were heard before that?' A: 'The people wept and screeched.'[33] Few other accounts put the time as short as that.

On occasion a *Sonderkommando* prisoner would recognize family or friends among the dead, and Höss – whose testimony must be seen through the prism of his unrepentant anti-Semitism – claimed that one had to drag his own wife to the furnace, and then sat down to lunch with his colleagues without displaying any untoward emotion. (Conversely, there is another story of a *Sonderkommando* member accompanying his mother into the gas chamber and then voluntarily remaining with her there to be gassed.) Unsurprisingly the *Sonderkommandos* were thought of by other Auschwitz inmates as the Nazis' henchmen, and as 'especially soulless and savage individuals'.[34] Primo Levi wrote that they existed on 'the borderline of collaboration' and it is true that the Nazis' job would have been far more difficult and laborious if the *Sonderkommandos* had not existed, although they would undoubtedly have found volunteers among the Ukrainian, Baltic or Belorussian auxiliary units to undertake the tasks.

Yet it should be remembered that the *Sonderkommandos* had no alternative except death, that they provided food for other inmates when they could, and that they were the only group of inmates to rise up against the Germans. When on 7 October 1944 it became clear that the *Sonderkommandos* of Crematorium IV were about to be selected, they attacked the SS with stones, axes and iron bars. The 'uprising' was over by nightfall, and no prisoner managed to escape, but they killed three SS guards and injured twelve, blew up Crematoria IV with hand-grenades smuggled to them by women prisoners, and tried to escape from the camp, with 250 dying in the attempt and 200 executed the next day. The Jewish women who had smuggled the explosives – Ester Wajcblum, Regina Safirsztajn, Ala Gertner and

1. General Werner von Blomberg, the German Defence Minister, in discussion with the newly elected Chancellor Adolf Hitler at Ulm in September 1933. The Pact made between these two men aboard the battleship *Deutschland* the following April cemented Hitler's power in the Reich and set Germany on the path to war.

. The Nazi–Soviet Pact was signed in the Kremlin at 2 a.m. on Thursday, 24 August 1939, by the two men on either side of Joseph Stalin, the German Foreign Minister Joachim bbentrop (*left*) and his Russian counterpart V. M. Molotov (*right*). Friedrich Gaus (*extreme eft*), head of the legal department of the Reich Foreign Ministry, drafted the agreement. It gave Hitler the diplomatic initiative and was Stalin's greatest blunder.

3. The Italian dictator Benito Mussolini, Hitler, Major-General Alfred Jodl and Field Marshal Wilhelm Keitel confer at Hitler's headquarters in East Prussia, the Wolfsschanze, on 25 August 1941, three days after Hitler had diverted troops southwards from the attack on Moscow towards Kiev.

4. Reichsmarschall Hermann Göring, Keitel and SS-Reichsführer Heinrich Himmler confer with Hitler on 10 April 1942.

The outspoken Field Marshal Gerd von
Rundstedt was appointed and sacked by Hitler
four times in his career. On 18 April 1944 he
was inspecting the Atlantic Wall as commander-
in-chief west.

6. Field Marshal Erich von Manstein,
the man responsible for the 'Sickle
Cut' manoeuvre that led to the fall of
France and the capture of the Crimea
and Kharkov, was the greatest German
strategist of the war, but even he could
not relieve Stalingrad.

7. General Heinz Guderian, Germany's
most talented tank commander, in
December 1940.

8. Field Marshal Walter Model
overseeing a German and
Hungarian counter-attack on the
southern Russian front. He was
sent to rescue difficult situations
so often that he was nicknamed
Hitler's Fireman.

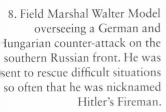

9. A French tank about to receive the full force of Blitzkrieg, as a Junkers Ju-8 Stuka dives to bomb it in northern Fran in 1940.

10. Refugees flee Paris in June 1940.

1. Operation Dynamo: Allied troops queuing along the evacuation beaches of Dunkirk in late May 1940, hoping for what Churchill was to call 'a miracle of deliverance'.

2. Huge quantities of Allied vehicles, arms, stores and ammunition had to be disabled and left behind in France. This was the scene on 27 May 1940.

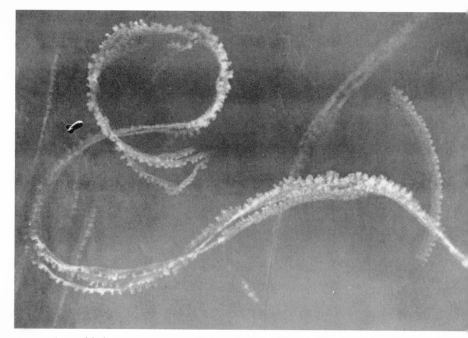

13. A terrible beauty: vapour trails from RAF and Luftwaffe planes battling over Kent on 3 September 1940. 'Both life and death had lost their importance,' wrote one British fighter ace. 'Desire sharpened to a single, savage purpose – to grab the enemy and claw him down from the sky'.

14. 'Scramble!' Pilots of 87 Squadron rush to their Hurricanes.

15. Hitler and Goebbels confer privately by a roaring fire in his Alpine retreat, the Berghof, in 1940.

16. Operation Barbarossa: the Wehrmacht in the Ukraine in the summer of 1941. Note the commandeered bus bringing up supplies.

17. Operation Typhoon, the German assault on Moscow, gets stuck in atrocious mud in October 1941. This assault gun is about to be abandoned.

18. Exhausted, freezing and demoralized, German soldiers start to surrender to winter-clad Russians as 1941 comes to a close.

Róza Robota – were hanged after a week of torture.[35] Each of the revolts that took place – in Sobibór, Treblinka and Auschwitz – in the six Nazi extermination camps were carried out by the *Sonderkommandos*, the only inmates with the physical strength to fight back. It was also they who tried to provide evidence of the genocide for the outside world, by burying accounts of it in tin cans in the soil near the crematoria, which have since been discovered and published.[36] One of these, written by Zalman Gradowski, asks, 'Why am I sitting here quietly instead of lamenting, weeping over my tragedy, and why instead are we frozen, numb, drained of all emotion?' The answer was that 'The continual systematic death, the only life of anyone who lives here, deadens, confuses and dulls your senses.'[37]

Several of the eighty *Sonderkommando* prisoners who survived the war submitted themselves to interview, and they attested that they turned themselves into automata in order to survive and bear witness against the Nazis. A sense of apathy and powerlessness, as well as the use of alcohol, helped push what has been described as 'the intrinsic moral quandary of the *Sonderkommando* phenomenon' into the background for these 'miserable manual labourers of the mass extermination'.[38] Surprisingly, suicide was rare among them. 'Although they knew what was about to happen,' records their historian, 'they could not rescue even one Jew.' That included the infants thrust into their arms by mothers entering the 'showers' who had divined that they would not emerge alive.[39]

Because the *Sonderkommandos* were *Geheimsträger* (bearers of secrets) they had to live together, could not resign their posts and could only hope that the war might end before they were themselves selected. Because they had the first access to parcels that the gassed Jews left in the undressing rooms, they ate better than any other prisoners, which because they were involved in such heavy manual labour suited the Germans. They were allowed to wear civilian clothes rather than prison uniform, had beds with mattresses in rooms over the crematoria, had time to rest and, beyond the daily roll-call, were not constantly overseen by the SS. 'We never ran short of anything,' recalled Sackar, 'clothes, food and sleep too.'[40] Their only distinguishing mark, other than their tattooed number, was a red cross on their backs. To differentiate the inmates, and dehumanize them, Jews were made to wear yellow Stars of David, and the rest of the inmates also wore colour-coded strips of fabric sewn on the prison uniform, thus Jehovah's Witnesses wore purple, homosexuals pink, criminals green, politicals red, Gypsies black, and Soviet POWs had the letters 'SU'. From 1943 prisoners were tattooed on arms or occasionally legs with numbers.

The utterly debased sadism and crudity of the German SS and their auxiliary-unit henchmen quite literally knew no bounds. Unremarkably representative was SS Staff Sergeant Paul Grot, at Sobibór, who was recalled by one of the only sixty-four survivors of that camp, Moshe Shklarek, for the way that he would 'have himself a joke; he would seize a Jew, give him a bottle of wine and a sausage weighing at least a kilo and order him to devour it in a few minutes. When the "lucky" man succeeded in carrying out this order and staggered from drunkenness, Grot would order him to open his mouth wide and would urinate into his mouth.'[41] As with any factory, the factory of death had shift labour, foremen (known as *capos*) and a conveyor-belt, time-and-motion attitude towards maximizing efficiency. The SS gave precise orders about what the *Sonderkommandos* were allowed to tell those about to be gassed, so that the victims went – at least for the most part – unknowingly to their deaths. Since it was unavoidable anyway, the *Sonderkommandos* did not want to terrify the victims more than they already were. 'I avoided looking them in the eye,' Sackar recalled of the people he escorted into the gas chambers. 'I always tried hard not to look them straight in the eye, so that they wouldn't sense anything.'[42] He admitted that he and his comrades had 'become robots, machines' but denied that he had been entirely desensitized to what was happening: 'We wept without tears . . . We had no time to think. Thinking was a complicated matter. We blocked everything out.' Sackar survived selection by the SS at Auschwitz by mingling with the other prisoners just as the Red Army was about to arrive in January 1945.

For those who survived the initial *Selektion* on the railway siding – known as the Ramp – there were plenty more. Regular barrack inspections would take place to ascertain whether prisoners still had the strength to work effectively, and those who could not, according to the most arbitrary criteria, were gassed. *Selektion* also took place in the prison hospital where SS doctors would regularly cull the 'hopelessly ill' patients. The historian Gideon Greig has identified seven areas of camp life where the absolutely pitiless phenomenon of *Selektion* regularly operated, against which there was no appeal.[43] *Selektion* officers would carry canes, which could be used as weapons but were more often used to direct inmates without having to come into physical contact with them. 'All those able to find a way out, try to take it,' recalled Primo Levi of the process, 'but they are in the minority because it is very difficult to escape from a selection. The Germans apply themselves to these things with great skill and diligence.'[44] Driven by thirst one day, Levi – *Häftling* (prisoner) number 174517 – opened the window of his hut to break off an icicle to drink, but a guard snatched it away. 'Why?' Levi asked, only to receive the reply, 'Hier ist kein warum' (Here, there is no why).[45] Yet in a sense there was; the SS did not want Levi to drink water because they did not want strong inmates, but rather weak, preferably dying ones as the numbers 'selected' could always be immediately replenished. Hearing a fellow prisoner thanking God that he was not selected, Levi recollected thinking: 'Can Kuhn fail to realize that next time it will be his turn? Does Kuhn not understand that what has happened today is an abomination, which no propitiatory prayer, no pardon, no expiation by the guilty, which nothing at all in the power of man can ever clean again? If I was God, I would spit at Kuhn's prayer.'[46]

To visit Auschwitz–Birkenau today is to be brought face to face with sights that bring home the horror as powerfully as any book or academic study ever could. Ladders were required to climb up the mountains of shoes that were taken from the victims. (In 2004, when 43,000 pairs were cleaned, some Hungarian money was found tucked into a pair, having somehow survived the official and unofficial looting of the camp.) Huge piles of shaving brushes, toothbrushes, spectacles, prosthetic limbs, baby clothes, combs and hairbrushes, and one million articles of clothing are displayed there. Most of the Jews' belongings had already long been expropriated and used by the Nazis, but these were left behind when the guards fled the Russians in January 1945. Seven tons of human hair were left, which otherwise would have been used in the German textile industry. Suitcases, of which there are thousands upon thousands in enormous piles, were chalked with the name and birthdates of their owners, such as 'Klement Hedwig 8/10/1898'. When the prams were taken away from Auschwitz, in rows of five rolling towards the railway station, it took an hour for them all to pass.[47] Writing to SS-Obergruppenführer Oswald Pohl in January 1943 about 'the material and goods taken over from the Jews, that is, the emigration of the Jews', Himmler even went into detail about what would happen to the crystals to be found in their watches, because in warehouses in Warsaw 'hundreds of thousands – perhaps even millions – are lying there, which for practical purposes could be distributed to the German watchmakers'.[48] On another occasion he (at least temporarily) saved five Jewish diamond jewellers from extermination because of their expertise in fashioning the Reich's highest decoration, the Knight's Cross with oak leaves and diamonds, which was only ever awarded to twenty-seven people.[49]

On 14 September 1942, Albert Speer authorized 13.7 million Reichsmarks to be spent on building huts and killing facilities at Birkenau as fast as possible.[50] Four gas chambers, numbered I to IV, were all fully operational by 1943, and were worked at full stretch by the time 437,000 Hungarians were brought there in the late spring of 1944 and killed in only a matter of weeks. A dozen German firms were used in the construction of the gas chambers and crematoria, and Oberingenieur Kurt Prüfer, representing the contractors Topf & Sons of Erfurt, was so proud of his incinerator system at Birkenau that he even had the gall formally to patent it.[51] 'From the chimneys shoot flames thirty feet into the air, visible for leagues around at night,' recalled a deportee from France, Paul Steinberg, 'and the oppressive stench of burnt flesh can be felt [sic] as far as [the synthetic-oil production facility of] Buna,' which was more than 3½ miles away. When bodies had to be burnt in open pits near by, either because the crematoria were working overtime or because they were being renovated through over-use, Höss recalled that 'The fires in the pits had to be stoked, the surplus fat drained off, and the mountain of burning corpses constantly turned over so that the draught might fan the flames.'[52] At the end of the war 7,500 inmates were liberated, of whom 600 were teenagers and children, mostly orphans who had no way even of discovering their own names.

At Auschwitz between 400 and 800 people could be packed into huts that had originally been designed for forty-two horses. Lice and fleas were endemic, although rats did not survive long because of the protein they provided. The standing cells in Prison Hut 11, which fitted four people at a time in a space 5 by 5 foot square, for up to ten days at a stretch, were used for starvation and suffocation, and the breaking of the human spirit, yet there were examples of great heroism and self-sacrifice. For example, Father Maksymilian Kolbe, a Roman Catholic priest from Warsaw, volunteered to take the place in a starvation cell of another Polish prisoner, Franciszek Gajowniczek, who had a wife and children. Of the ten in the cell, Kolbe was one of those still alive a fortnight later, and so was murdered by lethal injection.[53] He was canonized in 1982.

Viktor Frankl was an inmate of Türkheim, a satellite concentration camp of Dachau, between October 1944 and liberation in April 1945, where he was sent after a short stay at Auschwitz. 'I shall never forget how I was roused one night by the groans of a fellow prisoner,' he wrote,

who threw himself about in his sleep, obviously having a horrible nightmare. Since I had always been especially sorry for people who suffered from fearful dreams or deliria, I wanted to wake the poor man. Suddenly I drew back the hand that was ready to shake him, frightened at the thing I was about to do. At that moment I became intensely conscious of the fact that no dream, no matter how horrible, could be as bad as the reality of the camp which surrounded us, and to which I was about to recall him.[54]

It was true; for as Primo Levi put it: 'One wakes up at every moment, frozen with terror, shaking in every limb, under the impression of an order shouted out by a voice full of anger in a language not understood.'

The human nature of even the most noble people was warped in the struggle for existence. 'Only those prisoners could keep alive who . . . had lost all scruples in their fight for existence; they were prepared to use every means, honest and otherwise, even brutal force, theft, and betrayal of their friends, in order to save themselves,' recalled Frankl. 'The best of us did not return.'[55] Primo Levi, who somehow survived Auschwitz, likewise explained why it was useless to befriend the weak there, because 'one knows they are only here on a visit, that in a few weeks nothing will remain of them but a handful of ashes in some nearby field and a crossed-out name on a register.'[56] This was exemplified by a patient who was wheezing in one of the upper bunks near Levi in the camp hospital:

He heard me, struggled to sit up, then fell dangling, head downwards over the edge towards me, with the chest and arms stiff and his eyes white. The man in the bunk below automatically stretched up his arms to support the body and then realized he was dead. He slowly withdrew from under the weight and the body slid to the floor where it remained. Nobody knew his name.[57]

Anything approaching human dignity was next to impossible to retain; as Frankl recalled:

It was a favourite practice to detail a new arrival to a work group whose job it was to clean the latrines and remove the sewage. If, as usually happened, some of the excrement splashed into his face during its transport over bumpy fields, any sign of disgust by the prisoner or any attempt to wipe off the filth would only be punished by a blow from the *capo*. And thus the mortification of normal relations was hastened.[58]

It was because of experiences like this that another survivor, Elie Wiesel, later a Nobel laureate, was to say in 1983: 'Auschwitz defies perceptions and imaginations, it submits only to memory. Between the dead and the rest of us there exists an abyss that no talent can comprehend.'[59]

At the start of the Holocaust there was a good deal of confusion over the treatment of the people whom the Nazis eventually wished dead. At one moment Hitler wanted the Jews sent to south-east Poland, then it was earmarked as an area for *Lebensraum* for ethnic Germans to live in. Some German experts feared that allowing the Jews to die of starvation might mean that Germans might catch their diseases. Improvisation, rather than any solid blueprint, was the general rule, at least until a day-long conference held in a villa on the banks of Berlin's Lake Wannsee in January 1942. This did not inaugurate the Holocaust, as the mass killings at Auschwitz–Birkenau had been going on since the autumn. Nor was it simply a logistics meeting, as no railway or transport people were invited. Nor was it to discuss the fate of the *Mischlinge* (mixed blood) – such as half-Jews (who were to be vetted) and quarter-Jews (who were to be sterilized, if 'lucky') – although the last issue was indeed discussed. Instead its purpose was to place the thirty-seven-year-old Reinhard Heydrich, chief of the Security Police or SD, at the centre of the process, while also establishing undeniable collective responsibility. Afterwards, no department of the Reich could plead ignorance that genocide was official government policy, despite the sinister euphemisms employed in the circulated minutes, known as the Wannsee Protocol. These were not used at the meeting itself, however, for as Adolf Eichmann recorded in a 1961 memoir, 'one spoke openly, without euphemisms'. The historian of the conference Mark Roseman describes its Protocol as 'the most emblematic and programmatic statement of the Nazi way of doing genocide'.[60]

'Approximately 11 million Jews will be involved in the Final Solution of the European Jewish question,' the Protocol read, before listing every country where they were to be exterminated, from the Ukraine's 2,994,684 – the Nazis were nothing if not precise – down to the 200 who lived in Albania. Ireland's neutrality did not prevent Heydrich from adding her 4,000 Jews to the list, which is perhaps an indication of how seriously Nazi Germany would have taken Irish claims to sovereign independence in the event of their successful invasion of the rest of the British Isles. The Protocol also went into great detail about who exactly constituted a Jew, with paragraph 6 of section IV stating with regard to 'Marriages between Persons of Mixed Blood of the First Degree and Persons of Mixed Blood of the Second Degree' that 'Both partners will be evacuated or sent to an old-age ghetto without consideration of whether the marriage has produced children, since possible children will as a rule have stronger Jewish blood than the Jewish person of mixed blood of the second degree.'[61]

Genocide was industrialized rapidly after Wannsee, known at the time merely as the Conference of State Secretaries. The minutes of the meeting taken by Eichmann suggest that, although there were twenty-seven men present, Heydrich did at least three-quarters of the talking. Afterwards they drank brandy and smoked cigars. Wannsee, writes Roseman, was 'a signpost indicating that genocide had become official policy'. Before Wannsee, only 10 per cent of the total number of Jewish victims of Hitler had so far been killed, but in the next twelve months a further 50 per cent were liquidated. 'Not only did everybody willingly indicate agreement,' Eichmann testified in 1961, 'but there was something else, entirely unexpected, when they outdid and outbid each other, as regards the demand for a final solution to the Jewish question.' The experts discussed how the policy was to be carried out with minimum disruption to the war effort, and these bureaucrats were just as guilty as the medical orderlies who poured the Zyklon B crystals into the gas chambers. Conventional morality bypassed both sets of people, even though a majority of the state secretaries were cultured, educated men with academic doctorates who could hardly claim to have been desensitized by a brutal society. The Holocaust could not have been carried out without the willing co-operation of scientists, statisticians, demographers and social scientists supporting this 'radical experiment in social engineering', all operating in an utter moral vacuum. Here was an amoral caste of technocrats presenting learned papers that advocated 'population adjustments', the 'resettlement' of 'useless mouths' and the removal of 'inferior persons'.[62] It culminated in the *Generalplan-Ost*, a general plan for an eastern Europe populated according to Hitler's dream of German settler–farmer–warriors, with a servile workforce.

Although Hitler spoke ceaselessly of the two millennia of European civilization and culture that were threatened by the Jews, by far the most central aspect of that culture – indeed its *fons et origo* – was anathema to him. Goebbels recorded in his diary entry of 29 December 1939:

The Führer is deeply religious, though completely anti-Christian. He views Christianity as a symptom of decay. Rightly so. It is a deposit [*Ablagerung*] of the Jewish race. Both have no point of contact to the animal element, and thus, in the end, they will be destroyed. The Führer is a convinced vegetarian, on principle . . . He has little regard for *homo sapiens*. Man should not feel so superior to animals. He has no reason to.[63]

The destinies of Europe were therefore being run by a man who – when alone with his closest colleague – predicted that both Christianity and

Judaism 'will be destroyed' because of their lack of regard for animals, and who had 'little regard' for the human race. For those Christians who looked the other way during the Holocaust, or who tacitly supported it because of the supposed collective guilt of the Jews for the death of Christ – who was anyway crucified by Gentiles, in the shape of the Romans – there is some irony in the fact that, had Hitler prevailed, Christianity would eventually have faced its worst purges in Europe since the days of Ancient Rome. (As for Hitler's love of animals, some half a million horses died during his Operation Barbarossa.)

Himmler visited Auschwitz on 17 July 1942, telling SS officers openly that evening that the wholesale massacre of European Jewry was now Reich policy. Two days later he ordered the death of all Poland's Jews, with the exception of those few who were 'fit for work', who would be worked to the verge of death, and then gassed. 'The occupied Eastern zones are being cleansed of Jews,' wrote Himmler on 28 July. 'The Führer has laid the implementation of this very difficult order on my shoulders.' He certainly had an efficient and enthusiastic lieutenant in Reinhard Heydrich, whom Hitler called 'the man with the iron heart', meaning it as a term of praise. His victims called him 'the man with the icy stare'. His blond good looks, undoubted intelligence and utter fanaticism helped him to a position in the Third Reich whereby he might eventually have been Hitler's successor as the next Führer if he had survived and Germany had won the war.

Born in Halle of musical parents, and a gifted violinist himself, Heydrich was an able sportsman and seemingly model student. Yet, despite his cultured background, he joined the thuggish proto-Fascist organization the Freikorps in the 1920s, where he acquired a taste for street violence. In 1922, aged eighteen, he met the future spy chief Admiral Wilhelm Canaris, and through him joined the German Navy, rising to chief signals officer by 1930. Yet his naval career came to a sudden halt due to a sex scandal: he refused to marry the daughter of a steel magnate whom he had made pregnant, because he was engaged at the time to Lina von Ostau, whom he subsequently did marry. Dishonourably discharged in February 1931 for conduct unbecoming a German officer, Heydrich secured an interview, through Lina's help, with Heinrich Himmler, who had become head of the SS two years previously. Himmler was quickly impressed by Heydrich's cold efficiency, and offered him the chance to set up the SS's intelligence and security service, the Sicherheitsdienst (SD), which soon became feared for its utter ruthlessness.

In July 1934 Heydrich became a key figure in the Night of the Long Knives, thus bringing him to the admiring attention of both Hitler and Goebbels. By 1939, when the SD, Gestapo and Kripo (criminal police) were amalgamated as the Reichssicherheitshauptamt (RSHA), it was Heydrich who was appointed its first director. Hitler then entrusted him with creating the wholly invented 'border incident' at Gleiwitz which triggered the invasion of Poland. Once war had begun, Heydrich took charge of the brutal so-called housekeeping operations in Occupied Poland, with mass deportations of freezing victims in the dead of winter. After Germany had invaded Russia in June 1941, he was promoted to Obergruppenführer, and it was he who created the *Einsatzgruppen*.

Gaining the nickname the Hangman, Heydrich used the services of lieutenants such as Adolf Eichmann and Odilo Globocnik to kill the maximum numbers of Jews, and on 31 July 1941 he received written instructions from Göring to undertake the Final Solution. This was his prized chance to prove to the Führer that he rather than Himmler – whom he privately despised for weakness – would be the principal architect of the genocide programme. In September 1941, Hitler appointed Heydrich acting Reich protector of Bohemia and Moravia, that is dictator of the occupied Czech territories. Of course instead of 'protecting' anyone there, he ruled the region through torture and terror, sending hundreds of thousands to the concentration camps that he was busily converting into extermination centres. He soon earned the new soubriquet the Butcher of Prague.

On Wednesday, 27 May 1942, four British-trained Czech resistance fighters – Josef Valčik, Adolf Opálka, Jan Kubiš and Josef Gabčik – who had been parachuted into Czechoslovakia especially for the attempt, ambushed Heydrich's dark-green Mercedes at the bottom of the Kirchmayerstrasse in Prague. Although Gabčik's Sten gun jammed, Kubiš managed to hurl a grenade which blew a hole in the car's bodywork. The Czech anaesthetist who tended him recalled that

Heydrich's spleen had been punctured and his rib pierced by metal splinters and that horsehair from the car upholstery had entered his back on the left side above the diaphragm.[64] It took Heydrich seven days and twelve hours to die from septicaemia.

Heydrich received a state funeral in Berlin on 8 June; the city's Philharmonic Orchestra played a funeral march from Wagner's *Götterdämmerung* and Hitler laid a laurel wreath, although privately he blamed Heydrich's 'damned stupidity, which serves the country not one whit' for having driven publicly through the streets of Prague.[65] The four assassins of Heydrich were betrayed to the Germans, but none was captured alive, each fighting bravely to the death or committing suicide sooner than surrender. 'The Gestapo arranged for the identification of the dead in a particularly grue-some manner,' records Heydrich's biographer, 'the corpses being decapitated and the heads impaled on a stake, the relatives and friends then being invited to file past the display.'[66] It was a touch of which Heydrich would have been proud.

On the morning of 10 June 1942, units from the SD and Wehrmacht Field Police surrounded the mining village of Lidice, outside Prague. The entire population was rounded up. The 173 men and boys over the age of fifteen were shot there and then, and the 198 women and 98 children were taken off to extermination camps for subsequent execution. All the buildings in the village were burnt to the ground, and the village's name was erased from all records. Thirteen children were allowed to survive because they had blond hair; they were taken to Germany to be brought up as Aryans. In another village, Ležáky, seventeen men and sixteen women were shot and fourteen children gassed. An official statement was made to the effect that Lidice had been punished 'to teach the Czechs a final lesson of subservience and humility'.

At 06.00 hours on Monday, 19 April 1943, some 850 soldiers of the Waffen-SS entered the Warsaw Ghetto, intending first to 'evacuate' the remaining Jewish population there, and then to destroy it, under orders from Himmler. The Jews had been warned by the arrival of Ukrainian, Latvian and Lithuanian auxiliaries of what was about to happen, and the Żydowska Organizacja Bojowa (ŻOB, or Jewish combat organization) took up positions around the Ghetto, ready to make the SS pay as dearly as possible. The Ghetto Uprising came as a surprise to the Germans. On the first day they lost twelve killed as the ŻOB threw grenades and Molotov cocktails at their attackers, managing to set one tank alight. So serious a reverse was it that the chief of the SS in Warsaw was replaced, and SS-General Jürgen Stroop took over. 'The Jews and bandits defended themselves from one defence point to the next,' Stroop reported of one attack soon afterwards, 'and at the last minute escaped via attics or underground passages.'[67] It was to continue like that for nearly four weeks, as the SS and their auxiliary allies, as well as the German police and Wehrmacht and even the Jewish Ghetto police, had to fight hand to hand and street by street.

Vastly outnumbered in terms of fighters and outgunned in equipment, the Jews fought with a furious determination born of utter desperation, as Stroop slowly made his way into the centre of the Ghetto. 'One saw constant examples of how, despite the threat of fire, the Jews and bandits preferred to return into the flames than to fall into our hands,' Stroop reported to SS-Obergruppenführer Krüger in Kraków on 27 April. 'Yelling abuse at Germany and the Führer and cursing German soldiers, Jews hurl themselves from burning windows and balconies.'[68] The leader of the Uprising, Mordechai Anielewicz, and his closest comrades refused to surrender to the SS, which surrounded them in a bunker at 18 Mila Street; instead he and his comrades committed suicide on 8 May. Eight days later the Uprising reached its terrible denouement when at 8.15 p.m. on Sunday, 16 May Stroop blew up the Warsaw synagogue. By then he had captured or killed 55,065 Jews, and those Poles ('bandits') who had fought alongside them, who were executed on capture. Stroop had lost only sixteen men killed and eighty-four wounded, but Warsaw was a signal for Jewish resistance in Lvov, Częstochowa, Białystok and, on 2 August, even Treblinka and then twelve days later at Sobibór. With the huge preponderance of armaments enjoyed by the Germans, little useful militarily could be achieved, but much was won in terms of the pride of the Jewish people.

The deportation of Hungary's Jews to Auschwitz began in March 1944. SS-Obersturmbannführer (Lieutenant-Colonel) Adolf Eichmann led the special task force that deported 437,000 of them there over eight weeks. He later boasted to a crony that he would 'jump laughing into his grave' for his part in the deaths of four million Jews.[69] In a 1961 diary entry after his conviction in Israel of genocide, Eichmann wrote:

I saw the eeriness of the death machinery; wheel turning on wheel, like the mechanisms of a watch. And I saw those who maintained the machinery, who kept it going. I saw them, as they re-wound the mechanism; and I watched the second hand, as it rushed through the seconds; rushing like lives towards death. The greatest and most monumental dance of death of all time; this I saw.[70]

The trial and subsequent execution of Eichmann was very much the exception, however. The numbers of SS camp guards (*Lagerschützen*) at Auschwitz varied: very roughly in 1944 there were only 3,500 guarding the 110,000 inmates. There were also usually around 800 *Sonderkommando* prisoners at any one time. Out of the estimated 7,000 men and 200 women guards who served at Auschwitz during the war, only 800 were ever prosecuted. The rest merely disappeared into private life, and very many must have been able to escape with valuables stolen from the inmates. As the Russians advanced, Auschwitz was evacuated westwards in a terrible 'death march' of more than 50 miles in sub-zero temperatures. Those who could not keep up were shot and in all around 15,000 died. Nor was the horror over even when the camps were liberated. Despicably, Polish villagers even killed some Jews after the end of the war in Europe when they returned to reclaim their property, as happened at the village of Jedwabne.

The issue of whether the Allies ought to have bombed Auschwitz will long be with us. Although it was logistically possible by early 1944 – the USAAF and RAF were to supply the Polish Home Army during the Warsaw Uprising by air from Italy that summer – the decision was nonetheless taken not to bomb a camp that the Allies had known since 1942 was being used for the systematic extermination of Jews and Poles. While it was true that the unmarked underground gas chambers and crematoria might well have escaped, it is argued that it might have been possible to bomb the railway lines running to and from the camp, and would anyway have been worth the attempt. French railway lines, stations, depots, sidings and marshalling yards were principal targets during the pre-D-Day bombing operations, after all. The possibility of dropping arms to the inmates in the hope of an uprising, or even of landing paratroops there, was considered by the US War Refugee Board in its Weekly Report of 10 to 15 July 1944, but not passed on to the military.[71]

The fear of killing large numbers of inmates was a major consideration, of course, but a much more regularly used argument at the time was that the best way to help the Jews was to defeat the Germans as quickly as possible, for which the RAF and USAAF needed to bomb military and industrial targets instead. On 26 June 1944, the US War Department replied to a request from American Jewish organizations for the bombing of the Košice–Preskov railway line between Hungary and Auschwitz by saying that it 'fully appreciates the humanitarian importance of the suggested operation. However, after due consideration of the problem, it is considered that the most effective relief to the victims . . . is the early defeat of the Axis.'[72] By then the opportunity to save the remainder of Hungary's Jews had telescoped to only fifteen days, since all deportations were over by 9 July 1944 and photo-reconnaissance, weather analysis and operational planning would together have taken longer than that. Moreover, there were no fewer than seven separate railway lines which fed into the Lvov–Auschwitz route, of which Košice–Preskov was only one. (Auschwitz had initially been chosen precisely because it was a nodal point for eastern and southern-eastern European railway junctions.) 'Even if it had been successfully bombed,' concludes an historian of these various schemes to save the Hungarian Jews, 'Jews would simply have been transported over a different route.'[73] As the section covering the Holocaust in the modern Obersalzberg Documentation Centre's exhibition states above its entrance: *Alle Wege führen nach Auschwitz* (All roads lead to Auschwitz).

With the Allied Chiefs of Staff still concentrating on the aftermath of the Normandy invasion – Caen did not fall until 9 July – the bombing of Auschwitz was not likely to get high-level consideration. Nonetheless, the camp inmates – many of whom would have been killed – desperately wanted the camps to be bombed. When the nearby

IG Farben factory was attacked and forty Jews and fifteen SS were killed, the inmates inwardly celebrated, despite the nearly three-to-one ratio of deaths between oppressed and oppressor. The War Refugee Board officially called for the bombing of Auschwitz on 8 November 1944, drawing a comparison with the RAF Mosquito precision bombing of Amiens prison that February, during which 258 inmates had escaped, although 100 had died. By then it was almost too late, as the last gassings in the camp took place on 28 November, a mere twenty days later. With the autumn weather in southern Poland providing only patchy opportunities for bombing from bases many hundreds of miles away, good visibility was necessary for the kind of precision attacking that would be needed, very far removed from the kind necessary merely to bomb the nearby industrial plants. The post-war suggestion that de Havilland DH-98 Mosquito bombers should have attacked Auschwitz – no one came up with any such scheme during the war – has been exploded by a United States Air Force Historical Research Center archivist, Dr James H. Kitchens III, who has pointed out that 'flying over 620 miles in radio silence, crossing the Alps in some semblance of cohesion at low altitude, then sneaking through German air defenses with enough fuel to make a coordinated precision attack on five [gas chambers and crematoria] targets and return home beggars belief.'[74]

What might well have happened, given the inaccuracy of even so-called precision bombing – only 34 per cent of bombs dropped by the USAAF fell within a thousand feet of their targets – was that the gas chambers would have survived whereas thousands of innocents in the nearby huts would have perished. For this reason, some Jewish groups in Britain and America specifically opposed the bombing of the camps.[75] The decision not to attack was thus not a war crime, or a culpable moral failure – as some allege – nor even the dismal failure of the imagination that it might seem to modern eyes. For the past three decades aerial photographs of Auschwitz have been published which were taken by an Allied air crew on 25 August 1944 and which clearly show, once enlarged, the positions of the gas chambers and crematoria and even a line of people making their way to their deaths. It is therefore widely assumed that the Allied air forces could have destroyed the facilities with relative ease. In fact, however, these photographs were printed from the negatives for the first time only in 1978, and during the war the technology was not available to enlarge the photographs to the extent that the group of people would have been identifiable. The leading expert on Second World War photo-intelligence, Colonel Roy M. Stanley, has stated that 'This 1978 photo analysis contains an understanding and correlation of what was happening on the ground that would have been impossible for a 1945-vintage interpreter.'[76]

The supply of the Warsaw Uprising by air had been costly to the RAF: in twenty-two missions over six weeks to mid-August 1944, thirty-one out of 181 aircraft had failed to return. The British Foreign Office, as one of its officials minuted, was opposed to operations that 'would cost British lives and aircraft to no purpose'.[77] Various Foreign Office officials had reason to be ashamed of their notes on files, such as that of Armine Dew, who wrote of the Red Army's treatment of Romanian Jews in September 1944: 'In my opinion a disproportionate amount of the time of the Office is wasted on dealing with these wailing Jews.'[78] Nor was that an isolated example.

The American Assistant Secretary of War, John McCloy, rejected an appeal to bomb the gas chambers and crematoria on the grounds that it 'could only be executed by the diversion of considerable air support essential to the success of our forces now engaged in decisive operations elsewhere and would in any case be of such doubtful efficacy that it would not warrant the use of our resources'. Far less convincingly, McCloy also argued that any such action 'might provoke even more vindictive action by the Germans'.[79] The synthetic-oil and -rubber plant at Monowitz was bombed by the Fifteenth US Air Force on 20 August 1944, from Foggia in southern Italy, with the loss of only one out of 127 Flying Fortresses. Much damage was done, and the morale of the prisoners of Auschwitz–Birkenau was boosted, for as one of them, Arie Hassenberg, put it: 'We thought, they know all about us, they are making preparations to free us, we might escape, some of us might get out, some of us might survive.' He also declared: 'To see a killed German; that was why we enjoyed the bombing.'[80]

Rationality might have dictated that, once the war looked as if it might be lost, the rail, military and human resources put into the

Holocaust ought to have been immediately redirected to the military effort instead, and the Jews who could have been forced into contributing to the war effort ought to have been put to work rather than exterminated. Yet a quite separate, entirely Nazi, rationale argued that the worsening situation on the Eastern Front required if anything an intensification of the Holocaust, rather than a winding down. 'Whipping up anti-Jewish frenzy was, in Hitler's imagination,' writes Saul Friedländer, 'one of the best ways to hasten the falling apart of the enemy alliance,' because in his diseased imagination 'the Jews were the hidden link that kept Capitalism and Bolshevism together'.[81] Furthermore, if Fortress Europe was about to be invaded, the supposed domestic danger posed by the Jews needed to be eradicated as soon as possible.

Speaking at the Sportpalast on 18 February 1943, only days after Field Marshal Paulus' capitulation at Stalingrad, perhaps Germany's greatest single defeat of the war, Goebbels made a Freudian slip during his harangue against the supposed 'Jewish liquidation squads' that he claimed were stationed 'behind the onrushing Russian divisions' (a neat inversion of what the *Einsatzgruppen* had done behind the onrushing German divisions). 'Germany in any case has no intention of bowing to this threat,' Goebbels told his enormous, carefully chosen and wildly appreciative audience, 'but means to counter it in time and if necessary with the complete and radical extermin— [*Ausrott*—]' – he then corrected himself and said instead – 'elimination [*Ausschaltung*]'. This was greeted with applause, shouts of 'Out with the Jews' and laughter.[82] Broadcast live to tens of millions of Germans, the speech was Goebbels' best known, and was delivered under a huge banner stating: 'Totaler Krieg = Kürzester Krieg' (Total war = shortest war). Across the Reich, the man closest to Hitler could be heard hastily correcting 'Ausrottung' to 'Ausschaltung'. Germans took note.

Because Hitler did not spell out his thinking in regard to the relative importance of the Holocaust and victory on the Eastern Front, we can only surmise. It is not impossible that the reason that the Holocaust was intensified when defeat seemed likely, rather than halted as logic might imply – albeit to be reinstated after victory was won – goes to the heart of Hitler's view of his own place in history. Even if Germany lost the war, he believed, he would always be the man responsible for the complete extermination of the Jewish race in Europe. That would be his legacy to the *Volk*, even if the Allies managed to defeat the Reich. Putting his dream of a *Judenfrei* (Jew-free) world even before the need for victory was a measure of Hitler's fanaticism. He knew that German Jews had fought bravely for the Kaiser in the Great War, winning many Iron Crosses and producing impressive officers. Indeed it was largely down to the efforts of the Jewish adjutant of his own regiment, Second Lieutenant Hugo Gutman, that he received his own Iron Cross First Class. A Hitler who in 1933 had ditched anti-Semitism once he had come to power might have been able to harness millions of the brightest and the best-educated Europeans to the German war effort by 1939, including its award-winning nuclear scientists. A conservative nationalist German might possibly have achieved that, but Hitler's Nazism meant that he never wanted to.

8

Five Minutes at Midway

June 1942–October 1944

*Five minutes! Who would have dreamed that the tide of battle
would shift completely in that amount of time?*
Captain Mitsuo Fuchida and Commander
Masatake Okumiya of the Imperial Japanese Navy, 1955[1]

With the important exception of Burma, the next stage in the Allies'
war against Japan can be told largely in terms of aircraft carriers,
which became the key weapon in deciding whether the Japanese could
retain the sprawling empire they had won in the six months after Pearl
Harbor. Although the monsoon had halted the Japanese advance
towards India in May 1942 – at least for the time being – it was their
catastrophic loss of no fewer than four aircraft carriers at the battle
of Midway (to the Americans' one) the following month that evened
up the odds between Axis and Allies. Midway ended any hope of
Japan – whose carrier production lagged far behind that of the United
States – continuing her whirlwind progression in the east. Captain
Mitsuo Fuchida and Commander Masatake Okumiya subtitled their
1955 history of Midway *The Battle that Doomed Japan*; nor was this
unacceptable hyperbole.

The indecisive battle of the Coral Sea, fought 800 miles north-east
of Queensland on 7 and 8 May 1942, had resulted in the sinking of
the Japanese light carrier *Shoho*, which capsized after being hit by
thirteen bombs, seven torpedoes and a crashing dive-bomber, and of
the American carrier *Lexington*, which exploded two hours after the
last Japanese plane left, the victim of a spark from a generator that
was left running accidentally, with fires ignited by petrol fumes from

tanks ruptured in the attack. The evacuation of the *Lexington* was orderly and 2,735 crew members – over 90 per cent – survived. Two heavy Japanese carriers, the *Shokaku* and *Zuikaku*, were damaged, and so the plans to take Port Moresby in Papua New Guinea – from where Australia could be threatened – had to be abandoned. (Lieutenant James Powers won a posthumous Congressional Medal of Honor for bombing the *Shokaku*'s deck from only 300 feet, which along with his Dauntless dive-bomber comrades' efforts meant that aircraft could not land on it. As there was not enough room on *Zuikaku* for both carriers' aircraft, Japanese planes had to be physically manhandled over the side into the sea to make room. In all, 564 American sailors and airmen died and sixty-six aircraft were lost, compared to 1,074 Japanese and seventy-seven aircraft.[2] Crucially, the US carrier *Yorktown* had only been damaged in the battle rather than sunk, as Admiral Isoroku Yamamoto, the commander of the Japanese Combined Fleet, believed. He therefore assumed that his invasion of the atoll of Midway would not be opposed by American air power, and assembled 165 warships, the most powerful armada ever seen in the history of the Pacific Ocean, to take the island. With Midway in Japanese hands, Pearl Harbor could be bombed, and along with the Aleutian Islands, another part of the 'ribbon defence' of the Southern Resources Area could be protected.

Intelligence was key to the American victory at Midway, both the accurate and timely information that Admiral Chester W. Nimitz, the Commander-in-Chief in the Pacific, was given by his code-breakers, and the halting and inaccurate reports that Admirals Yamamoto and Nagumo got from their intelligence officers, who did not have the luxury of reading their enemy's signals. To make matters worse the Japanese failed to pool what little information they did have, partly because Nagumo's radio transmitter was weaker than Yamamoto's and partly because of the need for radio silence.[3] Nimitz knew that Nagumo had four aircraft carriers in service after the battle of the Coral Sea, with one damaged there and another stripped of aircraft, whereas Yamamoto did not know that Rear-Admiral Frank 'Jack' Fletcher had three carriers – *Enterprise*, *Hornet* and *Yorktown* – which by late May 1942 were stationed north of Midway. (It was estimated that it would take three months to repair the damage done to

Yorktown in the Coral Sea; it was miraculously achieved in forty-eight hours, a testament to American engineering efficiency and professional devotion.) In a sense the three islets of Midway, though only 2 square miles in size, themselves counted as a fourth – unsinkable – American aircraft carrier, with its complement of 109 planes.

Yamamoto split his invading force into three, which was an error as the squadrons were too far apart to support one another. As well as Nagumo's First Air Fleet, there was a Midway Occupation Force carrying 51,000 men, and his own main force comprising one carrier, four cruisers, seven battleships, twelve destroyers and eighteen submarines. As well as taking Midway, Yamamoto was hoping to lure the American Pacific Fleet into a massive engagement that it could not win. Nagumo's First Air Fleet approached the atoll under heavy cloud cover, masking it from Midway's reconnaissance planes, and was able to launch a dawn attack with 108 of its 201 planes. This was successful, although the runway was not attacked, as the Japanese wanted to use it as soon as they had captured the atoll. The ninety-three planes in the reserve were fitted with bombs and torpedoes in case of an appearance by the fifty-vessel American fleet. Through what Fuchida and Okumiya call 'a fantastic chapter of accidents and blunders', this was to be decisive.[4]

Having finally spotted Nagumo's fleet at 07.00 hours, Rear-Admiral Raymond Spruance, who commanded the *Enterprise* and *Hornet* battle group, sent 116 planes into an all-out attack from 175 miles away. (As in the battle of the Coral Sea, neither side's ships even came within sight of each other, in this new form of naval engagement.) At exactly the same time, Nagumo, having heard reports from Midway that another wave of attacks was needed, but nothing about the American fleet, which he had every reason to believe had sailed off north to deal with the diversionary attack against the Aleutian Islands, ordered his ninety-three reserve planes to be refitted with incendiary and fragmentation bombs. The change-over would take an hour to carry out, yet only fifteen minutes into the job a reconnaissance plane reported ten American ships to the north-east. 'For a *mauvais quart d'heure* he pondered the problem, and then decided to re-arm his reserve aircraft with torpedoes. Order; counter-order; disorder.'[5] Meanwhile, his first wave of bombers and fighters were on their way back from Midway. It was a pivotal moment in the war in the Pacific. With half of his reserve planes loaded with ordnance to attack Midway and the other half armed to attack the American carriers, Nagumo took the fateful decision to land his Midway first-strike planes before launching the others.

While the flight crews on the carriers were therefore struggling to detach the incendiary and fragmentation bombs and reattach the torpedoes, at 09.05 Nagumo turned 90 degrees east-north-east to engage the American task force. This had the effect of allowing him to evade, for the moment, the US dive-bombers and fighters from the *Hornet*, which had launched her planes at 07.00. *Yorktown*, to the east, launched half her planes at 07.30. Fifteen Devastator torpedo-bombers from the *Hornet* did spot Nagumo's force, and went straight into the attack. Much is made of the fanatical courage of the Japanese *kamikaze* (divine wind) airmen later on in the war, but to have flown unescorted into the anti-aircraft guns and Zeke fighters of Nagumo's fleet took tremendous bravery, and only one of the fifteen survived, with no hits scored. The torpedo-bombers of the *Enterprise* (nick-named 'the big E') and *Yorktown* were also badly mauled without any positive results, and at 10.24 hours the attack was broken off with only eight Devastators still in the air out of an initial attacking force of forty-one. 'For about one hundred seconds the Japanese were certain they had won the battle of Midway,' wrote the US Navy's official historian Rear-Admiral Samuel Eliot Morison, 'and the war.'[6]

Yet at 10.26, before the Zekes had time to regain altitude after devastating the Devastators, thirty-seven dive-bombers from the *Enterprise* appeared directly above Nagumo's four carriers. Cloud cover at 3,000 feet masked the American approach, but below that the visibility was ideal for the attackers. The hero of Pearl Harbor, Mitsuo Fuchida, believed that because the Japanese fighters had no time to regain altitude while they were shooting the US torpedo planes out of the sky, 'It may be said that the Americans' dive-bombers' success was made possible by the earlier martyrdom of their torpedo planes.'[7] Soon after the *Enterprise* dive-bombers attacked, planes from first the *Hornet* and then the *Yorktown* arrived. Thousands of feet below, the crews were still changing the bombers' armaments, and so were caught with the maximum amount of ordnance in the most exposed place possible. The carriers' decks were strewn with bombs, fuel and planes, with little stowed away, so when *Enterprise*'s dive-bombers hit the result was carnage. On board Nagumo's flagship, the *Akagi*, Zero fighters were just beginning to be launched. Fuchida, who could not fly at Midway because he had recently had his appendix out, and who was then wounded during the attack, recalled that:

[as] the first Zero fighter gathered speed and whizzed off the deck, at that instant a lookout screamed 'Hell-divers!' I looked up to see three black planes plummeting towards our ship. Some of our machine-guns managed to fire a few frantic bursts at them, but it was too late. The plump silhouettes of the American Dauntless dive-bombers quickly grew larger, and then a number of black objects suddenly floated eerily from their wings. Bombs! Down they came straight at me![8]

Akagi took two direct hits, the first on the aft rim of the amidship lift, the second on the port side of the flight deck, the effects of which might have been controlled if the deck had not been wing-tip to wing-tip full of burning planes loaded with exploding torpedoes. 'The entire hangar area was a blazing inferno,' wrote Fuchida, 'and the flames moved swiftly towards the bridge.' By 10.46 Nagumo – who had made one of the worst decisions in military history – was persuaded to transfer his flag to the light cruiser *Nagara*, which he did with reluctance. Below decks on the *Akagi*, survivors had to use hand-pumps and:

Fire-fighting parties, wearing gas masks, carried cumbersome pieces of equipment and fought the flames courageously. But every explosion overhead penetrated to the deck below, injuring men and interrupting their desperate efforts. Stepping over fallen comrades, another damage-control party would dash in to continue the struggle, only to be mown down by the next explosion.[9]

Not a single man from the engine room escaped from this Dantean hell. The ship was abandoned at 18.00 hours, except for Captain Taijiro Aoki, who lashed himself to an anchor 'to await the end'.

'We had been caught flat-footed in the most vulnerable position possible,' wrote Fuchida and Okimiya, 'decks loaded with planes armed and fuelled for an attack.'[10] Meanwhile, the aircraft carrier

Kaga slipped beneath the waves at 19.25, with 800 of her crew dead, and another carrier, *Soryu*, which had suffered three hits from thirteen planes in three minutes, sank at 21.13, with her captain Ryusaku Yanagimoto singing the 'Kimigayo', the Japanese national anthem. Nagumo ordered the fourth carrier, *Hiryu*, to sail off north-eastwards and send forty planes to attack *Yorktown* and, although only seven made it through the American defences, they were able, with 'skill, gallantry and determination', to land three bombs on her. Later on *Yorktown* was also hit by two torpedoes from planes returning from Midway, forcing the listing carrier to be taken in tow and set off back to Pearl Harbor and Fletcher to transfer to the cruiser *Astoria*, with Spruance taking over tactical command.[11] *Hiryu* was not going to escape retribution, however, for at 17.00 hours twenty-four planes from *Enterprise* and *Yorktown* sank her with four hits. On the way back to Pearl Harbor, *Yorktown* and an escorting destroyer were sunk by the Japanese submarine *I-168*, the only American vessels that were lost in the entire battle.

Midway between Japan and mainland America geographically, and coming almost midway during the Second World War (in the thirty-third of a seventy-one-month war), the battle wrecked the three-phase Japanese plan for Asian domination midway through its second phase. It was true that the two minuscule Aleutian Islands of Attu and Kiska had been captured by the northern diversionary force, but because of Allied code-breaking, that attack had failed to divert American forces away from Midway. The battle of Midway deserves its attribution as one of the most decisive battles of history, because against the American losses of one aircraft carrier and a destroyer, 307 men killed and 132 planes lost, the Japanese lost four aircraft carriers, a heavy cruiser, 3,500 men – including many experienced pilots – and 275 planes.[12] It was true that after Midway the Japanese still had five aircraft carriers in commission, with six being built or repaired, but by contrast the Americans had three large carriers, and no fewer than thirteen under construction. 'Until late 1943,' records an historian of the Pacific War, 'the US Pacific Fleet never possessed more than four aircraft carriers. Thereafter, however, American strength soared, while that of Japan shrank.'[13] The United States could now attack the perimeters of the Southern Resources Area at will. 'Midway was the most crucial battle of the Pacific War,' Nimitz was to conclude, 'the engagement that made everything else possible.'[14]

The British also took great heart from the victory. With the news only just starting to come in, Churchill told the War Cabinet, as noted by an assistant in the secretariat:

Losses at sea signs of fear on part of Japs – the Navy is a political force in Japan – which will perhaps be more inclined to a restrictive and cautious policy – this policy be in harmony with sending out submarine raiders – if we think of this as having an effect on the Japanese situation – think they will go for China and Chiang Kai Shek conquest. I don't think they'll try India or Australia. This gives us 2 or 3 months breathing-space. We must come to rescue of China – it would be an appalling disaster if China were forced out of the war – and a new government set up. The General Staff must think of attacking lines of communication in Burma. If carrier losses confirmed – review consequences of diminution of enemy forces. If Japan adopts conservative course it is a chance for us to get teeth into her tail.[15]

*

Midway made possible the landing on 7 August 1942 of US forces on the island of Guadalcanal in the southern Solomon Islands, the first offensive land operation undertaken by the Americans since Pearl Harbor nine months previously. Once it was known that the Japanese were attempting to build a runway there, which would have had the effect of interdicting air traffic between the United States and Australia, 18,700 men of the Marine Corps 1st Division under Major-General Alexander A. Vandergrift made an amphibious landing on Guadalcanal and also the nearby islands of Tulagi and Gavuth. Taken by surprise, the Japanese garrison of Guadalcanal fled into the thick jungle of the 'steamy, malaria-ridden, rain-sodden island', while 1,500 of them put up stiff resistance on Tulagi, but were almost all killed, at the cost of 150 Marines.[16] Having taken the runway on 8 August, which they named Henderson Field after a hero of the battle of Midway, the 11,145 Marines on Guadalcanal threw up a defensive perimeter of 2 by 4 miles, and dug in. That tiny area was about to receive a battering equal to any similarly sized battlefield in American history.

As the Marines were still bringing equipment ashore for Operation

Cactus, disaster overcame their naval escort when a Japanese force from Rabaul made a night attack, in what became known as the battle of Savo Island. Armed with new, liquid-oxygen-propelled Long Lance torpedoes which could carry a 1,000-pound warhead at 37 knots for up to 25 miles, the Japanese slipped past Captain Howard D. Bode's patrol south of the island – Bode was asleep in his bunk in the USS *Chicago* at the time – and attacked the cruisers under the command of the Australian Rear-Admiral Victor Crutchley VC, who was himself ashore on Guadalcanal. Four cruisers – the American *Vincennes*, *Astoria* and *Quincy* and the Australian *Canberra* – were sunk, as they and the *Chicago* were lit up by flares dropped by Japanese planes. (A guilt-stricken Bode later shot himself, proving that the Japanese had not entirely monopolized the honourable tradition of *hara-kiri*.)[17]

With more than a thousand Allied sailors dead, Crutchley's stricken flotilla was forced to leave the environs of Guadalcanal, from which Fletcher had already removed the aircraft carriers *Saratoga*, *Wasp* and *Enterprise* after losing twenty-two fighters out of ninety-eight. This meant that the Japanese based at Rabaul had an opportunity to reinforce the island and attempt to fling the Americans off it. The Henderson Field bridgehead was subjected to day and night bombardment from Japanese naval vessels as well as aerial bombing from Rabaul, and on one day – Dugout Sunday – there were no fewer than seven air raids. The Cactus Air Force of nineteen fighters and twelve torpedo-bombers of the 23rd Marine Air Group did what they could, but until they were reinforced they could not protect the airfield adequately. On 17 August Lieutenant-General Haruyoshi Hyakutake landed from Rabaul with 50,000 men of the Seventeenth Army to attack on the ground. Rear-Admiral Razio Tanaka also began a series of landings of men and supplies along the Slot, a channel of islands between Rabaul and Guadalcanal, in a six-month series of often night-time operations nicknamed the Tokyo Express by the Marines who found themselves on its painful receiving end.

Instead of attacking simultaneously, which was difficult to do in the light of his lack of reinforcements, Hyakutake sent in assaults on Henderson Field piecemeal, which in desperate fighting the Marines managed to fight off and occasionally to counter-attack. In the battle of Tenaru River (which was actually fought on the Ilu river), Colonel

Kiyono Ichiki's attack of 917 men ended on 18 August with the loss of almost every man in the unit. Ichiki himself burnt the regimental standard and committed *hara-kiri*. On 12 and 13 September, during the hard-fought battle of Bloody Ridge, a mile to the south-west of the airfield, the Japanese got to within 1,000 yards of the runway. Yelling 'Banzai!' (One thousand years!) and 'Marine, you die!', 2,000 Japanese rushed out of the jungle and overwhelmed the right flank of Lieutenant-Colonel Merritt A. 'Red Mike' Edson's Provisional Force of two battalions. Three Japanese even got inside Vandergrift's bunker, where they were killed by his clerks. Edson won the Congressional Medal of Honor for his valiant defence, in which 143 Americans were killed and 117 wounded, but 600 Japanese were killed and 500 wounded.

Although the Marines were finally reinforced by air on 20 August, Hyakutake received reinforcements via the Tokyo Express throughout September and October, and between 23 and 25 October his assaults were flung back with 2,000 killed against 300 American killed and wounded. After that Vandergrift felt he could expand the perimeter, and go on the offensive.[18] Although malaria in the fetid conditions badly affected the American forces, the Japanese were hit by malaria and severe hunger too, and once the US Navy had won a four-day battle off the island on 15 November – the last of seven major naval engagements in the six-month campaign – the Japanese were reduced to releasing drums of supplies from passing destroyers, hoping they would float ashore and be retrieved.

On 8 December, a year and a day after Pearl Harbor, Vandergrift, 'the Hero of Guadalcanal', and his Marines were finally relieved by Major-General Alexander M. Patch's US Army regulars, who forced the Japanese, in a 'desperate and well-conducted rearguard action', back to Cape Esperance in the east of the island, from where 13,000 of them, including Hyakutake, were miraculously evacuated by night on 9 February 1943 by Tanaka's Transport Group.[19] They were the lucky ones; Japanese left in the interior of Guadalcanal looted native villages to survive, and so 'The islanders exacted terrible revenge, and Japanese heads decorated the native long-houses for years afterwards.'[20] In the entire land campaign, the Japanese had lost 25,000 dead and 600 planes, the Americans 1,490 killed and 4,804 wounded.

Both sides lost twenty-four ships, but the Japanese far more tonnage. The first rung of the 'Solomons ladder' had been successfully trodden, and the Americans would now move north. Most importantly, though, just as Midway had proved that the Imperial Japanese Navy was far from invincible, Guadalcanal showed the same for the Imperial Japanese Army. In all 103,000 American lives were to be lost defeating Japan, as well as 30,000 British, Indian, Australian and Commonwealth. Guadalcanal was to be the first of several stations on a *via dolorosa* whose names – such as Kwajalein, Tarawa, Saipan, Guam, Luzon, Iwo Jima and Okinawa – are 'written in blood into American history'.[21]

The onset of the monsoon in May 1942 had halted the Japanese advance into India, and Commonwealth attempts to attack in the Arakan and retake Akyab came to naught in 1942 and 1943, so the British resorted to a new type of warfare for their forces in Burma in 1943: long-range penetration jungle fighting. This innovative strategy was the brainchild of one of the most glamorous, unconventional and controversial figures of the war: Brigadier (later Major-General) Orde Wingate. Churchill called him 'this man of genius who might well have become a man of destiny' and likened him to Wingate's relation Lawrence of Arabia, who had been a friend of Churchill's.

The Chindits, Wingate's British, Indian and Gurkha troops of the 77th Indian Brigade, fought deep behind Japanese lines in northern Burma. The heavy losses they suffered, on occasion having to abandon their wounded, makes Wingate's military legacy something that historians continue to debate.[22] There is disagreement over how the name Chindit originated; some believe it came from Wingate's mishearing of the Burmese word for lion, *chinthe*, others that it was after a figure of Hindu mythology, others after the Burmese word for griffin. Whatever its genesis, the force soon found great popularity with the British public, which appreciated the high courage shown in spending long periods of time operating far behind enemy lines.

Wingate could be unscrupulous, especially in leapfrogging senior officers by using his access to his admirer Churchill, and he made a fair number of enemies in the Fourteenth Army in building up his command from a brigade to a division, but for all the sometimes bitter criticisms of him he was undoubtedly one of the true originals. On 31 August 1940, lunching at the War Office, 'He said he had acquired quite a taste for boiled python, which tasted like chicken,' the Director of Military Operations Major-General John Kennedy recorded. 'His men kept remarkably fit – he thought chiefly because they knew they would fall into the hands of the Japanese if they didn't. He is a man of great character, a good talker and a very good writer too.'[23] A manic depressive who tried to commit suicide by cutting his throat with a knife in a hotel in Cairo in 1941 after the Ethiopian campaign; a nudist who frequently wore only a pith helmet and carried a fly-whisk in camp; someone who never bathed but instead cleaned himself by vigorous scrubbing of his body with a stiff brush, Wingate ate raw onions for pleasure and has been described as a 'neurotic maverick' and a 'foul-tempered, scruffily dressed egomaniac'.

Born in India when his father was fifty-one, Wingate was raised a strict Nonconformist, who was thus excused chapel at Charterhouse. He came sixty-third out of sixty-nine candidates entering the Royal Military Academy Woolwich in 1921, and hardly shone there either, graduating fifty-ninth out of seventy. It was actual experience of guerrilla warfare in Palestine and Ethiopia that convinced Wingate that a small force could wage a new type of long-range penetration warfare beyond the Chindwin river. 'If you're in the Army you have to do something extraordinary to be noticed,' he once said. He certainly achieved that in his comparatively short life. When fighting the Italians in Ethiopia and the Sudan or Arab terrorists in Palestine – Wingate was an ardent Zionist – or indeed the Japanese, Wingate often found himself also ranged against the British military High Command, who tended deeply to distrust his unconventional methods. He struck his own men in both the Sudan and Palestine, hardly adding to his popularity. Yet as the writer Wilfred Thesiger, who served under him, pointed out, the defeat of 40,000 Italian-led troops by two battalions of Ethiopians and Sudanese could have been achieved only with Wingate in command.

There were two separate Chindit expeditions, with many lessons learnt in 1943 that were put into operation in 1944. Their training in India was comprehensive, with bayonet practice at 6 a.m. followed by unarmed combat, jungle-craft lectures, use of the compass, map-reading, two hours of fatigues in the afternoon, latrine-building and jungle-clearing with machetes. On exercise the Chindits would concentrate on blowing up bridges, disabling airfields and especially staging ambushes. Brigadier Michael Calvert, one of Wingate's key lieutenants, later stated of this regime: 'Most Europeans do not know what their bodies can stand; it is the mind and willpower which so often give way first. Most soldiers never realized that they could do the things they did . . . One advantage of exceptionally heavy training is that it proves to a man what he can do and suffer. If you have marched thirty miles in a day, you can take twenty-five miles in your stride.'[24]

In the first Chindit sally, Operation Longcloth, Wingate crossed the Chindwin into Japanese-occupied northern Burma on the night of 13 February 1943 with 3,000 men. Using mules for transportation and air drops for supplies, he marched 500 miles in order to harass the Japanese and cut their rail links. Wingate's Order of the Day stated:

Today we are on the threshold of battle. The time of preparation is over and we are moving on the enemy to prove ourselves and our methods . . . The battle is not always to the strong, nor the race to the swift. Victory in war cannot be counted on, but what can be counted on is that we shall go forward determined to do what we can to bring this war to an end . . . Knowing the vanity of Man's effort and the confusion of his purpose, let us pray that God may accept our service and direct our endeavours, so that when we shall have done all we shall see the fruit of our labours and be satisfied.[25]

On 18 February the Chindits succeeded in cutting the railway link between Mandalay and Myitkyina for four weeks. Thousands of Japanese were being diverted from other operations, especially against China, to try to swat the small force. Then, on 6 March, the Chindits blew up three important railway bridges in the Bongyaung region. On 15 March two Chindit columns, under Calvert and Major Bernard Fergusson (later Lord Ballantrae), crossed the Irrawaddy river with plans to destroy the strategic Gokteik Gorge railway viaduct. The east bank of the Irrawaddy, however, with its lack of adequate cover, made it much more difficult to operate there than in the jungle on the west side of the river. Although they were successfully supplied by air occasionally, food and sustenance were limited and constant forced marches burnt up energy. The fighting was fierce, too, and almost always against heavy odds. By 26 March only three-quarters of the Chindits were left of the original 3,000-strong force, of whom 600 were badly emaciated. With three Japanese divisions advancing on them, they moved north towards India and eventual escape, crossing back over the Chindwin in the second half of April 1943. Before they returned, however, they set an ambush for the enemy in which a hundred Japanese were killed at the cost of one Chindit.

The fighting the Chindits had to undertake, and the appalling conditions they had to contend with in the jungle, made their two expeditions among the great military feats of the Second World War. A passage from Fergusson's war diary for his column dated 30 March 1943 underlines the harshness of the situation by the end of the first expedition:

Party now consists of 9 officers, 109 other ranks, of which 3 officers, 2 other ranks wounded. All weak and hungry in varying degrees. Addressed all ranks and told them: (a) only absolute discipline would get us out. I would shoot anybody who pilfered comrades or villages, or who grumbled (b) Anybody who lost his rifle or equipment I would expel from the party, unless I was satisfied with the excuse (c) Only chance was absolute trust and implicit obedience (d) No stragglers.[26]

Sentries who fell asleep could expect to wake up to a flogging.

For some of the wounded or simply exhausted men, the last 80-mile trek back to safety was simply too much. Sergeant Tony Aubrey of 8 Column recalled how one soldier, 'whose feet were in a very bad state, made up his mind he could go no further. He lay down. His mates, worn out as they were, tried to carry him. But he wouldn't allow them to. All he wanted was to be left alone with as many hand grenades as we could spare. So we gave him the hand grenades and left him. There wasn't anything else to do.' Stragglers got back as best they could. 'At first we worried about him,' Aubrey said of one such. ' "How's so-and-so making out?" we asked each other. But after a time we forgot him. He was just another piece of landscape. This may sound like man's inhumanity to man, but it wasn't you know. We were just too tired to care.'[27] Wingate himself, wearing the same corduroy trousers he had worn throughout the expedition, which were slashed to ribbons and his legs streaming with blood, swam back across the Chindwin. Once in camp he told the press that he was 'quite satisfied with the results. The expedition was a complete success.'

Of the 3,000 officers and men who crossed the Chindwin on 13 February, 2,182 were safely back in India by the first week in June. Nearly all the mules were dead, and most of the equipment had been lost or destroyed. The Japanese had killed 450 Chindits; 120 Burmese had been permitted to remain in the jungle, and most of the rest were taken prisoner. The 17th Battalion the King's Liverpool Regiment lost more than one-third of its complement. Fergusson's own estimation was that they had achieved:

not much that was tangible. What there was became distorted in the glare of publicity soon after our return. We blew up bits of railway, which did not take long to repair; we gathered some useful Intelligence; we distracted the Japanese from some minor operations, and possibly from some bigger ones; we killed a few hundreds of an enemy which numbers eighty millions; we proved that it was feasible to maintain a force by supply dropping alone.[28]

Yet the three-month expedition also proved that Allied troops could survive in the jungle just as well as could the Japanese, an important psychological factor. The first expedition therefore helped to dissolve the myth of the invincible Japanese superman, a necessary precursor to building up the morale necessary for eventual victory. The raid had nonetheless been very costly, and several regular soldiers questioned the value of the Chindits' incursions into the Japanese strongholds of Pinbon, Mongmit and Mianyang. Wingate was taken by Churchill as a prize exhibit (along with the leader of the daredevil Dambusters bombing raid Wing Commander Guy Gibson) to the Quebec Conference in August 1943, where he persuaded both Churchill and Roosevelt that light infantry brigades properly supplied from the air could fight hundreds of miles behind enemy lines, cutting lines of communication, creating mayhem, drawing off troops from the front line and generally, in his words, 'stirring up a hornets' nest'. It was therefore decided that the Chindits should be launched on a second expedition in the spring, only this time with treble the forces.

On 5 March 1944, three Chindit brigades comprising over 9,000 men and 1,000 mules launched Operation Thursday, entering Burma in three separate places, with some landing by glider deep behind Japanese lines. This was far more ambitious than Longcloth had been, and was intended to cut off the Japanese Army of Upper Burma, threatening its rear as it marched towards the Imphal Plain. It was also hoped to cut the communications of the Japanese forces fighting against the Chinese armies in Burma under the effective command of Chiang Kai-shek's chief of staff, the American Lieutenant-General Joseph 'Vinegar Joe' Stilwell. A fourth Chindit brigade had already set off the previous month on an exhausting land route from the Naga Hills, across the Chindwin and over precipitous, 6,000-foot mountain ranges.

Within ten days of its launch, Calvert's 77th Brigade succeeded in taking Mawlu, cutting Japanese road and rail links and getting his 'strongholds' supplied by air. Unfortunately Fergusson's 16th Brigade, after a fatiguing overland march from Ledo that was to take over a month, was unable to capture the Japanese supply base at Indaw. Wingate's Order for the Day for 13 March 1944 nonetheless read:

Our first task is fulfilled. We have inflicted a complete surprise on the enemy. All our columns are inside the enemy's guts. The time has come to reap the fruit of the advantage we have gained. The enemy will react with violence. We will oppose him with the resolve to conquer our territory of Northern Burma. Let us thank God for the great success He has vouchsafed us and we must press forward with our sword in the enemy's ribs to expel him from our territory. This is not the moment, when such an advantage has been gained, to count the cost. This is a moment to live in history. It is an enterprise in which every man who takes part may feel proud one day to say 'I was there.'[29]

Tragically, an air crash at Imphal on 24 March killed the forty-one-year-old Wingate, who had possibly been warned by the RAF that sudden rainstorms made flying too dangerous at that time. 'He died as he had lived,' concludes one account of his campaigns, 'ignoring official advice.' Other accounts vigorously deny this, claiming that the weather and flying conditions were not as treacherous as has been made out. Like much else about his life, his death is surrounded with mystery and controversy.

On 9 April the Chindits were reinforced by hundreds of extra troops flown in by glider in a daring operation. The conditions they faced were horrendous: monsoon rain that could turn a foxhole into something approaching a Passchendaele trench in minutes; constant attacks of diarrhoea, malaria and any number of other tropical diseases; ingenious booby-traps and the ever present fear of them; highly accurate enemy mortar and sniper-fire; inaccurate maps; leeches; bad communications; reliance on village rumours for intelligence; sick and obstinate mules; low-nutrition food and bad water; mile upon mile of thick jungle in which it could take an hour to cut through 100 yards; the abandonment of the wounded and stragglers. These are the factors in Chindit warfare that crop up time and again in the memoirs of the survivors.[30]

George MacDonald Fraser, who was not a Chindit but who did serve in Burma, explained what it was like when two men of his section died in a jungle skirmish:

There was no outward show of sorrow, no reminiscences or eulogies, no Hollywood heart-searchings or phoney philosophy . . . It was not callousness or indifference or lack of feeling for two comrades who had been alive that morning and were now names for the war memorial; it was just that there was nothing to be said. It was part of war; men died, more would die, that was past, and what mattered now was the business in hand; those who lived would get on with it. Whatever sorrow was felt, there was no point in talking or brooding about it, much less in making, for form's sake, a parade of it. Better and healthier to forget it, and look to tomorrow.[31]

Much the same would have gone for the Germans, Russians, Americans or Japanese. War is war and its personal, human element has changed remarkably little over the centuries.

One problem that the Chindits had, as well as the enemy and the terrible conditions, was the fact that the US commander in China, General Stilwell, considered them to be merely 'shadow-boxing' and a waste of time and effort. Yet on 27 June, Mike Calvert, by then a brigadier, took Mogaung with his Chindit 77th Special Force Brigade supported by two Chinese battalions. After fighting for Mogaung for an entire month, Calvert's force, once 800 strong, was down to 230 Gurkhas, 110 1st Lancashire Fusiliers and 1st Battalion the King's

Liverpool Regiment and 180 1st Battalion South Staffordshire men. They nonetheless took the key railway bridge, and thus cut off the Japanese 18th Division fighting against Stilwell.

Acts of individual bravery were commonplace. One case was that of Captain Jim Blaker of the 3rd Battalion 9th Gurkha Rifles who had taken more than five hours to climb up to the summit of Point 2171 outside Kamaing, only to find it ringed with mortars and machine guns, which scattered his small force back into the thick jungle. 'Come on C Company!' cried Blaker, who charged forward until hit in the stomach by machine-gun bullets. 'I'm going to die,' he called out as he expired. 'Take the position!'[32] The Gurkhas rose as one with fixed bayonets and kukri knives and captured the hillside. (They did not have the strength afterwards to bury him and his dead comrades, however, and three months later a Graves Registration Unit found tall bamboo growing through their skeletons, by which time Blaker had been awarded the Victoria Cross.)

The human cost of the Chindit operations was very high, but after the war Lieutenant-General Renya Mutaguchi, commander of the Japanese Fifteenth Army in northern Burma in 1943, stated that: 'The Chindit invasions did not stop our plans to attack [India], but they did have a decisive effect on these operations and they drew off the whole of 53rd Division and parts of 15th Division, one regiment of which would have turned the tables at [the coming battle of] Kohima.' Disgracefully, the *Official History*, written by Major-General S. W. Kirby, who shared the High Command's distaste for Wingate, published only the part of that sentence up to the first comma.

The last Chindits left Burma on 27 August 1944. Half were admitted to hospital on their return, but after rest and special diets the formation – once reinforced – began training for its third operation before it was officially disbanded in February 1945. The Chindits left an example of human endurance extraordinary even for a conflict such as the Second World War.

Western accounts of the war often minimize, to the point of sometimes ignoring it altogether, the experience of China, despite the fact that fifteen million of those who died in the conflict – a full 30 per cent – were Chinese. It was the Chinese who held down half of Japan's fighting strength throughout the war, and around 70 per cent of the effort was undertaken by the Kuomintang (Nationalist) forces under their generalissimo, Chiang Kai-shek, based at Chunking. By contrast the Communists under Mao Zedong were, as Max Hastings has put it, at best merely 'an irritant' to Japan.[33] The Chinese experience of war was terrible: in the great starvation caused by the Japanese, Chinese people 'hunted ants, devoured tree roots, ate mud'. In December 1937 the Japanese Army massacred 200,000 civilians and raped a further 20,000 women after the fall of Nanking. Yet the Chinese somehow stayed in the war, with the result that Japan had to divert vast forces to fighting in the interior of China, which she could otherwise have dedicated to the invasion of India, or Australia, or both.

China had been at war with Japan since 1937, and in the two years after the fall of Nanking, Chiang Kai-shek's capital, that December the Japanese established control across much of China's eastern seaboard, including many of her industrial centres. Russian support for the Kuomintang ended with the Russo-Japanese neutrality pact of April 1941, Japanese air superiority was near total, and the Communists would attack Chiang's forces as readily as Japan's. The Nationalists therefore fought a hand-to-mouth campaign until significant support began arriving from the United States after Pearl Harbor. Even then, the fall of Burma in 1942 meant that the overland route for supplies was cut off, and they instead had to be flown over the Hump of the Himalayas. After Operation Torch, the Allied invasion of North Africa in November 1942, US warplanes were withdrawn from Chiang, even though he was desperate for them. In any Allied allocation list, the Chinese, who had been forced back into Yunnan province by 1943, always seemed to come at the bottom.

It was, as so often and over so many theatres in the war, to be air power that made the difference, in this case the China Air Task Force (USAAF Fourteenth Air Force) under Major-General Claire L. Chennault. With the ear of FDR but having to fight running administrative battles against General Stilwell, Chennault achieved much in China, albeit with minimal resources stretched to capacity and beyond. At the end of the war, Chiang was badly positioned to take on the Communists, but he had done the Allies a great – and largely unreciprocated – service by tying down more than one million Japanese soldiers for four years, who therefore could not be used elsewhere. The Chinese had not defeated the Japanese by August 1945, but they had remained in the field, which for a country the size of China was all that was necessary to force the Japanese to expend huge resources trying to defeat them.

In January 1944 the Imperial Headquarters in Tokyo authorized Operation U-Go, a Japanese invasion of India under the command of Lieutenant-General Mutaguchi, hoping to forestall General Slim's own advance into Burma, to close the Burma Road to China and, through the use of Subhas Chandra Bose's Indian National Army, possibly to spark off a revolt against British rule in India. Of the 316,700 Japanese troops in Burma in March 1944, three divisions – the 33rd, 15th and 31st – were earmarked for the task, along with the (anti-British) Indian National Army, numbering more than 100,000 troops in all.[34] Owing to a lack of supplies and a relative weakness in air power, Mutaguchi depended on surprise and an early capture of the gigantic arms, food and ammunition depot at Imphal, the capital of the Manipur province. From there he hoped to march via the village of Kohima to capture Dimapur, which boasted a vast supply dump (11 miles by 1 in size) on the Ledo-to-Calcutta railway, and which was therefore the key to British India. Certainly, Slim would not be able to recapture Burma without the stores at Dimapur.

Slim's plans to capture Akyab in December 1942 had failed, as had an attack on Donbaik in March 1943, and for all its splendid effect on morale Operation Longcloth could not affect the course of the struggle in Burma. In September 1943 South-East Asia Command (SEAC) had been founded with Admiral Lord Louis Mountbatten as its supreme commander, and the following month Slim's Four-teenth Army, comprising Britons, Indians, Burmese, Chinese, Chins, Gurkhas, Kachins, Karens, Nagas and troops from British East Africa and British West Africa, was also set up. The intention for 1944 was for Lieutenant-General Philip Christison to take Akyab with XV Corps, Stilwell's Northern Combat Command to take Myitkyina, and Lieutenant-General Geoffrey Scoones' Central Front to take Tiddim. Before any of that could happen, however, the U-Go offensive had to be repulsed. Although Slim was expecting an attack, he did not think it would come with such speed and force and as early as it did. The Japanese Burma Area Army attacked in the Arakan in February 1944, but was defeated by the 5th and 7th Divisions, which were airlifted to Imphal on 19 March. They got back just in time, because it turned out that the Japanese were only 30 miles from the town. On 7 March 1944 the Japanese unleashed Operation U-Go: their 33rd Division struck in the south, a week later the 15th Division crossed the Chindwin river in the centre and the 31st Division, under Lieutenant-General Sato Kotuku, in the north. Slim ordered the 17th and 20th Divisions to hold the Imphal perimeter, while the 5th and 23rd fought on the Imphal Plain.

Because of the mountainous Naga Hill region in the north, with jungle paths and narrow ridges 8,000 feet high, Slim assumed that Sato would have to try to capture Kohima with only a regiment; in fact on 5 April the entire 31st Division arrived there, after marching 160 miles in twenty days, bringing large numbers of animals both for food and for carrying arms and ammunition over passes and ravines and through jungles. Kohima was considered the key to Imphal 80 miles to the south, Imphal to Dimapur and Dimapur the key to British India itself, which is why it was soon to see, in the writer Compton Mackenzie's view, 'fighting as desperate as any in recorded history'.[35]

At 17.00 hours on 5 April, Colonel Hugh Richards of the 1st Assam Regiment, some of whose rear details were stationed at Kohima, was informed by a Naga tribesman that the Japanese were approaching along the road from Imphal, and there was no time to waste if he wanted to defend the town. Sure enough, Major-General Shigesaburo Miyazaki of the 58th Infantry Regiment was approaching, his pet monkey Chibi on his shoulder, having cut the Dimapur–Imphal road that morning (the Kohima–Imphal road was to be cut soon afterwards).[36] Kohima, a village 5,000 feet above sea level surrounded by peaks 10,000 feet high to the west and 8,000 feet to the north and east, has been described as 'an ocean of peaks and ridges crossed by bridle paths'.[37] Richards had been trying to fortify the place for a month, stymied by a quartermaster in Dimapur who would not release barbed wire to him as there was an administrative regulation forbidding its use in the Naga Hills.

Defending the village perched on a ridge and soon completely surrounded by over 6,000 Japanese under Sato were 500 men of the 4th
Battalion of the Royal West Kent Regiment under Lieutenant-Colonel
John 'Danny' Laverty, some platoons of the Assam Rifles and Shere
Regiment, a small detachment from the 1st Assam Regiment and
some recruits from the Royal Nepalese Army, numbering around
a thousand in total.[38] The 1,500 non-combatant civilians proved a
problem: although the tiny area the British Commonwealth forces
were defending – effectively a triangle 700 by 900 by 1,100 yards –
was well supplied with food and ammunition, the Japanese cut off its
water supply early on in the siege, so that water had to be severely
rationed. Despite his formidable advantage in numbers at Kohima,
Sato had little faith in the success of U-Go in general. On the eve of
his attack, he drank a glass of champagne with his divisional officers,
telling them: 'I'll take this opportunity, gentlemen, of making something quite clear to you. Miracles apart, every one of you is likely to
lose his life in this operation. It isn't simply a question of the enemy's
bullets. You must be prepared for death by starvation in these mountain fastnesses.'[39] The Japanese obviously did pep-talks differently.

What happened next rates with the great sieges of British history,
such as that of Rorke's Drift in the Zulu War. The Japanese, having
taken positions above Kohima, bombarded the force inside the perimeter at dusk every day from 6 April onwards, before attempting to
overrun it night after night. Vicious hand-to-hand fighting took place,
with the Japanese capturing more and more of the village as the
dreadful fortnight wore on. Every building in the village – the General
Hospital, Garrison Hill, the Kuki Piquet, the Field Supply Depot
(FSD) and its bakeries, the Kohima Club, the Detail Issue Store and
the District Commissioner's bungalow – became a scene of death and
destruction, as some held out and others were captured by countless
determined Japanese assaults. Water had to be dropped in by parachute, and the defenders felt desperate when supplies fell on Japanese
positions instead, so small was the perimeter target area. They felt
even worse when ammunition originally intended for them was used
to bombard them.[40]

Scenes of great heroism on both sides were commonplace, though
none perhaps outdone by the nineteen-year-old Lance-Corporal John

Harman of D Company of the 4th Royal West Kents, who almost single-handedly cleared the tactically vital FSD bakeries of Japanese, taking direct part in the killing of forty-four Japanese, and winning a posthumous Victoria Cross in a series of feats that almost defy belief.[41] 'The actions were hand-to-hand combat, fierce and ruthless, by filthy, bedraggled, worn-out men, whose lungs were rarely free of the noxious smell of decaying corpses inside and outside the perimeter. Once the circle had closed, the wounded could not be evacuated, and were often wounded again as they lay, helpless, in the restricted space available to the frantically overworked medical officers.'[42]

With front lines sometimes only 15 yards from each other, as close as anything seen in the Great War, at one point fierce fighting took place across District Commissioner Charles Pawsey's tennis court which lay between the rubble of the Kohima Club and his destroyed bungalow.[43] 'Where tennis balls had been idly lobbed by the few Europeans in more placid times,' wrote Louis Allen, who served in intelligence in South-East Asia during the war, 'grenades whizzed back and forth across the width of the court.' It was true that 161st Brigade, part of the 5th Indian Division at Jotsama, kept up counter-battery fire against the Japanese shelling Kohima, but Sato had cut the road link at Zubza, which was only 36 miles from Dimapur, so reinforcement was impossible. The most dangerous moment of them all came on the night of 17 April, when the Japanese stormed the Kuki Piquet, thereby getting between Garrison Hill and the FSD, threatening at any moment to cut the perimeter in half, thus splitting the garrison. Richards had run out of reserves, and he and his men resolutely if fatalistically awaited the *coup de grâce* expected at dawn. Yet as the Indian *Official History* of the war states, 'The final vicious assault did not come.'[44] The Japanese, as exhausted and as hungry as the defenders, failed to press home the attack.

It was at this key moment, on Sunday, 18 April 1944, that 161st Brigade, part of Lieutenant-General Sir Montagu Stopford's XXXIII Indian Corps from Dimapur, managed to infiltrate a Punjabi battalion and tank detachment into Kohima, which relieved the General Hospital and the West Kents' position facing Kuki Piquet and Pawsey's bungalow. 'Most of its buildings were in ruins,' recorded Allen of the battered village of Kohima, 'walls still standing were pockmarked with shell bursts or bullet holes, the trees were stripped of leaves and parachutes hung limply from the few branches that remained.'[45] As the Punjabis took up position, ready to start the process of trying to prise the Japanese out of their immensely well-dug-in positions, they saw among the British and Indian survivors 'little groups of grinning and bearded riflemen standing at the mouths of their bunkers and staring with blood-shot and sleep-starved eyes as the relieving troops came in. They had not had a wash for a week.'[46] They had suffered over 300 casualties between 5 and 20 April 1944 – including three British brigadiers killed – but had held out.

Going on to the offensive, the next problem was how, in the words of Major Geoffrey White of the Dorsets, to 'get a medium tank on to the tennis court or manhandle a gun into such a position as to blow the devils out of their holes at very close range in support of an infantry attack'.[47] The Japanese were expert diggers and had dug themselves into the terraced ground in such a way that little could touch them from the air. Over the next two months, Shigesaburo Miyazaki's 58th Infantry Regiment was dislodged from its positions, terrace by terrace, ridge by hard-fought ridge, holding out the longest of the division, and covering the retreat. Its commander survived to hold high office in the Japanese Army.

Meanwhile at Imphal the RAF's Third Tactical Air Force kept the besieged town resupplied by air once Mutaguchi had cut the road to Kohima on 12 April. During the eighty-eight-day siege it moved 1 million gallons of petrol, 12,000 reinforcements and 14 million pounds of rations into the town, and flew 13,000 casualties out. Once again, Allied air superiority was the key. With weak air support and inadequate supplies, the entire Japanese offensive had stalled, and Mutaguchi's Fifteenth Army was starting to disintegrate. His whole plan had gambled on being able to supply his forces from captured supplies, and when Slim's 5th and 23rd Divisions broke the Japanese stranglehold, this was denied him. With Sato withdrawing from Kohima on 31 May, and the monsoon descending that month, the gamble had clearly failed. Mutaguchi was furious that Sato had committed so many troops to Kohima, rather than diverting at least one regiment to attacking Imphal, and when Sato arrived at Mutaguchi's headquarters he was solemnly handed a revolver and a white cloth, which he indignantly refused. He explained that he had saved his men from 'a meaningless annihilation' but was nonetheless accused of 'premeditated treason'.[48]

The first time that the Japanese abandoned a position without a fight came on 17 June at the Mao Songsan Ridge, and five days later the Imphal–Dimapur Road reopened. Some units, such as Lieutenant-General Masafumi Yamauchi's 15th Division, had been so stripped of manpower by illness, battle-losses and dispersal that they were down to the strength of one and a half battalions. (Yamauchi consoled himself writing haiku poetry.) 'The road dissolved into mud,' recorded Major Fujiwara Iwaichi, the officer who had trained the Indian National Army, 'the rivers flooded, and it was hard to move on foot, never mind in a vehicle . . . Almost every officer and man was suffering from malaria, while amoebic dysentery and *beri-beri* were commonplace.'[49] The time had come for Slim to exact a terrible revenge against the U-Go offensive. The number of Commonwealth casualties at Imphal was 12,603 versus 54,879 Japanese (including 13,376 killed). Some authorities give figures as high as 65,000 for the number of Japanese killed in the whole of the U-Go campaign.[50] Although miraculously the Japanese retreated in formation, keeping order throughout the ordeal and recrossing the Chindwin under constant harassment by the RAF, not one tank or heavy artillery piece could be saved, and over 17,000 mules and pack ponies perished too.

As a result of U-Go, which has been described as 'the biggest defeat the Japanese had known in their entire history', Mutaguchi was dismissed, along with the entire Fifteenth Army Staff, barring one officer. Hideki Tojo, the Japanese Prime Minister, resigned on 18 July 1944. Given that he was not told about the battle of Midway until six weeks after the event, he was clearly not the all-powerful dictator of popular Western mythology; power rested in the Supreme War Council. He was much more than a scapegoat, however, and was not surprisingly executed in 1948. Burma was now open for Allied reconquest, and the British Army recrossed the Chindwin on 19 November. 'The consequences of Imphal and Kohima', recorded their historian, 'far transcended any British achievement in the Far East since December 1941.'[51]

In protecting the Indian sub-continent from the ravages of Japanese rule, whose vicious cruelties had been apparent in Manchuria and

China since 1931 and which were extended to the whole of the Southern Resources Area between 1941 and 1945, the British Empire performed its greatest service to the people of India. Adolf Hitler had written in *Mein Kampf*: 'If anyone imagines that England would let India go without staking her last drop of blood, it is only a sorry sign of absolute failure to learn from the World War, and of total misapprehension and ignorance on the score of Anglo-Saxon determination.'[52] About this he was right, and yet only three years later the British did indeed withdraw from India without fighting for it. But there was a world of difference between granting independence to a dominion's own people in peacetime and having it wrested away by a foreign power in time of war.

When considering the horrific cruelties inflicted on European POWs by the Imperial Japanese Army during the Second World War, it is important to see them in the overall context of atrocities such as the Rape of Nanking.[53] Whereas 6.2 per cent of British Commonwealth prisoners of the Japanese died between 1941 and 1945, the figures were 23 per cent for the Dutch, 41.6 per cent for the Americans and a monstrous 77 per cent (230,000 out of 300,000) for Indonesian forced labourers.[54] As Pedro Lopez, the Philippine counsel at the Japanese War Crimes Tribunal, stated of the 131,000 documented Filipinos – the full figure was probably many times higher – murdered by the Japanese after 1941, there were 'hundreds who suffered slow and painful death in dark, foul and lice-infested cells'.[55]

The literature covering what one historian has called 'The Horror in the East' is voluminous, and the Kachanaburi death camp on the River Kwai, Unit 731's anthrax experiments, Changi Jail in Singapore, Korean 'comfort' women, the Bataan Death March and so on have particularly foul places in the long story of man's inhumanity to man.[56] There are many other, lesser-known aspects of the barbarity shown by the Imperial Japanese forces towards their captives, including that of the psychopathically sadistic behaviour of the Japanese Navy, and especially their Marines. Cold-blooded torture and the routine execution of prisoners seems to have been standard procedure. What happened to the SS *Tjisalak* was fairly normal practice, according to the evidence given at the Tokyo War Crimes Tribunal.[57] After the 5,787-ton Dutch merchant ship was torpedoed in the Indian Ocean on the way from Melbourne in Australia to Colombo in Ceylon on the morning of Sunday, 26 March 1944, the captain gave its seventy-six crewmen the order to abandon ship. Unbeknown to them, an official Japanese naval order of almost exactly a year earlier had authorized submarine commanders: 'Do not stop at the sinking of enemy ships and cargoes. At the same time carry out the complete destruction of the crews of the enemy ships.' What happened next was thus the officially condoned policy of the Japanese Admiralty.

The Japanese submarine *I-8* rose to the surface and its commander, Tatsunosuke Ariizumi, ordered it to move close to the three lifeboats full of survivors, which were fired upon with machine guns. Survivors of that ordeal were ordered to come up on to the submarine's deck, where they were disarmed and their hands tied. Within a few minutes the crowded foredeck was full of the *Tjisalak*'s Chinese, Indian and European crew. They then started to behead the Europeans, one by one. 'They'd just go up and hit a guy on the back and take him up front, and then one of the guys with a sword would cut off his head. Zhunk!' recalled the ship's radio operator. 'One guy, they cut off his head halfway and let him flop around on the deck. The others I saw, they just lopped 'em off with one shot and threw 'em overboard. They were laughing.'[58] Another survivor, a twenty-one-year-old British wireless operator called Blears, agreed. 'They were having fun, and there was a cameraman taking movies of the whole thing!' As he was led off to execution, Blears could see 'Two Japanese officers were waiting for us, one with a sword and the other with a sledgehammer.' Managing to free one of his bound arms, he dived into the water and swam to a raft from the wreckage of the *Tjisalak*, as two Japanese sitting on deckchairs fired at him. Fear of the sharks that were being attracted by the smell of blood from his comrades made him swim all the faster. Back on the submarine, the twenty-two seamen were all tied together by long ropes and the *I-8* then submerged, 'dragging the kicking and struggling men down into the depths, deliberately drowning them'. Miraculously, one Indian named Dhange managed to free himself, and also lived to bear witness alongside Blears and the radio operator.[59]

Sinking lifeboats was common practice among the Japanese, as was shooting survivors in the water. After the Japanese submarine *I-26* torpedoed the American Liberty ship *Richard Hovey* in March 1943, two days out of Bombay sailing towards the Suez Canal, it surfaced and opened up its 20mm anti-aircraft cannon into her small boats and rafts, and then rammed them. Lieutenant Harry Goudy recalled that the Japanese on deck 'were laughing and seemed to get quite a bit of sport out of our predicament'. These criminal actions were also being filmed.[60]

Similar treatment was meted out to the crew of the American Liberty ship *Jean Nicolet* on her way to Calcutta from California in July 1944. William Musser, a seventeen-year-old mess-room steward, was hauled up on to the Japanese submarine that had sunk his ship, and was 'immediately frogmarched towards the bows between two Japanese sailors. Suddenly, one of his captors turned and struck Musser a savage blow across his skull with a length of steel pipe. The Japanese laughed as Musser staggered about concussed and terrified. Taking careful aim with a pistol, the same Japanese pulled the trigger and blew the American boy's brains out. Musser's body was then kicked over the side like a bag of refuse.'[61] Ordinary Seaman Richard Kean, aged nineteen, was stripped of valuables and his lifejacket and had his hands tied behind his back. Before he got to the bow of the ship a Japanese sailor bayoneted him in the stomach, as another smashed a rifle butt down on the back of his head. His body was also kicked overboard. The other prisoners then had to hear a harangue from the captain, who told them, 'Let this be a lesson to you that Americans are weak. You must realize that Japan will rule the world,' and so on. From then on, Americans were dragged off the deck individually down the hatch into the submarine. 'The night air was soon rent with screams of agony and the sounds of violence,' the Tokyo War Crimes Tribunal was told, 'as the terrified survivors suffered untold mental anguish waiting to be snatched and led to an unknown fate.' On deck, the Japanese formed two lines, whereupon the Americans were forced to run the gauntlet, being hit with metal bars, rifle butts and lengths of chain, and slashed with bayonets and knives. Anyone still alive at the end of the line faced a large sailor 'whose job it was to lunge his bayonet deep into the bleeding and bruised Americans and heave them bodily over the side like a man heaving hay with a pitchfork'.[62]

Astonishingly, two men somehow survived this process. Assistant Engineer Pyle was cut with a sword but managed to fall into the sea, and Able Seaman Butler described how 'One tried to kick me in the stomach, another hit me over the head with an iron pipe, another cut me over the eye with a sabre,' but he too managed to release his hands and jump overboard. With thirty others tied up, the submarine's diving klaxon then sounded and the Japanese rushed down into the bowels of the vessel, slamming the hatches shut behind them. One American sailor who had secreted a penknife managed to free several of his comrades before the submarine dived; all the rest drowned.

Yet it was the behaviour of Japan's 17,000-strong Manila Naval Defence Force (MNDF) against innocent civilians in the capital of the Philippines in February 1945 that truly defies belief. Furious that the Americans were recapturing the islands, Vice-Admiral Denshichi Okuchi unleashed the MNDF to do anything they liked to the local population, who they (rightly) believed sympathized with the Westerners. In one incident, twenty Filipina girls were taken to an officers' club called the Coffee Pot, and later to the nearby Bay View Hotel, where they were 'Imprisoned in various rooms and over the next four days and nights Japanese officers and other ranks were given free access to the terrified girls, who were dragged from their rooms and repeatedly raped.'[63] One written order from the High Command of the MNDF from this period reads: 'When killing Filipinos, assemble them together in one place as far as possible, thereby saving ammunition and labour.' The diary of a warrant officer called Yamaguchi reads: 'All in all, our aim is extermination.' Civilians who had taken refuge in the German Club in Manila were burnt to death when Japanese naval troops surrounded the building, poured petrol over the exits and set fire to it. According to the historian of these horrors, those who tried to escape were:

impaled on bayonets, some also were shot dead. Women who made it through were dragged screaming into nearby ruined buildings where Japanese soldiers gang-raped them. Some were carrying children, but the Japanese bayoneted these babies in their mother's arms before assaulting the mothers. After being raped many times the Japanese soldiers often cut the women's breasts off with bayonets; some had petrol poured on their hair and ignited.[64]

Such utter bestiality was repeated 'on countless occasions' right across the city.

On 7 February 1945, advancing American forces discovered the mutilated corpses of forty-nine Filipinos on the corner of Juan Luna and Moriones Streets in Manila. One-third of the corpses were women and another third babies and infants. All had been shot, bayoneted or beheaded, and most of the females – of almost all ages – had been raped. Pregnancy was certainly no protection, as a mountain of contemporaneous evidence proves: 'In some cases, Japanese troops had cut the foetuses out of their mother's bellies before killing the victim.'[65] As well as bayonet wounds, some young female survivors of a separate massacre had had 'both of their nipples amputated from their breasts, and a 2-year-old boy had had both of his arms cut off by the Japanese. Some children as young as five were nursing bayonet stab wounds and severe burns caused by sadistic Japanese naval troops for no other reason than to inflict pain and suffering on infants.'

When the MNDF entered the Philippines Red Cross hospital in Manila, further foul scenes of wholesale massacre were enacted, and one survivor, its acting manager Modesta Farolan, recorded, 'From where we were, we could hear victims in their death agony, the shrill cries of children and the sobs of dying mothers and girls.' On leaving her hiding place, Farolan discovered that 'Women were raped and sliced with bayonets from groin to throat and left to bleed to death in the hot sun. Children were seized by the legs and had their heads bashed against the wall. Babies were tossed into the air and caught on bayonets. Unborn foetuses were gouged out with bayonets from pregnant women.'[66]

Nor was the deliberate attack on the Red Cross hospital out of character for the Japanese Navy. There were many occasions when hospital ships bearing clearly identifiable Red Cross marks were specifically targeted. Whenever doctors and nurses fell into Japanese hands, as in Hong Kong at Christmas 1941, they were particularly ill-treated, possibly because they were seen as responsible for getting wounded men back into action. The Japanese had agreed before the outbreak of war to abide by the provisions of the Geneva Convention regarding non-combatant status, which since 1907 had expressly protected the International Red Cross, but this was entirely ignored after the attack on Pearl Harbor. Hospital ships were bombed in harbour, torpedoed at sea and fired upon too often for it to be coincidental.

On occasion the Japanese Navy would go to some lengths to think up imaginative ways to murder people. At St Paul's College in Manila in February 1945, for example, 250 hungry and thirsty civilians were herded into the school hall and told that there was food and drink under three large chandeliers in one of the buildings. The Japanese then withdrew. The prisoners rushed to the trestle tables loaded with food, but they barely had a chance to take a bite before explosives in the booby-trapped chandeliers blew up. Then the Japanese threw hand grenades into the hall to finish off the survivors.

At La Salle College, a Catholic institution in the city, the rapes and massacres wound up, as the father superior later recalled, with 'bodies being thrown into a heap at the foot of the stairs. The dead were thrown over the living. Not many died outright, a few died within one or two hours, the rest slowly bled to death. The sailors retired and we heard them drinking outside. Frequently they returned to laugh and mock at our suffering.' Many Japanese even raped women and girls who were bleeding to death from gunshot and stab wounds. There were many other scenes described to the War Crimes Tribunal – and not denied by the perpetrators – that are simply too disgusting to recount here. Men of the Imperial Japanese Navy were undoubtedly every bit as depraved, sadistic and ruthless as their military counterparts.

9

Midnight in the Devil's Gardens

July 1942–May 1943

Rommel, Rommel, Rommel! What else matters but beating him?
            Winston Churchill to Brigadier Ian Jacob, August 1942[1]

General Sir Claude Auchinleck did not really deserve to be removed from his command in North Africa in August 1942. 'The Auk' had stopped Rommel's Panzer Army from breaking through his defensive lines based on the Ruweisat Ridge at the first battle of El Alamein in early July, taking 7,000 prisoners, and had laid sound plans for a full-scale counter-attack in the autumn, but had warned the High Command in London that this could not be launched until September at the earliest. Churchill and Brooke visited Cairo, and Auchinleck was rewarded for his caution by being offered the command of forces in the Middle East instead, a definite demotion, which he refused. Although after a year he was appointed to the post of commander-in-chief in India, he was never to see battlefield service again. Taking over the Near East command was General Sir Harold Alexander, with the brilliant Lieutenant-General William 'Strafer' Gott at the helm of by far its largest component, the Eighth Army, which had already suffered no fewer than 80,000 casualties during its short existence.[2] As a brigadier Gott had led the armoured strike force for Operation Brevity in May 1941, the first attempt to relieve Tobruk. Yet just as Gott flew back from the desert to meet Churchill in Cairo before taking up his command, travelling in a slow and unescorted Bristol Bombay passenger plane, it was attacked by six Messerschmitt Me-109s from Jagdgeschwader 27, and crash-landed in flames. Four of the twenty-one people on board survived, but not Gott. The second choice for the post had been Brooke's protégé, the fifty-five-year-old Lieutenant-General Bernard Montgomery, who was flown out post-haste, and took up the Eighth Army command at Ruweisat Ridge at 11 a.m. on Thursday, 13 August 1942.

There are a number of pitfalls in attempting to delve into the minds of generals at a distance of seven decades, and the results of doing so are often meaningless psychobabble. But if anyone makes a fascinating candidate for the psychiatrist's sofa, it is Montgomery. The fourth child of a vicar who became Anglican bishop of Tasmania, he cut off all contact with his unloving mother to the extent of boycotting her funeral.[3] After an academically undistinguished time at the London day school St Paul's, Montgomery went to the Royal Military College at Sandhurst, where he bullied a fellow cadet so badly by setting fire to his coat-tails that the young man required hospitalization.[4] He then served on the North-West Frontier of India with the Royal Warwickshire Regiment. Montgomery had a good First World War, leading an attack at Ypres in which he took one German prisoner by kicking him in the testicles. On another occasion a grave was dug for him at a dressing-station, so unlikely did it seem that he would survive his wounds, but instead of an early interment he won the Distinguished Service Order, and ended the war as a brevet lieutenant-colonel. After marrying in 1927 and having a son, his wife Betty died tragically in 1938 from septicaemia, from an insect bite on her foot which even the amputation of her leg had failed to halt. The emotional side of his life closed down after her death, and total concentration on soldiering took over; he even became teetotal (not in any sense a British Army tradition). The professor of military history at Oxford, Hew Strachan, has written that:

Montgomery's great strengths lay in training, careful preparation and method; above all, he integrated artillery into an all-arms battle. He accepted that battles swung on fire-power and the exploitation of ground, as much as on movement, and he emphasized that they were about killing and being prepared to be killed. He expressed all this in a language that was direct and even attritional.[5]

Disciplined, focused, adaptable, a meticulous planner, quick to dismiss the incompetent, respectful of the Germans' capacity for counter-attack, for all that Montgomery was irascible, opinionated and egotistical he was also the greatest British field commander since the Duke of Wellington. As one historian has noted, 'Generals should not be judged by their party manners.' If Montgomery was vain, he had plenty to be vain about.

Montgomery had performed well on the retreat to Dunkirk, and although he had been in part responsible for the initial planning of the disastrous Dieppe Raid of August 1942, he had at least suggested that it be abandoned before it was undertaken. By the time he got to the Western Desert he had worked out in what way he wanted to fight his duel with Rommel differently from the way his three predecessors – Alan Cunningham, Neil Ritchie and Claude Auchinleck – had fought theirs. Unlike them, he would not seek to chase the Desert Fox back and forth along the North African littoral between Egypt and Tunisia. Instead he would try to bring the Afrika Korps to a single great, Clausewitzian decisive battle, and break its power for ever. As he told his Eighth Army officer corps in a short speech on the evening of his first day in command:

I understand that Rommel is about to attack at any moment. Excellent. Let him attack. I would sooner it didn't come for a week, just to give me time to sort things out. If we have two weeks to prepare we will be sitting pretty; Rommel can attack as soon as he likes after that and I hope he does ... Meanwhile, we ourselves will start to plan a great offensive; it will be the beginning of a campaign which will hit Rommel for six right out of Africa ... He is definitely a nuisance. Therefore we will hit him a crack and finish with him.[6]

Such a pep-talk might today sound like absurd hyperbole from a hitherto minor commander speaking of a strategic giant who had not lost an important battle, and moreover was well inside Egypt. But, nine months later to the day, the Afrika Korps – which was to lose a total of 5,250 vehicles during 1942 – surrendered in Tunisia.[7]

The depredations of desert warfare were well described in the British propaganda film *Desert Victory*, and included boiling days but freezing nights; bathing in one's shaving mug for want of water; sandstorms that lasted many days (in some traditional Arab lore, murder was acceptable after the fifth); mosquitoes, flies and scorpions; and a landscape so desolate that a compass was as important a tool as to a sailor. Of the local inhabitants, one divisional history recorded: 'If they could have carried it away, they'd have stolen the air out of the tyres.'[8]

Rommel attacked the Alam el Halfa Ridge seventeen days after Monty's first speech, on 30 August, and destroyed sixty-seven British tanks for the loss of forty-nine of his own. But within twenty-four hours British minefields, warplanes and artillery had slowed his Panzers' advance to a crawl, and that day the Germans got as far eastwards in Africa as they were ever going to; their 3,000 casualties were almost twice the Eighth Army's 1,750. Rommel himself only narrowly avoided death when the Desert Air Force (DAF) bombed and strafed his *Kampfstaffel* (tactical headquarters).

For the rest of the summer and into the autumn of 1942 the two armies faced one another at the obscure desert railway stop of El Alamein, each being resupplied as best they could organize. Here lay the key to Montgomery's victory. Because both Benghazi and Tobruk could not be properly protected by the Luftwaffe, and were thus heavily bombed by the Allies, most of the Axis supplies came to Tripoli via Naples and Sicily. Yet whereas in 1941 the average monthly delivery of motor fuel to Axis forces in Africa had been 4,884 tons, because the Tripoli-to-El Alamein return journey was over 2,000 miles long, and German trucks consumed a litre of fuel for every 2 miles covered, the Afrika Korps required 5,776 tons of fuel per month by 1942 as a result of its extended supply lines.[9] With the DAF destroying lorries carrying fuel to Rommel along the only road that was worthy of the name, as Frederick von Mellenthin recorded, 'Petrol stocks were almost exhausted, and an armoured division without petrol is little better than a heap of scrap iron.'[10] One Afrika Korps divisional commander, General Hans Cramer, believed El Alamein to have been 'lost before it was fought. We had not the petrol.'[11]

Aircraft and submarines stationed at Malta ceaselessly harried the Axis lines of communication. An unsinkable Allied aircraft carrier, Malta now became the most heavily bombed place on earth. The island was awarded the George Cross in April 1942 for its stalwart courage under near-permanent attack, one of only 106 recipients between 1940 and 1947. (The only other collective recipient would be the Royal Ulster Constabulary, in 1999.) A problem developed when the devoutly religious Governor of Malta, Lieutenant-General Sir William Dobbie, would not allow the garrison to work on Sundays. In the view of the military historian John Keegan, this Sabbatarianism effectively allowed two of the few ships which succeeded in running the Axis blockade to be sunk with their cargoes at their moorings, a fact not mentioned in Dobbie's autobiography, entitled *On Active Service with Christ*.[12]

Yet if Rommel's supply routes were long at more than 1,000 miles, Montgomery's were twelve times longer. Most Allied troops and equipment had to come around the Cape of Good Hope, menaced all the way by U-boats, and the rest along the shorter but also dangerous air route across central Africa and up the Nile Valley. This was described in *Desert Victory* as the longest line of communication in the history of warfare. However, the proximity of the Middle Eastern oil meant that in the twelve months after August 1941 Commonwealth ground and air forces in Egypt received no less than 342,000 tons of oil products.[13] The logistics could be complicated: for example, the Allies' four types of tank – Shermans, Crusaders, Grants and Stuarts – ran on three different types of fuel. Yet, whereas in August 1942 Churchill had privately described the Eighth Army as 'a broken, baffled army, a miserable army', by October its huge reinforcement and strange but charismatic new commander had changed all that.

It has been argued that Rommel should never have offered battle at El Alamein, only 60 miles west of Alexandria, but ought instead to have withdrawn back along his extended lines of communication into Libya once it had become obvious that the interdictions of the Royal Navy and DAF meant that he was being resupplied at only a fraction of the rate of his antagonist. But Jodl's deputy General Warlimont had explained to Rommel's Staff in July the importance of remaining at El Alamein. He spoke of Kleist's plans to invade Persia and Iraq from the Caucasus and pointed out that it was essential to have the Allies tied up defending Egypt rather than sending troops to other parts of the Middle East.[14] Furthermore, the prizes of victory in Egypt were dazzling for Rommel. Alexandria was the headquarters of the Royal Navy's Mediterranean Fleet; Suez was the gateway to Britain's Indian Empire; Cairo was the largest city in Africa and the centre of

British power in the region, just as the Nile Delta was the route to Iran, Iraq and the oilfields of the Middle East. The Wehrmacht had pulled off astonishing coups regularly over the previous three years despite a growing paucity of men, equipment and fuel, so it was felt to be far too early to give up such hard-won ground.

The lull in fighting after the battle of Alam el Halfa allowed Montgomery – who with his taste for multi-badged service berets and eccentric dress was very consciously transforming himself into the much loved public figure known as Monty – to train his army. Detailed orders went out from his headquarters – a caravan in the desert which featured a postcard photograph of Rommel – concerning every aspect of the army's logistics, fitness, equipment, morale, organization and discipline. Many of the reinforcements he was being sent had never fought in the desert, and his belief in intensive training was put into full operation in the weeks of relative calm. This led Montgomery to take a firm stance with Churchill, who was pressing for an early attack. The best that Alexander would offer Downing Street was the promise of being sent a codeword – Zip – when the great assault finally began.[15] Alexander's determination to leave Montgomery alone might have frustrated the Prime Minister but it was the right thing to do. Alexander – who tap-danced in regimental talent shows – was a cool commander, who ran his Staff mess in a way that Harold Macmillan, the Minister Resident in North-West Africa, equated to an Oxford high table, where the war was 'politely ignored' as they instead discussed 'the campaigns of Belisarius, the advantages of classical over Gothic architecture, or the best ways to drive pheasants in flat country'.[16]

In hoping to drive Rommel back over the very flat country, special-forces attacks were made in mid-September against Tobruk (Operation Agreement) and Benghazi (Operation Bigamy). Operation Agreement was badly compromised from the start after a clash at a roadblock, and cost the lives of 750 men, the cruiser HMS *Coventry* and two destroyers with little to show for it. Bigamy was an attractive idea in theory, but ultimately turned out to be expensive and not worth the effort. Although the Long Range Desert Group did destroy twenty-five enemy aircraft at Barce, that was its only real success, and afterwards the Germans used second-line units to garrison their staging areas, freeing up first-class troops for the coming battle.[17] Meanwhile, Rommel fell ill with stomach and liver complaints, high blood pressure, sinusitis and a sore throat, and so on 23 September he flew back to Germany for a long period of leave, passing on his command to an Eastern Front veteran, the obese and unfit General Georg Stumme. He was therefore not even in Africa on 23 October 1942, when Montgomery launched Operation Lightfoot, the first phase of the second battle of El Alamein.

As we have already seen, after his fighting retreat of 400 miles earlier in the year Auchinleck had originally chosen El Alamein for his defensive lines because there was only a 40-mile gap between the Mediterranean Sea to the north and the impassable salt-marshes of the Qattara Depression, an area the size of Ulster, to the south. Yet this same narrowness now worked in Rommel's favour, when he was forced on to the defensive by sheer weight of numbers. Whoever attacked at El Alamein, it was always going to be a battle of attrition rather than movement, far more reminiscent of the Western Front of the First World War than the sweeping Blitzkrieg manoeuvres of the Second.

Montgomery hoped that the Germans would be distracted by a diversionary attack in the south of the battlefield by Lieutenant-General Brian Horrocks' XIII Corps, while full frontal infantry attacks by Lieutenant-General Oliver Leese's XXX Corps towards the Miteiriya and Kidney Ridges in the north were exploited by the 1st and 10th Armoured Divisions of Lieutenant-General Herbert Lumsden's X Corps driving through and rolling up the Axis defences from behind.

The Axis front line was defended by vast minefields of between 5,000 and 9,000 feet in depth, comprising half a million mines and nicknamed the Devil's Gardens by the Germans.[18] Teller anti-tank mines, packing 11 pounds of TNT, destroyed vehicles but were not set off by infantrymen (though they were by camels), while the Springen mines sprang to midriff-height after being stepped on, before exploding with 360 ball bearings. Hidden beneath the sand, they were hard to detect even in daylight. Clearing a path through the minefields for the infantry would be sappers using detection equipment that was in its infancy and involved poking the sand with bayonets, often while under artillery, mortar, machine-gun or small-arms fire. The cool nerve of the Allied sappers at El Alamein was equal to anything seen in any theatre of the war.

On 23 October, Stumme commanded some 50,000 German and 54,000 Italian troops, compared to Montgomery's 195,000 mainly Commonwealth soldiers. The Eighth Army had eighty-five infantry battalions compared to the Africa Korps' seventy-one (of which thirty-one were German), as well as 1,451 anti-tank guns to Rommel's 800, and 908 first-class field and medium artillery pieces to about 500 Axis, of which 370 Italian guns were temperamental Great War pieces, and not up to the coming task.[19] If one strips out the British light tanks, German Panzer Mark IIs and the Italian tanks, which Rommel called 'decrepit and barely fit for action', the figures for effective medium tanks at El Alamein were 910 Allied to 234 Axis, a ratio of four to one.[20] The disparity is striking, and a testament to Allied interdiction of Axis reinforcement attempts, as well as to the massive reinforcement of the Allied forces via the Gulf of Aden.

Although the morale of the Italians' air force, armour, artillery and, especially, paratroopers was generally high, this was not true of their regular infantry, who made up the great majority of the 1.2 million Italians stationed on foreign soil in 1942. As had been seen earlier in the war, the Italians could fight bravely if properly officered, equipped, trained and fed, but this was rarely the case in the latter stages of the Desert War. Some Italians units, such as the small but all-volunteer Folgore (Lightning) paratrooper and Ariete armoured divisions, were as solid as any on the battlefield. Rommel said of the Ariete that 'We always asked them to do more than they practically could, and they always did.' Nonetheless, some Italian infantry formations could not stand prolonged bombardment before they began to consider surrendering. Lack of food was also a major problem for the Italians, and as a history of El Alamein records: 'The only fresh meat was provided by the occasional camel that strayed into one of the Devil's Gardens and either set off a mine or came close enough to be shot.'[21] Moreover, Italian tanks were generally too light and mechanically unreliable, much of their artillery was wildly inaccurate at over 5 miles' range and their tanks' wireless sets barely functioned when in motion.[22]

'We have a very daring and skilful opponent against us,' Churchill controversially told the House of Commons of Rommel on 27 January

1942, 'and, may I say across the havoc of war, a great general.'[23] (Churchill had used his maiden speech in 1900 to praise the Boers as fighting men too.) The way that Rommel attempted to stiffen the morale of the Italian infantry was to 'corset' them close to crack German units, so for example the Italian Bologna Division would be stationed near to the elite German Ramcke paratroops, while the Italian Trento Division would be interspersed with the 164th (Saxon) Light Division. Much the same thing had been done by the Duke of Wellington at the battle of Waterloo, when he had placed British regiments among Belgian and Dutch units of more doubtful quality.

A vital aspect of the coming struggle was to be the air superiority that the Allies had by the time of Alam el Halfa established over the Luftwaffe, but which by the second battle of Alamein had almost turned into air supremacy. Montgomery attached Air Vice-Marshal Arthur Coningham's DAF headquarters to his own, and, although he gave him little credit in his writings later on, the two commands worked effectively together. The DAF could deploy 530 aircraft to the Luftwaffe's 350, but it had an edge that the difference in numbers would not seem to justify, for during the battle the DAF flew 11,600 sorties against 3,100 by the Luftwaffe.[24] By then the DAF consisted of nineteen British, nine South African, seven American and two Australian squadrons, including some supplied with Spitfires, which had begun to appear in Africa that March. By September 1942, the United States had also landed 1,500 aircraft in a theatre in which her ground forces were not yet engaged, and before Alamein the ratio of air reinforcement had been five to one in the Allies' favour.[25]

The sheer productive power of the United States – awakened and infuriated by Pearl Harbor – was thus already beginning to tell. Between December 1941 and September 1942, the Anglo-American alliance sent 2,370 single-engined fighters to the Middle Eastern theatre, against a total German production of 1,340 in that same period (only 25 per cent of which could be sent there).[26] Hitler was very soon to feel the folly of his declaration of war against America. 'Anyone who has to fight, even with the most modern weapons,' wrote Rommel, 'against an enemy in complete control of the air, fights like a savage against modern European troops, under the same handicaps and with the same chances of success ... We had to face

the likelihood of the RAF shortly gaining absolute air superiority.'
The days of Messerschmitt Me-109s based in Libya dominating the
skies, shooting down Tomahawks and Hurricane IIs with impunity,
were over. Rommel appreciated that he had, in his own words, to
'put our defences into such a form that British air superiority would
have the least effect . . . We could no longer rest our defence on the
motorised forces used in a mobile role . . . We had instead to try to
resist the enemy in field positions.'[27] For all Rommel's loose nomen-
clature about the RAF rather than the DAF, and the 'English'
rather than the Allies, the battle of El Alamein was not a British
victory so much as a British Empire one (despite the American planes
and Sherman tanks). As well as Major-General Douglas Wimberley's
51st Highland Division, for example, Leese's XXX Corps consisted –
from the sea southwards – of Major-General Leslie 'Ming the Merciless' Morshead's 9th Australian Division, Major-General Bernard
Freyberg's 2nd New Zealand Division, Major-General Dan Pienaar's
1st South African Division and Major-General Francis Tuker's 4th
Indian Division. A better roll-call of Empire could hardly be imagined,
missing Canadians only because 3,400 of them had been senselessly
sacrificed at Dieppe two months earlier.

South of the Ruweisat Ridge, Horrocks commanded a more British
line, including the north-countrymen of Major-General John 'Crasher'
Nicholls' 50th Division and Major-General Hector Hughes' 44th
(Home Counties) Division, as well as Major-General John Harding's
7th Armoured Division, whose nickname the Desert Rats – because
of the jerboa painted on the sides of their tanks – was gradually
to extend in popular parlance to the whole Eighth Army. Yet there
were also two important units entirely unconnected to Britain's
Commonwealth or Empire: the Free Greek Brigade held the Ruweisat
Ridge itself and Brigadier-General Marie-Pierre Koenig's Free French
Brigade guarded the gap between the 44th Division and the Qattara
Depression. With these forces fighting against Germans and Italians,
Alamein was thus almost as cosmopolitan a battle as it was possible
to have, and to characterize it as merely Britons versus Germans is
unwarrantably to caricature what happened. Rommel always said, for
example, that the New Zealanders were the finest troops in the Eighth
Army.

According to Montgomery's plan, it was the Commonwealth forces of Australia, New Zealand and South Africa who were, along with the 51st Highlanders, intended to break through the Axis lines in the first two days of fighting and open the gaps in the minefields through which Major-General Raymond Briggs' 1st and Major-General Alec Gatehouse's 10th Armoured Divisions of X Corps would flood. Montgomery's *Schwerpunkt* was going to be not on the coastal road to the north nor down by the Qattara Depression in the south – as it had been in almost all previous engagements over the past two years – but instead in the centre of the battlefield. In this, as with his insistence on a decisive battle and his return to attritional warfare, Montgomery was to prove both original and far-sighted. As Michael Carver, who served under him in the Western Desert, would later write: 'It may have been expensive and unromantic, but it made certain of victory, and the certainty of victory at that time was all-important. Eighth Army had the resources to stand such a battle, while the Panzerarmee had not, and Montgomery had the determination, will-power and ruthlessness to see such a battle through.'[28]

Nor can one belittle Montgomery's success at Alamein by pointing out his two-to-one superiority over Rommel in terms of artillery and men, and four-to-one superiority in effective tanks. The established view in military thinking was still – as it had been since Napoleon's day – that the attacker needed a three-to-one preponderance to be sure of victory. Moreover, as one of his officers, the military historian Peter Young, has pointed out: 'If, for once, a British general managed to get his army across the start line with a numerical superiority over the enemy, this should be a matter for praise rather than complaint!'[29]

Montgomery, while learning the lessons of the Second World War on which he had been at the receiving end at Dunkirk, had also not forgotten those of the Great War. With what he called '100% binge', Montgomery believed that a huge initial barrage and the attack of Leese's corps could begin a process of what he called 'crumbling', whereby the Axis forces – particularly the Italian infantry – would be demoralized and collapse, especially once Lumsden's tanks attacked them from the flanks and rear. British anti-tank guns and tanks pouring through the bridgehead would, he hoped, hold off the Panzers' inevitable counter-attack wherever the breakthroughs occurred.[30] (In writing military history – indeed history in general – it is impermissible to use the word 'inevitable', except when describing the Germans' swift and aggressive counter-attacking of Allied successes.) Panzers on the move would prove a far easier target both for the DAF and for the British tanks and anti-tank gunners. Unlike earlier desert commanders, Montgomery was positively looking forward to the Axis response, or claimed to be, for morale's sake. 'Having thus beaten the guts out of the enemy,' Montgomery told his divisional commanders, 'the eventual fate of the Panzerarmee is certain. It will not be able to avoid destruction.' Envisaging 'a dogfight lasting about twelve days', Montgomery predicted a crushing victory.[31]

The Eighth Army's massive artillery bombardment opened up at 21.40 hours on Friday, 23 October 1942, accompanied by aerial attacks from Wellington and Halifax bombers. In all, some 882 guns, manned by around 6,000 artillerymen, took part, with the field guns averaging 102 rounds per gun per day. An estimated 1 million shells were fired by the Allies during the battle.[32] In Cairo, Alexander cabled 'Zip' to a relieved and initially delighted Prime Minister in London. After twenty minutes of firing against Axis artillery, at 22.00 the target became the Axis front line, to soften it up for the infantry assault under a full moon. 'The peaceful stars were shaken in their heavens when nearly a thousand guns flashed and roared simultaneously against us that night,' recalled Second Lieutenant Heinz Werner Schmidt, who was serving in a reserve anti-tank battery. 'The earth from the Qattara Depression to the Mediterranean quaked. Far back from the front line, men were jarred to their teeth.'[33] The barrage could be heard in Alexandria, some 60 miles away. It continued for five hours, and then broke off at 03.00, only to be resumed at 07.00. Meanwhile sappers went forward to clear paths through the minefields for the infantry, marking them with white tape. The pipers played 'Highland Laddie' as the Highland and Commonwealth battalions tried to reach objectives along what was codenamed the Oxalic Line. By 08.00 Leese's corps had succeeded in taking roughly half of them, but at the cost of nearly 2,500 casualties, mostly from mines and booby-traps. (The Axis certainly had no monopoly on ingenious booby-traps: the American Office of Strategic Services (OSS) in Tunisia used to plant exploding mule droppings.)

The 'creeping barrage' had managed to keep Axis mortaring, sniping and machine-gunning to a minimum. Yet, potentially disastrously, Lumsden's X Corps had largely failed to break through, and was generally not in a position to protect the infantry from counter-attack. Only the 8th Armoured Brigade made it to the Miteiriya Ridge, but the rest of the corps got fouled up in gargantuan traffic jams along the narrow pathways through the minefields. 'Once a lane had been cleared, there was also the problem of congestion,' records one history. 'An overlooked mine which blew a track off could block a lane for hours and make a mockery of numerical superiority' – and an inviting target for the Luftwaffe.[34] An infuriated Montgomery remonstrated with Lumsden in person 'in no uncertain voice', threatening to relieve his divisional commanders, and possibly by implication Lumdsen himself. Feeling the full weight of Montgomery's ire cannot have been pleasant, and Lumsden ordered fresh attacks to try to relieve the infantry, who by then had to face elements of the Folgore Division and Ramcke Brigade.

Yet Montgomery had not one lucky break but three when it came to the higher direction of the German side of the battle. Not only was Rommel away in Germany when the offensive began, but his efficient chief of staff Fritz Bayerlein was on leave, and the overweight Georg Stumme then died of a heart attack on the first day, whereupon the Panzer general Wilhelm von Thoma took over. It was not until just before midnight on Sunday, 25 October that the signal could be relayed to the Afrika Korps: 'I have taken command of the army again. Rommel.' (Many units did not in fact receive this encouraging signal, as the great opening barrage had cut a number of telephone wires.) Rommel nonetheless quickly deduced that the attacks in the south of the battlefield were merely diversionary, so he withdrew the 21st Panzer Division from there and sent it northwards towards Kidney Ridge. Such was the shortage of petrol that he had to be certain, because if Montgomery was bluffing the division might not even have had enough fuel to return. The sinking of two Italian oil-tankers, *Proserpina* and *Louisiana*, in Tobruk harbour by the DAF on 26 and 28 October, before they could unload their fuel, was to be a particular blow.

On 25 October Montgomery abandoned attempts to get both the 10th and 7th Armoured Divisions through the Axis lines, and instead ordered the 9th Australian Division to start 'crumbling' operations in the north. Meanwhile, the 1st Armoured Division was sent to the area of Kidney Ridge. That night the Australians were mainly successful, but the 1st Armoured made no progress. The next day saw heavy Axis attacks on Kidney Ridge, but without much success. The 7th Motor Brigade (which included the 2nd Battalion of the Rifle Brigade and the 2nd Battalion of the King's Royal Rifle Corps) fought desperate actions to secure positions north and south of Kidney Ridge, jocularly codenamed Snipe and Woodcock, on 27 October. Heavy German shelling, much friendly fire and strong armoured counter-attacks by the 15th Panzer, 21st Panzer and Littorio Divisions failed to dislodge these units from those key positions during that day and night, and thirty-three Axis tanks, five self-propelled guns and other vehicles were destroyed on Snipe alone. Lieutenant-Colonel Victor Turner, who commanded the Rifle Brigade battalion there, won the Victoria Cross, mirroring his brother's posthumous achievement at the battle of Loos in the Great War, while others in the battalion received the DSO, DCM, MC and seven Military Medals. One recent history of El Alamein regards the gallantry on Snipe as one of the turning points of the battle, because it convinced Rommel that Kidney Ridge was the true *Schwerpunkt*, whereas Montgomery had in fact already turned his attentions further north in his desire to find a place for his armour to punch through the Axis lines. The British commander also knew that the coastal road and railway line in the north composed both Rommel's supply lines and his sole route of retreat.

Up in the north, the 9th Australian Division had already suffered more than a thousand casualties – only half of 51st Highland Division's losses, but twice those of the entire X Corps – yet it had succeeded in establishing what in military parlance was called a 'thumb' across the railway line and towards the sea, and was hoping thereby to trap Theodor Count von Sponeck's 90th Light Division and the 164th Saxon Division with their backs to the sea.[35] It was a success that Montgomery wanted to capitalize upon, and to protect against which Rommel was forced to send badly stretched Panzer reinforcements from the Kidney Ridge area. This move was necessary, but it both used up precious petrol and exposed the German armour – the most vulnerable part of any tank was its roof – to DAF attack once it had been spotted by aerial reconnaissance. 'No one can conceive the extent of our anxiety during this period,' Rommel later wrote:

That night I hardly slept and by 03.00 hours [on 29 October] was pacing up and down turning over in my mind the likely course of the battle, and the decisions I might have to take. It seemed doubtful whether we could stand up much longer to attacks of the weight which the British were now making, and which they were in any case still able to increase. It was obvious to me that I dared not await the decisive breakthrough, but would have to pull out to the west before it came.[36]

Nonetheless, Rommel decided 'to make one more attempt, by the tenacity and stubbornness of our defence, to persuade the enemy to call off his attack'. If it failed, he would order a general withdrawal to the town of Fuka, but he recognized that that would probably involve the loss of much of his non-motorized infantry, who were fighting at close quarters and had no means of escape. Meanwhile, Leese sent Royal Artillery 6-pounder anti-tank guns over to the Australians to try to help deal with the Panzers. Nothing could be afforded from the reserve, and no fewer than twenty-two of the thirty Valentine tanks that were also sent were destroyed with comparative ease. Sherman tanks, with 75mm guns in their turrets which were able to traverse 360 degrees, and Grant tanks might have made the difference, but they could not be spared.

Instead, Montgomery withdrew some of the heavy tanks from further south and ended the coastal thrust, bringing Operation Lightfoot to an end on 29 October. This caused immense consternation in London, where Anthony Eden persuaded Churchill that Montgomery was giving up the fight only halfway through. Calling Brooke out of a Chiefs of Staff meeting, the Prime Minister berated 'your' Montgomery for fighting 'a half-hearted battle', asking 'Had we not got a single general who could even win one single battle?' Brooke defended his protégé and was supported by the South African premier Field Marshal Jan Christian Smuts in protecting the man on the spot against the Whitehall strategists, and a row broke out in which harsh words were said on both sides. Privately, however, Brooke admitted that he had:

my own doubts and my own anxieties as to the course of events, but these had to be kept entirely to myself. On returning to my office I paced up and down, suffering from a desperate feeling of loneliness . . . there was still just the possibility that I was wrong and that Monty was beat. The loneliness of those moments of anxiety, when there is no one one can turn to, have to be lived through to realize their intense bitterness.[37]

Far from being 'beat', the Eighth Army commander, ending Lightfoot and the coastal approach, on the night of 1 November launched Operation Supercharge, under the command of Freyberg. Montgomery withdrew one brigade from each of the 44th, 50th and 51st Divisions for the assault, to be directed to the south of Kidney Ridge, largely against the Italian infantry. Once they had made the initial breakthrough, it was hoped that the 1st Armoured Division would debouch through the gap with its 39 Grant, 113 Sherman and 119 Crusader tanks, cross the north–south Rahman Track and engage the 15th and 21st Panzer Divisions to the west of it. The 15th Panzer Division was down to fifty-one tanks by this time and the 21st had only forty-four. By the time Supercharge took place, the Axis line was almost completely denuded of armoured and motorized reserves, with General Francesco Arena's armoured Ariete Division and General Francesco La Ferla's motorized Trieste Division now fully occupied against Leese's XXX Corps. The breakthrough moment had finally come.

After a short preliminary bombardment from 01.05 on 2 November, Supercharge went into operation. The Durham Brigade of the 50th Infantry Division, the battalions of Seaforth and Cameron Highlanders and a battalion of Maoris from the 2nd New Zealand Division captured all their objectives by 06.15, punching a 4-mile-wide gap in the Axis line beyond Kidney Ridge and almost up to the Rahman Track. The 9th Armoured Brigade, comprising the 3rd Hussars, the Royal Wiltshire Yeomanry and the Warwickshire Yeomanry, then poured through the gaps in the Axis line. When the commanding officer of the 3rd Hussars, Lieutenant-Colonel Sir Peter Farquhar, had told Montgomery that Supercharge would be 'suicide', Montgomery did not disagree, saying, 'If necessary, I'm prepared to accept 100% casualties in both personnel and tanks' in order to break through. Farquhar, a sixth baronet who was to be wounded thrice in the war and win the DSO and bar, took these *kamikaze* orders with commendable sangfroid. He later recalled: 'There was, of course, no more to be said.'[38] Overall, however, Montgomery husbanded the lives of his men extremely carefully, indeed to the point that he is often criticized for over-caution. 'Casualties are inevitable in war,' he would say, 'but unnecessary casualties are unforgivable.'[39]

Rommel's movement of German motorized and armoured units north to deal with the Australians, while it did limit Morshead's successes near the coast, also meant that the 'corset' system started to break down, leaving Supercharge with a superb opportunity in the Italian sector near Kidney Ridge. Of Rommel's concern about losing the coastal road, Montgomery wrote in 1958, 'He concentrated his Germans in the north to meet it, leaving the Italians to hold his southern flank. We then drove in a hard blow between the Germans and the Italians, with a good overlap on the Italian front.'[40] Because he had the invaluable advantage of being able to read Rommel's Enigma communications, Montgomery knew how short the Germans were of men, ammunition, food and above all fuel. When he put Rommel's picture up in his caravan he wanted to be seen to be almost reading his opponent's mind. In fact he was reading his mail. Rommel might have tried to 'persuade the enemy to call off his attack', but in reality that was never going to happen, whatever he hoped and Churchill and Eden feared. Otherwise Rommel fought the battle of El Alamein without mistakes, except insofar as he fought there at all. By the end of 2 November, despite spirited German counter-attacks and a thoroughgoing reorganization of new defensive positions, Rommel was persuaded by Thoma that air attacks, fuel shortages and the absence of reserves meant that withdrawal to Fuka was now unavoidable, and he prepared to give the order to retreat.

The bombardment had been going on, day and night, for ten days, and the shelling around an area near the Rahman Track codenamed Skinflint had been so intense that the 'whole place', in Carver's recollection, 'was knee-deep in dust. Nobody knew where anybody or anything was, where minefields started or ended.' Shells created 'a cloud of dust as dense as a smokescreen' when they landed, and visibility could get down to as little as 50 yards.[41] Of the 187 tanks still available to the Axis by then, all but thirty-two were Italian machines with calibres too small to face the Allies' Shermans.

The 9th Armoured Brigade under Brigadier John Currie made good advances under the cover of darkness on 2 November – night-time tank attacks were rare, and as such came as a surprise – but, in the words of one history, these troops 'were betrayed by the dawn. It came up behind them long before they were through the anti-tank guns, silhouetting their tanks as plainly as in a recognition manual.'[42] Only nineteen out of the brigade's ninety tanks survived intact, and 270 casualties were suffered, but it had destroyed thirty-five anti-tank guns along the Rahman Track, and once the 2nd Armoured Brigade joined the remnants of the 9th to take on the 15th and 21st Panzer Divisions, Africa's largest tank battle commenced, around a hillock named Tel el Aqqaqir. If Thoma, who relocated his *Kampfstaffel* there to supervise it, had won this battle-within-a-battle, it is not inconceivable that the Axis line might have continued to hold, leaving Montgomery with very few arrows left in his quiver.

In a pattern that was to be repeated very often in the war from then on – and especially in Russia – the Germans actually destroyed more tanks than their opponents, but not enough for overall victory. By the end of the Aqqaqir battle of 2 November, there were only fifty viable Axis tanks, against more than 500 Allied ones, leaving Rommel no alternative but to order a general retreat so that he might, as he put it in a message that was intercepted by the GCCS at Bletchley Park, 'extricate the remnants' of his army. This was to start at 13.30 hours on 3 November.

Yet Hitler – in another development that was often to be repeated as the war progressed – issued an immediate *Führerbefehl* (Führer-order) stating:

It is with trusting confidence in your leadership and the courage of the German–Italian troops under your command that the German people and I are following the heroic struggle in Egypt. In the situation in which you find yourself there can be no other thought but to stand fast, yield not a yard of ground and throw every gun and every man into the battle. The utmost efforts are being made to send you the means to continue the fight. Your enemy, despite his superiority, must also be at the end of his strength. It will not be the first time in history that a strong will has triumphed over the bigger battalions. As to your troops, you can show them no other road than that to victory or death. Adolf Hitler[43]

Rommel received this unequivocal 'Stand or die' order with bemusement. 'The Führer must be crazy,' he told a junior Staff officer.[44] Later he wrote that 'This order demanded the impossible. Even the most devoted soldier can be killed by a bomb.' Although the order was not officially rescinded until the 4th, in fact the Afrika Korps began a piecemeal withdrawal the previous night anyway. In Carver's estimation, if there was any attempt to put the *Führerbefehl* into effect it 'does not appear to have succeeded, even if it were seriously made'.[45] Five days later, on 9 November, Rommel noted in a letter that 'Courage which goes against military expediency is stupidity, or, if it is insisted upon by a commander, irresponsibility.' He blamed 'the custom at the Führer's HQ [of subordinating] military interests to those of propaganda'.[46] The irresponsibility of Hitler's 'Stand or die' demands had first been spotted by Rundstedt at Rostov in November 1941, but was destined to become the dominant leitmotiv of the rest of the war, as such *Führerbefehlen* were issued to commanders like confetti, preventing them from falling back, consolidating and adopting better defensible positions. Interestingly, however, Rommel was not reprimanded for ignoring the order. A darling of the Reich, recently raised to field marshal, his status meant that nothing more was heard of it. Only when Rommel was discovered to have shown disloyalty to Hitler politically, advocating the Führer's arrest by the Army, was he forced to commit suicide, on 14 October 1944. His death was ascribed to earlier wounds, and he was given a state funeral.

Faced with being outflanked from the south by the 7th Armoured Division, and with large sections of his army – especially the Italian infantry – surrendering in droves, Rommel withdrew to Fuka on 4 November. That night, Montgomery entertained the captured General von Thoma to dinner in his tent, in a scene reminiscent of the wars of earlier centuries. After a 'dogfight' that had indeed lasted the twelve days that Montgomery had predicted, the Afrika Korps quitted the field with as much equipment as its fuel supplies could extricate. This took place in comparatively good order, although those without motorized transport, including 20,000 Italians and 10,000 Germans, that is 29 per cent of Rommel's army, including nine generals, either surrendered on the field or were captured just behind it. In the desert, flight was not an option as on European battlefields; dying of thirst or starvation were the only alternatives to spending the rest of the war in captivity.

It has been argued that El Alamein need not have been fought at all, and that Rommel would have been forced to retreat once the Anglo-American landings began in North-West Africa the following month, and that 'Instead of a set-piece attack on a strongly fortified position, Eighth Army would have been better engaged in organising and training for the rapid pursuit and destruction of the retreating Axis forces.'[47] However, this does not take into account the British Commonwealth's desperate need for an authentic and major morale-boosting land victory over the Germans, to regain their military self-respect after three years of defeat and evacuation, and to dispel the myth of Rommel's invincibility. This El Alamein did. Yet it did more than just that; the Afrika Korps had been decisively defeated on the field of battle, the threat to Cairo ended and Rommel forced into headlong retreat.

In all, the Eighth Army suffered 13,560 casualties, or 8 per cent of its numbers, in the battle, against around 20,000 Axis killed or wounded, or 19 per cent.[48] The losses were 'by far the highest toll suffered by a British Army in the war so far'.[49] They fell heavily on the Commonwealth: one-fifth of them were Australians, and of the 16,000 New Zealanders who fought there, 3,000 were killed and 5,000 wounded. Yet Rommel was forced to leave around 1,000 guns and 450 tanks on the battlefield, and a further 75 tanks were abandoned during the retreat. In Carver's estimation, 'The Afrika Korps cannot have had more than 20 tanks, if that, left when they withdrew from Mersa Matruh on 8 November.' Malta was also now safe, at least once the Axis air bases at Martuba were overrun soon afterwards. Small wonder, then, that Churchill ordered the church bells of Britain to be rung out on Sunday, 15 November 1942 to celebrate the victory, the first time they had been heard since the invasion scares of thirty months earlier.

Montgomery's relatively tardy and cautious follow-up to Alamein – he took nine days to retake Tobruk – has been much criticized, but he understandably did not want to overreach himself, especially against an adversary like Rommel. Heavy rain at Fuka after 5 November ended the 2nd New Zealand Division's hopes of cutting off the Afrika Korps' long retreat back to Tripoli. 'Only the rain on 6 and 7 November saved them from complete annihilation,' wrote Montgomery afterwards. 'Four crack German divisions and eight Italian divisions had ceased to exist as effective fighting formations.'[50] Although Montgomery had fifteen times more tanks than Rommel on 5 November, and the ratio was to oscillate between 10:1 and 13:1 for the rest of the year, he wanted to take no risks with his victory.[51] 'The doom of the Axis forces in Africa was certain,' he wrote later, 'provided we made no mistakes.'[52]

No fewer than 500 Allied tanks had been put out of action in the battle, although only 150 irreparably. The fact that Rommel did not make a serious stand again for three months, and that was hundreds of miles to the west at the Mareth Line, shows how crushing El Alamein had been for him. The British Empire might have won its first land battle of the war against Germany, but it was to be the last major battle fought as an overwhelmingly imperial force. For, on the day that Rommel left Mersa Matruh, thousands of miles to the west an Anglo-American force was landing in Morocco and Algeria, under the aegis of Operation Torch. From now on the Allies would fight the war under joint command, with the supreme Allied commander more often than not an American.

Montgomery's victory at El Alamein should have provided a powerful inducement for the Vichy authorities in Africa to co-operate with the Allies during the invasions of Morocco and Algeria on Sunday, 8 November, codenamed Operation Torch. The landings represent the greatest amphibious operation since Xerxes crossed the Hellespont in 480 BC, outnumbering even the Gallipoli Expedition of 1915, which many feared it would emulate. The fighting nonetheless cost the French 3,000 casualties over three days, and the Allies 2,225. Small wonder that Torch's commander, the American general Dwight D. Eisenhower, wrote: 'I find myself getting absolutely furious with these Frogs.'[53] Torch was undertaken because the British refused to re-enter the European continent in north-west France, from where they had been ignominiously expelled in June 1940, until the Wehrmacht had been significantly weakened on the Eastern Front by the Russians, Germany had been heavily bombed, the Middle East was safe and the battle of the Atlantic unequivocally won. General Marshall's April 1942 plans for an early return to France – with either a nine-division assault codenamed Sledgehammer, or a forty-eight-division invasion codenamed Roundup – were both judged far too risky by General Brooke, since March 1942 the chairman of the British Chiefs of Staff as well as Chief of the Imperial General Staff. 'The plans are fraught with the gravest dangers,' he confided to his diary. 'The prospects of success are small and dependent on a mass of unknowns, whilst the chances of disaster are great and dependent on a mass of well established military facts.'[54]

General George C. Marshall, a courtly Pennsylvanian, and General Sir Alan Brooke, a flinty Ulsterman, were the primary military drivers behind Allied grand strategy in the war, alongside Roosevelt and Churchill. They had a fundamentally different view of how the war should be won, with Marshall arguing for an early cross-Channel assault in force and Brooke preferring to see German forces diverted and defeated piecemeal in North Africa, Sicily and Italy before the clash in north-west France was attempted. The meetings of the Anglo-American Combined Chiefs of Staff saw the arguments for each option debated aggressively from 1942 to 1944, with stand-up rows occasionally developing. Nonetheless the Allies' victory-by-committee approach was far superior to Hitler's supreme-warlord approach, in that it allowed for rational discussion, relatively open and logical argument and, ultimately, democratic control imposed by elected leaders. Marshall and Brooke furthermore respected each other as gentlemen, even when profoundly disagreeing over grand strategy.

President Roosevelt saw the political importance of striking against the Germans somewhere on land in 1942, and preferably before the mid-term Congressional elections, in order to protect the Germany

First policy from those American strategists who preferred to concentrate on the Pacific. On 25 July 1942, persuaded during a visit from Churchill to Roosevelt's country house Hyde Park, and galvanized by the fall of Tobruk on 20 June, the President came down firmly in favour of Operation Torch, which Marshall had to accept and then implement, despite having severe reservations about its practicality.[55] Marshall realized that a large-scale commitment to North Africa in late 1942 would effectively make an attack on France impossible in 1943. He resented this and was convinced that taking what he called 'side shots' in the Mediterranean had elongated the war, telling Brooke on more than one occasion that he considered the British had led the Americans down the garden path.[56]

It was nevertheless Marshall's clear duty to undertake Torch, and he hoped that its sheer size might minimize the massive risks involved. No fewer than 300 warships and 400 other vessels would carry more than 105,000 troops – three-quarters of them American and one-quarter British – from the eastern seaboard of the United States and the south coast of Great Britain to nine landing places up to 900 miles apart in Africa. Some 72,000 troops would leave from Britain and a further 33,843, in Task Force 34 under the overall command of Lieutenant-General George S. Patton, would cross the Atlantic Ocean from Hampton Roads, Virginia, with all the dangers that that entailed. Right up to the last moment, Rear-Admiral Henry Kent Hewitt wanted to put off the sailing of Task Force 34 for a week because an ebb tide was forecast for the Moroccan beaches at dawn on 8 November, and he preferred the landing craft to ride in on a rising one. Only Patton's force of personality ensured there was no delay from the agreed time.

George Smith Patton had been known to Americans ever since he had strapped the corpses of three bandits to his vehicle during the Punitive Expedition in Mexico in 1916. 'Old Blood and Guts' admitted to what he called 'the white-hot joy of taking human life', but he was prepared to risk his own too. 'If we are not victorious,' he told his men before one offensive in Tunisia, 'let no one come back alive.'[57] Other invocations to his troops included 'Grab those pusillanimous sons-of-bitches by the nose and kick 'em in the balls,' and '[Kill] lousy Hun bastards by the bushel.' At one dinner he toasted his officers' wives with the words: 'My, what pretty widows you're going to make.'[58] With his ivory-handled revolvers, polished steel helmet, riding boots and sharply creased breeches, and flamboyant and occasionally obscene language, Patton was clearly a showman, but he was also a Southern aristocrat who was fluent in French. His namesake grandfather was killed leading a Confederate brigade in 1864, and Patton was imbued with the belief that he had been reincarnated several times (always as a warrior). In his last incarnation he can be credited with formulating the US Army's first doctrine for armoured warfare, having commanded tanks in the Great War. Soon after Pearl Harbor, Patton was given command of the 1st US Armored Division, which despite being founded only in 1940 was nicknamed Old Ironsides. Every officer was expected to wear a necktie, every soldier to have his helmet buckled on tight. 'I'm going to be an awful irritation to the military historians,' General Patton once said, 'because I do things by sixth sense. They won't understand.'[59]

The supply for Patton's attack during Torch was meticulous, right down to the 6 tons of women's stockings and lingerie with which it was hoped that American commanders could bribe the local Arabs (and presumably also Vichy officials). Other essentials included 750,000 bottles of mosquito repellent, $100,000 in gold (to be signed for by Patton himself), 5 pounds of rat poison per company, 7,000 tons of coal, 3,000 vehicles, no fewer than 60 tons of maps and the new 2.36-inch M9 anti-tank rocket launcher (the bazooka). There were also 1,000 Purple Heart medals sent out in a secret crate, to be awarded to those wounded in action.[60] They would soon need more.

Overall control of Torch was exercised by (Acting) General Dwight David Eisenhower from the 30 miles of tunnels underneath the Rock of Gibraltar. 'Ike', as he was universally known, would jog the half-mile from the tunnel entrance to his bunker headquarters, and he had taken only one day's leave in the previous eleven months, which he had spent at the Army shooting range at Bisley in Surrey. So far Eisenhower had not seen a shot fired in anger during his entire military service, although later in the war he did fire at a rat in the bathroom at his Italian headquarters, missing it the first time but wounding it the second.[61] He nonetheless won the respect of Patton and Montgomery, although the former somewhat jealously noted in his diary that 'DD' stood for 'Divine Destiny', and the latter complained ceaselessly behind Eisenhower's back.

At times it must indeed have seemed like divine destiny that the third son of a failed Midwestern merchant, who had chosen a military career only because it afforded him a free education, who had never commanded so much as a platoon in combat, who had spent sixteen years as a major, and who thirty months before had been a mere lieutenant-colonel, could be placed in overall command of the largest amphibious operation of the past two millennia.[62] Yet Eisenhower's time in the Operations Division of the US War Department gave him a fine strategic sense, his mentor General George Marshall's stalwart support for him in Washington gave him political power, and his own charm and growing charisma gave him the ability to referee the increasingly bitter contests between the prima-donna generals who were to dominate the next stages of the western war, primarily Montgomery, Patton, Omar Bradley and Mark Clark. Squabbling schoolgirls could hardly have been as petty and bitchy as these senior Allied commanders. (Harold Alexander and William Slim were men of different temperaments, while Douglas MacArthur was 5,000 miles away.) One of Patton's biographers observes that he was 'obsessed with beating the British on the battlefield, both to satisfy his personal vanity and to demonstrate that the American soldier was second to none'.[63] Yet Patton was hardly any less hard on American rivals such as Mark Clark, and he recorded in his diary in September 1942: 'He seems to me more preoccupied with bettering his own future than with winning the war.'[64] The only consolation is that the German and Russian generals seem to have been just as vain, ambitious, backbiting and political as the British and American ones. The pretence of many generals to be bluff soldiers just doing their duty without regard to fame or promotion was for the most part just that.

Despite all the preparations at Gibraltar and elsewhere, and a need-to-know list numbering 800, somehow Torch achieved operational surprise. Both Vichy and the Abwehr assumed that such an attack was being considered, and the Italians even correctly predicted where it would land, but it was not spotted beforehand.[65] Task Force 34 was lucky that a U-boat wolf-pack off the Moroccan coast had moved off

THE STORM OF WAR

to attack a British convoy sailing from Sierra Leone, although a total of twelve merchant ships were not.

In all there were nine Torch landings at three ports in Africa, which met differing levels of resistance from the Vichy French forces. Those at Casablanca were unopposed on the beaches, which was fortunate because they were the riskiest in terms of high surf and heavy tides. Nevertheless immediately afterwards they met the fiercest resistance of all three. Meanwhile, Major-General Lloyd R. Fredendall's force attacked Oran over a 50-mile front, and met only 'hesitant and uncertain' resistance.[66] The briefest resistance of the three was faced by Major-General Charles W. Ryder's force at Algiers – the capital of the French Empire in North Africa – which attacked over a 25-mile front and suffered few casualties. The French Navy tended to be far more aggressive than the Army, recalling with undimmed fury the sinking of its fleet at Oran by the Royal Navy in July 1940. Yet its attempts at serious resistance collapsed after three days, once the sheer scale of the Allied offensive was revealed, especially at sea and in the air. Although Marshal Pétain issued orders for continued resistance against the Allies, the commander of all Vichy forces in Africa, Admiral Jean-Louis Darlan, whose great-grandfather had died at the hands of the British at the battle of Trafalgar and who Churchill said was 'a bad man with a narrow outlook and a shifty eye', nonetheless ordered a ceasefire on 10 November, just before Patton was about to storm Casablanca.[67] Pétain's actions were in part actuated by the knowledge that the Germans still had 1.5 million French soldiers in their POW camps. He did not save Vichy France, however, because the Germans invaded it that month, and soon afterwards Hitler congratulated Rundstedt, saying that he 'took timely, improvised countermeasures to ensure the integrity and sovereignty of the Reich in face of French armed forces that had broken their word'.[68] It seems that the French response to Torch satisfied neither the Allies nor the Axis. (As more Frenchmen bore arms for the Axis than for the Allies during the Second World War, it is unsurprising that there is still no official French history of the period.)[69]

By the morning of 11 November, Casablanca, Oran and Algiers were all in Allied hands. The Americans fronted the operation both because they provided larger numbers and because the French were thought to hate the British more, so each British soldier sewed the Stars and Stripes on to his sleeve. 'As long as it saves lives,' said a British officer, 'we don't care if we wear the bloody Chinese flag.'[70] Even after the success of Torch there continued to be gripes in Whitehall about various aspects of Eisenhower's command – such as the fact that after its move from Gibraltar his headquarters in Algiers, which he originally envisaged numbering about 150 officers, eventually ballooned to 16,000 – but his victory in Africa put him in pole position for future supreme commanderships as they arose, assuming they were not given to either Brooke or Marshall.

The French Admiral Jean Laborde's decision to scuttle three battleships, seven cruisers, twenty-nine destroyers, sixteen submarines and an aircraft carrier in Toulon on 27 November, rather than sail to Algiers, came as a serious blow to the Allies, as did the speed of the German response to Operation Torch. Two thousand troops were landed at Tunis as early as 9 November, and it soon became clear that Hitler intended to contest North Africa despite Rommel's defeat 1,000 miles to the east. In retrospect it would have been better had Eisenhower stuck to his original plans for landings deep inside the Mediterranean as far east as Bône on the Tunisian border, even though it was out of reach of air cover from Gibraltar. Marshall feared that this might over-extend the American forces, however, and invite retaliation from the Luftwaffe in Sicily, or even a German counterattack via Spain. Roosevelt therefore told Churchill on 30 August that he wanted to 'emphasize that under any circumstances one of our landings must be on the Atlantic'.[71] This meant that one-third of the task force would land 1,000 miles west of Tunis, the German capital in Africa and thus the ultimate objective, just in case the other two-thirds were sunk on their way to the Mediterranean or repulsed once ashore. 'Caution prevailed and audacity stole away,' rightly concludes a history of the campaign.[72] Although the commander of the British First Army, Lieutenant-General Kenneth Anderson, was to reach Bône by land by 12 November, thereafter the winter rains set in and he found himself at the end of a long supply line fighting on too wide a front – at 50 miles – to be able to seize Tunis.[73] Some units of the First Army got to within 15 miles of Tunis in early December, and 20 miles from Bizerta, but the Germans forced Anderson back with over a thousand casualties and the loss of seventy tanks. It was to take another six months for Tunis to fall.

Yet for two reasons it turned out to be fortunate for the Allies that the Germans in Africa did not collapse overnight in late 1942, and Eisenhower's order to Anderson to give up the drive on Tunis proved correct, however much consternation it created in the British High Command at the time about the Supreme Commander's fitness for the post. The first was that when they landed in Africa, as the American historian Rick Atkinson states, the soldiers of the US Army 'were fine men, but not yet a good army'. To defeat the Germans in north-west France they would need to be both, and the campaign in North Africa proved the best possible training ground for this. As Patton admitted over his capture of Casablanca, there would have been 'no victory to celebrate if his forces had been facing battle-hardened German defenders'.[74] The second reason was that Hitler's decision to continue to pour reinforcements into North Africa meant that the number of Axis troops captured – or 'bagged' in the British parlance of the day – was far higher than if he had ordered a withdrawal to Sicily immediately after Torch. Hitler actually sent far more men into Africa after Torch than Rommel had commanded in his initial struggle against Montgomery. In the campaigning after Torch, 8,500 Germans died, against around 10,000 Americans and 17,000 British killed, wounded and missing. Yet it was the 166,000 German and 64,000 Italian prisoners taken in Tunisia that puts that victory on a scale comparable with Stalingrad itself, a comparison that Goebbels himself privately made. And it was won at a fraction of the cost.

At a War Cabinet meeting on 16 November, Churchill said that Eisenhower had given a 'convincing' account of the political situation with regard to the French in North Africa, where after all they still had four divisions in Morocco, three in Algeria and one in Tunisia. Eisenhower's negotiations with Admiral Darlan had secured the cease-fire, at the price of establishing the recently pro-German Anglophobe in power in Algiers. Churchill described Darlan as a 'contemptible figure', pointing out that 'Whilst the French Navy was fighting, Darlan was negotiating.' Yet Churchill equally despised Darlan's rival, General Henri Giraud, who, he said: '1) signed a letter to Pétain saying he would behave, 2) then manoeuvred to get power for himself, 3) now he's accepted a commission from Eisenhower to fight.'[75] The discussion then moved on to American policy towards Darlan, which Eden said would outrage British public opinion; Churchill pointed out that Eisenhower was 'not our Commander-in-Chief' but added that the British 'Can't afford to upset Eisenhower just now ... Eisenhower is our friend – grand fellow – don't want to get across him.' The Foreign Secretary said that nonetheless Washington should be told 'fairly soon' that the Darlan position should not be stabilized, and that 'When [we] get [to] Tunis [we] ought to get rid of Darlan.' He did not specify whether he meant this in a political or a physical sense.

The assassination of Admiral Darlan by a young French patriot in Algiers on Christmas Day 1942 threw the already volatile political situation into turmoil, but it helped to make possible a public reconciliation between the (British-backed) Free French leader Charles de Gaulle and the (American-backed) Giraud. SIS involvement in the assassination has long been suspected, but never substantiated, although Lawrence Burgis' verbatim notes of what Anthony Eden said at the War Cabinet meeting only six weeks before can only further encourage speculation. The cordial mutual loathing of de Gaulle and Giraud did not prevent them from shaking hands (albeit reluctantly) at a conference that was held in January 1943 between the British and American High Commands at Casablanca. It was there that Roosevelt announced that the Allies would accept nothing less than unconditional surrender from the Axis, a decision that was agreed beforehand by the American Joint Chiefs of Staff and by the British War Cabinet. Although the President has been criticized for promulgating this position, as it was thought to strengthen the Nazis' commitment to fight on to the death, it had the effect of calming Soviet fears that the Western Allies might make a separate peace with Germany. It was also at Casablanca that Roosevelt and Churchill conferred on where to attack once the Germans were expelled from Africa. After much tough negotiation, it was concluded that the Germans would have been able to remove their troops from Corsica or Sardinia, which were anyway further from the Allies' African bases. So Sicily was chosen as the most direct route. Churchill had observed by 11 February that Hitler had a possibly fatal strategic blind spot, in that he was psychologically incapable of giving up ground once it had been won. 'It is, indeed, quite remarkable', he told the House of Commons that day,

that the Germans should have shown themselves ready to run the risk and pay the price required of them by their struggle to hold the Tunisian tip. While I always hesitate to say anything which might afterwards look like over-confidence, I cannot resist the remark that one seems to discern in this policy the touch of the master hand, the same master hand that planned the attack on Stalingrad, and that has brought upon the German armies the greatest disaster they have ever suffered in all their military history.[76]

*

'During the last weeks of January 1943,' records a history of Torch, 'Rommel was shepherded warily towards the Tunisian frontier by Montgomery's forces.'[77] Driven across that border early in February, the Afrika Korps prepared to make a stand at the Mareth Line, its first major attempt to halt Montgomery since El Alamein. As these units dug in, however, Rommel flew westwards to perform one of his stunning counter-attacks, in a series of five engagements collectively known as the battle of the Kasserine Pass. This struggle, between Rommel's Afrika Korps and Major-General Fredendall's II Corps through the Western Dorsal mountain range in Tunisia between 14 and 22 February, perfectly illustrates the formidable and apparently ubiquitous German capacity for counter-attack, and illustrates why Marshall's plan for an early attack on north-west France was probably impracticable.

The initial defence of the pass had to be carried out by the US 19th Combat Engineer Battalion, a construction unit that had not completed rifle training before being shipped overseas, and only one member of which had seen active service before, as well as an infantry battalion from the 1st Division and a four-gun French battery, barely 2,000 men all told.[78] 'Machine guns were badly sited, foxholes were too shallow, and barbed wire remained mostly on the spools. Nearly every man had entrenched on the floor of the pass, rather than the adjacent heights.'[79] Anti-tank mines had been dumped rather than buried and there were not enough sandbags or entrenching tools. This was no way to send green GIs into battle, especially against German veterans who had fought in Poland, France and Russia, and were now armed with the six-barrelled 75-pound high explosive Nebelwerfer ('fog-throwing') mortar.

Major-General Orlando Ward's 1st Armored Division was split into small units, and an Allied counter-attack was ambushed, with 'appalling' ground-to-air liaison and 'lamentable' co-operation between US armour, artillery and infantry, which led to more than 6,000 Allied casualties out of the 30,000 engaged, against 989 German casualties (of whom only 201 were killed), and 535 Italians captured. Fredendall's corps alone lost 183 tanks, 104 half-tracks, 200 guns and 500 trucks and jeeps.[80] Although Rommel's counter-attack finally petered out on the road to Thala called Highway 17, it was not before he had almost broken through to the straight roads and flat country which led to the Le Kef supply depots only 40 miles away. 'I felt strategic fear,' the highly competent commander of the French forces in the region, General Alphonse Juin, later admitted, 'for if Rommel broke through, all of North Africa was doomed.'[81] This included more than a touch of Gallic hyperbole: the 10th Panzer Division's fifty tanks, thirty guns and 2,500 infantry were not about to thrust the Allies all the way back to Casablanca, but they could possibly have turned the tide in Tunisia. Instructed therefore to hold the town 'at all costs', Brigadier Charles Dunphie of the British 26th Armoured Brigade ordered 'every cook, driver and batman in Thala to the [front] line'.[82] A tank fight developed in the dark of night at 20 yards' range, with Dunphie losing twenty-nine of his fifty tanks before midnight. The arrival at 08.00 hours the next day of Brigadier-General Stafford Le Roy Irwin of the US 9th Infantry Division with, as one historian has put it, '2,200 men, 48 guns and a killer's heart', was critical in persuading Rommel not to press on further that morning, and instead an intensive artillery duel developed through the day.[83]

With four days' rations and only enough fuel to drive 200 miles, and intelligence reports of the reinforcement of Thala, Rommel appeared 'depressed' to Field Marshal Albert Kesselring, who as commander-in-chief south had overall responsibility for the Mediterranean Basin and who visited Kasserine to confer with him. 'Rommel was physically worn out and psychologically fatigued,' thought Kesselring, noting that 'he had undoubtedly turned into a tired old man'. In the event, the outskirts of Thala was the furthest the Axis were ever to get in North-West Africa, and on the night of Monday, 22 February 1943 the Afrika Korps turned back, with the 21st Panzer Division acting as rearguard. It took three days for the Americans and British to reach the pass, and to organize Italian POW burial parties to bury the many corpses found there.

Fredendall had been forced back 85 miles in seven days, and Eisenhower's amanuensis Harry Butcher noted that his 'proud and cocky' countrymen 'today stand humiliated by one of the greatest defeats in our history'.[84] The blame for Kasserine must be shared by Anderson, Eisenhower and Fredendall, and the last was swiftly replaced by Patton, but the German assault had nonetheless petered out, leaving the Desert Fox exhausted and blown. Co-operation between the British, French and Americans had been dire, at least until Eisenhower's deputy Harold Alexander arrived the next month to take over command of the 18th Army Group, comprising the British First and Eighth Armies, the French XIX Corps and the US II Corps. (When Patton arrived to take up command of II Corps, General Omar Bradley later recalled the 'procession of armoured cars and half-tracks [that] wheeled into the dingy square opposite the schoolhouse headquarters at Djebel Kouif on the late morning of 7 March. In the lead car Patton stood like a charioteer. He was scowling into the wind and his jaw strained against the web strap of a two-starred general.')[85]

The defeat at the Kasserine Pass – and the humiliating sight of 4,026 Allied POWs being marched from the Colosseum through Rome – ended any mood of over-confidence, and reminded each component of the Western alliance of the importance of close co-operation. 'Our people from the very highest to the very lowest have learned that this is not a child's game,' Eisenhower reported to Marshall on 24 February. Yet it must be remembered that the Kasserine Pass was recaptured only days after the defeat. Despite having fallen back more than 1,000 miles, Rommel was still not getting the supplies he needed. He estimated that he required 140,000 tons of supplies a month to sustain him, and by early 1943 was receiving only one-quarter of that. Furthermore, almost every request to Kesselring in Rome was – unbeknown to him – landing on Eisenhower's desk via Ultra, often within six hours of transmission.

By 17 March Patton was ready to advance, and he delivered this message to his troops:

Fortunately for our fame as soldiers, our enemy is worthy of us. The German is a war-trained veteran – confident, brave and ruthless. We are brave. We are better equipped, better fed, and in the place of his blood-glutted Woten, we have with us the God of our Fathers, Known of Old . . . If we die killing, well and good, but if we fight hard enough, viciously enough, we will kill and live. Live to return to our family and our girl as conquering heroes – men of Mars.[86]

While Patton attacked Rommel's rear – and with fine covering artillery support defeated the veteran German 10th Panzer Division at El Guettar – the Eighth Army attacked the Mareth Line on 20 March, but got bogged down in the minefield. Montgomery nonetheless took the port of Sfax shortly afterwards. The nutcracker effect of Patton and Montgomery on each side of Rommel was one that was to lead to a ludicrous competitiveness – culminating in outright enmity – between the two men. 'God damn all British and all so-called Americans who have their legs pulled by them,' Patton wrote in his diary. 'I would rather be commanded by an Arab. I think less than nothing of Arabs.'[87] Montgomery's vanity has already been noted, but this is what Patton wrote in his diary before sailing on Torch: 'When I think of the greatness of my job and realise that I am what I am, I am amazed, but on reflection, who is as good as I am? I know of no one.'[88] Yet there was a sentimental side to the bruiser too: Patton wept at his ADC's funeral and put flowers on his grave before leaving the North African theatre.

The final part of the campaign from March 1943 saw Mark Clark's II Corps – Patton had passed on the command in order to plan for the invasion of Sicily – attacking the northern sector of the Axis defensive position, and some particularly tough fighting by the US 34th Division for a defensive position called Hill 609. Only twenty months earlier, that division had been composed merely of National Guard units from Iowa and Minnesota. Anderson's First Army and Montgomery's Eighth Army also played crucial roles, which were reallocated by Alexander to ensure that the British and Americans jointly took the glory for expelling the Axis from Africa.

Constantly refusing Rommel's reasonable and strategically sound requests to extricate his forces from Africa, Hitler proceeded in early 1943 to make precisely the same mistake that he had at Stalingrad in late 1942, reinforcing defeat and issuing 'Stand or die' orders that amounted to demands for suicidal resistance for no appreciable gain. Yet Bradley took Bizerta on 7 May, the same day that the British finally entered Tunis. The British suffered heavily in the Tunisian campaign: of the 70,000 Allied casualties in Tunisia, more than half were British and, of those, two-thirds were suffered by the First Army.[89] The Eighth Army has taken much of the glory and the attention of history, but the First Army deserves recognition too.

For there was plenty of glory to be shared by the end of the campaign. Although an ill Rommel was himself evacuated from Tunis back to Germany on 9 March, his successor General Hans-Jürgen von Arnim was captured on 13 May, along with no fewer than 230,000 other POWs, 200 tanks and 1,200 guns. 'The Tunisian campaign is over,' Alexander cabled Churchill. 'We are masters of the North African shore.' Six days later Churchill chose the opportunity of his speech to the US Congress to underline the point about 'the military intuition of Corporal Hitler' that he had made in London back in February. To be an object of fear and hatred was perfectly acceptable to Hitler, but Churchill wanted to transform him into one of derision and mirth. The master of parliamentary ridicule had spotted a way of mocking 'Corporal Hitler', as he increasingly took to calling him, and he unerringly grasped it. 'We may notice', he said of German strategy in Africa, 'the touch of the master hand. The same insensate obstinacy which condemned Field Marshal von [sic] Paulus and his army to destruction at Stalingrad has brought this new catastrophe upon our enemies in Tunisia.'[90]

10

The Motherland Overwhelms
the Fatherland

January 1942–February 1943

Animals flee this hell; the hardest stones cannot bear it for long; only men endure.
A lieutenant in the 24th Panzer Division at Stalingrad, 1942[1]

In their original conception the plans for Operation Barbarossa had not even mentioned the city of Stalingrad (present-day Volgograd). Hitler's idea was to reach a line running from Archangel in the north to Astrakhan on the Caspian Sea, with Leningrad, Moscow and the Volga river, upon which Stalingrad lies, well within the German-occupied zone. Yet because by the summer and autumn of 1942 Leningrad and Moscow still held out, and indeed the Soviets had been launching counter-offensives since December 1941, Stalingrad was to loom large in Hitler's calculations. In January and February 1942, Russian attacks along the line from Finland down to the Crimea had seen several notable successes. Although Leningrad and Sevastopol could not be relieved, nor Kharkov recaptured, Rostov was retaken and the immediate threat to Moscow was lifted by the recapture of Kallinin and Kaluga and the elimination of German salients close to the city. By the time the great thaw set in between March and May, the Russians had advanced their front westwards by 120 miles near Rostov and up to 150 miles further north, bringing it close to Smolensk.

The Wehrmacht's response was the second German summer offensive, Fall Blau (Operation Blue), intended to achieve in 1942 what they had seemed so close to grasping in 1941. It was launched on 8 May with no fewer than fifty-one divisions, including many from the satellite countries of Italy, Romania, Hungary and Slovakia, as well as a division of Spanish volunteers. There was something of a Faustian compact involved in the use of these non-German troops, for although they made up the numbers necessary for warfare in Russia, they were not always as reliable or as effective as German and Austrian troops. Nonetheless, Blau won early and significant successes: Sevastopol fell to amphibious attack on 2 July and the Russians were then expelled from the rest of the Crimea. Field Marshal Fedor von Bock, who had commanded Army Group Centre in the invasion, was sacked and replaced by Kluge in December 1941 for failing to take Moscow, but was recalled to command Army Group South in February 1942. He had captured Voronezh by 7 July and the Eleventh Army of the newly created field marshal Erich von Manstein took the Kerch peninsula, from which it could cross into the Caucasus. At this key moment, on 13 July 1942, Hitler took the vital decision to try to capture Stalingrad and the Caucasus in the same campaigning season. He therefore sacked Bock again and split Army Group South into two, giving the separate parts different but complementary tasks. Army Group B in the north under General Baron Maximilian von Weichs was to clear the Don and Donets valleys and capture Stalingrad. This would provide cover for Army Group A in the south, under Field Marshal Wilhelm List, to capture first Rostov and then the whole of the oil-rich Caucasus. 'If we do not capture the oil supplies of the Caucasus by the autumn,' Hitler said, 'then I shall have to face the fact that we cannot win this war.'[2] When autumn came, it was not a remark of which anyone was to remind him.

On 22 July 1942, having been transferred from Army Group B to Army Group A five days earlier, the Fourth Panzer Army crossed the Don east of Rostov. Hitler believed that Stalingrad could be taken by the Sixth Army alone, so he sent the Fourth Panzer Army southwards. Yet only a week later, on 29 July, he countermanded this order, and the Fourth Panzer Army was instead directed to attack Stalingrad from the south. Few things disorientate and demoralize troops more than the countermanding of recently issued orders, as it implies confusion at the very highest level of command. As Hitler's power depended on seeming omniscient, even 1,000 miles behind the lines, this was dangerous. Paul von Kleist, whose First Panzer Army led the drive into the Caucasus, believed Hitler had made a fatal error, writing later of this incident:

The Fourth Panzer Army was advancing on my left. It could have taken Stalingrad without a fight at the end of July, but was diverted south to help me in crossing the Don. I did not need its aid. It merely congested the roads I was using. When it turned north again a fortnight later, the Russians had gathered just enough forces at Stalingrad to check it.[3]

The OKH Chief of Staff, Franz Halder, continually warned against Hitler's over-confidence, pointing out the presence of Russian divisions that had not existed even the previous autumn, and predicting disaster for the Sixth Army in its thrust towards Stalingrad. On 23 July, Halder confided to his (fortunately well-hidden) war diary, about how the Führer, when faced with his realism,

explodes in a fit of insane rage and hurls the gravest reproaches against the General Staff. This chronic tendency to underrate enemy capabilities is gradually assuming grotesque proportions and develops into a positive danger ... This so-called leadership is characterized by a pathological reacting to the impressions of the moment and a total lack of any understanding of the command machinery and its possibilities.[4]

Halder told Lieutenant-General Kurt Dittmar of OKH that Hitler 'was a mystic, who tended to discount, even when he did not disregard, all the rules of strategy'.[5] A week later, on 30 July, Halder recorded that Jodl 'announces pompously that the fate of the Crimea will be decided at Stalingrad and that, if possible, it would be necessary to divert forces from AGp.A to AGp.B, if possible, south of the Don'.[6] The diversion of such forces meant that neither army group was able to achieve its objectives under Operation Blau, and on 9 September Hitler dismissed List and took personal command of Army Group A, a post for which he was entirely unqualified, not least because he intended to stay in East Prussia directing its operations from his headquarters, codenamed the Wolfschanze (Wolf's Lair).

Though over-optimistic, the desire to take the important industrial city of Stalingrad was perfectly understandable. With its capture, the oil terminal of Astrakhan would be within reach, and the Russians would be denied the use of the Volga for transportation. Furthermore,

Army Group A in the Caucasus would be safe from another Soviet winter offensive, attacks northwards could be launched again, and the fall of Stalin's own name-city would be as good for German morale as it would be bad for Russian. Its capture therefore seemed to make sense at the time. What made less sense was the way that Manstein's Eleventh Army, which was badly needed in the south as a reserve in case Blau did not go according to plan, was suddenly reallocated to Leningrad.

Although the British and Americans initially had little faith that the Russians could survive Operation Barbarossa, and privately feared the worst until the Germans were turned back from Moscow in December 1941, by mid-1942 the Western Allies recognized that they could give the Russians invaluable help by drawing off German units. Stalin certainly underlined this point in his meetings with Churchill in Moscow between 12 and 15 August 1942, and did not hide his ire that no Second Front – as a large-scale assault in the west was (rather inaccurately) named – would be in the offing that year. Although General Marshall wanted to launch such an operation as soon as practicable, President Roosevelt, Churchill and Brooke all believed that an over-hasty return to the Continent might be suicidal. The most that Churchill would offer was a small-scale amphibious assault, designated a 'reconnaissance in force', on the French port of Dieppe, on the Channel coast.

This attack, which was undertaken on 19 August 1942, was not large enough to require any German forces to be diverted from the Eastern Front, yet was easily large enough for its failure to be a shattering blow to the 5,100 Canadians and 1,000 British Commandos and American Rangers who had to carry it out. Supported by 252 ships (though none larger than a destroyer, and thus unable to provide heavy gunfire from the sea) and sixty-nine squadrons of aircraft (which nonetheless gave only intermittent air support), Operation Jubilee was also large enough to be spotted in the Channel by a German coastal convoy, yet not large enough to achieve anything of consequence once it landed, even had it been a success. The intelligence was faulty, the planning – undertaken by the Director of Combined Operations, Lord Mountbatten – was profoundly flawed, and the results were little short of catastrophic. Within six hours of landing, three-quarters of the Canadian forces had been killed, wounded or captured, and all seven battalion commanders wounded. The Commandos and Rangers also suffered heavily.

Efforts were made, both at the time and since, to present the Dieppe Raid as having taught the Allies valuable lessons about the way the French coast could be assaulted, which were subsequently put to invaluable use in Normandy in June 1944. In fact sheer common sense ought to have told the Combined Chiefs of Staff that Mountbatten's plan was misconceived from the outset, that tanks could not attack up shingle beaches with high esplanade walls, that proper sea and air support was required and that surprise was essential.

Meanwhile in the east General Friedrich Paulus' Sixth Army was designated to take Stalingrad (he had a force of around 280,000 men at the start of the battle), and by Sunday, 23 August the 16th Panzer Division had crossed the steppe to reach the Volga just north of the city. Once there, however, the Germans could do little to interdict the river traffic because they had no naval weaponry or river-mines. They had brought along their exterminatory ideology, however, so when the Wehrmacht – there were no SS involved in the battle of Stalingrad – reached the hospital for mentally handicapped children in the city, they promptly shot all the ten- to fourteen-year-old patients.[7]

In the short term, Army Group A did well in the Caucasus. Rostov fell on 23 July, Kleist's First Panzer Army captured Stavropol on 5 August, and the Germans seemed about to grasp the region. At their furthest point, elements of the First Panzer Army almost reached Ordzhonikidze and were less than 50 miles from Grozny and only 70 miles from the Caspian Sea. The loss of the Caucasus, from where the Russians took 90 per cent of the oil that fuelled their tanks, planes, ships and industry, would have been catastrophic for the Allied cause. The Russians could not retake it except by crossing the 1,300-yard-wide River Volga, and by the late summer Stalingrad, on the west bank on the bend of that river, seemed about to fall. 'What's the matter with them?' Stalin asked of the local military commanders there. 'Don't they realize that this is not only a catastrophe for Stalingrad? We would lose our main waterway and soon our oil too.'[8] The stakes could therefore hardly have been higher.

*

The battle of Stalingrad is deservedly considered to be the most desperate in human history. The German Sixth Army was sucked into a house-by-house, street-by-street, factory-by-factory struggle often even more attritional than the trench warfare of the Great War. The city is 25 miles long and hugs the western bank of the River Volga, confusingly called the right bank because the river flows southwards towards the Caspian. Visiting Volgograd today, and viewing the city-length battlefield, one is immediately struck by the problems faced by the Germans in their assault. To the north lie three huge factories – from north to south, the Dzerzhinsky Tractor Factory, the Barrikady (Barricades) Arms Factory and the Krasny Oktyabr (Red October) Factory. In the centre is the 300-foot-high Mamayev Kurgan, the highest hill in the city (originally the burial mound of the Tatar Duke Mamayev) and all the southern approaches to the city are dominated by an enormous reinforced-concrete Grain Elevator, which stayed in Russian hands for much of the siege, supplied by trenches and gullies connecting it to the Volga. The Wehrmacht had to capture these formidable obstacles in order to take the city.

The Red October Factory specialized in recycling metal, the Barrikady Factory in military hardware, and the Tractor Factory, named after the monstrously cruel 'Iron' Felix Dzerzhinsky, founder of the Bolshevik secret police, makes tractors to this day, which roll past his larger-than-life-sized statue there. In 1942 it had been turned over to making tank chassis. These three brick and concrete buildings – each half a mile long and between 500 and 1,000 yards wide – were originally erected for industrial production rather than defence, of course, but their sturdy structures might just as easily have been designed specifically for keeping out enemy armies. Although the three great factories and their adjacent Settlements (that is, workers' tenement blocks) were well spaced, they were connected by roads that were not metalled in 1942. 'In Russia,' the old saying goes, 'we have no roads, only directions.'

As well as reaching the Volga north of Stalingrad, on 23 August the Germans bombed the city's giant oil storage tanks, setting them alight. The *Krasnaya Zvezda* (Red Star newspaper) journalist Vasily Grossman, who specialized in reporting the activities of *frontoviki* (front-line troops), wrote of how:

The fire rose thousands of feet, carrying with it clouds of vaporized oil that exploded into flame only high in the sky. The mass of flame was so vast that the whirlwind was unable to bring enough oxygen to the burning molecules of hydrocarbon; a black, swaying vault separated the starry sky of autumn from the burning earth. It was terrible to look up to see a black firmament streaming with oil.[9]

The oil burnt for more than a week, and the pillars of heavy smoke could be seen throughout the region. At one point a spillage caused the Volga itself to catch fire. The battlefield commander of the Russian forces in the city, General Vasily Ivanovich Chuikov, recalled that 'clouds of thick black smoke hung over us. Flakes of ash and soot descended on us all the time, so that everything at the command post turned black and looked black.' The Luftwaffe dropped not just conventional bombs, but any random pieces of metal that could do damage such as plough-shares, tractor wheels, harrows and empty metal casks, which Chuikov remembered 'whistled about the heads of our troops'.[10] Grossman interviewed many of the leading figures in the defence of Stalingrad, including Chuikov, and he recorded in his 1964 novel *Life and Fate*: 'An iron whirlwind howled over the bunker, slicing through anything living that raised its head above the earth's headquarters.'[11]

Chuikov had joined the Red Army in 1918 aged eighteen. He fought in the Civil War and the Russo-Polish War and attended the elite Frunze Military Academy, before becoming Soviet military attaché to China for eleven years after 1926, thereby escaping some of the worst years of the purges. A protégé of Zhukov, he had fought in the Polish and Finnish campaigns of 1939–40 before being given command of the Soviet Sixty-second Army in Stalingrad. 'He was a tough street-fighter, described by one of his staff officers as a "coarse" man – *gruby* – who had been known to hit officers whose performance displeased him with a big stick he carried.'[12] For all that, he was a leader, who staked everything on the Red Army remaining on the right bank of the Volga.

The Luftwaffe's initial bombing policy, which had the effect of turning Stalingrad almost into a lunar moonscape, eventually worked in the Soviet defenders' favour. The rubble had to be fought over brick by brick, exactly the kind of warfare that benefited the far larger but less well-equipped Russian Army. Before the Germans' arrival, Stalingrad had been inadequately fortified, with Chuikov observing that the barricades outside the city could be pushed over by a truck. Both K. A. Gurov, the Sixty-second Army's senior commissar, and General N. I. Krylov, its chief of staff, agreed that the defences were 'laughable', and Chuikov accurately told Grossman that 'In the defence of Stalingrad, divisional commanders counted more on blood than barbed wire.'[13] Chuikov coined the expression 'the Stalingrad Academy of Street-Fighting' and, for all the Germans' martial skill and bravery in that school, it was the Russians who graduated *summa cum laude*. The Germans called the brutal, hand-to-hand, no-quarter-given fighting in cellars and sewers, with rifles, bayonets, grenades and even spades, *Rattenkrieg* (rat warfare). Grossman cited an occasion when a German and a Russian patrol were both in the same house, unaware of the other's proximity. When the Germans wound up a gramophone on the floor below, betraying their presence, the Soviet troops made a hole in the floor and fired through it with a flame-thrower. So close-quarter was the combat at times that when Major-General V. Zholudev's 37th Guards Infantry Division broke into houses in *Shturmovaya* (storming groups), their weapon of choice was the knife.[14]

The Germans on the right bank had the advantage of heavy weaponry, but when the Russians were able to get hold of long-barrelled anti-tank guns, and use them on the flanks of Panzers sent into Stalingrad, they could be highly effective. 'When you've hit it,' a thirty-eight-year-old rifleman called Gromov told Grossman, describing the destruction of a German tank,

'you see a bright flash on the armour. The shot deafens one terribly, one has to open one's mouth. I was lying there, I heard shouts: "They're coming!" My second shot hit the tank. The Germans started screaming terribly. We could hear them clearly. I wasn't scared even a little. My spirits soared. At first, there was some smoke, then crackling, then flames. Evtikhov had hit one vehicle. He hit the hull, and how the Fritzes screamed!' (Gromov has light green eyes in a suffering, angry face.)[15]

Once Soviet reinforcements arrived at the railway station on the left bank during the battle, they were ferried across the Volga, on boats that took appalling punishment from the Luftwaffe. Grossman described how 'Those launches that did get through to Chuikov were holed fifty to seventy times in only a few minutes. They arrived at the right bank with their decks covered in blood.'[16] The journalist, who himself crossed the river under fire, fortified by 'a huge amount' of cider from a nearby collective farm, found the Volga 'terrifying like a scaffold'.[17] Most crossings took place after nightfall, when the Stukas could no longer operate, and sometimes the smaller launches were buried under the sand of the beaches during the day, ready to be dug up and used the following evening. The 10th NKVD Rifle Division policed the crossing points, shooting deserters and preventing civilians from escaping. Stalin believed that the presence of civilians would make the troops fight harder, but after the air raids of 23 August 300,000 were evacuated, nonetheless leaving 50,000. Of these, only around 10,000 survived the battle, including 904 children, a mere nine of whom could be reunited with their parents.[18]

On 28 August, responsibility for the overall defence of the Stalingrad sector was given to General Georgi Zhukov, a commander who fully deserves the subtitle of his recent biography: *The Man Who Beat Hitler*.[19] Born of peasant parents, Zhukov was conscripted into the Russian Army in 1914 and joined the Red Army in October 1918, serving first in the cavalry and then in armoured mobile units before joining the High Command. At the battle of Khalkin Gol in August 1939, Zhukov proved that even a decapitated Red Army could defeat the modern, efficient Japanese. Commanding in Mongolia also kept Zhukov away from the Winter War against Finland, in which few Russian generals shone. After June 1941 he assisted Voroshilov in the defence of Leningrad, being brought back to Moscow by Stalin to co-ordinate the great 1941 winter counter-offensive. He was therefore a natural choice for the overall command of the Stalingrad campaign. Although much of the war was spent at the Stavka, the Russian High Command in Moscow, Zhukov's driver estimated that he covered more than 50,000 miles by road and wore out three aircraft visiting the various fronts. Decisive, tough, energetic, personally brave, occasionally cruel – he would strike officers and occasionally attended the executions of subordinates – Zhukov was a meticulous planner and always showed complete confidence in ultimate victory. High casualty rates never unnerved him in the slightest. It was always going to take such a commander – one who displayed the military equivalent of Stalin's political ruthlessness – to win this existential struggle.

Meanwhile, Franz Halder's diary entry for 30 August illustrates Hitler's highly strung nature as he committed the cardinal error of fighting according to the enemy's strengths rather than his own: 'Today's conferences with [the] Führer were again the occasion of abusive reproaches against the military leadership of the highest commands. He charges them with intellectual conceit, mental non-adaptability, and utter failure to grasp essentials.'[20] The next day Hitler declared that it was all a 'Problem of toughness! The enemy will need his strength sooner than we do ... So long as the enemy suffers losses in his approach, let him run; someone will collapse; not us. By [the time of the fall of St] Petersburg [that is, Leningrad] six to eight divisions are free.' He later spoke of 'World War I circumstances. Heavy barrages' – that is, precisely the war of attrition he most needed to avoid, and probably the only type of warfare which the Soviets could win against the Wehrmacht.[21] Hitler's error in not fighting a war of manoeuvre in Russia, but instead contesting with maximum mutual attrition cities such as Stalingrad, is all the more reprehensible from one who had himself fought in the trenches of the Great War.

Understanding the propaganda blow that would follow its fall, Stalin told the Stavka on 12 September that his name-city – later one of the 'hero-cities' of the Soviet Union – had to stay in Russian hands at all costs.[22] Yet at dawn the next morning the Sixth Army launched its major offensive, with the 295th Infantry Division driving straight for the Mamayev Kurgan, which today contains the graves of 35,000 soldiers of both sides. By the evening of 13 September the German 71st Infantry Division had broken into the city centre. On the 14th the main railway station changed hands five times in one day, and was to change hands another thirteen times over the next three days.[23]

The battle of Stalingrad is suffused with legends and, as with all great battles, some events are blown out of proportion – often by the veterans themselves – whereas other moments that might in truth have been equally important are minimized by posterity, sometimes because of the sheer lack of survivors. Fierce historiographical battles have also inevitably been fought over the fiercest battle ever contested.

Generals became jealous of each other's fame, and politicians of generals, thus further blurring the testimony. Finally, political ideology during the Cold War also badly skewed the history. One undeniably extraordinary moment in the battle, however, came at 17.00 hours on 14 September during the crossing of the Volga by the 13th Guards Rifle Division, under the Spanish Civil War hero General Alexandr Rodimtsev, which charged up the steep bank to engage the Germans, who had reached to within 200 yards of the river. Rodimtsev's division of over 10,000 men was reduced to only 320 survivors by the end of the battle.

Grossman vividly recorded the many perils of the river crossing:

'He's diving, the louse!' someone shouted. Suddenly, a tall and thin bluish column of water sprang up about fifty metres from the barge. Immediately after another column grew and collapsed even closer, and then a third one. Bombs were exploding on the surface of the water, and the Volga was covered with lacerated foamy wounds; shells began to hit the side of the barge. Injured men would cry out softly, as if trying to conceal the fact of being wounded. By then, rifle bullets had already started whistling over the water.[24]

The story of Stalingrad is also indelibly linked to the phenomenon of snipers, the more successful of whom, such as Anatoly Chekhov and Vasily Zaitsev, became heroes throughout the Soviet Union. With near-destroyed buildings littering the city, well-hidden sharp-shooters on both sides could keep up an accurate and debilitating fire against almost anyone moving anywhere. Counter-sniper actions became part of the Stalingrad myth, too, since flushing snipers out was costly and difficult. 'I killed forty Fritzes in eight days,' claimed Chekhov, who served in the 13th Guards Rifle Division. Even though Zaitsev began as a sniper only on 21 October, his supporters claimed that he shot 149 people; and another sniper, Zikan, allegedly killed 224.[25] When the Germans persuaded starving Russian children to fill their water bottles from the Volga, in return for a crust of bread, Red Army snipers shot these 'traitors to the Motherland' as they returned from the river. The extent to which the (notoriously untruthful) Soviet propaganda machine exaggerated the snipers' totals can never now be checked, but reports of exploits such as Zaitsev's were good for morale, and today he is buried in pride of place on the Mamayev

Kurgan. Women also made good snipers, and Tanya Chernova of the 284th Siberian Division claimed eighty kills in three months.

During the battle of Stalingrad, the NKVD shot around 13,500 Russian soldiers – the size of an entire fully manned division – for treachery, cowardice, desertion, drunkenness and 'anti-Soviet agitation'. The condemned men were ordered to undress before execution, so that their uniforms could be reissued 'without too many discouraging bullet-holes'.[26] Stalin's 'Not One Step Back' Order No. 227 of July 1941 had made provision for each army command to detail up to one thousand men to 'combat cowardice'. In circumstances as terrible as those at Stalingrad, any lesser punishment would probably have led to mutinies and mass desertion. 'The only extenuating cause for withdrawing from a firing position', Komsomol (Young Communist League) members were told, 'is death.'[27]

Burials during the battle took place at night, with volleys fired not into the air, but at the German lines. Chuikov ordered that the no man's land between the front lines should be kept as small as possible, both to wear down the enemy's nerves and to give the Luftwaffe as little opportunity as possible to strafe the Russian lines, for fear of killing their own troops. (Ever-present Russian black humour was at its sharpest during Soviet friendly-fire incidents, with jokes such as 'Here we go, the Second Front has opened at last!')[28] The close proximity of the lines meant that soldiers could call out to each other. 'Rus,' one German joked about the Russians' supposedly unreliable Uzbecki troops, 'do you want to swap an Uzbeck for a Romanian?' There were incidents of grenades being tossed such short distances that they could be tossed back before they exploded.

Coming at right angles from the Volga is a succession of deep, narrow *balkas* (gullies), which can still be seen today and which were fought over with particular fierceness as they provided good cover for both defenders and attackers, who could turn each other's flanks if they won possession. 'Command posts or mortar units use it,' Grossman wrote of the series of *balkas*. 'It is always under fire. Many people have been killed here. Wires go through it, ammunition is carried through it.' Describing the German onslaught of 27 September 1942 in the first volume of his memoirs, *The Beginning of the Road*, Chuikov recalled that telephone communication broke down, constant smoke hampered visual reconnaissance, Staff and signals officers were killed and his command post was under attack the entire time, and he remembered concluding: 'One more attack like that and we'll be in the Volga.'[29] There were in fact plenty more attacks just like that, with Chuikov's headquarters having to move once more, but the Red Army somehow managed to hold on to at least parts of the right bank throughout the battle.

The failure to dislodge the Soviets was one of the reasons that Hitler dismissed Halder as chief of the General Staff on 24 September. 'After [the] situation conference,' wrote Halder, 'farewell by the Führer. My nerves are worn out; also his nerves are no longer fresh. We must part. Hitler talked of the necessity for educating the General Staff in fanatical faith in The Idea. He is determined to enforce his will also onto the army.'[30] Hitler appointed in Halder's place the recently promoted Brigadier-General Kurt Zeitzler, who had 'a reputation for brutality towards subordinates and subservience to superiors', and certainly showed lickspittle servility towards Hitler.[31]

'There were daily quarrels all summer,' Halder later told his Nuremberg interviewer about his relations with Hitler.

The point upon which we had our final disagreement was the decision of an offensive on the Caucasus and Stalingrad – a mistake, and Hitler didn't want to see it. I told him the Russians would put in another million men in 1942 and get another in 1943. Hitler told me I was an idiot – that the Russians were practically dead already. When I told Hitler about Russian armament potentials, especially for tank materials, Hitler flew into a rage and threatened me with his fists. Hitler issued several orders to the Eastern Front, contrary to military advice. This caused the setback. Then he blamed the army group for the defeat and claimed that they were purposely at fault. At that point I became furious, struck my fists on the table, made scenes, et cetera . . . those arguments were provoked by me because in twenty years of general staff work I have served with many superior officers and have not had arguments and I have always got along.[32]

A fundamental cause of the defeat on the Eastern Front was the continual tension between the OKH and the OKW. Hitler resented the supposed snobbery, suspected the loyalty and despised the caution of his generals. Instead of a permanent consultative body of experts preparing situation reports and future possible operations, such as the Stavka in Moscow, the Chiefs of Staff in London and the Joint Chiefs in Washington, Nazi Germany just had the noontime *Lagevortrag* (situation conference), at which Jodl submitted Warlimont's daily assessments. Hitler worked through Jodl and Keitel, whom he trusted but whom the OKH generals came to despise for their cowardice before the Führer. Orders were not debated with the Commander-in-Chief, Brauchitsch, who was simply expected to carry them out. It was a system that almost deliberately failed to use the best brains in the Wehrmacht hierarchy.

On 30 September, Hitler made a radio broadcast promising the German *Volk* that Stalingrad would fall. Yet from nightfall that evening the 39th Guards Infantry Division under Major-General Stiepan Guniev was ferried across the Volga to defend the Red October Factory, an operation which Guniev continued 'even when the grenades of German tommy-gunners were bursting at the entrance' to his command post. The next day, 1 October, the situation in Chuikov's headquarters was such that with the 'Fumes, smoke – we could not breathe. Shells and bombs bursting all around us. So much noise that however loud you shouted no one could hear you . . . Many times the radio operator would be killed with the microphone in his hands.' When the Front HQ asked their whereabouts, Chuikov's command post answered: 'We're where the most flames and smoke are.'[33] Yet all this came before Paulus' most powerful offensive.

The three huge factories and their adjacent Settlements were turned into a hecatomb during the fighting of early October 1942. Chuikov estimated that the 308th Infantry Division under Colonel L. N. Gurtiev fought off 'not less than a hundred ferocious attacks' in the course of the battle.[34] At the Tractor Factory, north of the Barrikady complex, one regiment, commanded by a Colonel Markelov, had just eleven men left standing after only twenty-four hours of fighting.[35] Yet right up until Paulus' great offensive of 14 October, artillerymen and engineers at the Tractor Factory were still repairing tanks and guns with the help of workers from the Barrikady. Within the factory itself individual areas such as the sorting shop, calibration shop, warehouse and foundry became mini-battlefields in themselves,

9. US Navy Douglas Dauntless dive-bombers during the attack that crippled the Japanese fleet at the battle of Midway. Note the Japanese ship on fire below.

20. The aircraft carrier USS *Yorktown* burns after being hit by Aichi D34 'Val' dive-bombers at Midway shortly after 13.30 hours on 4 June 1942.

21. Generals Sir Claude Auchinleck and Sir Archibald Wavell confer in Egypt in 1941. Churchill removed both men from their commands in his quest for more aggressive leadership.

22. General Sir Harold Alexander speaking to soldiers of the 18th Army Group in Tunisia in early 1943.

3. General Erwin Rommel, the 'Desert Fox', at the scene of his greatest triumph, when he captured Tobruk and almost all its defenders and stores in June 1942.

24. The battle of El Alamein: soldiers of the 9th Australian Division firing a captured Italian 47mm Breda anti-tank gun on a beach in the northern sector.

25. The Holocaust: Jews from sub-Carpathian Rus undergoing 'selection' for work details (for those queuing on the left) or immediate gassing (for those on the right), after disembarking onto the ramp at Auschwitz-Birkenau in late May 1944.

26. A fraction of the corpses discovered by the US Seventh Army at the Dachau concentration camp on 1 May 1945.

. A scene from Stalingrad in late 1942, where desperate and often hand-to-hand fighting over several months saw areas of the factory district change hands many times.

28. Russian artillery at the Red October Factory in Stalingrad, early 1943.

29. Victory by committee: behind President Franklin Roosevelt and Winston Churchill at the Casablanca Conference in January 1943 stand the Combined Chiefs of Staff: (*left to right*) Admiral Ernest J. King, General George C. Marshall, Admiral Sir Dudley Pound, Air Chief Marshal Sir Charles Portal, General Sir Alan Brooke, Field Marshal Sir John Dill, Vice-Admiral Lord Louis Mountbatten and General Henry 'Hap' Arnold.

30. General Charles de Gaulle (*centre*), self-proclaimed saviour of France, takes the salute of a guard of honour on arrival in Algiers on 30 May 1943. The next day he and General Henri Giraud (*left*) assumed the joint presidency of the Committee of National Liberation, without letting it affect their mutual detestation.

31. The battle of the Atlantic: a destroyer, the smaller ship alone in the rear (*right*), shepherds a convoy of merchantmen across the ocean in June 1943.

32. The captain of a U-boat at his periscope.

33. The battle of Kursk, July 1943. The crack 3rd SS Panzer Totenkopf (Death's Head) Division advances to fight the largest tank battle in history. This attack was part of what later dubbed 'the Death Ride of the Fourth Panzer Army'.

34. German soldiers pass a burning Soviet T-34/76 tank during the battle.

changing hands several times during the struggle. On 5 October alone, 2,000 enemy sorties were counted by the Russians, with the communal bath-house of the Red October Settlement changing hands five times. Chuikov could not find time to wash for an entire month. He took the terrible losses philosophically, saying that the experience gained in fighting the Germans 'compensated for our physical losses. Of course, the loss of men is a bitter thing – but war is war.'[36]

Dawn on Monday, 14 October 1942 saw the massive Sixth Army offensive by which Paulus tried finally to force the Sixty-second Army off the right bank of the Volga. Three whole infantry divisions and more than 300 tanks were thrown against the factory district. Chuikov sent all the women and wounded back across the Volga, and on the night of 15 October many of the 3,500 wounded had to crawl towards the medical centres because there were no longer enough medical orderlies and stretchers to carry them.[37] A building has been preserved at one of the ferry crossings near the factory district, called Crossing 62, and there is hardly a brick of it that does not contain a bullet or artillery scar of some kind. The heroism of the forty-day defence of the Barrikady Settlements by Colonel L. Lyudnikov's 138th Red Banner Rifle Division, as it was pushed back to a 700-yard perimeter on the Volga and surrounded on three sides by the Germans at this crossing, was one of the epics of a battle that was full of them.

'Women soldiers proved themselves to be just as heroic in the days of fighting as men,' recorded Chuikov. For all the ferocity of the battle, at Stalingrad women served on or near the front line, in their capacity as doctors carrying out operations, medical orderlies as young as fifteen carrying wounded men (and especially their weapons) off the battlefields, telephonists (one of whom was buried twice under the rubble in one day but kept on working once freed), radio operators, sailors in the Volga Fleet, anti-aircraft gunners, and especially pilots, known by the Germans as the Flying Witches. Most doubled as blood-donors. Stalingrad might have been an abattoir, but it was an equal-opportunities one. Around 490,000 women fought in front-line roles in the Soviet armed forces during the Great Patriotic War, and a further 300,000 in other roles.[38] This was something Nazi ideology would never have permitted the Wehrmacht to copy, yet it significantly contributed to the Soviet war effort. Some 40 per cent of all Red Army front-line doctors were women; graduates of the Central Women's School for Snipers were credited with killing 12,000 Germans; three regiments of the 221st Aviation Corps were women, as were thirty-three Heroes of the Soviet Union.[39]

One act of particularly extraordinary heroism seen in the factory district was that of Marine Mikhail Panikako, who was about to throw a Molotov cocktail at a tank when a bullet hit it, drenching him with the burning liquid. 'The soldier burst into a living sheet of flame,' wrote Chuikov. 'Despite the terrible pain he did not lose consciousness. He grabbed the second bottle. The tank had come up close. Everyone saw a man in flames leap out of the trench, run right up to the German tank and smash the bottle against the grille of the engine-hatch. A second later an enormous sheet of flame and smoke engulfed both the tank and the hero who had destroyed it.'[40] Today, Panikako's self-sacrifice can be seen as part of the superb 160-foot-long panorama in the Stalingrad Military Museum in Volgograd. Even when strained through the sieve of wartime and Cold War propaganda, such acts of courage were clearly outstanding, on both sides.

Also synonymous with Stalingrad heroism was the defence under-taken by Sergeant Jakob Pavlov and his *Shturmovaya* (storming groups), from 28 September for fifty-eight consecutive days, of a four-storey house 300 yards from the river.[41] With machine guns and long-barrelled anti-tank guns, and their tactic of denying Panzers any easy targets, this platoon of the 42nd Guards Regiment held out valiantly under Pavlov, their lieutenant having been blinded. 'Pavlov's small group of men, defending one house,' recalled Chuikov proudly, mischievously but accurately, 'killed more enemy soldiers than the Germans lost in taking Paris.'[42] It helped their subsequent fame that they came from a very wide geographical cross-section of the Soviet Union – including Russians, Ukrainians, Georgians, an Uzbecki, a Tajik, a Tatar and an Abkhazian – and therefore seemed to symbolize the unity of the Motherland as well as her courage. What little remained of Pavlov's House, as it is called, has been preserved.

Chuikov described the Sixth Army's offensive of 14 October as having brought 'fighting of unprecedented ferocity. Those of us who had already been through a great deal will remember the enemy attack all our lives. We recorded 3,000 sorties by every type of aircraft on that day! . . . It was a sunny day, but the smoke and dust cut visibility down to a hundred yards.' The German attacks on the Tractor and Barrikady Factories numbered 180 tanks, which broke through Zholudev's 37th Division at 11.30 hours and went on to attack Colonel V. A. Gorishny's 95th and Gurtiev's 308th Divisions and the 84th Armoured Brigade. In the course of the day Zholudev had to be excavated from his dug-out, where he had been buried by a direct hit. By midnight the Germans had cut off the Tractor Factory on three sides and had entered the workshops. The fate of Stalingrad hung in the balance.

The story of how the Red Army soldiers hung on to the right bank through Paulus' assault of mid-October is one of quite extraordinary heroism, appalling self-sacrifice and complete lack of alternative considering what the NKVD was doing to anyone who left his post. Courage was uppermost, however, as German six-barrelled mortars kept the Volga under constant bombardment. With the thousands of wounded crawling back towards the ferries, 'We often had to step over bodies,' Chuikov recalled, and 'Everything on the bank was covered in ash and dust.'[43] Yet the Germans took the Tractor Factory on 16 October, and by the end of the 18th only five men from the thousands-strong workers' detachment of the Barrikady Factory were still alive. By 23 October the Soviets were finally forced out of the Red October Factory, too, but not for long. Eight days later they advanced a hundred yards in the environs of Novoselskaya Street and won back the factory's open-hearth, calibration and profiling shops, and soon afterwards the finished-products warehouse as well. Chuikov was greatly helped by the Soviet artillery on the left bank – 250 guns of 76.2mm calibre and fifty heavy guns – which kept the Germans under constant fire and which had been heavily reinforced by 203mm and 280mm guns in mid-October.[44] On the right bank, however, the lorries carrying the Katyusha rockets had to be reversed right back into the Volga itself in order to give them the necessary elevation of fire, so close had the Germans got to the river.

After the war there was a good deal of ill-tempered argument about which Russian units had fought hardest, even though there was plenty of glory to go around. Whenever possible, Chuikov was sent reinforcements, and in the course of the battle the Sixty-second Army was bolstered by a total of seven infantry divisions, one infantry brigade and an artillery brigade, all of which were flung into the human meat-grinder almost as soon as they arrived. The general paid tribute to the activities of the Red Army outside the city, which drew off considerable German forces, writing that 'They held Paulus back by the ears.' As for the Wehrmacht: 'Some inexplicable force drove the enemy to keep on attacking. It seemed as though Hitler was prepared to destroy the whole of Germany for the sake of this one city.'

Tsaritsyn (which was Tatar for 'yellow river' and had nothing to do with the tsars) had changed its name to Stalingrad in 1925 in recognition of Stalin's successful defence of the city during the Civil War. Important though it was strategically for both sides, it is impossible to escape the conclusion that they would not have committed the resources they both did – at one point in October neither had any tactical reserves left whatsoever – had the city been called Tsaritsyn or Volgograd, as in its earlier and later incarnations. The *mano a mano* nature of the struggle between the two dictators was personalized in a way that Hitler publicly acknowledged when on 8 November 1942 he again broadcast about capturing Stalingrad, in a speech from Munich, the birthplace of National Socialism. 'I wanted to reach the Volga, to be precise at a particular spot, at a particular city,' he said. 'By chance it bore the name of Stalin himself.' The battle had thus taken on a symbolic significance far removed from its strategic one. In his speech Hitler claimed that 'Time was of no importance,' but in fact winter was fast closing in, just as it had been when he had failed to take Moscow the previous year. The Sixth Army's next great offensive began at 18.30 hours on Wednesday, 11 November – coincidentally the anniversary of the Great War Armistice – with five infantry divisions as well as the 14th and 24th Panzer Divisions attacking on a 3-mile-wide front between Volkhovstroyevskaya Street and Banna Gully, just south of the Barrikady Factory warehouse. 'Exceptionally heavy fighting went on all day for every yard of ground,' wrote Chuikov, 'for every brick and stone. Fighting with hand grenades and bayonets went on for several hours.'

Simultaneously, attacks were made on the Mamayev Kurgan, whose height made it such a commanding position that neither side could allow the other to position artillery there, and which thus saw so much bombardment that its actual underlying physical shape was transformed during the battle. It was also said that shellfire was so unremittingly hot there that winter that snow never had a chance to settle on its slopes.[45] Certainly the fighting around the huge water-tanks on the hillside was continuous for 112 days from the second half of September to 12 January 1943. Historians simply cannot say, or even estimate, how often the summit changed hands, for, as Chuikov notes, there were no witnesses who survived all through the whole battle for it, and in any case no one was keeping count. At one point the life expectancy of soldiers there was between one and two days, and to see a third day made one a veteran. Rodimtsev's, Gorishny's and Batyuk's divisions all fought there with distinction (and to near-annihilation). At one point, when telephone communication was lost between Chuikov's headquarters and Batyuk's divisional command post at the Mamayev Kurgan, a signaller called Titayev was sent to re-establish it. His corpse was found with the two ends of the wire clamped tightly together between his teeth, after he had used his own skull as a semi-conductor.[46]

The German attack of 11 November succeeded in reaching the Volga along a front of 600 yards, splitting the Russian forces for the third time during the battle. But as Chuikov crowed, 'Paulus had been unable to capitalize on his superior strength, and had not achieved what he intended. He had not thrown the 62nd Army into the icy Volga.' With Paulus' Sixth Army and the Fourth Panzer Army in possession of three-quarters of the city, but Chuikov's Sixty-second Army still holding out on the right bank and receiving heavy reinforcements, the Germans decided to pour yet more forces from the Don and the south into the city, their places being taken by the Romanian Third Army and Italian Eighth Army along the Don to the north-west and the Romanian Fourth Army to the south of Stalingrad. This was to give the Russians their great chance.

At a two-and-a-half-hour meeting of generals at the Führer's office in Berlin during the planning of Barbarossa back in March 1941, at which Hitler spoke about German goals in Russia and the means of attaining them – 'Commanders must make the sacrifice of overcoming their personal scruples' – he had said that he was under 'No illusions about our allies! Finns will fight bravely . . . Romanians are no good at all. Perhaps they could be used as a security force in quiet sectors behind very strong natural obstacles [rivers] . . . The fortunes of large German units must not be tied to the uncertain staying power of the Romanian forces.'[47] Yet he did not take his own advice, for that is precisely what now happened at Stalingrad. It was Zhukov who masterminded the double envelopment of Stalingrad from north and south which, once successfully completed on 23 November 1942, was no less successfully defended from Manstein's counter-attack in December and then developed into an unbreakable stranglehold in January 1943, ending with the German surrender there the following month. Chuikov was left as the tethered goat in the city, to distract the German wolf, and for four days after Thursday, 19 November Zhukov flung four army groups (called fronts) into the great assault, codenamed Operation Uranus. The secret logistical buildup had been impressive: in the first three weeks of November, 160,000 men, 430 tanks, 6,000 guns and mortars, 14,000 vehicles and 10,000 horses had been ferried across the Volga and Don rivers. By then, over 1.1 million men were ready to take part in both Uranus (the encirclement of Stalingrad) and Operation Saturn (a wider swing all the way to Rostov). In Uranus, the Voronezh, South-west and Don Fronts attacked north of Stalingrad and the Stalingrad Front came around the south in a classic pincer movement. The initial bombardment by 3,500 Russian guns, mortars and rockets at 07.30 hours on Thursday, 19 November woke up German soldiers more than 30 miles away. From 1944, that day was ever after known in Russia as Artillery Day, in commemoration of the salvoes launched before the infantry assault at 08.50. German minefields had been cleared by Russian engineers working through the night before the offensive.

The Romanians fought bravely, but Soviet T-34 and KV-1 tanks of the South-west Front soon created a 7-mile gap in the lines of General Petre Dumitrescu's Third Romanian Army, and five divisions were swiftly trapped in the bend of the River Don. Every gap was exploited and expanded, and it was fitting that it had to fall to Kurt Zeitzler to break the news to Hitler, because three weeks earlier it had been he who had confidently assured the Führer that the Soviets were 'in no position to mount a major offensive with any far-reaching objective'.[48] On Friday, 20 November, the southern pincer ripped into the Fourth Romanian Army, where these forces too met with quick success, and forged an even larger, 17-mile gap, through which the IV Cavalry and IV Mechanized Corps were poured. Wide, sweeping, confident cross-country tank movements characterized Uranus just as they had the opening phases of Barbarossa, and Weichs' Army Group B outside the city was pushed back westwards. The Russians closed the ring around Stalingrad at Sovietskiy village near Kalach-on-Don on the night of Monday, 23 November. 'Dwarfed by the vastness of the landscape, they fired green flares periodically so that they did not miss each other, or think the other force were Germans.'[49] The troops from the two connecting units came together with such speed, and at night, that they had to re-enact the whole scene the next day with cheering and mutual hugging for the propaganda footage.[50]

In a sense it was not the Germans who lost the battle of Stalingrad; they had taken the whole city except for a Russian toe-hold on the right bank; rather it was the Romanian Third Army and the Italian Eighth Army to the north and the Romanian Fourth Army in the south of the city who were comprehensively outfought. When the encirclement was completed, around 275,000 of Paulus' army were trapped. Yet the pincers were still thin, in places only a few miles deep, so at this point Hitler ought to have ordered Paulus to attempt an immediate breakout. He did not, believing that Manstein, then flying down from Leningrad, could command yet another regrouping of the Wehrmacht in southern Russia and break through from the south-west, during which the Luftwaffe could keep Paulus provisioned with food and equipment.

Göring – against advice from the Luftwaffe generals on the spot – promised the Führer that he could fly 550 tons of supplies per day into Stalingrad.[51] Yet that was based on having 225 Junkers Ju-52s serviceable every day, whereas in fact there were only about eighty serviceable at any one time, supported by two squadrons of Heinkel He-111s which could carry only 1.5 tons each.[52] Admittedly, Göring hoped to bring in other planes from different theatres, but it would never have been enough to service an army of a quarter of a million men indefinitely. The statistics were discouraging for the Sixth Army's hopes for survival: Paulus requested 750 tons a day, Göring promised 550, the Luftwaffe generals said 350 were possible, but the planes available could actually manage only half that, even before the bad weather closed in, after which an average of only 100 tons per day were delivered.[53]

Paulus needed to move fast to escape the giant trap that had been sprung around him, and to meet Manstein coming north-eastwards to his relief, but Hitler refused him permission to move, and Paulus himself did not want to attempt it. 'I gave the order finally for the Sixth Army to break out,' Manstein told his interviewer at Nuremberg in June 1946, 'but then Paulus said it was too late and not possible. Hitler did not want the Sixth Army to break out at any time, but to fight to the last man. I believe that Hitler said that if the Sixth Army tried to break out, it would be their death.'[54] A decade after the war, and thus with the benefit of both hindsight and little likelihood of being gainsaid, Zeitzler claimed that, back in November 1942, 'I had told Hitler that if a quarter of a million soldiers were to be lost at Stalingrad, then the backbone of the entire Eastern front would be broken.'[55] The Führer hardly needed to be told of the importance of Stalingrad, himself exhorting the troops of the Sixth Army and the Fourth Armoured Army on 26 November:

The battle around Stalingrad is reaching its climax ... My thoughts and those of the German people are with you in these grave hours! Whatever the circumstances, you must hold on to the Stalingrad position which has been won with so much blood under the leadership of resolute generals! Your resolve must be so unshakeable that, as at Kharkov in the spring, this Russian breakthrough too will be annihilated by the measures that have been put in hand. Everything that lies in my power is being done to help you in your heroic struggle.[56]

Earlier that same month Hitler had issued a similar 'Stand or die' order to Rommel at El Alamein; henceforth there were to be many such messages, in which the Führer forsook strategic manoeuvre, replacing it with a blind, unyielding test of willpower, one in which flesh and blood were set against steel and fire.

Stalingrad was an important transport hub, industrial city and oil refinery, but not so important as to justify the emphasis the Nazis put on its capture, in fighting that still today results in mines and shells and especially bones being uncovered every springtime. Hitler was not merely being hubristic when he ordered Paulus to stay in Stalingrad, however. He also needed to withdraw Army Group A from the Caucasus, which had to be covered by Stalingrad.

'Hitler's veto on any breakout appears incredibly rash when one considers the forces involved,' wrote Mellenthin. 'For this was no ordinary army invested at Stalingrad; the Sixth Army represented the spearhead of the Wehrmacht, in what was intended to be the decisive campaign of the war.'[57] Stalingrad certainly was that, but not for the reason Hitler intended, for in the event Manstein's rescue bid was stopped short of its destination. With a fraction of the necessary supplies being dropped by the IV Luftflotte Junkers of Luftwaffe Field Marshal Baron von Richthofen – a cousin of the Great War ace the Red Baron – whose aircraft were put out of action by Russian fighters, anti-aircraft guns and the weather conditions, Paulus' army started to die on its frostbitten feet. Casualties, disease, exhaustion, starvation and above all the debilitating cold later rendered a breakout impossible anyway. (Richthofen developed a brain tumour in 1944, and died the next year.)

Chuikov now faced a renewed danger on the ground, since the Volga had started to freeze over on 12 November. Stalingrad lies on the edge of the windy, treeless steppes and was thus particularly vulnerable to temperatures that could reach as low as –45 Celsius. It was not unknown for German soldiers to build walls of frozen corpses behind which to hide from the elements. The freezing of the river speeded up once the temperature dropped to –15 Celsius in late November, but was not complete until 17 December. Before then, the ice floes made any river crossing impossible even for armoured boats, so the Sixty-second Army had to stay on short rations until trucks were able to cross the river. 'We were going to have to fight on two fronts,' recorded the Russian commander, 'against the enemy and the Volga.' With ammunition and food supplies dropping off dangerously, Chuikov recalled how the 'ice-floes piled up and formed obstructions, and made a disgusting crunching noise which made our flesh creep and sent shudders up our spines, as if someone were sawing into our vertebrae'.[58] Once the ice was thick enough, however, 18,000 trucks and 20,000 other vehicles crossed over to resuscitate the still-besieged Red Army.[59] Meanwhile, the desperate hand-to-hand fighting in the factory district continued unabated.

By mid-December, the dire position of the Sixth Army could only possibly be alleviated by Manstein coming to the rescue. His Army Group Don looked effective on paper, consisting of two Panzer divisions, one infantry division, Hoth's headquarters and some Romanians, and it set out on 12 December to try to cross the 62 miles to the city in Operation Wintergewitter (Winter Tempest). 'I have considered one thing, Zeitzler,' Hitler said of Stalingrad at the Wolf-schanze that same afternoon,

Looking at the big picture, we should under no circumstances give this up. We won't get it back once it's lost . . . To think that it would be possible to do it a second time, if we go back there and the matériel stays behind, is ridiculous. They can't take everything with them. The horses are tired, and they don't have any more strength to pull. I can't feed one horse with another. If they were Russians, I'd say 'One Russian eats up the other one.' But I can't let one horse eat the other horse.[60]

It is unclear whether he reached this conclusion on practical or humanitarian grounds. Talking of the heavy artillery in the city, especially howitzers, Hitler added: 'We can't replace what we have in there. If we abandon it, we abandon the whole purpose for the campaign. To think that I will come back here next time is madness . . . We won't come back here, so we can't leave.'

Manstein's plan was for Paulus to break out once Hoth's tanks came to within 20 miles of the perimeter. However, on 16 December Zhukov unleashed Operation Little Saturn to turn Hoth back. Once again, it was their allies who proved the bane of the Wehrmacht: the Soviet South-west Front destroyed the Italian Eighth Army on the middle Don, opening a 60-mile gap and allowing the Russians to attack Manstein's right flank towards Rostov. The loss of Rostov would have cut off Kleist, who in November had been named commander of Army Group A in the Caucasus, so Hoth's force was weakened to prevent this happening, thereby wrecking his chances of getting close enough to Stalingrad to prise the Sixth Army out.

On 19 December Manstein ordered Paulus to break out to the

south-west, but Paulus now preferred to follow Hitler's orders to stay put. ('Dear Field Marshal,' Paulus had replied in a postscript to an earlier request, 'In the circumstances I hope you will overlook the inadequacy of the paper and the fact that this letter is handwritten.'[61]) Manstein's under-strength divisions nonetheless got to within 35 miles of Stalingrad, but the whole momentum of Winter Tempest stalled when on 23 December Hoth's armour was forced to halt on the River Mishkova, unable to make any further headway in the face of tough Russian opposition and the monstrous weather conditions. The irony of the operation's codename was not lost on anyone. If Stalingrad was the turning point of the war, the halt on the River Mishkova was what prevented it from turning back again. By 28 December Manstein had to pull Hoth's force back in order to prevent its encirclement.

Yet, even if Manstein had got the whole way to Stalingrad, it is not certain that Paulus could have been rescued. On one day 180 tons of supplies got through, but for three weeks he had received only 120 tons a day, and after Christmas the nightly average was down to only 60 tons.[62] It is hard to imagine the despair felt when the starving Germans opened a container that had been successfully parachuted into the city only to find that it held a kilo of ground pepper and a case of condoms.[63] Once the airfields at Morovskaya and Tatsinskaya on the Don had fallen to the Russians at Christmas, the closest German-held airfields to Stalingrad were even more distant, further cutting down the number of possible flights.

The first German death by starvation within what they were calling the Kessel (cauldron) was recorded on 21 December. In early December the daily bread ration for the encircled forces was 200 grams per head, which was cut further at Christmas. They were also given, recalled a survivor, Colonel H. R. Dingler, 'watery soup which we tried to improve by making use of bones obtained from horses we dug up'. The lack of petrol meant that tanks had to be kept in the rear of infantry, with the result that 'when the Russians broke in – as later on they did – counter-thrusts lacked every vestige of momentum.'[64] Paulus' army was disintegrating, and probably could not have crossed the 20 miles back to safety even if Hoth had broken the stranglehold.

Lice infections broke out because it was too cold to wash; the frozen bodies of horses littered the roads; sentries who fell asleep at their posts didn't wake up; with petrol being hoarded by the commissariat for the breakout, there was no fuel to turn the abundant snow into desperately needed water; bread that had frozen solid, called *Eisbrot* (ice bread), provided a taunting reminder of how close they were to salvation if only they could find fuel. 'The men were too weak to dig fresh emplacements or communication trenches,' records one historian of the Sixth Army's plight in the Kessel that Christmas; 'when forced out of their old positions they would simply lie on the ground behind heaped-up snow "parapets", numb with cold and the inevitability of death. To be wounded might be lucky, more often it was a stroke of hideous misfortune among comrades too exhausted to lift a man onto a stretcher; where medical services had no anaesthetic other than artificially induced frostbite.'[65]

There were terrible scenes at Pitomnik airport as Junkers attempted to fly the wounded and others away to safety. Soldiers who rushed to get on to planes without documentation were shot, and there were two cases of men hanging on to the tail wheels of planes, who soon afterwards fell to their deaths. The self-discipline of the Wehrmacht collapsed at Pitomnik, as desperation to escape overcame the most famed Teutonic virtue of the Army. When the cratered runway proved too badly damaged by Russian artillery fire to use, and twenty men had to be unloaded from one plane, a Lieutenant Dieter recalled:

At once there was a terrific din, everyone shouting at once, one man claimed that he was travelling by order of the Army Staff, another from the SS that he had important Party documents, many others who cried about their families, that their children had been injured in air raids, and so on. Only the men on stretchers kept silent, but their terror showed in their faces.[66]

It was understandable; those wounded men whose stretchers were offloaded and placed too far away from the stoves in the makeshift shanties at the perimeter of the airfield simply froze to death.

On Christmas Day the Germans were finally expelled from the Tractor Factory, and an ingenious method was used to get them out of the main office building of the Red October Factory, when a storming group of Lieutenant-General V. P. Sokolov's division carried a 122mm howitzer into the factory piece by piece, which they then reassembled inside the walls. After a few rounds at point-blank range, 'the German garrison in the factory ceased to exist.' The next day Paulus received only 70 tons of supplies, less than 10 per cent of what he knew he needed for survival. A German soldier, Wilhelm Hoffman of the 267th Regiment of the 94th Infantry Division, made a last entry in his diary, writing: 'The horses have already been eaten. I would eat a cat; they say its meat is also tasty. The soldiers look like corpses or lunatics, looking for something to put in their mouths. They no longer take cover from Russian shells; they haven't the strength to walk, run away and hide. A curse on this war . . .'[67] It was about this time that Dingler and his comrades 'began to discuss what to do if the worst came to the worst. We talked about captivity. We talked about the question of committing suicide. We discussed the question of defending what we held to the last bullet but one . . . There was no compulsion from above in any direction. These things were left to be decided by the individual himself.'[68]

On 8 January 1943, the commander of the Don Front, General Konstantin Rokossovsky, dropped leaflets offering the Germans an honourable surrender, sufficient rations, care for the wounded and repatriation to Germany after the war, all on the condition that their military equipment be handed over undamaged. Tempting as it was, this was refused, because – so Dingler told Mellenthin – they did not trust the Russians, still hoped against hope that they might escape and wanted to give Army Group A enough time to withdraw from the Caucasus. Rokossovsky therefore opened up a major offensive against the southern and western parts of the perimeter on 10 January, code-named Operation Ring. 'The cover of the tomb is closing over us,' was the perceptive judgement of a Colonel Selle at that time, and so many German soldiers were now committing suicide that Paulus had to issue an order forbidding it as dishonourable.[69] As the so-called Marinovka nose, the south-western protuberance of the Kessel, came under Russian attack, some German troops found that their fingers were so badly swollen from frostbite that they could not fit inside their rifles' trigger guards. Summary execution was resorted to in order to keep the German troops fighting, in conditions so cold that mortar shells 'rebounded off the frozen earth and exploded as air bursts, causing more casualties'.[70] Yet once the Marinovka had fallen, it was even worse for the defenders, as they were now forced out into the open. 'There were no trenches and no places for the riflemen,' recalled Dingler; 'the decimated troops, overtired, exhausted, and with frostbitten limbs, simply lay in the snow.' All heavy weaponry had to be disabled – often by means of a grenade down the barrel – and then abandoned. The Kessel's last contact with the outside world came on 23 January when Gumrak airfield – 'a snowy desert filled with aircraft and vehicles' – fell to the Russians. 'Everywhere lay the corpses of German soldiers too exhausted to move on,' Dingler wrote. 'They had just died in the snow.'

Saturday, 23 January also saw the Führer issuing another rather predictable order to Paulus: 'Surrender is forbidden. Sixth Army will hold their positions to the last man and the last round, and by their heroic endurance will make an unforgettable contribution to the establishment of a defensive front and the salvation of the Western world.'[71] One week later, Hitler appointed Paulus a field marshal, in order to prevent him from surrendering, because no German field marshal had ever before surrendered his forces in the field. There's a first time for everything, however, and at 07.35 hours on Sunday, 31 January Paulus was captured in his bunker, and his (southern) pocket of forces in the Kessel collapsed. The basement under the 1937-built Univermag (central department store) where Paulus and his chief of staff General Arthur Schmidt made their makeshift headquarters, is one of the few places where Germans did not suffer from chilblains and frostbite. On display there today are Paulus' drawings dated November 1942 of red elephants outside the city trampling on the German flag in their march to Stalingrad, pictures which imply a severe lack of confidence in ultimate victory.

Hitler was disgusted and sarcastic at his Führer-conference at the Wolfschanze at 12.17 the next day, 1 February, equating the Sixth Army with a suicidal rape victim, to the Army's disadvantage. 'True to form,' he told Zeitzler,

they surrendered themselves. Because otherwise, you gather yourselves together, build an all-round defence, and shoot yourself with the last cartridge. If you can imagine that a woman, after being insulted a few times, has so much pride that she goes out, locks herself in, and shoots herself dead immediately – then I have no respect for a soldier who shrinks back from it and prefers going into captivity.[72]

At least Hitler was to practise what he preached in that respect. Meanwhile, on 15 January, the Red Army reintroduced gradations of rank signified by epaulettes and other such badges of seniority, for reasons of discipline, morale and ease of recognition during battle. Some thought this step reminiscent of tsarism, although it was not a view that was expressed too vocally.

Two days after Paulus' capture, the northern pocket surrendered too. Paulus, Schmidt, twenty-two other generals and a further 91,000 soldiers shuffled off into Soviet captivity, the only survivors of the 275,000 or so (estimates vary) Germans, Romanians, Italians and Russian anti-Soviet volunteers who had been cut off within the Kessel on 23 November 1942.[73] An even greater percentage of German prisoners died in two years of Russian captivity before the end of the war than Russians died in four years of German captivity. Of the more than 90,000 Wehrmacht soldiers who surrendered at Stalingrad, only 9,626 ever returned to Germany, and some of them not until 1955.

The Soviets meanwhile lost 479,000 killed or captured in the Stalingrad campaign between 17 July 1942 and 2 February 1943, and a further 651,000 sick or wounded, a total of 1.13 million.[74] 'Stalingrad had become a symbol of resistance unparalleled in human history,' wrote Chuikov. Such hyperbole is often written by old soldiers about their past battles, but in his case it was true. Chuikov's memoirs were written with some bitterness during the Cold War, in 1959; the general was angry with Western historians downplaying the importance of his battle. Specifically attacking J. F. C. Fuller, Winston Churchill, Omar Bradley, Heinz Guderian, Kurt von Tippelkirsch 'and other apologists of imperialism', he went to great pains to point out the differences between El Alamein and Stalingrad. 'At El Alamein the British were faced by four German divisions and eight Italian divisions,' he argued,

and what is more, the main German and Italian forces managed to avoid being defeated in battle; on the Volga and the Don, however, in the period of the counter-attack by the Soviet armies from 19 November 1942 to

2 February 1943, thirty-two divisions and three brigades belonging to Nazi Germany and her satellites were destroyed. Sixteen more of the enemy's divisions suffered serious defeat ... In the battle of Stalingrad, Humanity saw the dawn of victory over Fascism.[75]

Chuikov was only slightly exaggerating the figures, and it is worth pointing out that little humanity was shown by the defenders of Humanity, even towards their own citizens. It is not known how many Russians – deserters or prisoners, known as Hiwis, short for *Hilfswillige* (volunteer helper) – fought for the Germans. No fewer than 150,000 served with the SS alone during the war, which was probably merely 'the tip of the iceberg'.[76] It was an embarrassing subject for the post-war Soviet authorities, so details about their service are sketchy, but it is estimated that over 20,000 Hiwis surrendered or were captured at Stalingrad. It is still not known what the NKVD did to them, although there are accounts of their being worked to death in camps, and of others 'being beaten to death, rather than being shot, to save ammunition'.[77] With the NKVD, it is best to err on the most brutal side of estimates.

A total of twenty German divisions – thirteen infantry, three Panzer (the 14th, 16th and 24th), three motorized and one anti-aircraft – had been lost by the Wehrmacht, as well as two Romanian divisions, a Croat regiment, service troops and members of the German construction unit known as the Organisation Todt. 'The destruction of these divisions was bound to alter the whole balance of power on the Eastern Front,' commented Mellenthin with some understatement. Zeitzler agreed, writing in 1956 that Stalingrad 'was the turning point of the entire war'.[78] The historian Nigel Nicolson considered Stalingrad to be 'even worse than 1812, for at least Napoleon's army was retreating: from Stalingrad there was no retreat. The nearest comparison might be if the British Expeditionary Force had been totally destroyed at Dunkirk.'[79] With the remains of the Sixth Army in captivity, German strength in southern Russia was halved; moreover, the half-million men whom Zhukov had detailed to besiege Stalingrad were now available for other duties, and would be directed against Manstein, who was busy withdrawing, often asking for permission from the OKW only after he had given his orders. Manstein owned a pet dachshund that raised its paw when it heard the command 'Heil Hitler', but he himself showed a more independent spirit.

Stupidly, the Nazis attempted to pretend that the Sixth Army had not been captured at all, but had died fighting the Bolsheviks. 'True to its oath of allegiance to fight to the last breath,' a communiqué from the OKH announced on 3 February, 'the Sixth Army under the exemplary command of Field Marshal Paulus has succumbed to the superiority of the enemy and unfavourable circumstances ... Generals, officers, non-commissioned officers and men fought shoulder to shoulder down to the last bullet.' Nonetheless, 'the sacrifice of the Sixth Army was not in vain.'[80] As the truth filtered back, especially after the Soviets paraded the POWs through the streets of Moscow in front of the world's media, the credibility of German communiqués was further undermined.

Superlatives are unavoidable when describing the battle of Stalingrad; it was the struggle of Gog and Magog, the merciless clash where the rules of war were discarded. Merely staying alive in the frostbitten winter of 1942/3 was an achievement, but the two vast armies fought each other hand to hand and house to house throughout it, with a desperation and on a scale never before seen in the annals of warfare. Around 1.1 million people died in the battle on both sides, with only a few thousand civilians still there out of the half-million who had lived there before the war.

Charles de Gaulle's (necessarily very private) comment when he visited the area in November 1944 on his way to Moscow to meet Stalin – 'Un grand peuple' – referred to the Germans, for having got that far and endured that much.[81] Today it is impossible not to agree with him, however appalling the decision-making of their High Command, and especially their Supreme Warlord. Yet in the street battles of Stalingrad it had been the Russian fighting man who had prevailed, defending his Motherland. The unbelievably dogged resistance shown by the ordinary Russian soldier had delivered victory. Operation Barbarossa had indeed, as Hitler had predicted, made 'the world hold its breath' and it was only after Stalingrad that it could finally begin to exhale.

I I

The Waves of Air and Sea

1939–1945

*Such is the U-boat war – hard, widespread and bitter, a war
of groping and drowning, a war of ambuscade and stratagem,
a war of science and seamanship.*

Winston Churchill in the House of Commons,

26 September 1939[1]

The British politician the 2nd Viscount Hailsham once said that 'The
one case in which I think I can see the finger of God in contemporary
history is Churchill's arrival at the premiership at that precise moment
in 1940.'[2] Another candidate for the intervention of the Almighty in
the Second World War might be the Allied cracking of the German
Enigma codes, producing a stream of decrypts known by their British
special security classification, Ultra. This allowed the Allies for much
of the war to read many of the communications sent and received by
the OKW, OKH, Wehrmacht, Luftwaffe, Kriegsmarine, Abwehr, SS
and Reichsbahn (railways), amounting in total to several million items
of intelligence.[3] From the correspondence of the Führer himself right
down to that of the harbour-master of Olbia in Sardinia, messages
were routinely decoded by the Allies. It made the Second World War,
as Michael Howard has put it, 'like playing poker with marked cards,
albeit against an opponent with a consistently better hand than you'.
Its importance can be gauged from the jokey acronym 'BBR' that the
Americans gave to Ultra, which stood for Burn Before Reading.

For those who would prefer other explanations to divine intervention, the story of the cracking of the Enigma machine is also full
of secular miracles. The design was patented by a Dutchman, H. A.

Koch, in 1919, and by 1929 had been bought by the German Army and Navy (which used different versions of it). Looking like a normal typewriter but with three, four or five twenty-six-spoke rotor wheels attached, as well as lights and plugs that resembled a telephonist's board, the machine had the ability to transform a typed message into a code so complicated that the Germans assumed it could never be broken. 'To give an idea of how secure these machines are,' General Franco's intelligence officer Commander Antonio Sarmiento wrote in a 1936 report, when the Nationalists were buying ten Enigma machines from the Germans at the start of the Spanish Civil War, 'suffice to say that the number of combinations is a remarkable 1,252,962,387,456.'[4]

The technical side of the Enigma story is ferociously complex, and involves specialist terms such as the Banburismus procedure, Caesar reflector, Dolphin, Porpoise, Shark and Triton nets (that is, sub-codes), the Eins catalogue, Cillis, the Herivel Tip, codes-within-the-code, Gamma wheels, perforated sheets and plugboard connections, rodding, Bigram tables, bombes, cross-ruffing, straight-cribs and a related code entitled *Geheimschreiber* (secret writer).[5] The cracking of Enigma and its related codes – such as the Japanese diplomatic cipher Purple which was transformed into decrypts codenamed Magic – was a genuine Allied operation, involving the secret services of Poland, France, Britain, Australia and the United States. It began as early as 8 November 1931, when a traitor working in the German Cipher Office called Hans Thilo Schmidt allowed the French Deuxième Bureau (secret service) to photograph the Enigma operating manuals, which he had momentarily spirited out of a safe in the War Ministry. The French told the British, who subsequently told the Poles about the machine, but none could crack the code without building a replica of the machine itself. This was achieved by the Polish cryptographer Marian Rejewski in December 1932, although the Poles did not initially inform the French and British that this had happened. From that point on, the Poles could read Wehrmacht and Kriegsmarine radio traffic, although when in 1937 the latter changed its Enigma indicating key (the setting on a vital cog) the naval side fell silent, and was to remain so for the next three crucial years. Changes in the machines instituted by the Germans in December 1938 (installing an extra two rotor wheels, bringing the total to five) and January 1939 (doubling the number of plugboard sockets) also plunged the Poles into darkness. In late July 1939 they finally told the French and British secret services that they had been reading the German traffic until late 1938.

Ultra was not the sole means by which the Allies gathered intelligence, of course. Prisoners were captured and interrogated; simpler signals intelligence (sigint) codes used by front-line communications were eavesdropped upon and decoded by a British organization known as the Y Department; aerial photo-reconnaissance was interpreted at Medmenham on the Thames; resistance groups in Occupied Europe passed on information; SIS produced human intelligence (humint) from its own sources, although many were compromised early on in the war during the disastrous incident when in November 1939 two SIS officers, Captains Stevens and Best, were kidnapped at Venlo on the Dutch–German border by Gestapo agents posing as Resistance figures; German generals in British captivity were eavesdropped upon when they discussed important subjects such as rocketry. Nonetheless, Ultra was by far the most important intelligence source and, because of its direct nature, the least corruptible in analysis. The Bletchley code-breakers were, as Churchill put it, 'the geese who laid the golden eggs' and who, just as importantly, 'never cackled'. They were also almost all amateurs, recruited from civilian life, although their contribution was far to outweigh that of the career intelligence officers of the day.[6]

After the invasion of Poland in September 1939, several senior Polish cryptographers escaped with their replica Enigma machine and were installed by the Deuxième Bureau in a château near Paris, where they began – with British and French help – to decode messages, although at the time it took them two months to do so, meaning that the information they divulged had usually been long superseded by events. On 12 February 1940, however, the German submarine *U-33* was attacked off the west coast of Scotland and two of the extra rotor wheels used by the naval Enigma were captured. Five weeks later, a brilliant, eccentric, accident-prone, homosexual Cambridge mathematics don called Alan Turing installed something known as a bombe machine, an electro-mechanical device which made hundreds of computations every minute, at the Government Code and Cypher School at Bletchley Park in Buckinghamshire, 40 miles north-west of London. Other heroes of Bletchley were to include the mathematicians Stewart Milner-Barry and Alfred Dilwyn ('Dilly') Knox. In modern computing parlance, while the Poles provided the Enigma hardware, the assorted civilian geniuses stationed at Bletchley provided the software that produced Ultra.

Far from being a school, Bletchley was a department of SIS, operating from a Victorian mansion that housed 150 workers in 1939, before expanding into huts in the grounds to fit 3,500 people by 1942 and no fewer than 10,000 by the end of the war. (Several of the huts can still be seen today, including the ones where the most important work was done, along with captured Enigma machines and the bombe predecessors of the computer.) Huts 6 and 3 deciphered, translated, annotated and passed on Wehrmacht and Luftwaffe signals, while Huts 4 and 8 (run by Turing and subsequently the chess champion Hugh Alexander) did much the same thing for the Kriegsmarine, sending reports to the Naval Intelligence Division of the Admiralty. Hut 4 also analysed sudden increases and decreases of signals traffic volume, which could suggest possible enemy intentions. On 4 April 1940, five weeks before Hitler unleashed Blitzkrieg on the West, same-day decoding of the German Army codes first became possible, but on 1 May the British at Bletchley and Poles in France were 'blinded' for three weeks when the Germans altered their indicating systems.[7] Overall, however, Wehrmacht and Luftwaffe signals were decoded between three and six hours after they were sent, and naval signals during the battle of the Atlantic could be read as swiftly as one hour after transmission.[8]

Before May 1940 the cracking of the codes depended upon chance factors such as the transmission of flaws and errors, as with one German unit reporting every morning the same phrase, *Verlauf ruhig* (situation unchanged), thus giving the Cambridge mathematics don in Hut 6, Gordon Welchman, who had improved Turing's bombe machine in 1940, a vital clue about several letters.[9] The major expansion of the Luftwaffe before the war meant that its signallers were generally less well trained and disciplined, and more sloppy, than their Army and Navy counterparts. The fact that there were only twenty-six letters in the alphabet, the key flaw in the machine that no letter could represent itself in the code, and the absence of number keys meaning that every number had to be spelt out, also encouraging replication, were the major aids to decryption. The vast number of permutations – just under 1,253 trillion – that the Enigma code depended upon could therefore be narrowed down considerably by Turing's and Welchman's bombes.

It was not until the beginning of April 1941 that the German naval Enigma codes were broken – except for a very brief period in April 1940 – although there had been no shortage of plans to try to obtain German codebooks to help the process along, with the scheme of the intelligence officer and future Bond author Ian Fleming to crash a captured aircraft into the English Channel, and then ambush the rescue boat, being the most hare-brained.[10] It turned out to be the capture off Norway of the German trawler *Krebs* that yielded up the vital settings list that Bletchley needed to operate Turing's Banburismus procedure for decryption. Although all German skippers were under strict instructions to destroy or throw overboard all codebooks at all costs, with the capture by HMS *Bulldog* and HMS *Broadway* of soaking codebooks from Julius Lemp's *U-110* on 9 May 1941 by Sub-Lieutenant David Balme – they were dried over a stove on a British destroyer by Lieutenant Allon Bacon from the Naval Intelligence Division – Bletchley was able to discover future settings, the so-called Offizier procedure. This meant it could pick up announcements of future settings changes. By the autumn of 1941, evasive routing of convoys due to Ultra meant that the U-boats were sinking far fewer merchantmen; and as one historian has put it, 'Bletchley Park had gone from being stymied by maddening cryptanalytic obstacles to being overwhelmed by its own success.'[11] Yet it was not to last long.

Although the Abwehr set up regular investigations into the security of Enigma, and the commander of the U-boat branch of the German Navy, Karl Dönitz, had himself questioned whether it could have been broken, the Germans only continued to refine the existing machine settings rather than institute a brand-new communications system. *Geheimschreiber*, for example, was a non-Morse cipher that had up to ten rotary wheels, against the Enigma's maximum of five. Its product was codenamed Fish at Bletchley and was far harder to crack, but it was not universally employed. Had a suspicious Reich turned to it instead of relying upon Enigma, the story of the Second World War might have been very different. Sir Harry Hinsley, the historian of British wartime intelligence, calculated that without Ultra the Normandy landings could not have been launched until 1946 at the earliest.[12]

Although the Allies could not be seen to rely on it too much, for fear that the Germans would realize it had been compromised, information gleaned from Ultra was used to great advantage at many key moments of the war – for example, it brought about the battle off Cape Matapan, enabled the sinkings of the *Bismarck* and *Scharnhorst*, disclosed Rommel's weaknesses and shortages prior to El Alamein, simplified Montgomery's advance into Tunisia in March 1943, made the planning for the invasions of Sicily and southern France much easier, exposed the whereabouts of German divisions before D-Day and revealed Hitler's orders for a counter-attack at Falaise in August 1944. (The day before the Mediterranean battle of Cape Matapan, Admiral Cunningham strode ashore at Alexandria carrying his golf clubs, so as to lull the suspicions of the Japanese consul-general there. The next day, 28 March 1941, he sank three Italian destroyers and two cruisers whose whereabouts and intentions he knew from the Ultra decrypts he had received.)[13] Yet it was undoubtedly in the battle of the Atlantic that Ultra was put to greatest use. Hut 8 of Bletchley Park succeeded in decoding about 1.12 million of the 1.55 million Kriegsmarine signals that were intercepted during the Second World War.

The battle of the Atlantic has been described as 'one that really did threaten Britain's survival just as surely as would panzer divisions roaming through the Home Counties'.[14] In his memoirs Churchill wrote: 'The only thing that ever really frightened me during the war was the U-boat peril ... I was even more anxious about this battle than I had been about the glorious air fight called the Battle of Britain.'[15] The UK had to import two-thirds of all her food during the war, 30 per cent of her iron ore, 80 per cent of her soft timber and wool, 90 per cent of her copper and bauxite, 95 per cent of her petroleum products and 100 per cent of her rubber and chrome.[16] It is a moot point whether, in the event of the U-boats closing down her imports completely, Britain's armaments industry would have ground to a halt before or after mass starvation struck every urbanized area. Yet that was unlikely to happen, for Hitler saw only too late the potential war-winning capacity of the U-boat, despite its almost bringing Britain to her knees in 1917. If the Nazis had started the war with as many submarines operational in September 1939 as they had in March 1945 – that is, 463 instead of only 43 – they might have won it. As it was, they did not come close to strangling British imports at any point, and once they had invaded Russia instead of the Middle East, and declared war against the United States, Britain was effectively safe from a naval and supply point of view. 'The decisive point in warfare against England lies in attacking her merchant shipping in the Atlantic,' Dönitz had long argued, but he believed he needed a minimum of 300 U-boats to be sure of victory, and he had less than one-sixth of that total in 1939.[17] Once Hitler finally recognized their potential, a huge increase in U-boat production took place, but it was too late to win the all-important battle of the Atlantic. With only one-third of submarines operational at any one time, the others needing crew training and boat refitting, a massive building effort should have been instituted by Hitler by 1937 at the very latest, but he missed the opportunity.

Churchill agreed with Dönitz's thesis, writing after the war: 'The U-boat attack was our worst evil. It would have been wise for the Germans to stake all on it.'[18] However, Dönitz was not the important figure when war broke out that he later became (indeed he ended the war as Führer of Germany). Although he was *Führer der Unterseeboote* at the outbreak of war, he only held the same rank as a cruiser captain.[19] Born in September 1891 at Grünau near Berlin, he served as first watch officer under the U-boat ace Walter Forstmann in the Great War, before being given his own command in the Mediterranean, only for his boat to surface out of control while attacking a convoy. As a POW aboard a British cruiser in Gibraltar, he witnessed the armistice celebrations on the Rock in November 1918, and gestured to the ship's captain at all the flags of the Allied powers flying from the ships, before asking what pleasure could be gained 'from a victory attained with the whole world as allies'. The Briton replied pathetically, 'Yes, it's very curious,' thus missing out on teaching Dönitz a valuable lesson about what would happen when Germany declared war against a global alliance.[20]

Karl Dönitz became a proponent of submarine warfare long before the moment when the Reich threw off its restraints under the Versailles Treaty, which banned it from having any submarines. Under the 1935 London Treaty, all signatories, including Germany, agreed to build a submarine fleet of no more than 52,700 tons, with no individual boat of more than 2,000 tons, but Germany used Spanish and Finnish yards to circumvent these restrictions. Yet Germany needed a tonnage vastly larger than she was building even illegally in order to destroy British maritime trade in wartime; and even if Dönitz had held greater sway in the German Naval Ministry than he actually did, it would probably have made little difference, as Admiral Erich Raeder was also making these arguments, with only intermittent interest from Hitler. 'On land I am a hero,' the Führer once said, 'but at sea I am a coward.'[21]

Hitler was fascinated by the great surface ships such as the battleships *Bismarck* and *Tirpitz*, the pocket battleships *Deutschland*, *Admiral Graf Spee* and *Admiral Scheer*, the battle cruisers *Scharnhorst* and *Gneisenau* and the heavy cruiser *Prinz Eugen*, but he understood very little of naval strategy and the influence of sea-power. He certainly failed to spot the potential of a massive U-boat campaign, and largely ignored his admirals' pleas for more ships and submarines during 1940, preferring to concentrate resources on the Wehrmacht and Luftwaffe. It was to be one of his greatest blunders of the war.

The deeply religious, handsome Dr Erich Raeder was born in Hamburg, the son of a languages teacher. He had been the navigation officer aboard the Kaiser's yacht *Hohenzollern*, then served as a Staff officer under Admiral von Hipper during the Great War. He took an honours doctorate from Kiel University afterwards, writing a dissertation on cruiser warfare that he later published as a book. Naval chief of staff from 1928 and commander-in-chief of the Kriegsmarine from 1935, Raeder's naval building programme, Plan Z, presupposed a war that began in 1944, which implies very poor co-ordination with the Führer. When it actually began five years too early, the German

Navy did not yet have the balance – specifically in the areas of aircraft carriers and U-boats – to deliver victory against the Royal Navy. On the outbreak of war, Germany had only two modern battle cruisers – *Scharnhorst* and *Gneisenau* – three pocket battleships, two heavy cruisers, six light cruisers, twenty-two destroyers and only forty-three submarines, so on 24 September 1939 Raeder spent several hours trying to persuade the Führer of the attractions of a major, immediate U-boat building programme.[22] Hitler said that he sympathized, but the necessary manpower and steel were not subsequently allotted to the Kriegsmarine in anything like the quantities required.

After a series of sharp engagements against the Royal Navy, by the end of 1940 Germany only had twenty-two U-boats left, and only twenty were built between the outbreak of war and the summer of 1940. Yet the twenty-five U-boats that were operating in the Atlantic by then had sunk no less than 680,000 tons between them.[23] On 17 October 1940 a group of seven U-boats attacked Convoy SC-7 near Rockall, which numbered thirty-four merchantmen but had only four escorts. No fewer than seventeen ships were sunk, and no U-boat was damaged. U-boat captain Otto Kretschmer chalked up sinkings in the Atlantic that were to amount to more than a quarter of a million tons. As a result, Hitler slowly recognized the submarines' potential and on 6 February 1941 he issued Führer Directive No. 23, which emphasized that 'The wider employment of submarines . . . can bring about the collapse of English resistance within the foreseeable future . . . It must therefore be the aim of our further operations . . . to concentrate all weapons of air and sea warfare against enemy imports . . . The sinking of merchantmen is more important than attack on enemy warships.'[24] Yet by then he was already deep into the planning stage for Operation Barbarossa, which was severely to undermine the U-boat offensive. Had he concentrated on knocking Britain out of the war first, he could then have turned eastwards at his leisure, with all the forces of the Reich and no prospect of having to draw off forces into Africa or the Mediterranean, and no aid coming to Russia from Britain either.

The Kondor was the Focke-Wulf 200 maritime reconnaissance bomber and had a range of up to 2,200 miles; it carried a 4,626-pound bomb load, flew at 152mph but lacked significant armour. It could be an invaluable spotter for U-boats, but when Dönitz asked Göring for more Kondors he was refused them, and for all the inspiring language of Directive No. 23 he had to rely on the twelve Kondors of Squadron KG40. These were nothing like enough, and as he later noted: 'Here the flaw in the conduct of the war was revealed with painful clarity.'[25] The call-up of 25,000 skilled dockyard workers to fight on the Eastern Front was another blow to Raeder and Dönitz, and when two years later Hitler announced the total scrapping of the capital-shipbuilding programme, Raeder resigned, to be replaced by Dönitz.

The battle of the Atlantic was a grim affair. 'Seas the size of houses would come from every side,' recalled one who fought in it, 'so that on duty or off one could rarely rest, was always bracing the body, bending body and knees like some frozen skier to meet the motions of the ship.'[26] Able Seaman Edward Butler, who served on an Atlantic convoy escort ship, told of how cold the crossings could get, when the ice was 'freezing everything on the upper deck and the captain had to turn all hands to chip it off because it was becoming over top weight and there was a very severe danger of the ship capsizing. So we had to work during the night, in complete darkness, to get the ice off.'[27] The best fictional account of the battle is Nicholas Monsarrat's 1951 autobiographical novel *The Cruel Sea*, which was later made into a fine movie starring Jack Hawkins and Denholm Elliott. The story of the 1,000-ton, 88-man corvette HMS *Compass Rose*, from her commissioning in 1940 to her torpedoing in 1942, and then of the frigate HMS *Saltash*, the book covers the U-boat war, the Murmansk convoys and D-Day. Monsarrat particularly expresses his unstinting admiration of the men of the merchant marine who sailed in oil-tankers: 'They lived, for an entire voyage of three to four weeks, as a man living on top of a keg of gunpowder: the stuff they carried – the life-blood of the whole war – was the most treacherous cargo of all; a single torpedo, a single small bomb, even a stray shot from a machine-gun, could transfer their ship into a torch.'[28] The logistics of organizing a convoy were also well described; at any one time there might be more than 500 British ships at sea in a dozen or so convoys, and each ship:

would have to be manned, and loaded at a prescribed date, railage and docking facilities notwithstanding ... their masters would have to attend sailing conferences for last-minute orders: they would have to rendezvous at a set time and place, with pilots made available for them: and their readiness for sea would have to coincide with an escort group to accompany them, which itself needed the same preparation and the same careful routing. Dock space had to be waiting for them, and men to load and unload: a hundred factories had to meet a fixed dispatch-date on their account: a railway shunter falling asleep at Birmingham or Clapham could spoil the whole thing, a third mate getting drunk on Tuesday instead of Monday could wreck a dozen carefully laid plans, a single air raid out of the hundreds that had harassed the harbours of Britain could halve a convoy and make it not worth the trouble of sending it over the Atlantic.[29]

A major problem with British strategy at the start of the war was that too much attention was paid to taking the offensive against the U-boat threat, and not enough to protecting convoys, which the Great War had proved was the best way of keeping the sea-lanes open. 'Instead of employing the maximum number of vessels in the escort role,' Vice-Admiral Sir Peter Gretton believed, the Royal Navy 'wasted a great deal of energy in hunting for submarines in the open ocean'.[30] When the captain of the unarmoured, converted passenger liner HMS *Jervis Bay*, Edward Fogarty Fegen, bravely but suicidally attacked the pocket battleship *Admiral Scheer* in November 1940, thereby allowing convoy HX-84 to scatter in a smokescreen at dusk, she had been the only escort vessel accompanying thirty-seven merchantmen. (*Scheer* nonetheless sank five of them. Fegen won a posthumous Victoria Cross.)

It was not until May 1941 that convoys were escorted all the way across the Atlantic, and very often they were woefully under-protected even then. Although Liberator bombers from Britain had the range to search the Eastern Atlantic for enemy submarines on the surface, and then attack them before they could dive to safety, Bomber Command would release only six squadrons to Coastal Command, which was not enough to make a serious difference. Air cover was generally scanty, and completely non-existent in the mid-Atlantic 'Ocean Gap', the area several hundred miles wide which planes could not reach from Iceland, Britain or Canada. (The Gap was closed in 1943 by the introduction of Very Long Range Liberators.) RAF Coastal Command entered the war badly under-equipped, under-staffed and under-trained, considering that its main role was to search for surface ships rather than submarines. There was also an absurd rivalry between the Admiralty and the Air Ministry that stymied efficiency in the opening stages. The Americans took even longer to institute a proper convoy system. On the eastern seaboard of the United States, failure to douse lights in the ports, and the relocation of much of the US Navy to the Pacific after Pearl Harbor, led to the sinking of no fewer than 485 ships totalling 2.5 million tons by August 1942.[31]

The battle of the Atlantic provided some nerve-wracking moments for British strategists: in March 1941 alone, U-boats sank forty-one ships. Yet that same month three of Dönitz's best U-boat captains were neutralized. Germany's top ace Otto Kretschmer – who had sunk forty-six ships totalling 273,000 tons – was captured after his *U-99* was depth-charged and forced to the surface. Günther Prien, who had torpedoed the British battleship *Royal Oak* in Scapa Flow in October 1939, was killed when his *U-47* was sunk by the destroyer HMS *Wolverine*. Finally Joachim Schepke was killed in an attack by an escort group commander, Captain Donald MacIntyre. An even greater blow fell that month when – in an escalation of 'neutral' America's aggression – the United States announced that the waters between Canada and Iceland would thenceforth be protected by her Navy, thus allowing the Royal Navy to concentrate on protecting convoys. In September 1941, Roosevelt gave American ships permission to fire on German submarines wherever they saw them. 'So far as the Atlantic is concerned,' the American Chief of Naval Operations Admiral Harold Stark noted privately of the shooting war, 'we are all but, if not actually, in it.'

After Enigma had been cracked in April 1941, between July and December 1941 Allied convoys were re-routed so expertly that not one was intercepted in the North Atlantic.[32] Although there were still significant losses – over 720,000 tons were sunk in that period – experts calculate that more than 1.6 million tons were saved. Of course, if the Germans had started the war with enough U-boats, thereby closing the gaps in the ocean between them, no amount of re-routing could have saved the convoys. In May 1941 Churchill warned Roosevelt that if 4.5 million tons of shipping were lost during the next year, with the USA building 3.5 million and Britain 1 million, they would be 'just marking time and swimming level with the bank against the stream'.[33] Yet that month was the first that a west–east convoy was given escorts that sailed the whole way across the Atlantic with them. By September 1941, however, Hitler's belated submarine-building programme had started to bear fruit, and Dönitz now had no fewer than 150 U-boats in commission, with which he would try to wrest victory in the battle of the Atlantic.

When the war broke out, both the British and German Admiralties assumed that the great German surface ships would be crucial in deciding whether Britain survived or starved. It was thought by London and Berlin that if these capital ships could dominate the Ocean Gap, the New World would be incapable, to adopt Churchill's phrase in his 'fight on the beaches' speech, of stepping 'forth to the rescue and liberation of the Old'. If, on the other hand, the Royal Navy and its Canadian and later American counterparts could sink these huge vessels, the danger was thought to be far less great. On the outbreak of war *Graf Spee* and *Deutschland* were already stationed to attack the trade routes, and *Scharnhorst* and *Gneisenau* put to sea in November 1939.

As recounted in Chapter 1, the forced scuttling of *Graf Spee* outside Montevideo harbour on 17 December 1939, the victim of a brave naval action at the battle of the River Plate but also a brilliant British deception operation, dented the myth of invincibility that had begun to surround the big German raiders. Similarly, although it was successful the German invasion of Norway in April 1940 cost the German Navy dear – almost half its entire destroyer force. But the fall of France in June allowed the Kriegsmarine to establish itself right along France's Atlantic seaboard, with major bases at Lorient, Brest, La Rochelle and Saint-Nazaire. October 1940 saw *Admiral Scheer* break into the Atlantic Ocean, followed two months later by the heavy cruiser *Admiral Hipper*. The British Admiralty seemed incapable of preventing German raiders from sailing through the Denmark Straits between Greenland and Iceland. 'For the first time in our history,'

Vice-Admiral Günther Lütjens told the crews of *Scharnhorst* and *Gneisenau* in January 1941, as they passed through the Faeroes–Iceland gap, 'German battleships have today succeeded in breaking through the British blockade. We shall now go forward to success.'[34] He was right in the short term: in two months the two ships together sank 116,000 tons of Allied shipping.

Yet both Admiralties were wrong in assuming that the big battleships would be decisive. In fact, it very soon became clear that the U-boats posed the primary threat, especially during what their crews were later to dub 'the happy times' of 1939–41. U-boats were often faster than their prey, averaging 17 knots on the surface, where they often sailed at night (they managed only 3 knots when submerged). Long after the war, Dönitz enumerated the advantages of the U-boat, which were more manoeuvrable than their Great War predecessors and:

had only a small silhouette consisting only of the conning tower and that is why the submarine could only be seen with difficulty during a night attack. Gradual development in communications meant the submarines were no longer obliged to fight alone, but they could attack together. This enabled us to develop the 'wolf-pack' tactics that became very useful against the convoys.[35]

After April 1941 Dönitz pioneered *Rudeltaktik* (herd tactics), by which the first U-boat to spot a convoy shadowed it while sending out signals to headquarters and other U-boats in the area, prior to a concerted night-time, surface, close-range torpedo attack by them all, acting as a wolf-pack. Monsarrat described how the U-boats took the upper hand in 1941:

The enemy was planning as well as multiplying. At last, the U-boats were co-ordinating their attack: they now hunted in packs, six or seven in a group, quartering a huge area of the convoy route and summoning their full strength as soon as a contact was obtained. They had the use of French, Norwegian and Baltic ports, fully equipped for shelter and maintenance: they had long-range aircraft to spot and identify for them, they had numbers, they had training, they had better weapons, they had the spur of success.[36]

By March 1941 the Allies had lost over 350,000 tons of shipping in the Atlantic, but the following month this rose to 700,000 tons.

Since in 1939 Britain's entire merchant marine totalled a gross tonnage of 17.5 million, the largest in the world, the danger to her from losing more than 1 million tons in two months was obvious.[37] Setting up the Battle of the Atlantic Committee on 6 March 1941 to co-ordinate ministers, civil servants and the services, Churchill announced that 'the Battle of the Atlantic has begun . . . We must take the offensive against the U-boat and the Focke-Wulf wherever we can and whenever we can. The U-boat at sea must be hunted, the U-boat in the building yard or in the dock must be bombed.'[38]

Yet it was the Germans who took the initiative, unleashing the battleship *Bismarck* and the new heavy cruiser *Prinz Eugen* into the Atlantic shipping lanes, in the hope of asphyxiating Britain and forcing her to sue for peace. *Bismarck* had been launched in Hamburg by the Iron Chancellor's granddaughter, Dorothea von Löwenfeld, on 14 February 1939, and Göring, Goebbels, Hess, Ribbentrop, Himmler, Bormann, Keitel and of course Raeder were all present; the Führer gave a speech. The ship was one-sixth of a mile long, recalled the British writer Ludovic Kennedy, who was a junior reserve lieutenant when he took part in the operation to try to sink her,

120 feet wide, designed to carry eight 15" guns and six aircraft, with 13" armour made of specially hardened Wotan steel on her turrets and sides. Listed as 35,000 tons to comply with the London Treaty, she would in fact be 42,000 tons standard displacement and over 50,000 tons fully laden. There had never been a warship like her: she symbolized not only a resurgent Navy but the whole resurgent German nation . . . Warships combine uniquely grace and power, and *Bismarck*, massive and elegant, with the high flare of her bows and majestic sweep of her lines, the symmetry of her turrets, the rakish cowling of her funnel, her ease and arrogance in the water, was then the most graceful, most powerful warship yet built. No German saw her without pride, no neutral or enemy without admiration.[39]

Furthermore she had twelve boilers, her four gun turrets each weighed 1,000 tons – they were nicknamed Anton, Bruno, Caesar and Dora – she could sail at 29 knots and her crew numbered 2,065. *Prinz Eugen*, meanwhile, displaced 14,000 tons, had eight 8-inch guns and a speed of 32 knots.

These two warships left port at Gotenhafen (present-day Gdynia)

at 21.30 hours on Sunday, 18 May 1941 in Operation Rheinübung (Rhine Exercise), a break for the Atlantic. Because several Polish labourers had been killed by oil fumes while cleaning her tanks, *Bismarck* sailed 200 tons of fuel short, something which her captain, Ernst Lindemann, was later bitterly to regret. *Bismarck* and *Prinz Eugen* skirted as far as possible away from the major British naval base of Scapa Flow and sailed through the Denmark Straits, where on the afternoon of Friday, 23 May they were shadowed with radar by the Royal Navy heavy cruisers HMS *Norfolk* and HMS *Suffolk*, until HMS *Prince of Wales* and HMS *Hood* were able to intercept them at dawn the next day. 'If any one ship could be said to have been the embodiment of British sea-power and the British Empire between the wars,' wrote Kennedy, 'it was "The mighty *Hood*", as Britain and the Navy called her.' Built on Clydeside in 1916, she was, at 860 feet, 38 feet longer even than the *Bismarck*. Like *Bismarck* she had eight 15-inch guns in four massive turrets. With her maximum speed of 32 knots – she was the fastest ship of her size afloat – a ton of oil only got her half a mile. She had everything except upper-deck armour, because she had been built just before the battle of Jutland, when three British battle cruisers had been lost from shells falling vertically through their decks. Despite this, she had not been reconditioned.

When the *Hood* and *Prince of Wales* exchanged fire, at a range of 13 miles, with *Bismarck* and *Prinz Eugen* at 06.00 on Saturday, 24 May 1941, *Norfolk* and *Suffolk* were not close enough to provide support. In his fine memoir *Pursuit: The Sinking of the Bismarck*, Kennedy described how 'For a moment the world stood still, then the guns spoke with their terrible great roar, the blast almost knocked one senseless, thick clouds of cordite smoke, black and bitter-smelling, clutched at the throat, blinded the vision, and four shells weighing a ton apiece went rocketing out of the muzzles at over 1,600 miles per hour.'[40]

Without the *Norfolk* and *Suffolk* to harry *Bismarck* from the rear, there was nothing to draw her fire from *Hood*, which was also taking fire from *Prinz Eugen*, and because the two German ships had swapped places since the last visual report, *Hood* was firing at the wrong target – *Prinz Eugen* rather than *Bismarck* – as the two looked alike at that distance despite their very different displacements.[41] The

Germans also had the weather gauge working in their favour, so that the British range-finders on the forward turrets were drenched with spray and other, less accurate instruments in the control tower had to be used instead. Furthermore, only the front turrets could be engaged as the British ships sailed towards the Germans, whereas their antagonists were able to deploy every high-calibre weapon they had.

Nonetheless, what happened next could not have been avoided whichever range-finders were used, whatever *Norfolk* and *Suffolk* had done, and however many guns *Hood* had managed to deploy. Only a thorough re-armouring of *Hood*'s upper deck in the inter-war years could have saved her. For a shell from *Bismarck*, in Kennedy's phrase,

came plunging down like a rocket, hit the old ship fair and square between centre and stern, sliced its way through steel and wood, pierced the deck that should have been strengthened but never was, penetrated the ship's vitals deep below the water-line, exploded, touched off the 4″ magazine which in turn touched off the after 15″ magazine. Before the eyes of the horrified British and incredulous Germans a huge column of flame leapt up from *Hood*'s centre.[42]

No one who witnessed that flame ever forgot it, as *Hood* exploded and then sank, with only three survivors out of a crew of over 1,400. Captain John Leach of the *Prince of Wales* continued firing at *Bismarck*, hitting her twice but only on the seventh salvo, yet once he was himself hit by German 5- and 8-inch shells, he was forced to escape under smoke cover. In an engagement lasting only twenty minutes, the Germans had sunk the maritime pride of the British Empire. Thereafter, their luck changed. One of the two 14-inch shells that the *Prince of Wales* landed on *Bismarck* had ruptured her fuel tanks, and she started leaking oil, which, because she had also sailed under-oiled and had not been resupplied when she might have been, meant that her skipper had to try to reach her supply ships and, he hoped, lead his antagonists into a wolf-pack.[43] Meanwhile, *Prinz Eugen* broke off westwards, covered by an attack by *Bismarck* on *Norfolk* and *Suffolk*.

At sunset on 24 May, nine Fairey Swordfish torpedo-bombers from the aircraft carrier HMS *Victorious* braved *Bismarck*'s sixty-eight anti-aircraft guns and scored a hit with their 18-inch torpedoes. With the battleship still leaking oil steadily, it changed course for Brest. Then Enigma made its vital contribution, when a senior Luftwaffe officer in Athens using the Lufwaffe Enigma code enquired of his son serving in *Bismarck* where he was headed, and received the reply 'Brest.' Had it not been for *Bismarck* breaking radio silence in a code that Bletchley had cracked, she might have reached the port. She almost escaped anyway after her bearings were incorrectly plotted, but at 10.30 on 26 May she was spotted by a US Navy patrol pilot called Leonard Smith in a Consolidated Catalina flying-boat, part of RAF Coastal Command (and seven months before America entered the war).[44]

Force H, based in Gibraltar, and including the battle cruiser HMS *Renown* and the aircraft carrier HMS *Ark Royal*, attacked that afternoon. Planes from *Ark Royal* landed two hits with contact-detonating torpedoes, one of them entering the starboard steering compartment, exploding, and thrusting the starboard rudder against the central propeller. This jammed *Bismarck*'s steering and wrecked her chances of getting to Brest. Nevertheless, German aircraft and submarines operating out of French Atlantic ports might still have saved her, had it not been for the attacks made at 08.47 the following day, Tuesday, 27 May, by the battleships *King George V* and *Rodney*, firing at 16,000 yards, with *Norfolk* taking part too, and the cruiser *Dorsetshire* finished *Bismarck* off with torpedoes. At 10.36 she sank, killing all but 110 of her crew. It seems that she was also scuttled, evidence for which was discovered when she was found on the seabed 300 miles off south-west Ireland in 1989.

Hitler learnt the lesson of the vulnerability of great surface raiders to air attack. On 19 June 1943 he told Martin Bormann that although he had once 'planned to construct the most powerful squadron of battleships in the world' – which he was going to name after the great sixteenth-century poet–adventurers Ulrich von Hutten and Götz von Berlichingen – now 'I am very pleased that I abandoned the idea.' The reason was that 'it is now the infantry of the sea which assumes the prime importance,' and submarines, corvettes and destroyers 'are the classes that carry on the fight'. To illustrate the point, the Führer said that although the Japanese had the greatest battleships in the world, 'it is very difficult to use them in action. For them, the greatest danger comes from the air. Remember the *Bismarck*!'[45]

The sinking of the *Bismarck* – although of course it cost the *Hood* – saw the last of the German surface-fleet raiders threatening the Atlantic sea-lanes, and in that sense marked a major turning point in the battle. *Bismarck*'s and *Prinz Eugen*'s supply ships were immediately targeted, using the German Home Waters key of the naval Enigma code called Dolphin, and hardly any made it back to port.[46] That meant that the Germans had henceforth to rely on underwater tankers and supply carriers, which had much smaller capacities and slower speeds.[47] Although there were other major battles to be fought against vessels such as the battle cruiser *Scharnhorst* (sunk off the Northern Cape of Norway on 26 December 1943), Bismarck's sister ship the *Tirpitz* (sunk by Lancaster bombers with 12,000-pound Tallboy bombs on 12 November 1944), the battle cruiser *Gneisenau* (scuttled at Gotenhafen on 28 March 1945) and the *Prinz Eugen* (which ended her days as a nuclear-test target in the Pacific), none of these ships posed the same level of danger during the battle of the Atlantic.

Tirpitz did, however, play a major – if not actually operational – part in the tragedy that overtook Convoy PQ-17 in July 1942. The Arctic convoys had started very soon after Operation Barbarossa. On 12 August 1941, even while Churchill and Roosevelt were still meeting at Placentia Bay in Newfoundland discussing how to help Russia, two squadrons of British fighters comprising forty aircraft left Britain on board HMS *Argus* bound for Murmansk, the first of the supplies shipped to Russia by the Arctic route. Under the command of a New Zealander, Wing Commander Ramsbottom-Isherwood, they reached the Soviet naval base at Polyarnoe, near Murmansk, which was to become a huge receiving depot for Allied supplies over the next four years. Although the RAF needed every aircraft it could get for home defences and North African operations in the summer of 1941, nonetheless it transported planes to help the USSR in its hour of trial.

The first regular convoys, which all had the codename PQ followed by a consecutive number, started out from Iceland to Murmansk and Archangel via Bear Island. On 28 September, PQ-1 set out packed with military supplies and large quantities of the vital raw materials that Stalin had asked for personally, including rubber, copper and aluminium. Soon afterwards, Churchill announced that Britain's entire tank production for the month of September was going to be despatched to Russia. The tanks were badly needed, for on 2 October the Nazis launched Operation Typhoon on Moscow. The horrific winter of 1941/2, which did so much to destroy Hitler's dreams of turning European Russia into an Aryan colony, also badly affected the Arctic convoys. The route taken was a hazardous one that comprised seventeen nerve-wracking days sailing around the Northern Cape above Norway and Finland, through the potentially lethal ice-floes, through German air strikes, U-boat attacks, marauding surface ships and the constant freezing Arctic storms. Monsarrat wrote: 'One of the seamen, who'd taken off his gauntlets to open an ammunition locker, had torn off the whole of the skin of one palm and left it stuck to the locker like half a bloody glove, with him staring at it as if it were something hanging up in a shop. But that wasn't as bad as what happened to the poor bastards that got dropped into the drink.'[48] They froze to death within three minutes. By 1942, after three years of war, Monsarrat recalled how the sailors of the Royal Navy had:

developed – they had to develop – a professional inhumanity towards their job, a lack of feeling that was the best guarantee of efficiency: time spent in contemplating this evil warfare was time wasted, and rage or pity was something that could only come between them and their work. Hardened to pain and destruction, taking it all for granted, they concentrated as best they could on fighting back and on saving men for one purpose only – so they could be returned to the battle as soon as possible.[49]

One of the most serious setbacks of the naval war occurred on 4 July 1942, three days after Convoy PQ-17 had been spotted by German submarines and aircraft. It was hard to miss, comprising thirty-five merchant ships (twenty-two American, eight British, two Russian, two Panamanian and one Dutch), protected by six destroyers and fifteen other armed vessels. That same morning, four merchantmen were sunk by Heinkel torpedo-bombers, and, fearing that four powerful German warships – including the *Tirpitz* – were on their way, Admiral Sir Dudley Pound, the First Sea Lord, ordered the convoy to scatter, overriding the C-in-C Home Fleet Admiral Sir John

Tovey and the Admiralty's Operational Intelligence Centre. It was a virtual death sentence.

The German warships had indeed been ordered to intercept the convoy, but, unbeknown to Pound, Hitler had told them to turn back. Instead, the scattered convoy was picked off from the air and by submarines. Only thirteen ships reached Archangel; of the 156,500 tons loaded on board the convoy in Iceland back on 27 June, 99,300 tons were sunk, with the loss of no fewer than 430 of the 594 tanks and 210 of the 297 planes on board. It was astonishing that not more than 153 sailors were drowned. Further tragedy was to follow three days later, when the returning convoy QP-13 ran into a British mine-field off Iceland through bad navigation, and a further five merchant ships were sunk. There were further serious setbacks during the war, including Convoy PQ-18, thirteen of whose forty ships were sunk in September 1942, although it did at least manage to take a severe toll on its attackers, destroying four German submarines and forty-one aircraft. This led to the War Cabinet temporarily suspending convoys to Russia altogether, an action which Churchill told the War Cabinet on 14 September had left the Russian Ambassador to Washington, Maxim Litvinov, 'squealing' but the Ambassador to London, Ivan Maisky, 'plaintive'.[50] It was not until late in 1943 that the Allies began to win the Arctic campaign: in November and December three eastbound and two westbound Arctic convoys reached their destinations without any loss.

Major scientific and technical developments during the war helped in the struggle against the U-boat. The Royal Navy used Asdic, the echo-sounding device for tracking U-boats, and 180 ships were fitted with it. It was not foolproof, however, so ships constantly zig-zigged hoping to escape submarines. As the battle of the Atlantic progressed, there were a number of factors that secured victory for the Allies, including the vast expansion of the Canadian Escort Force based at Halifax, Nova Scotia; side-firing as well as back-firing depth-charges; the new high-frequency, direction-finding (HF/DF) apparatus; Anti-Surface-Vessel radar, which the Germans greatly overestimated and often blamed for intelligence coups that actually derived from Ultra; Very Long Range bombers that reported U-boat positions, bombed them and closed off the Ocean Gap; powerful Leigh floodlights for spotting conning towers and periscopes; airborne centrimetric radar; and the alteration of the Royal Navy codes in June 1943 which plunged the German decrypters in the dark (although they were still able to read the Merchant Navy's ciphers).

As so often it was the Commonwealth that played a vital, if largely unsung, part in winning the battle. The Royal Canadian Navy grew fifty-fold in the course of the conflict, and its anti-submarine arm, the Canadian Escort Force, contributed almost as much to victory as the Royal Navy. Protecting the HX (Halifax-to-Britain) and SC (Sydney- or Cape-Breton-to-Britain) eastbound convoys in one direction, and the westbound ONF (fast outbound-from-Britain) and the ONS (slow outbound-from-Britain) convoys in the other, they were invaluable.

Part of the explanation for the heavy losses on the Atlantic and Arctic convoys was that the British convoy code had been cracked by German intelligence, something that was not discovered until after the war. In February 1942 the German Beobachtungdienst (radio monitoring service) managed to crack about 75 per cent of Naval Cipher No. 3 which since June 1941 had routed convoys.[51] The Germans were reading Royal Navy codes, although only 10 per cent of the intercepts could be used operationally because of the time taken to decipher them.[52] Nonetheless, when the size, destinations and departure times of convoys did become known to the Germans, they could draw up an accurate picture of the whole operation. If they had achieved real-time decryption, as Turing was to do, it could have been potenti- ally as decisive an advantage to the Germans as the cracking of the Enigma code was for the Allies. Instead of recognizing the danger, the Admiralty put the U-boats' remarkable success in intercepting convoys down to the advanced hydrophone equipment they used, which it was thought could detect propeller noise for over 80 miles. When marvelling at the Germans' continuing trust in Enigma, therefore, one must also consider the British faith in the Royal Navy's own compromised codes. Naval Cipher No. 3 was not replaced with No. 5, which the Germans never cracked, until June 1943.

Coincidentally, the worst moment for the Allies in the battle of the Atlantic came in the same month as the Beobachtungdienst cracked Naval Cipher No. 3. On 1 February 1942, OKM (the

Supreme Command of the Navy) introduced an extra rotor wheel to the Enigma machines used by U-boats in the Atlantic, thus enormously increasing the number of solutions to any Enigma-encrypted texts. The new code was dubbed Shark at Bletchley, and every effort was made to crack it, initially by producing four-rotor bombes.[53] Hitherto the Royal Navy had been able to foil ambushes and divert convoys away from danger areas. Suddenly, for more than ten months – almost for the whole of 1942 – Bletchley was thrust into the dark, its bombes producing only gibberish. With the Navy unable to re-route convoys away from peril, sinkings increased dramatically.

In 1940 U-boats had sunk 1,345 Allied ships totalling 4 million tons for the loss of twenty-four submarines, and in 1941 slightly more, 1,419 totalling around 4.5 million, for the loss of thirty-five. Yet in 1942, with Shark unbroken, U-boats sank 1,859 ships totalling over 7 million tons, albeit for the loss of eighty-six U-boats.[54] In November 1942 alone over 860,000 tons of Allied shipping were sunk, 88 per cent of it by more than a hundred submarines that the Germans had at sea.[55] Although the church bells were rung to celebrate the victory at El Alamein that month, they could just as well be tolling the news that the Allies were now for the first time in the war losing more tankers than they were building.

Yet salvation was at hand. At 22.00 hours on Friday, 30 October 1942, *U-559* was forced to the surface after no fewer than 288 depth-charges were dropped on her by four British destroyers in the eastern Mediterranean. Her captain opened her stopcocks to scuttle the vessel and the entire crew abandoned ship, but Lieutenant Francis Fasson, Able Seaman Colin Grazier and a sixteen-year-old Naafi assistant Tommy Brown (who had lied about his age to join the Navy) from HMS *Petard* stripped off their clothes and swam over to it.[56] Getting into the captain's cabin, they used a machine gun to break into a locked cabinet and retrieve the codebooks and documents. After Brown had made three journeys delivering these to another party from the destroyer, the U-boat suddenly sank, drowning Fasson and Grazier. Although their gallantry had been up to the standard required for the Victoria Cross, as it was not 'in the face of the enemy' as the criteria stipulate they were awarded the George Cross posthumously, and Brown received the George Medal.

No decorations were more deserved: once Bletchley received the documents on 24 November they were found to include the all-important indicator list, code and weather tables that allowed the code-breakers to break into Shark on Sunday, 13 December. When the Shark code was used for weather signals, it was discovered, the fourth rotor was always set at neutral, so the old three-bombe rotor could be used to decrypt them, allowing the rest of the code to be reconstructed with relative ease.[57] It was a massive breakthrough. 'Although Dönitz did not know it,' records an historian of the secret intelligence war, 'the tide had turned, this time for good.'[58] (Meanwhile, Tommy Brown GM was discharged from the Navy for volunteering while under age.)

There were other periods of the war when one or more codes – including Shark – went suddenly blank owing to the Germans upgrading or changing aspects of Enigma, but not for so long as to cause insuperable difficulties. Even though the Abwehr learnt from a captured Deuxième Bureau agent about the treachery of Hans Thilo Schmidt – who committed suicide in September 1943 – still they did not connect the facts and adopt a new communications system. Nor did they realize that the sinking of the Scharnhorst on 26 December 1943 had been partly the result of the reading of the Kriegsmarine's codes. If at any stage the Germans had recognized the truth it could have proved catastrophic for the Allies, but the cracking of Enigma turned out to be the best-kept secret of the twentieth century.

At the Casablanca Conference in January 1943, Churchill and Roosevelt gave as high a priority to the defeat of the U-boat threat as they gave to the invasion of Sicily, their other immediate strategic objective. With seventeen new U-boats now being commissioned every month, Dönitz had no fewer than 400 by the spring of 1943, although only one-third were operational. Yet they were not to be enough, for in the first four months of 1943 the battle of the Atlantic turned heavily in the Allies' favour. New tactics in dealing with U-boats, by peeling off escorts to attack in groups, once allied to scientific and technological advances, more aircraft and escort numbers, increasing ranges of bombers, the closing of the Ocean Gap, and the re-cracking of the Ultra naval code the previous December, all helped to tip the balance.

In 1943, the Germans sank only 812 ships totalling over 3 million tons, for the loss of 242 submarines.[59]

In the first five months of 1943 – the *Schwerpunkt* of the battle of the Atlantic – RAF Coastal Command and Royal Navy escort carriers managed to provide the all-important air support for convoys, and in April the battle was taken to Dönitz's own bases in the Bay of Biscay with combined sea and air attacks. Ever since 1943 dawned there had been heavy bombing of the Biscay ports despite the effect on the civilian population, with Churchill summarized as telling the War Cabinet on 11 January that it was an 'Important point of principle. The First Lord makes out his case ... No doubt about gravity of the U-Boat War ... Warn the French population to clear out. It is no longer touch and go with France.'[60] Eden said he had gone into the issue, and 'hitherto our policy was based on effect on French National Army if there was a great slaughter of French people. In this case we can't possibly refuse. But they must have 3 or 4 days' warning.' Sir Charles Portal, Chief of the Air Staff, pointed out that warning the local population would greatly increase the risk to his bombing crews because of the increased anti-aircraft measures taken, which would leave the 'effectiveness of attack imperilled'. Churchill thought a general warning 'to leave coastal areas' would suffice, and asked the service departments to get the co-operation of the United States over the policy. In naval matters, meanwhile, he said that the 'Germans run away whenever they meet our surface ships ... most discreditable in German history.'

Victory in the battle of the Atlantic was heralded by the fate of Peter Gretton's Convoy ONS-5, which was attacked in atrocious weather off the south coast of Iceland during the spring of 1943. The convoy of forty ships had sailed out of Londonderry on 23 April at 7 knots in bad weather with an escort of two destroyers, one frigate and four corvettes, which went more slowly than surfaced U-boats. On 28 April the first U-boat attacked the convoy off the coast of Iceland, and for the next nine days there were constant running battles – on one night there were twenty-four separate attacks – until 09.15 hours on 6 May when Dönitz called off the action. In all fifty-nine U-boats from four wolf-packs – Group Star, Group Specht, Group Ansel and Group Drossel – had engaged the convoy, losing eight and with seven more damaged, for the loss of thirteen Allied merchantmen. 'The convoy was still together,' wrote Gretton later, 'and the longest and fiercest convoy action of the war had ended with a clear-cut victory.'[61] In his review of Dönitz's memoirs, the naval historian Captain Stephen Roskill noted that the convoy's struggle 'is marked only by latitude and longitude and has no name by which it will be remembered; but it was, in its own way, as decisive as Quiberon Bay or the Nile'.[62] In the single month of May 1943 forty-one U-boats – 30 per cent of the total force at sea – were sunk at a heavy cost in German lives (including that of Dönitz's youngest son Peter on U-954).[63]

On 24 May Dönitz was forced to withdraw all his U-boats from the North Atlantic, and report to Hitler in Berlin. 'There can be no let-up in submarine warfare,' Hitler told him at a conference also attended by Keitel, Warlimont and Karl-Jesko von Puttkamer, the Führer's naval adjutant, on 5 June. 'The Atlantic is my first line of defence in the West, and even if I have to fight a defensive battle there, that is preferable to waiting to defend myself on the coast of Europe.'[64] No longer did Germany see the Atlantic as a potential means of strangling Britain; now it was somewhere to hold off the coming invasion of north-west Europe. Yet Dönitz was powerless to obey his Führer – though he wisely did not admit as much then or subsequently – and on 24 June Allied ships capable of sailing 15 knots or faster were allowed to sail across the Atlantic without convoy protection for the first time in four years. June 1943 was the first month of the war in which not a single Allied convoy was attacked in the North Atlantic. June also saw the British introduce a new code for ship-to-shore radio traffic, Naval Cipher No. 5, to replace the one that the Germans had been listening into since 1941.

It was ironic that just as Albert Speer, who had been appointed armaments minister after the death in a plane crash of Fritz Todt in April 1942, found a way of rationalizing the manufacture of U-boats – using time-and-motion studies prevalent in the pre-war motor-car industries – down from forty-two weeks to only sixteen, there were fewer places for them to be deployed.[65] Although twenty-eight U-boats did return to the North Atlantic in September 1943, they sank only nine of the 2,468 ships that crossed in the next two months. Despite large numbers of U-boats being put into service – there were never fewer than 400 between the summer of 1943 onwards, of which one-third were operational – the battle of the Atlantic had been decisively lost by Germany. Shipping losses of over 7 million tons in 1942 fell to 3 million in 1943.[66] It was not negligible, but it was survivable. In August 1943 more U-boats were destroyed than merchant ships were sunk, 'a piece of news which stirred a thousand hearts, afloat and ashore', recalled Monsarrat. 'For the first time in the war, the astonishing balance was struck.'[67]

Between January and March 1944 Germany lost twenty-nine U-boats while sinking only three merchantmen. They were thus incapable of interdicting the D-Day landings, although by the start of 1944 they had perfected the Schnorchel, a hinged air mast which permitted the U-boats' diesel engines to suck in air and expel exhaust while fully submerged. Batteries could therefore be recharged underwater without having to surface and U-boats could increase their speed while submerged to 8 knots.[68] Yet by August 1944 Dönitz had given up attempting to prevent resupply of the Allied armies on the Continent, especially after more than half of the U-boats in the Channel had been sunk.

In June 1944, just in time for the Normandy landings, Turing's greatest invention of all, the Colossus II, came on stream. The world's first digital electronic computer, it was able to decode Fish as well as Enigma messages in real time, and also decrypted the correspondence between OKW and the Commander-in-Chief West. As one who worked on Colossus, Donald Michie, has recalled: 'At the end of hostilities 9 new-design Colossi were operational and 63 million characters of high-grade German messages had been decrypted.'[69] Turing's reputation for eccentricity seemed confirmed by his practices of bicycling around wearing a gas mask, and chaining his coffee mug to a radiator, but one of those who worked at Bletchley, WAAF Sergeant Gwen Watkins, later explained that 'If you had a china mug and it was "borrowed", you could replace it only by an enamel one, which made tea taste horrid. And cycling to work in your gas mask, if you had hay fever, was a good idea.'[70] Eccentric or not, Turing's contribution to victory was enormous, making his OBE a paltry reward and his cyanide-by-apple suicide in 1954 correspondingly tragic.

*

As the Russians made their way along the Baltic coast, the Germans had to relocate their U-boat fleet to Norway. Although their number peaked at the huge figure of 463 in March 1945, it was far too late for them to be able to make a difference. In total, throughout the war Germany deployed 1,162 U-boats, of which 785 were destroyed (over 500 by British ships and planes). Altogether they sank 145 Allied warships and 2,828 Allied and neutral merchantmen totalling 14,687,231 tons.[71] In the course of the war, the Royal Navy lost 51,578 men killed and the Merchant Navy 30,248, mainly to U-boats.[72] The U-boat crewmen were immensely brave, and at 75 per cent suffered among the highest death rates of any branch of service in the Reich, in what they themselves dubbed iron coffins. As the war progressed, the U-boat sailors' life expectancy decreased, as is superbly portrayed in the German movie *Das Boot*. Furthermore, heavy Allied bombing of U-boat construction and marshalling yards meant that the newest-pattern U-boat – once hailed as a super-weapon – did not slide down the slipway until 3 May 1945, just as Dönitz was negotiating peace terms with the Allies.

For all that the battle of the Atlantic could have been disastrous for Britain had the Nazis built up a large submarine fleet before the war, nonetheless it was very unlikely that Britain could have lost, for the simple reason that the United States' entry into the war meant that, even when the Shark code went suddenly silent in February 1942, the vast American production of merchant shipping was always ready to make up the losses, almost however bad. Thus whereas the amount of Allied tonnage sunk totalled 4.01 million against the 0.78 million built in 1940, and 4.355 million sunk against 1.972 million built in 1941, and the totals were almost equal at 7.39 million versus 7.78 million in 1942, in 1943 only 3.22 million were sunk against 15.45 million being built, in 1944 1.04 million were sunk against 12.95 million being built, and in 1945 0.437 million tons were sunk against 7.592 million being built.[73] The overwhelming majority were being built by America, by a factor of over five to one.

Moreover, despite the losses, the size of the British merchant fleet stayed almost level throughout the war at between 16 and 20 million tons, making up tonnage through purchase, requisition, chartering from neutrals and other means. Even when the U-boats were sinking large quantities of shipping from 1939 to 1941, therefore, the British merchant fleet actually increased in size by three-quarters of a million tons. The statistics for U-boat and all other sinkings as a percentage of the net tonnage of incoming cargo docked in the United Kingdom are conclusive throughout: in 1939–40 it was 2.0 per cent; thereafter 1941: 3.9 per cent; 1942: 9.7 per cent; 1943: 2.7 per cent; 1944: 0.3 per cent and 1945: 0.6 per cent. Of course imports were wildly below the 91.8 million tons of pre-war levels – and were down to 24.5 million tons in 1942 – but by 1944 they had risen to 56.9 million tons.[74] This means that, in the absence of a huge U-boat fleet in 1939 such as the one Germany belatedly had in 1945, and after America had entered the war, however vicious and bitter the battle of the Atlantic undoubtedly was Britain's survival was never really in doubt, even though for most people on both sides it certainly did not look that way at the time.

12

Up the Wasp-Waist Peninsula

July 1943–May 1945

Here is this beautiful country suffering the worst horrors of war, with the larger part still in the cruel and vengeful grip of the Nazis, and with the hideous prospect of the red-hot rake of the battle-line being drawn from sea to sea right up the length of the peninsula.

Winston Churchill, House of Commons, 24 May 1944[1]

The invasion of Sicily, codenamed Operation Husky, had been agreed at the Casablanca Conference in January 1943, once the alternatives of Sardinia and Corsica were discarded, and then confirmed at the Trident Conference in Washington that May. However, the Americans had not agreed to invade mainland Italy once Sicily had fallen, and were not to do so until the Quadrant Conference in Quebec in August 1943, while the fighting was actually taking place on the island. The Italian campaign thus grew naturally out of the Sicilian, yet the delay in officially authorizing it had the disastrous effect of allowing large numbers of Germans to escape capture in Sicily, which an early landing on the toe of the Italian boot at Reggio could probably have prevented.

Although the Allies wanted to capture Naples and take the airfields around Foggia, hoping thereby to relieve the pressure on the Russians on the Eastern Front, General Marshall recognized that landing on the Italian mainland could only further delay the eventual invasion of north-west France, which he always saw as the most important step towards extinguishing the Third Reich. Although the Oxford-educated German General Fridolin von Senger und Etterlin believed that the Allies should have invaded Sardinia and Corsica instead of Sicily, thereby leap-frogging Italy altogether, this would not have achieved the objective of tying down as many German units in Italy as possible. The German Military Cemetery outside Cassino contains the remains of 20,057 men, buried six to a grave, who represent less than 5 per cent of the casualties that the Reich was to suffer in Italy.

Sicily was invaded at dawn on Saturday, 10 July 1943 by 160,000 men of General Alexander's 15th Army Group, comprising Patton's US Seventh Army and Montgomery's Commonwealth Eighth Army, landing in 3,000 vessels on the southern coast in stormy weather, but with the advantages of surprise and heavy naval gunfire. The Axis had 350,000 troops stationed in Sicily, but only one-third were German. In all, the Allies were to pour 450,000 troops on to the island during the thirty-eight-day campaign. Although the Italian Sixth Army fought back bravely as soon as the Allies landed, and German divisions at Gela and Licata nearly reached the invasion beaches in counter-attack, western Sicily was conquered in the week after 15 July.

Because the Eighth Army was halted for a week at Catania by fierce German defence, the US 3rd Division reached Messina first, on 17 August. By then, however, 53,545 German troops, 50 tanks and 9,185 vehicles plus 11,855 tons of stores had been successfully evacuated off the island, which Eisenhower later privately admitted had been a severe strategic error of the Allies.[2] The Sicilian campaign saw 7,319 American casualties and 9,353 British, but 132,000 Italians and 32,000 Germans were killed, wounded and (mainly) captured there.[3] The Mediterranean and Suez Canal could now be opened up as an Allied sea route, ending the necessity of taking supplies via the Cape of Good Hope. This, General Brooke estimated, was to free up a million tons of Allied shipping for use elsewhere.[4]

The landings in Sicily also had the effect of overthrowing Mussolini, whose Fascist Grand Council passed a vote of no confidence in him by nineteen votes to seven a fortnight later. (His own son-in-law and foreign minister, Count Ciano, voted with the majority, and along with four of the others was to pay for it with his life later on.) It seems somewhat unFascist of the Council even to call a vote, and even more unFascist of Mussolini to take any note of its democratic will, but when he visited the King to report what had happened, he was arrested. His replacement, Marshal Pietro Badoglio, publicly committed Italy to fighting on against the Allied invader, in order to reassure Hitler, while secretly entering into peace negotiations with Eisenhower. Even before the Sicilian campaign was over, Hitler sent Rommel, commander of a new Army Group B, to contest the peninsula with eight and a half divisions. (After Rommel left for France on 6 November 1943, this army group was reconstituted as the Fourteenth Army.)

The Sicilian campaign saw the equally egocentric Generals Patton and Montgomery fighting together in the same campaign. Their rivalry was as pathetic as it was probably unavoidable, and when later the egos of Generals Mark Clark and Omar Bradley were added to the ever combustible mix, it did the Allied war effort no good. While much is made of Montgomery's and Patton's vanity and ceaseless self-promotion, however, it is often forgotten how Clark, in the words of one history:

became obsessed with public relations and soon had fifty men working to ensure that his efforts, and those of his Army (and particularly the American part of it), were given maximum publicity. Ensuring this he ordered a 'three to one rule'. Every press release was to mention Clark three times on the front page and at least once on all other pages – and the General also demanded that photographs be only taken of him from his left side. His public relations team even came up with a Fifth Army song: 'Stand up, stand up for General Clark, let's sing the praises of General Clark . . .' He was very fond of that song.[5]

Patton's ambitions for a major command in Italy were ended prematurely after he slapped two hospitalized, shell-shocked soldiers. In two separate incidents, he called Private Charles H. Kuhl an 'arrant coward' and a week later Private Paul G. Bennett a 'yellow bastard', adding, 'I won't have those cowardly bastards hanging around our hospitals. We'll probably have to shoot them some time anyway, or we'll raise a breed of morons.'[6] Although on Eisenhower's insistence Patton had to apologize to his troops – most of whom vocally supported him – Patton felt no genuine repentance, except insofar as the incidents had damaged his hitherto meteoric career. (In both the German and Russian armies, needless to say, the two privates would have been shot.) Eisenhower's relegation of his old friend Patton led to Omar Bradley leapfrogging him, and becoming commander of the US First Army in the invasion of France. When Bradley paid a final courtesy call on Patton on 7 September 1943, at his palace in Palermo, he found him 'in a near-suicidal state . . . This great proud warrior, my former boss, had been brought to his knees.'

To counter the general impression of George Patton it is worth considering the testimony given many years after the war to the US Army's Senior Officer Oral History Program by General John 'Ed' Hull, one of George Marshall's right-hand men at the Pentagon, who knew Patton well and worked with him closely in the planning stages of three campaigns. 'General Patton was in a way a two-faced individual,' Hull stated.

At heart he was very gentle, he was modest, very friendly, not at all superior in his attitude towards you, but very kindly, very considerate. But he put on the other face – well, we've had a lot of generals in history that were people of that kind . . . but that face was the rough and ready face. Curse a little bit at times and he knew all the words; but when he left a formation where he bawled somebody out, he might sit down and write a prayer . . . So, all in all he was quite a character, interesting and very likeable if you knew him.[7]

Field Marshal 'Smiling Albert' Kesselring was in overall charge of German troops in Italy, superior even to Rommel. A bourgeois gunner turned airman from Bavaria, he was looked down upon socially by the aristocratic Prussians under his command, but he was obeyed. Kesselring assumed that the Allies' next step would be to make amphibious landings at the Gulf of Salerno, just south of Naples, which was as far north as Allied air cover from Sicily could stretch. Sure enough, at 03.30 hours on Thursday, 9 September 1943, forty-seven-year-old Mark Clark's Fifth Army landed on the Gulf in Operation Avalanche, and dug in on four narrow, unconnected beachheads. They were vigorously counter-attacked by the German Tenth Army, commanded by General Heinrich von Vietinghoff, who had commanded a Panzer division in Poland, a Panzer corps in Yugoslavia and Russia and the Fifteenth Army in France and was now to prove an equally formidable opponent in Italy. 'Shells were flashing in the water,' recalled an American journalist, Jack Belden, 'flames were yellowing the sky, and bullets were slapping into the boat. They snapped over our heads, rattled against the boat sides like hail and beat at the ramp door . . . The boat shuddered and the ramp creaked open . . . I stepped down . . . At last I was on the continent of Europe.'[8]

Montgomery had landed almost unopposed on the tip of Italy five days earlier in Operation Baytown. Nonetheless the Germans concentrated their efforts further north at Salerno, hoping to fling Clark's Fifth Army – comprising Major-General Richard McCreery's British X Corps to the north of the Sele river and Major-General Ernest Dawley's US VI Corps to the south – back into the sea. If they had succeeded, which they almost did on 13 September amid bitter fighting, it would have had a profound effect on the plans to invade Normandy the following year. At the same time as Avalanche, the 1st Airborne Division of the Eighth Army landed at the instep of the Italian boot at Taranto. In Berlin, Goebbels was reading Richard Llewellyn's 1939 novel about Wales, *How Green was my Valley*. 'It is very informative about English mentality,' he noted in his diary on 20 September. 'I don't believe that England is in any present danger of becoming Bolshevized.'[9]

Sailing to Salerno, the men of the Fifth Army had been informed that Italy had signed an armistice, formally dropping out of the war. It made no difference to the reception that Clark's men received from the Germans when they landed, of course, and Kesselring later claimed that Badoglio's defection had meant that 'Our hands were no longer tied' and that he could now requisition anything he needed without tiresome negotiations with the Italians over compensation.[10] There was a viciousness to Kesselring that was to come to the fore in March 1944 when, with his full prior knowledge, following the killing of thirty-two SS men in Rome by partisans, 335 Romans were taken to the Ardeatine Caves on the southern side of the city and shot in the back of the neck in groups of five. He could also undertake wholesale reprisals against the partisans, sending out an order on 17 June 1944 that 'The fight against the partisans must be carried out with all means at our disposal and with utmost severity. I will protect any commander who exceeds our usual restraint in the choice of methods . . . Wherever there is evidence of a considerable number of partisan groups a pro-portion of the male population of the area will be arrested, and in the event of an act of violence being committed these men will be shot.'[11] Churchill and Alexander nonetheless called for the commutation of Kesselring's death sentence in 1947, and he was released in 1952.

Although the Germans disarmed and interned all Italian forces in their vicinity, much of the Italian Navy sailed from Spezia to Malta, allowing Admiral Sir Andrew Cunningham on 11 September 1943 to make his splendid signal to the Admiralty Board in London: 'Be pleased to inform Their Lordships that the Italian Battle Fleet now lies at anchor under the guns of the fortress of Malta.'[12] In all five battleships, eight cruisers, thirty-three destroyers, thirty-four submarines and scores of other war vessels surrendered, as well as 101 merchant ships totalling 183,591 tons. A further 168 merchant ships were scuttled to avoid capture by the Germans. On their arrival in Spezia, the Germans shot all Italian captains responsible. 'That's the way to treat your late Allies!' remarked Cunningham. The Italian Navy was subsequently used against Germany, especially its brave special underwater section, the 10th MAS Flotilla, with no less an authority than Admiral Cunningham paying tribute to their 'cold-blooded bravery and enterprise'.

Although Clark showed personal bravery on the beach-head at Salerno, nonetheless in the words of Anzio's historian, 'He had a momentary wobble and had to be dissuaded from re-embarking VI Corps,' although Clark denied this in his memoirs.[13] With German artillery observation points in the hills surrounding the beach-heads, and attacks from no fewer than six German divisions, it took the dropping of three battalions of the US 82nd Airborne almost on the water's edge, the bombardment of German positions by strategic bombers from the North-west African Air Force, and close supporting fire from the 15-inch naval guns of specially diverted naval forces, but above all the grim determination of the Fifth Army on the beach-heads, to stay in place. 'If the Germans had pushed on to the sea', Alexander commented with characteristic sangfroid, 'their arrival might have caused us some embarrassment.'[14] The position was not secured until 16 September, and it was only four days later – once the Germans had successfully extricated their forces from the south of Italy – that the attacks abated, and a further eleven days after that before the Allies could enter an abandoned Naples. By then the Fifth Army had got 170,000 troops and 200 tanks ashore, and Montgomery was coming up from the south. The Salerno operation in all had cost 15,000 Allied casualties against 8,000 German, and it is hard to take issue with the historian who concludes that 'The outstanding feature of the battle had been the foresight, skill and initiative of Kesselring, and the efficiency of his troops.'[15] It was a phenomenon that was to be repeated as the fighting moved northwards up the peninsula.

Meanwhile, on the other side of Italy, the 1st Canadian Division of the Eighth Army took the Foggia airfields on 27 September and reached the Adriatic Sea on 3 October. From those flat plains, General Ira C. Eaker's Mediterranean Allied Air Forces could then dominate the air war in the south of Europe. Within three weeks the USAAF Fifteenth Air Force was roaming at will all over southern Germany, Austria and the Balkans, and in particular they could bomb the Romanian oilfields of Ploesti, from where much of the Reich's fuel flowed. The US 12th Air Support Command bombed the German forces in Italy itself, forcing them to move largely at night. From the spring of 1944, the Allies had more than ten times as many warplanes in Italy – at 4,500 – as the Luftwaffe.[16]

The situation in Naples was appalling, with bread riots, typhus, Mafia crime, water shortages, totally corrupt local authorities, prosti-tution-for-food (special military VD hospitals had to be set up) and a general breakdown in law, order and morality. Even the papal legate's car was found to be driving on stolen tyres.[17] Most serious for future operations further north, the German scorched-earth policy had dev-astated the docks. Allied military experts, engineers, police and admin-istrators moved in en masse under the auspices of the Allied Military Government of Occupied Territories, but it was to be months before anything approaching normality or decency could return to the stricken city.

With Rome the next major objective – more for political and morale than for military reasons, since it was designated a demilitarized open city by both sides – the Allies had to fight their way northwards, taking booby-trapped and sharply contested towns and villages, cross-ing rivers whose bridges had been destroyed and driving down roads expertly laid with Tellermines, mushroom-shaped circular metal boxes a foot in diameter which packed a 12-pound charge of TNT.

The terrible weather in the autumn of 1943, combined with the topographical opportunities for defence provided by the 840-mile-long, 80-mile-wide Apennine mountain range with its 4,000-foot peaks, meant that Vietinghoff had myriad opportunities for tenacious rearguard actions, with the effect of Allied air superiority often negated. Churchill had injudiciously likened Europe to a crocodile, with the Mediterranean as its 'soft underbelly'. As Mark Clark told the TV programme *The World at War*, 'I often thought what a tough old gut it was instead of the soft belly that he had led us to believe.'[18] Montgomery agreed. 'I don't think we can get any spectacular results,' he reported to Brooke, 'so long as it goes on raining; the whole country becomes a sea of mud and nothing on wheels can move off the roads.'[19] The rain, sleet and frequent blizzards during the winter of 1943/4 led to pneumonia, dysentery, respiratory diseases, fevers, jaundice and the debilitating fungal infection called trench foot, which arises from wet socks that are not removed for days on end. As well as Fifth Army's 40,000 battle casualties by the end of 1943, there were 50,000 non-combat casualties and perhaps as many as 20,000 deserters.[20]

The first meeting of what became known as the Big Three – Roosevelt, Stalin and Churchill – took place at the Teheran Conference (codenamed Eureka) from 28 November to 1 December 1943. Roosevelt was under the mistaken but surprisingly widespread impression that personal intercourse could mollify Stalin, and he deliberately set out to try to charm the Russian dictator, if necessary by making Churchill the butt of his teasing. For his part Stalin insisted on the invalid Roosevelt flying halfway around the world to meet in the Iranian capital, and placing him in the Russian Legation as his guest, thus separating him from Churchill. On Stalin's insistence, Chiang Kai-shek was also excluded from the conference altogether, so as not to ruffle the sensibilities of the Japanese, with whom the USSR had a non-aggression pact. In the first session of the Teheran Conference, however, Stalin announced his willingness to declare war against Japan after Germany had surrendered, which was greeted with undisguised pleasure by the Western Allies.

Less happy was the reception given to Churchill's strategy of using

Italy as a springboard from which to attack the Germans in south-eastern France and Austria and Hungary via Yugoslavia. Not wishing to see a powerful Allied force in his south-eastern European backyard, Stalin opposed the scheme, and was supported by Roosevelt, so it fell through, much to Churchill's chagrin. Although Stalin would have preferred to see an earlier date for the cross-Channel invasion, he accepted that it would take place on 1 May 1944. (It later had to be put back five weeks for lack of landing craft after fighting in Italy went on for longer than planned.)

Other discussions on the eastern border of Poland, which was to be compensated with German territory for the loss of land to the USSR to its east, ran directly contrary to the promise made in the Atlantic Charter for 'no territorial changes that do not accord with the freely expressed wishes of the peoples concerned', but at least Stalin agreed to the outlines of a United Nations Organization with vetoes for Britain, Russia, the United States and China. There was also agreement on Yugoslavia, where Marshal Tito's Communist partisans would be given support rather than the pro-monarchist Chetniks, because it was clear from Ultra decrypts that the Chetniks were in league with the Italians, and the Germans feared the partisans much more than the Chetniks. Meanwhile, also at Teheran, on Stalin's insistence it was decided that Germany was not to be split up into five autonomous countries, as Roosevelt and Churchill had envisaged. Teheran saw the high-water mark of Allied co-operation in the war, and was hard fought though generally good natured. Roosevelt's overt keenness to charm Stalin, however, allowed the Marshal to spot a gap between the two democracies that he was to seek to exploit over the coming months. Nothing got past him. Each of the Big Three left Teheran with something he wanted, but each had to give up something too, although it is hard to escape the conclusion that Churchill was forced to give up the most.

'The army's advance up the spine of Italy,' wrote John Harris in his novel *Swordpoint*,

had been that of a bull, wearied yet still willing, butting its way head-down in assault after assault. The pattern had rarely changed. Plains were few and far between and no sooner had one river or mountain been crossed than another barred the route. They'd battled across the Creti, but behind the Creti was the Agri, and behind the Agri was the Sele, and behind the Sele was the Volturno ... The whole country, every river, every town, every hill, had shown them how useless machines could be when climate and terrain conspired to make them so. 'Oh yes,' the current joke ran, 'the Germans are retreating all right. Unfortunately, they're taking the last ridge with 'em.'[21]

The terrain has been described as one 'that goats would find difficult to negotiate'.[22]

The Fifth Army crossed the swollen Volturno river, whose bridges the Germans had destroyed, in mid-October, after which Alexander ordered a short rest for regrouping and recuperation. The way ahead, over seemingly endless mountain passes through atrocious weather, could not but depress the most enthusiastic spirits. As the Germans withdrew, they adopted a scorched-earth policy against all types of food supplies and public utilities. This was only intensified when the Badoglio Government, ruling from the safety of Bari having judici- ously fled Rome, declared war on Germany on 13 October.

With the Eighth Army – commanded by Montgomery's protégé Oliver Leese after 1 January 1944 – to the east of the Apennines, and Clark's Fifth Army to the west, there was precious little meaningful mutual support. As the Germans retreated northwards, they pro- vided their countrymen with as much time as possible to perfect the Bernhard, Barbara, Winter and especially the Gustav Lines of defence. The last stretched right across Italy from the Gulf of Gaeta in the Tyrrhenian Sea to just south of Ortona in the Adriatic.

Informed via Ultra of Hitler's decision of 4 October to support Kesselring's plans to fight south of Rome, Eisenhower and the 15th Army Group commander Harold Alexander concocted a plan that would use the Fifth and the Eighth Armies in unison to take Rome. The Eighth Army would capture Pescara and swing westwards, while the Fifth Army advanced up the Liri Valley, aided by a bold am- phibious landing just south of Rome at Anzio that would take reserves off the Gustav Line and draw away any strategic reserves further north. Although Alexander had eleven divisions in Italy by December 1943, Kesselring had nine south of Rome, and another eight in reserve to the north. Whereas the Wehrmacht was an homogeneous army in Italy, no fewer than sixteen nationalities fought on the Allied side, including Poles, New Zealanders, Algerians, South Africans, Moroccans, a Jewish contingent and even a Brazilian expeditionary force – many of them speaking different languages and using different weapons and ammunition. Moreover, the Anglo-American rivalries that had been seen in the 'race' to capture Messina in Sicily – convincingly 'won' by Patton – resurfaced and multiplied in the bid to capture the Eternal City. In general the British, exhausted after the North African and Sicilian campaigns, seemed slow and over-cautious to the Americans. On the reverse side of the same coin, some of the fresh American units seemed raw and naive to the British. There were undoubted tensions between the senior officers, though fewer among the other ranks. Mark Clark in particular became obsessed with the glory of being the general who marched into the first Axis capital, as Alexander's chief of staff Major-General John Harding later stated: 'If I may put it diplomatically, I think General Clark was overwhelmed by the wish to be the first into Rome, which he would have [been] anyhow.'[23]

Clark made a key error in not moving straight on to the nearby Gustav Line as soon as the Winter Line was broken in mid-December 1944. Instead the Fifth Army only reached the Sangro, Rapido and Garigliano rivers and the Gustav Line between 5 and 15 January 1944. The Germans were thus given almost another month to prepare the (already formidable) defences of the Gustav Line after the fall of Mounts Camino and Lungo and the medieval town of San Pietro Infine. These had been formidable obstacles, and the scars of the house-by-house fighting in San Pietro, in three separate assaults by the 36th Texas National Guard Division against the 15th Panzergrenadiers, can still be seen today, in the town which has been kept just as it was in 1944. 'The name of San Pietro will be remembered in military history,' reads the Operations Report of the 143rd Infantry Regiment of the 36th Division, which finally took the town from the rear on 18 December 1943 after two previous attacks had been flung back.

We picked our way through fields ripped by mortars and shells and the still bodies of doughboys [GIs] who fell in the bloody, savage fighting ... [in]

this gray little town overlooking the valley approaches to Cassino. The soldiers call it Death Valley because death was on the rampage ... as they stormed this enemy fortress ringed by fortifications, dug into terraced slopes commanding the Liri valley.

The German garrison of San Pietro could not merely be bypassed, isolated and hemmed in, as the Fifth Army moved on towards the Gustav Line, because their observation posts in the town would have directed incessant and accurate artillery fire on to the advancing forces and their logistical support. Just as with Camino, Lungo and the great monastery hill of Monte Cassino itself, there was no alternative to holding the high ground.

Between the attack on Camino on 6 December and the Germans finally being expelled from San Pietro on the 18th, the fierce fighting left the Fifth Army spent, and the driving sleet and hail further blunted enthusiasm for an assault on the Gustav Line during the shortest days of the year. The snow and low clouds also meant that little air support could be expected in the period before planes could land by instrumentation alone. The hiatus before the renewed Allied offensive therefore allowed Senger a vital month in which to dig in, bring up reinforcements from Rome, reposition his forces and make his contingency plans. The (anti-Nazi) Senger had commanded the withdrawal of German troops from Sicily, Sardinia and Corsica, and was a master of the rearguard action. The Winter Line was only ever an outpost, a delaying position in front of the Gustav Line, just as the Hitler Line was yet another one behind it.

Since it was deemed impossible for troops untrained in mountain warfare to operate to the east of the 5,000-foot Mount Cairo, where there was a continuous range of peaks right across the centre of the peninsula, the attack on Cassino had to take place from the west and south of the town. Then, as now, the town formed a horseshoe around the 1,700-foot-high hill on the peak of which the abbey rests. Founded in the early sixth century by St Benedict himself, it was the mother church of the Benedictine Order. Cassino was the strongest part of the Gustav Line, nestling under Mount Cairo. 'There was something titanic about the scene,' wrote Harris, 'frightening in its vastness, sombre under the low cloud and drizzling rain that blurred outlines and gave the slopes a menacing appearance of evil.'[24] By the time the Allies reached it, the Gustav Line bristled with deep, reinforced concrete bunkers, anti-tank ditches, tunnels, barbed wire, minefields, hidden gun emplacements, 60,000 defenders and scores of secret observation posts from which withering artillery fire could be directed. Not for nothing did N. C. Phillips, the official historian of the New Zealand forces in Italy, point out that 'On its military merits alone, no competent soldier would have chosen to assault Cassino in March 1944. He would have looked askance at the very notion of trying to carry by storm the strongest fortress in Europe at the dead of winter by a single Corps unsupported by diversionary operations.'[25] Yet considering the forces at hand, the lack of geographical alternatives and the pressing need to take Rome before the Normandy landings, that was what had to happen.

From Cassino to the Tyrrhenian Sea lies a succession of rivers, principally the Gari, the Garigliano and the aptly named Rapido, which provided major obstacles for the Allies. It was here, just as much as at Cassino, that the Fifth Army fought and bled trying to break the Gustav Line during the four months after January 1944. Between 17 and 21 January, X Corps tried to attack across the Garigliano, but was blocked by the Fourteenth Army's reserves, although 46th Division's assault caused Senger some concern. Meanwhile to the east, the US 36th Division was thrown back ignominiously from the fast-flowing, freezing Rapido, with such heavy losses that a Congressional inquiry was later held. The British 46th and 56th and US 36th Divisions desperately attempted to establish a toe-hold on the northern side of these three rivers, but in vain. The sheer topographical majesty of Monte Cassino has overawed historians as much as today it continues to overawe tourists, but in fact the battles to the south and west were equally important and costly; since crossing the Volturno, Fifth Army had suffered 26,000 casualties. Had any bar been awarded for the Italy Star medal, it ought to have read 'Garigliano' rather than 'Cassino', for all the iconic status that was awarded to the latter due to its geographical prominence.

The prize – either by crossing the rivers or by taking Cassino, or both – was the Liri Valley, a flat, wide and direct route straight through to Rome down which the Allied armour could drive at speed. (Once

Cassino finally fell on 17 May, the Fifth Army was in Rome within three weeks.) It might be that the Allies put too much emphasis on the importance of armour in the advance on Rome, since their tanks – though more numerous – had been inferior to the Germans' throughout the war so far. The Sherman tank was nicknamed the Ronson by the Allies because in the words of the contemporary advert 'It lights first time, every time', and the Tommy-cooker by the Germans because a hit from an 88mm shell tended to create enough kinetic energy to ignite its engine fuel. Until later in 1944, the Germans retained a lead over the Allies in creating tanks with a better combination of firepower, mobility and protection. Allied tanks often had such restricted vision that driving them was likened to driving a semi-detached house looking through its letterbox. If the Allies had been less fixated on the Liri Valley, they might have broken the Gustav Line elsewhere earlier.

On 11 December 1943 Kesselring assured the Vatican that the abbey of Monte Cassino would not be occupied by his forces, but most of its movable treasures were taken to Rome nonetheless (today they can be seen in the monastery's museum). At 09.30 on Tuesday, 15 February 1944, the entire abbey was flattened by 239 bombers dropping 500 tons of bombs, destroying the immovable but arthistorically important frescos in the process. This Allied vandalism was a propaganda coup for Dr Goebbels, although it was good for the morale of the troops preparing to attack the monastery, at least until they discovered that few Germans had died in the bombing and that rubble was almost as easily defended as entire buildings. 'I say that the bombing of the Abbey was a mistake, and I say it with the full knowledge of the controversy that has raged round this episode,' wrote Mark Clark in his autobiography *Calculated Risk*, in 1951. 'Not only was the bombing an unnecessary psychological mistake in the field of propaganda, but it was a tactical military mistake of the first magnitude. It only made our job more difficult, more costly in terms of men, machines and time.'[26] Though he later denied responsibility for it, in fact Clark had been personally involved in and approved of Alexander's and Freyberg's decision to destroy the abbey.[27] Certainly the commander of the Cassino defenders, Senger, later claimed that 'The bombing had the opposite effect of what was intended. Now we would occupy the abbey without scruple, especially as ruins are better for defence than intact buildings ... Now Germany had a mighty, commanding strongpoint, which paid for itself in the subsequent fighting.'[28] The defensive superiority of ruins over intact buildings had already been seen at Stalingrad, and was to be so again at Caen. Yet it is hard to believe that during the Allied attacks the Germans would not have abandoned their moral 'scruple' and defended the abbey room by room.

Visitors to the magnificent rebuilt structure will immediately be impressed by how completely the abbey dominates the hilltop, which in turn dominates the Liri Valley. It was effectively doomed as soon as Kesselring chose it as the hinge of the Gustav Line, which a glance at the landscape from the top of the hill looking south shows was unavoidable. Churchill could never understand why Cassino could not simply be outflanked, and why three divisions had to 'break their teeth' on a front only 3 miles wide, and it is indeed difficult to comprehend on two-dimensional maps. The folds of the land, the overlaps of the rivers, above all the heights of the mountains protecting the Liri Valley are best studied *in situ*, and make the tactical difficulties instantly comprehensible. As for Monte Cassino itself, Harding believed that 'It was necessary to bomb it from the point of view of the morale and the confidence of the troops. Everybody thought the Germans were using it for military purposes ... It's part of my military philosophy that you must not put troops into battle without giving them all possible physical and military support to give them the best chance for getting a success.'[29] The political price of attacking the abbey without first having flattened it was felt to be too high, especially in New Zealand, whose troops were to form the first wave, and Freyberg, Clark and Alexander all approved its destruction. Of course it was paradoxical that, in the crusade for civilization against Nazi barbarism, a prominent jewel of that very civilization should have been destroyed by the Allies, but such was the nature of the Total War unleashed by Hitler, who must therefore bear ultimate responsibility for the aesthetic and cultural tragedy.

By the end of January, the French Mountain Corps had made considerable advances between Monte Cairo and Monte Cassino, and the US 34th 'Red Bulls' Division had reached Point 593 behind the monastery hill. Snake's Head Ridge, of which Point 593 was a part, saw bitterly contested fighting, reminiscent of the Great War, as the Allies attempted to outflank Cassino from the north; indeed as many men fell there as in the full-frontal assaults up Monastery Hill itself.

The four battles of Monte Cassino were fought by Germans, Americans, British, French, Poles, Australians, Canadians, Indians, Nepalis, Sikhs, Maltese and New Zealanders, although not by the Italians themselves, the majority of whom had by now largely adopted a *che sara, sara* attitude to their national fate, apart from (mainly Communist-dominated) partisans who fought against the Germans further north. 'We do not want Germans or Americans,' one representative piece of Italian graffito read. 'Let us weep in peace.'[30] The four battles have been likened to the Somme: at the first battle after 12 February, for example, the Fifth Army suffered 16,000 casualties, above all in the 34th Division. In the second battle between 15 and 18 February it was the New Zealanders who suffered, and between 15 and 23 March further losses were sustained in the third.

The Luftwaffe barely made it into the air for routine reconnaissance during the struggle for the Gustav Line, such was the Allies' preponderance, and in late 1943 it had only 430 aircraft in the whole of Italy.[31]

In the Vatican, meanwhile, the British Ambassador to the Holy See, Sir D'Arcy Osborne, reported to the Foreign Office on 26 January 1944 that 'The Cardinal Secretary of State sent for me today to say that the Pope hoped that no Allied coloured troops would be among the small number that might be garrisoned at Rome after the occupation. He hastened to add that the Holy See did not draw the colour line but it was hoped that it would be possible to meet the request.'[32] The role of Pius XII in the Second World War remains highly controversial, because he took the deliberate decision not to denounce publicly the Nazis' war against the Jews, despite having detailed information about its nature and extent (and indeed that of the persecution of the Catholic Church in Poland). This decision was based on his belief – proved well founded with regard to the Protestant Church in Holland – that the Germans would viciously punish ecclesiastical authorities who spoke up for the Jews, thereby lessening their opportunities to help in other, more clandestine ways. (The Pope himself harboured thousands of Jews at his own properties in Rome and at Castel Gandolfo outside the city.) Yet although it would not have derailed or perhaps even slowed down the Holocaust, which by its nature was not undertaken by genuinely pious people, it was in retrospect of course part of the Pope's moral duty to draw global attention to what was taking place. It is quite untrue, as has been alleged, that the Pope himself was anti-Semitic or held any brief for the Nazis or that he was in any way, as the title of one book has it, 'Hitler's Pope'.[33]

After the second battle of Cassino in February 1944, the commander of its defence, General Fridolin von Senger und Etterlin, reported to Hitler at the Berghof to receive the oak leaves to his Knight's Cross, an honour that left him unimpressed 'now that hundreds of people wore the decoration'. Senger was even less impressed by the sight of the Führer himself, which he found 'utterly depressing' and wondered what effect it would have on the other soldiers receiving medals that day. 'He wore a yellow military blouse with a yellow tie, white collar and black trousers – hardly a becoming outfit!' recorded the Roman Catholic Rhodes Scholar:

His unprepossessing frame and short neck made him appear even less dignified than usual. His complexion was flabby, colourless and sickly. His large
blue eyes, which evidently fascinated many people, were watery, possibly due
to his constant use of stimulating drugs. His handshake was soft, his left arm
hung limp and trembling by his side. Yet a striking feature, contrasting with
his notorious screaming fits during speeches or fits of rage, was the quiet and
modulated voice that almost inspired compassion since it barely concealed
his despondency and weakness.[34]

The trembling left hand has been put down to incipient Parkinson's disease, from which it is thought that Hitler might have suffered. Even taking into account Senger's anti-Nazism and the fact that this account was written long after the war, it seems that Hitler was ailing even before the Normandy landings in June, the assassination attempt on 20 July or the destruction of Army Group Centre in Russia later that month.

On 15 March more than 1,000 tons of bombs were dropped on

Cassino from 500 bombers, yet too often the USAAF, which flew two-thirds of the sorties and dropped 70 per cent of the bombs, failed to co-ordinate closely enough with the commanders on the ground, who often did not know when the raids were scheduled to end. This meant that, however heavy the bombardments, the Germans in the many arched cellars of the abbey always had time to take up positions in the rubble of the monastery before the assault waves moved in. 'I had climbed every single hill that offered a long view,' recalled Senger of his 50-mile-wide sector based at Cassino, 'and this gave me a complete picture of the fissured mountain terrain. I could thus appreciate fluctuations in the situation from changes in artillery fire and air activity.'[35] The Germans managed to avoid being outflanked in the first battle of Cassino in February, retaking Point 593, but the hill succumbed in subsequent engagements in February and March. Fighting between the 8th Indian Division and German *Fallschirmjäger* (paratroopers) was particularly harsh, and on the rocky outcrop known as Hangman's Hill a company of Gurkhas somehow clung like limpets for ten days under constant German bombardment and sniping. To visit the spot is to appreciate both units' extraordinary achievement and courage.

'What exceeded all expectations was the fighting spirit of the troops,' Senger later wrote of his 1st Parachute Rifle Division, which had relieved the 90th Panzer Grenadier Division on 15 March and was engaged against the New Zealanders in the town. 'The soldiers crawled out of the shuttered cellars and bunkers to confront the enemy with the toughest resistance. Words can hardly do them justice. We had all reckoned that those who survived the hours of bombing and the casualties would be physically and morally shaken, but this was not so.' He put this down to their being trained, as paratroopers, in fighting in isolated, surrounded areas of resistance. Senger particularly liked the way they didn't bother to report the loss of small amounts of ground 'because they hoped soon to recover it'.[36] Visiting 3rd Paratroop Regiment at the divisional headquarters of General Richard Heidrich, the commander of I Parachute Corps, Senger recalled the 'jarring explosion of shells, the whistling of splinters, the smell of freshly thrown-up earth, and the well-known mixture of smells from glowing iron and burnt powder', which vividly reminded him of his time on the Somme. 'Hitler was right when he told me that here was the only battlefield of this war that resembled those of the First,' he wrote after the war. In fact there were plenty such battlefields, especially in Russia, but Führers are not on oath when awarding oak-leaf clusters to brave commanders.

The gradient of the Monastery Hill slope up to the abbey is 500 yards up for every thousand horizontal, that is 26 degrees, and the other places where the fighting was fiercest in the town – the Continental Hotel (which had a German tank concealed inside its foyer), Castle Hill, the botanical gardens and the railway station – sound like sites in a Baedeker guide, but they all saw vicious hand-to-hand combat. The fighting in the town of Cassino, recalled a veteran, 'was at such close quarters that one floor of a building might be held by a defender while the next was occupied by the attackers. If the latter wished to use their artillery to soften up the building before storming it, they would have to evacuate this floor!'[37]

'The Cassino front cost the Allies three whole months for an advance of 15 kilometres,' boasted a proud Senger years afterwards. By early 1944 the Germans had twenty-three divisions in Italy, fifteen of which formed the Tenth Army holding the Gustav Line against Alexander's by now eighteen divisions. If the Allies were able to make amphibious hops up the coast of Italy, 'like a harvest bug' in Churchill's typically arresting simile, they needed to get behind the Germans' east–west defensive lines. This was the thinking behind the attack on Anzio, Operation Shingle, although the need for landing craft – principally Landing Ships Tank (LSTs) – for the operation meant that the timing for the Normandy landings (codenamed Overlord) had to be postponed for five weeks from the date of 1 May 1944 that had been agreed at the Trident Conference in Washington.

The amphibious attacks on Anzio and Nettuno, small holiday ports on the west coast of Italy 30 miles south of Rome, by the US VI Corps under the corncob-pipe-smoking, fifty-three-year-old Major-General John Lucas, was intended to cut communications between Rome and Cassino, forcing the German Tenth Army to weaken or even abandon the western part of the Gustav Line, and outflank the Cassino position. Task Force 81 comprised 374 vessels and sailed the 100 miles from

Naples under the overall command of Rear-Admiral Frank Lowry, with Rear-Admiral Thomas Troubridge commanding the Royal Navy element. As Ultra had suggested they would, the landings achieved complete surprise, and many Germans – nicknamed Teds by the Allies, a shortening of the Italian word for Germans, *Tedeschi* – were caught with their trousers down, in some cases literally so. 'As our squad entered a gloomy narrow street,' an American private later recalled, 'I could see a pair of fleshy white buttocks wobbling in the opposite direction and I shouted "Halt!" as loud as I could. The man stopped, raised his hands and walked towards us . . . His thin legs were shivering below a great pot belly. It was my first encounter with the Master Race.'[38]

Within two days of the first landings at 02.00 on Saturday, 22 January 1944, some 50,000 Allied troops and 5,200 vehicles were ashore, establishing a perimeter 3 miles deep. If Lucas had pushed inland to seize the towns of Aprilia (nicknamed the Factory), Campoleone and Cisterna, he could have cut both the main railway and Route 7, which ran southwards to the Gustav Line. Instead he waited for tanks and heavy artillery, and within seventy-two hours had lost the opportunity, which was not to recur for four pain-filled months. Whereas there were only a few thousand Germans in the area on 23 January, by the evening of the next day there were over 40,000. Lucas was the wrong man to command Shingle, not least because he believed, as he vouchsafed to his diary, that 'The whole affair has a strong odour of Gallipoli and apparently the same amateur was still on the coach's bench.'[39] Intended by Churchill as a campaign-winning coup, the battle of Anzio turned into a drawn-out, costly failure. The German capacity for counter-attack was undimmed as Kesselring rushed troops from the Gustav Line, France, northern Italy and the Balkans to try to snuff out what Hitler described as an 'abscess'. Since Ultra gave Clark good warning of this, Lucas was able to dig in on his beach-head, albeit under constant fire from the Alban Hills (Colli Laziali) and direct attack from the German Fourteenth Army under the aristocratic General Eberhard von Mackensen. Digging in at the beach-head was uncomfortable work: deep trenches were impossible because the water table was too high, and as one veteran recalled, 'Dig a slit trench, leave it for an hour, and the bottom would be black with beetles trying to get out.'

Anzio was where the Emperor Nero reputedly played the fiddle while Rome burned in AD 64. The German Commander-in-Chief South showed no such lassitude when the Allies began landing there in 1944. Kesselring had signalled the warning code 'Case Richard' to all units by 04.30 on 22 January, and forces started arriving fast. The Allies had slightly expanded their beach-head by 1 February on narrow and exposed fronts, but their further attacks were comprehensively repulsed at both Campoleone and Cisterna. Although soon after the landings Churchill had told Alexander, 'Am very glad you are pegging out claims rather than digging in beach-heads,' he had spoken too soon.[40] Alexander and Clark both landed at Anzio at 09.00 on the first day, yet neither ordered Lucas to take Campoleone and Cisterna post-haste at all costs. (On visiting a 5th Battalion, Grenadier Guards anti-tank platoon, an 88mm shell-burst covered Alexander's fur-lined jacket with earth. 'He brushed off the soil as he would the drops of water having been caught in a shower of rain,' recalled a guardsman, 'and continued on his way chatting to his aide, who looked as though he'd seen a ghost.')[41]

'Daddy' Lucas, who was also known to his men by the hardly inspiring nickname Foxy Grandpa, set up VI Corps headquarters in underground cellars in the via Romana in Nettuno, close to where he had got off the boat. He then kept them there, far from the British sectors, and at one point a practice evacuation was even carried out. 'Slow in movement and speech,' records Anzio's historian, 'Shingle's pilot was as far removed from a dynamic, charismatic leader as could be imagined.'[42] The British war correspondent Wynford Vaughan-Thomas wrote that Lucas had 'the round face and the greying moustache of a kindly country solicitor'. Lack of progress meant that Lucas was replaced on 23 February by the altogether more dashing Major-General Lucian Truscott, who wore a silk scarf around his neck that was part of an airman's escape kit. Both Alexander and Clark, who rubber-stamped all Lucas' decisions but escaped censure, were affected by what today is called legacy-thinking. They refought the battle of Salerno at Anzio, without taking into account the key differences between the two operations, the main one being that the latter had the inestimable advantage of total surprise. Alexander, who had to be a mediator as much as a commander with his multi-national force, ought to have set out far more specific objectives than he did, allowing both Clark and Lucas less leeway. They were nonetheless right not to have made a dash for the Alban Hills just south-east of Rome on landing, as some now argue they ought to have. With his forces strung out from Anzio to the mountains it would have been simple for the counter-attacking Germans to cut Lucas off, and the heights would have turned into the largest POW camp in Italy. Equally, had he pushed on northwards to Rome, he would have had, in his own picturesque phrase, 'one night in Rome and eighteen months in PoW camps'. Dick Evans, the adjutant of the 1st Battalion King's Shropshire Light Infantry, agreed wholeheartedly with this assessment: 'In the first two days we could have driven straight into Rome. Then we would have been slaughtered.'

The harbours of Anzio and Nettuno, and the armada needed to keep the beach-head resupplied, took a severe battering from the Germans once Kesselring put the aerial side of Case Richard into operation. In the ten days after the landings he summoned a force of 140 long-range bombers from outside Italy, and sixty more from southern French bases. The ships supplying the Anzio beach-head had to face E-boat torpedoes, bombs and the terrifying new invention of radio-operated, rocket-powered glider bombs, although all the human torpedo attacks failed miserably. The cruiser *Spartan*, destroyers *Janus*, *Jervis* and *Plunkett* and minesweeper *Prevail*, as well as a hospital ship and troop transporter, were all lost. Nonetheless, over 68,000 men, 237 tanks and 508 guns came ashore in the first week, a great inter-Allied and inter-service achievement. In all, no less than half a million tons of supplies were landed at Anzio, which for a brief moment became the world's fourth busiest port. Those who landed in that first week faced 71,500 Germans, including 7,000 crack troops from the 26th Panzer Division defending Cisterna.

The British attack on the key railway station at Campoleone failed. Major-General W. R. C. Penney's 1st Infantry Division began its assault on 28 January, badly delayed because of an ambush of some key Grenadier Guards officers. Only one man, from the 2nd Battalion, the Sherwood Foresters, got across the railway line, but he was subsequently killed, along with 244 other comrades from his regiment in the space of only ten minutes. Campoleone was not to fall for over three months. In all, 23,860 American and 9,203 British Commonwealth casualties had to be taken off the beaches in the Anzio operation, apart from around 7,000 who had been killed there. The life expectancy of a forward observation officer was a mere six weeks.[43] Those who fought at Anzio saw the full horrors of the Second World War close up. An army surgeon called James A. Ross, who later became president of the Royal College of Surgeons of Edinburgh, recalled the scene in a casualty clearing station inside the Anzio perimeter:

The wounded lay in two rows, mostly British but some American as well in their sodden filthy clothes . . . soaked, caked, buried in mud and blood; with ghastly pale faces, shuddering, shivering with the cold of the February night and their great wounds . . . some (too many; far too many) were carried in dying, with gross combinations of shattered limbs, protrusions of intestines and brain from great holes in their poor frames torn by 88-millimetre shells, mortar and anti-personnel bombs.[44]

By 7 February 1944 it was clear that the British War Cabinet had severe reservations about the way the Italian campaign – especially at Anzio – was progressing. 'The battle in Italy is approaching its climax,' Churchill reported, according to the notes of the War Cabinet Secretariat:

Two weeks ago we had high hopes of a military success – now we still have hopes of an uphill slogging match, which may nevertheless succeed . . . The 5th Army not yet delivered its attack – force not yet engaged and may at any moment advance on enemy's front – Enemy troops stretched, no relief. No reason to suppose possibility of decisive victory has faded away. But the strategic principles on which the operations were founded are sound and persist in bringing their rewards in spite of tactical disappointments. The German attempt to crush the bridgehead failed . . . Advisers not alarmed . . . We have a front engaging 19 divisions of the enemy. Hitler evidently on impulse had 6 or 7 divisions sent down. Our duty is to fight and engage all our forces with the enemy. Hitler does not want all his forces engaged on the peninsula. Our battle must be nourished. Disappointing not to gain tactical success.[45]

Churchill then said something that Lawrence Burgis took down as 'US asked us for an appreciation . . . In US may say Eisenhower removed.' This is capable of the interpretation that Eisenhower's job would be on the line in the United States if victory was not won in Italy, and when the Minister of Labour Ernest Bevin said that he should send Alexander a message of encouragement, Churchill said, 'I'll think about it,' which was hardly a ringing endorsement.

The great German counter-attack, Operation Fischfang (Catch Fish), came on 16 February, with Mackensen's intention to drive down the via Anziate to Anzio and throw the Allies back into the sea. Supported by a 452-gun bombardment, Mackensen flung his 125,000 troops against the Allies' 100,000, but Allied artillery and naval guns fired no fewer than 65,000 rounds on the first day alone. Fierce engagements developed at the road's flyover at Campo di Carne on 18 February, with craters formed, mines laid and concrete-laden lorries blocking the underpass below. 'Cooks, drivers and clerks fought side by side with infantry,' records the battle's historian as the Germans reached what was ominously designated 'the Final Beachhead Line'.[46] Close co-operation between the Allied artillery and infantry – it is estimated that they fired around fifteen times more shells during the battle than the Wehrmacht – made all the difference in a struggle where the air forces could not operate because of the low visibility. Light reconnaissance aircraft were used, however, to devastating effect. In all at Anzio, 10 per cent of German losses were due to Allied infantry, 15 per cent to aerial bombardment, but no less than 75 per cent to the artillery – figures which, as the Royal Military Academy Sandhurst historian Lloyd Clark has pointed out, are virtually identical to the statistics for the Western Front in the Great War.[47]

Mackensen's offensive, broken up by artillery bombardment and tenacious resistance on the ground, failed to reach closer than 7 miles from Anzio, and petered out by the evening of 19 February. It had cost the Fourteenth Army 5,400 casualties, against VI Corps' 3,500. From then on there were nearly three months of almost continuous fighting in what were known by the British Army as the wadis, the sunken marshlands and mosquito-ridden tributaries of the upper Moletta river. Although the front lines were broadly static in the areas nicknamed Starfish, the Bloody Boot, North Lobster Claw, South Lobster Claw, Shell Farm, Mortar Farm and Oh God Wadi, there were constant costly trench raids and counter-attacks. Battalions typically spent six days in and eight days out of the line. In his superb diary of the wadi fighting entitled *The Fortress*, the twenty-year-old subaltern in the Green Howards, Raleigh Trevelyan, recorded the experience of his battalion being surrounded by the Germans on three sides:

I find it bewildering the way our own and the Jerries' positions are so interwoven. There is no hard and fast straight line as the front between us . . . The men keep asking why we don't press forward and drive the enemy back – any risk is better than our present conditions. The answer is that there are more wadis beyond, and at the expense of much blood we would only be in exactly the same predicament, but with lengthier lines of communication.[48]

Walking the wadis today – it is advisable to do so only with a guide as there is still some unexploded ordnance there – one can see how close-quarter the fighting was, with trenches less than 50 yards from one another along waterlogged ditches, and man-sized holes dug out in the side of mud-banks for protection and makeshift accommodation. The 1st Battalion, Irish Guards took 94 per cent casualties in the wadis in only five days serving there, while the 2nd Battalion of the Sherwood Foresters was reduced from 250 officers and men down to a mere thirty in a similar period.[49] Yet the Germans failed to break through either there or at the nearby Flyover.

'I had hoped that we were hurling a wild cat on to the shore,' Churchill complained to the Chiefs of Staff on 31 January, 'but all we got was a stranded whale.'[50] It was true that the Anzio operation had not succeeded in its objectives, largely owing to the German capacity for counter-attack. In his novel of Anzio, *Seven Steps Down*, the war correspondent John Sears Barker describes the Ranger attack on Cisterna on the night of 29 February, carried out along one of the main drainage ditches of the Mussolini Canal that came close to the town:

The Rangers considered it a sheltered alley . . . That 800 yards would be over unprotected open land but the Rangers, advancing through the early morning shadows, counted on surprise. What they didn't count on was the Hermann Göring Division, which had set up a three-point ambush. Machine gun emplacements, mortars, anti-tank guns, depressed anti-aircraft guns, and Tiger tanks, hidden in farmhouses, ditches and haystacks, rimmed the ditch on all sides.[51]

The attack was disastrous: of the 767 men of the 1st and 3rd Ranger Battalions who took part, twelve were killed, thirty-six wounded and almost all of the rest were captured.

In the event, instead of VI Corps saving X Corps trapped on the Gustav Line, it turned out to be X Corps breaking through the Line in Operation Diadem in mid-May that finally opened up the opportunity to save the trapped VI Corps. With a proportion of Eighth Army brought back across the Apennines in support, Diadem saw Allied superiority of three to one, and an opening barrage of 1,500 guns at 23.00 hours on Thursday, 11 May 1944.[52] General Alphonse Juin's Free French Corps performed impressive feats of specialist mountain soldiering in turning the German flank. Meanwhile, II Corps of Fifth Army made good progress, and on 16 May Alexander could finally report to a hugely relieved Brooke that the Gustav Line had 'definitely' been breached. After initial rebuffs, XIII Corps of Eighth Army broke through, and it turned out to be the Polish II Corps which took Monastery Hill on 18 May. (Their charismatic commander, General Władysław Anders, died in exile in 1970, and his grave can be seen among those of his comrades at the Polish cemetery there.)

As the Tenth Army reeled back from the Gustav Line, and tried to defend the Hitler and Caesar Lines behind it, the opportunity arrived for Alexander to use VI Corps at Anzio to cut off the Germans' retreat. Having missed capturing large numbers of the Wehrmacht in Sicily and Salerno, here was a third chance to put a great many German soldiers, then streaming up Highway 6 towards Valmontone, 'in the bag', as had happened in Tunisia. Yet at a press conference at 20.00 hours on Monday, 22 May Clark told reporters: 'I intend to take Rome, and to take it soon – nothing will stand in my way.'[53] It was assumed at the time that he was just referring to the Germans. When the very next day, Alexander – informed of enemy intentions via Ultra – ordered Clark to break out of the Anzio pocket, cross the Alban Hills and swing his Fifth Army eastwards, thereby trapping the retreating Tenth Army at Valmontone as it tried to escape northwards, his subordinate was in no mood to comply.

Admittedly, breaking out of the Anzio perimeter was still no easy task. By the end of 23 May, 3rd US Infantry Division of VI Corps had lost 955 men, the largest number of any US division on any single day during the whole war.[54] German losses were equally heavy, however. By the evening of Wednesday, 24 May, Truscott's VI Corps was making good progress towards Valmontone, and the prospect beckoned of the Tenth Army being trapped in the valley on Route 6, with many forced to surrender. Contact was finally made between the two Allied forces at 07.30 on Thursday, 25 May, more than four months after the Anzio landings, and Cisterna also fell later that day.

Yet, instead of obeying his orders from Alexander, on Friday, 26 May Clark deliberately reduced the force Truscott needed to capture Valmontone – the true *Schwerpunkt* – with the result that the Germans were able to keep their retreat route open all the time between 26 May and 4 June, and so the Tenth Army escaped. Clark kept the greater part of his force to make a dash for Rome – which Kesselring had anyhow evacuated – taking it largely unopposed on 5 June, the day before D-Day and therefore just early enough for him to bask in global approbation for a full twenty-four hours before attention turned elsewhere. (He understandably kept a large *Roma* traffic sign, complete with a bullet hole, in his office as a souvenir.) 'Alexander never gave orders not to take Rome,' was Clark's *ex post facto* rationalization, dripping with double negatives, special pleading and Anglophobia:

I know he was concerned about my maintaining my thrust to Valmontone, but hell when we were knocking on its door we had already destroyed as much of the German Tenth Army as we could ever have expected . . . One thing I knew was that I had to take Rome and that my American army was going to do it. So in all the circumstances I had to go for it before the British loused it up . . . We had earned it you understand.[55]

As a result of Clark's orders on 26 May 'to leave the 3rd Division and the Special Force to block Highway 6 and mount that assault . . . to the north as soon as you can', the US 34th and 45th Divisions broke off their march to Valmontone and instead headed for Rome, covered by the 36th Division. Truscott was 'dumbfounded' and protested that 'We should pour our maximum power into the Valmontone Gap to ensure the destruction of the retreating German army,' but he was overruled.[56] For the rest of his life he was convinced that, as he put it, 'To be first in Rome was a poor compensation for this lost opportunity.' Clark's divisional commanders – especially Major-General Ernest N. Harmon of 1st US Armored Division and Brigadier John W. O'Daniel of 3rd Division – were equally angry about the change of plan, and Alexander himself was informed only after it had been made, when it was too late to countermand. Short of instantly replacing Clark with Truscott, there was little the commander of 15th Army Group could do, and he was reduced to asking Clark's chief of staff, Major-General Alfred M. Gruenther, 'I am sure the army commander will continue to push towards Valmontone, won't he?'[57] He would indeed, but not with anything like the force necessary to trap Vietinghoff, seven of whose divisions now managed to withdraw north-east of Rome.

Between the opening of Operation Diadem and the fall of Rome, 15th Army Group had lost 44,000 casualties, a sacrifice that might have been easier to justify if the German army had not been permitted to escape in relatively good order to continue the struggle in central and northern Italy, and especially on the Gothic Line. General von Vietinghoff himself had no doubts that 'If the Allies, as in previous days, had directed their attack against Valmontone, the initially weak forces of the Hermann Göring Panzer Division would not have been able to prevent a breakthrough. The fall of Rome, the separation of both German armies, and the bottling up of the bulk of their units would have been unavoidable.'

Alexander confined himself in his memoirs to the caustic comment that he could 'only assume that the immediate lure of Rome for its publicity persuaded Mark Clark to switch the direction of his advance', and Harding agreed, saying: 'By diverting his axis to advance from almost due east to north-east he missed an opportunity of cutting off some forces, but he was attracted, I think, by the magnet of Rome.'[58] To make matters worse, Clark actually informed Alexander that, if the British tried to approach Rome before the Americans, he would order 'his troops to fire on the Eighth Army', and once Rome had fallen – or rather was evacuated in relatively good order by the retreating Germans – American Military Police refused British units permission to enter the city.[59] It was, Harding recalled, the nearest that the British ever got to 'coming to blows' with General Mark Clark.

Churchill told Roosevelt and Stalin at the Teheran Conference of November 1943 that 'He who holds Rome holds the title-deeds to Italy,' but he was wrong. The fall of Rome proved to be just another step on the long and bloody journey up the peninsula. If Rome had fallen in the autumn of 1943 it might have been a significant moment in the history of the Second World War, but coming so late, and so soon before D-Day, it makes little more than a footnote. Thereafter the entire Italian campaign became a sideshow, kept alive by Churchill's faith that victory there could open up opportunities in Yugoslavia, Austria and France, each of which was heavily discounted by Marshall and the Joint Chiefs of Staff. Alexander's pursuit of the Germans northwards, where the Gothic Line had been constructed between La Spezia and Pesaro, has been described as 'wooden and hesitant', leading one historian to state, with reference to North Africa as well as Italy, that 'This failure in the pursuit was the most marked feature of the Western Allies in the Second World War.'[60] It is true that the Germans managed to get their forces up to the Gothic Line without being overtaken, but Harding estimated that on 1 July 1944 the Germans had between eighteen and twenty-one divisions, against the Allies' fourteen infantry and four armoured, and moreover they had mini-defensive lines such as the Albert Line behind Perugia and Chiusi, and lines in front of Arezzo and Siena, and the Arno Line centred on Florence and Bibbiena. All these had to be mastered before the Allies even reached the Gothic Line itself.

It was to be a phenomenally hard slog up the Apennines before reaching the plains of the Po Valley. Small wonder that the fellow officers of Coldstream Guards Lieutenant (later Professor Sir) Michael Howard, who won the Military Cross at Salerno, wondered whether the General Staff had used a map that featured contours when they had planned the campaign. Alexander's chances of a glorious breakthrough of the Gothic Line were severely weakened when six divisions were withdrawn from his command in order to take part in the invasion of southern France on 15 August 1944, while Kesselring was simultaneously being reinforced. The Fifth Army crossed the Arno on

2 August, and the Eighth Army took Rimini on 21 September, but the focus of the Second World War had long since moved to north-west Europe, where the life or death of the Third Reich would be decided, rather than in northern Italy. By the time Romagna fell on 20 September 1944, Eighth Army had been fighting in the mountains of Italy for a year, and the autumnal rain brought more dreadful weather conditions that would shock present-day visitors to Italy who confine their tours of Tuscany and Umbria to the summer months. Even once the Allies reached north-eastern Italy, there was a series of east–west-running rivers to cross if they were to achieve Alexander's plan to destroy the twenty German divisions in front of the Alps. Even as late as December 1944, Hitler was capable of putting together a twenty-six-division surprise attack in the Ardennes without having to remove troops from Italy, although he did remove Kesselring in March 1945 to defend western Germany.

The last stage of the Allied campaign was easily its best tactically, with the Gothic Line breached with vigour and a pursuit of the Germans that has been described as 'tactically superb'.[61] Much of the credit for this must go to Clark, who commanded 15th Army Group, Truscott of the Fifth Army and Sir Richard McCreery, who in November 1944 had taken over command of the Eighth Army from Oliver Leese. Refusing Vietinghoff permission to retreat into the Alps, but instead ordering his troops to 'Stand or die', Hitler condemned the by then demoralized German forces to fight north of the Po, where they were comprehensively defeated between 14 and 20 April 1945. Vietinghoff surrendered German Army Group South-west to Alexander, who was by then supreme commander Mediterranean, on Wednesday, 2 May 1945.

Although the attritional warfare on the slim peninsula – which might have been specifically designed for a long retreat – had cost the Fifth Army 188,746 casualties and the Eighth Army 123,254, a total of 312,000, it had cost the Germans as many as 434,646.[62] Yet despite constant inferiority of numbers in the air, and being always on the defensive, Kesselring and Vietinghoff had held up the Allies for nineteen months before the final collapse. It is hard to see what the continued Allied assaults from Rome to the Po Valley really achieved considering the cost, except that they kept many German divisions away from the Western Front, and some historians assert that 'The Allied Italian campaign was a necessary component of the giant ring that squeezed the life out of the Nazi state.'[63]

The Italian campaign also provides a perfect illustration of how well the Germans could fight when not interfered with strategically by Hitler. Kesselring, Vietinghoff, Mackensen and Senger hardly made a serious error in their masterly withdrawal northwards up the entire length of Italy, and had Hitler permitted a retreat into the Alps they could have extricated their armies further. From the spring of 1944 the Allies had more than ten times as many warplanes in Italy as the Luftwaffe, but had the Nazis organized aircraft and tank production efficiently enough for the Luftwaffe and Wehrmacht to be able to contest the skies and plains, there is no reason to suppose that they would have been expelled from the country in the first place. 'May I give you a word of advice?' the urbane General Senger joked to Michael Howard ten years after the war ended. 'Next time you invade Italy, do not start at the bottom.'[64]

Back on 12 September 1943, Mussolini had been rescued on Hitler's orders from the mountainside hotel in which he was being held, in a sensational German glider operation commanded by Colonel Otto Skorzeny. 'The liberation of the Duce has caused a great sensation at home and abroad,' crowed Goebbels to his diary two days later. 'Even upon the enemy the effect of his melodramatic deliverance is enormous.'[65] After meeting Hitler, Mussolini was set up as dictator of the so-called Republic of Salò, ruling from Gargagno on Lake Garda for nineteen months until the German collapse. Attempting to escape across the Swiss border on 26 April 1945, Mussolini and his mistress Clara Petacci, her brother Marcello and fifteen others were captured by the Italian partisans. On Saturday the 28th Mussolini and Petacci were executed by sub-machine gun in front of a low stone wall by the gates of a villa outside the village of Giulino di Mezzegra on Lake Como, one of the loveliest beauty-spots in Italy. (It seems rather unItalian to murder an attractive and apolitical mistress, but such is war.) Their bodies were added to those of the other captured Fascists, loaded in to a removal van and driven to Milan, the birthplace of Fascism.[66] There, the corpses of Mussolini and Petacci were kicked, spat upon, shot at and urinated over, and then hung upside-down from a metal girder in front of the petrol station in the Piazzale Loreto, with their names on pieces of paper pinned to their feet. It was remarked with surprise by the women present, who were joking and dancing around this macabre scene, that Clara Petacci wore no knickers and that her stockings were unladdered. (It was hardly her fault; she had not been given time to put her knickers on before she was taken away and shot.)

It is all too easy at this distance of time to forget that each casualty listed in these campaigns represents a tragic human story. In the Beach Head Cemetery 3 miles north of Anzio, for example, lies the grave of the twenty-five-year-old Sergeant M. A. W. Rogers of the Wiltshire Regiment, who won the Victoria Cross taking a German position on the north side of the Moletta river by bomb and bayonet on 3 June 1944, advancing alone against an enemy that occupied the high ground. The *London Gazette* recorded how, under intense fire, Rogers had penetrated 30 yards before he was:

blown off his feet by a grenade, and wounded in the leg. Nothing daunted, he ran on towards an enemy machine-gun post, attempting to silence it. He was shot and killed at point-blank range. The NCO's undaunted determination, fearless devotion to duty and superb courage carried his platoon on to their objective in a strongly defended position.[67]

For all the glory of winning Britain's greatest gallantry medal, his gravestone tells of the grief of his wife: 'In memory of my beloved husband. May we be together soon, dear. Peace at last.'

PART III

Retribution

The winning war was over, the losing war had begun. I saw the white stain of fear growing in the dull eyes of German officers and soldiers . . . When Germans become afraid, when that mysterious German fear begins to creep into their bones, they always arouse a special horror and pity. Their appearance is miserable, their cruelty sad, their courage silent and hopeless. That is when the Germans become wicked.

Curzio Malaparte, *Kaputt*, 1948

13

A Salient Reversal

March–August 1943

We have severely underestimated the Russians, the extent of the country and the treachery of the climate. This is the revenge of reality. General Heinz Guderian, July 1943[1]

Between Field Marshal Paulus' surrender at Stalingrad in early February 1943 and the battle of Kursk five months later, the Soviets forced their way across the Donets river. Yet despite his men being massively outnumbered, sometimes by seven to one, Field Marshal Erich von Manstein counter-attacked between 18 February and 20 March, winning the third battle of Kharkov and recapturing the city on 14 March in one of the great military achievements of the war.[2] Although the Soviet winter offensive had regained much of the territory lost the previous year, and inflicted around one million German casualties, Manstein had halted it.

Erich von Manstein was born in 1887, the tenth son of an aristocratic Prussian artillery officer, General Eduard von Lewinski, but he was given away at birth to his mother's childless brother-in-law, the aristocratic Prussian infantry lieutenant-general Georg von Manstein, whose surname he took. Since both his grandfathers and an uncle had also been Prussian generals, and Paul von Hindenburg was married to his aunt, it was a natural career path for Erich to be commissioned into the cadet corps aged thirteen, and six years later into the 3rd Regiment of Foot Guards. His study at the Berlin War Academy was interrupted within a year by the outbreak of the Great War, in which he served bravely on both fronts, and he was severely wounded in Poland in November 1914. He then took a series of Staff positions until the end of the war, and stayed on in the Regular Army into peacetime, becoming head of the Operations Section of the General Staff (OKH) in 1935. The following year, by then a *Generalmajor* (brigadier-general), he became deputy to the Chief of Staff, General Ludwig Beck.

In the purge of the Army following the dismissal of General von Fritsch in February 1938, Manstein – who was known to despise the Nazis, largely on social grounds – was relieved of his post in the Staff and given command of the 18th Infantry Division. It was as chief of staff to General von Leeb that he took part in the occupation of the Sudetenland in 1938 and as chief of staff to General Rundstedt in the invasion of Poland the following year that he first distinguished himself as a fine strategist. By then he had also, much to Beck's chagrin and contempt, stopped criticizing the Nazis, arguing that soldiers should stay out of politics, a stance that was to serve his promotion prospects well.

As has already been seen in Chapter 2, it was Manstein who, as chief of staff of Rundstedt's Army Group A, in May 1940 masterminded the *Sichelschnitt* manoeuvre, also known as the Manstein Plan, which, by concentrating on attacking through the Ardennes, crossing the Meuse and fighting in the ideal tank country of the rolling plains of northern France, brought such a rapid victory in the west. Hitler showed his gratitude by promoting him to full general and awarding him the Knight's Cross. In March 1941 Manstein was given the command of LVI Panzer Corps for Operation Barbarossa, in which he led the advance on Leningrad, advancing more than 50 miles a day and capturing vital bridgeheads. When in September 1941 a vacancy occurred for the command of the Eleventh Army in the Crimea – the previous occupant's plane having crashed in a Russian minefield – Manstein was the obvious choice, and he captured Sevastopol on 4 July 1942 after a long and gruelling siege. Hitler telephoned 'The Conqueror of Sevastopol', as he called him, to announce his promotion to *Generalfeldmarschall* (field marshal).

It was as commander of Army Group Don in November and December 1942 that Manstein tried but failed to relieve Stalingrad, but he was appointed to command Army Group South nonetheless. 'He was arrogant and intolerant at times, and something of a martinet,' wrote the British field marshal Michael Carver, 'but he was highly intelligent, with a clear, quick brain. Beneath a cold, reserved exterior, he was an emotional man, who kept his feelings under strict control ... He was respected for the speed and sharpness with which he analysed the essentials of a problem, for the brevity and clarity of his orders, and for the calm, cool calculation by which he arrived at his decisions.'[3] The greatest of all the strategists of the Third Reich, Manstein had a better understanding of mechanized weaponry than any of the German generals outside the tank school itself, and Keitel thrice urged Hitler to give Manstein his own job as chief of staff of OKW.[4] This was ignored, but was one of the best pieces of advice the Führer ever received.

The city of Kursk lies 315 miles south of Moscow and straddles the main Moscow–Rostov railway line. By the spring of 1943 it was the centre of a Russian-held protuberance, or salient, jutting 120 miles wide and 90 miles deep into the German lines. Kursk had once been famed for its nightingales; bird-singing competitions had been hosted there since the nineteenth century. In July 1943, however, all that could be heard in the city were the decibels of war. Kursk had been captured by the Germans on 2 November 1941, after which the Wehrmacht shot 15,000 people, transported 30,000 for slave labour in Germany, destroyed 2,000 buildings and generally stripped the region bare, even transporting back to Germany thousands of tons of the region's sticky, jet-black, highly fertile soil. Kursk was recaptured by the Russians soon after Paulus' surrender.

After Stalingrad, Manstein had stabilized Army Group South's front, and Army Group Centre under Field Marshal von Kluge, who had replaced Bock in December 1941, had retained Orel to the north. Mutually exhausted, both sides settled into a period of little activity, as fresh troops were brought up for the coming summer offensive. Yet time was not on the Germans' side, with Lend-Lease distributing large quantities of equipment to the Russians, totalling by the summer of 1943 some 2,400 tanks, 3,000 planes and 80,000 trucks.[5] An historian of the Eastern Front estimates that Western aid contributed 5 per cent of the USSR's war effort in 1942 and 10 per cent in 1943 and 1944, invaluable help in such a close-run fight.[6] The Americans provided the Russians with 15 million pairs of boots, for example.

Unfortunately for the Germans, even the most cursory glance at the map made it completely obvious where they would attack. A pincer movement directly to the north and south of Kursk would pinch off the salient, and thus lead to the capture of Rokossovsky's Central Front in the north and General Nikolai Vatutin's Voronezh Front to the south. That was certainly what would have happened in 1941, when the Germans were still capable of pulling off such coups. Hitler flew to see Manstein on the front line at Zaporozhe for three days on 17 February 1943, coming so close to the enemy that some T-34 tanks even got to within firing range of the airfield.[7] Yet the Führer was now a very different man from the Supreme Warlord of the days before Stalingrad. As Guderian recorded of a meeting four days later: 'His left hand trembled, his back was bent, his gaze was fixed, his eyes protruded but had lost their former lustre, his cheeks were flecked with red. He was more excitable, easily lost his composure and was prone to angry outbursts and ill-considered decisions.'[8] This description matched Senger's impressions during the Monte Cassino battle. Because the next move was so obvious to all, Manstein wanted to undertake it as early as possible, ideally in early March, but the go-ahead for Unternehmen Zitadelle (Operation Citadel) was postponed by Hitler until the ground had thoroughly thawed, and Zeitzler had called a Staff conference at OKH headquarters, which on 11 April submitted a plan for General Walther Model's Ninth Army to attack from the north simultaneously with Hoth's Fourth Panzer Army from the south of the salient. Yet Hitler, who had put Manstein's recapture of Kharkov largely down to the new Tiger I model E tank, of which he thought one battalion was worth a division of Panzers, wanted to wait until the Tiger had come fully on stream before launching the offensive. As only twelve were being produced per week at that time, this was a major impediment to the early action for which Manstein was pushing.

Internal dissension in OKH and OKW further exacerbated the problem, leading to further postponements of Zitadelle. Jodl opposed it outright because of the impending danger of Allied landings in the Mediterranean. Guderian, who was then inspector-general of tanks, responsible for overhauling Germany's armoured forces, was equally opposed because he knew that the Russians were expecting and preparing for it. Kluge – who hated Guderian and in May even asked the Führer if he could challenge him to a duel – was very much in favour, as was Zeitzler who claimed it was his brainchild, at least until it went wrong. Model was dubious, but when he argued that the Stavka knew it was coming, Zeitzler responded with a weirdly circular argument, saying that the very fact that the Russians expected it 'was an admission that the area chosen was of vital importance, and would result in a substantial part of the Russian armour being brought to battle', where it could be destroyed.[9] As time dragged on, Manstein slowly turned against the whole operation. Frederick von Mellenthin's estimation was the correct one: that if it had been undertaken early it might have worked, but by the time of its actual launch Zitadelle had become 'an operation in which we had little to gain and probably a great deal to lose'.[10]

At yet another conference on 3 May, Guderian and Speer spoke out against Zitadelle, Zeitzler and Kluge enthusiastically in its favour, and Manstein stated that it was hard to say whether its moment had not passed. Only a hundred Panthers had been delivered to the front, despite Speer having promised 324 by the end of May. Nonetheless, 13 June was agreed as the date the operation would take place. A week later a famous exchange took place between Hitler and Guderian, when the Inspector-General asked, 'My Führer, why do you want to attack in the East at all this year?' and Hitler replied: 'You are quite right. Whenever I think of this attack, my stomach turns over.'[11] Although Keitel believed that Germany needed to attack Kursk, which was by then one of the best-defended fortresses in the world, out of prestige, Guderian pointed out that few people had even heard of the city.[12] As Keitel ought to have learnt from Stalingrad, prestige is rarely a good enough reason for conducting a military operation.

Meanwhile, at the end of April the Stavka had sent Zhukov to the city to assume day-to-day control of the battle, always a sign that Stalin took a particular front extremely seriously. Zhukov had sent a report warning about the salient's vulnerability on 8 April, but had persuaded Stalin not to follow his initial instinct of striking first. Writing to Stalin (codenamed Comrade Vasil'ev), Zhukov (codenamed Konstantinov) said: 'I consider it inexpedient for our forces to mount a preventative offensive in the near future. It will be better if we wear out the enemy in our defence, destroy his tanks, and then, having introduced fresh reserves, by going over to an all-out offensive, we will finish off the enemy's main grouping.'[13] That was the plan the Stavka adopted, and it was substantially what was to happen.

Marshal Alexandr Vasilevsky went down to Kursk with Zhukov and together they easily spotted that the *Schwerpunkt* for the Germans was going to be the point between Belgorod and Kursk defended by Vatutin's Voronezh Front, which they reinforced with the Twenty-first and Sixty-fourth Armies (renamed the Sixth and Seventh Guards Armies) that had been blooded at Stalingrad, and one of the best Soviet tank formations, the First Armoured Army. To the north, Rokossovsky's Central Front was massively reinforced as well, until it consisted of no fewer than five infantry armies. As well as the 1.3 million men under Vatutin and Rokossovsky, leaving nothing to chance Zhukov created a half-million-man Stavka Reserve Force under General Ivan Konev, later called the Steppe Front, consisting of five tank armies, several tank and mechanized corps and a number of infantry divisions.[14] This front was, in the view of one historian of the Eastern Front, 'the most powerful reserve accumulated by the Soviet Union at any time during the war'.[15] If for any reason the Germans did manage to pinch off the salient, it would be able to form an entirely new front, preventing them from exploiting their victory eastwards.

With the attack postponed yet again from 13 June, by early July the Germans faced a forbidding task. In some sectors of the Russian defence, artillery regiments outnumbered infantry by five to one, with more than 20,000 guns trained on the oncoming Wehrmacht. These included over 6,000 anti-tank guns of 76.2mm calibre and 920 Katyusha multiple rocket launchers. Furthermore the cannon and armour-piercing bombs of Shturmovik ground-attack aircraft posed a mortal peril for the German tanks. By employing the entire civilian population of the Kursk region, as well as the Army, 3,000 miles of trenches were dug, and 'countless miles of barbed wire and obstacles, some of which were electrified', put in place, along with automatic flame-throwers.[16] Overall, around 2,700 German tanks – more heavily armed and usually of higher-calibre weaponry – faced around 3,800 Russian. But it was down to the German tanks – as well as the huge Ferdinand self-propelled assault guns (*Sturmgeschütze*) – to try to break through the formidable Soviet defences. 'The main defensive zones were three to four miles deep,' recorded one historian,

consisting of battalion defence areas, anti-tank areas and support points, and systems of obstacles, consisting of three lines of trenches (up to five lines in most important sectors), interconnected by communication trenches. Second zones, six to eight miles from the leading edge of the zone, were laid out in similar fashion. Rear defence zones were situated at about twenty-five miles from the leading edge of the defence zones ... The whole system consisted of no fewer than eight defensive belts existing over a depth of between 120 and 180 miles.[17]

Furthermore, 2,200 anti-tank and 2,500 anti-personnel mines had been laid across every single mile of the front, a density four times that which had defended Stalingrad and six times that of Moscow. In all, 503,993 anti-tank mines and 439,348 anti-personnel mines were laid by the Red Army prior to the battle of Kursk. Lieutenant Artur Schütte, a tank commander in the Grossdeutschland Division, was pardonably exaggerating when he said that the minefields he had to cross were laid so densely 'that it would have been impossible to put even a medal between them'.[18] Mellenthin recorded that the Russians could lay 30,000 mines in two or three days and that 'it was no rare thing to have to lift 40,000 mines a day in the sector of a German Corps'.[19] This was laborious, time-consuming and dangerous work for the German engineer corps but vitally necessary, though it could never be 100 per cent successful.

The hundred days of waiting before the German attack also gave the Red Army plenty of time to build miniature fortresses, reconnoitre the battlefield, gauge the depths of fords and strengths of bridges, and to train day and night. By the time they had finished, noted the chief of staff of XLVIII Panzer Corps, they had 'converted the Kursk front into another Verdun'.[20] Furthermore, Mellenthin complained that the terrain in the southern sector across which his 300 tanks and 60 assault guns had to attack was not good tank country, with 'numerous valleys, small copses, irregularly laid out villages and some rivers and brooks; of these the Pena [river] ran with a swift current between two banks.' Walking the battlefields of Kursk and taking the journey known as the Death Ride of the Fourth Panzer

Army alert one to the fact that Mellenthin slightly exaggerated the 'valleys', which are little more than undulations. As he himself admitted elsewhere, 'It was not good "tank country", but it was by no means "tank proof".'[21] The ground rises slightly to the north between Belgorod and Kursk, further aiding the defender.

It was an unusual luxury for the Russians to be able to prepare to this extent. 'At the beginning of the war everything was done in a hurry,' commented a Red Army tank captain, 'and time was always lacking. Now we go calmly into action.'[22] The Luftwaffe's aerial reconnaissance, even allowing for Russian camouflage, ought to have been enough for Hitler to have stuck to his original instincts and look for somewhere else to fight, especially as Manstein hardened his view against the attack as time went on. Yet the all-powerful 'Greatest Warlord of All Time', as Goebbels' propaganda machine was still describing Hitler, seems to have been persuaded by Keitel, Zeitzler and Kluge to set H-Hour for dawn on 4 July. 'Independence Day for America', complained Mellenthin afterwards, 'and the beginning of the end for Germany.' As a tank purist and theorist, Mellenthin could not bear to see the way that the Wehrmacht was fighting to Russian strengths, in the same way that had led to Stalingrad, rather than to its own, in the way that had led to the sweeping victories of 1941. 'Instead of seeking to create conditions in which manoeuvre would be possible,' he complained, 'by strategic withdrawals or surprise attacks in quiet sectors, the German Supreme Council could think of nothing better than to fling our magnificent Panzer divisions against Kursk, which had now become the strongest fortress in the world.'[23] It was as though they had chosen deliberately to attack the Maginot Line head-on in 1940, rather than skirting around it. Like Napoleon, who by the time of Borodino no longer cared about the lives of his men, too many decision-makers at OKW – principally of course Hitler himself – had given up worrying about how to husband troop numbers. A *Materialschlacht* (war of attrition) was precisely what the Germans had to avoid after Stalingrad, but it was what they got with their constant postponements of Zitadelle. Before Hitler kept putting off the attack, Kursk was an undefended town set in hundreds of miles of virgin countryside; by the time it took place it was indeed a citadel.

*

The 'bad news' of the death of the Polish Prime Minister General Sikorski as well as his liaison officer, the Tory MP Victor Cazalet, in a plane crash at Gibraltar was broken to the War Cabinet by Churchill on 5 July 1943. Portal reported that the Czech pilot was still alive, but it was 'impossible to say at the moment what happened' beyond the fact that it was a 'very serious loss to Poland and to us'. Churchill said it was the 'Moment [for the Poles] to try and patch it up with the R[ussians]', but the Minister Resident in the Middle East, the Australian diplomat Richard Casey, thought General Anders, though a good soldier, had 'no political sense' and so was unlikely to do this. 'I'll say something in the House,' said Churchill, 'quite out of the ordinary.'[24] The fact that the War Cabinet privately thought Sikorski's death a blow implies that the conspiracy theory that SIS had assassinated him (along with a Conservative MP) is absurd.

'Soldiers of the Reich!' read the Führer's message to his troops for Zitadelle on Monday, 5 July 1943. 'This day you are to take part in an offensive of such importance that the whole future of the war may depend on its outcome. More than anything else, your victory will show the whole world that resistance to the power of the German Army is hopeless.'[25] Although probing attacks did begin on the afternoon of 4 July, the main German assault in the south was not finally unleashed until 05.00 the next day, and in the north half an hour later. The Russians had already heard from a Czech deserter from an engineering battalion of LII Army Corps that all ranks had been issued with a five-day schnapps and food ration, so the Germans did not even enjoy the advantage of tactical surprise. The Lucy spy ring operating from Switzerland had also furnished the Stavka with reasonably accurate reports of German capabilities and intentions, as did Ultra decrypts from Bletchley Park delivered in a suitably opaque form by the British Ambassador to Moscow. Vatutin could thus further disrupt the opening stage of Zitadelle by ordering a bombardment of the areas where the Germans were forming up, just prior to the assault.

The German attacks above and below the salient were almost mirror images of each other. In the north, Model's Ninth Army drove southwards from Orel towards Kursk on a 35-mile-wide front against

Rokossovsky's Central Front. In the south, Hoth's Fourth Panzer Army attacked northwards from Belgorod towards Kursk on a 30-mile-wide front against Vatutin's Voronezh Front. Zhukov decided deliberately to allow the attack to get well under way before counter-attacking its exposed flanks. The German Army elsewhere in Russia had been denuded of armour in order to provide the seventeen Panzer divisions necessary to spearhead this formidable fifty-division assault, leaving Hoth's Panzer army 'the strongest force ever before put under a single commander in the German Army'.[26] Yet their hopes for victory due to the combination of Stuka dive-bombing, fast tank advances and close infantry support – Blitzkrieg, in effect – failed to take into account the fact that by July 1943 their enemies had finally learnt all about the tactics that had proved so devastating against Poland in 1939, France in 1940 and Russia herself in 1941–2. Furthermore, one of the essential elements of Blitzkrieg – surprise – was entirely missing from the mix.

Because the Red Army had learnt to fight on even when penetrated by Panzer formations, the Germans were forced to adopt a *Panzerkeil* (armoured wedge) tactic of having the heaviest tanks, such as Tigers and Panthers, in the middle of a formation with the others, such as Mark IVs (by then the majority of Panzers), on the wings, supported by infantry, grenades and mortars behind the centre of the wedge. The Russians responded to *Panzerkeil* tactics with what the Germans termed *Pakfront*, where up to ten Russian guns welded into a single unit would concentrate all their fire on one tank before moving on to the next. 'Neither minefields nor Pakfronts could be detected until the first tank blew up,' recalled Mellenthin, 'or the first anti-tank gun opened fire.'[27] Red Army mortar operators were particularly feared: a skilled one could put a third bomb into the air before the first and second ones landed.

The sheer numbers involved, as well as its crucial outcome, make Kursk a remarkable battle. The Germans had around 900,000 troops, 2,700 tanks and self-propelled guns, 10,000 artillery pieces and 2,600 aircraft.[28] Facing them, Rokossovsky, Vatutin and Konev had around 1.8 million men, 3,800 tanks and self-propelled guns, 20,000 artillery pieces and 2,100 aircraft.[29] Kursk therefore fully justifies its popular designation as the greatest tank battle in history. Despite their two-to-one superiority in numbers of troops, it was nonetheless a terrifying sight for the Red Army when the German tanks, in Alan Clark's words, 'clambered out from the sunken lanes and dried-up *balkas* where they had been lying and moved slowly forward, hatches closed, across the billowing yellow-green corn of the upper Donets valley'. (The heat inside the tanks in Russia's summer weather was stifling.) Hoth deployed no fewer than nine of the best Panzer divisions in the German Army – from west to east the 3rd Panzer, Gross Deutschland, 11th Panzer, SS Leibstandarte (Lifeguard) Adolf Hitler, SS Das Reich, SS Totenkopf (Death's Head), 6th Panzer, 19th Panzer and 7th Panzer – all across a mere 30 miles of front.

'The whole front was a girdle of flashes,' recalled a Tiger tank radio operator Sergeant Imboden; 'it seemed as if we were driving into a ring of flame . . . We thanked the Fates for the strength of our good Krupp steel.' When German tanks were disabled by mines or by special Red Army squads hiding in slit trenches in the middle of minefields, their crews were ordered to stay inside and give covering fire for the rest of the battle. This was a virtual death sentence for them, as their becalmed tanks were almost always hit only a matter of minutes afterwards. Those Waffen-SS Panzer crewmen who did get out immediately ripped the death's-head insignia off their uniforms, as those wearing it were almost never allowed the luxury of being taken prisoner.

Although the long, slim 76.2mm Russian anti-tank gun could knock out a Tiger's frontal armour only at point-blank range, it was effective against the Mark IVs, and anyway there was plenty of point-blank-range fighting at Kursk. Mines accounted for many German tanks, and there was only so much the *Panzergrenadiere* – who fought throughout the night – could do against well-entrenched Russian anti-tank groups that no longer turned and ran as in earlier days. As Konstantin Simonov recorded in his novel *Days and Nights*, Red Army veterans had learnt by experience that 'Under mortar fire it is no more dangerous to move forward than to stay where you are. They knew that tanks most often kill soldiers who are running away from them, and that German automatic rifle fire from two hundred metres away is always intended more to frighten than to kill.'[30]

Although Hoth broke through the first line of Soviet defence on the first day of the assault, fire from the second and strongest line had been pre-ranged and self-propelled guns had been dug in so that their hulls were pointing down, hidden by the terrain and camouflage. Between 6 and 7 July, Hoth's force was reduced in the fierce fighting from 865 operative vehicles to 621.[31] Lieutenant Schütte complained to his commander after capturing a village only to take heavy losses from pre-registered artillery fire that 'Having driven Ivan out, we should have withdrawn ourselves and let him bomb the place out of existence. Then we could have moved the armour forward relatively safely.'[32] This is what Schütte did successfully at a hamlet the following day, though losing several tanks to mines because there was 'no time for laborious mine-clearing'. Schütte recalled this period before the Soviet counter-attack as being characterized by a desolate battlefield, with 'miles of devastated corn, dozens of destroyed tanks and dead bodies swelling obscenely in the summer heat'. On one occasion his company commander looked up in a small copse to see the face of what he thought was an enemy sniper. He fired a full clip of his pistol into what turned out to be 'a bodiless head, which had been blown off by an artillery blast and tossed up into the tree, where it had lodged'.[33]

After a week of continual fighting, Hoth could boast only a rectangular salient 9 miles deep by 15 across in the Voronezh Front's line, and no immediate prospect of breaking through to Kursk itself. As Alan Clark noted of the Waffen-SS: 'These men were face to face with the *Untermensch* and finding to their dismay that he was as well-armed, as cunning, and as brave as themselves.'[34] On 9 July the Soviets went on to the counter-offensive, having drawn in the Germans across their defences in a way most expensive to the Wehrmacht, with a barrage so long and heavy that Schütte said it felt like 'a continual earthquake'. Meanwhile, in the northern part of the salient, Model's Ninth Army managed only to penetrate the 6 miles to Ponyri, and had ground to a halt by the night of 11 July, with the Soviets counter-attacking the next day. A major problem overtook the vast Ferdinand assault gun, which XLVII Panzer Corps had hoped would be a battle-winning weapon. Although they had very thick armour-plating, these monsters had no machine guns, and were therefore defenceless against Russian soldiers who would bravely run up to them, board them with flame-throwers and incinerate everyone inside through the engine's ventilation shafts. Guderian had spotted that using Ferdinands to fight infantry was akin, in his words, to 'going quail-shooting with cannons', but the requisite changes had not been made.[35] In the first two days of fighting at Kursk, forty of the seventy Ferdinands were destroyed, and, because they failed to silence Russian machine-gun emplacements, Lieutenant-General Helmuth Weidling's infantry could not support those that did break through. It was a classic example of a foreseeable design defect leading to disaster, and the assault guns had to be refitted with machine guns before being sent to Italy to oppose the Anzio landings.

The Russian assault against the Orel salient to the north of the Kursk bulge, Operation Kutuzov, led by General Marian Popov's Bryansk Front and General Vasily Sokolovsky's West Front, which Zhukov had held off until the most opportune moment, forced Kluge to withdraw four divisions from the spearhead of the Ninth Panzer Army, thereby effectively condemning its chances of breaking through. Zhukov was thus in the enviable position one week into Zitadelle of having blocked Model in the north and slowed Hoth in the south, and so was able to send an elite part of his uncommitted mobile reserve, the 793 tanks of General Pavel Rotmistrov's Fifth Guards Tank Army, into action against XLVIII Panzer Corps and SS-General Paul Hausser's II SS Panzer Corps, which were working their laborious way across the Donets river to the rail junction at Prokhorovka, hoping to outflank Vatutin and find a way to Kursk north-eastwards. The crossing of the Donets by Lieutenant-General Werner Kempf's detachment with two Panzer corps has been described as 'the only element of surprise in the entire operation'.[36] 'Success at Prokhorovka', writes an historian of Zitadelle, 'would ensure the encirclement and destruction of the two main Soviet group-ings in the southern half of the salient and open a new road to Kursk, bypassing the stronghold of Oboyan to the east.'[37]

Yet motoring towards Prokhorovka just as fast as the Germans was Rotmistrov, who vividly recalled the first day of his army's 200-mile drive up to the front line:

It grew hot as early as 08.00 hours and clouds of dust billowed up. By midday the dust rose in thick clouds, settling in a solid layer on roadside bushes, grain fields, tanks and trucks. The dark red disc of the sun was hardly visible through the grey shroud of dust. Tanks, self-propelled guns and tractors (which towed the artillery), armoured personnel carriers and trucks were advancing in an unending flow. The faces of the soldiers were darkened with dust and exhaust fumes. It was intolerably hot. Soldiers were tortured by thirst and their shirts, wet with sweat, stuck to their bodies.[38]

It was about to get an awful lot hotter.

It was the eight-hour tank battle of Prokhorovka on Monday, 12 July that was described by Mellenthin as the 'veritable death ride of the 4th Panzer Army'. The army had begun Zitadelle with 916 mission-capable vehicles, but was down to 530 by 11 July. The II SS Panzer Corps meanwhile had dropped from 470 to about 250. The numbers of tanks involved in the battle of Prokhorovka is a complex historical problem, as sources differ, politics and propaganda become involved, and the geographical extent of the battlefield is disputed, but the best estimate is that 600 Soviet tanks fought 250 German.[39] If one includes the units in the areas of Prokhorovka and Jakovlevo, not all of which saw action that particular day, the numbers swell to 900 German (including about 100 Tigers) versus just under 900 Russian, which does indeed make it the largest tank battle in history.[40] Whereas the Germans had been fighting for a week, found it hard to refuel under fire and were having engineering problems with the Panther tanks' propensity to break down, the Russians were fresh into battle, and as well as T-34/76 tanks they deployed the SU-85, a self-propelled gun with an 85mm armour-busting shell built on the chassis of the T-34. Fighting with one basic make of tank meant spare parts were far easier to find, whereas the Germans had five different types – the Panzers Marks III and IV, the Panther, Ferdinand and Tiger – with all the concomitant supply problems which that implied. Many Panther tanks at Kursk 'went into action belching flame from unproven engine systems', and others broke down with transmission problems.[41] In all, as many as 160 tanks of the Fourth Panzer Army simply broke down on the battlefield, which with German output numbering only 330 tanks a month – much less than the 1,000 Speer had promised the Führer – was disastrous, and a far cry from the much lauded Teutonic industrial miracle of wartime and post-war myth.

A vast dust cloud was flung up by the hundreds of tanks and self-propelled guns on both sides as they clashed head-on at the rail junction at Prokhorovka, a battlefield of only 20 square miles. 'We found ourselves taking on a seemingly inexhaustible mass of enemy armour,' recalled Sergeant Imbolden; 'never have I received such an overwhelming impression of Russian strength and numbers as on that day. The clouds of dust made it difficult to get help from the Luftwaffe, and soon many of the T-34s had broken past our screen and were streaming like rats all over the old battlefield.'[42] The T-34s and some KVs needed to get into close quarters as soon as possible with the larger, more powerful German tanks – especially considering the 88mm gun on the Tiger – and there are accounts of Russian tanks deliberately ramming into German ones.[43] 'Once at close range with scores of machines churning about in individual engagements,' writes John Erickson, 'front and side armour was more easily penetrated, when the tank ammunition would explode, hurling turrets yards away from shattered hulls or sending up great spurts of fire.'[44]

The Luftwaffe failed to support the tanks enough during this vicious, pell-mell, close-quarter battle; indeed, when considering the campaign as a whole one historian has noted that its 'loss of supremacy in the air is as important and interesting as the Wehr-macht's loss of supremacy in armour'.[45] Occasionally almost lunatic bravery was shown by the Russian Air Force: on 6 July, Lieutenant Alexei Gorovets, flying an American Airacobra, single-handedly engaged twenty German aircraft, destroying eight (or possibly nine) before being shot down himself.[46] His impressive memorial can be seen today near the spot where he crashed on the battlefield. In all, the Germans lost 702 planes over the Eastern Front in July and August 1943, a number they could ill afford.

Kursk was the first major engagement where the Russians were able to put up more aircraft than the Luftwaffe, which showed, as with so many other aspects of that battle, the shape of things to come. The Second and Seventeenth Air Armies flew 19,263 sorties from Kursk over the southern sector, in much larger formations than hitherto. One author has subtitled his chapter on the battle 'A New Profession-alism', and in many ways it did exemplify how much the Soviet armed forces had adapted and learnt from the débâcles of 1941.[47] For all that, however, II SS Panzer Corps (comprising the Leibstandarte, Totenkopf and Das Reich Divisions) inflicted more damage than it received in the mêlée at Prokhorovka – indeed the Soviet tank force suffered more than 50 per cent casualties – but by then it did not matter.[48] By the end of the day the Russians had lost around 400 tanks against around 300 German (including 70 Tigers).[49] What was later dubbed the *Prokhorovskoe poboische* (slaughter at Prokhorovka) by Russian propaganda had been mutual, but anything less than a stunning breakthrough was now a disaster for the Germans by that stage of the conflict; pyrrhic victories were of no use to the Reich. The Germans kept possession of the field until ordered to retreat from it, but Zitadelle had clearly completely fizzled out, and the salient was in no danger of being 'pinched out'. The 3rd, 17th and 19th Panzer Divisions started the operation with 450 tanks, and now had barely 100 between them.[50] Like a boxer who has won his last bout on points but is unable to fight another because of the battering he has received, the Wehrmacht was too damaged after Prokhorovka to undertake another major offensive.

Hitler summoned Manstein and Kluge to Rastenburg on 13 July and ordered Zitadelle to be closed down. The Allies had landed in Sicily three days earlier and part of II SS Panzer Corps, including the Leibstandarte Adolf Hitler, needed to be transferred to Italy forthwith. This was easier to order than to carry out, for as Mellenthin put it: 'We are now in the position of a man who has seized a wolf by the ears and dare not let him go.'[51] Kluge, in the words of Liddell Hart, 'had sufficient moral courage to express his views frankly to Hitler, yet he also refrained from pressing his views to the point of being troublesome.'[52] In that he was not unlike a number of German generals, who knew that there were always many well-qualified men eager to take their places.

Manstein believed that, since Zhukov had now committed his mobile reserves in the shape of the Fifth Guards Tank Army, the offensive should be carried on, but he was overruled by Hitler. By 23 July, Army Group South – weakened by the loss of the Grossdeutschland Division being sent to Kluge – had been forced back to its starting lines for Operation Zitadelle.[53] Konev's fresh Steppe Front took over the positions held by the heroic but exhausted Voronezh

35. General Sir William Slim inspects a captured Japanese sword in Burma in 1944.

6. Major General Orde Wingate, whom
n described as a 'strange, excitable, moody
eature, but he had a fire in him. He could
ignite other men'.

37. General Tomoyuki Yamashita, the
brutal but brilliant conqueror of Malaya.

38. General George S.
'Old Blood and Guts'
Patton Jr: tough and
crude, but curiously
sensitive too, on occasion.

39. General Mark Clark (*front seat, le*
got his day of glory liberating Rome o
5 June 1944, but at great strategic cos

40. D-Day: Piper Bill Millin of the 1st Special Service Brigade of the British Second Army prepares to disembark on Sword Beach at 08.40 hours on 6 June. Their commander, Brigadier Lord Lovat DSO MC, can be seen wading through the water to the right of his column of men.

41. The longest day: American troops pinned down behind anti-tank obstacles on Omaha Beach.

42. Mussolini takes his leave of Hitler, Göring and Ribbentrop two days after Colonel von Stauffenberg's 20 July 1944 Bomb Plot explosion at the Wolfsschanze in East Prussia. Hitler right arm had been slightly injured in the blast, hence his shaking the Duce's hand with his l

43. General Dwight D. Eisenhower, Supreme Commander of the Allied Expeditionary Forc pointing the way forward to an American officer and General Montgomery in 1944. 'Ike' was loved by his men, but could also keep his commanders' egos under control.

4. Over the top: Russian infantry charge out of a trench in Belorussia during Operation gration, the massive Soviet assault launched on 22 June 1944 which resulted in 381,000 Germans killed, 158,000 captured and the destruction of Army Group Centre.

5. The Ardennes Offensive: American troops crouching in snowy woods near Amonines n Belgium in December 1944 during the great German counter-attack they dubbed the Battle of the Bulge.

46. The aftermath of the Allied bombing of Dresden, on the night of 13/14 February 194

47. Field Marshal Sir Alan Brooke, the Chief of the Imperial General Staff (behind the gu
General Sir Miles Dempsey, commander of the 2nd Army, and an ebullient Winston Churc
cross the Rhine in an amphibious vehicle on 25 March 1945.

48. Red Army troops ride on a T-34/85 tank towards Berlin, April 1945.

Marshal Georgi Zhukov – 'the man who
⁃at Hitler' – enters Berlin in May 1945.

50. Marshal Ivan Konev: tough peasant
soldier and fanatical Communist who
became one of the great commanders of
the war.

51. The city obliterated: Nagasaki after the atomic bomb dropped on 9 August 1945. Note the bridge that lay directly under the epicentre of the blast.

52. Japan's Foreign Minister Mamoru Shigemitsu and Gene Yoshijiro Umezu, the Chief of Imperial Japanese Army Gener Staff, finally surrender aboard the battleship USS *Missouri* on 2 September 1945, six years and a day after the outbreak of the second world war.

Front on 3 August, and confused tactical fighting took place until 17 August, with the Germans withdrawing to the Hagen Line across the base of the Orel salient in the north and the Soviets pushing on in the south to recapture Kharkov – the most fought-over city in the Soviet Union – which fell on 23 August when Manstein finally abandoned it (against Hitler's orders) and fell back to the Dnieper river.[54] Four distinct and bloody battles over one city emphasizes the nature of war on the Eastern Front, and by the time of Kharkov's last fall the Voronezh and Steppe Fronts had suffered over 250,000 casualties.[55] This places in stark perspective the battles that were taking place in Sicily at the time, which were all puny by comparison.

In a war of men and machines, the Russians were out-producing the Germans in both. German, Hungarian, Italian and Czech factories produced a total – when added to the tanks captured in France – of 53,187 tanks and self-propelled guns of all kinds throughout the war, whereas between 1941 and 1945 the USSR produced 58,681 T-34s alone, 3,500 IS-2s (which had a 122mm cannon with a 2.5-kilometre accurate range) and 3,500 SU-100 self-propelled guns, not including the KV range of tanks. By 1943 the Russians were also turning out huge numbers of the excellent 122mm M-30 howitzers, and their standard hand grenade was as good as Germany's M-24 classic stick grenade, which had not undergone any major improvement since 1924.

The Russian performance at Kursk, especially in the area of co-operation between different arms, brought the losses down to tolerable levels (albeit still much higher than the German). It created a new military theory and ethos for Russia, one that afforded her a glimpse of victory. The casualty rate at Kursk was half that of the Moscow battles of late 1941, and the rates for 1944 were to be one-quarter of it. 'The reconstruction of an almost entirely new army on the ruins of the collapse of 1941', reckons Richard Overy, 'ranks as the most remarkable achievement of the war.'[56] The Soviets had combined their arms, applied new techniques to offensive operations, exploited successes quickly and learnt how to defeat Blitzkrieg. They were still losing more men than the Germans, it was true, but they had reduced the ratio to three for two, at which proportion it was to stay until the end of the war. As a result, 'German defeat simply became a matter of blood and time.'[57] The Germans had little of either; the Russians now had plenty of both.

In the two months of fighting at Kursk, it is estimated that the Germans lost half a million men killed, wounded, taken prisoner or missing, as well as 3,000 tanks, 1,000 guns, 5,000 motor vehicles and 1,400 planes.[58] Soviet losses were half as heavy again, at three-quarters of a million men, but the German retreat from Prokhorovka meant that it was a defeat, since the Russian population and levels of production ensured that the USSR could absorb the losses in a way that the Reich no longer could. Konev was thus right to describe Kursk as 'the swan-song of the German armoured force'.[59]

A growing problem for the Germans was getting matériel to the front line. By the end of 1942 the pro-Soviet partisans – hitherto almost ignored by the Stavka – were being supplied with officers, mine-experts and engineers, who were parachuted in to them with orders to disrupt the German lines of communication. With thousands of miles of railway track between German factories and regimental depots deep inside Russia, the partisans were able to cause massive dislocation of supplies. They meanwhile invented instruments which could adjust Russian machine-gun barrels to the size of captured German ammunition, and special steel bars that could be welded on to railway tracks in order to derail trains, examples of which can be seen in the Armed Forces Museum in Moscow today. In the month of June 1943, against Army Group Centre alone, partisans blew up forty-four railway bridges, damaged 298 locomotives and 1,233 wagons and disrupted rail traffic 746 times.[60] This had severely hampered the Germans' ability to reinforce their fronts just prior to Kursk, and afterwards it was to get much worse, despite the extremely harsh German reprisals against local populations. By contrast, Russian matériel was flooding into the Red Army by 1943. That calendar year the Soviets produced 24,000 tanks, twice the number of Germany, and the firepower they deployed in the Kursk salient that summer underlined their immense achievement in taking losses but surviving them and replenishing their numbers.[61] They had 3,800 tanks when the German attack began on 5 July, and were down to 1,500 when it was called off on 13 July, yet by 3 August the Red Army was up to 2,750 in that sector.

The outcome of the battle of Kursk was superb for Russian morale, and correspondingly bad for German. Zhukov and the Stavka had timed and placed their counter-punch perfectly. German invincibility had been shown to be a myth at Stalingrad, but at Kursk the Russians turned back a fifty-division, full-scale attack. Not only had the Germans shown that they were capable of losing the war, but just as crucially the Russians had demonstrated that they – despite their appalling losses of experienced combat commanders – were developing the tactics necessary to win it. Zhukov's strategy in the immediate aftermath of Kursk of not over-extending a counter-attack so much as to invite a counter-counter-attack is still taught in military colleges as a model example. 'The three immense battles of Kursk, Orel and Kharkov, all in the space of two months,' wrote Churchill, 'heralded the downfall of the German army on the Eastern Front.' Germany had lost the initiative on by far the most important front of the war, and was never to regain it. Intelligent Germans, and even some not so intelligent ones such as Keitel, recognized that the war in the east could not now be won. On the walls of the Hall of Glory in the Museum of the Great Patriotic War in Moscow there are the names of no fewer than 11,695 Heroes of the Soviet Union, winners of the Red Star medal.

Rumours about what was happening to Russian POWs in German captivity had percolated back to the Red Army, were sedulously spread by Soviet propaganda and left the Russian soldiers understandably disinclined to surrender whatever the circumstances. This was yet another example of how Nazi fanaticism actually weakened Germany's military position.

To visit the battlefield of Prokhorovka today, and see the furthest point that the German armour reached on their final great offensive on the Eastern Front – the last gasp of Nazi aggression, as it were, before the Reich was turned on to the defensive – is a profoundly moving experience. These undulating fields saw the furthest expansion that Hitler ever achieved in his dreams of world conquest. Its forces having been turned back at Moscow, then defeated at Stalingrad, for Nazism Prokhorovka was the beginning of the end. The bell atop a tall campanile that today tolls six times every twenty minutes on those windy flat cornfields effectively tolled the death knell of Operation

Zitadelle. OKW hoped Kursk would be a turning point for them, but on the battlefield of Prokhorovka – although the Russians lost more men and machines than the Germans – history failed to turn.

14

The Cruel Reality

1939–1945

From the flak tower, the air raids on Berlin were an unforget-
table sight, and I had constantly to remind myself of the cruel
reality in order not to be completely entranced by the scene:
the illumination of the parachute flares ... followed by the
flashes of explosions which were caught by the clouds of
smoke, the innumerable probing searchlights, the excitement
when a plane was caught and tried to escape the cone of light,
the brief flaming torch when it was hit. No doubt about it,
this apocalypse provided a magnificent spectacle.

Albert Speer, *Inside the Third Reich*, 1970[1]

Along with the decision to use nuclear weapons against Japan, the
most controversial aspect of the Allies' war has been the area, strategic
or – more emotively – carpet or terror bombing of German cities and
civilians. For most in the west at the time it was considered a perfectly
legitimate way to bring a satanic enemy to its knees once Total War
had been unleashed by Hitler, but for some – especially after the war
had been safely won – it was a morally unacceptable war crime.
This chapter will seek to establish simply whether or not it worked
strategically, whether it was necessary and whether there was any
alternative.[2]

Proponents of air doctrine in the bomber wings of the German,
British and American air forces in the 1920s and 1930s all believed
that it was possible to win wars through bombing alone, with navies
relegated to a blockading role and armies primarily used for mopping
up and occupation. 'It is well also for the man in the street to realize

that there is no power on earth that can protect him from being bombed,' the former and future British Prime Minister Stanley Baldwin, then lord president of the council, told the House of Commons in November 1932. 'Whatever people might tell him, the bomber will always get through.'[3] He spoke before the invention of radar, the Spitfire and the mass-production of the 4.5-inch anti-aircraft gun, but the message certainly got through so that by 1939 it was assumed that general aerial bombardment would lead to massacre and the breakdown of civilization.

When war broke out, the Luftwaffe's bombing of Warsaw in September 1939 and of Rotterdam and Louvain in May 1940 made it clear that Germany did not intend to abide by the 'civilized' view of warfare that confined targets to military assets attacked in daylight. Further raids on Coventry (on 15 November 1940), Belgrade (in April 1941, when 17,000 people were killed), Hull and even unarmed beauty spots like Bath (where more than 400 people died over three nights in April 1942) confirmed this. As the Luftwaffe bomber General Werner Baumbach later recalled: 'Hitler talked about "extirpating" the English towns, and propaganda coined the word "coventrizing" for the maximum degree of destruction which was deemed to have been inflicted on Germany.'[4] Yet simply because the Nazis had adopted ruthless methods of warfare, it did not follow that their foes ought to have as well.

The RAF's Bomber Command was founded in 1936, based in High Wycombe in Buckinghamshire and at the outbreak of war it consisted of thirty-three squadrons comprising 488 aircraft. Initially these were planes with too short a flying range to reach even the Ruhr industrial basin – the closest German targets worth bombing – and with bomb-loads too small to cause much damage even if they had managed to get there and back. Even worse, in the words of Richard Overy:

There were no effective bomb-sights; there were few bombs bigger than 250 pounds; only a handful of bases in Britain could handle the larger aircraft; and there was even a shortage of maps for navigating in north-west Europe. Bombing trials betrayed a wide margin of inaccuracy even when bombing in bright sunlight from a few thousand feet with no enemy interference.[5]

It was an unpromising start from which to try to force the Third Reich to its knees. With a general lack of navigational aids, target-marking and aiming equipment and carrying capacity, Bomber Command was initially forced into the strategy of attacking cities, effectively through the lack of a realistic alternative. After a raid on Berlin in which most of the bombs fell on farms in the surrounding countryside, rather than on the capital itself, Berliners joked: 'Now they are trying to starve us out!'

Once Bomber Command had suffered unacceptably high – sometimes as much as 50 per cent – losses in daylight raids on largely coastal targets such as Heligoland and Wilhelmshaven at the start of the war, it switched to night-time bombing instead, with a serious reduction in accuracy. Bomber Command pilots had not expected or been intensively trained for night-bombing, and the navigational aids were basic, yet after victory was won in the battle of Britain in the autumn of 1940 the emphasis turned from Fighter Command defence to Bomber Command attack. By then an altogether more offensively minded Churchill had replaced Chamberlain, whose government had even discouraged the bombing of Germany's Black Forest on the ground that 'so much of it was private property'.[6] The bombing of Germany – even if inaccurate and at night – gave an immense morale boost to Britons, who felt that they were at last taking the war directly to the enemy. There was also a tangible sense that after Dunkirk and the battle of Britain the bombing offensive was the only possible way for Britain to show that she was still in the war and keen to continue to fight.

While Bomber Command did attempt throughout the war to pinpoint specific German production facilities for bombing – never devoting less than 30 per cent of bombing efforts to those types of targets – in a short space of time the general policy widened to destroying huge, heavily populated industrial areas in order to 'de-house' the workers, dislocate production and demoralize the population. The Commander-in-Chief of Bomber Command, Air Chief Marshal Sir Arthur 'Bomber', 'Bert' or 'Butch' Harris, was convinced that the policy he had inherited when he took over in February 1942 could win the war. In the words of one historian, 'four years of arms production had given Britain the four-engined heavy bombers . . . and little else with which to fight ... Counter-city strategy was his only option if Britain, unable to face the disaster that might ensue from invading a defended Europe with inferior forces, and under attack in Africa and threat in the Far East, was to show any signs of fighting at all.'[7] Harris tended to decry precision attacks on individual industries such as ball-bearing or synthetic-oil factories, as favoured by the Americans, dismissing them as 'panacea targets' in the belief that the Germans could perfectly well compensate through dispersed production, alternative technologies, foreign purchases and stockpiling. While he was right to take this stance at the beginning of the war, when few bombs came close to landing on their targets, advancing technology meant that by the end of the war he was starting to be proved wrong. Yet he was not overruled when he continued to pursue his strategy.

De-housing certainly had an effect on Germany's industrial production because, as one study has concluded, in many cases after a raid 'workers did not turn up for work as they were either looking after their families, or physically could not reach their workplaces. Many left the devastated city for the countryside, where food was more available, and stayed with relatives.'[8] In the BMW factory in Munich, for example, some 20 per cent of the workforce were absent in the summer of 1944, and in the same year absenteeism rose to 25 per cent in the Ford plant in Cologne and the Ruhr.[9] In 1939 Göring had addressed the Luftwaffe, saying: 'No enemy bomber can reach the Ruhr. If one reaches the Ruhr, my name is not Göring. You can call me Meyer.' (They did not, at least not to his face.)

The distinction between area and precision bombing was often blurred by the fact that German armaments, ball-bearing and synthetic-oil factories, as well as submarine dockyards, railway marshalling yards and other targets deemed morally acceptable by post-war armchair strategists, were very often located in built-up areas and near schools, hospitals and the tenement housing of their workers. As a senior USAAF officer joked at a post-war seminar, 'The RAF carried out precision attacks on area targets, while the USAAF carried out area attacks on precision targets.'[10] The difference, as the campaign's official historian Noble Frankland discovered, was often marginal. Specially coloured incendiary bombs were used to illuminate and differentiate targets, but photographic evidence showed that many night-dropped bombs in the first two and a half years of war missed their intended targets by thousands of yards. The development of night photographic equipment and post-operational photo-reconnaissance helped ram this point home, but there seemed little genuine alternative at the time.

Harris's personality has long been held up for vilification, with the Labour politician Richard Crossman equating him with the Great War Commander-in-Chief Sir Douglas Haig. The controversy continued; in 1994, there were angry demonstrations when the Queen Mother unveiled a statue of Harris at the RAF church, St Clement Danes in London. In March 1948 the wartime head of the Air Force, Marshal of the RAF Lord Portal, Harris's immediate (indeed only) superior, spoke to the BBC correspondent Chester Wilmot, complaining that 'The trouble with Harris was – off the record – that he was a cad, and would not hesitate to go behind your back to get something he wanted.' Portal believed that, had there ever been a 'showdown' between him and Harris, Portal would have won because 'my hold over the PM was stronger than his'. Portal accused Harris of being 'a limelighter', 'a trouble-maker', 'particularly difficult to control' and – possibly incorrectly in view of Portal's own remarks – 'his own worst enemy'. Portal despised the way that Harris would ring him in the morning to say: 'We had 800 bombers over Munich last night and this morning we've only got two inches in *The Times* and Coastal Command got four. If this sort of thing goes on the morale of Bomber Command will be ruined.'[11]

Harris was unquestionably a tough man, but as the scientist Professor R. V. Jones used to ask: 'Who else could have stood up to what he had to do?'[12] His refusal to indulge in pleasing euphemism – 'kill the Boche, terrify the Boche,' he would say openly – led to his post-war demonization, but he was a loving father and privately a warm individual, kind to his bull-terrier Rastus and popular with both his men and the British public. He was a single-minded individual who thought he knew how to shorten the war, and a realist who despised cant about what his airmen were doing night after night. He also had a sharp tongue, asking civil servants, 'What are you doing to retard the war effort today?' and telling Air Chief Marshal Sir Trafford Leigh-Mallory, who had complained before D-Day that he didn't want to go down to posterity as the killer of thousands of Frenchmen: 'What makes you think you're going to go down to posterity at all?'[13] Certainly Harris had absolutely no moral qualms about what he was doing to the Germans, telling the newsreels in 1942: 'They sowed the wind and now they are going to reap the whirlwind. There are a lot of people who say that bombing can never win a war. Well, my answer to that is that it has never been tried yet, and we shall see.'[14] Yet he was not a monster, and two days after VE Day he wrote to Portal to say: 'I regret indeed occasions on which I have been crotchety and impatient. I was the closest to the urgencies of my command, and, frankly, borne down by the frightful inhumanities of war.'[15]

By the end of 1941 Bomber Command had dropped 45,000 tons of bombs over military targets in Germany, though without much to show for it. One reason why the High Command put so many resources into the bombing offensive was to try to help the Russians. Churchill and Roosevelt were very conscious of not doing enough for the USSR – a feeling Stalin sedulously encouraged – operationally in the west. When the British Commonwealth was fighting twelve Axis divisions at El Alamein, as we have seen, the Russians were engaging 186 on the Eastern Front. The postponing of the so-called Second Front attack in north-west France led to a powerful desire to help draw off German forces elsewhere, and the bomber offensive was thought to be one way of doing that which did not involve an over-hasty return of ground troops to France. Rather like the Arctic convoys to Murmansk, the bombing offensive was conceived almost as a kind of displacement therapy. In the end, helping Russia was indeed to be its chief value to the war effort.

The losses suffered by Bomber Command were monstrous. Soon after taking over, Harris ordered the bombing in March and April 1942 of the ports of Lübeck and Rostock, which were badly damaged for the loss of only twenty-four aircraft, but overall Bomber Command lost 150 aircraft in the month of April alone. No fewer than 55,573 members of Bomber Command lost their lives during the Second World War, 47,268 on operations, but a further 8,305 on training and other non-combatant missions, representing in all one-quarter of all British military dead. Out of 199,091 Bomber Command aircraft despatched on raids during the war, 6,440 (or 3.2 per cent) failed to return.[16] The death toll was roughly the same number as British officers killed in the Great War or American soldiers killed in Vietnam, although it represents a far higher attrition rate than either. The USAAF lost 26,000 men, or 12.4 per cent of its bomber crews. The heroism of the men who flew hundreds of miles over many hours in the noisy, dark, cramped, freezing, unpressurized bombers filled with cables and sharp-edged objects, being fired at by anti-aircraft flak and attacked by fighter aircraft, was immeasurable. Often defensive action could not be taken against flak over the targets, as the bombardiers (or bomb aimers) needed a steady platform to achieve accuracy.

Germany had 50,000 anti-aircraft guns protecting the Reich. Mid-air explosions, collisions and crash-landings were usually lethal, sitting as close as the air crew were to hundreds of gallons of high-octane fuel and tons of high explosive. Fighters could come from any angle, were always far faster than the bombers and could often see their prey caught in searchlights below or by flares above the bombers. The RAF's Cyril March vividly recalled what it was like in his Avro Lancaster on the way to bombing Böhlen when 'suddenly a string of flares lit up above us, lightening the sky into daylight . . . they continued until there was a double row for miles on our track. We knew fighters were dropping them, but where were they, behind, above or below the flares? Our eyes must have been like saucers looking for them. It was like walking down a well-lit road in the nude.'[17]

One of the only defences the pilot of a heavy bomber had against the attentions of a fighter coming from astern was to corkscrew the plane into a 300mph diving turn that the fighter could not follow, before dragging it up sharply in the other direction. 'It was a testament to the strength and aerodynamic qualities of the heavies that they could be thrown about the sky with a violence that, if they were lucky, could shake off their smaller, nimbler pursuers long enough to escape into the darkness beyond the fighter's limited onboard radar range.'[18]

Bullet-holes through fuel tanks could lead to disastrous leakages, and air crew were often lynched on the ground – as 'pirate-pilots' in Hitler's phrase – by German civilians, always supposing they managed to use their parachutes. On returning to base, ball-turret gunners under the planes were sometimes crushed to death when mechanical malfunctions trapped them inside their plastic cages and the planes' wheels could not be lowered owing to damaged electrical systems.[19] Horror and heroism were in abundant supply, with no fewer than nineteen Victoria Crosses being won by Bomber Command in the course of the war.

An indication of the amount of time spent in the air on operations can be seen from the flight logbook of an Avro Lancaster rear-gunner, Bruce Wyllie, who served in Bomber Command's 57 Squadron based in East Kirkby in Lincolnshire. The twenty-two-year-old Wyllie's first operation was none other than the Dresden raid of 13 February 1945, which involved a 10¼-hour round-journey. The very next night he bombed Rositz (9 hours 50 minutes), then on 19 February Böhlen (8 hours 25 minutes), then the following night Mittland (6 hours 50 minutes), and on 24 February he took part in the daylight bombing of Ladbergen, which took 4 hours 50 minutes.[20] In the space of only eleven days, therefore, this young Bomber Command 'tail-end Charlie', as rear-gunners were nicknamed – whose service record has been chosen entirely at random – took part in no fewer than five operations totalling over forty hours' flying time. On top of nearly sixteen hours' daytime and six hours' night-time training flights since 3 February 1945, Wyllie was in the air an average of nearly three hours a day for three weeks, with about two-thirds of that time spent in mortal danger. Wyllie and the 125,000 members of Bomber Command who volunteered for active service, 44.4 per cent of whom died on it, were truly heroic.

In 1942 fewer than half of all heavy-bomber crews survived the thirty sorties required of their first tour of duty, and only one in five of those made it through their second. By 1943 the odds had shortened yet further: only one in six survived the first tour, and one in forty a second. The crews were self-selecting and built up intense bonds of comradeship living in the flat eastern counties of East Anglia, Yorkshire and Lincolnshire, and surprisingly few of them claimed mechanical failure or ditched their bombs on suburbs before reaching the target (the so-called fringe merchants).

The heavy losses in Bomber Command led to Churchill calling for press censorship in the War Cabinet on 21 September 1942. After Portal had given an extensive summary of the war in the air, the Prime Minister was recorded as arguing that 'losses of bombers continue to be announced. Enormous convenience to Germany. Say we've done it for a long time but since it's a great advantage to enemy after such and such a date we'll not do it any more.'[21] He didn't mind the RAF knowing the figures, and would tell the House of Commons in secret sessions, but he didn't see why the totals should be announced after each raid. Yet such was the commitment to press freedom, BBC independence and free speech as cornerstones of what Britain was fighting for, that the Cabinet preferred to rely on responsible self-censorship by news organizations rather than impose control centrally. For the most part their trust was justified, and information did not tend to be broadcast that was of use to the enemy, in terms either of morale or of operations.

The bombing offensive had its opponents within the British High Command, not simply because of its high cost in air crew but also because the resources it took up were enormous, and many strategists thought these could be better employed elsewhere, specifically in the immediate support of military operations on land and sea. On 15 February 1942 – the day that Singapore fell – for example, the Director of Military Operations at the War Office, Major-General John Kennedy, recommended simply ending the bombing of Germany and instead using the planes this freed up 'for essential air reinforcement' in Ceylon, Burma, Australia, New Zealand, India and the eastern Mediterranean. He considered the bombing campaign against Germany to be 'ineffective and ... beyond our means'.[22] A month later on 12 March there was a major allocations debate in the War Cabinet's Defence Committee, chaired by Churchill, which was summed up (with evident bias) by Kennedy: 'The Air Ministry want to go on with their main bombing policy and leave the other services, particularly the Army, in their present lamentable state.' At no stage did Kennedy, Brooke or anyone else in the decision-making reaches of the High Command ever employ humanitarian considerations among their reasons for why the aerial bombardment policy was mistaken. Brooke's fear was that by diverting resources, raw materials (especially iron and steel), money, manpower and fuel on such a huge scale for the bombing offensive over Germany, the RAF was denuding equally worthwhile causes, such as tank production. If bombers were to be produced in such large quantities, he and others also thought, then more ought to be used against U-boats in the battle of the Atlantic and against Rommel in North Africa rather than in just bombing German cities night after night. That said, nearly one-third of all German ships sunk in European waters were by mines laid by plane.

The first two significant heavy bombers used early in the war, the Short Stirling and Avro Manchester, were rather sub-standard aircraft; certainly neither was as good as the pre-war medium two-engined Vickers Wellington, which was the major aircraft used in the first Thousand-Bomber Raid, launched against Cologne on the night of Saturday, 30 May 1942. The Handley Page Halifax provided some good service, but in the last six months of 1942 the Avro Lancaster became fully operational, which enormously increased the RAF's bombing power and range. By the end of the war sixty out of Bomber Command's eighty squadrons flew these sturdy giants. In ninety minutes over Cologne, 1,046 planes – including trainee crews roped in to make up the talismanic four-figure number – dropped 1,455 tons of high explosive and 915 tons of incendiary bombs, destroying thirty-six factories, killing 500 civilians and injuring 5,000. Some 45,000 civilians were also made homeless.[23] As only forty-one planes, in the phrase of the day, 'failed to return', it was considered a tremendous success and trumpeted as such in the press. *The Times*, with pardonable inaccuracy, thundered, 'Biggest Air Attack of the War. 2,000 Tons of Bombs in 40 Minutes' and posters were produced with the caption: 'British Bombers Now Attack Germany a Thousand at a Time!', so popular was the campaign with the public. It was popular with Churchill too: on 1 June he told the War Cabinet that he congratulated Portal and Harris on the fact that 'over a thousand [bombers] left this island and almost as many go tonight – Great manifestation of air power. The United States like it very much. Give us bigger action early next month.'[24] Eleven days after the Cologne raid, Harris was knighted.

Albert Speer and the Director of Air Armament, Field Marshal Erhard Milch, met Hermann Göring at his Veldenstein Castle in Franconia the morning after the raid on Cologne. They heard Göring being put through on the telephone to the city's Gauleiter, Joseph Grohé, and telling him: 'The report from your police commissioner is a stinking lie! I tell you as the Reichsmarschall that the figures cited are simply too high. How can you dare report such fantasies to the Führer!' He insisted that the number of incendiary bombs reported was 'many times too high. All wrong!' and demanded that a new one be sent to Hitler which agreed with his own, much lower estimates. After this rant he showed Speer and Milch – who knew the truth as well as he did – around the Castle, pointing out the 'magnificent citadel' he intended to build there. 'But first of all he wanted to have a reliable air-raid shelter built,' noted Speer. 'The plans for that were already drawn up.'[25] Göring certainly did not want to be on the receiving end of what had apparently not just happened to Cologne.

The US Eighth Air Force started its major daylight bombing campaign on 17 August 1942, using twelve 1,200hp-engined Boeing B-17 Flying Fortresses to attack Rouen's railway marshalling yards. The raid was led by Brigadier-General Ira C. Eaker flying Yankee Doodle and in-cluded Major Paul W. Tibbets Jr, who was later to fly the B-29 which dropped the atomic bomb on Hiroshima. Planes could fly much closer together in daylight, and could thus protect each other better. The system whereby the British bombed at night and the Americans during the day meant that the Germans had no respite round the clock, with all the greatly increased worry, fear, exhaustion and trauma that that implied. French targets, where fighter cover could be provided, proved easier than the more distant German ones, where it could not always be. Despite their having formidable defences which were constantly being improved – rising to a total of thirteen 0.5-inch machine guns in the B-17G model which bombed Berlin in March 1944 – the Flying Fortresses were in constant danger from German fighters. Nonetheless the B-17G could fly at 287mph at 25,000 feet and carry 3 tons of bombs up to 2,000 miles. Its gunners were protected against sub-zero temperatures with electrically heated boots and gloves, and wore 'flak aprons' of manganese steel squares for protection.

After serious initial disagreements over the prioritization of targets, the Casablanca Conference of January 1943 envisaged the un-ambiguously codenamed Operation Pointblank, a joint bombing pro-gramme designed to intensify 'the heaviest possible bombing offensive against the German war effort', to be known as the Combined Bomber

Offensive (CBO).[26] This established the priority targets as (in descending order): Germany's U-boat pens, her aircraft industry, railways and roads, her oil industry and then other targets such as Berlin, north Italian industry and warships in harbour. General Eaker, who took over Eighth Air Force from General Carl 'Tooey' Spaatz in December 1942, assumed that this meant precision bombing would also be adopted by the RAF, but Portal and Harris continued to pursue their policy of night-time area bombing of the Ruhr, Berlin and other major cities. The directive was ambiguous, in that it was clearly necessary to bomb cities in order to bring about what the Combined Chiefs of Staff ordered should be 'the progressive destruction and dislocation of the German military, industrial and economic system, and the undermining of the morale of the German people to a point where their capacity for armed resistance is fatally weakened'.[27] That could not be achieved by precision attacks on ball-bearing and synthetic-oil factories, Portal and Harris argued, and could clearly only be done by the kind of bombing they were already pursuing. The Chiefs of Staff were ready to will the end and provide the means; they ought therefore to be fully included in the denunciations that have instead been concentrated almost solely on Harris.

Attacks on the U-boat yards at Lorient and Brest were regularly made in force after Casablanca, without inflicting any worthwhile damage on the massive reinforced concrete submarine pens. Once Dönitz withdrew from the Atlantic in May 1943, this first priority fell further down the list. At the Trident Conference in Washington that month, Pointblank was redefined to concentrate more on the destruction of the Luftwaffe's fighter arm in the air, on the ground and in production, as this was 'essential to our progression to the attack of other sources of the enemy war potential'.[28] Yet for all that the Combined Chiefs might want precision attacks, which the Fifteenth Air Force did undertake from the Foggia air bases in Italy later that year, Harris was given enough leeway to continue with the general area bombing that he fervently believed would bring victory soonest. If the High Command, including Churchill, Brooke and Portal, who all complained privately about Harris, had wanted to pursue precision bombing, they could have simply ordered him to alter his targeting policy, to the point of sacking him if he refused. They did not.

Bomber Command certainly did hit precision targets, such as the rocket factories at Peenemünde in August 1943 and the *Tirpitz* on several occasions from September to November 1944, and on the night of Sunday, 16 May 1943 Wing Commander Guy Gibson's 617 Squadron breached the Möhne and Eder dams of the Ruhr, dropping specially designed bouncing and spinning Upkeep bombs with incredible precision from only 60 feet above the water. As the actor and writer Stephen Fry has said of that raid:

It was about practice, practice, practice (for they knew not what). Then, on the day, it was about the constant monitoring of data – glide paths, magnetic compass deviations, dead reckoning pinpoints, calculations of fuel according to atmosphere and so on. These men were not just beefy brave chaps; they had real brains. Lancasters cannot take off at night in formation and fly low for hundreds of miles, drop an enormous bomb that is spinning at 500 revolutions per minute from exactly the right height and then move on to *another* target before returning home – all the time under fire from enemy anti-aircraft batteries – without a particular kind of steady, unblinking courage, tenacity and will that is out of the ordinary.[29]

The loss of no fewer than eight bombers out of nineteen and fifty-three air crew on the 'Dambusters' raid was a high price to pay, but Churchill was right when he told Harris that 'The conduct of the operations demonstrated the fiery gallant spirit which animated your aircrews, and the high sense of duty of all ranks under your command.'

The bombing of the Ruhr and Hamburg suddenly brought the monthly growth in German armaments production – which had been averaging 5.5 per cent since February 1942 – crashing down to 0 per cent from May 1943 to February 1944.[30] As the leading expert on the Nazi economy records: 'For six months in 1943 the disruption caused by British and American bombing halted Speer's armaments miracle in its tracks. The German home front was rocked by a serious crisis of morale.'[31] Although the Nazi war economy was still producing as much in 1944 as it had in May 1943, indeed production was slightly higher, the miracle that had more than doubled armaments production between February 1942 and May 1943 was over and the all-important rates of increase were never to recover.

Between March 1943 and April 1944 the Krupp factory in the Ruhr lost 20 per cent of production, which was 'far below' what British propaganda was making out at the time, but very significant nonetheless.[32] Yet that was only one site, and overall the results were mixed: in Essen, although 88 per cent of its housing had been destroyed or badly damaged, and 7,000 inhabitants killed, the intensive post-war investigations discovered that production had somehow continued, through German bravery and ingenuity, until March 1945, when it was overrun. At the end of January 1945 Albert Speer found that in 1944 Allied bombing had meant that Germany produced 35 per cent fewer tanks than he had wanted to build and Germany required, as well as 31 per cent fewer aircraft and 42 per cent fewer lorries.[33] In a sense those figures alone justify the Allies' CBO, as we have already seen what the Wehrmacht and Luftwaffe were capable of achieving in counter-attack when they had enough tanks and aircraft.

The debate about strategic bombing has all too often centred on its failure significantly to lessen actual German armaments production, but that is based on a false premise. What the campaign needed to do was to curtail the *rate of increase* in armaments production by which the Germans could have prolonged, or even won, the war, and this it achieved triumphantly, as is shown in Figure 1. The tragic reality was that area as well as precision bombing was necessary to halt Speer's miracle, although by 1944 the RAF ought to have switched to concentrating more on Luftwaffe factories, which could be targeted with a far higher degree of accuracy than in 1940. The estimation that the entire Combined Bomber Offensive of 1944 reduced German gross industrial production by only 10 per cent seems damning, in view of the sacrifice in Allied servicemen's lives, the cost in resources in building the 21,000 bombers that were destroyed and of course the deaths by bombing of around 720,000 German, Italian and French civilians throughout the war.[34] Yet the entire campaign took up only about 7 per cent of Britain's war effort, and so was militarily justified.

In late July and early August 1943, four bombing raids on Hamburg over ten days codenamed Gomorrah led to the deaths of between 30,000 and 50,000 people.[35] On 27 July a navigational error sent 787 RAF planes 2 miles to the east of the intended target, Hamburg's city centre, and over the closely packed tenement buildings of its working population instead. The release of thousands of strips of aluminium

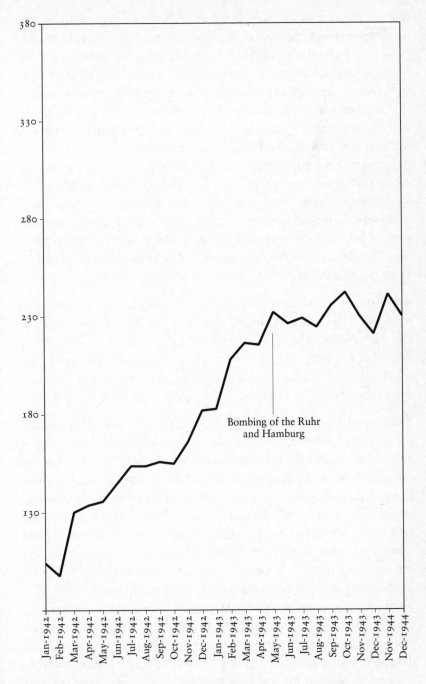

Figure 1: German armament production, 1942–1944 (Jan 1942 = 100)

foil, codenamed Window, blinded the radar on which the German night-fighters and anti-aircraft artillery depended, allowing the raiders more time to do their work. Hamburg had been experiencing a freak heatwave and the hot, dry weather, when combined with the flames from high-explosive and incendiary bombs, created a firestorm inferno that reached 1,600 Celsius and reduced to ashes all in its path. It was said that the orange luminosity from fires that raged, largely unfought, for forty-eight hours could be seen 120 miles away.

The surviving population of 1.8 million fled the city, spreading panic throughout the region. 'Hamburg had put the fear of God in me,' admitted Speer, who predicted to Hitler that 'a series of attacks of this sort, extended to six more major cities, would bring Germany's armaments production to a total halt.' The Führer merely replied: 'You'll straighten all that out again.'[36] Goebbels was as worried as Speer, writing in his diary of the:

most serious consequences both for the civilian population and for armaments production. This attack definitely shatters the illusions that many have had about the continuation of air operations by the enemy. Unfortunately we shot down very few planes – twelve, all told . . . It is a real catastrophe . . . It is believed that new quarters must be found for about 150,000 to 200,000. I don't know at this time of writing how we are going to solve that problem.[37]

Yet six more such attacks proved beyond the capacity of the already overstretched Allies. On 17 August 1943 an Eighth Air Force raid of 376 planes against the ball-bearing factories of Schweinfurt attracted the attentions of 300 German fighters around Frankfurt. Twenty-one Flying Fortresses were shot down before the air armada even reached Schweinfurt, and overall the raid led to the loss of sixty B-17s, 16 per cent of the total, and the damaging of a further 120 (most beyond repair), a further 32 per cent, some of them through air-to-air rocket fire for the first time.[38] On 14 October the Americans bravely, if foolhardily, decided to return to Schweinfurt with nearly 300 bombers, only to suffer yet heavier carnage from rockets, air bombing from above, heavy anti-aircraft fire and then fighter action, with another sixty bombers (20 per cent) destroyed and 138 (46 per cent) damaged. In the aftermath of this defeat, the USAAF was forced to suspend daylight raids until it developed a long-range fighter that could escort its bombers and protect them from German fighters. German ball-bearing production was badly hit – dropping 38 per cent by Speer's estimates after the first raid and 67 per cent after the second – but was made up after a few weeks by using different bearing types, slide rather than ball, and buying in more from the ever helpful (and well-paid) Swedes and Swiss.

By late 1943 the Americans had got their fighter, and began to mass-produce – total production topped 15,500 – the single-seater, 437mph, P-51B Mustang to escort their bombers as far as Berlin and back, and take on anything the Luftwaffe had at the time. Auxiliary fuel tanks that could be jettisoned were the key to flying the long distances, and the fastest version, the P-51H, could reach 487mph. Although Mustangs had been used operationally by the RAF since before America entered the war, by 1944 the constant updating of the prototype (the D model with its bubble canopy was the most recognizable) had produced a plane that could tip the balance of the air war over Germany. Once the Mustangs established dominance over the German skies, shooting down large numbers of Messerschmitts flown by experienced Luftwaffe pilots, thereby allowing Allied bombers to destroy Luftwaffe factories, the next stage was to destroy the synthetic-oil factories without which new German pilots could not even complete their air training.

Even the very existence of these American super-fighters with improved fuel capacity produced a stand-up row between Göring and his Fighter Arm commander General Adolf Galland. After Galland had warned Hitler that the Mustangs would be able to escort American bombers far deeper into German territory than ever before, Göring 'snapped' at him, saying: 'That's nonsense, Galland, what gives you such fantasies? That's pure bluff!' Galland replied: 'Those are the facts, Herr Reichsmarschall! American fighters have been shot down over Aachen. There is no doubt about it!' 'That is simply not true,' retorted Göring. 'That's impossible.' When Galland suggested that he inspect the wreckages for himself, Göring replied that they might have glided 'quite a distance further before they crashed'. Galland then pointed out that the planes would hardly have glided further into the Reich, as opposed to away from it, whereupon Göring left the meeting on his special train, saying: 'I officially assert that the American fighter planes did not reach Aachen.' Galland's reply was simply: 'Orders are orders, sir!'[39]

The Mustang would have faced a mighty competitor, however, if Hitler had concentrated on producing the twin-engine Messerschmitt Me-262, which has been described as 'the plane with which the German air force could have reclaimed the skies over Germany'.[40] The speed of this jet-powered fighter, along with its relative stability in flight, suggests that it offered the best possibility 'of Germany driving the Allied bombers out of the sky'. Hitler saw the Me-262 for the first time at Insterburg airfield after the Berlin raids of late November 1943, in the company of Göring, Milch, Speer, the warplane designer and manufacturer Willy Messerschmitt, Galland and others, and his Luftwaffe adjutant Nicolaus von Below. (Below was a devout Nazi until his death in 1983, and his recollections of working beside Hitler between 1937 and 1945 provide an invaluable and reliable source for historians.[41] He was a Christian Prussian from an old Junker soldiering family, thus personifying an entire menagerie of Hitler's *bêtes noires*, but he and his wife Maria loved the Führer, and Maria was also close to his girlfriend Eva Braun.) At the Insterburg meeting, Below recorded, Hitler 'called Messerschmitt over and asked him pointedly if the aircraft could be built as a bomber. The designer agreed, and said that it would be capable of carrying two 250kg bombs.' Hitler replied, 'That is the fast bomber,' and insisted on its being developed as such exclusively, rather than as a fighter. He saw it as part of the campaign against London and the southern English invasion ports, rather than as a fighter that could protect Germany from the Allied bombing offensive. Yet the conversion and the development of new bombing mechanisms took up valuable production time, while the acquisition of bomb-loads drastically slowed down the plane's top speeds. Hitler saw it as a new Stuka, rather than an entirely new kind of warplane, which potentially it was.

As a result of German air production being dispersed into smaller units, and the alterations Hitler had ordered, the Me-262 did not arrive until March 1944, and even then in numbers that were far too small to make a difference. With the Americans' destruction of oil facilities and Luftwaffe targets, the Reich did not have the fuel to train the pilots, and many brand-new models were destroyed on the ground anyway. A similarly promising warplane project, the Arado 234, which could reach speeds of 500mph, saw only 200 produced before the Red Army captured the factory where its production had been moved to in the east, for fear of bombing from the west.[42]

After the big raids of late 1943, Albert Speer drove around the factory districts of Berlin. Buildings were still burning and a cloud of smoke 20,000 feet high hung above the city, which 'made the macabre scene as dark as night'. When he tried to describe this to Hitler, he was interrupted every time, almost as soon as he began, with questions about, for example, the next month's tank production figures.[43] By the end of that year the Allies had dropped 200,000 tons of bombs on Germany.[44] Their effect in at least blunting the rate of increase in aircraft production can be seen in Figure 2.

The word Nuremberg meant many things in the relatively short period covered by the Nazi experiment. Originally it denoted the vast rallies held there in the late 1930s, then the anti-Semitic Nuremberg Laws, then a city that was devastated by Allied bombing, and finally the place where the International Military Tribunal brought the worst of the surviving Nazis to justice.[45] On the night of 30 March 1944, some 795 Allied aircraft devastated the city centre, but at very serious loss – including 109 Canadians – with ninety-five aircraft shot down and seventy-one damaged. After this reversal, the policy of heavy night-time raids on Germany was suspended, which was due to happen anyway in order to help prepare for the invasion of Normandy.

Although the Germans did manage to jam the Allies' Gee radio-based navigational device after its introduction in March 1942, improved technologies such as Oboe, by which a control station in Britain could broadcast a radar beam that would lead Pathfinder bombers to the target, were operational from November 1942, and by the end of 1943 airborne H2X radar sets were guiding USAAF daylight bombers to enemy targets in all weathers. Pathfinder target-making squadrons (later No. 8 Group), the *corps d'élite* of Bomber Command, had been founded in July 1942, their specially selected crews identifying and marking the targets. Pathfinders' tour of duty expired only after forty-five 'straight-through' operational sorties,

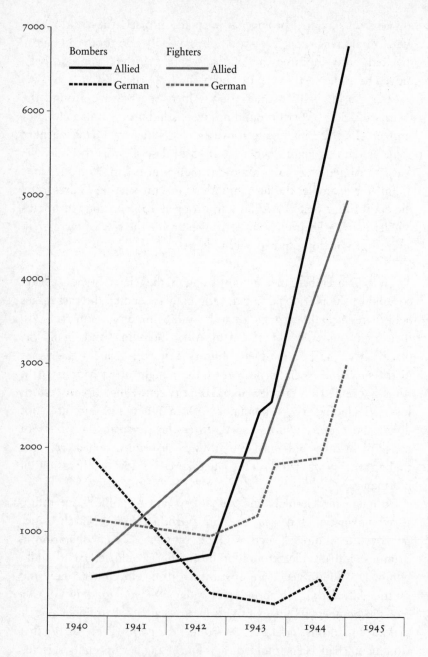

Figure 2: Allied and German aircraft production, 1940–1945

and the bravest of the brave were the crews of the master bombers, who flew the aircraft that led the entire attack. These men determined the accuracy of the target indicators that had been dropped by the primary visual markers, and decided what further illumination was required. They would tell the rest of the force which colour markers to bomb and which to ignore, sometimes flying over the target area for more than an hour.[46]

The policy on bombing Germany and her allies also affected – some said skewed – grand strategy. A principal argument for landing on mainland Italy, besides capturing Rome, tying down eighteen German divisions and keeping Allied forces occupied with a successful land campaign prior to D-Day, was to capture the Foggia air bases in eastern Italy from where southern European targets could be more easily bombed than from England and Sicily. On 28 September 1943, General George Marshall wrote to President Roosevelt to explain that 'The fall of Foggia has come exactly at the time when it is needed to complement our Bomber Offensive now hammering Germany from bases in the UK. As winter sets in over northern Europe, our heavy bombers operating from the dozen or more (13) air bases in the Foggia Area will strike again and again at the heart of German production, not only in Germany proper but in Austria, Hungary and Romania. For our bombers operating from England, this aerial "Second Front" will be a great assistance.'[47]

Differences between the RAF and USAAF emerged occasionally, but not to the extent that they affected operations. On 1 November 1943 Trafford Leigh-Mallory, reporting from Washington, indeed writing on USAAF HQ paper, told Charles Portal about a lunch he had had with the Chief of the US Air Staff, Henry 'Hap' Arnold. After registering his shock at the way 'We were waited on by two Negro servants before whom matters of the highest secrecy were freely discussed,' Leigh-Mallory reported that Arnold could not understand why with air superiority the RAF had not destroyed the Luftwaffe in France. 'I managed to keep my temper and explain to General Arnold how air operations are carried out and how the German Air Force fights.' Arnold claimed that the British figures were 'hopelessly inaccurate', and 'also delivered a tirade against the short range of the Spitfire, and seemed to think we lacked vision in the design of our fighters and were not alive to the developments of the war. I did my best to overcome this prejudiced outlook.'[48]

The very next day Air Marshal Sir William Welsh also wrote to Portal, this time from the British Joint Staff Mission in Washington: 'I feel sure that the fundamental misunderstanding between us and the Americans is the constant feeling in their minds that they are always "outsmarted" by us and that we do not recognise what a great country theirs is.' Roosevelt's closest confidant Harry Hopkins had dinner with Welsh and spoke about Arnold, explaining that he 'was not a great staff officer or strategist, that he was lost when dealing with the Chiefs of Staff, but that he was a born leader and a terrific fighter who had the whole of the air force behind him'. He said that Arnold was 'bitter against the British Air Force, because we had all the important commands – in the United Kingdom, Mediterranean and India', and added that Arnold 'was determined to get one of these for an American, and it was only natural that he should, because America was building the greatest Air Force in the world and . . . her production far outstripped ours . . . All this was constantly drumming in Arnold's mind.' Welsh replied by saying that the RAF bomber force based in the UK was only 45 per cent larger than the Eighth Air Force, yet it had dropped 237 per cent more bombs in September.[49] But these were the inevitable turf wars found in any great conflict, and not evidence of a genuine rift between the RAF and USAAF, whose division of labour between daylight and night-time bombing automatically solved a number of possible operational problems.

On 6 March 1944 the Americans began daylight raids on Berlin, which was now being pounded almost round the clock. Its strong air defences meant that the cost of attacking the capital was always high, however, and on the night of 24 March 1944 losses of almost 10 per cent of Bomber Command's planes were suffered, and much damage was caused to those that managed to limp home. Although it cannot be conclusively proven either way, there are those who believe that the decision to concentrate on softening-up targets for D-Day was as much an admission of defeat by Bomber Command over its attempts to destroy Berlin as a necessity in aiding D-Day. Whatever the true reason, and of course both might have been true, from mid-1944 there was a significant diversion of the bombing effort away from hitting

German cities towards supporting the Normandy landings, and in particular trying to cut off German retaliation by road and rail. This was given the hardly impenetrable codename of Transportation Plan. After the war, Air Chief Marshal Tedder published a book entitled *Air Superiority in War* which featured a graph (see Figure 3) emphasizing how exponentially the weight of bombs dropped on Germany increased as the war progressed.

At a meeting at St Paul's School in Hammersmith, London, on 15 May 1944, when the entire Allied top brass met to go over the plans for the invasion of France, Operation Overlord, the First Sea Lord and Chief of the Naval Staff Admiral Sir Andrew Cunningham, who sat between Churchill and Admiral Stark, recalled that 'Bomber Harris complained what a nuisance this Overlord operation was and how it interfered with the right way to defeat Germany, i.e. by bombing.'[50] Harris was also characteristically blunt about Churchill's scientific adviser Solly Zuckerman, who on another occasion had proposed a plan to suspend the area-bombing campaign altogether for three months, describing him as 'a civilian professor whose peacetime forte is the study of the sexual aberrations of the higher apes'.[51]

The massive bombing of targets in north-west France, many of them far from Normandy, as a feint to convince the Germans that the attack was going to come further north, is estimated to have cost between 80,000 and 160,000 (mainly French civilian) casualties. After a War Cabinet on 3 April 1944 Cunningham wrote of how there had been 'Considerable sob stuff about children with legs blown off and blinded old ladies but nothing about the saving of risk to our young soldiers landing on a hostile shore. It is of course intended to issue warnings beforehand.'[52] Ten days later the Defence Committee returned to the theme, prompting Cunningham to report again to his diary: 'The expected casualties were grossly exaggerated but apparently it is all right to kill 1,100 French people per week. Still I agree with the RAF policy for want of having a better and more useful one propounded.'[53]

By 30 May, less than a week away from the proposed landings, Anthony Eden told the War Cabinet that there was a worrying reaction from the French and Belgians about the heavy pre-Overlord bombing campaign. Portal reported to the War Cabinet that '95% of RAF

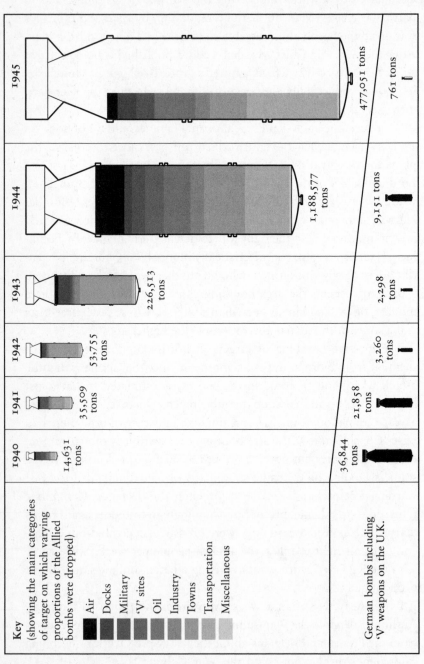

Figure 3: The Allied and Axis bombing campaigns, 1940–1945

Key
(showing the main categories of target on which varying proportions of the Allied bombs were dropped)

Air
Docks
Military
'V' sites
Oil
Industry
Towns
Transportation
Miscellaneous

German bombs including 'V' weapons on the U.K.

1940
14,631 tons
36,844 tons

1941
35,509 tons
21,858 tons

1942
53,755 tons
3,260 tons

1943
226,513 tons
2,298 tons

1944
1,188,577 tons
9,151 tons

1945
477,051 tons
761 tons

show finished; US got 50% to do.' Lord Cherwell, the government's scientific adviser, pointed out that Swiss newspapers which had hitherto been consistently friendly towards Britain were now full of denunciations. 'I don't think it was the right policy,' said Churchill, in one of the few times that he was recorded saying such a thing in the verbatim reports.[54] This seems to have represented the start of a process by which Churchill subtly distanced himself from what were later to be considered by many the 'excesses' of Bomber Command. Since he normally would not have cared a hoot for the views of the Swiss press, the subject must have been weighing on him. On 30 November 1944 – incidentally his seventieth birthday – Churchill interrupted Portal's report to criticize the bombing of Holland: '800–900 German [casualties] against 20,000 Dutch – awful thing to do that.'[55] Back on 27 June 1943, watching a film of Germany being bombed with Richard Casey, the Australian representative in the War Cabinet, Churchill had 'sat bolt upright and said to [Casey] "Are we beasts? Are we taking this too far?"' It was probably meant rhetorically at that stage of the war, but he soon got the answer when Casey replied that 'We hadn't started it, and that it was us or them.'[56]

After D-Day further efforts were made by the Americans – with large numbers of B-24 bombers now joining the B-17s – to shift concentration towards attacking German synthetic-oil supplies. Harris opposed this too, yet by then the Luftwaffe was somehow surviving on 10,000 tons of high-octane fuel a month, when 160,000 had once been required.[57] Harris won, and between October 1944 and the end of the war more than 40 per cent of the 344,000 tons of bombs dropped by the RAF on Germany hit cities rather than purely military targets, even though the Allies had complete aerial superiority and the RAF could bomb their targets in daylight once again. This led to a row between Portal and Harris, with Harris spiritedly protecting his policy. Portal now wanted Bomber Command to concentrate on oil and transportation targets, which Harris still considered mere 'panacea targets'. Yet the debate was only ever about the efficacy of the bombing offensive, not its morality, over which neither man had any doubts. Nor did Portal feel strong enough simply to order Harris to alter his targets, in the face of his immensely popular lieutenant's opposition. In the last years of the war, Bomber Command continued to be hugely enlarged. Despite losses, the thirty-three squadrons with which it had begun the war had expanded to ninety-five by its end. As usual Canada made a disproportionate contribution to the war effort: RCAF squadrons made up the entirety of No. 6 Bomber Group, for example, which comprised fourteen squadrons and in 1944 flew 25,353 operational sorties, dropping 86,503 tons of bombs and mines with the lowest loss percentages of four-engined aircraft in the whole of Bomber Command. In all, one in four members of Bomber Command came from the overseas dominions, of whom no fewer than 15,661 did not live to see their native Australia, Canada, New Zealand or South Africa again.

From February 1945, German west-to-east troop movements were being disrupted at the Russians' urgent request by the Western Allies bombing the nodal points of Germany's transportation system, including Berlin, Chemnitz, Leipzig and Dresden. But it was to be the raid on Dresden ten nights later that was to cause the most furious controversy of the entire CBO, which lasts to this day. During the Yalta Conference of 4 to 11 February 1945, the Chiefs of Staff meetings were held at Stalin's headquarters, the Yusupov Villa at Koreiz, 6 miles from the Livadia Palace at Yalta where FDR stayed and where the plenary sessions took place. The British delegation stayed in 'the slightly odd Moorish–Scottish baronial style' Vorontsov Villa Palace overlooking the Black Sea at Alupka, 12 miles from the Livadia Palace.[58] Alan Brooke was chairing the Chiefs of Staff meeting at the Yusupov Villa the day after the opening session when the Russian Deputy Chief of Staff Alexei Antonov and the Soviet air marshal Sergei Khudyakov 'pressed the subject of [bombing German] lines of communication and entrainment, specifically via Berlin, Leipzig and Dresden'. In the view of one of those present at Yalta, Hugh Lunghi, who translated for the British Chiefs of Staff during these meetings with the Russians, it was this urgent request 'to stop Hitler transferring divisions from the west to reinforce his troops in Silesia, blocking the Russian advance on Berlin' that led to the bombing of Dresden only two days after the conference ended.[59] (Of course this did not prevent the Soviets denouncing the bombing as an inhumane Anglo-American war crime forty years later during the Cold War, until it was pointed out to them that it had been they who had requested it.) At the time, however, the bombing of Dresden was not a major issue.

The massive attack on Dresden just after 10 o'clock on the night of Tuesday, 13 February 1945 by 259 Lancaster bombers from RAF Swinderby in Lincolnshire as well as other nearby airfields – flying most of the way in 10/10ths (that is, total) cloud – and then by 529 more Lancasters a few hours later, and then by 529 Liberators and Flying Fortresses of the USAAF the next morning, has proved particularly controversial, but possibly for the wrong reasons. It has long been assumed that a disproportionately large number of people died in a vengeance attack that had little or no strategic or military purpose. Yet though the attack on the beautiful, largely wooden, medieval city centre – 'the Florence of the Elbe' – was undeniably devastating, there were many war industries centred in this architectural jewel of southern Germany.[60]

The 2,680 tons of bombs dropped laid waste to over 13 square miles of the city, and many of those killed were women, children, the old and some of the several hundred thousand refugees fleeing from the Red Army, which was only 60 miles to the east. 'They were . . . suffocated, burnt, baked or boiled,' writes the military historian Allan Mallinson.[61] Nor was 'boiled' an exaggeration: piles of corpses had to be pulled out of a giant fire-service water tank where people had jumped to escape the flames but instead were boiled alive. The American novelist Kurt Vonnegut was a POW in Dresden the night it was bombed, and had to dig corpses out of the ruined city the morning afterwards. In his novel *Slaughterhouse Five*, which can be described only as semi-autobiographical because he is abducted by aliens and travels through time, the hero Billy Pilgrim nonetheless recalls how before the raid he had been 'enchanted by the architecture of the city. Merry amoretti wove garlands above windows. Roguish fauns and naked nymphs peeked down at Billy from festooned cornices. Stone monkeys frisked among scrolls and seashells and bamboo.'[62] Yet when Pilgrim and his German guards emerged at noon the day after the bombing, 'the sky was black with smoke. The sun was an angry little pinhead. Dresden was like the moon now, nothing but minerals. The stones were hot. Everybody else in the neighborhood was dead.' Pilgrim notices what seemed like 'little logs lying around', which had been people who had been caught in the firestorm. Houses were just 'ashes and dollops of melted glass'. Digging corpses out of the rubble, 'They didn't smell bad at first, were wax museums. But then the bodies rotted and liquefied, and the stink was like roses and mustard gas.' After a while, bodies were no longer excavated, 'They were cremated by soldiers with flame-throwers right where they were. The soldiers stood outside the shelters, and simply sent the fire in.'[63]

Vonnegut claimed that 'around 130,000' people died in the bombing of Dresden, but he took his figures from the former historian David Irving's 1964 book *The Destruction of Dresden*, which have long been disproven. The true figure was probably around 20,000, as a special commission of thirteen prominent German historians, headed by the respected Rolf-Dieter Müller, has concluded.[64] Claims by the Nazis at the time, and by post-war neo-Nazis since, that human bodies completely disappeared in the high temperatures have been shown by the commission to be false.

By February 1945 the Allies had discovered the means to create firestorms, even in cold weather very different from that of Hamburg in July and August 1943. Huge 'air mines' known as 'blockbusters' were dropped, designed to blow out doors and windows so that the oxygen would flow through easily to feed the flames caused by the incendiary bombs. High-explosive bombs both destroyed buildings and just as importantly kept the fire-fighters down in their shelters. 'People died not necessarily because they were burnt to death,' records one writer, 'but also because the firestorm sucked all the oxygen out of the atmosphere.'[65] In Dresden, because the sirens were not in proper working order, many of the fire-fighters who had come out after the first wave of bombers were caught out in the open by the second.

Yet this in itself does not make the raid the war crime that Labour's Richard Stokes MP and Bishop George Bell described it as at the time and many have since assumed it to have been. For as the foremost historian of the operation, Frederick Taylor, has pointed out, Dresden 'was by the standards of the time a legitimate military target'. As a nodal point for communications, with its railway marshalling yards and conglomeration of war industries – its pre-war industry based on porcelain, typewriters and cameras had been converted into an extensive network of armaments workshops, particularly in the vital optics, electronics and communications fields – the city was always going to be in danger once long-range penetration by bombers with good fighter escort was possible. 'Why is it legitimate to kill someone using a weapon', one historian has asked, 'and a crime to kill those who make the weapons?'[66]

Nor was it the Allies' fault that the Nazi authorities in Dresden, and in particular its Gauleiter Martin Mutschmann, had failed to provide proper air-raid protection. There were inadequate shelters, sirens failed to work and next to no anti-aircraft guns were stationed there. When Mutschmann fell into Allied hands at the end of the war he quickly confessed that 'A shelter-building programme for the entire city was not carried out', because 'I kept hoping that nothing would happen to Dresden.' He nonetheless had two deep reinforced-concrete shelters built for himself, his family and senior officials, just in case he had been mistaken.[67] Even though the previous October 270 people had been killed there by thirty USAAF bombers, the Germans thought Dresden too far east to be reached, since the Russians left the bombing of Germany almost entirely to the British and Americans. Quite why Mutschmann thought that, almost alone of large cities, Dresden should have been immune to Allied bombing is a mystery, for the Germans had themselves designated it 'a military defensive area'.

With his honed political instinct, Churchill could see that the Combined Bomber Offensive would provide a future line of attack against his prosecution of the war, and on 28 March 1945 he wrote to the Chiefs of Staff to put it on record that:

It seems to me that the moment has come when the question of bombing German cities simply for the sake of increasing the terror, though under other pretexts, should be reviewed. Otherwise we shall come into control of an utterly ruined land. We shall not, for instance, be able to get housing materials out of Germany for our own needs because some temporary provisions would have to be made for the Germans themselves. The destruction of Dresden remains a serious query against the conduct of Allied bombing ... I feel the need for more precise concentration upon military objectives ... rather than on mere acts of terror and wanton destruction, however impressive.[68]

This minute has been described as sending 'a thunderbolt down the corridors of Whitehall'. Harris, who had had considerable misgivings about the operation because of the long distances involved, was none-theless characteristically blunt in defending the destruction of a city that once produced Meissen porcelain: 'The feeling, such as there is, over Dresden could be easily explained by a psychiatrist. It is con-nected with German bands and Dresden shepherdesses. Actually Dresden was a mass of munition works, an intact government centre and a key transportation centre. It is now none of those things.'[69] One argument made since the war, that the raid was unnecessary because peace was only ten weeks off, is especially ahistorical. With talk of secret weaponry, a Bavarian Redoubt, fanatical Hitler Youth 'were-wolf' squads and German propaganda about fighting for every inch of the Fatherland, there was no possible way of knowing how fanatical German resistance might be, and thus when the war would end.

Although the Blitz on London and other British cities in 1940–41 did not break civilian morale as it was in part intended to do – indeed it stiffened it – the bombing was far lighter and shorter-lived than the retribution against Germany from 1940 to 1945, which certainly did leave very many Germans in despair. Defeatism was ever present, especially after D-Day, but unsurprisingly kept private in a totalitarian state where spreading it was a capital offence. A total of 955,044 tons of bombs were dropped by Bomber Command during the war, and this was bound to have a demoralizing effect, but overall it was the dawning knowledge that Germany not only was not going to win the war after all, but was instead going to be defeated, that wrecked morale in the Reich.[70]

The second major reason why the Combined Bomber Offensive was justified, as well as ending the rate of increase in German armaments production, was because of the vast number of fighter aircraft that it forced Hitler to keep stationed on the defensive in Germany, when they would have proved invaluable in other places, primarily the all-important Eastern Front. The night before Albert Speer died in 1981, in a hotel room in London, he told the historian Norman Stone that the Allied bombing campaign 'had caused so many German fighters simply to patrol the skies that there was not enough air power left for the Eastern Front'.[71] This was true: by the spring of 1943, just as the Germans needed every weapon they could use for the Kursk offensive, no fewer than 70 per cent of all German fighter aircraft were stationed in the west.[72] The Allied bombing campaign also forced the Germans to divert from offensive use as much as one-third of their artillery in anti-aircraft guns, two million men for anti-aircraft defence plus repairing, rebuilding and restoration, building air-raid bunkers and flak towers, and 20 per cent of all ammunition, just in order to protect the Reich from aerial assault.[73] 'German air power declined steadily on the Eastern Front during 1943 and 1944, when over two-thirds of German fighters were sucked into the contest with the [Allied] bombers,' records Richard Overy. 'By the end of 1943 there were 55,000 anti-aircraft guns to combat the air offensive – including 75 per cent of the famous 88mm gun, which had doubled with such success as an anti-tank weapon on the Eastern Front.'[74] This meant that the Luftwaffe was forced to produce fewer bombers – 18 per cent of the total aircraft produced in 1944, against over 50 per cent in 1942 – even though bombers had hugely aided Hitler in his eastern victories of 1941–2, with their devastation of Russian aerodromes, industry and military installations.

In his 1969 autobiography, *Inside the Third Reich*, Speer denied that Allied bombing had weakened the German public's morale, and that the 9 per cent loss of production capacity in 1943 might even have been 'amply balanced out by increased effort', but he accepted that the 'ten thousand anti-aircraft guns [whose barrels] were pointed towards the sky' in Germany and the west instead 'could have well been employed in Russia against tanks and other ground targets'.[75] More rounds of 88mm or higher-calibre ammunition were produced in 1941–3 for non-tank than for anti-tank purposes, and one-third of Germany's optical industry and half her electronics industry was engaged in producing gun-sights, radar and communications networks for defence against bombing, leaving front-line troops without infantry walkie-talkies and artillery sound-ranging apparatus, such as the Western Allies were developing.[76]

The fact that more than ten times the number of Germans died – some 600,000 in all – in the retaliation against the Blitz than Britons who actually died in the Blitz itself echoes the biblical phrase about David multiplying the numbers killed by Saul. (A further 120,000 French and Italians perished as well.) Whereas the Luftwaffe flattened

400 acres of London, the RAF and USAAF turned 6,247 acres of Berlin into little more than rubble. Total War did not allow for what is today called 'a proportionate response'. No fewer than sixty major German industrial cities suffered colossal material damage during the Second World War. Yet Germany is today such a model democracy, and so pacific in her foreign policy, partly because of the terrible retribution that that war visited upon her. If the Second World War had not seen civilian casualties on German soil, just as the Great War had not, a new spirit of revanchism might have been rekindled there. As it was, the Germans looked into the face of Armageddon, and it has instilled an aversion for foreign military intervention that might occasionally frustrate NATO policy-makers today, but is overall a very welcome development for the world.

15

Norman Conquest

June–August 1944

My dear friend, this is much the greatest thing we have ever attempted.
Winston Churchill to Franklin Roosevelt, 23 October 1943[1]

'What's your most valuable possession?' General Montgomery asked a soldier just before D-Day. 'My rifle, sir,' came the reply. 'No, it isn't,' Monty replied; 'it's your life, and I'm going to save it for you.'[2] Although of course any large-scale amphibious landing on the heavily defended coastline of north-western Europe would be a major risk, the Allies did everything they possibly could to minimize military casualties through the employment of overwhelming force. This had the effect of hugely increasing the already high stakes, because a major defeat in Normandy in June 1944 would almost certainly have had the effect of the United States abandoning the Germany First policy, and turning to the Pacific War instead. Amphibious operations had not had a rosy history in the Second World War so far, let alone earlier. The 1940 attempted landing at Dakar and the 1942 attack on Dieppe had been disasters; Salerno and Anzio had been near-disasters; Torch had been extremely lucky with the tides and anyway had not been undertaken against the Germans. Further back, Gallipoli haunted the minds of many, not least its prime author, Churchill.

Yet the Normandy landings were going to be different because the planners – initially under Lieutenant-General Sir Frederick Morgan at COSSAC (the London-based organization of the Chief of Staff to the Supreme Allied Commander) – would ensure total air and sea supremacy, would interdict German counter-attack through bombing and airborne assault, and would land truly vast numbers of men – twenty-five divisions by the end of June 1944 and a further fourteen on their way – along with a massive preponderance of war matériel. American war production would be displayed to full effect. Even on top of all that, however, luck would be required. 'We shall require all the help that God can give us,' the commander of all naval forces for the operation, Admiral Sir Bertram Ramsay, noted in his diary the night before. 'I cannot believe that this will not be forthcoming.'[3] In Führer Directive No. 51 of 3 November 1943, Hitler had stated:

The danger in the East remains, but a greater threatens to the West – the Anglo-Saxon landings. In the East, in the worst scenario, the vast size of the territory allows a loss of ground even on the large scale without delivering us a mortal blow. But it is different in the West! . . . It is there that the enemy has to attack, there – if we are not deceived – that the decisive landing battles will be fought.[4]

These battles, he told his Führer-conferences from the summer of 1943 onwards, would be decisive not only for the invasion itself, but for the outcome of the war. 'We have to be on guard like a spider in his web,' he said on 20 May 1943, adding, 'Thank God, I have a good nose for such things and can usually anticipate these developments beforehand.'[5] Enormous amounts of work had already been put into the German fortifications in France known as the Atlantic Wall over the previous eighteen months, with an estimated two million slave labourers working for two years, pouring 18 million tons of concrete to create deep bunkers and impressive fortifications, many of which can still be seen today. Mines were laid in the water and on the beaches, anti-glider poles made from tree trunks, known as Rommel's asparagus, were dug into fields. Rommel had been given command of Army Group B in January 1944, charged with defending France from invasion. This role clashed with that of Rundstedt, Commander-in-Chief West, who moreover took a fundamentally different view from Rommel, who advocated a concentration of defensive forces on the coast.

The one person who rarely wavered in his conviction that the Allies would land in Normandy was Hitler himself. 'Watch Normandy,' he said to Rundstedt many times, injunctions which both Rundstedt and his chief of staff General Günther Blumentritt confirmed to Basil

Liddell Hart after the war.[6] From March 1944 onwards, Blumentritt recalled, Rundstedt's staff 'received repeated warnings about it, starting with the words "The Führer fears . . ."' Neither man knew what had led Hitler to his conclusion, but, as Liddell Hart acknowledged, 'It would seem that Hitler's much derided "intuition" was nearer the mark than the calculations of the ablest professional soldiers.'[7]

To mislead the enemy about one's intentions, capabilities and operations is a strategy as old as military theory itself: the ancient Chinese strategist and philosopher Sun Tzu himself taught that 'All warfare is based on deception.' Even if a great deal of the Allied deception activity relied on flummery as much as it did on genuinely worthwhile activity, nothing can detract from the triumph of Operations Fortitude North and Fortitude South in the months before D-Day, which left Hitler stationing hundreds of thousands of men in Norway, Holland, Belgium and the Pas de Calais, rather than on the Normandy beaches where the blow was always going to come, ever since its first inception as a serious plan in the spring of 1942. The two Fortitude operations constitute the most successful deception plan in the history of warfare.[8] These elaborate operations had been put in place by the Allies years earlier. Twice as many reconnaissance flights, interdiction raids and bombing missions took place over the Pas de Calais as over Normandy. The First US Army Group (FUSAG), commanded by General Patton and visited by King George VI, was simply invented and stationed across the Channel from Calais. It came complete with dummy tanks (made from rubber by Shepperton film studios' set designers), false headquarters, fabricated landing-craft, camp stoves that smoked and even concealed lighting on the airfields.[9] The Germans could not believe that a commander of Patton's eminence would have been wasted by the Allies on a ruse (indeed Patton could not believe it himself). Very soon his period of disgrace over the slapping incident would be over, however.

By May 1944, the Abwehr estimated there were seventy-nine divisions stationed in Britain, when the true figure was forty-seven. False wireless traffic was sent out in East Anglia. An armada of dummy landing craft and tanks was assembled in the Thames Estuary. An actor was sent to Gibraltar prior to the Normandy landings to pose as Montgomery – complete with the initials BLM monogrammed on to his khaki handkerchiefs. He made a special study of the general he was impersonating, and noticed what a consummate actor Monty was too. (A very observant Axis agent in Gibraltar might, however, have spotted that Monty's double was missing a middle finger.) On D-Day itself the chaff codenamed Window was dropped off the Pas de Calais in such a way that it seemed to German radar that a massive armada was approaching. These many, varied, sometimes convoluted yet often brilliant schemes saved tens of thousands of lives.

In trying to predict the place where the Allies would land, the Abwehr assumed that a major port would be required to bring in all the necessary logistical supplies, such as petrol, whereas in fact two vast artificial quays known as Mulberry Harbours were going to be shipped out from Devon and sunk in the sea off two of the Normandy invasion beaches. 'They required 600,000 tons of concrete (the weight of more than two thousand two storey houses) and 1.5 million yards of steel shuttering,' records Martin Gilbert. 'To build them, 20,000 men were employed working in eight dry docks.'[10] Furthermore steel and lead pipes codenamed PLUTO (for Pipeline Under The Ocean) would pump petrol from the Isle of Wight 80 miles along the floor of the English Channel to Cherbourg. In all, 172 million gallons were to flow down it.

There were nerve-wracking moments for British intelligence as well as the Abwehr, however. On 1 June an answer to the *Daily Telegraph*'s crossword puzzle clue 'Britannia and he hold the same thing' was 'Neptune', because the Roman personification of Britain and the god of the sea Neptune both hold tridents. Yet Neptune was also the codename for the naval part of Overlord. Since 2 May, other answers had included 'Utah' and 'Omaha' (the codenames of the two beaches the Americans were to land on), as well as 'Overlord' and 'Mulberry'. The crossword setter, Leonard Dawe, a fifty-four-year-old headmaster of Strand School, which had been evacuated to Effingham in Surrey, had a brother-in-law serving in the Admiralty, and it took MI5 some time before they accepted the surprising truth that the choices had been entirely serendipitous. 'They turned me inside out,' recalled Dawe in a BBC interview in 1958. Various pupils of his have since claimed to have inspired the clues, using words they had overheard at a nearby Canadian military base.

'The tide has turned!' stated Eisenhower's exclamation-mark-studded Order of the Day on Tuesday, 6 June 1944, distributed to all Allied troops by SHAEF (Supreme Headquarters Allied Expeditionary Force). 'The free men of the world are marching together to victory! I have full confidence in your courage, devotion to duty and skill in battle. We will accept nothing less than full victory! Good luck! And let us beseech the blessing of Almighty God upon this great and noble undertaking.'[11] Along with the surprise they achieved, the sheer size of the Normandy landings was key to their success. Although the first day itself – codenamed D-Day, the D simply standing for Day – involved fewer troops going ashore than Husky had in Sicily, overall they were the largest amphibious landings in world history by far, altogether comprising 6,939 vessels – of which around 1,200 were warships and 4,000 were 10-ton wooden landing craft capable of an upper speed of 8 knots – 11,500 aircraft and two million men. On the first day 5,000 vessels sailed, including five battleships, twenty-three cruisers, seventy-nine destroyers, thirty-eight frigates and other warships, as well as a reserve of 118 destroyers and other warships.[12] Meanwhile over 13,000 sorties were flown, and 154,000 Allied troops (70,500 Americans, 83,115 British and Canadian) alighted on French soil on the first day alone, 24,000 of them by parachute and glider.[13]

The timing of the invasion was one of the greatest challenges faced by the Allied High Command during the war. Because it took no fewer than forty-five troopships, cargo ships and escorts to move a single armoured division across the Atlantic Ocean, because safety from U-boats was not assured until mid-1943, because the English Channel is impassable for amphibious assault from September to February inclusive, earlier opportunities were severely limited. The plans had been undergoing revisions and regular updating ever since the first Joint Planning Staff meetings of September 1941, when one of the earliest American planners to study the problem had been a one-star general in the US War Department's Operations Division called Dwight D. Eisenhower. In December 1943 Eisenhower was appointed supreme commander of the Allied Expeditionary Force in western Europe and soon afterwards went to London to establish his SHAEF headquarters to oversee and direct the invasion, with

Montgomery as his overall land commander. Both Marshall and Brooke had been considered for the post of supreme commander, but the former had effectively turned it down by not asking for it and the latter ruled himself out through his lack of enthusiasm for the operation, though he also felt that by 1944 the invasion needed to be commanded by an American.

The planners' general scheme – for a massive invasion via Normandy – survived the intense personal examination and interrogations of George Marshall, Alan Brooke, Franklin Roosevelt and Winston Churchill, although Churchill and Brooke never threw off presentiments of disaster for the operation.[14] Churchill often spoke of seeing the Channel full of Allied corpses as a result of the defeat of Overlord and Brooke noted in his diary as late as 5 June 1944, the day it was originally due to take place: 'I am very uneasy about the whole operation. At the best it will fall so very very short of the expectation of the bulk of the people, namely all those who know nothing of its difficulties. At the worst it may well be the most ghastly disaster of the whole war. I wish to God it were safely over.'[15] That same night Churchill said to his wife Clementine: 'Do you realize that by the time you wake up in the morning, 20,000 men may have been killed?'[16]

In part because of Churchill's and Brooke's deep pessimism about the chances a cross-Channel invasion had of success, the British had prevented an early return to the Continent at a moment they had considered too early by insisting on a North African, Mediterranean and then Italian series of campaigns undertaken to weaken and disperse German forces, while the Wehrmacht was bled white on the Eastern Front. By June 1944, however, the Germans were about to be comprehensively defeated in Russia, and so there was no time to be lost by the Western Allies in attacking the Reich from the west. By then Britain had 57 million square feet of storage area filled with supplies for the operation, including nearly half a million tons of ammunition, much of it brought over from the United States under Operation Bolero, which had been instituted as soon as America had entered the war.

Eisenhower did make some important alterations to the COSSAC plans when he took over in London early in 1944, as did Montgomery. Typically Eisenhower kept quiet about his input, whereas Montgomery boasted insufferably about his, with slight additions of self-pity. In a (hitherto unpublished) letter to Air Vice-Marshal Harry Broadhurst of 31 January 1944, Montgomery wrote:

I have been terribly busy ever since I got back here. The whole plan was a complete bullock and had to be changed; very like Husky over again. I am becoming a sort of 'enfant terrible' who goes round knocking things down and getting all the mud slung at one!! However so long as we win the war it does not matter to me. I shall retire to my garden – and the evening of life – when the party is all over.[17]

Although the beaches of the Cotentin peninsula were retained as the target, the initial assault force was increased from three divisions to five and the front was widened from 25 miles to 40. Montgomery also pushed back the invasion date from 1 May to the first week of June, to get the Anzio landing craft back from Italy and to allow more time for the bomber forces to destroy the roads, railways, bridges and tunnels down and across and through which the German reserves would counter-attack.

'In the better days that lie ahead,' went Montgomery's Order of the Day for D-Day, 'men will speak with pride of our doings.' He divided his 21st Army Group into two armies. Bradley's US First Army, split between Joseph Collins' US VII Corps and Leonard Gerow's US V Corps, would assault the westward beaches codenamed Utah and Omaha. Meanwhile, Miles Dempsey's Second Army, split between G. C. Bucknall's British XXX Corps and John Crocker's Anglo-Canadian I Corps, would assault Gold, Juno and Sword beaches. The British 6th Airborne Division would land on the eastern extremity of the battlefield to try to disrupt the German counter-attack and silence the German batteries on the high ground at the mouth of the River Orne, while two American airborne divisions, the 82nd and 101st, would land on the western extremity of it behind Utah beach to secure roads through the marshland behind the dunes that had been deliberately flooded by the Germans. The American parachutists landed in Normandy even more heavily laden than the infantry, each man carrying almost his own weight including jump suit, camouflage helmet, main and reserve parachutes, boots, gloves, combat uniform, life-jacket, Colt .45 pistol, Browning automatic rifle plus ammunition, knives, first-aid kit, blanket, food and change of socks and underwear. Corporal Dan Hartington of C Company, the 1st Canadian Parachute Battalion in the British 6th Airborne Division recalled:

We were loaded to the hilt with grenades, Gammon bombs, flexible Bangalore torpedoes around our necks, two-inch mortar bombs, ammunition, weapons and water bottles. Our exposed skin was blackened with charcoal, the camouflage netting on our helmets was all tied up with burlap rags, and the space above the harness in our helmets was crammed with cigarettes or with plastic explosive.[18]

As soon as the beach-heads were secure, troops would pour into Normandy, principally Patton's US Third Army and Lieutenant-General Henry Crerar's Canadian First Army. The plan was to establish the 21st Army Group from the Loire to the Seine, take Cherbourg and Brest, and then liberate the rest of France and march to Germany. It was bold and imaginative and would be backed up by enormous air power, co-ordinated by Eisenhower's deputy supreme commander, Air Chief Marshal Sir Arthur Tedder. One of the keys to victory was command of the air: whereas the Luftwaffe flew only 309 sorties on D-Day, the Allies flew 13,688. 'The scene in the Channel was quite amazing,' recalled Lieutenant-Commander Cromwell Lloyd-Davies of HMS *Glasgow*. 'It was almost like Piccadilly Circus – there were so many ships there and it was incredible to us that all this could be going on without the Germans knowing anything about it. But we never saw a German aircraft the whole time.'[19] In fact only a dozen German fighter-bombers ever made it to the beaches, and they could only stay long enough for a single strafing attack each before being chased off. Similarly, the German Navy posed next to no danger to the invasion, as it would have at any period before Dönitz withdrew his U-boats from the Atlantic ports on 24 May 1943. By D-Day, such was the success of the Allies' naval war in the west that the Kriegsmarine was completely incapable of inflicting significant damage on the invasion armada. What surface ships the Germans had were concentrated on protecting the Pas de Calais area and no U-boats made any attacks against Allied shipping. On 4 July four German destroyers made a sally from Brest, but all were sunk or forced back into port. The Royal Navy's Home Fleet meanwhile closed off any threat from

Scandinavian and Baltic ports, and the Kiel Canal was mined as a precaution in Operation Bravado.[20] Although three E-boats under Lieutenant Heinrich Hoffmann, based at Le Havre, made it through the Allies' smokescreen to loose off eighteen torpedoes, a Norwegian escort destroyer was their only victim.

One major problem was the shortage of landing craft. So few were available that Operation Anvil, an attack in the south of France originally scheduled for the same day as Overlord, had to be postponed until 15 August, by which time the Germans had largely withdrawn their forces from the region. Quite why the US Maritime Commission was capable of building a 10,500-ton Liberty cargo ship in under a week (and 2,700 of them in total) but not enough basic, wooden, 10-ton landing craft is a continuing mystery of the war. Marshall suspected a Navy plot at the Bureau of Yards and Construction. Overlord did in the end deploy the necessary number of landing craft, but only at the cost of a diversionary operation that might have been strategically useful in early June but was largely obviated by mid-August.

Meteorology was in its infancy in the 1940s and, as the weather in the Channel was never predictable, Eisenhower had to order a postponement of the attack from Monday, 5 June to Tuesday the 6th, on the advice of his chief meteorological officer, a twenty-nine-year-old civilian called James Stagg who had been awarded the rank of group captain in order to give him some weight among the much more senior officers. With too many clouds and too strong winds, the crucial aerial part of the operation could have been compromised, with disastrous results. Yet as Stagg later pointed out, with the Navy wanting onshore winds of not more than Force 3 or 4, as well as good visibility for bombarding coastal defences, and the Air Force also wanting specific cloud cover and heights, 'When I came to put them together I found that they might have to sit around for 120 or 150 years before they got the operation launched.'[21]

Had Overlord not been launched on 6 June, considerations of fuel, moonlight and tidal flows would have meant that the whole invasion would have had to have been postponed for a fortnight, with concomitant problems regarding the troops' morale and the security of keeping so vast an operation secret. Fortunately Stagg was able to report at

04.15 on 5 June the approach of a new, favourable weather front. Pausing only to pen a resignation letter for release in the event of defeat – 'If any blame or fault attaches to the attempt it is mine alone' – late that day Eisenhower gave the final go-ahead, with the hardly morale-boosting remark to his Staff: 'I hope to God I know what I'm doing.'[22]

The Pas de Calais, as the shortest route across the Channel, would have had the best cover from fighter aircraft from the RAF's Kentish airfields. The Abwehr also believed the information supplied by its spy network in the United Kingdom, centred on an anti-Fascist Catalan called Juan Pujol García, who lived in a safe house in Hendon and was codenamed Garbo by the Allies (who awarded him the MBE) and Arabel by the Germans (who awarded him the Iron Cross), his twenty-four fictitious sub-agents and other German spies who had been infiltrated into Britain, every single one of whom had been successfully 'turned' by MI5. These included the real and imagined agents Gelatine, Hamlet, Meteor, Brutus (Roman Garby-Czerniawski), Cobweb (Ib Riis), Beetle (Petur Thomsen), Bronx (Elvira Chaudoir), Tricycle, Artist, Freak, Tate, Mullet, Puppet and Treasure.[23] As they fed the Abwehr with reports about FUSAG's activities, all co-ordinated by Garbo (so called because he was such an accomplished actor), the spy network became completely trusted by the Germans.[24] Meanwhile Ultra built up a picture of the enemy's order of battle and command structure in France, helped by the French Resistance destroying land-line connections, thus forcing the Germans to resort to wireless communications. It took the Germans nearly a week after the Normandy landings had begun to appreciate that they were not a southern feint, but the true invasion itself, and even up to 26 June half a million troops of the German Fifteenth Army stayed stationed around the Pas de Calais, guarding against an invasion that would not come.

At 00.16 hours on D-Day, Staff Sergeant Jim Wallwork landed his Horsa glider a mere 50 yards from the road bridge over the Caen Canal, now known as Pegasus Bridge, and only 500 yards from the bridge over the River Orne. These two coastal road bridges were strategically vital, because any German counter-attack from the east would need to cross them, as would any Allied breakout to the plains east of Caen. 'The Horsa seemed to skim the tall trees at the end of the field,' recalled one of those on board, 'and came in to land with an ear-splitting crash that shook us all to our bones.'[25] One minute later, at 00.17, a second glider landed and then at 00.18 a third. The pilots had flown 5 miles by moonlight with only a stopwatch and a flashlight attached to a finger to guide them, yet they landed precisely where the French Resistance had pinpointed, through the perimeter-wire defences of the bridge.

Ninety men from D Company of the 2nd Battalion, the Oxford and Buckinghamshire Light Infantry, under the command of Major John Howard, debouched from the gliders and captured Pegasus Bridge without difficulty, so total was the Germans' surprise. They then held it until relieved by Lord Lovat's Commandos, who marched from the beach up the canal tow-path at 13.00 hours to the sound of bagpipes played by Lovat's piper, Bill Millin, 'blowing away for all he was worth'.[26] Less accurate in their landing zones were the American 82nd and 101st Airborne Divisions, some units of which landed as far as 35 miles off target. Yet this, and the practice of dropping dummy parachutists, had the added advantage of so confusing German intelligence that it estimated that 100,000 Allied troops had landed by air, more than four times the true number. The majority of parachutists landed in the correct drop-zones, however, and were to play an invaluable part in attacking the beaches from the rear and holding back the inevitable German counter-attack.

The French Resistance had been ordered to ready itself for the invasion by the BBC broadcast on 1 June of the first line of the poem 'Autumn Song' by Paul Verlaine, which went: *Les sanglots longs des violons de l'automne* (The long sobs of the autumn violins). The Abwehr had tortured a Maquis leader and learnt that when the second line – *Blessent mon coeur d'une langeur monotone* (wound my heart with monotonous langour) – was broadcast, it meant that the invasion was imminent. So when it was duly broadcast at 23.15 on 5 June, the commander of the Fifteenth Army in the Pas de Calais put his troops on alert, but no one warned the Seventh Army in Normandy. At Army Group B's château headquarters at La Roche-Guyon it was assumed that it must be mere disinformation, as the Allies would hardly have announced the invasion over the BBC.[27]

When shortly before 05.00 the Seventh Army's chief of staff warned Army Group B that the attack was indeed taking place, Rommel himself was unavailable as he was in Germany celebrating his wife Lucie's birthday which fell that day. He only made it back to La Roche-Guyon at 6 o'clock that evening. His chief of staff, Lieutenant-General Hans Speidel, ordered the 12th SS Hitler Youth Panzer Division to counter-attack at Caen at first light, but some of the 4,500 bombers that the Allies fielded that day severely blunted this assault. As Rommel later pointed out:

Even the movement of the most minor formations on the battlefield – artillery going into position, tanks forming up, etc. – is instantly attacked from the air with devastating effect. During the day fighting troops and headquarters alike are forced to seek cover in wooded and close country in order to escape the constant pounding of the air. Up to 640 [naval] guns have been used. The effect is so immense that no operation of any kind is possible in the area commanded by this rapid-fire artillery, either by infantry or tanks.[28]

Interrogated after the war, Speidel quoted Rommel as having said, very perceptively:

Elements which are not in contact with the enemy at the moment of invasion will never get into action, because of the enormous air superiority of the enemy . . . If we do not succeed in carrying out our combat mission of warding off the Allies or hurling them from the mainland in the first 48 hours, the invasion has succeeded and the war is lost for lack of strategic reserves and lack of Luftwaffe in the west.[29]

Although Hitler was not woken at Berchtesgaden with the news of the Normandy landings – he had been up with Goebbels until 3 o'clock the previous night, 'exchanging reminiscences, taking pleasure in the many fine days and weeks we have had together', recorded Goebbels; 'the mood is like the good old times' – it made very little difference. Even by the lunchtime conference OKW was unsure that this was the true attack rather than a diversion. Rundstedt was not certain either. So by the time two Panzer divisions were sent against the beaches 100 miles away, much valuable time had been lost.[30] This was not the fault of the adjutants who failed to wake the Führer, so much as evidence of the success of the Allies' deception operation in confusing the minds of the OKW and OKH about where the main attack was going to take place, and of the difference of opinion between Rundstedt and Rommel about what should be done. Rundstedt thought the Allies could not be prevented from landing and so needed to be flung back into the sea in a counter-attack; Rommel felt they had to be stopped from getting ashore, telling his Staff that 'The first twenty-four hours will be decisive.'[31] In all there were fifty-nine German divisions in the west at the time of D-Day, of which eight were in Holland and Belgium. More than half that total were mere coastal-defence or training divisions, and of the twenty-seven field divisions only ten were armoured, with three of these in the south and one near Antwerp. Six divisions, four of them coastal defence, were stationed along the 200 miles of Normandy coast west of the Seine where the Allies attacked. 'These dispositions would more truly be described as "coast-protection" rather than as defence!' stated Blumentritt later.

At 05.50 a massive naval bombardment opened up on the German beach fortifications and the villages along the Normandy coast. At H-hour, 06.30, the main American landings took place on Utah and Omaha beaches, with the British and Canadians arriving on their three beaches an hour later. The crossings had taken several hours in some cases. It had been feared that the Germans would use gas on the beaches, and the anti-gas chemical with which uniforms were sprinkled smelt so disgusting that, once added to the landing crafts' tossing about in the waves, it induced vomiting in many troops who had not already been seasick.

At Utah 23,000 men got ashore with only 210 killed and wounded, partly because the current swept the 4th Division's landing craft some 2,000 yards south of the original area designated for attack, on to a relatively lightly defended part of the coastline, and twenty-eight of the thirty-two amphibious Duplex Drive (DD) Sherman tanks got ashore. The one regiment facing them from the German 709th Division surrendered in large numbers once the 101st Airborne had secured at least four exits from the beaches.

On Omaha beach, however, where two-thirds of the American effort that day was to land, it was a very different state of affairs. The veteran US 1st Division (known as the Big Red One from its shoulder flash) and the 29th Division, which had never seen combat before, were to suffer ten times the losses as did the 4th Division at Utah.[32] Despite all the intense preparation, with tourists' photo albums pored over by Staff officers for years, the ground had been seemingly ill chosen for attack. However, once the decision had been taken to expand the lodgement area (that is, the territory to be secured by Overlord from which further operations could be conducted) as far as Utah beach to the west, Omaha beach was the only feasible landing area between Utah and the British and Canadian beaches. The cliffs and bluffs at Omaha were in some places more than 150 feet above the sea wall at the end of the dunes; the inward curvature of the coast at that stretch helped German fields of fire to overlap; underwater sand bars and ridges snagged landing craft; the powerful and well-placed fortifications (which can still be seen today) were not silenced by naval shelling; the anti-personnel mines, barbed wire and huge steel anti-tank 'hedgehogs' proved murderous obstacles; accurate German artillery fire, and above all a regiment of the 716th Infantry Division and units from the crack German 352nd Infantry Division, caused havoc. Ultra had conveyed that there would be eight enemy battalions at Omaha, rather than the four that had been planned for, but it was too late to alter the entire plan because of them. These battalions provided, in the words of Overlord's historian Max Hastings, 'by far the greatest concentration of German fire on the entire invasion front'. This nearly led to disaster for the Americans on Omaha.[33]

'With unbelieving eyes we could recognize individual landing craft,' recalled Franz Gockel of the 726th Infantry Regiment of the 716th Division. 'The hail of shells falling on us grew heavier, sending fountains of sand and debris into the air.'[34] The opening scene of the movie *Saving Private Ryan* is the best cinematographic representation of those first monstrous minutes of the American landings on Omaha beach, but even that cannot begin to show the extent of the chaos and carnage on the beaches. This would have been even worse had Rommel been right about the Allies arriving at high tide, as every gun had been fixed for that eventuality. As it was they came in at low tide in order for the obstacles to be more visible.[35] This had its own disadvantages, however, for as Signal Sergeant James Bellows of the 1st Battalion of the Hampshire Regiment recalled of the men he had landed with on Sword: 'A lot of them had been overridden by their landing craft as they came off. The landing craft became lighter as men came off and as it surged up the beach, and many who were in front went straight underneath.'[36]

The 6,000 yards of Omaha beach along which the Americans landed were soon a scene of confusion and destruction. American soldiers – whose age averaged twenty and a half, far younger than the British twenty-four or Canadian twenty-nine years – had to leap out of their landing craft into a hail of machine-gun and mortar fire loaded down with 68 pounds of equipment, including gas-mask, grenades, TNT blocks, two ammunition bandoliers, rations, water bottle and related kit. Many simply drowned when the water they jumped into proved deeper than expected.

Although the British beaches were in part cleared of German killing apparatus by a series of specialized tank-based gadgets, known as Hobart's funnies after Major-General Sir Percy Hobart of the 79th Armoured Division, which employed inventions such as giant thrashing metal chains to set off mines, Generals Bradley and Gerow preferred massive frontal assault. Because of heavy seas and being transferred from their transport vessels 11½ miles out, ten landing craft and twenty-six artillery pieces sank on the way to the beaches. 'I never saw water that bad,' recalled Sergeant Roy Stevens, 'the seas were rolling and rolling, and there were whitecaps way out where we were, twelve miles from the coast.'[37] Most of the troops had been seasick on the three-hour journey in choppy seas. The British transferred only 6½ miles out, and suffered fewer sinkings as a result in less turbulent weather. The loss of twenty-seven of the twenty-nine DD 'floating' tanks, which were launched 6,000 yards from the Omaha shore but then sank when the waves came over their canvas screens, denied the Americans the necessary firepower to get off the beach early. 'We could see a shambles ahead of us on the beach,' recalled Leading Aircraftman Norman Phillips of the RAF who landed there, 'burning tanks, jeeps, abandoned vehicles, a terrific crossfire.'[38]

The official account of what happened to Able Company of the 116th Infantry, 29th Division, after its landing craft hit Omaha beach at 06.36 gives a sense of the horror of those next few minutes:

Ramps are dropped along the boat line and the men jump off in water anywhere from waist deep to higher than a man's head. This is the signal awaited by the Germans atop the bluff. Already pounded by mortars, the floundering line is instantly swept by crossing machine gun fire from both ends of the beach . . . The first men out . . . are ripped apart before they can make five yards. Even the lightly wounded die by drowning, doomed by the water-logging of their overloaded packs . . . Already the sea runs red . . . A few move safely through the bullet swarm to the beach, then find they cannot hold there. They return to the water to use it for body cover. Faces turned upwards, so that their nostrils are out of the water, they creep towards the land at the same rate as the tide. This is how most of the survivors make it . . . Within seven minutes after the ramps drop, Able Company is inert and leaderless.[39]

It was not until 13.30, after seven hours being pinned down on the beaches, that Gerow could signal to Omar Bradley, who was on board a ship trying to make out what was going on through binoculars, that 'Troops formerly pinned down on beaches' were finally 'advancing up heights behind beaches'. Although there were 2,000 Americans killed on Omaha beach, by nightfall a total of 34,000 men had made it ashore, including two Ranger battalions that had silenced the German coastal battery at Pointe du Hoc to the west after scaling cliffs with rope ladders.[40] At one point the 5th Rangers had to don gas-masks in order to charge through the dense smoke coming from the under-growth of a hillside that suddenly caught fire.

There were no high cliffs at Gold, Juno and Sword beaches, and more time for the naval bombardment to soften up the German defences; however, by late afternoon part of the 21st Panzer Division attacked in the gap between Juno and Sword beaches and almost made it to the Channel before being turned back by naval fire. The British suffered over 3,000 casualties, but by the end the Canadians, who lost 1,074, got the furthest inland on the first day, with their 9th Brigade advancing to within 3 miles of the outskirts of Caen.

At 16.00 hours Hitler, who had dithered about the best way to react to what he still suspected was a diversionary attack, finally agreed to Rundstedt's request to send two Panzer divisions into the battle in addition to the 12th SS and 21st Panzer Divisions already committed. But as the historian Gerhard Weinberg has pointed out:

The reinforcements dribbled into the invasion front were never enough, and the Allied air forces as well as the sabotage efforts of the French resistance and Allied special teams slowed down whatever was sent. The German armoured divisions, therefore, arrived one at a time and quite slowly, were never able to punch through, and ended up being mired in positional warfare because they continued to be needed at the front in the absence of infantry divisions.[41]

Allied aerial supremacy over the battlefield made it impossible for the German tanks to be committed better than piecemeal in daylight. Yet five armoured divisions of the reserve in France, and no fewer than nineteen divisions of the Fifteenth Army 120 miles to the north, simply stayed in place waiting for the 'real' attack on the Pas de Calais. Meanwhile, Rundstedt and Rommel became increasingly certain that Normandy was indeed the true *Schwerpunkt*, whereas the Führer continued to doubt it.

D-Day itself saw around 9,000 casualties, of whom – very unusually – more than half were killed. The dead comprised 2,500 Americans, 1,641 Britons, 359 Canadians, thirty-seven Norwegians, nineteen Free French, thirteen Australians, two New Zealanders and one Belgian: 4,572 soldiers in total. Although Air Chief Marshal Tedder had predicted that the airborne troops would lose 80 per cent of their number, the actual figure was 15 per cent; still high, but not catastrophically so.[42] The American cemetery at Colleville-sur-Mer above Omaha beach bears noble witness to the sacrifice.

The Germans were critically under-reinforced at Normandy, partly because of the success of the Allies' elaborate but never suspiciously uniform deception plans. 'The 7th Army had thrown into battle every major unit that stood in the Cotentin,' records a history, 'and committing units from Brittany and elsewhere would take time.'[43] Yet time was a commodity of which the Germans were rapidly running out, because if the invasion was not flung back into the English Channel immediately, such were the reinforcements alighting from the Arromanches Mulberry Harbour – only one, as the one off Omaha was rendered largely inoperable by a storm on 19 June – that by 1 July they would exceed a million men, 150,000 vehicles and 500,000 tons of supplies.[44]

D-Day once again saw a determined German counter-attack on

the ground being staved off by Allied air power. The capacity and willingness of the Wehrmacht to try to push the Allies back into the sea were still there, but were overwhelmed by the ability of the RAF and USAAF to attack the unprotected armour from above, where it was weakest. The bombing campaign against Luftwaffe factories and the attritional war against German fighters once they had been built had paid off spectacularly. (There had been an effort to build German aircraft factories underground before the war, but not enough resources had been devoted to it.)

The news of D-Day gave sudden, soaring hope to Occupied Europe. 'The invasion has begun!' wrote the German-Jewish Anne Frank, who was about to celebrate her fifteenth birthday, in a diary that she kept while living in her family's hidden attic in Amsterdam. 'Great commotion in the Secret Annexe! Would the long-awaited liberation that has been talked of so much but which still seems too wonderful, too much like a fairy-tale, ever come true? Could we be granted victory this year, 1944? We don't know yet, but hope is revived within us; it gives us fresh courage, and makes us strong again.' In her case the hope was misplaced: the Frank family were betrayed to the Gestapo in August 1944 and Anne perished at Bergen–Belsen in early March 1945.

Having got into the countryside behind the beaches, the Americans in particular were dismayed to find themselves among the *bocage* – high and wide, ancient (sometimes Viking-built) thick hedgerows that provided ideal cover for defence. German resistance around Carentan on 13 June and Caen on 18 June prevented Montgomery from taking either town, although the US VII Corps under Major-General J. Lawton Collins took Cherbourg on 27 June after five days' heavy fighting and the destruction of the harbour by the Germans, which could not be used until 7 August. The Germans in Caen, which Montgomery called the 'crucible' of the battle, held out until 9 July, and the town was little more than rubble when it finally fell. (This hadn't prevented the London *Evening News* from proclaiming its capture on D+1.) Basil Liddell Hart was thus right in his description of Overlord as having gone 'according to plan, but not according to timetable'.[45]

From the German perspective, General Blumentritt wrote to a correspondent in 1965, saying that the German soldier had 'bled to death through wrong politics and dilettante leadership of Hitler'. In particular, Normandy was lost because 'Hitler ordered a rigid defence of the coasts. That was not possible over 2,000 kilometres,' especially when considering 'the Allied mastery of the air, the Allied masses of matériel, and the weakened German potential after 5 years of war.' Rundstedt, he believed, was 'a cavalier, gentleman, grand seigneur' with a wider view than Hitler and Rommel. Rundstedt wanted to give up the whole of France south of the Loire and fight a fast-moving tank battle around Paris instead, but was prevented by Hitler and Rommel who 'intended to carry out the defence with all forces on the beach and to use all tank-corps right in front, at the coast'.[46]

Timetables were vital to the Germans too, and in reinforcing Normandy as quickly as possible they were severely hampered by the destruction of road and rail routes by the bombing campaign and by heroic acts of resistance by the French Maquis, who attacked the Germans and destroyed bridges and railways in the path of the Panzers. This led to horrific reprisals, the best known of which were carried out by the 15,000-strong 2nd SS Das Reich Panzer Division, frustrated by losses and delays as it attempted to drive from Montauban in southern France to repel the invader in Normandy. The 450-mile journey lasted three weeks after they had set out on 8 June, as opposed to the few days it would have taken had they been left unharried. In retaliation for the killing of forty German soldiers in one incident, Das Reich exacted widespread reprisals in the town of Tulle in the Corrèze. 'I came home from shopping on 9 June 1944 to find my husband and my son hanging from the balcony of our house,' recalled a woman from the town. 'They were just two of a hundred men seized at random and killed in cold blood by the SS. The children and wives were forced to watch while they strung them up to the lamp-posts and balconies outside their own homes. What is there for me to say?'[47]

Yet worse was to come the next morning at the small village of Oradour-sur-Glane, where Major Adolf Diekmann's unit murdered 642 people, including 190 schoolchildren; the men were shot, the women and children were burnt alive in the church, and the village was razed. Max Hastings cannot entirely rule out as ghoulish exaggeration the reports that the SS burnt a baby alive in an oven. The village can be visited today, a stark reminder of man's inhumanity to man. Yet as Hastings has pointed out, 'It is important to remember that if Oradour was an exceptionally dreadful occurrence during the war in the West, it was a trifling sample of what the German Army had been doing on a national scale in the East, since 1941.' As one of Diekmann's officers – an *Ostkämpfer* (Eastern Front veteran) – confidentially told a former officer of the SS Totenkopf Division, 'in our circles, Herr Muller, it was *nothing*.'[48]

'I am certainly not a brutal man by nature,' Hitler told his lunch guests on 20 August 1942, 'and consequently it is cold reason that guides my actions. I have risked my own life a thousand times, and I owe my preservation simply to my good fortune.'[49] The black angel hovering over him certainly never performed a better service of protection than on the afternoon of Thursday, 20 July 1944. Hitherto, Hitler had believed that 'In the two really dangerous attempts to assassinate me I owe my life not to the police, but to pure chance.' These had been when he had left the Bürgerbräu beerhall ten minutes before a bomb went off there on 9 November 1939, and when a Swiss stalked him for three months at the Berghof.[50] Hitler took all the normal precautions against assassination, saying, 'As far as is possible, whenever I go anywhere by car I go off unexpectedly and without warning the police.' His chief security officer SS-Standartenführer (Colonel) Hans Rattenhuber and his chauffeur Erich Kempka had 'the strictest orders to maintain absolute secrecy about my comings and goings', however high up the official making enquiries about them. Nonetheless, if he felt safe anywhere it would have been at his command headquarters deep in the pine forests of East Prussia (now in Poland) known as the Wolfschanze (Wolf's Lair), from his long-term Nazi Party codename of Wolf.

'Here in the Wolfschanze,' Hitler said on the night of 26 February 1942, 'I feel like a prisoner in these dug-outs, and my spirit can't escape.'[51] That might be why, when one visits the destroyed buildings today, they resonate with sinister echoes. Jodl called the Wolfschanze 'somewhere between a monastery and a concentration camp'. The size of twenty-one football pitches and staffed by 2,000 people, it housed Hitler for more than 800 days of his 2,067-day war. The *Führerbunker*, Hitler's own quarters where he paced backwards and forwards in the card room – 'In that way I get my ideas' – boasted 6-foot-thick concrete walls, a sophisticated ventilation system, electric heating, running hot and cold water and air conditioning. As well as two airfields, a power station, a railway stop, garages and an advanced communications system, the headquarters possessed saunas, cinemas and tea rooms.

'In consequence of the defeat of the submarine,' Dönitz stated years after the war, 'the Anglo-American invasion of Normandy in July [*sic*] 1944 was now a success and now we knew clearly that we had no more chance to win the war. But what could we do?'[52] The answer for some in the German High Command – though certainly not the ultra-loyal Dönitz himself – was to try to assassinate Hitler. There had been some latent hostility between Hitler and his generals, except in those periods at the start of the war when victories came as easily as the subsequent mutual admiration. 'The General Staff is the only Masonic Order that I haven't yet dissolved,' Hitler said on one occasion, and on another: 'Those gentlemen with the purple stripes down their trousers sometimes seem to me even more revolting than the Jews.'[53] From the time of the rebuff at Moscow in late 1941, these antipathies resurfaced and, once the war looked as if it was going to be lost, some of the braver generals decided it was time to act. Far from acting out of democratic values, however, the majority of the Plotters were simply trying to remove an incompetent corporal who they realized was the major impediment to a negotiated peace, which objectively speaking was Germany's only hope of preventing a Soviet occupation.

At 12.42 p.m. on Thursday, 20 July 1944, a 2-pound bomb planted by the Swabian aristocratic war hero Colonel Count Claus von Stauffenberg ripped through one of the conference huts at the Wolf-schanze only 6 feet from where Hitler was studying an air-reconnaissance report through his magnifying glass. Stauffenberg used British fuses because they did not make a tell-tale hissing sound. A series of accidents had meant that the meeting was transferred to a different room outside the bunker, the bomb was moved away from close to Hitler to behind a heavy table leg, and only one rather than two bombs were primed, otherwise the assassination attempt – one of seventeen made against him – would probably have succeeded. 'The swine are bombing us!' was Hitler's first thought after the explosion, which burst his eardrums, hurt his right elbow, scarred his forehead, cut his face, set his hair and clothes alight, shredded his trousers and left more than a hundred splinters in the lower third of both thighs, but nothing more serious than that. 'Believe me,' he told his private secretary Christa Schroeder at lunch that day, 'this is the turning point for Germany. From now on things will look up again. I'm glad the *Schweinhunde* have unmasked themselves.'[54] At 2.30 that afternoon Hitler, Himmler, Keitel, Göring, Ribbentrop and Bormann all arrived at the railway station to greet Mussolini, with Hitler shaking hands with his left hand. By that time, a corporal had recalled a one-armed colonel leaving the hut in a hurry without his yellow briefcase, shreds of which were being found in the wreckage. Hitler's Army adjutant, General Rudolf Schmundt, was blinded and horribly burnt in the blast, finally dying from his injuries on 1 October. 'Don't expect me to console you,' Hitler told Frau Schmundt, somewhat insensitively in the circumstances. 'You must console me for my loss.'[55] The situation room where the bomb went off itself no longer exists, though there is a memorial stone to Stauffenberg where it once stood. (His remains were dug up by the SS after his execution at 1 a.m. on 21 July, and his final resting place is thus unknown.)

Churchill described the July Plotters as 'the bravest of the best', but there were not many of them, and most were extreme German nationalists rather than the idealistic democrats depicted by Hollywood.[56] Although 5,764 people were arrested for complicity in the Plot in 1944, and an almost identical number the following year, fewer than a hundred were genuinely involved in it to the extent that they knew what was about to happen, although they did include soldiers as senior as Field Marshal von Witzleben, General Erich Hoepner, General Friedrich Olbricht and Field Marshal Günther von Kluge.[57] It was a myth that the Plotters were hanged with piano wire, but true that the film of their execution (by strangulation from meat hooks at the Ploetzensee prison in Berlin) was sent to the Wolfschanze for Hitler's delectation. What is unclear is whether the Plotters really spoke for many more than themselves. Count Helmuth von Moltke's ideas for post-war democracy involved elections for local councils only. Claus von Stauffenberg and Carl Goerdeler wanted Germany to return to her 1939 borders, which included the remilitarized Rhineland as well as the Sudetenland. (Stauffenberg was far from the model democrat: he despised 'the lie that all men are equal', believed in 'natural hierarchies' and therefore resented being made to swear an oath to the 'petit bourgeois' Hitler whom he disdained on class grounds. As a Staff officer in a light Panzer division in Poland in 1939, he described Poles as 'an unbelievable rabble' of 'Jews and mongrels' who were 'only comfortable under the knout'. He even got married carrying his steel helmet.)[58] Other Plotters, such as Ulrich von Hassell, considered Germany's 1914 imperial frontiers desirable, yet they included parts of the very country, Poland, for which Britain and France had ostensibly gone to war. The future orientation of Alsace-Lorraine was another point of contention.

The hopes of the Plotters that they could make peace with Britain suffered from the flaw that such decisions were no longer up to Britain alone. Once the war was being fought by an Anglo-Russo-American coalition, and especially after President Roosevelt's January 1943 insistence on Germany's unconditional surrender, it was unthinkable that Britain should enter into negotiations with any Germans behind her allies' backs. As one of the senior officials in the German Department of the Foreign Office, Sir Frank Roberts, put it in his autobiography: 'If Stalin got the impression we were in contact with the German generals, whose main aim was to protect Germany against Russia, he might well have been tempted to see whether he could not again come to terms with Hitler.'[59]

The British Government's stance had been succinctly summed up by Sir D'Arcy Osborne, who when told by Pope Pius XII that the German Resistance groups 'confirmed their intention, or their desire, to effect a change of government' answered, 'Why don't they get on with it?' It is anyway also questionable what genuine aid the Allies could actually have given to the Plotters. Logistical support was hardly needed and moral support was of little practical help. Any promises about their attitude towards a post-Hitler Germany would necessarily have been contingent on its nature, and British decision-makers had seen quite enough of the Prussian officer class between 1914 and 1918 not to place too much faith in its commitment to democracy. For them, Prussian militarism was almost as unattractive as full-blown Nazism, and national-conservative Germans were nearly indistinguishable from national-socialist ones. One can understand why Eden should have said that the July Bomb Plotters 'had their own reasons for acting as they did and were certainly not moved primarily by a desire to help our cause', however harsh that may seem in retrospect.

Seen in this light, the offhand attitude of Sir Alec Cadogan, the permanent under-secretary at the Foreign Office ('As usual, the German Army trust us to save them from the Nazi regime') becomes explicable. After Goerdeler had asked for Danzig, colonial concessions and a £500 million interest-free loan before deposing Hitler in December 1938, Cadogan had been equally scathing, writing in his diary: 'We are to deliver the goods and Germany gives the IOUs.'[60] The Foreign Secretary of the day agreed. On the subject of what Neville Chamberlain termed 'Hitler's Jacobites', Lord Halifax complained, 'The Germans always want us to make their revolutions for them.'

An assassinated Hitler might also have provided the ideal *Dolchstosslegende* (stab-in-the-back myth) once Germany was defeated in 1945, or later if the Wehrmacht had directed the war. Like the myth of 1918, which blamed the loss of the Great War not on the German Army in the field but on defeatists, capitalists, Jews, socialists, aristocrats and traitors at home, so a new myth would have developed that argued that just as Hitler was about to launch his war-winning secret weapons to destroy the Allied armies, which he had spent six months purposely luring towards Germany, he was murdered by a clique of aristocrats, liberals, Christians and cosmopolitans whose treachery was evident since they were working in tandem with British intelligence. It would have been a potent recipe for revanchism which might have resonated in Germany for years to come.

The war had to be won by the Allies, of course, but it also needed to be lost, comprehensively and personally, by Hitler himself. His suicide in the bunker after the total collapse of his dreams had to be the last chapter of the tale, the crucial prerequisite for the decent, peace-loving Germany we know today.[61] If Hitler had been killed by the generals in 1944 – with or without British help – and a compromise peace had been arranged that way, present-day Germans would always have wondered whether the Führer might have won the war. There would always be the nagging doubt that Hitler was about to pull off his greatest master-stroke in a career that had hitherto been full of them. Furthermore, if a post-Hitler German government had been allowed to escape Allied occupation as part of the peace settlement, it is even uncertain whether the full facts about the Holocaust would ever have been revealed in the dramatic, undeniable way that they were.

It is also doubtful that the death of Hitler in the summer of 1944 would have necessarily shortened the war. The historian Peter Hoffmann has written that 'Göring would have sought to rally all the state's forces by an appeal to *völkisch* and national-socialist ideals, by vowing to fulfil the Führer's legacy and to redouble the efforts to fight the enemy to a standstill.' If Göring, or more probably Himmler – who controlled the SS – had taken over and not made the many strategic blunders perpetrated by Hitler in the final months, Germany might even have fought on for longer. Before June 1944, Germany had wreaked far worse damage on the Allies than they had on her. A negotiated peace would have let the German people off the hook, although it would have saved millions of lives in Europe and, by presumably shortening the war against Japan, in the Far East too. Yet to have concluded an armistice on the demonstrable fallacy that the war was begun and carried on by one man's will, rather than through the wholehearted support and enthusiasm of the German people, would hardly have produced the most durable and profound period of peace Europe has ever known.

On 24 July 1944 Churchill warned the War Cabinet that 'Rockets may start any minute,' referring to the Germans' 'wonder-weapon', the supersonic V-2 missile. The V-2's sister-weapon, the V-1 flying bomb, had been terrorizing southern England for six weeks, even though fifty-eight of the ninety-two V-1 launching sites had been damaged. After Brooke's encouraging report on the Normandy campaign, Churchill reported on his trip to Cherbourg, Arromanches and

Caen over the previous three days, saying that he 'Saw great many troops – never seen such a happy army – magnificent looking army – only want good weather. Had long talks with M[ontgomery] – has outfit of canaries – two dogs – six tame rabbits – play with dogs – frightful bombing of Caen . . . remarkable clearing of mines in Cherbourg harbour.'[62] Amid all this talk of Monty's menagerie, Admiral Cunningham diarized that 'PM full of his visit to France and was more inclined to talk than to listen.'[63] But one difference between Churchill and Hitler was that Churchill was capable of listening to – indeed asking for – news and advice he did not like. After the Bomb Plot, Hitler became highly suspicious of the veracity of what he heard from his generals, suspecting that many more of them were involved than in fact had been.

By 24 July the Allies had lost 122,000 men killed, wounded or captured in France, to the Germans' 114,000 (including 41,000 taken prisoner). The highly competent, robust and aggressive Günther von Kluge – who by the summer of 1944 had recovered from injuries sustained in a bad car-crash in Russia – took over control of the defence, having been given Rundstedt's job by Hitler, and he also temporarily inherited Rommel's job on 17 July when the latter's car was strafed from the air and he fractured his skull. Overlord having now ended, the next phase of the invasion was codenamed Operation Cobra and was intended to break out from the linked beach-heads and strike south and east into central France. The hinge was to be the British Second and Canadian First Armies in the area east of Caen, which kept the main weight of the German Army occupied while bold thrusts were made across country by Omar Bradley's US First Army and Patton's US Third Army.

The Allied offensive began with the carpet bombing of Saint-Lô and areas west of it in which 4,200 tons of high explosive were dropped by Spaatz's heavy bombers. (Shortfall bombs killed around 500 Americans, including Lieutenant-General Lesley J. McNair, chief of US Army ground forces, whose body could be identified only by the three stars on his collar.) Despite Hitler giving Kluge some of the Fifteenth Army's divisions on 27 July, the Americans poured forward through gaps in the German defences created by the bombing, and by the end of the month Collins' VII Corps had taken Avranches. This allowed US forces to attack westwards into Brittany and eastwards towards Le Mans, proving the value of Patton's eve-of-battle observation to his Third Army that 'flanks are something for the enemy to worry about, not us'.[64] A counter-attack at Mortain that Hitler demanded of Kluge, and insisted on his carrying on for two days after it had been stopped by the RAF on 8 August, petered out and left a large body of troops in danger of being surrounded by the Americans from the south-west and the British and Canadians from the north, in an area 18 miles wide by 10 deep known as the Falaise–Argentan pocket, whose mouth was called the Falaise Gap.

Better communications – and indeed better personal relations – might have led to a greater victory at the Gap even than the one gained by Montgomery, Bradley and Patton between 13 and 19 August. On 16 August Kluge had ordered a general retreat out of the pocket, warning Jodl at OKW, 'It would be a disastrous mistake to entertain hopes that cannot be fulfilled. No power in the world can realize them, nor will any orders which are issued.'[65] Panzer Group West, comprising the Seventh and Fifth Panzer Armies, sustained around 50,000 killed, wounded or captured, to the loss of 29,000 Allies at Falaise.[66] Eisenhower visited the pocket forty-eight hours after the battle, and later described it as 'unquestionably one of the greatest "killing grounds" of any of the war areas. Roads, highways and fields were so choked with destroyed equipment and destroyed men that passage through the area was extremely difficult.' This was due to 'scenes that could be described only by Dante. It was literally possible to walk for hundreds of yards, stepping on nothing but dead and decaying flesh.'[67] With Allied fighter-bombers flying 3,000 sorties a day, those who did escape were merely the shattered remnants of the hitherto formidable German Fifth and Seventh Panzer Armies and Panzer Group Eberbach.

Yet 20,000 German troops did escape, along with their 88mm guns, although this did not save Kluge from being replaced by Field Marshal Model on 17 August. After the war Bradley blamed Montgomery for over-caution at Falaise, and vice versa, but Kluge's defeat there allowed the Allies to make for the Seine and to liberate Paris – which had risen on 23 August – by the 25th. Out of the thirty-nine divisions that took part in the Normandy invasion, just one was French, the 2e

Division Blindée (2nd Armoured Division) under the command of General Leclerc (the *nom de guerre* of Vicomte Jacques-Philippe de Hautecloque). It fought very bravely in the battle to close the Falaise Gap, and as part of the US Fifth Army it was given the honour of entering Paris first, although this did not elicit any noticeable gratitude from the Free French leader, General de Gaulle.

In 1956, de Gaulle went on a Pacific cruise with his wife and an entourage that included the Agence France Presse journalist Jean Mauriac, son of the Nobel Prize-winning Catholic novelist François Mauriac. When asked by Mauriac *fils* whether he knew the most beautiful of Charles Trenet's songs, 'Douce France' (Gentle France), de Gaulle retorted '"Douce France"? There is nothing *douce* about *la France*!'[68] There had certainly been nothing gentle about de Gaulle's declamations in defence of France, a country he redeemed virtually alone by his courage and determination. It was perfectly true that *les Anglo-Saxons* could find him to be a monster of intransigence and ingratitude, but he had his nation's self-respect to protect, which he did superbly. Although Churchill never said that the heaviest cross that he had to bear during the war was the Cross of Lorraine, it was indeed said by de Gaulle's liaison officer, General Louis Spears, who knew de Gaulle better than any other Englishman.[69] Yet even Spears emerged with great admiration for de Gaulle, albeit tempered with constant irritation.

Examples of de Gaulle's ingratitude towards his British wartime hosts are legion. 'You think I am interested in England winning the war,' he once told Spears. 'I am not. I am only interested in French victory.' When Spears made the logical remark: 'They are the same,' de Gaulle replied: 'Not at all; not at all in my view.' To a Canadian officer who just before D-Day had asked him whether he could join the Free French, but declared himself pro-British, de Gaulle shouted: 'I detest the English and the Americans, you understand, I detest the English and the Americans. Get out!'[70] De Gaulle's staple diet between 1940 and 1944 was the hand that fed him. He set foot in France for the first time since 1940 on 14 June, more than a week after D-Day, and only then for a one-day visit to Bayeux, after which he left for Algiers and did not return to French soil until 20 August. In the meantime General George Patton's Third Army had broken out of

Avranches at the end of July and had driven through Brittany. The French Resistance, the *résistants* and *maquisards* – a separate organization from de Gaulle's Free French forces – was doing brave and vital work in support of the Allied forces, especially in hampering German armoured retaliation, but de Gaulle played little part in any of this from his base in North Africa.

Meanwhile in Paris, the German commander General Dietrich von Choltitz took the historic and humane decision not to set fire to the city. 'Paris must be destroyed from top to bottom,' the Führer had demanded of him, 'do not leave a single church or monument standing.' The German High Command then listed seventy bridges, factories and national landmarks – including the Eiffel Tower, Arc de Triomphe and Notre-Dame Cathedral – for particular destruction. Hitler later repeatedly asked his chief of staff: 'Is Paris burning?' Yet Choltitz deliberately disobeyed these barbaric instructions, and the Germans did not therefore fight in the French capital the battle of extirpation that they were even then fighting in Warsaw, at the cost of over 200,000 Polish lives and the utter devastation of the city. Choltitz instead surrendered and went into captivity as soon as he decently could once regular Allied forces arrived, telling the Swedish diplomat who negotiated the agreement that he did not wish to be remembered as 'the man who destroyed Paris'.

In all General Leclerc lost only seventy-six men killed in the liberation of Paris, although 1,600 inhabitants had been killed in the uprising, including 600 non-combatants. Today the places where the individual soldiers and *résistants* fell are marked all over the city, and none would wish to belittle their great bravery and self-sacrifice, yet the fact remains that the only reason that Leclerc was assigned to liberate the city was that Eisenhower could spare the French 2nd Division from far greater battles that were taking place right across northern and southern France, battles fought against crack German units by British, American and Canadian forces. For political and prestige reasons, de Gaulle had begged Eisenhower to allow French troops to be first into the capital, and the Supreme Commander was as good as his word, giving the order to General Leclerc to advance on the city on 22 August. De Gaulle instructed Leclerc to get there before the Americans arrived, and, because he did not wish to detract from de Gaulle's limelight, Eisenhower did not visit the capital himself until 27 August.

There is some truth in the suggestion that, as with Rome, the Allies did not see Paris as a prime military objective, as opposed to a political one, and they were right not to. As the historian Ian Ousby wrote in his history of the Occupation: 'Paris's concentration of both people and cultural monuments ruled out aerial bombardment and heavy artillery barrages, so taking the city would soak up time and lives in a campaign already behind schedule and high in casualties. Besides, the capture of Paris was not tactically essential.' For his part, Omar Bradley in his memoirs dismissed Paris as 'a pen and ink job on the map'.

The first of Leclerc's (American-donated Sherman) tanks rolled up the rue de Rivoli at 9.30 on the morning of Friday, 25 August. In the surrender document signed that same afternoon by Leclerc and Choltitz, there was no mention of either Britain or the United States; the German forces formally surrendered to the French alone. Similarly, once de Gaulle arrived in Paris soon afterwards to make a speech at the Hôtel de Ville, he proclaimed that Paris had been 'liberated by her own people, with the help of the armies of France, with the help and support of the whole of France, that is to say of fighting France, that is to say of the true France, the eternal France'. A sub-phrase summed up the Allied contribution. The next morning, Saturday, 26 August 1944, de Gaulle led a parade from the Arc de Triomphe down the Champs-Elysées to a thanksgiving service in Notre-Dame. When the head of the National Council of Resistance, Georges Bidault, came up abreast of him in the parade he hissed, 'A little to the rear, if you please.'[71] The glory was to be de Gaulle's alone.

16

Western Approaches

August 1944–March 1945

When Herr Hitler escaped his bomb on July 20th he described his survival as providential; I think that from a purely military point of view we can all agree with him, for certainly it would be most unfortunate if the Allies were to be deprived, in the closing phases of the struggle, of that form of warlike genius by which Corporal Schickelgruber has so notably contributed to our victory.

Winston Churchill in the House of Commons, 28 September 1944[1]

It took eleven months from D-Day for the Western Allies to force the Germans to surrender in the west, fighting against often fanatical resistance and at least on one occasion – the Ardennes offensive – having to face a convincing, formidable counter-attack. Yet any thinking German knew that the war was lost from about the time of the destruction of Army Group Centre in the east and the fall of Paris in the west. Some of the German generals themselves had indicated the way they thought the war was progressing, by launching the Bomb Plot, which they had shown little inclination to do when Germany was winning the war. It was the news of a large Allied invasion of the south of France on 15 August 1944, Operation Anvil, with 86,000 troops going ashore on the first day alone, that had persuaded Field Marshal von Kluge to withdraw from the Falaise pocket. While talk of secret super-weapons sometimes now enthused the ordinary soldier, the officer corps generally knew better than to trust to it; indeed a belief in the Führer and ultimate victory seems to have been held in the German armed forces in directly inverse proportion to seniority, except for a very few fanatically Nazi generals such as Walther Model, Ferdinand Schörner and Lothar Rendulic.

The Nazis' argument that they had to fight on to prevent Soviet barbarity being unleashed on their wives and daughters was true as far as it went, but it only went as far as the east. In attempting to explain why the High Command nonetheless kept on fighting so hard on both fronts after Overlord, Max Hastings argues that whether they were SS officers, Prussian aristocrats, career soldiers or mere functionaries, the German generals 'abandoned coherent thought about the future and merely performed the immediate military functions that were so familiar to them'.[2] It was certainly a great deal easier than acting for themselves, at least once the Bomb Plot had brought suspicion upon them all, just as the Plot's failure seemed to underline the Führer's indestructibility. They also knew how heavily implicated they were in the crimes of the Nazi regime.

The extent to which the German generals knew about and collaborated in war crimes, particularly on the Eastern Front, was revealed by a massive clandestine operation undertaken by the British Secret Intelligence Service between 1942 and 1945. A section of SIS called MI19 secretly recorded no fewer than 64,427 conversations between captured German generals and other senior officers, all without their knowledge, indeed without their ever suspecting anything. These explain what the German High Command privately thought of the war, Hitler, the Nazis and each other. They also comprehensively explode the post-war claim of senior Wehrmacht officers that they did not know what was happening to the Jews, Slavs, Gypsies, mentally disabled and other so-called *Untermenschen*, crimes which they exclusively blamed on the SS.

The Combined Services Detailed Interrogation Centre (CSDIC) was based in Trent Park, a magnificent estate once owned by the Sassoon family near Cockfosters in north London. Captured German senior officers were brought there for internment, including General Wilhelm von Thoma, who had been captured at El Alamein, General Hans-Jürgen von Arnim, who had been 'bagged' in Tunisia, and General Dietrich von Choltitz from Paris. It was a huge top-secret operation, numbering several hundred stenographers, transcribers, interpreters and recording technicians, not to mention stool-pigeons and agents provocateurs whose job it was to stimulate conversations among the captive generals, brigadiers and colonels.[3]

Everything was done to get the Germans to speak to each other in one of the twelve rooms in the common areas of the house that were expertly wired for sound. Luftwaffe commanders were mixed with Wehrmacht generals; newspapers and radios passed on snippets of news from the front; occasionally Lord Aberfaldy – a CSDIC agent posing as the Park's welfare officer – would bring up subjects British intelligence hoped might provoke debate once he had left the room. The astonishing success of the operation can be measured in the sheer number as well as the extreme candour of the conversations that ensued. Of course British intelligence hoped to discover operational secrets by this eavesdropping, believing that it might yield results that face-to-face interrogations would not, but they also heard evidence of sustained atrocities, especially in the east. Although most of the generals at Trent Park were captured in North Africa, Italy and France, it became clear that they knew perfectly well what was happening throughout the Third Reich and its occupied territories.

No fewer than 10,191 German and 567 Italian prisoners passed through Trent Park and its two related listening centres. Some of the conversations originally recorded on gramophone discs covered only half a page in transcribed length – the longest was twenty-one pages – but out of their own mouths these officers were condemned. Even Choltitz, who has had the reputation of being a 'good' German since refusing to carry out Hitler's orders to destroy Paris, was implicated in killing Jews in the Crimea.[4] A few generals come out acceptably well, though far from heroic. In January 1943 Thoma, who commanded a Panzer division in Russia before being captured in Africa, said to the pro-Nazi General Ludwig Crüwell, who had been shot down behind British lines, 'I am actually ashamed to be an officer.' He related how he had spoken to Franz Halder about the atrocities, only to be told, 'That's a political matter, that's nothing to do with me.' So he put it in writing to Army Commander-in-Chief General Walther von Brauchitsch, who said, 'Do you want me to take it further? Listen, if you want me to take it further anything might happen.' Thoma said of those who believed the Führer was ignorant of what was happening: 'Of course he knows all about it. Secretly he's delighted. Of course, people can't make a row, they would simply be arrested and beaten if they did.'[5] That would not have happened if they had simply resigned their commissions, however, which is not something Thoma or any of the others did.

The truth about what was happening to Poles, Russians and especially Jews was common currency in the 'private' conversations at Trent Park. In December 1944, to take one of any number of examples, Lieutenant-General Heinrich Kittel, the former commander of the 462nd Volksgrenadier Division, told Major-General Paul von Felbert, the former commandant of Feldkommandantur (military administration unit) 560: 'The things I've experienced! In Latvia, near Dvinsk, there were mass executions of Jews carried out by the SS. There were about fifteen SS men and perhaps sixty Latvians, who are known to be the most brutal people in the world. I was lying in bed early one Sunday morning when I kept on hearing two salvoes followed by small arms fire.' On investigating, Kittel found 'men, women and children – they were counted off and stripped naked. The executioners first laid all the clothes in one pile. Then twenty women had to take up their position – naked – on the edge of the trench, they were shot and fell down into it.' 'How was it done?' asked Felbert. 'They faced the trench and then twenty Latvians came up behind and simply fired once through the back of their heads, and they fell down forwards into the trench like ninepins.'[6]

Kittel gave an order forbidding such executions 'outside, where people can look on. If you shoot people in the wood or somewhere where no one can see,' he told the SS, 'that's your own affair. But I absolutely forbid another day's shooting here. We draw our drinking water from deep springs; we're getting nothing but corpse water there.' 'What did they do to the children?' asked Felbert. Kittel – who, the report states, sounded 'very excited' – answered: 'They seized 3-year-old children by the hair, held them up and shot them with a pistol and then threw them in. I saw that for myself. One could watch it.' Another general, Lieutenant-General Hans Schaefer, commander of the 244th Infantry Division, asked Kittel: 'Did they weep? Have the people any idea what's in store for them?' 'They know perfectly well,' replied Kittel; 'they are apathetic. I'm not sensitive myself, but such things turn my stomach.' Later on, however, he mused: 'If one were to destroy all the Jews of the world simultaneously there wouldn't remain a single accuser,' and 'Those Jews are the pest of the east!' 'What happened to the young, pretty girls?' asked Felbert when the conversation turned to the concentration camps. 'Were they formed into a harem?' 'I didn't bother about that,' Kittel answered. 'I only found that they did become more reasonable . . . The women question is a very shady chapter. You've no idea what mean and stupid things are done.'[7] In another conversation later that same day, Kittel told Schaefer about Auschwitz: 'In Upper Silesia they simply slaughtered the people systematically. They were gassed in a big hall. There's the greatest secrecy about all those things.' Later still he said: 'I'm going to hold my tongue about what I do know of these things.' He little suspected that his every word was in fact being recorded, transcribed and translated.

The following February, Major-General Johannes Bruhn, commander of the 533rd Volksgrenadier Division, discussed the Holocaust with Felbert, saying: 'I must assume, after all I have read about the Führer, that he knew all about it.' 'Of course he knew all about it,' replied Felbert. 'He's the man who is responsible. He even discussed it with Himmler.' 'Yes,' said Bruhn, 'that man doesn't care a hoot if your relatives are annihilated.' 'That man doesn't care a damn,' agreed Felbert. They saw the Holocaust, therefore, primarily in terms of the retribution the Allies would visit on the Fatherland once it was uncovered. In March 1945 Bruhn, one of the very few generals to emerge with credit from these conversations, said he believed that Germany did not deserve victory any longer, 'after the amount of human blood we've shed knowingly and as a result of our delusions and blood lust. We've deserved our fate.'[8] In reply, Lieutenant-General Fritz von Broich said: 'We shot women as if they had been cattle. There was a large quarry where 10,000 men, women and children were shot. They were still lying in the quarry. We drove out on purpose to see it. It was the most bestial thing I ever saw.' It was then that Choltitz spoke of the time he was in the Crimea and was told by the CO of the airfield from where he was flying to Berlin, 'Good Lord, I'm not supposed to tell, but they've been shooting Jews here for days now.' Choltitz estimated that 36,000 Jews were shot in Sevastopol alone.

'Let me tell you,' General Count Edwin von Rothkirch und Trach told General Bernhard Ramcke on 13 March 1945, 'the gassings are by no means the worst.' 'What happened?' asked Ramcke. 'To start with people dug their own graves, then the firing squad arrived with tommy-guns and shot them down. Many of them weren't dead and a layer of earth was shovelled in between. They had packers there who packed the bodies in, because they fell in too soon. The SS did that. I knew an SS leader there quite well and he said: "Would you like to photograph a shooting? They are always shot in the morning, but if you like we still have some and we can shoot them in the afternoon some time."' Three days later at Trent Park, Colonel Dr Friedrich von der Heydte told Colonel Eberhard Wildermuth about the Theresienstadt concentration camp in Czechoslovakia: 'Half a million people have been put to death there for certain. I know that all the Jews from Bavaria were taken there. Yet the camp never became over-crowded. They gassed mental defectives too.' 'Yes, I know,' replied Wildermuth. 'I got to know that for a fact in the case of Nuremberg; my brother is a doctor at an institution there. The people knew where they were being taken.'[9] 'We must uphold the principle of only having carried out orders,' suggested Lieutenant-General Ferdinand Heim on another occasion. 'We must stick to that principle if we are to create a more or less effective defence.'

As the war progressed, the Trent Park internees divided between true Nazis, who still practised the Heil Hitler salute, and the anti- or at least non-Nazis. The Nazis' fanaticism was undimmed by the way the war was going. 'What do I care about Good Friday?' asked Major-General Wilhelm Ullersperger, who had been captured during the Ardennes offensive. 'Because a filthy Jew was hanged umpteen years ago?' Major-General Walther Bruns recalled the attitude of the members of the firing squad who killed thousands of Jews in Riga: 'All those cynical remarks! If only I had seen those tommy-gunners, who were relieved every hour because of over-exertion, carry out their task with distaste, but not with nasty remarks like: "Here comes a Jewish beauty!" I can still see it all in my memory; a pretty woman in a flame-coloured chemise. Talk about keeping the race pure. At Riga they first slept with them and then shot them to prevent them from talking.' Meanwhile, Colonel Erwin Josting of the Luftwaffe recalled an Austrian friend being asked by a lieutenant: '"Would you like to watch? An amusing show is going on down here; umpteen Jews are being killed off." The barn was bunged full of women and children. Petrol was poured over them and they were burned alive. You can't imagine what their screams were like.'[10]

Of course once in captivity in Nuremberg and subsequently in their autobiographies in the 1950s and 1960s, the generals both blamed Hitler for everything and used the now notorious excuse that they were only obeying orders. 'It is interesting but it was tragic,' Kleist told the US Army psychiatrist Leon Goldensohn in June 1946, in a statement typical of the entire officer corps. 'If you receive a military order you must obey. That is where the big difference between a military and a political order comes in. One can sabotage a political order but to disobey a military command is treason.'[11] Kesselring put it equally succinctly when he told Goldensohn, 'A soldier's first duty is to obey, otherwise you might as well do away with soldiering . . . A military leader often faces a situation he has to deal with, but because it was his duty, no court can try him.' The evidence from Trent Park suggests that the Wehrmacht officer corps fought on with such resilience even after the war seemed certainly lost not just out of the soldierly virtues of loyalty and obedience, but because they hoped against hope to escape judicial retribution afterwards.

On 1 September 1944, Eisenhower took over day-to-day control of all ground forces from Montgomery, much to the latter's chagrin. Eisenhower's plan was for a broad advance into Germany, whereas Montgomery wanted a narrow 'single thrust' into the heart of the Reich, spearheaded by his 21st Army Group. On the same day that Montgomery put forward this plan, Patton produced one in which his Third Army led the way instead, with characteristic immodesty calling it 'the best strategicall [sic] idea I've ever had'.[12] Writing twenty years after the war, General Günther Blumentritt, who was commander of the Fifteenth Army from December 1944 onwards, admitted, 'We had the highest respect for General Patton! He was the American Guderian, an excellent and bold tank corps leader.'[13] Omar

Bradley, meanwhile, felt that his drive on Frankfurt ought to be the centre of operations. It is sadly impossible to believe that the best demands of grand strategy, rather than their own egos, actuated these soldiers, and Eisenhower had the difficult task of holding the ring between them and imposing his own view. His greatness – doubted by some, like Brooke and Montgomery – stems partly from his success in achieving that.

There were a number of major problems with Montgomery's scheme, which would have needed flank protection from the largely undamaged German Fifteenth Army to the north, and would have required the Scheldt estuary to have been used as a direct supply route, though the Germans continued to hold it until long after the fall of Antwerp in September. Montgomery's plan to strike off across the North German Plain towards Berlin, crossing important rivers such as the Weser and Elbe in the process, made little military sense considering the level of resistance that the Germans were still offering even comparatively late on in the war. The 1,500 bodies in the British Military Cemetery at Becklingen, between Bergen–Belsen and Soltau, are testament to how hard the fighting was between the Weser and the Elbe as late as April 1945. Moreover, it would have reduced the American forces, especially the Third Army, to the minor role of flank protection. Eisenhower had to ensure a rough equality of glory, in order to keep the Western alliance on track. It is likely that the plan to reduce Patton's role to mere tactical support of himself was one of the reasons it commended itself to Montgomery, but Eisenhower was later gently to belittle the scheme as a mere 'pencil thrust' into Germany.[14]

Instead, the Supreme Commander adopted the less risky 'broad front' approach to the invasion of the Reich, which he believed would 'bring all our strength against the enemy, all of it mobile, and all of it contributing directly to the complete annihilation of his field forces'.[15] Partly because of the efficacy of the V-weapon flying-bomb and rocket campaign against Britain – which could be ended only by occupying the launching sites – the main part was still to be the 21st Army Group's advance through Belgium north of the Ardennes forest and into the Ruhr, which would also close off Germany's industrial-production heartland, and thus deny Hitler the wherewithal to carry on the fight.

The 12th Army Group, which had been commanded by Bradley since August and was the largest force ever headed by an American general, was split by Eisenhower. Most of Lieutenant-General Court-ney Hodges' First Army was sent north of the Ardennes to support Montgomery, leaving Patton's Third Army to march on the Saar, covered to his south by Lieutenant-General Jacob Devers' 6th Army Group which had made its way up from the Anvil landings in the south of France. Even though Patton had crossed the Marne by 30 August 1944 and was soon able to threaten Metz and the Siegfried Line, lack of petrol along his 400-mile supply lines to Cherbourg – he had only 32,000 gallons but needed 400,000 for his planned advance – held him back, to his intense frustration. Patton's personality was immense, but his battlefield achievements matched it. 'I want you men to remember that no bastard ever won a war by dying for his country,' he told his troops. 'He won it by making the other dumb bastard die for his country . . . Thank God that, at least, thirty years from now, when you are sitting around the fireside with your grandson on your knee and he asks you what you did in the great World War II, you won't have to say, "I shovelled shit in Louisiana." '[16] To the widow of Second Lieutenant Neil N. Clothier, who was shot through the heart at Morville on 16 November leading his platoon towards a German machine-gun position, Patton wrote: 'I know that nothing I can do can assuage your grief except to point out to you that since all of us must die, there is comfort in the fact that your husband died gloriously doing his duty as a man and a soldier.'[17]

Brussels fell to the Canadians of the 21st Army Group on 3 September and Antwerp the next day, but here Montgomery made a significant error. Antwerp was next to useless to the Allies until the River Scheldt was free of Germans, but clearing its banks was to cost the Allies – mainly Crerar's Canadian First Army – as many as 13,000 casualties, because it was not concentrated upon immediately. Allied ships did not reach Antwerp until 28 November 1944. Until that point supplies still had to reach the 21st Army Group via Normandy, an absurdly long route. (Dunkirk wasn't liberated until 9 May 1945.) For Churchill, who had understood the vital importance of Antwerp in the Great War so clearly that he had led a mission there as first lord of the Admiralty in 1914, and for Brooke, Montgomery, Eisenhower and others so to underestimate the inland port's strategic value is hard to understand even today.

Clearing the estuary was always going to be tough work; this is John Keegan's description of a day in the life of Peter White's platoon in the 4th Battalion, the King's Own Scottish Borderers, part of the 52nd Lowland Division whose job it was to open the mouth of the Scheldt in late 1944:

To get up each morning, after a day that had been itself an escape from death, to swallow tinned bacon, hard tack and chlorine-flavoured tea, to plod forward across soaked fields in which every footstep might set off a lethal explosive charge, to lie for hours in freezing water while shells raked the landscape, to rise as darkness fell in the hope of finding a dry spot to shelter for the night after a mouthful of bully beef and hard biscuit.[18]

By contrast with Antwerp, Churchill's tardiness over liberating the Channel Islands was understandable – for, as he told the War Cabinet on 26 November, now that it had 'Come to [the] crunch' the issue was 'food'. There were 28,000 Germans stationed there who 'can't get away', whereas 'if [they came] over here [we would] have to feed them.'[19]

The food situation in liberated Europe was dire, especially in Holland where the destruction of transport, flooding of several dykes and continued disorganization as a result of continuing operations created fears of mass starvation. As late as 12 March 1945 Churchill had to tell the War Cabinet that 'Some of the inhabitants will need to take their food intravenously.' When he had been read a report on how the Americans expected primarily British food reserves to be used in saving Holland, the Prime Minister exploded in anger and launched this (hitherto unpublished) tirade:

The United States are battening on our reserves, accumulated by years of self-denial. I am resisting that: but for an acute emergency we can and should use our reserves . . . Now is the time to say firmly that the US soldier eats five times what ours does. US civilians are eating as never before. We will never be behindhand with them in sacrifices: but let them cut down themselves before presuming to address us.[20]

In September 1944 – two months after his sacking – Rundstedt was recalled as commander-in-chief west, a post he was to hold until

March 1945 when his urging of Hitler to make peace earned him his third dismissal. Nicknamed *der alte Herr* (the old gentleman), he was sixty-eight at the time of his final appointment. Watching the Hitler Youth Division retreating over the River Meuse near Yvoir on 4 September, Rundstedt said what many German officers were thinking, but few dared state: 'It is a pity that this faithful youth is sacrificed in a hopeless situation.'[21] A week later, on 11 September, the Allies set foot on German soil for the first time, when American troops crossed the frontier near Trier, yet Hitler still had armies numbering several million men, albeit far too widely dispersed. His West Wall – also known as the Siegfried Line – seemed formidable, and his reappointment of Rundstedt as commander-in-chief west was good for the Wehrmacht's morale, with Field Marshal Model remaining in charge of Army Group B, Rommel and Kluge both having committed suicide after being tangentially implicated in the Bomb Plot. Later that month, Churchill, by now convinced that Hitler was a hopeless strategist, ridiculed him in the House of Commons:

We must not forget that we owe a great debt to the blunders – the extraordinary blunders – of the Germans. I always hate to compare Napoleon with Hitler, as it seems an insult to the great Emperor and warrior to connect him in any way with a squalid caucus boss and butcher. But there is one respect in which I must draw a parallel. Both these men were temperamentally unable to give up the tiniest scrap of any territory to which the high-water mark of their hectic fortunes had carried them.[22]

He went on to liken Napoleon's strategy of 1813–14 to that of Hitler, who 'has successfully scattered the German armies all over Europe, and by obstination at every point from Stalingrad and Tunis down to the present moment, he has stripped himself of the power to concentrate in main strength for the final struggle'. Yet even while the House of Commons was laughing at the Führer's strategic blunderings, Hitler was planning for a concentration of German force in the Ardennes such as would once again astonish the world – but for the last time.

Montgomery's bold scheme to use the British 1st and the US 82nd and 101st Airborne Divisions to try to capture the bridges over the great rivers of the Maas (Meuse), Waal (Rhine) and Neder Rijn (Lower Rhine), and thereby help the land forces to encircle the Ruhr to the north, came to grief in mid-September 1944 in and around the Dutch towns of Eindhoven, Nijmegen and Arnhem. Despite heroism of the highest order, mistakes were made in the planning stages – principally by Lieutenant-General F. A. M. 'Boy' Browning, on the intelligence side – which meant it was doomed before it began. It was the largest airborne assault in history, but intelligence that should have warned the 1st Airborne Division of two Panzer divisions that were refitting near Arnhem was given insufficient weight, and it therefore did not take enough anti-tank weaponry to the drop-zones.[23] Operation Market, the airborne assault of Friday, 17 September, was initially successful, but the simultaneous ground attack by General Dempsey's British Second Army and XXX Corps, codenamed Operation Garden, reached Eindhoven on the 18th and Nijmegen on the 19th but could not break through determined German resistance in time to relieve the paratroopers at Arnhem. Montgomery's orders to Dempsey to be 'rapid and violent, without regard to what is happening on the flanks', seems not to have been taken sufficiently to heart.[24] XXX Corps suffered 1,500 casualties compared with five times that number of Britons and Poles at Arnhem, who were massacred on the Lower Rhine by tank, mortar and artillery fire, with their food and ammunition exhausted. Treacherous flying conditions prevented reinforcement or resupply by air, and on the night of 25 September around 3,910 of the 11,920 men of the 1st Airborne Division and Polish Independent Brigade Group managed to withdraw to the south side of the river, the rest being either killed, wounded or captured.[25] The 1st Airborne Division's casualty figures were twice as high as the combined totals of the 82nd and the 101st Divisions. It was, nonetheless, to be the British Army's last defeat.

What became known jointly as Operation Market Garden used up scarce Allied resources, manpower and petrol at precisely the moment that Patton was nearing the Rhine without insuperable opposition. Once the Allied armies stalled for lack of supplies, however, they would be unable to cross the borders of the Reich for another six months. The Germans meanwhile used the breathing space bought by their temporary victory in Holland to rush defenders to the Siegfried

Line, which had previously been under-defended. Between late September and mid-November, Eisenhower's forces found themselves fighting determined German counter-attacks in the Vosges, Moselle and the Scheldt and at Metz and Aachen. Hoping to cross the Rhine before the onset of winter, which in 1944/5 was abnormally cold, Eisenhower unleashed a massive assault on 16 November, supported by the heaviest aerial bombing of the entire war so far, with 2,807 planes dropping 10,097 bombs in Operation Queen. Even then, the US First and Ninth Armies managed to move forward only a few miles, up to but not across the Roer river.

Hopes that the war might be over in 1944, which had been surprisingly widespread earlier in the campaign – Admiral Ramsay wagered Montgomery £5 on it – were comprehensively extinguished just before dawn on Saturday, 16 December 1944, when Field Marshal von Rundstedt unleashed the greatest surprise attack of the war since Pearl Harbor. In Operation Herbstnebel (Autumn Mist), seventeen divisions – five Panzer and twelve mechanized infantry – threw themselves forward in a desperate bid to reach first the River Meuse and then the Channel itself. Instead of soft autumnal mists, it was to be winter fog, snow, sleet and heavy rain that wrecked the Allies' aerial observation, denying any advance warning of the attack. Similarly, Ultra was of little help in the early stages, since all German radio traffic had been strictly *verboten* and orders were only passed to corps commanders by messenger a few days before the attack.

Suddenly on 16 December no fewer than three German armies comprising 200,000 men spewed forth from the mountains and forests of the Ardennes. Rundstedt and Model had opposed the operation as too ambitious for the Wehrmacht's resources at that stage, but Hitler believed that he could split the Allied armies north and south of the Ardennes, protect the Ruhr, recapture Antwerp, reach the Channel and, he hoped, re-create the victory of 1940, and all from the same starting point. 'The morale of the troops taking part was astonishingly high at the start of the offensive,' recalled Rundstedt later. 'They really believed victory was possible. Unlike the higher commanders, who knew the facts.'[26] The highest commander of them all, however, believed that the Ardennes offensive might be the longed-for *Entscheidungsschlacht* (decisive battle) as prescribed by Clausewitz.

The German disagreements over the Ardennes offensive were really three-fold, and more complex than Rundstedt and others made out after the war. Guderian, who was charged with opposing the Red Army's coming winter offensive in the east, did not want any offensive in the west, but rather the reinforcing of the Eastern Front, including Hungary. Rundstedt, Model, Manteuffel and other generals in the west wanted a limited Ardennes offensive that knocked the Allies off balance, and gave the Germans the chance to rationalize the Western Front and protect the Ruhr. Meanwhile, Hitler wanted to throw the remainder of Germany's reserves into a desperate attempt to capture Antwerp and destroy Eisenhower's force in the west. As usual, Hitler took the most extreme and thus riskiest path, and as always he got his way.

Eisenhower had left the semi-mountainous, heavily wooded Ardennes region of Belgium and Luxembourg relatively undermanned. He cannot be wholly blamed for this, since he was receiving intelligence reports from Bradley stating that a German attack was 'only a remote possibility' and one from Montgomery on 15 December saying that the enemy 'cannot stage major offensive operations'.[27] Even on 17 December, after the offensive had actually begun, Major-General Kenneth Strong, the Assistant Chief of Staff (Intelligence) at SHAEF, produced his Weekly Intelligence Summary No. 39 which offered the blithe assessment that 'The main result must be judged, not by the ground it gains, but by the number of Allied divisions it diverts from the vital sectors of the front.'[28] For all the débâcle of 1940, the Ardennes seemed uninviting for armour, and important engagements were being fought to the north and south. With Wehrmacht movement restricted to night-time, and the Germans instituting elaborate deception plans, surprise was complete. Although four captured German POWs spoke of a big pre-Christmas offensive, they were not believed by Allied intelligence. Only six American divisions of 83,000 men protected the 60-mile line between Monschau in the north and Echternach in the south, most of them under Major-General Troy Middleton of VIII Corps. They comprised green units such as the 106th Infantry Division that had never seen combat before, and the 4th and 28th Infantry Divisions that had been badly mauled in recent fighting and were recuperating.

The attack took place through knee-high snow, with searchlights bouncing beams off the clouds to create artificial illumination for the troops. Thirty-two English-speaking German soldiers under the Austrian-born Colonel Otto Skorzeny were dressed in American uniforms in order to increase the confusion behind the lines. Two of the best German generals, Generaloberst der Waffen-SS Josef ('Sepp') Dietrich and General der Panzertruppen Baron Hasso-Eccard von Manteuffel, led the attacks in the north and centre respectively, with the Seventh Army providing flank protection to the south. Yet even seventeen divisions would not be enough to dislodge the vast numbers of Allied troops who had landed in north-west Europe since D-Day. 'He was incapable of realising that he no longer commanded the army which he had had in 1939 or 1940,' Manteuffel later complained of Hitler.[29]

Both the US 106th and 28th Divisions were wrecked by the German attack – some units broke and ran to the rear – but the US V Corps in the north and 4th Division in the south managed to hold on to their positions, squeezing the German thrust into a 40-mile-wide and 55-mile-deep protuberance in the Allied line whose shape on the map gave the engagement its name: the battle of the Bulge. The Sixth SS Panzer Army failed to make much progress against the 2nd and 99th Infantry Divisions of Gerow's V Corps in the north, and came close but never made it to a giant fuel dump near the town of Spa. They did, however, commit the war's worst atrocity against American troops in the west when they machine-gunned eighty-six unarmed prisoners in a field near Malmédy, a day after executing fifteen others. The SS officer responsible, SS-General Wilhelm Mohnke, was never prosecuted for the crime, despite having also been involved in two other such massacres in cold blood earlier in the war.[30]

In the centre, Manteuffel's Fifth Panzer Army surrounded the 106th Division in front of St Vith, and forced its 8,000 men to surrender on 19 December – the largest capitulation of American troops since the Civil War. St Vith itself was defended by the 7th Armored until 21 December, when it fell to Manteuffel. Although the Americans were thinly spread, and caught by surprise, isolated pockets of troops held out for long enough to cause Herbstnebel to stumble, and to give time for Eisenhower to organize a massive counter-attack. By midnight on the second day, 60,000 men and 11,000 vehicles were being sent as reinforcements, and over the following eight days a further 180,000 men were moved to contain the threat.[31] Because the 12th Army Group had been geographically split to the north and south, on 20 December Eisenhower gave Bradley's US First and Ninth Armies to Montgomery's 21st Army Group, in the former's case for four weeks and in the latter's until the Rhine crossing. It was a sensible move that nonetheless created lasting resentment. 'General Eisenhower acknowledges that the great German offensive which started on December 16 is a greater one than his own,' blared out German loudspeakers to troops of the US 310th Infantry Regiment. 'How would you like to die for Christmas?'

With Ultra starting to become available again after the assault, confirming the Meuse as the German target, the Supreme Commander could make his dispositions accordingly, and prevent his front being split in two. It fell to Patton's Third Army in the south to break through General der Panzertruppen Erich Brandenberger's Seventh Army. 'Sir, this is Patton talking,' the general peremptorily told Almighty God in the chapel of the Fondation Pescatore in Luxembourg on 23 December. 'You have just got to make up Your mind whose side You're on. You must come to my assistance, so that I might dispatch the entire German Army as a birthday present to Your Prince of Peace.'[32] Either through divine intervention or human agency, the 101st Airborne Division had already arrived in the nick of time at the town of Bastogne, only hours before the Germans reached its vital crossroads. With 18,000 Americans completely surrounded there on 20 December, the commander of the 47th Panzer Corps, General Heinrich von Lüttwitz, gave Brigadier-General Anthony C. McAuliffe, a veteran of Overlord and Market Garden who was acting commander of the division, the opportunity to surrender. McAuliffe's single-word reply – 'Nuts!' – was a slang term that the Germans nonetheless understood perfectly well. Christmas Day thus saw a massed German attack on Bastogne, which had to hold out until the US Third Army could come to its rescue from the south. 'A clear, cold Christmas, lovely weather for killing Germans,' joked Patton, 'which is a bit queer, seeing whose birthday it is.'

On 22 and 23 December he had succeeded in turning the Third

Army a full 90 degrees from driving eastwards towards the Saar to pushing northwards along a 25-mile front over narrow, icy roads in mid-winter straight up the Bulge's southern flank. 'Brad,' the ever quotable Patton had said to his commander, 'the Kraut's stuck his head in a meat-grinder. And this time I've got hold of the handle.'[33] Even Bradley had to admit in his memoirs that Patton's 'difficult manoeuvre' had been 'One of the most brilliant performances by any commander on either side of World War II'.[34] Less brilliant was the laxity of Patton's radio and telephone communications staff, which allowed Model to know American intentions and objectives.

After surviving a spirited German attack that broke through the defensive perimeter on Christmas Day, Bastogne was relieved by Patton's 4th Armored Division on Boxing Day. By then Manteuffel's Fifth Panzer Army had started to run short of fuel, and although its 2nd Panzer Division got to within 5 miles of the town of Dinant on the Meuse, Dietrich had not committed his mechanized infantry reserves in support of Manteuffel, 'because such a manoeuvre was not in Hitler's orders and he had been instructed to obey his instructions to the letter'.[35] It was true: contrary to Model's advice, Hitler had insisted that Dietrich, described by one historian as 'Hitler's SS pet', should deliver the decisive blow, even though he had not got a quarter as far as Manteuffel.[36] By then the Germans had run out of yet another precious resource – time – as better weather allowed the Allies to harry their Panzer columns from the air, with 15,000 sorties flown in the first four days after the skies had cleared. When being debriefed by Allied interviewers, Rundstedt put the defeat down to three factors: 'First, the unheard-of superiority of your air force, which made all movement in daytime impossible. Second, the lack of motor fuel – oil and gas – so that the Panzers and even the Luftwaffe were unable to move. Third, the systematic destruction of all railway communications so that it was impossible to bring one single railroad train across the Rhine.'[37] All three of these factors involved air power to a greater or lesser extent.

The great offensive petered out by 8 January 1945, with the US First and Third Armies linking up on the 16th and the German order to retreat finally being given on the 22nd. By 28 January there was no longer a bulge in the Allied line, but instead a large one developing in the Germans'. 'I strongly object to the fact that this stupid operation in the Ardennes is sometimes called the "Rundstedt Offensive",' Rundstedt complained after the war. 'This is a complete misnomer. I had nothing to do with it. It came to me as an order complete to the last detail. Hitler had even written on the plan in his own handwriting "Not to be Altered".'[38] Rundstedt said he felt it should instead be called 'the Hitler Offensive'.[39] In fact, neither man's name was to be appended.

'I salute the brave fighting man of America; I never want to fight alongside better soldiers,' Montgomery told a press conference at his Zonhoven headquarters on 7 January. 'I have tried to feel I am almost an American soldier myself so that I might take no unsuitable action to offend them in any way.'[40] This encomium made no mention of his fellow generals, however, and his press conference served to inflame tensions among the Anglo-American High Command. Patton and Montgomery had long mutually loathed one another – Patton called Monty 'that cocky little limey fart', Monty thought Patton a 'foul-mouthed lover of war' – and as the United States overhauled Great Britain in almost every aspect of the war effort, Montgomery found himself unable to face the new situation, and became progressively more anti-American as the United States' preponderance became more evident. So when on 7 January SHAEF lifted the censorship restrictions it had imposed nearly three weeks before, Montgomery gave his extensive press briefing to a select group of war correspondents. It was a disgraceful performance by anyone's estimation, including that of his personal staff who were shocked by his ineptitude, or some thought his malice. 'General Eisenhower placed me in command of the whole northern front,' boasted Monty. 'I employed the whole available power of the British group of armies. You have this picture of British troops fighting on both sides of American forces who had suffered a hard blow. This is a fine Allied picture.' Although he spoke of the average GIs being 'jolly brave' in what with studied insouciance he called 'an interesting little battle', he claimed he had entered the engagement 'with a bang', and left the impression that he had effectively rescued the American generals from defeat.

Saying that Montgomery was 'all-out, right-down-to-the-toes mad', Bradley told Eisenhower that he could not serve with him, but would prefer to transfer back to the United States. Patton immediately made the same declaration. Then Bradley started courting the press himself, and he and Patton subsequently leaked to the American press information damaging to Montgomery. In the words of one of Bradley's (many) press officers, the ex-editor Ralph Ingersoll, Bradley, Hodges and Lieutenant-General William Simpson of Ninth Army began 'to make and carry out plans without the assistance of the official channels, on a new basis openly discussed only among themselves. In order to do this they had to conceal their plans from the British and almost literally outwit Eisenhower's Supreme Headquarters, half of which was British.'[41] The British and American generals in the west from 1943 to 1945 did indeed have a special relationship: it was especially dreadful.

Montgomery certainly ought to have paid full tribute to Patton's achievement in staving in the southern flank of the Ardennes offensive, but Patton was not a wholly attractive man. The obverse side of his intense racial pride in himself was his anti-Semitism, and his belief in the Bolshevist–Zionist conspiracy was in no way lessened after the liberation of the concentration camps. By the end of his career, the US Army had placed a psychiatrist on his staff to keep an eye on him, and were monitoring his phone calls. He was to die in his sleep on 21 December 1945, twelve days after fracturing his neck in a collision with a truck near Mannheim, in which no one was speeding. 'The God of War, whom Patton worshipped so devotedly, clearly has a wry sense of humour,' wrote one reviewer of his biography, and Patton himself acknowledged beforehand that it was 'a helluva way to die'.[42] Perhaps the Almighty had not appreciated Patton's impertinence in being told to make up His mind and take sides in the struggle between civilization and barbarism.

The battle of the Bulge cost the Germans 98,024 battlefield casualties, including over 12,000 killed, but also 700 tanks and assault guns and 1,600 combat aircraft, against Allied (the great majority American) casualties of 80,987, including 10,276 killed, but a slightly larger number of tanks and tank-destroyers lost.[43] The great difference was that in matériel the Allies could make up these large losses, whereas the Germans no longer could. The effect on Allied morale was powerful. 'The Germans were going to be defeated,' concluded a

British tank commander who had fought in the battle, 'and not only in their Ardennes adventure but in their whole mad attempt to dominate the world.'[44] The time-frame was another matter: on 6 February Lieutenant-General Brian Horrocks wagered Montgomery £10 'that the German war will be over by 1 May 1945'. He lost by a week.

Hitler had been warned by Rundstedt and Model that the offensive would achieve only a drastic weakening of the Reich's power to resist the Russians on the Eastern Front, without any concomitant advantage in the west. Nonetheless, he was willing to gamble all, as so often before in his career. The hopes of many Germans that the Red Army could be kept back were thus sacrificed for an offensive in the west, against an enemy far less vicious and rapacious than the one bearing down on the *Heimat* (homeland) from the east. 'Only Hitler's personal folly maintained the Ardennes battle,' records Max Hastings, 'encouraged by Jodl, who persuaded him that maintaining pressure in the west was dislocating the Anglo-Americans' offensive plans.'[45] So it was, but only at a greater cost to Germany's defensive plans, and Hitler was never able to undertake a major offensive again.

It was unusual for Hitler to have been influenced by Jodl, the Chief of the Operations Staff of OKW throughout the war, whose attitude towards his Führer can be gleaned from his speech about the coming victory to Gauleiters in Munich in November 1943, when he said: 'My most profound confidence is based on the fact that at the head of Germany there stands a man who by his entire development, his desires, and striving can only have been destined by Fate to lead our people into a brighter future.'[46] At Nuremberg Göring told Leon Goldensohn that he thought Wilhelm Keitel should not even be on trial because 'although he was a field marshal, [he] was a small person who did whatever Hitler instructed'.[47] Head of the OKW throughout the war, Keitel, in the estimation of the British post-war historian of the German High Command, John Wheeler-Bennett, had 'ambition but no talent, loyalty but no character, a certain native shrewdness and charm, but neither intelligence nor personality'.[48] He was far more sycophantic – Hitler called him 'as loyal as a dog' – even than Jodl. Yet he certainly did deserve his Nuremberg punishment: he presided over the so-called Court of Honour that condemned the July Plotters to death; he signed the order to shoot all Soviet commissars on capture, as well as the notorious *Nacht und Nebel* (night and fog) Decree of 7 December 1941 by which more than 8,000 non-German civilians were kidnapped and executed; he encouraged the lynching of Allied airmen by civilians; and gave the order of 16 December 1942 that in the east and the Balkans 'Any consideration for the partisans is a crime against the German people.'[49] Keitel nonetheless resented his nickname, Hitler's Lakaitel, taken from the word *Lackai* (lackey).

'Why did the generals who have been so ready to term me a complaisant and incompetent yes-man fail to secure my removal?' Keitel wrote in his self-pitying memoirs before he was hanged at Nuremberg. 'Was that all that difficult? No, that wasn't it; the truth was that nobody would have been ready to replace me, because each one knew that he would end up as much of a wreck as I.' There is some justification to this; certainly Kleist felt that because 'Hitler wanted a weak general in that powerful position in order to have complete control of him,' other generals could not have borne the job. 'If I had held Keitel's position under Hitler,' Kleist later claimed, 'I wouldn't have lasted two weeks.'[50] Yet had Keitel and Jodl shown more backbone with the Führer, as Guderian did, they might have been able to instil a sense of proportion into his strategy, but Keitel's attitude was summed up in his remark to his Nuremberg psychiatrist in May 1946, when he said: 'It isn't right to be obedient only when things go well; it is much harder to be a good, obedient soldier when things go badly and times are hard. Obedience and faith at such time is a virtue.'[51] Hitler had plenty of people still willing to give him obedience and faith, the human nullity Wilhelm Keitel at their head, when what he most needed were constructive criticism and sound advice.

Late in 1942 Hitler decided that every word spoken at his military conferences needed to be preserved for posterity. He accordingly ordered six (and eventually eight) of Germany's parliamentary stenographers, who had been idle since the Reichstag was mothballed that April, to take down in shorthand and then transcribe everything that was uttered at these meetings. If the Germans had won the war, this book would today be the equivalent of Nazi holy writ. Verbatim, unvarnished and contemporary, the pure raw material of history, they reveal the Führer as a painstaking, calculating, inquisitive dictator, with a phenomenally good memory and a great interest in the mechanics of armaments, and even as rather a good listener. At least three-quarters of the meetings were taken up with the answers given to his incisive questioning by such senior Reich figures as Rundstedt, Rommel, Guderian, Keitel and Jodl, Zeitzler, Dönitz, Göring and Goebbels.

Because the verbatim reports open on 1 December 1942, with the battle of Stalingrad effectively lost, and end on 27 April 1945, three days before Hitler's suicide, the picture is one of Germany in retreat and eventual defeat, although it is impossible to tell from the Führer's remarks exactly when it dawned upon him that he would lose the war, and with it his own life. It possibly came at the end of the battle of the Bulge at the close of 1944, for on 10 January 1945 he had the following conversation with Göring over the problems with the production of secret weaponry:

HITLER: It is said that if Hannibal, instead of the seven or thirteen elephants he had left as he crossed the Alps . . . had had fifty or 250, it would have been more than enough to conquer Italy.

GÖRING: But we did finally bring out the jets; we brought them out. And they must come in masses, so we keep the advantage . . .

HITLER: The V-1 can't decide the war, unfortunately.

GÖRING: . . . Just as an initially unpromising project can finally succeed, the bomber will come, too, if it is also—

HITLER: But that's still just a fantasy!

GÖRING: No!

HITLER: Göring, the gun is there, the other is still a fantasy![52]

The use of a surname between people on close terms is a sure sign of intended emphasis. Hitler knew what was coming.

Although there were often up to twenty-five people in the room during these Führer-conferences, Hitler usually had only two or three interlocutors. There is no noticeable sycophancy in their answers to his ceaselessly probing questions. Gun calibres, oilfields, plastic versus metal mines, Panzer driver training, encirclement strategies: little escaped his attention. 'Can't we make a special supply of flame-throwers for the west?' he asked just before D-Day. 'Flame-throwers are the best for defence. It's a terrible weapon.' He then made a telephone call to order a trebling of the monthly flame-throwing production, ending the conversation: 'Thank you very much. Heil! Happy holidays.' There are several moments of unintended humour – 'One always counts on the decency of others. We are so decent,' Hitler said – but the atmosphere was uniformly businesslike, even towards the very end. There was of course no mention of the Holocaust in front of the stenographers. Other things were not transcribed, such as his paeans about his German shepherd dog Blondi and his constant asking of the time – Hitler never wore a watch – but otherwise his every word was taken down. He only really started rambling incoherently towards the end, as the Red Army advanced on his bunker and he took refuge in nostalgia, *Schadenfreude*, accusations of betrayal (many of them perfectly justified) and blind optimism.

It was after a Führer-conference in February 1945 that Albert Speer tried to explain to Dönitz how the war was certainly lost, with the maps there showing 'a catastrophic picture of innumerable breakthroughs and encirclements', but Dönitz merely replied, 'with unwonted curtness', that he was only there to represent the Navy and 'The rest is none of my business. The Führer must know what he is doing.'[53] Speer believed that had Göring, Keitel, Jodl, Dönitz, Guderian and himself presented the Führer with an ultimatum, and demanded to know his plans for ending the war, then 'Hitler would have had to have declared himself.'[54] Yet that was never going to happen, because they suspected – half of that group correctly – that there was soon to be only a rope at the end of it. When Speer approached Göring at Karinhall soon after he had spoken to Dönitz, the Reichsmarschall readily admitted that the Reich was doomed, but said that he had 'much closer ties with Hitler; many years of common experiences and struggles had bound them together – and he could no longer break loose'.

Hitler knew too: on 2 March 1945, criticizing a proposal by Rundstedt to move men south from the sector occupied by the 21st Army Group, he perceptively pointed out: 'It just means moving the catastrophe from one place to another.'[55] When five days later an armoured unit under Brigadier-General William M. Hoge from the 9th Armored Division of Hodge's US First Army captured the Ludendorff railway bridge over the Rhine at Remagen intact, and Eisenhower established a bridgehead on the east of the Rhine, Hitler's response was to sack

Rundstedt as commander-in-chief west and replace him with Kesselring. Few chalices could have been more heavily poisoned than that appointment at that time, with American troops swarming over the bridge into Germany, and Patton crossing on 22 March, and telegraphing Bradley to say 'For God's sake tell the world we're across . . . I want the world to know 3rd Army made it before Monty.'[56] Montgomery's crossing of the Rhine the next day, codenamed Operation Plunder, was watched by Churchill and Brooke and established a 6-mile-deep bridgehead within forty-eight hours. When 325,000 men of Army Group B were caught in the Ruhr pocket and forced to surrender, Field Marshal Walther Model dissolved his army group and escaped into a forest. Having recently learnt that he was to be indicted for war crimes involving the deaths of 577,000 people in Latvian concentration camps, and after hearing an insanely optimistic radio broadcast by Goebbels on the Führer's birthday, he shot himself on 21 April.

A few days earlier, Churchill had proposed a triple proclamation from the Big Three 'giving warning to Germany not to go on resisting. If [the Germans] carry on resistance past sowing time then [there] will be famine in Germany next winter . . . we take no responsibility for feeding Germany.'[57] As usual Churchill was advocating the most extreme measures, but like several others he put forward this was not adopted. Despite the Allies encountering some fierce resistance from fanatical units, but not the supposed *kamikaze* 'Werewolf battalions' that were threatened by Goebbels' propaganda machine, the outcome of the war in the west was not in doubt in the minds of rational Germans. For the more optimistic of Hitler's subjects, however, propaganda about his so-called wonder weapons kept the faith alive, but on Thursday, 29 March 1945, six days after Montgomery's Second Army and the US Ninth Army had crossed the Rhine, anti-aircraft gunners in Suffolk shot down the last of the V-1 flying bombs launched against Britain in the Second World War. Called the *Vergeltungswaffe-Eins* by the Germans, meaning (Vengeance Weapon-1), they were nicknamed doodlebugs or buzz bombs by the Britons whom they were intended to kill, maim and terrify.

The V-1, for which Hitler announced high hopes on its inception on Christmas Eve 1943, was certainly an horrific weapon. Powered by a pulse-jet mechanism using petrol and compressed air, it was 25 feet 4 inches long with a 16-foot wingspan, and it weighed 4,750 pounds. Its warhead was made up of 1,874 pounds of Amatol explosive, a fearsome mixture of TNT and ammonium nitrate. Launched up 125-foot concrete ramps stationed right across Occupied France, from Watten in the north to Houppeville to the south, they flew at up to 360mph, which was slow enough to have a proportionately greater surface-blast effect for its warhead size than its equally fiendish sister weapon the V-2 rocket bomb (known to the Germans as the A-4). 'The English will only stop when their towns are destroyed,' Hitler told a Führer-conference in July 1943, 'nothing else will do it . . . He'll stop when his towns are destroyed, that much is clear. I can only win the war by destroying more on the enemy's side than he does on ours – by inflicting on his the horror of war. It has always been that way and it's the same in the air.'[58] With the Luftwaffe unable to escort bombers over England due to British fighter protection, the V-1 was a sign of Hitler's desperation rather than his strength.

As the V-1's maximum range was 130 miles, London and south-east England were its main targets, and they suffered heavily. Flown by autopilot from a preset compass, the flying bomb contained in its nose propeller a log which measured the distance flown. Once it reached the correct range, the elevators in the wings were fully deflected and it dived, cutting out the engine as it did so. Part of the terror that V-1s inspired came from the sinister way that the noise of their propulsion suddenly stopped at this preset moment, meaning that they were about to fall on the people below. To hear the noise continue meant that the V-1 would carry on flying overhead, but to hear it stop brought the certainty of an imminent, devastating explosion. It is estimated that about 80 per cent of V-1s landed within an 8-mile radius of their targets.

Between 13 June 1944 – a week after D-Day – and 29 March 1945, no fewer than 13,000 V-1 bombs were launched against Britain. Because their cruising altitude of between 3,500 and 4,000 feet was too low for heavy anti-aircraft guns to be able to hit them very often, yet too high for light guns to reach them, it was often the RAF that had to deal with this grave new threat. Radar-guided fighter aircraft tried either to shoot them down or to tip them over by lightly tapping their wings. It took outstanding courage to fly so close to a ton of explosives, yet that was the way it was often done. Barrage balloons were also employed to try to stop them with trailing metal chains.

'I was eleven or twelve when I had my first experience of a doodle-bug raid,' recalled Thomas Smith, who lived in Russell Gardens in north London during the last two years of the war, along with his mother and eight brothers and sisters. 'It was 6.30 a.m. on Friday, 13 October 1944. We were all lying in bed, when we heard the flying bomb come over. We knew it could drop anywhere as we could hear it flying over the house. We were terrified. I was sharing a bed with my four brothers and we all huddled together under the bedclothes.' His father was abroad, serving in the British Army, which was at that time attacking and shutting down launch sites in northern France in the aftermath of the Normandy invasion. (This did not end the attacks, however, as some V-1s were launched from modified Heinkel He-111 bombers after the fall of the northern France launch sites.) 'The bomb missed the house,' recalled Smith, 'but it dropped 120 yards away, in Russell Gardens. The force of the bomb caused the roof and ceilings of our house to fall in and the windows were also blown out by the blast. Despite the bomb, my mum still sent me to school.' They were a tough generation, and the Smith family was fortunate; in all, more than 24,000 Britons were casualties of the Führer's vicious 'secret weapon', with 5,475 of them dying. One of the most nerve-wracking aspects of the campaign for Britons was the way that the attacks came round the clock, allowing for no respite. Whereas the Luftwaffe had long since confined its attacks to night-time, when its bombers could be cloaked in darkness and hidden from RAF fighters, the pilotless bombs came all through the day and night. At one point during the initial assault in July and August 1944 10,000 homes were damaged every day. By late August over 1.5 million children had been evacuated from the south-east.

The huge ground-space that the V-1 could devastate – a single flying bomb might damage an area covering a quarter of a square mile – made it a particularly dangerous weapon, although the defenders quickly adapted. Between June and September 1944, for example, 3,912 were brought down by anti-aircraft fire, RAF fighters and barrage balloons. It soon became clear that Hitler, who had hoped that V-1s might destroy British morale and force the Government to sue for peace, was wrong about the weapon's potential. He therefore placed hopes in the V-2, which had been devised at the Peenemünde research centre in Pomerania and which comprised ground-breaking rocket technology. It was a supersonic ballistic missile, flying faster than the speed of sound, so the first thing its victims heard was the detonation. No air-raid sirens could be sounded or warnings given, which added to the terror, and there was no possibility of interception because it flew at 3,600mph, ten times faster than the Spitfire.

The gyroscopically stabilized fin guided this huge, 13-ton machine for distances of up to 220 miles. It was originally intended to be loaded with poison gas, and only had its 1-ton high-explosive warhead attached later. Its astonishing speed came from a mixture of alcohol and liquid oxygen being pumped into the motor by two centrifugal pumps driven by turbines and heated to 2,700 Celsius. It could fly at a maximum height of 100,000 feet. The V-2 was enormous: 46 feet high, with a diameter of over 5 feet in the middle, and 12 feet down by the fins, it was by far the biggest weapon of its kind. Launched from an upright position from vehicles that simply drove off after firing, it did not even have launch-pad installations – as most V-1s needed – that the Allies could bomb and overrun. (Both V-weapons can be seen today at the Imperial War Museum in Lambeth, London.)

With production at full capacity in the autumn of 1944, Hitler hoped that London could be bombed into submission before the Allies could reach Germany and destroy the Third Reich. Yet it was largely his own fault that the V-2 came on stream so late. If he had given high priority to it in 1942, its teething problems might have been sorted out in time to mass-produce it in 1943 rather than 1944.[59] Of course increased rocket production would have had to take the place of some other weapon programmes, be they for warplanes, tanks or submarines. There were a high proportion of misfires, and half the rockets built were defective, but this might not have been the case if the Führer had supported the project much earlier and more emphatically.

It was at 6.40 p.m. on 8 September 1944 that the first V-2 landed on Britain, fired only five minutes earlier after being unloaded from a converted lorry in a suburban road in The Hague. Staveley Road in Chiswick, west London, was another such quiet residential street before the warhead exploded there, killing three people and injuring six. Where once six suburban houses had stood, there was now only an immense crater. In the beginning, in order to prevent panic, the authorities made no announcement about the V-2, encouraging people to believe that the loud explosion heard across west London had been a 'gasworks explosion', but by November it became clear that the Government had to be more honest about the new threat.

Over the five months of the campaign, a total of 1,359 rockets were fired at London, killing 2,754 people and injuring 6,523. In reply to German propaganda claims that London was being 'devastated', Winston Churchill told the House of Commons on 10 November 1944 that 'The damage and casualties have not so far been heavy. There is no need to exaggerate the danger.' Yet when a single rocket hit the Woolworth's store in New Cross, south-east London, on 25 November, 160 people were killed and a further 200 injured, and four rockets landing on Croydon, Surrey, on 29 December had rendered as many as 2,000 houses uninhabitable.

'Things were still falling out of the sky,' recalled a young girl who survived the New Cross blast,

bits of things and bits of people. A horse's head was lying in the gutter. There was a pram hood all twisted and bent and there was a little baby's hand still in its woolly sleeve. Outside the pub there was a crumpled bus, still with rows of people sitting inside, all covered in dust and dead. Where Woolworth's had been, there was nothing, just an enormous gap covered by clouds of dust. No building, just piles of rubble and bricks, and underneath it all, people screaming.

In all, 3,225 such weapons were launched, costing 100,000 Reichsmarks each. Antwerp was also heavily hit by V-2s, with more than 30,000 casualties inflicted there. The Germans even had a plan to launch V-2s against America, fired from converted U-boats. The last V-2 rocket to land on Britain was fired from The Hague just like the first; it landed on a block of flats in Whitechapel at 7.21 p.m. on 27 March 1945, killing 134 people. There was no possible defence from them, and they penetrated deep shelters too. As well as killing people when they landed, the V-2s also killed people while they were being made. It is estimated that up to 20,000 people died in the horrific slave-labour conditions while manufacturing the rockets. Life in the factories, which were scattered over the Reich, was appalling: starvation, disease, maltreatment and accidents were rife.

Although the V-weapon flying bombs and rockets were to cause thousands of casualties in Britain, and many more in Holland and Belgium, they could not have changed the balance of the struggle even if they had caused ten times that amount of devastation, because Hitler did not begin firing them until a week after D-Day. By that time the Americans, British and Canadians were ashore and there was no prospect of their coming to terms with Hitler, pretty much however successful the V-weapon campaign. The concentration of technological research, money, raw materials, skilled labour, slave labourers' lives and general effort that went into creating the V-weapons was thus in no way justified by their results. Good for rhetoric, but short on results, Vengeance weaponry turned out to be yet another error of the Führer's strategic judgement.

17

Eastern Approaches

August 1943–May 1945

We no longer fought for Hitler, or National Socialism, or for the Third Reich, or even our fiancées or mothers or families trapped in bomb-ravaged towns. We fought from simple fear. We fought for ourselves, so that we didn't die in holes filled with mud and snow. We fought like rats.
A veteran of the Grossdeutschland Division in 1945[1]

For all the advances made against the Germans in the west between D-Day on 6 June 1944 and the crossing of the Rhine in March 1945, postponed by the disaster at Arnhem in mid-September and the Ardennes counter-offensive in the winter, it was on the Eastern Front that the war against Germany was won. Between Operation Barbarossa and December 1944, the Germans lost 2.4 million men killed there, against 202,000 fighting the Western allies.[2] The cost of inflicting such casualties was uneven: between D-Day and VE Day (Victory in Europe Day, 8 May 1945), the Russians suffered more than 2 million casualties, three times that of the British, Americans, Canadians and French fighting forces put together. It is worth considering whether democracies could ever have tolerated that level of sacrifice, or whether – as seems likely – it required the whole horrific apparatus of the NKVD and domestic terror to keep the Soviet Union in the war.

After the Wehrmacht's convincing defeat at Stalingrad and the capture of Field Marshal Paulus' Sixth Army in February 1943, and then the withdrawal with unacceptable losses – albeit fewer than the Russians suffered – at the battle of Kursk six months later the scene was set for a series of enormous Soviet offensives across the eastern part of the Eurasian land mass that were only to end with Germany's surrender in Berlin in early May 1945, after Hitler's suicide there on 30 April. In its 1943 summer offensive after the successful defence of Kursk, the Red Army recaptured Orel, Kharkov, Tagonrog and Smolensk, forcing the Germans back to the Dnieper river and cutting off the Seventeenth Army in the Crimean peninsula. Hitler came under pressure from Field Marshal Erich von Manstein and the Romanian dictator Marshal Ion Antonescu to evacuate the German and Romanian forces from the Crimea, which could have been used in the defence of Romania and Bulgaria, but his obstinate refusal to do so meant the fall of both countries in short order, and the eventual destruction of the army group there. Hitler had a scheme for the Crimea to become a solely Aryan colony from which all foreigners would be permanently banned, and he hung on to his dream for it long after military considerations dictated that they needed to be – at the very least – postponed.

Nicolaus von Below wrote of this period: 'Hitler foresaw threatening developments on the Eastern Front earlier and with greater clarity than his military advisers, but he was determined with great obstinacy not to accede to the request of his army commanders to pull back fronts, or would do so exceptionally only at the last minute. The Crimea was to be held at whatever cost, and he refused to entertain Manstein's arguments in the matter.'[3] A quarter of a million troops were therefore lost to the German line. It did not affect the outcome of the war, of course, and perhaps only meant, as one historian has argued, 'that large numbers of German soldiers ended up in Soviet captivity instead of being killed in the fighting'.[4] Nonetheless, according to its own lights it was a strategic error. Like the decision to leave German troops on the Kerch peninsula in order to try to recapture the Caucasus one day, it was actuated by Hitler's hope for a new assault on the southern USSR, long after such an attack was rationally possible.

For the German soldiers on the ground, in their long, bitter withdrawal from their high-water mark at Kursk, survival took on greater meaning than any lingering hopes of victory. For the Russians, liberating their cities and towns involved discovering the horrors of the

German occupation. At Orel, which was a typical example, half the buildings and all the bridges had been destroyed, and there were only 30,000 survivors from a pre-war population of 114,000, the rest having been sent to Germany as slave labour or shot, or having died of disease or starvation.[5] For sheer ghoulishness, little could beat the discovery of eighty-two headless corpses and eighty-nine human heads in Danzig's Anatomical Medical Institute, however, where soap and leather had been manufactured from Russian, Polish, Jewish and Uzbecki corpses. The nearby Stutthof concentration camp had little problem providing the bodies – 16,000 prisoners died of typhoid there in one six-week period, for example – and human soap was in production when the Institute received official visits from the Reich education and healthcare ministers.[6] Small wonder that the Red Army hardened its already rock-like heart still further against the enemy, encouraging it to see them as subhuman, and instilling a determination to punish all Germans – civilians as well as military – now that the jackboot was on the other foot. The innocence or otherwise of individual Germans was immaterial, because it was not so much they who were being punished as their husbands, fathers and sons. Human pity was now beside the point.

'A series of withdrawals by adequately large steps would have worn down the Russian strength, besides creating opportunities for counter-strokes,' General Kurt von Tippelskirch stated of this immediate post-Kursk period. 'The root cause of German defeat was the way her forces were wasted in fruitless efforts, and above all, fruitless resistance at the wrong time and place.'[7] Manstein did his best with a mobile defence across southern Russia – often at odds of seven to one – that seems to have been too subtle for Hitler, who constantly issued 'Stand or die' orders freezing the defensive lines, such as at Kharkov after the Soviets broke through on 3 August 1943.[8]

It took no fewer than seven conversations – often face to face after long flights – for Manstein to get Hitler's permission to retreat to the line of the Dnieper.[9] Falling back there, Manstein ignored Hitler and allowed Kharkov to fall on 23 August, putting his loyalty to his troops and the German people higher than that to OKW and his Führer. This was felt further down the line of command: Major-General Frederick von Mellenthin, Chief of Staff of the 48th Panzer Division which was retreating to the Dnieper, complained bitterly of the way that 'During the Second World War the German Supreme Command could never decide on a withdrawal when the going was good. It either made up its mind too late, or when a retreat had been forced upon our armies and was already in full swing.'[10]

Given enough warning, the Wehrmacht was in fact excellent at strategic withdrawals. It made thorough preparations improving roads, bridges and river crossings; it camouflaged assembly areas and made precise calculations about what equipment could be moved and the amount of transport necessary, and about what needed to be destroyed; then command posts, headquarters, medical and veterinary posts were established to the rear before the withdrawal began; telephone lines were removed; supplies, rations and night-traffic control were organized; demolitions, roadblocks and mines were readied, and lines of resistance mapped out. (The problems were of course multiplied once the Wehrmacht was forced back on to German soil, because millions of panicky refugees wanted to escape the Red Army too.) The Wehrmacht was also expert in the policy of scorched earth, of which Army Group South's retreat to the Dnieper between the end of August and October 1943 was the exemplar, and for which Manstein received an eighteen-year jail sentence in 1949. (He served only four years.) 'The wide spaces of Russia favour well-organized withdrawals,' recalled Mellenthin. 'Indeed if the troops are properly disciplined and trained, a strategic withdrawal is an excellent means of catching the enemy off balance and regaining the initiative.' Yet, for all its expertise, Hitler gave the Wehrmacht as little time as possible to organize such retreats, on those rare occasions when he authorized them at all.

The Kuban bridgehead on the Taman peninsula fell in October 1943, leaving the Caucasus safe for the Soviets and effectively turning the Sea of Azov into a Russian lake once more. 'Towards the end of 1943 at the latest it had become unmistakably clear that the war had been lost,' wrote General Halder. 'Would it not have been possible even so to beat off the invasion and thus provide the basis for a tolerable peace? Had the "Fortress Germany" no hope of consuming the enemy's strength on its walls? No! Let us once and for all have done with these fairy tales.'[11] He was right; having taken on four of the world's six greatest powers, Germany was doomed. Yet it was to take a further eighteen months of unimaginable horror and slaughter before the war finally came to an end. The blame for this can largely be put down to the efficiency, determination and obedience of the Wehrmacht. Had Hitler passed over ultimate decision-making to a committee of its best brains, and appointed Manstein as supreme commander of the Eastern Front, all that it would have meant at that stage was that the defeat would have taken longer and cost many more German and Russian lives.

Almost throughout this period the Germans inflicted higher casualties on the Russians than they received, but crucially never more than the Soviets could absorb. Attacks were undertaken by the Red Army generals without regard to the cost in lives, an approach which German generals could not adopt because of a lack of adequate reserves. 'The Russians were five times superior to us poor but brave Germans, both in numbers and in the superiority of their equipment,' complained Kleist from his Nuremberg cell in June 1946. 'My immediate commander was Hitler himself. Unfortunately, Hitler's advice in those critical periods was invariably lousy.'[12] In Hitler's defence, Alan Clark has pointed out that from December 1943 the Führer had been aiming at breaking the Allied coalition through emphasizing 'the apparent impossibility of its task and the incompatibility of its members', and that seen in this context his defence of every inch of territory in the east was perfectly explicable.[13] Yet ever since November 1941 Stalin had been making speeches about Hitler's aim of using fear of Communism as a way of splitting the Grand Coalition against Germany. The Soviet Information Buro (Sovinform) had been issuing statements since June 1942 lauding Russia's alliance with the Western Allies, and there is plenty of evidence for how fully this was reciprocated in Britain and America.[14] If Hitler had had a better understanding of the true nature of the alliance against him, he would have realized that its desire to extirpate him and his New Order would always be greater than any mutual suspicions and antipathies within it. To believe anything else was mere desperation, for as he had written in *Mein Kampf*: 'Any alliance whose purpose is not the intention to wage war is senseless and useless.'

For all Kleist's other legitimate complaints about his supreme commander, it was untrue that German equipment was inferior, except in sheer numbers. Guderian, who wrote the 1936 work *Achtung-Panzer!*, believed that two different types of tank were necessary in any attack, one to deal with tanks and the other with infantry. The five-man Panzer Mark III, produced from 1936, was used against other tanks, but its 37mm gun was not powerful enough against the British Matilda tanks in Africa, so Rommel used 88mm anti-aircraft guns against them there instead. In 1940 Hitler ordered the production of a 50mm, 350hp Mark III, which the manufacturers watered down to a 47mm gun. These, as well as *Sturmgeschütze* (self-propelled assault guns), were used in Operation Barbarossa, along with the far less powerful Panzer Marks I and II. Up to 1944, around 6,000 Mark IIIs were produced by different manufacturers. Twelve thousand Mark IVs were built with 76mm guns, which the Soviets thought 'good for bad European weather, not for bad Russian weather'.[15] In 1942 the Germans started producing Mark VI (Tiger) and then in 1943 Mark V (Panther) tanks.

Although the Russian tanks and self-propelled guns used diesel, only one German tank (the enormous Maus) did so, all the others being petrol-fuelled. Petrol was far more costly, flammable and rapidly consumed, yet Germany – which had the technology as Messerschmitts flew on diesel – for some reason stuck to petrol for her tanks. The Panther was a bigger and heavier copy of the Russian T-34, with a sloped front that encouraged ricochets. It entered the front line in July 1943 at Kursk, but faced a number of problems, mainly electrical and hydraulic. Weighing 45.5 tonnes with a crew of five and top speed of 46mph, it had 110mm of front armour (it was also covered with zimmerit cladding to foil magnetic mines and grenades), a 75mm cannon 15 feet long and a Daimler-Benz copy of the T-34's engine. Some 6,400 were produced; along with the Panzer VI, known as the Tiger I, of which the Henschel company made 1,355, these were formidable weapons indeed.

The Tiger I weighed 58.9 tonnes, had an 88mm gun, five crew and a cruising speed of 24mph. At the Museum of Tank Construction at Kubinka, 40 miles south of Moscow, one can see a Tiger tank that has been fired upon by a T-34 at around 300 yards' range, which merely left a 2-inch dent in its frontal armour. Except at point-blank range, or firing at its side-tracks, or unless a lucky shot hit the area between the hull and turret, the Tiger tank was well placed to smash the T-34.

The heaviest tank deployed in combat during the Second World War, at 68 tonnes, was the Tiger II. This had a five-man crew, a maximum speed of 22mph, no less than 150mm of armour (180mm on the front) and an 88mm cannon. By January 1944 some 487 Panzer VIB Tiger II or King Tiger tanks had been produced, using the same chassis specifications as the Panther. Unfortunately for the Germans, these therefore inherited many of the problems of the Panther. The 88mm gun could be found on the Elefant or Ferdinand assault gun (named after Ferdinand Porsche), which had also been deployed for the first time at Kursk. Fortunately for the Russians, only ninety of these were ever built. In response to the Panthers and Tigers, the Soviets produced the very heavy KV-85, which was the same as a KV-1 except for having an 85mm cannon. This was enough to penetrate German middle-sized tanks such as the Panzers Mark III and IV, but could also destroy Tigers and Panthers.

At a meeting with General von Thoma on 23 December 1940, Halder was told that the OKH had 'Scanty information on Russian tanks', which nonetheless were felt to be 'Inferior to ours in armour and speed. Maximum thickness of armour 30mm. The 4.4cm Ehrhard gun penetrates our tanks at range of 300 metres: effective range 500 metres; safe at over 800 metres. Optical sights very bad; dim, limited range of vision. Radio control equipment bad.'[16] Yet none of that was true of the new T-34 tank. Just as the Spitfire and Hurricane can be said to have saved Britain in 1940, so the T-34 tank saved Russia at Kursk and thereafter. First coming off the production line in 1938, the T-34/76 was easy to produce because the designer had created a welding tool for its armour sheets that women and children could also use. Its 6,000 parts were also reduced to 4,500 over the coming years. Before 1943, the T-34/76, the standard Soviet medium tank, had to get within 250 yards of a German tank with its 76mm gun and hit it from the side, whereas a German Tiger tank could destroy T-34s at a range of over a mile. (The T stands, rather unimaginatively, for Tank. Today, the Russians are up to the T-90.)

After Kursk, however, where the Russians took heavy losses before they were able to close with the enemy, they changed the calibre of the T-34's 76mm gun to 85mm, which made a considerable difference because the 76mm gun could penetrate only 50mm thickness of enemy armour at 600 yards, whereas the 85mm could penetrate 90mm at that range. Keeping the same chassis, and thus the same powerful 500hp engine and most of the same spare parts, the T-34/85 also had five rubber wheels on each side rather than two, and, crucially, an enlarged turret that allowed the crew to be increased to five. This permitted the commander to direct operations, without having to double as a loader as in the T-34/76. This allowed the T-34/85 to fire from six to eight times per minute. The length and height of the two T-34 models were much the same, but every T-34/85 had a radio, whereas only the command tanks of the original version had been equipped with one. Although the 45mm armour thickness on its sides and 90mm on the front made the T-34/85, at 32 tonnes, 3½ tonnes heavier than the earlier model, its powerful engine meant that it could reach a top speed of 20mph, not much slower than the 21.4mph of the T-34/76. The later model also had two 7.62mm machine guns, and could drive 235 miles on a full tank of 690 litres of diesel (including the barrels attached to its outside). It carried seventy-four shells, 2,500 bullets and ten grenades inside, only marginally fewer than the ninety-two shells that fitted into the T-34/76's magazine.[17] When it was produced in enough numbers, therefore, Stalin finally had a campaign-winning weapon for 1944.

The lack of armour on the top of tanks – even Tigers had only 18mm – made them highly vulnerable to air attack and in built-up areas where they could be attacked from rooftops, as the Germans discovered in Stalingrad and the Russians in Berlin in 1945 (and fifty years later in Grozny). The 20mm SHAK-20 cannon on Soviet fighter planes could penetrate tank roofs, although the planes needed to attack almost vertically downwards in order to do so. With the Luft-waffe swept from the skies of Belorussia in the latter part of 1943, the German tanks there were immensely vulnerable. Tank for tank, however, they were still the best in the world. Had Hitler started the war much later, in 1943 or 1944, and if tank- and aircraft-production factories had been better protected and dispersed in a way that the Allies found harder to destroy, especially with Me-262 jet fighters protecting them from the Allies' Combined Bomber Offensive, the Wehrmacht would have stood a far better chance of winning the war.

Between 22 and 30 October 1943, Russian forces crossed the River Dnieper in several places along a 300-mile stretch from the Pripet Marshes to Zaporozhe, and when Kiev fell on 6 November the northern flank of Army Group South's defence of the river's great bend was threatened too. On 27 and 28 December Manstein begged Hitler that the bend be given up, thereby shortening his line by over 125 miles, but he was refused permission to do so. 'I am worrying myself sick for having given permission for retreats in the past,' Hitler replied.[18] By 2 January 1944, the Russians had advanced north of Kiev and were about to cross the pre-war borders of Poland.

Up in the north of the country, the Red Army launched a major offensive to relieve Leningrad south of the city on 15 January 1944, when General L. A. Govorov's Leningrad Front and General Kirill A. Meretzkov's Volkhov Front took advantage of the freezing weather to cross the Gulf of Finland and the iced-up lakes and swamps to attack the German Eighteenth Army on both flanks. After the bloodiest siege in human history, lasting 900 days, during which 150,000 shells and 100,000 bombs had fallen on the city and more than 1.1 million people had died, Leningrad was finally liberated on Monday, 17 January 1944. Novgorod fell two days later as the Germans recoiled rapidly. When General Georg von Küchler withdrew Army Group North from its forward positions, Hitler replaced him with Model, who managed to persuade the Führer that a *Schild und Schwert* (shield and sword) strategy should allow minor withdrawals as part of a larger, planned counter-offensive. Nevertheless, by 1 March the Red Army had reached a line from Narva to Pskov to Polotsk. (Govorov attacked Finland in June, which came to terms in September, promising no longer to aid the hard-pressed German war economy.)

Model was able to persuade Hitler of things, such as the withdrawal, that other generals could not because the Führer admired him and was utterly convinced of his loyalty. He argued with Hitler to his face, but only on matters of military policy, and would not allow any criticism of Hitler at his HQ. Because he led from the front, constantly being seen in the front line, Model was popular with the troops in the way that a number of other German château-generals were not.

In January 1944 Hitler set a problem for OKH planners which threw light on the severe manpower problems that Germany was facing by then. Between the outbreak of war and late 1943 the standard German infantry division had consisted of three regiments totalling nine rifle battalions. Each regiment had twelve rifle and heavy-weapons companies, and a howitzer and anti-tank company, and the division itself also had a separate anti-tank and reconnaissance battalion too, which brought the average division size up to 17,000 men. In October 1943, however, divisions were reorganized to comprise three regiments of only two battalions each, bringing the average size down to 13,656 men. Yet only three months later Hitler was forced to ask OKH how divisions could be cut back to 11,000 men each, without its affecting firepower and overall combat strengths. The planners recognized that this was impossible, and put forward a compromise solution of divisions of 12,769 in size. This '1944-type' infantry division had a higher proportion of combat to service troops – at anything up to 80 per cent – but the swingeing reductions in supply personnel and others were sorely felt. With Germany simply running out of soldiers by January 1944, while divisions still had to hold their sections of many miles of crumbling fronts, such demoralizing reorganizations were a potent foretaste of her coming disaster.

Manstein was attacked on the Dnieper on 29 January 1944 by the 1st Ukrainian Front under Zhukov and the 2nd Ukrainian Front under Konev, perhaps the best two Russian generals since Vatutin had been assassinated by Ukrainian nationalist partisans. A fierce struggle developed, called the battle of Korsun but scarcely heard of in the West; it lasted three weeks, during which two German army corps were cut off in a salient and were extricated by Manstein only at the cost of 100,000 casualties.[19] The Russians then just moved on ahead, crossing the Bug and Dniester rivers. Such was its vast preponderance in both men and matériel that the Red Army could afford to engage the entire German force along a line, and then wait to see where the gaps appeared before striking again and again. Yet throughout this losing battle the Germans' camaraderie and esprit de corps allowed them to continue to make withering counter-attacks, which any less resilient soldiers than the Russians could probably not have withstood. If Russian troops had broken and run in the way that Western troops sometimes did, for example in the opening stages of the battle of the Bulge, they would have been shot by the NKVD. 'Who but us could have taken on the Germans?' asked Konstantin Mamerdov, a Soviet soldier at this time.[20] It was meant rhetorically, because the answer was: probably no one.

March saw Army Group South suffer a series of reversals, although these were not the fault of Manstein, who did the best he could under the thoroughly adverse circumstances. On the 4th his northern flank was battered by Zhukov, who over the next three days advanced 100 miles to the Warsaw–Odessa railway line. Nikolayev on the Bug fell on the 28th and two days later, on 30 March, Hitler dismissed Manstein, who in Basil Liddell Hart's view, and that of many other military historians, had the finest strategic brain on the German – or perhaps any – side in the war. 'You can almost look at the Soviet/German war during the period between 1942 and 1944 as a duel between Manstein and Zhukov,' the distinguished historian of these campaigns John Erickson has stated. 'It takes in Stalingrad, then Kursk and it all comes to a head in January and March 1944 when Manstein and Zhukov again duel in the Eastern Ukraine ... These are the two striking, outstanding strategic thinkers, strategic planners, and strategic commanders of the first rank.'[21] But whereas Stalin had the sense to retain Zhukov, Hitler dismissed Manstein, who had been pressing for the creation of the post of commander-in-chief of the Eastern Front, and ought to have been given it himself, but instead he was never to see active command again. 'I was in constant feud with Hitler about leadership ever since I took command of the army group until the end,' Manstein later told his Nuremberg interviewer, blaming Himmler's and Göring's influence on Hitler, before also saying of Hitler in virtually the next sentence: 'He was an extraordinary personality. He had a tremendously high intelligence and an exceptional willpower.'[22]

Manstein's command of Army Group South – from early April 1944 renamed Army Group North Ukraine – was given to Model, who had been in command of Army Group North only since January and who was also promoted to field marshal, at fifty-three the youngest after Rommel. Kleist, who had been forced back into Romania by Konev and General Rodion Malinovsky's 2nd Ukrainian Front, was dismissed as commander of Army Group South Ukraine, and replaced by the brutal and unpopular Ferdinand Schörner on the same day that Manstein was sacked. Kleist diagnosed Hitler's mentality at that stage as 'more of a problem for a psychiatrist than for a general'. Speaking at Nuremberg, he gave the standard line that 'I'm just a plain soldier and not given to analysing temperaments. He was the chief of state and I accepted that as enough.'[23] He claimed to have suggested that Hitler give up the supreme command back in December 1943, and was sacked after 'a very severe argument' on 29 March 1944, and that 'When Hitler shouted [at] me, I shouted twice as loud.' True or not, he did diagnose an interesting trait of Hitler's that others mentioned too, and which must have been dispiriting to those who worked closely with him, namely that 'If you talked for two hours and you thought that finally you had convinced him of something, he began where you started just as if you had never said a word.'[24] Such self-centredness and utter certainty in his own will and destiny might have been necessary to Hitler in becoming Führer, but it served his country – and thus ultimately himself – badly when it came to fighting a world war, which his enemies proved was done better according to a collegiate format than a dictatorial one.

A classic example of this phenomenon came on 8 March 1944 when Hitler promulgated an order embodying his concept of 'fortified localities'. Instead of retreating and remaining as part of the overall front line, he ordained that troops should defend themselves in cities and towns and be supplied by the Luftwaffe until they were relieved:

Fortified localities are intended to discharge the same functions as fortresses in the past. German army commanders therefore must allow themselves to become encircled, and in this way tie down the largest possible number of enemy forces. In this way they will also play a part in creating the prerequisite for successful counter-operations ... The Commandants of the fortified localities should be selected from the very toughest soldiers, if possible of general's rank.[25]

Although this strategy was attempting to make a virtue out of a necessity in some places, its main effect was simply to prevent troops from giving up untenable areas and staying within the main body of the army when a front collapsed. While it might have worked as a desperate measure in medieval times, in modern warfare it allowed precisely the mass encirclement that had led the Soviets to such a series of disasters during Barbarossa three years earlier. A Soviet disinformation campaign could not have put out instructions more helpful to their cause than this.

April 1944 – a month when the Luftwaffe was down to 500 combat aircraft on the Eastern Front, versus 13,000 Soviet warplanes – saw Marshal Fedor Tolbukhin clearing the Germans from the Crimea, with the fall of Sevastopol on 19 May, at a cost to the Reich of nearly 100,000 men.[26] The Russians had reached the Dnieper in January, but by April they were over the Dniester and Prut rivers, into Romania and Poland and threatening the borders of Hungary. Odessa was evacuated on 10 April. In the spring of 1944, and especially after D-Day, Hitler completely failed to rationalize his line in the east, preferring to issue 'Stand or die' orders to his battlefield commanders. 'His shrinking armies straggled along a front of 1,650 miles,' records Max Hastings. 'In the centre, divisions averaging only 2,000 men were holding sixteen-mile sectors of the line. Between July 1943 and May 1944, Germany lost 41 divisions in Russia – almost a million casualties between July and October 1943 alone, 341,950 men between March and May 1944.'[27] Yet all this was merely a prelude to the disaster that was to overtake Army Group Centre in Operation Bagration, an engagement that can lay claim to be one of the most decisive campaigns in history.

This huge Russian summer offensive, timed for the moment when attention in the Reich would be most concentrated on events in Normandy, was launched on Thursday, 22 June 1944, the third anniversary of Barbarossa. The codename was chosen by Stalin personally, to commemorate his fellow Georgian, the great Marshal Peter Bagration of the 1812 campaign. The attack was supported by no fewer than 400 guns per mile along a 350-mile front connecting Smolensk, Minsk and Warsaw. Bagration was intended utterly to destroy Army Group Centre, thus opening the way to Berlin itself. The 3rd and 2nd Russian and 1st Belorussian Fronts had almost total air superiority, much of the Luftwaffe having been flown off westwards to try to deal with D-Day and the Combined Bomber Offensive. Rokossovky achieved surprise on 24 June when the tanks and guns of his 1st Belorussian Front suddenly appeared out of the swamps of the northern Pripet Marshes, supposedly impassable to heavy vehicles, but which his engineers had diligently prepared with wooden causeways.[28]

Much of the Third Panzer Army was destroyed in a few days. The hole created in the by then wildly overstretched German line was soon no less than 250 miles wide and 100 miles deep, allowing major cities to be recaptured such as Vitebsk on 25 June and Minsk – where 300,000 Germans were encircled and captured – on 3 July. Hitler's strategy of 'fortified localities' had to be put into operation imme- diately at Mogilev, Bobruysk and elsewhere, with the predictable result that the Russians merely bypassed them and left them to be besieged by reserve troops, rather as the Americans were doing in the Pacific by 'island-hopping'. By 3 July the Russians had moved forward 200 miles from their start lines. Army Group Centre had effectively ceased to exist except on paper, and instead a vast gap had appeared between Army Group South and Army Group North. For the Ger- mans, Bagration has accurately been described as 'one of the most sudden and complete military disasters in history'.[29] Its importance cannot be overestimated. 'Even in the months following the Allied invasion in Normandy,' records an historian, 'German casualties in Russia continued to average four times the number in the West.'[30]

Although they were exhausted by constant combat over many months, under-equipped, outnumbered and largely unsupported from the air, Army Group Centre might have remained intact had it not been saddled with tactics as illogical and untutored as that of 'fortified localities' and other related concepts that Hitler invented. Had the Führer visited the front more often, he might have seen for himself how Order No. 11, which called for 'stubbornly defended strong points in the depth of the battlefield in the event of any breakthrough', was a recipe for denuding the German line yet further, merely permit- ting further such breakthroughs.

Field Marshal Walther Model, by then nicknamed 'Hitler's fire- man', was appointed to Field Marshal Ernst Busch's command of the 1.2 million men of Army Group Centre, while continuing to command

Army Group North Ukraine, but he could do little to hold back the Russians. By 10 July, twenty-five of the thirty-three divisions of Army Group Centre were trapped, with only a small minority able to extricate themselves. The choice of the third anniversary of Barbarossa for the launch of Bagration was instructive: the destruction of Army Group Centre was in many ways the mirror image of what had happened in the early stages of Barbarossa, with strongpoints being encircled with bewildering speed by swarms of highly mobile opponents. Bagration lasted for sixty-eight days, and saw average German casualties of more than 11,000 per day. In the course of this vast *Kesselschlacht* (cauldron battle), the Russians punched the Wehrmacht in its solar plexus, regained Belorussia and opened the way to attack East Prussia and the Baltic States. Small wonder the year 1944 is regarded as an *annus mirabilis* in today's Russia. During Bagration, the Soviets claimed to have killed 381,000 Germans, wounded 384,000, captured a further 158,000 and destroyed or captured 2,000 tanks, 10,000 guns and 57,000 motor vehicles.[31] For all that is made of the Anglo-American victory in the Falaise pocket, this victory was over ten times the size, yet is hardly known in the West beyond the cognoscenti of military history.

On 14 July 1944, the Russians attacked south of the Pripet Marshes, capturing Lvov on the 27th. The Germans were therefore now back to their Barbarossa start lines of three years earlier. The offensives north and south of the Pripet Marshes meant that the Red Army was able to cross the pre-war borders of Poland and recapture Kaunas, Minsk, Białystok and Lublin, and by August they had crossed the River Bug. They stopped on the Vistula, outside Warsaw, because Model managed to check Rokossovsky's 1st Belorussian Front to the east of the Polish capital. It is often assumed that the Russians stopped on the Vistula on 7 August for entirely political reasons, in order to allow the Germans to crush the Warsaw Uprising, but they had a good excuse to do so, for their 450-mile advance since 22 June had stretched their supplies and lines of communication to the limits.

At the celebrations in Moscow soon afterwards, 57,000 German POWs were paraded through Red Square, with many of the twenty-five captured generals at their head. The war correspondent Alexander Werth reported:

The Moscow people looked on quietly without booing and hissing, and only a few youngsters could be heard shouting, 'Hey, look at the Fritzes with their ugly snouts,' but most people only exchanged remarks in soft voices. I heard a little girl sitting on her mother's shoulders say: 'Mummy, are these the people who killed Daddy?' And the mother hugged the child and wept. The Germans had finally arrived in Moscow. When the parade was over Russian sanitation trucks disinfected the streets.[32]

Churchill used the occasion of the destruction of Army Group Centre to make another quip at Hitler's expense in the House of Commons, saying on 2 August, the tenth anniversary of Hindenburg's death and thus of Hitler becoming undisputed master of Germany, 'It may well be that the Russian success has been somewhat aided by the strategy of Herr Hitler – of Corporal Hitler. Even military idiots find it difficult not to see some faults in some of his actions . . . Altogether, I think it is much better to let officers rise up in the proper way.'[33]

There were a few scrawny scraps of comfort for Hitler, however. With the Red Army only 15 miles from the borders of East Prussia on 1 August, Model – outnumbered and outgunned, especially in the air – had nonetheless managed severely to maul the Second Tank Army and force the Soviets back 30 miles. During the 'hurricane of fire' from German assault guns, the following Russian wireless conversation was intercepted by the Abwehr:

A: Hold your position!

B: I am finished.

A: Reinforcements are moving up.

B: To hell with your reinforcement. I am cut off. Your reinforcement won't find me here any more.

A: For the last time, I forbid you to speak openly over the wireless. I would prefer you to shoot your own people than allow the enemy to shoot them.

B: Comrade No. 54, perhaps you will grasp the situation when I tell you that I have nobody left I can shoot, apart from my wireless operator.[34]

Model's victory, though relatively small-scale in the context of the overall situation, nonetheless earned him his Führer's encomium as 'the saviour of the Eastern Front'.[35] On 31 August Hitler said at a conference: 'I really think one can't imagine a worse crisis than the one we had in the East this year. When Field Marshal Model came, the Army Group Centre was nothing but a hole.'[36] Yet rather than giving him greater responsibilities there, or even perhaps command over the entire front, Hitler moved Model on to the Western Front later that same month, and there was yet another change of army group commanders.

The approach of the Red Army encouraged the anti-Communist Armia Krajowa (Polish Home Army) in Warsaw to attempt an uprising at 5 p.m. on Tuesday, 1 August 1944 under their indomitable Generals Tadeusz Bór-Komorowski and Antoni Chruściel. The Poles understandably wanted to wrest control of their capital, and with it, they hoped, the sovereignty of their country, away from the Germans before the arrival of the Russians, who they correctly assumed had no more desire for genuine Polish independence than the Nazis. So while the Uprising was aimed militarily against the Germans, it was also aimed politically against the Russians, something that Stalin well understood.[37] The result was as desperate and tragic for the Warsaw Poles as the Warsaw Ghetto Uprising had been for the Polish Jews in April 1943. The Uprising was crushed with maximum ferocity by the SS in sixty-three days, in scenes that can be seen in powerful contemporary film footage at the Uprising Museum in Warsaw today. When it began, only 14 per cent of the Home Army were even armed, with only 108 machine guns, 844 sub-machine guns and 1,386 rifles.[38]

On 26 August Churchill met the Polish Commander-in-Chief General Władysław Anders at his HQ in Italy. Anders had been imprisoned in Moscow's Lubyanka prison in his time, and was under no illusions: as he told Churchill, 'Stalin's declarations that he wants a free and strong Poland are lies and fundamentally false.' Anders then spoke about the way the Soviets had treated Poland in 1939 and about the Katyń massacre before exclaiming, 'We have our wives and children in Warsaw, but we would rather they perish than have to live under the Bolsheviks.' According to the minutes taken by Anders' aide-de-camp, Lieutenant Prince Eugene Lubomirski, Churchill replied: 'I sympathize deeply. But you must trust [us]. We will not abandon you and Poland will be happy.'[39] He probably meant it at the time, but was no longer really in a position to make such a promise considering that a Red Army of 6.7 million men was poised to march right across Poland.

The courage and ingenuity of the Poles during the Uprising were truly remarkable. When the Germans cut off the water supply to the city, the Poles bored wells by hand. On 1 September 1,500 defenders had to retreat from a position at Stare Miasto (Old Town), using the sewers accessible from a single manhole in Krasinski Square. 'A few gas-bombs through the manholes or an outbreak of panic in the tunnels would be enough to prevent anyone getting out alive,' recorded Bór-Komorowski. 'Besides, how could the entry of 1,500 into the sewers be concealed when the manhole by which they must enter lay concealed only some 220 yards from the enemy positions?'[40] He nonetheless gave the order, since the defenders 'had nothing more to lose'. So, leaving the Old Town completely defenceless in the event of a German surprise attack, the entire force, along with 500 civilians, their wounded and 100 German prisoners, went down the manhole. 'Slowly, very slowly, the queue of waiting people disappeared,' wrote Bór-Komorowski,

Each person held on to the one ahead. The human serpent was about 1½ miles in length. It moved slowly. There was no time for rest periods, because room had to be made for the others who were waiting by the manhole. It was only with the greatest difficulty that the line moved forward, for the water had now almost completely drained away and the mud had been replaced by a thick slime which gripped their legs up to the calf. The soldiers had had no sleep at all for several days and their only food had been dry potato flakes. The rifles slung round their necks seemed unbearably heavy and kept clattering along the tunnel walls . . . The last soldier in the queue entered the manhole just before dawn.[41]

When the Stukas, artillery, tanks and finally infantry attacked the positions the next morning, initially believing the Poles' silence to be merely a ruse to conserve ammunition, the Germans found their quarry gone. The Poles had escaped, at least for the present.

The Uprising led to the systematic destruction of 83 per cent of the city of Warsaw by the Waffen-SS, yet when in early September the Red Cross arranged an evacuation, only 10 per cent of the population of one million elected to leave the city. Although they initially had only seven days' supply of ammunition, the Home Army fought for more than nine weeks, until 5 October. Since the destruction of any future opposition to a Communist regime in Poland suited Stalin well, he refused the USAAF and RAF permission to land in Soviet-held territory, thus severely hampering their ability to drop supplies of food and arms to the Poles, although efforts were nonetheless made. In all 15,200 insurgents were killed and 7,000 wounded before Bór-Komorowski was forced to surrender. Yet German losses were high too: some reports claim as many as 17,000 died.[42] Himmler's revenge was to send 153,810 Polish men, women and children to the concentration camps, from where only a handful were to emerge alive.[43]

Only after the Uprising had been completely crushed in early October did the SS withdraw from Warsaw, and it was not until mid-January that the Red Army crossed the river and took over the smoking ruins of the city. It had been an epic struggle, which sometimes tends to be skated over in Anglo-American histories of the war. As an historian of Poland, Norman Davies, has pointed out, however, the Warsaw Uprising 'engaged twice as many [soldiers] as did the attack on Arnhem; it lasted ten times longer; and it caused five times as many casualties. What is more, the fate of an Allied capital was at stake. And three times as many civilians were killed as in the entire London Blitz.'[44]

On 27 December 1944 Stalin wrote to Roosevelt to complain that the Western Allies were effectively supporting Polish democrats, whom he characterized as 'a criminal terrorist network against Soviet officers and soldiers on the territory of Poland. We cannot reconcile with such a situation when terrorists instigated by Polish emigrants kill in Poland soldiers and officers of the Red Army, lead a criminal fight against Soviet troops who are liberating Poland, and directly aid our enemies, whose allies they in fact are.' To describe Polish democrats as the allies of the Nazis shows Stalin's attitude towards Poland at the time, only two months before the Yalta Conference at which Roosevelt and Churchill took at face value his promises for Polish self-determination.[45] Of course Stalin was not fighting the war for democracy; indeed, as Richard Overy points out: 'The greatest paradox of the Second World War is that democracy was saved by the exertions of Communism.'[46] Stalin was fighting to protect the October

Revolution and Mother Russia, and lost twenty-seven million Soviet citizens in the process. Yet before sympathy is invoked for the USSR, as opposed to the long-suffering Russian people, one should recall the terrible, cardinal errors made by her leadership. The Nazi–Soviet Pact itself, the dispositions of troops far too close to the new border, the refusal to believe myriad warnings of Barbarossa from a myriad different sources: all these blunders and many more can be laid directly at the door of Stalin and his Politburo. Hitler had done quite enough in his career to prove how utterly untrustworthy he was long before the Nazi–Soviet Pact was signed in August 1939, yet as Alexander Solzhenitsyn pointed out: 'Not to trust anybody was very typical of Josef Stalin. All the years of his life did he trust one man only, and that was Adolf Hitler.'

While the Poles were being crucified in Warsaw, on 20 August 1944 Marshal A. M. Vasilevsky began his drive to clear the Germans out of the Balkans, which saw spectacular successes as the 2nd and 3rd Ukrainian Fronts crossed the Prut river and attacked Army Group South Ukraine in Romania. With Hitler desperate to retain control of the Romanian oilfields, without which his tanks and planes would be forced to rely on failing synthetic-fuel production within the Reich, he could not withdraw the Sixth Army (reconstituted in name after Stalingrad), twenty divisions of which were therefore entrapped in a giant pocket between the Dnieper river and the Prut by 23 August. On that same day, Romania surrendered, and soon afterwards changed sides and declared war on Germany: 100,000 German prisoners and much matériel were taken and by 31 August the Red Army was in Bucharest. Despite having advanced 250 miles in ten days, it then actually speeded up, crossing 200 miles to the Yugoslav border in the next six days, and to within striking distance of Budapest by 24 September.

On 25 August Model was posted off to the west to replace Kluge both as commander of Army Group B and as commander-in-chief west, the posts Rommel and Rundstedt had held on D-Day. In the calendar year 1944, therefore, Hitler had appointed his 'fireman' to command each of the three major army groups in the east, and for a short period the Army Group North Ukraine too, as well as the two senior posts in the west. It was an extreme example of how Hitler tended not to leave his generals in commands for long enough for them to grasp more than the essentials. Only one month into Model's command in the west, he was relieved of it when Rundstedt was recalled from disgrace, although he retained his command of Army Group B, in which position he defended the Scheldt estuary for eighty-five days, defeated the British and Poles at Arnhem and commanded the Ardennes offensive.

Rundstedt's career was equally pitted with examples of the Führer's caprice. His first forced retirement had taken place before the war even started, in October 1938 after he had supported non-Nazi generals during the Wehrmacht rearmament programme that he headed. Recalled to command Army Group South in June 1939, he was one of the twelve field marshals appointed on 19 July 1940. When in December 1941 he refused to obey Hitler's 'Stand or die' order at Rostov, he was dismissed. Four months later he was appointed commander-in-chief west, but was removed from command on 6 July 1944 after trying to persuade Hitler to adopt a mobile defence rather than fighting for every town and village in France. After his recall that September, and being given his old job back, he was sacked once again after advising one of Hitler's Staff officers to 'Make peace, you fools!' in March 1945. Rundstedt's four dismissals were exceptional, but Guderian was sacked twice, in December 1941 and March 1945, and the movement of senior personnel on the Eastern Front in 1944 resembled a merry-go-round, made more complicated by the renaming of the army groups as the geographical situation worsened.

Bulgaria, which up to this point had been attempting not to fight anything more than a nominal war against Russia, nonetheless had war declared against her on 5 September 1944, only to collapse within twenty-four hours after the Russians crossed the Danube. She then joined the Allies on 8 September. Further south, Marshal Tolbukhin's 3rd Ukrainian Front marched on Belgrade, aided by Marshal Tito's Yugoslav partisans, taking it on 20 October. 'The results of Nazi barbarity, by now sickeningly familiar, greeted Russian liberators and more than 200 mass graves had been filled with slaughtered Slovaks.'[47]

Hitler insisted on Army Group F staying in Greece for as long as possible, which meant that it could not help much in the defence of

Yugoslavia, where, in order to avoid being cut off, Field Marshal Maximilian von Weichs, the German Supreme Commander in south-east Europe, was forced westwards via Sarejevo as the Russians established a bridgehead over the Danube on 24 November and encircled Budapest on Christmas Eve. The Hungarian capital held out bravely, if in vain, through terrible privations until mid-February 1945. The frustrations of the Red Army besiegers were taken out on the women of Budapest, with mass rape in scenes that were to be repeated across eastern Europe, and especially in Germany.

Meanwhile, the Baltic States of Estonia, Latvia and Lithuania were liberated from Hitler's yoke between 10 October and Christmas 1944, only to fall beneath Stalin's for the next forty-four years. Guderian, who had been appointed OKH chief of staff in June, attempted to get the twenty veteran divisions of Army Group North – a powerful manoeuvrable striking force – out of west Latvia so that it could reinforce the hard-pressed German units defending East Prussia to the south, but he was prevented from doing so by Hitler. So when the Russian 1st Baltic Front reached the Baltic Sea and took Memel, Army Group North was trapped, with no land route back to East Prussia. Hitler had effectively created a 'fortified locality' out of the whole western part of Latvia. Between September and November 1944 the German Sixteenth and Eighteenth Armies were forced to retreat into Baltic enclaves at Memel and Kurland, but Hitler would not evacuate them, because he said he needed the Baltic coastline to continue to import Swedish iron ore and to test a new generation of undetectable, indefinitely submersible U-boats that were faster underwater than the Allies' convoys. Hitler now hoped to win the war by marooning the Anglo-American armies on the Continent without supplies. He later insisted that, although some divisions could evacuate, the Kurland bridgehead must be held by an entire army. Thus his forces were trapped in the Kurland pocket, which the Red Army perceptively came to regard as a gigantic POW camp maintained for them by the Wehrmacht, and so did not force it to surrender until the end of the war.[48] (The U-boats never came on stream in sufficient quantities either.) As 1944 ended, it was understandably hailed as 'The Year of Ten Victories' by the Soviets, who had seen an unbroken run of success since the relief of Leningrad that January.

On 12 January 1945, the Russians unleashed a massive offensive along the entire front from the Baltic Sea in the north down to the Carpathian mountains in the south, against what was left of the new German Central Front, made up of the seventy divisions of Army Group Centre and Army Group A. Planned by Stalin and the Stavka, but particularly by Zhukov, this giant offensive primarily comprised, from south to north: Konev's 1st Ukrainian, Zhukov's 1st Belorussian, Rokossovsky's 2nd Belorussian, Ivan Chernyakovsky's 3rd Belorussian, Ivan Bagrayan's 1st Baltic and Andrei Yeremenko's 2nd Baltic Fronts, no fewer than 200 divisions in all.[49] Faced with this onslaught, wildly outnumbered and outgunned, the Germans conducted an impressive fighting retreat of almost 300 miles, losing Warsaw on 17 January and leaving isolated garrisons at Thorn, Poznań and Breslau that had no real hope of relief.

Almost one million German citizens were sheltering in or around the pleasant city of Breslau in Lower Silesia, which was not a fortress in the conventional sense despite attempts after August 1944 to build a defensive ring at a 10-mile radius from the city centre. 'Women and children must leave the city on foot and proceed in the direction of Opperau and Kanth!' blared loudspeakers on 20 and 21 January 1945, effectively expelling the civilian population into 3-foot snowdrifts and temperatures of –20 Celsius. 'The babies were usually the first to die,' records the historian of Breslau's subsequent seventy-seven-day defence.[50] For all the horrors of the siege – 26 per cent of Breslau's fire brigade perished, for example – the Aviatik cigarette factory somehow continued to make 600,000 cigarettes a day, which was good for morale. Ammunition and supplies were parachuted in by the Luftwaffe, but these often fell into the Oder or behind the Russian lines. Lower Silesia's famously brutal Gauleiter, Karl Hanke – who executed Breslau's mayor for suspected defeatism – chose the cellars under the University Library to use as his bunker. He wanted to blow up the library to provide additional cover above him, but feared that the flames from its 550,000 books might spread dangerously.[51] (A Gauleiter perishing from the burning of books would have had its own pleasing irony.) In the event Breslau surrendered only on 6 May 1945, with troops throwing their weapons into the Oder and changing into civilian clothes. The siege had cost the city the lives of 28,600 (that is, 22 per cent) of its 130,000 soldiers and civilians. A few days before Breslau's capitulation, Hanke – whom Hitler appointed as Himmler's successor as Reichsführer-SS in his will – changed into an NCO's uniform and flew in a Fieseler Storch plane from the Kaiserstrasse airstrip. He was shot by Czech partisans when trying to escape in June 1945.

Zhukov reached the Oder river on 31 January 1945 and Konev the Oder–Neisse Line a fortnight later, before finally halting due to their long lines of supply and communications. 'Logistics is the ball and chain of armoured warfare,' Guderian used to say, and, having long worked to their advantage, these long lines would now occasionally work in the Soviets' disfavour. Hitler's dispositions continued to make Germany's strategic situation worse. Guderian recalled after the war that the Führer had refused his advice to bring the bulk of the Wehrmacht stationed in Poland back from the *Hauptkampflinie* (front line) to more defensible positions 12 miles further back at the *Grosskampflinie* (defensive line), out of range of Russian artillery.[52] Disastrously, Hitler's orders meant that the new defensive lines, only 2 miles behind the front, were badly hit by the Soviet guns, wrecking hopes for a classic German counter-attack to develop. 'This was in absolute contradiction of German military doctrine,' notes an historian of the campaign.[53] Hitler's insistence on personally approving everything done by the Staff was explained to Guderian with words so hubristic as to invite retribution from the gods: 'There's no need for you to try and teach me. I've been commanding the Wehrmacht in the field for five years and during that time I've had more practical experience than any gentlemen of the General Staff could ever hope to have. I've studied Clausewitz and Moltke and read all the Schlieffen papers. I'm more in the picture than you are!'[54]

A few days into the great Soviet offensive in the east, Guderian challenged Hitler aggressively over his refusal to evacuate the German army in Kurland, which had been completely cut off against the Baltic. Speer vividly recalled walking across the heavy, hand-woven rug in Hitler's massive office in the Reich Chancellery to the table top of blood-red Austria marble, 'striated with the beige and white cross sections of an ancient coral reef'. When Hitler refused Guderian's request to evacuate the trapped army across the Baltic, as 'he always did when asked to authorize a retreat', the OKH Chief of Staff lost his temper and addressed his Führer with what Speer described as 'an openness unprecedented in this circle'. Speer thought that Guderian might have been drinking with the Japanese Ambassador Hiroshi Oshima beforehand, but whatever the reason he stood facing Hitler across the table, 'with flashing eyes and the hairs of his moustache literally [sic] standing on end', saying, in 'a challenging voice': 'It's simply our duty to save these people, and we still have time to remove them!' Hitler stood up to answer back: 'You are going to fight on there. We cannot give up these areas!' 'But it's useless to sacrifice men in this senseless way,' continued Guderian. 'It's high time! We must evacuate those soldiers at once!' According to Speer, 'Hitler appeared visibly intimidated by this assault,' more by its tone than by the arguments themselves, and although the Führer of course got his way, 'The novelty was almost palpable. New worlds had opened out.'[55]

In January 1945, as the Red Army's Vistula–Oder operation rolled forward and Warsaw was about to fall, three senior members of Guderian's OKH planning Staff – a colonel and two lieutenant-colonels – were arrested by the Gestapo and interrogated about their seeming questioning of orders from OKW. Only after Guderian spent much time and energy intervening were the lieutenant-colonels freed, although the colonel was sent to a concentration camp. 'The essence of the problem lay in Hitler's Führer-system of unquestioning obedience to orders clashing with the General Staff's system of mutual trust and exchange of ideas, against a background of Hitler's class consciousness and genuine distrust of the General Staff following the failed putsch.'[56]

At a two-and-a-half-hour Führer-conference starting at 4.20 p.m. on 27 January 1945, Hitler explained his thinking with regard to the Balkans, and in particular the oilfields of the Lake Balaton region in Hungary. Attended by Göring, Keitel, Jodl, Guderian, five other generals and fourteen other officials, he ranged over every front of the war, with the major parts of the agenda covering weather conditions, Army Group South in Hungary, Army Group Centre in Silesia, Army Group Vistula in Pomerania, Army Group Kurland, the Eastern Front in general, the west, ammunition allotments, Allied advances in Italy, the north, the situation at sea, and political and personnel questions.[57]

'Our main problem is the fuel issue at the moment,' Guderian told Hitler, who replied: 'That's why I'm concerned, Guderian.' Pointing at the Balaton region, he added, 'If something happens down there, it's over. That's the most dangerous point. We can improvise everywhere else, but not there. I can't improvise with the fuel.'[58] He had been speaking of the importance of keeping hold of the Balkans, largely for its copper, bauxite and chromium deposits, as well as oil, since mid-1943.[59] The Sixth Panzer Army, reconstituted after its exertions in the Ardennes offensive, was ordered to Hungary, from where it could not be extracted.

Defending Hungary accounted for seven of the eighteen Panzer divisions still available to Hitler on the Eastern Front, a massive but necessary commitment. By January 1945, the month that the battle of the Bulge was lost, Hitler had only 4,800 tanks and 1,500 combat aircraft in the east, to fight Stalin's 14,000 and 15,000 respectively.[60] The Red Army's 12 January offensive finally came to an end a month later on the lower reaches of the River Oder, a mere 44 miles from the suburbs of Berlin. It had been an epic advance, but had temporarily exhausted the USSR. Yet his troops' proximity to the German capital gave Stalin a greatly increased voice at the Yalta Conference in the Crimea, called to discuss the endgame in Europe, and to try to persuade the Soviets to undertake a major involvement in the war against Japan.

Franklin Roosevelt and Josef Stalin met only twice, at the Teheran Conference in November 1943 and the Yalta Conference in February 1945, although they maintained a very regular correspondence. The first letter was sent by Roosevelt soon after Hitler had invaded the Soviet Union in the summer of 1941, and the 304th, also sent by him, was dated 11 April 1945, the day before he died. By the time of Yalta it was Roosevelt who was making all the running attempting to keep the alliance together. With the Red Army firmly in occupation of Poland, and Soviet divisions threatening Berlin itself when the conference opened, there was effectively nothing that either FDR or Churchill could have done to safeguard political freedom in eastern Europe, and both knew it. Roosevelt certainly tried everything – including straightforward flattery – to try to bring Stalin round to a reasonable stance on any number of important post-war issues, such as the creation of a meaningful United Nations, but he overestimated what his undoubted aristocratic charm could achieve with the homicidal son of a drunken Georgian cobbler.

Addressing Congress in March 1945, Roosevelt reported that Yalta 'spells the end of the system of unilateral action, the exclusive alliances, the spheres of influence, the balance of power, and all the other expedients that have been tried for centuries – and have always failed.' This was a quite exceptionally idealistic, or perhaps naive, way to have interpreted Yalta, but it is quite possible that Roosevelt believed what he was saying when he said it. A far more realistic approach to dealing with Stalin had been adopted by Churchill in Moscow in October 1944, when he took along what he called 'a naughty document' which listed the 'proportional interest' in five south-east European countries. Greece would be under 90 per cent British influence 'in accord with the US' and 10 per cent Russian; Yugoslavia and Hungary were 50–50; Romania would be 90 per cent Russian, 10 per cent British; and Bulgaria 75 per cent Russian and 25 per cent 'the others'. Stalin signed the document with a big blue tick, telling Churchill to keep it, and generally stuck to the agreements.[61]

Despite his attempts to charm Stalin at Yalta, FDR could also be sharp with the marshal if necessary: on 4 April 1945 he wrote to Stalin: 'I have received with astonishment your message of April 3 containing an allegation that arrangements which [sic] were made between Field Marshals Alexander and Kesselring at Berne, "permitting the Anglo-American troops to advance to the East and the Anglo-Americans promised in return to ease for the Germans the peace terms".' Stating that no such negotiations had taken place, Roosevelt concluded: 'Frankly I cannot avoid a feeling of bitter resentment towards your informers, whoever they are, for such vile misrepresentations of my actions and those of my trusted subordinates.'[62] (Yet representatives of Alexander and Kesselring were indeed meeting in Berne, and indeed the British War Cabinet held a meeting on 12 April where the first item on the agenda was proposals from Berne concerning British POWs.[63] It was understandable if Stalin, who had no representatives present, was nervous lest deals were being done between the Germans and the Anglo-Americans behind his back.)

Within a fortnight Roosevelt was dead, and Harry S. Truman took on the burdens of the war presidency, but any hopes this raised in the breasts of the Germans, especially Goebbels, were dashed when it soon became clear that Truman would listen to the advice of the same man who had been directing American military strategy since 1939, General George C. Marshall.

By mid-March 1945, Hitler had found a new scapegoat to blame for the coming victory of the Jewish–Bolshevik hordes: it was all the fault of the German *Volk* itself. By that stage he positively invited the retribution that the Aryan race was about to undergo at the hands of the Russians, believing that it had been the people's weakness as human beings that had led to the disaster, rather than his own strategic errors. He even said as much, at least according to Albert Speer's later testimony, stating with consummate nihilism on 18 March:

If the war should be lost, then the *Volk* will also be lost. This fate is unavoidable. It is not necessary to take into consideration the bases the *Volk* needs for the continuation of its most primitive existence. On the contrary, it is better to destroy these things yourself. After all, the *Volk* would then have proved the weaker nation, and the future would exclusively belong to the stronger nation of the east. What would remain after this fight would in any event be inferior subjects, since all the good ones would have fallen.[64]

Mere survival by then was, for Hitler, Darwinian *a priori* proof of *Untermensch* status, and the utter destruction of Germany was preferable to her domination by Stalin. Although there must be some doubt that Speer interpreted Hitler correctly about the Soviets, whom he had only ever referred to with contempt as 'barbarians' and 'primitives', there was none about the order the Führer gave to his Gauleiters, Reichskommissars and senior commanders the very next day, 19 March, entitled 'Demolitions on Reich Territory', in which he commanded that 'All military transport, communication facilities, industrial establishments, and supply depots, as well as anything else of value within Reich territory that could in any way be used by the enemy immediately or within the foreseeable future for the continuation of the war, be destroyed.'[65]

Fortunately this order was not carried out by Speer at all, and by Nazi officials only sparingly according to the level of their fanaticism.

THE STORM OF WAR

If it had been carried out to the letter, the German people could hardly have survived the winter of 1945/6, which was harsh enough for them as it was. 'I think the Wagner ideology of *Götterdämmerung* [Twilight of the Gods] had an influence on Hitler during the last few months,' Walther Funk told his Nuremberg psychiatrist in May 1946, 'and everything had to go down in ruins with Hitler himself, as a sort of false *Götterdämmerung*.'[66] Yet Speer should not be commended too highly on the back of this one action, or rather inaction. It had been he who commanded the vast army of slave labourers that produced German armaments in barbarous conditions. 'Just as the Nazi state rested on a basis of total brutality and corruption,' recorded Alan Clark, 'so the parts of the army machine, the actual weapons with which the soldiers fought, Tigers, Panzers, Nebelwerfers, Solothurns [anti-tank rifles], Schmeissers, came from the darkened sheds of Krupp and Daimler-Benz; where slave labour toiled eighteen hours a day, cowering under the lash, sleeping six to a "dog kennel" eight feet square, starving or freezing to death at the whim of their guards.'[67] Although Speer's deputy, Fritz Sauckel, was hanged at Nuremberg, the life of the urbane, middle-class but above all seemingly apologetic Speer was spared.[68]

It was extraordinary, considering that the war's outcome had not been in doubt since the destruction of Army Group Centre in the summer of 1944, that the Wehrmacht continued to operate as an efficient, disciplined fighting force well into the spring of 1945. As many as 400,000 Germans were killed in the first five months of 1945 – entirely unnecessarily, as the chances of Germany winning the war were negligible for the whole of that time.[69] General Schörner's newly re-created Army Group Centre, for example, was still fighting around the town of Küstrin on the Oder in April 1945. Similarly the 203,000 men representing the remnants of Army Group North, renamed Army Group Kurland, kept fighting into May, showing astonishing resilience in the face of utter hopelessness and retaining military cohesion until the moment that they were marched off into a ten-year captivity spent rebuilding the infrastructure of the Soviet Union that they had destroyed. If one visits the railway stations of Kursk, Volgograd and other Russian towns and 'hero-cities' today, one can still see their handiwork.

The Sixth Panzer Army halted the Russian advance down the Hungarian valleys into Austria for as long as its fuel could last out during March 1945, but finally Vienna fell to Malinovsky's 2nd Ukrainian Front on 13 April. Hitler's headquarters had by then adopted a policy of lying to army group commanders, as General Dr Lothar Rendulic, the last commander of Army Group South (a term revived the previous September), discovered when he received orders on 6 April to hold Vienna at all costs. Rendulic was given to telling his troops: 'When things look blackest and you don't know what to do, beat your chest and say: "I'm a National Socialist; that moves mountains!"'[70] Since that wasn't working on this occasion, he asked OKW 'how the continuation or termination of the war was envisaged', only to 'receive the answer that the war was to be ended by political measures'.[71] This was clearly untrue, and Rendulic surrendered near Vienna in May. (Further to illustrate how much Hitler moved his senior officers around, in the first five months of 1945 Rendulic commanded Army Group North in East Prussia in January, Army Group Centre the same month, Army Group Kurland in March and Army Group South in Austria in April.)

In the north on the Baltic coast, the Germans were in a dire situation because of Hitler's refusal to countenance Guderian's pleas to rescue Army Group Centre in East Prussia and Army Group Kurland (formerly Army Group North) in Latvia. Yet with both Zhukov and Rokossovsky bearing down on more than 500,000 trapped Germans after 16 February 1945, the German Navy – at tremendous cost – pulled off an evacuation that was far larger even than that of Dunkirk in 1940. No fewer than four army divisions and 1.5 million civilian refugees were taken from the Baltic ports of Danzig, Gotenhafen, Königsberg, Pillau and Kolberg by the Kriegsmarine, and brought back to Germany. Under constant air attack, which claimed every major ship except the cruisers *Prinz Eugen* and *Nürnberg*, the German Navy had pulled off a tremendous coup. The Soviet Navy was surprisingly enough a grave disappointment throughout the Second World War, but one of its submarines, the *S-13*, sank the German liner MV *Wilhelm Gustloff* in the Baltic Sea on 31 January 1945, and around 9,000 people – almost half of them children – perished, representing the greatest loss of life on one ship in maritime history.

Taking overall command of the great final offensive against Berlin itself, Marshal Zhukov gave up his 1st Belorussian Front to Vasily Sokolovsky, and took over an army group combining both that and Konev's front, reaching Berlin on 22 April 1945 and encircling it three days later. On Wednesday, 25 April, units from the US First Army, part of Bradley's 12th Army Group, and from the 1st Ukrainian Front met up at Torgau on the Elbe. With the lines of demarcation between the Allies having been agreed even before the Yalta Conference, but reconfirmed there, it fell to the Russians to fight the battle of Berlin. It is perfectly possible that Simpson's US Ninth Army, which was on the Elbe only 60 miles west of Berlin on 11 April, eleven days before the Russians reached it, could have attacked the city first. It had crossed 120 miles in the previous ten days, and the Germans were not putting up the level of resistance in the west that they were in the east.[72] But, for all the theorizing after the war – and Montgomery's and Patton's complaints during it – that the Western Allies should have taken Berlin instead of the Russians, the British, Americans, Canadians and French did not have to suffer such a vast number of casualties in that final desperate struggle (although had it come to it they would have fought the engagement in a less costly way).

Bradley's assessment to Eisenhower was that a Western attack on Berlin would cost 100,000 casualties, which he considered 'a pretty stiff price for a prestige objective'.[73] This figure is almost certainly too high. Konev later stated that the Red Army lost 800 tanks in the battle for Berlin, and it is thought that Russian casualties amounted to as many as 78,291 killed and 274,184 wounded, although these figures could probably have been smaller – not least through fewer friendly-fire incidents – if Stalin had not been in such a hurry to capture the capital as soon as possible, regardless of the human cost involved,[74] and it also encompasses all the fighting from the Baltic to the Czech border including the crossings of the Oder and Neisse rivers.[75] One of the main reasons for Stalin's haste was that his spy chief, Lavrenti Beria, had discovered that the Kaiser Wilhelm Institute for Physics in Dahlem, a south-western suburb of Berlin, housed the German atomic research programme, where they hoped to find scientists, equipment, many litres of heavy water and several tonnes of uranium oxide.[76] Stalin therefore promoted an ill-concealed race between the rivals Zhukov and Konev as to who would take south-west Berlin first.

Berliners love black jokes and during the terribly deprived and dangerous Christmas of 1944 their Yuletide advice was 'Be practical: give a coffin'; another was 'Enjoy the war while you can, the peace will be terrible.' The constant Allied air raids were bad, but worse was the knowledge that a 6.7 million-strong Red Army was massed on the Reich's borders from the Baltic to the Adriatic, with their city as the ultimate goal. This was significantly larger than the army with which Hitler had invaded the Soviet Union in 1941, an awesome achievement of the Stavka, albeit greatly aided by the United States' Lend-Lease scheme, under which more than 5,000 aircraft, 7,000 tanks, many thousands of lorries, 15 million pairs of boots and prodigious quantities of food, supplies, arms and ammunition were shipped to the Soviet Union. Valued at $10 billion in total and representing 7 per cent of the USSR's total output, this allowed the Russians to concentrate production on areas where they were most efficient. (The debt was finally repaid in 1990.)[77] So, when they wished one another *Prosit Neujahr!* (Happy New Year!) for 1945, few Berliners clinked glasses. The irony was not lost on them that, before the war, their liberal city had been the most anti-Nazi place in Germany, yet now it faced destruction because of its most prominent resident, who had returned from the Wolfschanze on 20 November 1944 and since 16 January had been living in the bunker beneath the Old Chancellery in the Wilhelmstrasse. (Although the bunkers under the New Chancellery were more spacious, the Old Chancellery ones 50 feet below street level were chosen as they were deemed safer.) Once there, Hitler indulged himself in fantasies about the Allies falling out with each other once their armies met.[78] Although he has often been accused of moving phantom armies around on maps in the bunker, and making hollow declarations of coming victory, this was in part the fault of the sub-standard communications centre. Unlike the well-appointed Wolfschanze, his Berlin bunker had only a one-man switchboard, one radio transmitter and one radio telephone, and even that depended on a balloon suspended over the Old Chancellery.[79] Officers were reduced to telephoning numbers taken at random from the Berlin telephone directory, the Soviet advance being plotted by how many times the calls were answered in Russian rather than German.

'What troops and subordinate commanders appreciate is that a general should be constantly in personal contact with them,' Wavell wrote in his book *Generals and Generalship* in 1941, 'and should not see everything simply through the eyes of his staff. The less time a general spends in his office and the more with his troops the better.' Although of course Hitler was a head of state rather than merely a general, for the last two and a half years of the war, ever since Stalingrad, the German people had seen almost nothing of him. He took most of his information from his Staff and from personal meetings with hard-pressed generals who almost all had to visit him rather than he them, in contrast to Churchill and Brooke who regularly flew out to talk with Allied commanders. In equally stark contrast to Churchill, Hitler never visited a bomb-site; instead the curtains in his Mercedes-Benz were closed as it sped past them. The last time Hitler appeared in semi-public was on his fifty-sixth and last birthday on 20 April 1945, when he congratulated a line-up of Hitler Youth fighters who had distinguished themselves in fighting. One of these children, Arnim Lehmann, recalls the Fuhrer's weak voice and rheumy eyes as he squeezed their ears and told them how brave they were being. Analysis of the film footage with modern, computer-assisted lip-reading techniques for speech recognition confirms that he went down the line with an exhortation such as 'Well done', 'Good' and 'Brave boy' for most of the fighters, who look as if they were barely in their teens.

'I have the impression that a very heavy battle lies ahead of us,' said Stalin as he opened the last planning session for the capture of Berlin, and he was right. Yet he had 2.5 million troops, 6,250 tanks and 7,500 aircraft to throw into this enormous final assault, and on Monday, 16 April 1945 around 22,000 guns and mortars rained 2,450 freight-car loads of shells at the German lines, which were also blinded by a mass of searchlights shone at them.[80] The Russian gunners had to keep their mouths open when they fired, in order to stop their eardrums bursting. Within six days the Red Army was inside Berlin, but the desperate fighting in the streets and rubble there cut down their advantages, and increased the Germans'. The Wehrmacht's lack of tanks mattered less in the built-up areas, and hundreds of Soviet tanks were destroyed in close fighting by the Panzerfaust, an anti-tank weapon that was very accurate at short range. The German Ninth Army under General Theodor Busse in the south of Berlin and the Eleventh Army under General Felix Steiner in the north would now try to defend a city with no gas, water, electricity or sanitation. When Steiner, who was outnumbered ten to one, failed to counter-attack to prevent Berlin's encirclement, he was subjected to a tirade from Hitler.

The last direct order to be personally signed by Hitler in the bunker was transmitted to Field Marshal Ferdinand Schörner at 04.50 on 24 April. Now in private hands, the original reads:

I shall remain in Berlin, so as to play a part, in honourable fashion, in the decisive battle for Germany, and to set a good example to all the rest. I believe that in this way I shall be rendering Germany the best service. For the rest, every effort must be made to win the struggle for Berlin. You can therefore help decisively, by pushing northwards as early as possible. With kind regards, Yours, Adolf Hitler[81]

The signature, in red pencil, looks remarkably normal, considering the circumstances. Four days earlier, Hitler's birthday had found Schörner – who was admired by Hitler as 'a political soldier' – speech-ifying to a group of officers at his command HQ in a Czech hotel called Masarykov Düm near Königgrätz, about how they needed to live up to the Führer's great trust. Schörner, who had large numbers of men shot for cowardice, was named in Hitler's will as the new head of the Wehrmacht, but nine days later he deserted his army group and flew off in a small aircraft in civilian clothes to surrender to the Americans. He was handed over to the Russians and kept in captivity until 1954. In all about 30,000 death sentences for cowardice and desertion were handed down by the Germans on the Eastern Front in the last year of the war, two-thirds of which were carried out.

The Red Army had long been shooting anyone captured in SS uniform, and those SS men who had discarded it nonetheless could not escape the fact that their blood group was tattooed on their left arms, one inch below the armpit.[82] John Erickson speculates that it was this knowledge of certain death 'which kept many formations at their post during the dark days of the battles for Berlin, but, just in case, the military police remained vigilant to the last, ready to hang or shoot suspected deserters'.[83] Spreading defeatism was also a capital offence: after a short mockery of a trial by the SS or Gestapo, those suspected of it for whatever reason were hanged from the nearest lamp-post, with signs around their necks stating 'I have been hanged because I was too much of a coward to defend the Reich's capital', or 'I am a deserter; because of this I will not see the change in destiny', or 'All traitors die like this one'.[84] It is thought that at least 10,000 people died in this manner in Berlin – the same as the number of women who died (often by suicide) after having been raped by the Red Army there.[85]

Because of this horror, the Germans fought on with an efficiency that was utterly remarkable given the hopelessness of the situation. Yet at Berlin, as at Stalingrad and Monte Cassino, the indiscriminate artillery and aerial bombardment created fine opportunities for the defenders, of whom the city had 85,000 of all kinds. As well as the Wehrmacht, Waffen-SS and Gestapo contingents, there were several foreign volunteer forces (especially French Fascists) and the desperately under-armed *Volkssturm* (home guard) battalions made up of men of over forty-five and children under seventeen. Many of the 3,000 Hitler Youth who fought were as young as fourteen, and some were unable to see the enemy from under their adult-sized coal-scuttle helmets.

The looting, drunkenness, murder and despoliation indulged in by the Red Army in East Prussia, Silesia and elsewhere in the Reich – especially Berlin – were the inevitable responses of soldiers who had marched through devastated Russian towns and cities over the previous twenty months. 'Red Army troops loathed the neatness they found on the farms and in the towns of East Prussia: the china lined up on the dressers, the spotless housekeeping, the well-fenced fields and sleek cattle.'[86] The women of Germany were also about to pay a high personal price for the Wehrmacht's four-year ravaging of the Soviet Motherland. 'Altogether at least 2 million German women are thought to have been raped,' records the historian of Berlin's downfall, Antony Beevor, 'and a substantial minority, if not a majority, appear to have suffered multiple rape.'[87] In Berlin alone, 90,000 women were raped in the last few days before the city surrendered.[88] As one Red Army veteran joked, he and his comrades used to 'rape on a collective basis'.

Not only German women suffered. Polish women, Jewish con-
centration-camp survivors, even released Soviet female POWs were
raped at gunpoint, often by up to a dozen soldiers. Because Order
No. 227 had decreed that Russians who had surrendered to the
Germans were traitors, gang rapes of Russian female POWs were
permitted, even actually arranged.[89] Age, desirability or any other
criteria made virtually no difference. In Dahlem, for example, 'Nuns,
young girls, old women, pregnant women and mothers who had just
given birth were raped without pity.' The documentary and anecdotal
evidence is overwhelming and indisputable; the Red Army, which had
behaved so heroically on the battlefield, raped the women of Germany
as part of their reward, with the active collusion of their officers up
to and including Stalin. Indeed he explicitly excused their behaviour
on more than one occasion, seeing it as part of the rights of the
conqueror. 'What is so awful in his having fun with a woman, after
such horrors?' Stalin asked Marshal Tito about the ordinary Russian
soldier in April 1945. 'You have imagined the Red Army to be ideal.
And it is not ideal, nor can it be ... The important thing is that it
fights Germans.'[90] As well as for the sexual gratification of the soldiers,
mass rape was intended as a humiliation and revenge on Germany. If
the men of the Wehrmacht had sown the wind in Operation Barbarossa, it was their mothers, sisters and daughters who were forced to
reap the whirlwind. Yet it is perfectly possible that the Red Army
would have brutalized the Germans even if they had not envied their
enemies' prosperity and wanted revenge. When the Red Army entered
Manchuria in August 1945 there was widespread rape of Japanese
and non-Japanese people, even though the USSR had not been at war
with Japan and had not been invaded by her.[91]

It was not the Red Army alone that indulged in this form of warfare
against innocents. In North Africa and western Europe, the US Army
stands accused of raping an estimated 14,000 civilian women between
1942 and 1945, and although there were arrests and convictions,
nobody was ever executed for raping a German woman. Furthermore,
what punishment was meted out seems to have been decided on racial
lines; although blacks made up only 8.5 per cent of the US Army in
the European theatre, they accounted for 79 per cent of those executed
for rape. Yet, for an overall perspective, Russian soldiers were not

reprimanded for rape and 14,000 rapes over three years of war hardly equates with two million in one campaign.[92]

The issue of how many Russians – military and civilian – died during their Great Patriotic War was an intensely political one, and the true figure was classified as a national secret in the USSR until the fall of the Berlin Wall. Instead of exaggerating the numbers in order to excite the sympathy of the West, as might be expected of someone so well attuned to the use of propaganda, Stalin in fact minimized them in order to hide Soviet post-war weakness, and his own gross profligacy with human life, especially after making such monstrous errors in the early stages of the struggle.[93] In 1946 he gave a figure of only seven million dead. As part of his deStalinization programme, Nikita Khrushchev admitted in the 1960s to a number 'in excess of twenty million'. A General Staff commission in 1988–9 reported that the 'irrecoverable losses' of the Red Army alone – that is, those who died in action or from wounds, illness or accidents or were killed as POWs or shot for cowardice – had numbered 8,668,400, with a further eighteen million medical casualties from wounds, illness, frostbite and so on. Yet even this figure has been called into question by the leading scholar of the Russian war, John Erickson, over 'methodology, the genuineness and objectivity of data, the manner of its interpretation and much else'.[94] Figures compiled by General G. F. Krivosheev in 1997 seem to be much more reliable. These indicate that the Soviet Union mobilized 34.476 million people in the years 1941–5, including those already under arms in June 1941. Of that vast figure, 11.444 million died.[95] In the chaos of June 1941 many were slaughtered but few records were kept. The evacuation and displacement of such immense populations meant that the local military commissariats could not keep their card-indexes up to date, and with unregistered partisan activity, multiple counting for complex administrative reasons and many people dying of their wounds soon after the end of hostilities it is next to impossible, even free of political pressure, to arrive at an accurate final figure so long after the event. The ones chosen by Richard Overy, of eleven million military losses, eighteen million other casualties and civilian losses of around sixteen million killed, are probably as good as any and better than most. The aggregate figure of around twenty-seven million Russians killed is therefore probably best, which in a conflict that claimed the lives of fifty million people means that the USSR lost more than the whole of the rest of the world put together.

How would such genocide be punished? At 3.30 p.m. on 12 April 1945 the British War Cabinet discussed how to deal with German war criminals. The (hitherto unpublished) notes taken of this meeting by the Additional Cabinet Secretary, Norman Brook, became available in 2008 and show that the Minister of Aircraft Production, Labour's Sir Stafford Cripps, disagreed with the policy that the Foreign Secretary, Anthony Eden, set out for a large-scale trial, saying that it 'mixes politics and judicial decision with disadvantage to both'. Preferring the summary execution without trial of the senior Nazis, Cripps argued that either the Allies would be criticized for not according Hitler a real trial, or they would 'give him a chance to harangue' with the result being 'neither proper trial nor political act' but the 'worst of both worlds'. The Secretary for War, P. J. Grigg, pointed to the 'very large numbers, hundreds of thousands' of suspected war criminals who had fallen into British hands, whereupon Churchill suggested a 'Trial of [the] Gestapo as a body first. Then proceedings against selected members,' adding that it was 'Not proposed to arraign them all.' The Lord Chancellor, Lord Simon, then said that Roosevelt's Special Counsel, Samuel Rosenman, had made it clear that the US 'won't agree to penalties without trial', prompting Churchill to say, 'And Stalin insists on trial.' The historian in Churchill was unconvinced, however, and advanced the idea of a 'Bill of Attainder not an impeachment', such as that used to execute Charles I's adviser the Earl of Strafford in 1640 without the need for a trial.

The Home Secretary, Herbert Morrison, believed that 'This mock trial is objectionable. It really is a political act: better to declare that we shall put them to death.' Churchill agreed, insisting that 'The trial will be a farce.' Turning to the wording of the indictments, and the the defendants' right to be given access to defence barristers, the Prime Minister argued: 'All sorts of complications ensue as soon as you admit a fair trial. I agree with the Home Secretary that they should be treated as outlaws. We should however seek agreement of our Allies . . . I would take no responsibility for a trial – even though the

United States wants to do it. Execute the principal criminals as outlaws – if no Ally wants them.'[96] Field Marshal Smuts thought that Hitler's summary execution might 'set a dangerous precedent' and that there was an 'Act of State needed to legalise Hitler's execution'. Churchill added that allowing Hitler the right to make judicial arguments against his own execution 'apes judicial procedure but brings it into contempt', upon which Morrison interjected, 'And makes certain that he will be a martyr in Germany.'

Lord Simon then pointed out that, as the Americans and Russians wanted a trial, 'We must therefore compromise or proceed unilaterally.' By that stage of the war the latter option was almost unthinkable, yet he proposed publishing a document that put the British case against Hitler and then executing him 'without opportunity of reply'. This would be based upon the Allied pronouncement of 13 March 1815 that had declared Napoleon beyond the law, which he recalled having taken place after the battle of Waterloo rather than three months before it. Churchill then stated that he 'Will not agree to [a] trial which can only be a mock trial', and the Secretary of Air, Sir Archibald Sinclair, asked whether 'If Hitler is a soldier, we can refuse to give him quarter?' Churchill concluded the discussion by saying that Simon should liaise with the Americans and Russians 'to establish a list of grand criminals and get them to agree that these may be shot when taken in the field.'[97] In the event this expedient was not adopted, and instead the long process of putting the senior surviving Nazis on trial was established by the International Military Tribunal at Nuremberg, which for all its drawbacks did lead to justice being seen to be done.

The circumstances and macabre atmospherics of Hitler's death in his bunker were truly weird, made weirder by his decision to marry his girlfriend just before they killed themselves.[98] 'It's lucky I'm not married,' Hitler had said on the night of 25 January 1942. 'For me, marriage would have been a disaster ... I'd have had nothing of marriage but the sullen face of a neglected wife, or else I'd have skimped my duties.'[99] Eva Braun felt the same, having before the war sighed to the *Daily Telegraph*'s Berlin correspondent, 'It is too bad that Hitler became Reich Chancellor – or else he might have married me.'[100] The official who conducted his wedding to Eva Braun on Sunday, 29 April 1945 was Walter Wagner, the deputy surveyor of rubbish collection in the Pankow district of Berlin.[101] One of the many bizarre aspects of the ceremony was Wagner's asking the couple, in accordance with Nazi marriage law, whether they were both Aryan.[102] (They answered in the affirmative.) When she signed the register, Eva began her surname with a B, before it was pointed out to her 'that her new name begins with H'.[103] In more than one sense it was a shotgun wedding: Eva was worried about what people would make of her if Hitler didn't marry her, so in order to conform to bourgeois sensibilities she finally got her man. Just before the wedding the groom had dictated his Last Will and Testament to his secretary Traudl Junge, a predictable spew of anti-Semitism and self-justification. Junge was at the wedding reception, and recalled thinking to herself: 'What will they raise their champagne glasses to? Happiness for the newly married couple?'

After testing a cyanide capsule on their Alsatian bitch Blondi – who they obviously felt did not want to live in a post-Nazi Germany either – Eva swallowed one and Hitler shot himself at about 3.30 p.m. on Monday, 30 April 1945. The bunker's guards first guessed that Hitler was dead when they saw his Staff's cigarette smoke coming out of the ventilation shafts; he had been a fanatical anti-smoker.[104] When Winston Churchill was told the next day of the German official broadcast stating that Hitler had died 'fighting with his last breath against Bolshevism', his comment was: 'Well, I must say that he was perfectly right to die like that.' Lord Beaverbrook, who was dining with him at the time, observed that the report was obviously untrue.[105] By coincidence, the issue of *The Times* of 1 May that carried the news of Hitler's death had a small report mentioning that the Americans had reached the small Austrian border town of Braunau, where the Hitler story had begun fifty-six years earlier.

It took units as hardened as Zhukov's 1st Belorussian Front to force their way into the capital of the Reich, which was defended street-by-street all the way up to the Reichstag and the Reich Chancellery. Vasily Ivanovich Chuikov – the hero of Stalingrad, commander of the Eighth Guards Army and now of Soviet forces in central Berlin – recalled the Germans' attempted capitulation, which took place at his command post on May Day. 'At last, at 03.50 hours, there was a knock at the door, and in came a German general with the Order of the Iron Cross around his neck, and the Nazi swastika on his sleeve.'[106] General Hans Krebs, whom the Führer had appointed chief of the OKH General Staff in Guderian's place the previous month, was indeed straight out of Nazi central casting. 'A man of middle height, and solid build, with a shaven head, and scars on his face,' recalled Chuikov. 'With his right hand he makes a gesture of greeting – in his own, Nazi, fashion; with his left he tenders his service book to me.' Speaking through an interpreter, although it later turned out he was fluent in Russian from his three postings as a military attaché in Moscow (where he had once been embraced by Stalin), Krebs said: 'I shall speak of exceptionally secret matters. You are the first foreigner to whom I will give this information, that on 30 April Hitler passed from us from his own will, ending his life by suicide.' Chuikov recalled that Krebs paused after that, expecting 'ardent interest in this sensational news'. Instead Chuikov replied calmly: 'We know this.' In fact he had not known it at all, but was 'determined that I would meet any unexpected moves calmly, without showing the least shadow of surprise, and without drawing any hasty conclusions'. Since Krebs had brought only an offer of a negotiated surrender with a new government of which Dönitz was president and Goebbels chancellor, Chuikov – under orders from Zhukov and the Stavka – refused and demanded an unconditional surrender. Krebs then left to report to Goebbels, but just before leaving he said, 'May Day is a great festival for you,' to which Chuikov answered, 'And today why should we not celebrate? It is the end of the war, and the Russians are in Berlin.'[107] After Krebs had told Goebbels the news, they both committed suicide, their remains being thrown in with those of Mr and Mrs Hitler. (Goebbels' corpse was identified by the Russians from the special boot be wore for his club foot.) The next day, on 2 May, Berlin surrendered, and six days later so did all German forces throughout the now defunct Reich.

The famous photograph of the red flag being waved over the Reichstag in 1945 was taken by the twenty-eight-year-old Ukrainian Jew Yevgenny Khaldei with a Leica camera. The flag was actually one of three red tablecloths that the photographer had, in his words, 'got from Grisha, the bloke in charge of the stores at work. He made me promise to bring them back.' The night before he left Moscow for Berlin, Khaldei and a tailor friend of his father's had 'spent all night cutting out hammers and sickles and sewing them onto the cloths to make Soviet flags.' It was thus a tablecloth that was flown, somewhat precariously, over the devastated Berlin that day. 'What do you mean, you left it on the Reichstag?' Grisha cried when Khaldei explained to him what had happened. 'Now you're really going to get me into trouble!' The Tass picture editor spotted that the young soldier, 'a boy from Dagestan', who was propping up his flag-waving comrade, had watches on both wrists, clear indication of Red Army looting, and he made Khaldei airbrush that detail out of the photo.[108]

Although Zhukov was relegated after the war to a series of minor commands by a suspicious and jealous Stalin, his eminence and popularity in the West did at least allow him to escape the fate of 135,056 other innocent Red Army soldiers and officers, who were condemned by military tribunals for 'counter-revolutionary crimes'. A further 1.5 million Soviet soldiers who had surrendered to the Germans were transported to the Gulag or labour battalions in Siberia.

On 24 June 1945 an enormous victory parade was held in Red Square, in which over 200 captured Nazi standards were laid on the ground outside Lenin's tomb, with Stalin standing on the balcony above. The scene outdid anything from Ancient Rome, with the mass of enemy banners – which can be seen today in the Museum of the Great Patriotic War in Moscow – laid at the feet of the all-powerful conqueror. There can be no doubt, despite the numbers killed, who was the greatest territorial victor of the Second World War. For Britain, the victory brought near-bankruptcy, national exhaustion and years of grinding austerity. The British Empire, until then the proudest on earth since Ancient Rome, and for which Churchill himself had explicitly fought, had to be dissolved, with India being granted independence exactly two years after the end of the war against Japan. France also lay in the dust for over a decade. Nor did the war add any territorial acquisitions to the United States, which wished for none. Yet the war left the USSR battered but militarily supreme, in control not only of the whole of her pre-war territory, but also that of Latvia, Estonia, Lithuania, Poland, Hungary, Czechoslovakia, Bulgaria,

Romania, the eastern half of Germany and large parts of Austria, including Vienna. Yugoslavia and Finland were effectively client states, and a Communist insurgency in Greece might easily have turned that country into one too. When Stalin visited the tomb of King Frederick the Great of Prussia during the Potsdam Conference of July 1945, well inside the Russian zone of control, it was pointed out to him that no tsar had ever extended the Russian Empire so far westwards. His gruff reply: 'Alexander I rode through Paris.'

Germany, a nation that had unleashed no fewer than five wars of aggression in the seventy-five years after 1864, needed to have the warlike instinct burnt out of her soul. Only the horrors and humiliations of 1945 – Germany's 'Year Zero' – could achieve that. The macabre final scenes had to be played out, with Goebbels reading Thomas Carlyle's *Frederick the Great* to Hitler in the bunker as the Red Army closed in. Joachim von Ribbentrop, Heydrich's successor Ernst Kaltenbrunner, the propagandist Julius Streicher, Alfred Rosenberg and the six others could be hanged at Nuremberg, but Hitler could only die by one hand to make his defeat complete: his own. 'The destruction and human misery in 1945 is barely describable in its scale,' the historian of the German war economy records.[109] Some 40 per cent of German males born between 1920 and 1925 were dead or missing when the war ended; eleven million Wehrmacht soldiers were in POW camps, and some of those in Russia were not destined to return for up to twelve years; 14.16 million ethnic Germans were forced out of their homes in eastern and central Europe, with 1.71 million dying in the process. In some major German cities, over half the housing stock had been rendered uninhabitable; hunger hit a population that until the autumn of 1944 had not wanted for food.[110] Hitler would not have cared about any of this, of course, as the German people had by their very defeat shown themselves unworthy of his leadership. Had he not warned them in his recorded radio address of 24 February 1945: 'Providence shows no mercy to weak nations, but recognizes the right of existence only to sound and strong nations'?

The remains of Hitler, Eva Braun and the Goebbels family (Joseph and Magda had murdered their six children) were at last physically destroyed during the night of 4 April 1970. The bodies had been buried at a Smersh (military counter-intelligence) base in Magdeburg in East Germany in February 1946, which twenty-four years later was about to be turned over to the locals as surplus to requirements, and construction work was due to take place there. So potent a symbol were the mortal remains thought to be for neo-Nazi revanchists – even though the 'skulls, shin-bones, ribs, vertebrae and so on' were in 'an advanced state of decay, especially those of the children' – that the USSR's Chairman of State Security Yuri Andropov ordered that they be burnt with charcoal, crushed to dust, collected up and then thrown into a river.[111] So the remains were reincinerated and the ashes gathered into a canvas rucksack. 'We walked to a nearby hillside,' Vladimir Gumenyuk, the leader of the three-man detail charged with the task, told Russia's NTV television station years later. 'It was over in no time at all. I opened up the rucksack, the wind caught the ashes up into a little brown cloud, and in a second they were gone.'[112]

18

The Land of the Setting Sun

October 1944–September 1945

*Armchair strategists can look at the last stages of a campaign
and say there's nothing left but mopping up, but if you're
holding the mop it's different. The last Jap in the last bunker
on the last day can be as fatal to you personally as the biggest
battle at the height of the campaign, and you don't look or
think much beyond him – wherever he is.*
George MacDonald Fraser, *Quartered Safe Out Here*, 1992[1]

The collapse of Japan within four months of Hitler's death was a
powerful vindication of the Germany First policy adopted by the
Allies after Pearl Harbor. Had the Allies pursued a Pacific First policy
– as advocated by the US Navy in the wake of Pearl Harbor – it would
have allowed Hitler considerably more time and resources with which
to defeat the Soviet Union, and establish himself as master of the
Greater European land mass. There had always been a tension between
the US Army (which believed in the German First policy) and the US
Navy (which tended to believe in Pacific First, preferring the theatre
where it would play a far greater role). It took the Solomonic judgement of General Marshall to keep the United States committed to the
former, supported as he was in this by President Roosevelt and the
British.

Despite this, the United States had devoted a significant portion of
her armed forces to preventing Japan from consolidating her newly
won empire. The massive air superiority established by the Americans
in particular allowed them to pound the Japanese forces to a terrible
degree. The blows that rained down on Japan's Army, Navy, Air

Force and cities smashed each of them before the atomic bombs delivered the *coup de grâce*. On 12 October 1944, for example, Task Force 38 began its assault on Formosa, in which the Americans flew more than 2,300 sorties, whereas the very few planes that the Japanese managed to get into the sky were mostly intercepted and destroyed. Soon afterwards General Walter Krueger's Sixth Army was transported to Leyte in the Philippines by Admiral Thomas Kinkaid's Seventh Fleet, and in one day more than 130,000 troops were put ashore, almost as many as on D-Day. General MacArthur thereby redeemed the promise he had made to the Filipino people on 11 March 1942 when he had said: 'I shall return.'

As the Americans moved inexorably towards the Japanese mainland they often adopted a policy – as with the Palau Islands in October 1944 – of 'island-hopping', simply missing out engaging the Japanese forces on islands that were cut off and thus had no means of counter-attacking, in order to conserve troops' energy for assaults on those that did. The counter-attack at Leyte Gulf in late October 1944, with a carrier force from Japan and strike forces from Brunei, turned into the largest naval engagement in world history, with 216 United States Navy (and two Royal Australian Navy) vessels comprising 143,668 men doing battle with sixty-four Japanese vessels totalling 42,800 sailors and airmen. It was the last action fought between battleships, and was decisively won by the Americans, who by the end of the four separate engagements over three days had established unquestioned dominance over the Pacific Ocean for the first time since Pearl Harbor. Four Japanese aircraft carriers, three battleships, six heavy and four light cruisers and a submarine were sunk and scarcely another ship in their Navy emerged unscathed; more than 10,500 sailors and airmen and 500 planes had been lost. By contrast, Admiral William Halsey had lost one light carrier, two destroyers, 200 aircraft and about 2,800 killed and 1,000 wounded.[2] Then on 5 November Vice-Admiral John McCain, who commanded the carrier Task Force 38 of the Third Fleet, attacked Luzon, with the result that the Japanese lost a further 400 aircraft and a carrier for the loss of twenty-five American aircraft and the damaging of the carrier USS *Lexington* by *kamikaze* suicide-bombers. The *kamikaze* were a sign of Japanese fanaticism by that stage of the war, but also of their desperation. (They also deployed

Kaiten manned torpedoes later that month.) John McCain was a supremely successful air commander whose pilots once sank forty-nine Japanese ships in a single day and who were to destroy no fewer than 3,000 grounded Japanese planes in the last five weeks of war after 10 July 1945.[3]

The punishment that the Imperial Navy took in mid-November 1944 was devastating – four destroyers, a minesweeper and four transports carrying 10,000 troops were sunk on 11 November, a cruiser and four destroyers on the 13th, the aircraft carrier *Junyo* on the 17th, still more vessels on the 19th – yet still it fought on. Nor were there any signs that the Philippines could be recaptured without a long and debilitating land battle. Japanese stoicism in the face of half the world might have been strategically crazy but must inspire admiration. By the end of November, thirty-five B-29 bombers had raided Tokyo by night, the start of a destruction of the cities of the Japanese mainland that was to mirror that of Japan's naval, military and air forces. (In mid-February 1945 aircraft from Task Force 38 would conduct 2,700 sorties against Tokyo and Yokohama, for the loss of only eighty-eight aircraft, or 3 per cent.) Yet with no allies left, and ultimate defeat certain, still the Japanese fought on with seemingly undiminished ardour, genuine obedience to the perceived wishes of the Emperor playing an important part. Whatever the reason, it led directly to the deaths of over 1.5 million Japanese servicemen and 300,000 civilians during the Second World War.[4]

Although the bombing of Hiroshima and Nagasaki were not among them, some war crimes were committed by the Allies on the Japanese. George MacDonald Fraser, who fought in the 17th (Black Cat) Indian Division at the siege of Meiktila and the battle of Pyawbwe in Burma, described in his autobiography *Quartered Safe Out Here* how between twenty and fifty wounded Japanese soldiers had had rocks dropped on them in cold blood by an Indian unit, and explained his own feeling that 'the notion of crying for redress against the perpetrators (my own comrades-in-arms, Indian soldiers who had gone the mile for us, and we for them), on behalf of a pack of Japs, would have been obnoxious, dishonourable even.'[5] American Marines had to face the sight of their dead comrades' penises having been cut off by the Japanese and stuffed into the corpses' mouths. This kind of atrocity invited occasional barbaric reprisals, for even those fighting in a good cause can be brutalized by war, but in the view of the military historian Victor Davis Hanson there was 'a certain American exceptionalism that such barbarism should and usually was to be condemned as deviance rather than accepted as the norm – quite different from the Japanese'.[6]

On 13 December 1944, the heavy cruiser USS *Nashville*, on her way to the amphibious assault on Mindanao in the Philippines, was badly damaged by Japanese air attack. This did not halt the vast and successful operation at Cape San Augustin in the north-west of Luzon two days later, however, which was carried out by no fewer than thirteen carriers and eight battleships, as well as cruisers and destroyers. The Americans also established beach-heads at Lingayen Gulf on Luzon on 9 January 1945.

While these great land and sea battles were taking place further east, General Sir William Slim's British–Indian army was steadily making progress in expelling the Japanese from Burma. A landing on Akyab Island in the Arakan was scarcely opposed on 3 January 1945, and inland XXXIII Corps was marching towards the Irrawaddy river, while IV Corps was west of the Chindwin. On 23 January the British crossed the Irrawaddy – a river thrice the width of the Rhine in places – as Slim feinted towards Mandalay when all the time his ultimate prize was Rangoon much further south. Four days later the Burma Road to China was cleared. Meiktila was not to fall to the 17th Indian Division until early March, but, when it did, Japanese forces further north were effectively cut off. The 17th – which saw the longest period of continuous action of any British unit in the Second World War, at more than three years – was itself almost cut off in Meiktila by Japanese counter-attacks, but was resupplied from the air. The scale of defeat of the Japanese can be gauged from the fact that whereas the 100 miles from the Irrawaddy to Pyawbwe had taken the Fourteenth Army two months to cover, the next 260 miles down the Rangoon road took only twelve days.

Mandalay fell to the 19th Indian Division on 20 March, after Slim's brilliant strategy wrong-footed the Japanese on several occasions. 'Uncle Bill' Slim was, in the words of one of his veterans, 'large, heavily built, grim-faced with that hard mouth and bulldog chin; the rakish Gurkha hat was at odds with the slung carbine and untidy trouser bottoms . . . His delivery was blunt, matter-of-fact, without gestures or mannerisms, only a lack of them.'[7] When a British soldier thoughtlessly decorated his jeep with a skull he'd found – assuming it to be Japanese – Slim snapped at him to remove it, and then added gently: 'It might be one of our chaps, killed on the retreat.' Slim's 600-mile retreat out of Burma in 1942, the victory over Operation U-Go at Imphal from April to June 1944 and subsequently the advance down Burma outmanoeuvring the Japanese continually were each masterpieces of the military art. In the endless debate about who was the best battlefield commander of the Western Allies, in which the names of Patton, Bradley, Montgomery and MacArthur continually arise, that of the unassuming but immensely talented William Slim ought to feature much more than it does. Rangoon finally fell on 3 May, allowing the British to look beyond Burma to Malaya.

The US landings on the small but strategically vital island of Iwo Jima, starting on 19 February 1945, also proved that the Japanese had no intention of giving up simply because they could no longer win the conflict. The Americans needed Iwo Jima from which to fly fighter escorts protecting bombers, and as a place to where damaged bombers could return after smashing the Japanese mainland. In order to maximize American losses, the 21,000 defenders permitted 30,000 US Marines to land unopposed on the south-east of the island before they suddenly opened fire after they were ashore. The capture of the island, which was finally completed on 26 March, saw some of the most bitter hand-to-hand fighting of the Pacific War, in which no quarter was given or received, and where the Japanese made a number of suicide attacks by land, sea and air. The Anglo-American Lethbridge Commission, set up to study the tactics and equipment required to defeat Japan, even recommended the use of mustard and phosgene gas against underground enemy positions, and was supported in this by Army Chief of Staff George Marshall and Supreme Commander General Douglas MacArthur, but it was vetoed by President Roosevelt.

At the end of the battle for Iwo Jima, only 212 defenders – that is, 1 per cent of the original garrison – were still alive to surrender. Meanwhile, the US 3rd, 4th and 5th Marine Divisions had lost 6,891 dead and 18,070 wounded. Yet these terrible figures need to be placed beside the fact that by the end of the war 24,761 US airmen's lives had been saved by American possession of the island, receiving the 2,251 B-29s that had to make emergency, and on occasion crash, landings on the only viable runway in the region for planes of that size.[8] Yet even the bloodletting of Iwo Jima saw a fraction of the number of Japanese killed on Okinawa, the landings on which began only five days after Iwo Jima finally fell. Okinawa is the largest island of the Ryuku Islands group, midway between Formosa and Kyushu (Japan's southernmost island). It was therefore a crucial springboard for the invasion of the mainland, and the Japanese resolved to defend it to the last. On Easter Sunday, 1 April 1945, no fewer than 1,300 Allied vessels took part in the invasion of Okinawa, landing 60,000 troops under a huge bombardment, the first part of Lieutenant-General Simon Bolivar Buckner's Tenth Army, which was 180,000 strong (with more reserves available in New Caledonia), made up of XXIV Corps and III Marine Amphibious Corps. Although the Marines got ashore and established secure beach-heads on the first three days, the process of clearing the island of Japanese, which involved breaking through the strongly held Machinato and Shuri Lines of interlocking mountain-ridge defence systems, proved one of the epic tasks of America's war. For Buckner's opponent, Lieutenant-General Mitsuru Ushijima, commander of the Thirty-second Army, had around 135,000 well-armed and well-hidden men on the island.

Marine E. B. 'Sledgehammer' Sledge, a private in K Company, 3rd Battalion, 5th Marine Regiment of the 1st Marine Division, wrote an excellent memoir of his time on Okinawa entitled *With the Old Breed*, in which he recalled the weeks of constant fighting. Of one typical attack he wrote:

As the seconds ticked slowly toward 09.00, our artillery and ships' guns increased their rate of fire. The rain poured down, and the Japanese took up the challenge from our artillery. They started throwing more shells our way . . . The shells whistled, whined and rumbled overhead, ours bursting out in front of the ridge and the enemy's exploding in our area and to the rear. The noise increased all along the line. Rain fell in torrents, and the soil became muddy and slippery wherever we hurried around the gun pit to break out and stack our ammo. I looked at my watch. It was 0900. I gulped and prayed for my buddies.[9]

Flung back by 'a storm of enemy fire from our front and left back', Sledge's company 'all wore wild-eyed, shocked expressions that showed only too vividly they were men who barely escaped chance's strange arithmetic. They clung to their M1s, BARs [Browning automatic rifles], and Tommy guns and slumped to the mud to pant for breath before moving behind the ridge toward their former foxholes. The torrential rain made it all seem so much more unbelievable and terrible.' Company K had already suffered 150 killed, wounded or missing taking the island of Peleliu the previous autumn, and many more were to perish on Okinawa.

Meanwhile, furious *kamikaze* attacks sank two destroyers and two ammunition ships and damaged twenty-four other vessels off the shore of Okinawa on 7 April, for the cost of 383 planes. Five days later the *kamikaze* returned, and over the next forty-eight hours they sank twenty-one ships, damaged twenty-three and put a further forty-three permanently out of action, albeit at the cost of 3,000 of their own lives.[10] The Imperial Navy there suffered a near-mortal blow at 16.23 hours on 7 April when the 72,000-ton battleship *Yamato*, with its nine 18.1-inch guns, generally considered the most powerful battleship ever built, was sunk by 380 American aircraft, slipping beneath the waves along with 2,488 of her crew.[11] In the same engagement a Japanese cruiser and four destroyers were also sunk, at a total loss of 3,655 Japanese lives to the Americans' eighty-four sailors and airmen.

Yet, despite such punishment, Japan fought on in Luzon, Burma, Borneo and especially on Okinawa, where even American flame-throwers and heavy armour made slow progress against determined Japanese counter-attacks in early May. 'No one underestimated Jap,' wrote George MacDonald Fraser with a fine and characteristic disregard for political correctness; 'he might be a subhuman creature who tortured and starved prisoners of war to death, raped women captives, and used civilians for bayonet practice, but there was no braver soldier in the whole history of war.'[12] The surrender of Germany seems to have had little or no effect on the Japanese, even though it meant that they would soon face the combined wrath of the Allies. (Stalin had promised at Yalta to declare war on Japan three months to the day after VE Day, and was as good as his word.) While Germans were surrendering at the rate of 50,000 a month in late 1944, the Japanese were fighting on, often virtually to the last man. 'Even in the most desperate circumstances,' recorded Major-General Douglas Gracey, commander of the Indian 20th Division in Burma, '99% of the Japs prefer death or suicide to capture. The war is more total than in Europe. The Jap can be compared to the most fanatical Nazi youth and must be dealt with accordingly.'[13]

The last significant naval action of the war took place in the Malacca Straits on 15 May 1945, where five Royal Navy destroyers sank the Japanese cruiser *Haguro* by torpedoes. Yet, despite no longer having a fleet capable of defending the mainland, the Japanese Government decided to fight on.[14]

The Strategic Air Offensive against Japan had been as pitiless as that against Germany, particularly the firestorm created by the great Tokyo Raid of 10 March 1945, in which 334 B-29s flattened 16 square miles of the capital, killed 83,000 people, injured 100,000 and rendered 1.5 million more homeless. It is regarded as the most destructive conventional bombing raid in history, and even bears some comparison with the nuclear bombs that were to come, although it has excited nothing like the amount of moralizing.[15] With Mustang P-51s escorting the B-29s from Iwo Jima, the USAAF was able to establish almost complete air superiority in the skies over Japan for the last three months of the war; indeed major raids were undertaken from there even while there were still Japanese holding out in different parts of the island. Yet, although the bombing left ordinary Japanese – especially of course the city-dwellers – terrified and demoralized, there was no appreciable pressure put on the Government to end the war which all rational Japanese (including, it is alleged, Emperor Hirohito) could see was suicidal and unwinnable. The military clique that ran the Japanese Government felt no inclination to surrender, a course of action which they considered dishonourable.

Almost half of the residential area of Tokyo was destroyed by the end of the war, aided by the flammability of much of the paper and wooden housing. No fewer than 750,000 incendiary bombs were dropped at very low altitudes by 500 US bombers on the single night of 23 May, and a similar number the next night too. Yet Japan's reaction, or at least that of her Government, was to fight on, and a resigned but obedient population, which had little practical alternative, went along with the decision. It was not until 22 June 1945 that resistance on Okinawa ended, nearly three months after the US forces had landed on an island that was 60 miles long but rarely more than 8 wide. On the very eve of victory, Buckner was fatally wounded by an artillery shell at an observation post on the front line, the most senior Allied officer to be killed by the enemy in the whole war. Four days later, Lieutenant-General Ushijima committed *hara-kiri* just as his command post was finally overrun. In all, 107,500 Japanese were known to have died in the battle, an additional 20,000 were buried underground in their caves during the fighting, and only 7,400 surrendered. To set against these numbers, the US Tenth Army lost 7,373 killed and 32,056 wounded, with a further 5,000 sailors killed and 4,600 wounded, a total of nearly 50,000 American casualties for one Pacific island.[16] In the skies the ratios were much the same: some 8,000 Japanese planes had been lost in combat and destroyed on the ground, against 783 US naval aircraft.[17] Japan's Navy and Air Force were now in no position to oppose an American landing on the mainland, but, as her Army had shown, this was expected to be a bloodbath, for both sides.

The collapse of the Imperial Japanese Navy, as well as the mining of Japanese ports by B-29s, meant that the American naval blockade that had been in effect since 1943 would eventually starve the overcrowded island into surrender, though not for many months or possibly longer. No fewer than 4.8 million tons of Japanese merchant shipping were sent to the bottom by US submarines in the course of the war, 56 per cent of the total, and that did not include 201 warships, comprising a further 540,000 tons.[18] It came at the grievous cost of fifty-two US submarines, however, and thus the worst death rate of any branch of the US armed forces, even higher than the bomber crews of the Eighth Air Force.[19]

The situation that beckoned General MacArthur, Admiral Nimitz and General Marshall's operations planning Staff at the Pentagon in the summer of 1945 was an unenviable one. They had to consider a

Japan that by any rational criteria was defeated, but which was not only refusing to surrender but seemed to be preparing to defend the sacred soil of her mainland with the same kind of fanaticism seen on Saipan, Luzon, Peleliu, Iwo Jima, Okinawa and many other places. Few doubted that Operation Olympic – a strike against Kyushu slated for November 1945 – and Operation Coronet, an amphibious assault in March 1946 against the Tokyo plain on Honshu, would lead to horrific loss of Allied life on the ground, however well the B-29s of the Twentieth Air Force and carrier-based task forces managed to soften up the mainland first. Estimates of expected casualty rates differed from planning Staff to planning Staff, but over the coming months – perhaps years – of fighting anything in the region of 250,000 American casualties were thought to be possible. 'If the conflict had continued for even a few weeks longer,' believes Max Hastings, 'more people of all nations – especially Japan – would have lost their lives than perished at Hiroshima and Nagasaki.'[20]

It was against that background of looming dread that on 30 December 1944 General Leslie Groves, the head of the Manhattan Project, reported that the first two atomic bombs would be ready by 1 August 1945. At last an end to the war was in sight, and one that did not involve having to subdue the Japanese mainland. The means to be employed had not existed before, and were scientific, but it was hoped that the very newness of the technology might give the peace party in Tokyo – assuming there was one – an argument for why Japan could not fight on. 'Wars begin when you will,' wrote Niccolò Machiavelli in *The Prince*, 'but they do not end when you please.'

In the peroration of his 'finest hour' speech of 18 June 1940, Winston Churchill conjured up the vision of a nightmare world in which a Nazi victory produced 'a new Dark Age made more sinister, and perhaps more protracted, by the lights of perverted science'. The Nazis did indeed pervert science for their ideological ends, but then of course both sides tried to harness scientific developments for victory. Lieutenant-General Sir Ian Jacob, the military secretary to Churchill's War Cabinet, once quipped to the author that the Allies won the war largely 'because our German scientists were better than their German scientists', and in the field of atomic research and development he was undoubtedly right. Werner Heisenberg's atomic programme for Hitler thankfully lagged far behind the Allies', codenamed the Manhattan Project and based at Los Alamos in New Mexico. Because Hitler was a Nazi, he was unable to call upon the best scientific brains to create a nuclear bomb. Between 1901 and 1932 Germany had twenty-five Nobel laureates in Physics and Chemistry, the United States only five. Then came Nazism. In the fifty years after the war, Germany won only thirteen Nobel Prizes to America's sixty-seven. The list of those émigrés from Fascism – not all of them Jewish – who went on to contribute to the creation of the nuclear bomb, either at Los Alamos or in some other significant capacity, is a very long one, including Albert Einstein, Leo Szilard and Hans Bethe (who all left Germany when Hitler came to power in 1933), Edward Teller and Eugene Wigner (who left Hungary in 1935 and 1937 respectively), Emilio Segré and Enrico Fermi (who both left Italy in 1938), Stanisław Ulam (who left Poland in 1939) and Niels Bohr (who escaped from Denmark in 1943). By denying himself the scientific brains necessary to create a Bomb of his own, Hitler's Nazism meant that he had persecuted the very people who could have prevented his own downfall.

Nonetheless, Hitler's scientists did come up with an impressive array of non-atomic scientific discoveries during the war, including proximity fuses, synthetic fuels, ballistic missiles, hydrogen-peroxide-assisted submarines and ersatz rubber. Rabelais wrote that 'Science without conscience is the ruin of the world,' and all too often Hitler's scientists – such as the rocket engineer Wernher von Braun – ignored the suffering that their work created, including, as in Braun's case, tens of thousands of people working under slave-labour conditions to build the installations for his weaponry. (After the war, Braun headed President Kennedy's space programme, his career in rocketry saved by the fact that he had once briefly been arrested by the SS when Himmler had wanted to take over one of his projects.)

When in August 1939 Albert Einstein had written to President Roosevelt to inform him of the incredible potential of uranium, FDR's instinctive response was 'This requires action.' Sure enough, with huge investment in people and resources, and close collaboration between the American, British, Canadian and European anti-Nazi scientists, the Allies built two atomic bombs, codenamed Little Boy and Fat Man (supposedly references to Roosevelt and Churchill, though why FDR was little or a boy is anyone's guess). These scientists had discovered the secret to the vast force that held together the constituent particles of the atom, and how to harness it for military purposes. President Truman had few qualms in deploying a bomb that would undoubtedly kill tens of thousands of Japanese civilians, but would also, it was hoped, bring to a sudden halt the war.

At 08.15 on Sunday, 6 August 1945 (local time), the 9-foot 9-inch-long, 8,000-pound Little Boy was dropped from 31,600 feet over the city of Hiroshima, some 500 miles from Tokyo. It had been flown from the island of Tinian in the Mariana Islands in the B-29 Super-fortress *Enola Gay*, named after the mother of its pilot, Lieutenant-Colonel Paul W. Tibbets Jr, commander of the USAAF 509th Composite Group. The gigantic bomb detonated forty-seven seconds later 1,885 feet above the centre of the city which was home to a quarter of a million people, generating a blast of 300,000 Celsius for 1/10,000th of a second. Every building within a 2,000-yard radius of the hypocentre was vaporized, and every wooden building within 1.2 miles. Altogether 5 square miles of the city were destroyed, or 63 per cent of the city's 76,000 buildings.[21] A huge, mushroom-shaped cloud then rose 50,000 feet over the city. In all, including the civilian deaths of 118,661 and perhaps another 20,000 military deaths, and many who died of radiation sickness afterwards, around 140,000 people were killed.

The scenes in Hiroshima in the aftermath were truly hellish. The Rev. Kiyoshi Tanimoto, pastor of the Hiroshima Methodist Church, told a correspondent from the *New Yorker* magazine how he tried to ferry some survivors over the river to hospital:

He drove the boat on to the bank and urged them to get on board. They did not move and he realised that they were too weak to lift themselves. He reached down and took a woman by the hands, but her skin slipped off in huge, glove-like pieces. He was so sickened by this that he had to sit down for a moment. Then he got into the water and, though a small man, lifted several of the men and women, who were naked, into his boat. Their backs and breasts were clammy, and he remembered uneasily what the great burns he had seen during the day had been like: yellow at first, then red and swollen, with the skin sloughed off, and finally, in the evening, suppurated and smelly ... He had to keep repeating to himself, 'These are human beings.'[22]

To those who argued that the enemy ought to have been warned about the destructive power of the atomic bombs, or even had one demonstrated in a desert or an atoll beforehand, General Marshall succinctly noted: 'It's no good warning him. If you warn them there's no surprise. And the only way to produce shock is surprise.'[23] With only two bombs available, to risk wasting one to no effect was inconceivable. President Truman made a radio broadcast soon afterwards, explaining that the bomb had been atomic, and thus unlike anything that had ever been seen before. 'That bomb had more power than 20,000 tons of T.N.T.' (that is, 20 kilotons), he told his listeners, which included the Japanese Government. 'It had more than two thousand times the blast power of the [22,000-pound deep-penetration] British "Grand Slam", which is the largest bomb ever used in the history of warfare.'[24] (It was long thought that Truman was accurate, and that the bomb dropped on Nagasaki was roughly the same size in terms of TNT, but in 1970 the British nuclear pioneer Lord Penney proved that Hiroshima's blast had in fact been about 12 kilotons, while the Nagasaki blast had been around 22 kilotons.)[25]

George MacDonald Fraser's views on the morality of what had happened at Hiroshima echoed those of the vast majority of Britons and Americans at the time, both civilian and military. He pointed out that:

We were of a generation to whom Coventry and the London Blitz and Clydebank and Liverpool and Plymouth were more than just names; our country had been hammered mercilessly from the sky, and so had Germany; we had seen the pictures of Belsen and of the frozen horror of the Russian Front; part of our higher education had been dedicated to techniques of killing and destruction; we were not going to lose sleep because the Japanese homeland had taken its turn. If anything, at the time, remembering the kind of war it had been, and the kind of people we, personally, had been up against, we probably felt that justice had been done. But it was of small importance when weighed against the glorious fact that the war was over at last.[26]

Almost, but not quite. In fact the Japanese Government decided to fight on regardless, hoping that the Allies had only one such weapon and believing that the home islands could be successfully defended from invasion and the dishonour of occupation.[27] So three days after Hiroshima, the city of Nagasaki was similarly devastated by Fat Man, with 73,884 people killed, 74,909 injured and similarly debilitating long-term mental and physical effects on the population as at Hiroshima, owing to the radiation released.[28] (It almost didn't happen; the B-29 pilot Major Charles 'Chuck' Sweeney nearly ran out of runway on Tinian with his 5-ton bomb on board, and a crash would have wiped out much of the island.)[29]

Not knowing that the Americans had no more atomic bombs to drop, and shocked by Russia's intervention in the Pacific War on 8 August, which they were unable effectively to counter, the Japanese did finally surrender on 14 August, with the Emperor Hirohito admitting to his people in a broadcast at noon the next day that the war had gone 'not necessarily to Japan's advantage', especially in view of 'a new most cruel bomb'.[30] Even as he prepared to broadcast, a group of young officers invaded the palace grounds in an attempted coup intended to prevent him from doing so.[31]

A fortnight later, on Sunday, 2 September, six years and one day after Germany had invaded Poland, General Douglas MacArthur and Admirals Chester Nimitz and Sir Bruce Fraser and representatives of the other Allied nations took the formal Japanese surrender, which was signed by the one-legged Foreign Minister Mamoru Shigemitsu and the Army Chief of Staff General Yoshijiro Umezu, aboard the battleship USS *Missouri*, by then moored in Tokyo Bay. (She was chosen because she had served at Iwo Jima and Okinawa and was Nimitz's flagship; it was mere coincidence that she was named after President Truman's home state.) MacArthur concluded the ceremony by saying: 'Let us pray that peace be now restored to the world and that God will preserve it always. These proceedings are closed.'

Conclusion

Why Did the Axis Lose the Second World War?

'But all the same,' Lockhart went on, 'we are *in it, and we are fighting; and even if we don't consciously give it a melodramatic label like "fighting for democracy" or "putting an end to fascist tyranny", that's precisely what we're doing and that's the whole meaning of it.'*

Nicholas Monsarrat, *The Cruel Sea*, 1951[1]

With all military histories it is necessary to remember that war is not a matter of maps with red and blue arrows and oblongs, but of weary, thirsty men with sore feet and aching shoulders wondering where they are.

George MacDonald Fraser, *Quartered Safe Out Here*, 1992[2]

And some there be which have no memorial, who are perished as though they had never been.

Ecclesiasticus 44:9

'This war', Hitler told the Reichstag in 1942, 'is one of those elemental conflicts which usher in a new millennium and which shake the world.'[3] He was right, of course. Far from a Thousand-Year Reich, Germany today is a pacific, law-abiding, liberal democracy, as is Italy. Poland and Russia are proud and independent Slavic states. France is restored and plays a leading role in Europe. The Jewish people have not only survived and multiplied, but today have their own democratic nation-state, partly because of the Holocaust. The United States, which Hitler loathed because he thought it ruled by blacks and Jews, is the greatest world power and at the time of writing has a black man at its head. China is a powerful independent state and Japan a neutral, anti-militarist democracy. The British Empire has gone, but its Commonwealth is thriving across the continents. The realization of Hitler's hopes for a 'Pan-European Economic Area' does not conform to his scheme for a giant life-support system for the Aryan race, which never won its *Lebensraum* after all. Hitler's war was indeed therefore 'one of those elemental conflicts which usher in a new millennium', but it was precisely the opposite kind of millennium to the one he had in mind.

The Second World War lasted for 2,174 days, cost $1.5 trillion and claimed the lives of over 50 million people.[4] That represents 23,000 lives lost every day, or more than fifteen people killed every minute, for six long years.[5] At the Commonwealth Beach Head Cemetery just north of Anzio in Italy lie some of the men who fell in that campaign, in row after row of perfectly tended graves. The bereaved families were permitted to add personal messages to tombstones, below the bald register of name, rank, number, age, unit, and date of death. Thus the grave of Corporal J. J. Griffin of the Sherwood Foresters, who died aged twenty-seven on 21 March 1944, reads: 'May the sunshine you missed on life's highway be found in God's haven of rest'. Gunner A. W. J. Johnson of the Royal Artillery, who died the following day, has: 'In loving memory of our dear son. Forever in our thoughts, Mother, Joyce and Dennis'. That of twenty-two-year-old Lance-Corporal R. Gore of the Loyal Regiment, who died on 24 February 1944, reads: 'Gone but not forgotten by Dad and Mam, brother Herbert and sister Annie'. The gravestone of Private J. R. G. Gains of the Buffs, killed on 31 May 1944 aged thirty, says: 'Beautiful memories, a darling husband and daddy worthy of Everlasting Love, His wife and Baby Rita'. Even two-thirds of a century later, it is still impossible not to feel fury against Hitler and the Nazis for forcing baby Rita Gains to grow up without her father, Annie and Herbert Gore without their brother, and for taking her nineteen-year-old boy away from Mrs Johnson. If one then multiplies each of those tragedies by 50,000,000, one can begin to try to grasp the sheer extent of the personal side of the composite world-historical global cataclysm that was the Second World War.

*

On the morning of Saturday, 31 August 1946, the 216th day of the trials at Nuremberg, General Alfred Jodl addressed his judges and posterity. Knowing that his fate was going to be death by hanging, the former OKW operations chief directed his remarks to 'later historians' as much as to the President and bench of the International Military Tribunal. Speaking for the German High Command – or 'the higher military leaders and their assistants', as he put it – Jodl effectively set out their case, arguing that they had been:

confronted with an insoluble task, namely, to conduct a war which they had not wanted under a Commander-in-Chief whose confidence they did not possess and whom they themselves only trusted within limits; with methods which frequently were in contradiction to their principles of leadership and their traditional, proved opinions; with troops and police forces which did not come under their full command; and with an Intelligence service that was in part working for the enemy. And all this in the complete and clear realization that this war would decide the life and death of our beloved Fatherland. They did not serve the powers of Hell and they did not serve a criminal, but rather their people and their Fatherland.[6]

To what extent was Jodl right? It was certainly true that few in the High Command wanted war with Britain and France in 1939, although they were happy enough to fight Poland, which led inexorably to it, given the British guarantee to that country of April 1939. It was also true that the generals did not possess Hitler's confidence, but understandably so considering that some of them tried to kill him on 20 July 1944. The 'methods' the German officer corps permitted to be used against civilian populations, especially on the Eastern Front, were far worse than Jodl's weasel words implied, and those officers were almost universally deeply implicated in monstrous abuses of every canon of the rules of war, written and unwritten. Jodl's explanation that the partisans 'used every – yes, every – single means of violence', and that the Allies ensured that 'hundreds of thousands of women and children were annihilated by layers of bombs' cannot excuse the Axis methods of warfare. Every German general knew that the war in the east was to be one of extermination rather than a conventional military engagement; the oral and in some cases written orders, and indeed the very notion of *Lebensraum*, brooked no alternative explanation.

Jodl was also right that the fragmented nature of authority in the Nazi state – with the SS and other state institutions in particular being kept deliberately separate from the Wehrmacht – could be operationally frustrating for the generals. It was also true that Admiral Wilhelm Canaris, head of the Abwehr, thought Hitler a 'madman' and had been in communication with the Allies towards the end of the war, although his organization did not systematically aid the enemy, as Jodl alleged.[7] If Jodl had known the true story of why Allied intelligence so regularly outwitted the OKW – owing to the Ultra information gained from decrypting the Enigma codes – he would undoubtedly have added another line of defence for the High Command. Ultimately, however, Jodl's excuses do not convince: the German generals did indeed serve 'the powers of Hell' and 'a criminal', as well as the *Volk* and Fatherland.

The reasons why so many outwardly dignified professional officers served the Nazis so efficiently and seemingly enthusiastically were many and complicated. Their fathers and grandfathers had shot French *francs-tireurs* without mercy in the Franco-Prussian War and had ill-treated Belgian and French civilians in the Great War, so the supposedly noble Prussian military tradition was always something of a myth. The oath they swore to Hitler personally could not excuse them. Their motives included natural ambition, criminal complicity, genuine patriotism, lack of an alternative, professional pride, an understandable desire to protect their loved ones from Bolshevik vengeance, a desperate hope for unexpected victory, Nazi faith in many cases, but probably above all simple loyalty to their men and brother officers.

Yet the German generals who argued with, stood up to or even disobeyed Hitler were not particularly ill-treated, unless of course they had been involved in the Bomb Plot. They were dismissed, reassigned or retired for a few months, but they did not face the ultimate sanction, as anyone who displeased Stalin certainly did. On 21 February 1945 Albert Speer wrote to Otto Thierack, the Nazi Minister for Justice, saying that he wanted to testify as a character witness for General Friedrich Fromm, who had 'maintained a passive stance' towards the Bomb Plot and not warned the authorities about it.[8] It is inconceivable that anyone other than a would-be suicide would do such a thing in Soviet Russia. (It did no good: Fromm was executed by firing squad in March 1945.) Just as no one was shot for refusing to execute a Jew, so German generals put only their jobs, rather than their lives, on the line when they crossed Hitler on a point of military principle. Very often they were brought back from enforced retirement to serve again, as happened to Rundstedt three times. They might therefore have been 'only obeying orders', but they were not doing so out of a well-founded fear for their lives.

Of course there was a good deal of bluster at the Nuremberg Trials, with defendants distancing themselves from Hitler and Nazism. A man is not required to be truthful when pleading for his life. Walther Funk claimed actively to have opposed scorched-earth policies; Ribbentrop cited his work for Anglo-German amity and said that he had told Hitler that POWs 'should be treated according to the Geneva Convention'; Göring said, 'I was never anti-Semitic. Anti-Semitism played no part in my life,' 'I helped a great many Jews who appealed to me for help,' and claimed that he 'had no knowledge of the atrocities committed against Jews and the brutalities in concentration camps'; camp commandant Rudolf Höss said, 'I thought I was doing the right thing, I was obeying orders, and now, I see that it was unnecessary and wrong. But . . . I didn't personally murder anybody. I was just the director of the extermination programme in Auschwitz. It was Hitler who ordered it through Himmler and it was Eichmann who gave me the order regarding transports'; Sepp Dietrich even claimed that, with regard to POWs captured on the Eastern Front, 'We didn't shoot Russians'; Alfred Rosenberg, the Reich Minister of the Eastern Occupied Territories, somewhat bizarrely wanted the Agrarian Reform Act of February 1942 to be taken into consideration at his trial, for the way it had eased the lot of farm workers; Albert Speer tried to argue that 'the activities of the defendant as an architect were of a non-political nature' (despite his being from 1942 also minister for armaments and war); Erhard Milch complained about the lack of a free press in Nazi Germany, stating that he had 'never approved' of National Socialism; Ernst Kaltenbrunner proudly announced, 'I never killed anyone,' which in his case was strictly speaking true, but entirely beside the point; Wilhelm Keitel declared, 'I was never really close to the Führer,' with whom he lived cheek-by-jowl and saw almost every day for six years; Karl Dönitz apparently 'knew nothing about the plans for an offensive war' even in the U-boat arm he commanded; Goebbels' radio director Hans Fritzsche stated, 'I got to know, in 1923–25, men like Mussolini and Hitler and kept at a distance from them'; Paul von Kleist even came out with the classic line, 'I can only say that some of my best friends were Jews'; Julius Streicher could hardly claim that, but he did believe that his proposal that the Jews be sent to Madagascar should operate in his favour; Hjalmar Schacht spoke of 'my activities against Hitler after I had recognized his bad intentions', despite having remained a Nazi minister until 1943; Artur Seyss-Inquart, who had been responsible for mass deportations, summary executions and organizing slave labour in Holland, claimed he had 'tried everything to prevent violations against the provisions of international law', and ingeniously tried to argue that 'The starting of a war without a declaration of war also still does not make this into a war of aggression.'[9]

Nuremberg testimony therefore needs to be treated with extreme caution, especially such claims as that of Dönitz's that National Socialism probably 'would have collapsed soon after a German victory'.[10] It was perhaps inevitable that the survivors should have blamed everything upon Hitler, Goebbels, Himmler, Bormann, Heydrich and Ley, who were conveniently all dead by the start of the trials. Admittedly some of the Nazis, such as Julius Streicher, who pronounced that Jesus Christ was 'born of a mother who was a Jewish whore', conformed precisely to type.[11] Mainly, however, they argued vehemently that they had known nothing about the Holocaust, would have resigned if they had known that Hitler planned war, but could not do so after it had broken out, for moral and patriotic reasons. Yet for all their lies and claims to have stood up constantly to Hitler – as we have seen, Kleist even claimed to have outshouted him regularly at meetings – the fact remains that virtually no one resigned a position of power unforced, even when the war was clearly going to be lost.

Just as the Nuremberg defendants attempted to place total blame on the dead Führer for all the crimes of the Nazi state, so a slew of books written by the German generals in the 1950s and 1960s attempted to attribute the military defeat solely to him and his closest acolytes Keitel and Jodl. The phrase *Lost Victories* was even used by Manstein for his autobiography, a book that has – along with Guderian's memoirs *Panzer Leader* – rightly been condemned as 'arrogant' and 'self-serving'.[12] The general thrust of this historical and autobiographical genre was succinctly summed up in the letter written in 1965 by General Günther Blumentritt, who had been purged from the General Staff in September 1944, despite not having been involved in the Bomb Plot:

Hitler was militarily speaking no genius. He was a dilettante, interested in small details, and he wanted to hold everything, stubborn, dour, 'hold everything to the last'. He had no doubt also good military ideas. *Sometimes* even *he* was right! However he was after all a layman and acted following his feeling or intuition, not his reason. He did not know what was realistically possible and what was impossible.[13]

Stalin once described Hitler to Harry Hopkins as 'a very able man', but this was something that the German generals denied in a large body of literature that was published after the war.[14] It has been suggested that the criticisms of Hitler's strategy made by Franz Halder and Walter Warlimont stemmed from 'the professional jealousy of a successful amateur', and that the generals' memoirs, taken together, constitute 'the alibi of the incompetent corporal meddling in military matters he did not understand and preventing them from winning the war'.[15]

Although the German generals spoke much of their duty and honour after the war, in the event only a small number of them made one attempt to destroy Hitler with a 2-pound bomb, otherwise the vast majority served him with remarkable loyalty. Even Count von Stauffenberg's plot seems to have been more concerned with getting rid of a useless strategist than a bold attempt to introduce democracy, equality and peace to Germany. Individually, the generals had good reason to carry on fighting to the end: Manstein ordered the massacres of civilians, Jews and POWs; Rundstedt sat on the Court of Honour; Guderian accepted cash payments and an attractive Polish estate from Hitler, and so on. The German people nicknamed Nazi Party functionaries 'golden pheasants', but none were more heavily gilded than the Wehrmacht generals. 'Nor could they plead ignorance about what was involved,' points out David Ceserani in relation to their refusal to apply the Geneva Convention on the Eastern Front and elsewhere, because Hitler 'regularly briefed his party followers, ministers and military men about his racial goals. Occasionally some demurred ... but most cooperated. By 1939, thanks to Hitler's successes, his popularity and his style of rule, there were no alternative centres of power capable of stopping him or willing to try.'[16]

The German generals were for the most part corrupt, morally debased, opportunistic and far removed from the unideological knights of chivalry that they liked to portray themselves as. To eavesdrop on their private conversations when they thought no one was listening, read their exchanges at Trent Park at the beginning of Chapter 16. However, that did not mean that they were necessarily wrong when they complained about the incessant interference from a military amateur, aided and abetted by Keitel and Jodl. Although they were arrogant, self-serving and often untruthful about the extent of their adulation of Hitler while things were going well, their overall analysis is not wholly incorrect. For it is impossible to divorce Axis strategy from the centrality of Adolf Hitler: of the 650 major legislative orders issued during the war, all but seventy-two were decrees or orders issued in his name or over his signature.[17]

While the knowledge that one is going to be hanged in a fortnight is said to concentrate a man's mind wonderfully, the dawning certainty that it was going to happen at some unspecific point in the future certainly helped to derange that of Adolf Hitler. It would have had that effect on almost anybody, and can hardly be held against him. Yet it should not be for the unhinged dispositions of his troops in the last ten months of his life that the Führer should be principally arraigned, so much as for the disastrous decisions he took when he was (relatively speaking) rational. These were so heinous that he should have committed suicide out of sheer embarrassment over his myriad errors, rather than out of fear of being humiliated by the Russians before his execution.

The war ought not to have started in 1939 at all, but at least three or four years later, which is what he had originally promised the leaders of the Wehrmacht, Luftwaffe and Kriegsmarine. If he had started the war with the same number of U-boats with which he ended it – 463 – rather than the twenty-six operational ones he had in 1939, Germany might have stood a chance of asphyxiating Britain, especially if every effort had been bent towards developing the Walther U-boats (propelled by hydrogen peroxide and armed with homing torpedoes) and the Schnorchel as early as possible.

If Luftwaffe factories had been diversified away from major industrial areas, and protected underground, or if there had been large-scale early manufacture of the jet-engine Messerschmitt Me-262, which was capable of knocking American Mustangs out of the skies over Germany, then the air war might have gone differently. By October 1944 the Me-262 jet was finally deployed as a fighter. It was not to change the course of the war, as it was too unwieldy on take-off and landing and too high in fuel consumption, but these teething troubles might have been dealt with had not the Führer insisted on developing it as a bomber for far too long, against the advice of General Galland. The defeat of the Allied bombing campaign by Me-262s would have released a major part of the Luftwaffe's fighter force back into combat in the east, whereas 70 per cent of it was on protection patrol in the west.

In November 1939 Hitler halted the V-rocket development programme at Peenemünde, believing that the victory in Poland had shown it to be unnecessary. It was not reactivated until September 1941, and received priority status only in July 1943, after Speer had warned him that six more raids like those on Hamburg would mean defeat for the Reich. (He refused to visit Hamburg or even to receive a delegation from the city.) The rocket programme should either have been continued or not have been reactivated at all, as it took up a huge amount of resources for a weapon that came on stream too late to make any great difference.

In May 1940 Hitler should have supported those generals who wanted to overrule Rundstedt's Halt Order outside Dunkirk, thereby capturing the BEF en masse and preventing it escaping from the Continent. The military maxim ascribed to Frederick the Great, *L'audace, l'audace, toujours l'audace*, certainly applied to Hitler's career from the Beerhall Putsch of 1923 until the defeat at Stalingrad twenty years later. He was a gambler, taking ever greater gambles throughout his career; yet at the meeting with Rundstedt in the Maison Blairon caution overtook him, with ultimately disastrous results. After Göring had failed to destroy the BEF at Dunkirk in 1940, as he had promised he would, he should have been moved to a less vital post. Instead, he was allowed to continue in command of as important an arm as the Luftwaffe. He then failed to stop the bombing of Berlin in 1940 as he publicly promised he would, and then again failed to resupply Stalingrad from the air in anything like the quantities necessary. Since the Reichsmarschall was unquestioningly loyal to Hitler until almost the very end, his fidelity as a Nazi mattered more to the Führer than his competence as an air commander. Furthermore, after Rudolf Hess's flight to Scotland, to lose one deputy Führer might be considered unfortunate, but to lose two might look like carelessness. Hitler regularly kept proven incompetents in place – such as the chief of Luftwaffe intelligence, Colonel 'Beppo' Schmid, whose ludicrously over-optimistic reports of RAF strength helped lose the battle of Britain – if they told him what he wanted to hear.

Hitler learnt the wrong lessons from the Russians' Winter War against Finland, assuming that the Red Army was weak, rather than that defenders in atrocious weather in a country of lakes, forests and bad roads can be strong. In his invasion of Russia, despite the glaring example of Finland, he failed to make proper winter provision for his troops. Nor does the explanation most often made for this – that he thought the campaign would be over in four months – convince: four months from 22 June is 22 October, when the season of mud has already passed into the season of snow. In April 1941 he delayed the invasion of Russia by six weeks by invading the comparatively unimportant Yugoslavia, where the pro-Allied Government threatened his prestige but posed no appreciable threat to his southern front. Even in that hugely successful campaign – Yugoslavia fell faster than France had, and Greece and Crete soon followed – Hitler learnt the wrong lesson about airborne assault. Because Karl Student's paratroop attack on Crete had been relatively costly at over 4,000 casualties among the 22,000 dropped on the island, Hitler told their commander: 'The day of parachute troops is over.'[18] Because the raids on Saint-Nazaire and Dieppe had not included airborne forces he persuaded himself that the Allies were not developing them, and he failed to use them himself against Malta, Gibraltar, Cyprus or Suez as Student repeatedly urged. Instead paratroopers were used as elite infantry units, and Hitler was surprised when on D-Day an arm first used to great effect by the Axis proved to have been perfected by the Allies.

In June 1941 Hitler launched Operation Barbarossa, his cardinal error of the war. Considering that Rommel took Tobruk and got to within 60 miles of Alexandria by October 1942 with the twelve-division Afrika Korps, a fraction of the force that was thrown against Russia could have swept the British from Egypt, Palestine, Iran and Iraq long beforehand. Taking Cairo would have opened up four glittering prospects, namely the capture with relative ease of the almost undefended oilfields of Iran and Iraq, the expulsion of the Royal Navy from its major base in the Mediterranean at Alexandria, the closing of the Suez Canal to Allied shipping, and the prospect of attacking India from the north-west just as Japan threatened her from the north-east. Stationed in the Middle East, the Germans would have cut Britain off from her oil supplies, and posed a threat against British India from the west, but also against the Soviet Union and the Caucasus from the south. Even if Britain had fought on, from metropolitan United Kingdom, Canada and India, importing her oil from the United States, any British threat to Germany's southern flank would have been over.

Hitler could then have undertaken his invasion of Russia in his own time with Army Group South moving only a few hundred miles from Iraq to Astrakhan, rather than more than 1,000 miles as it had to in 1941 and 1942. Considering how much Stalin decried the idea that Hitler would ever attack him in 1941 – despite the eighty intelligence reports from dozens of unrelated sources from all over the world that Barbarossa was impending, some of which furnished the precise date – there is no real reason to suppose that the USSR would have been on any better war footing in the summer of 1942, or 1943, than she was in 1941. Army Group South should have taken the Caucasus from the south rather than the west. Marching between the Black and the Caspian Seas, a German invasion of the Caucasus and southern Russia would have cut the USSR off from the main part of her non-Siberian oil supply, and, as Frederick von Mellenthin noted in the context of El Alamein, a motorized division without fuel is mere scrap iron.

It was incredibly fortunate for the Allies that the Axis never co-ordinated their war efforts, and even failed to exchange information on basic equipment such as anti-tank weapons. The Japanese Foreign Minister Yosuke Matsuoka resigned in July 1941 because he wanted to attack Russia from the east at the same time that Hitler unleashed Operation Barbarossa on her from the west. By the time that Stalingrad fell and Hitler desperately needed such an attack, the Japanese were on the retreat from the point which they had reached the previous spring, when they had controlled 20 million square miles of the earth's surface. Close military co-ordination between Berlin, Rome and Tokyo should have ensured that the Japanese attacked not the Americans but rather the Russians as soon as Germany was ready. The oil Japan desperately needed for her war machine could have been taken from Siberia rather than the Dutch East Indies. Yet Hitler showed absolutely no interest in allowing Japan to take part in Barbarossa, and her leaders did not even inform him of the impending attack on Pearl Harbor, any more than Mussolini warned Hitler of his attack on Greece, or Hitler told Mussolini of his invasion of Yugoslavia.

Similarly, Hitler should have studiously ignored all provocations from Franklin Roosevelt, especially in the Atlantic, in the knowledge that the President did not have the political power to declare war against a Germany that was professing friendship and sympathy towards the United States. In the absence of a declaration of war against America after Pearl Harbor, something Hitler was under no treaty obligation to furnish – as though he cared about treaty obligations anyhow – it would have been well-nigh impossible for Roosevelt to have committed the United States to invading North Africa in 1942. Instead the Führer unnecessarily declared war on the uninvadable United States, giving Roosevelt the excuse for the Germany First policy. It was the second greatest error of his life, and came within six months of the first. Yet it hardly excited any opposition from the German generals, let alone the admirals who positively looked forward to this suicidal move. Instead, Hitler ought to have dissolved the Tripartite Pact, which had hitherto done so little for him, after Pearl

Harbor, and dismissed Ribbentrop whose ludicrous misreading of America's capabilities and intentions are detailed in Chapter 6. With Britain effectively neutralized, if not knocked out of the war altogether, and America fully committed in the Pacific fighting Japan, only then should Operation Barbarossa have been put into effect, with Germany fighting on one front rather than the traditionally suicidal two.

The Nazis' contempt for all Slavs meant that they were incapable of following the obvious beneficial course of action during Barbarossa. Putting *Lebensraum* and ethnic cleansing to the bottom of the agenda – to be pursued only after victory – the Germans ought to have striven to make allies of the Greater Russian subject peoples against their Bolshevik oppressors, allowing Ukraine, Belorussia, the Baltic States, the Crimea, the Caucasian republics and elsewhere the widest possible degrees of autonomy consistent with German hegemony in Europe, not unlike that enjoyed by Vichy France. The deliberate mass-starvation policies adopted by Moscow towards Ukraine in the 1920s and 1930s left a legacy of hatred towards the Soviet central Government, and it was clear from their initial welcoming of the Wehrmacht in 1941 that many nationalists would have enthusiastically seized the opportunity of limited independence within the Reich.

A single supreme commander on the Eastern Front from the very start – with Erich von Manstein easily the best choice, but several others possible – would have done far better than Hitler did when he replaced Walther von Brauchitsch with himself in December 1941. The Führer thereafter listened to senior generals less and less. (He even acknowledged this to his secretary, Christa Schroeder: she recalled asking him whether she could rephrase a sentence he had dictated, and 'he looked at me, neither angry nor offended, and said: "You are the only person I allow to correct me!"')[19] Instead he used their perceived failures to add to the preferential resourcing of the Waffen-SS which led to deprivations for Wehrmacht units. Instead of constant changes in policy and personnel, a single strategic brain that was advised and encouraged by Hitler, but was not Hitler, might have settled on a single campaign push that would surely have ignored the Kiev operation which diverted too much of the armour of Army Group Centre southwards in August 1941, thereby taking the marginal Ukrainian capital instead of the all-important Russian one.

Once it was clear that the Russians not only were not going to collapse but were actively counter-attacking, from Zhukov's 6 December 1941 offensive onwards, Hitler began to issue the 'Stand or die' orders that substituted his own willpower – or at least his soldiers' willingness to die for him – for genuine strategy. 'It is the common soldier's blood', went the eighteenth-century saying, 'that makes the general a great man.' Some, such as Wilhelm Keitel and Alan Clark, have argued that these orders made good military sense in bad weather conditions when retreats could be conducted only at 3 or 4mph and heavy equipment could not be saved. On occasion that might have been correct, but soon Hitler proved himself psychologically incapable of ever giving up any ground once won. This betrayed a First World War trenches mentality from a corporal who had never attended Staff college, combined with the fear of an ideologue who believed that it showed lack of willpower, as well as the fury of the professional gambler who is faced with indisputable proof that after a twenty-year winning streak his luck had finally turned.

Instead of seeing retreat as a geographical and strategic concept that, as Frederick von Mellenthin pointed out in Chapter 10, often opened up useful opportunities for counter-attack, Hitler saw it entirely in propaganda and morale – that is, political – terms, as symptomatic of defeat, and thus of being proved wrong dialectically. Ever the revolutionary, Hitler equated withdrawal from a military position as equivalent to backing off from a political one, something his pride and need for both prestige and momentum could not allow. He could not bear even tactically justifiable retreats, seeing them as an affront to the spirit of eternal advance on which he had built his political movement. With his 'Stand or die' orders, as Norman Stone puts it, 'Hitler hit the same note on the piano with increasing shrillness and persistence from the start to the gruesome finish.'[20] This attitude was all the more reprehensible in view of the fact that if anything the Wehrmacht was sometimes even better at counter-attacking than at attacking – as shown by Rommel at the Kasserine Pass, Manstein taking Kharkov after Stalingrad, Vietinghoff at Anzio, Senger at Cassino, Model in Belorussia and Manteuffel almost reaching the Meuse during the Ardennes offensive.

In naval matters, Hitler managed to drive the best German strategist since Tirpitz, Grand Admiral Erich Raeder, out of the Kriegsmarine. In February 1942, he was so convinced that the Allies were about to attack Norway that he threatened Raeder that if *Prinz Eugen*, *Scharnhorst* and *Gneisenau* did not escape from Brest he would remove their guns for coastal artillery. There was no credible Allied threat to Norway, and although the capital ships did make a successful dash down the Channel they were no longer of any great use, and certainly not as the Atlantic raiders that they always could have been when operating out of Brest. Hitler admitted to being 'a coward at sea', but never allowed Raeder to be a lion, and by the time Dönitz took over the Navy it had been chased out of the all-important Atlantic ports.

In his Memorial Day Address of 15 March 1942, Hitler promised listeners that the Red Army would be destroyed by the summer of 1942, another brazen, soon-to-be-broken promise. For from 13 July, when he redirected Army Group B to Stalingrad, there began a series of absurd changes in disposition – especially regarding the Fourth Panzer Army as documented in Chapter 10 – which were the stuff of any planner's nightmares. The cumulative effect of these changes of mind and of direction was fatally to slow the momentum towards Stalingrad, which was never worth the amount of men flung into it anyway, and probably would not have had its talismanic power for either dictator had it not been for its unfortunate change of name from Tsaritsyn in 1925.

Of course Hitler's true crises with the generals only began once events had very definitely taken a negative turn, in September 1942, just after the battle of Stalingrad had begun. The German generals were as guilty as their Führer of fetishizing that struggle, thereby destroying the opportunity for a controlled withdrawal which was the Sixth Army's only hope. On 24 September 1942, as we saw in Chapter 10, Hitler dismissed General Franz Halder for criticizing his personal involvement in the Eastern Front, and replaced him with the more subservient General Kurt Zeitzler. He then sacked Field Marshal Wilhelm List and took personal command of Army Group B, without the precaution of leaving the Wolfschanze and actually visiting the army group's headquarters himself. For a dictator whose word was law, it would always be difficult to get objective advice, but to sack those who did give it was yet another blunder. With Keitel and Jodl in their key posts at OKW, the last thing the Führer needed in late 1942 was any more sycophancy.

Having received Rommel's news, during El Alamein, that his tanks could not prevent a breakthrough by Montgomery, Hitler issued another 'Stand or die' order, which was largely disregarded by Rommel – who doubted the Führer's sanity when he received it – but which nonetheless reveals the mentality of Hitler, whose regard for human life was reflected in the Nazi ideology that whereas the nation was all, the individual – barring the Führer himself – was worthless. The entire battle of Stalingrad was fought on that basis.

Hitler's disagreements with the generals – particularly Manstein – over the withdrawal of the Seventeenth Army from the Kerch Straits bridgehead in late 1942 and early 1943 reflected a deeper dichotomy over future strategy. Hitler wanted to leave the force in place so that the Caucasus could be recaptured when the tide of fortune turned; the generals had written off the oil-rich region, wanting to use the saved Seventeenth Army to plug the growing gaps in the Ukrainian front. If the Caucasus had not fallen in 1941 or 1942, it was hardly likely to in 1943, yet to recapture the Kerch peninsula would be very costly. Similarly Hitler wanted to leave large German and Romanian forces in the Crimea rather than evacuate them while there was still time, in the hope that the land connection with them could be re-established even after it was cut off by the Red Army.

Hitler's strategic arguments were not unsound – the Crimea would be used to bomb the Romanian oilfields, Turkey might join the Allies if she fell – but this was not a case of Hitler's optimism versus the generals' realism.[21] Instead it sprang from a completely different *Weltanschauung*. Hitler felt that every risk must be taken to win the war, because losing it meant certain death for him, whereas a structured withdrawal leading to ultimate defeat signalled only lengthy prison terms for his generals, even those directly connected with war crimes, like Manstein. They were thus playing for drastically different stakes. (In the event, despite the long official sentences they received, Kesselring served only five years, Manstein and List four, Guderian, Blumentritt and Milch three and Zeitzler eighteen months.)

Very often, of course, the policy choices were not clear cut between Hitler on one side and his generals on the other, but were debated between the generals on both sides of the argument with Hitler deciding. Even though Hitler very often came down on the wrong side, he was rarely ever reminded of this. In September 1942, after Jodl had recalled the Führer's error with regard to the width of front given to List in the Caucasus, he was temporarily snubbed. Hitler avoided Jodl's company at mealtimes, 'refused ostentatiously to shake hands' and gave orders that he be replaced, though this did not happen. 'A dictator, as a matter of psychological necessity, must never be reminded of his own errors,' Jodl concluded to Warlimont, 'in order to keep up his self-confidence, the ultimate source of his dictatorial force.'[22] Since Hitler was also the ultimate – indeed sole – source of their prestige and power, it was not in Keitel's or Jodl's interests to undermine that self-confidence, and it does not seem to have happened again. As a result the Führer never learnt from his mistakes, and so continued to make much the same ones for two and a half years after Stalingrad. This would have been inconceivable in the Western Alliance, where Generals Brooke and Marshall felt under no obligation to refrain from pointing out earlier errors made by Churchill and Roosevelt, and vice versa.

Between March and July 1943, Hitler delayed the Operation Zitadelle attack on Kursk for a hundred days, partly because of Speer's promises that the new Panther tanks would be coming on line in large numbers by then. The complete loss of surprise, formerly the Germans' best weapon in the days of Blitzkrieg, was disastrous. The Russians knew where and roughly when they would attack, and prepared accordingly.

Although Hitler can hardly be blamed for sleeping through the D-Day landings, Rundstedt's defence of Normandy in June 1944 was badly hampered by him. Indeed he could hardly have helped the Allies better had he been working for them. The compromise he effected between Rundstedt's desire to deploy inland and Rommel's to fight on the beaches created the worst of both worlds, by muddying the response and separating the commands disastrously. Even in mid-July Hitler was still convinced that the main Allied attack was to be expected at the Pas de Calais, and refused to allow his powerful forces there to be transferred southwards. He therefore completely fell for both the Norwegian and the Calais parts of the Allied deception plans, Operations Fortitude North and South.

On 17 June 1944, at a meeting with Rommel and Rundstedt, Hitler blamed his troops in France for weakness and cowardice, refused to allow withdrawals and announced that secret weapons would win the war instead. Yet he had also spent the war undermining the secret-weapon programmes, by ordering the jet-aircraft programme to concentrate on producing bombers rather than fighters, and by stop-starting the V-1 and V-2 weapons programmes.

Hitler's continual merry-go-round of sackings and reinstatements of senior generals was bewildering for the High Command and demoralizing for the troops, who could only conclude that they were being badly led by their generals, which was not generally the case. The sacking of Manstein, instead of giving him complete control of the Eastern Front, was a significant blunder. Yet even subservience could not protect some commanders: on 28 June 1944 Hitler sacked Field Marshal Ernst Busch as commander of Army Group Centre, replacing him with Model. A week later he replaced Rundstedt with Field Marshal von Kluge, who was convalescing after a car crash. Then on 10 July he refused Model assistance from Army Group North to strengthen his attempts to keep the Russians out of the Baltic, and on 5 September he reappointed Rundstedt as commander-in-chief west, only a few weeks after his replacement by Kluge. Some field marshals commanded all three army groups in Russia in the course of a few months; for a man who prided himself on his 'unalterable will', Hitler changed his mind all the time.

The 20 July Plot made Hitler understandably wary about the loyalty of his generals, but also made him unwarrantably certain of his own destiny and indestructibility, a disastrous combination. By Christmas Day 1944, despite the Ardennes offensive having recaptured 400 square miles, it was clear that Antwerp would not fall and that the attack could not move much further. In yet another 'Stand or die' order, Hitler insisted that there would be an Alsace offensive in the New Year, which never materialized. By refusing Model the possibility of retreating from the area around Houffalize, the German Army was once again left powerless to reconstitute itself further to the east. By the end of the offensive, the US First Army had crossed into the Fatherland itself, east of St Vith.

March 1945 saw Hitler sack Rundstedt as commander-in-chief west yet again, after the US III Corps had succeeded in crossing the Ludendorff Bridge over the Rhine at Remagen. He then visited the Eastern Front on 12 March, at Castle Freienwalde on the River Oder, where he told his commanders that 'Each day and each hour is precious,' because he was about to unleash a new secret weapon, without disclosing its nature.[23] This was because he had run out of them – the last V-2 landed a fortnight later – unless he meant the new U-boats that were still far from seaworthy. (It was probably just another morale-boosting lie.) By that time he had indeed decided to unleash a new secret weapon, on the German people themselves for betraying him by losing the war, because on 19 March he ordered the destruction of all factories and food stores on all fronts, a policy that was thankfully ignored by Albert Speer and all but the most fanatical Nazis. Nine days later Hitler again dismissed perhaps the best of his battlefield commanders, Heinz Guderian, and replaced him with the utterly undistinguished General Hans Krebs. Charlie Chaplin's Great Dictator could hardly have done better than that. Towards the end of the war fanatical Nazi generals such as Krebs, Schörner and Rendulic were promoted, not so much for their military competence as for their ideological loyalty.

If Hitler had not been a National Socialist he would probably not have unleashed the Second World War, but equally he might possibly have won it. There was nothing inevitable about the Allies' victory in the conflict of 1939–45, for as John Stuart Mill observed in *On Liberty*: 'It is a piece of idle sentimentality that truth, merely as truth, has any inherent power denied to error of prevailing against the dungeon and the stake.' Many of his worst strategic blunders were the result of his ideological convictions rather than military necessity. As Kleist told Liddell Hart after the war, 'Under the Nazis we tended to reverse Clausewitz's dictum, and to regard peace as a continuation of war.' It is not difficult to construct a narrative of the Second World War in which a Chiefs of Staff committee of German generals did not make the blunders Hitler did, and it makes somewhat chilling reading.

Of course it is easy today to fight the Second World War with 20/20 hindsight, ridiculing Hitler for errors that at the time might have seemed – especially in the absence of critical advice – like the best options available. He did not have all the intelligence and information we do; he was not privy to the enemy's thinking as we are. But even Stalin allowed himself to be persuaded in the Stavka, so long as it did not look as if he was being overruled. A Chiefs of Staff committee over which Hitler and Göring had little influence, but which drew on the collective talents of generals such as Manstein, Halder, Brauchitsch, Rundstedt, Rommel, Guderian, Student, Senger, Vietinghoff, Bock and Kesselring, should have directed Germany's strategy after 1939, and Raeder and Dönitz her naval strategy, with Hitler concentrating on visiting the fronts, the wounded and bomb-sites, threatening neutrals, making morale-boosting speeches and doing everything in his diplomatic power to prevent the United States from declaring war.

It is impossible to say whether the German generals would have made the same or perhaps some quite different but no less disastrous errors. Perhaps the subjugation of 193 million Russians by 79 million Germans was simply a mathematical impossibility, and so Germany could never have won the war under any circumstances. If Hitler had taken a junior role after Barbarossa, it is likely that all that would have happened would have been that the war would have gone on even longer and claimed yet more lives. Hitler's defeat was intimately tied up in the political nature of Hitlerism, in particular his refusal to retreat, his belief in the power of his unfettered will and his constant upping of the stakes, which had worked well for him in Weimar domestic politics in the 1920s and in his international brinksmanship in the 1930s. Boldness, unpredictability and Blitzkrieg had served him superbly until late 1941, but were not enough, especially once his blunders ensured that his willpower came up against Allied air power and Russian armoured power. 'Allied air power was the greatest single reason for the German defeat,' claimed Albert Kesselring, with Blumentritt and others agreeing.[24] They were wrong, of course, as Russian ground-based power in fact tolled the death knell of Nazism. But together these two factors found the limits of how far fanaticism and Blitzkrieg could get a nation. And the answer, as we saw in Chapter 10, was the windy cornfields outside the village of Prokhorovka. But no further.

Of course, having declared war against the United States in December 1941 Hitler had no hope of winning the war anyway, because a nuclear bomb was being successfully developed in New Mexico, and Germany was far from achieving one. With the United States effectively uninvadable, however long the war took the side which possessed atomic weaponry first would perforce win, and that was always going to be the Allies. Had D-Day failed, as it easily might have, the horrific prospect beckoned of the Allies being forced to win the war in Europe the same way as they ultimately had to in Japan, with German cities being obliterated as fast as new bombs could be produced, until the Nazis – or their successors – eventually surrendered.

In the two areas where pure intellect had an appreciable influence on the outcome of the war, the cracking of codes at Bletchley Park and in the Far East and the creation of a nuclear bomb at Los Alamos, the Allies won the battle of the brains. 'It is comforting to be reassured', as John Keegan has put it, 'that our lot were cleverer than the other lot.'[25]

In December 1941, Germany, with her population of 79 million, Japan (73 million), Italy (45 million), Romania (13.6 million) and Hungary (9.1 million), faced the combined onslaught of the USSR (193 million), USA (132 million), Great Britain (48 million), Canada (11.5 million), South Africa (10.5 million), Australia (7.1 million) and New Zealand (1.6 million). These figures do not count India and China, which both made very significant contributions to the Allied victory, or the French, who did not.[26] After Italy had changed sides in 1943, that left roughly 175 million Axis facing 449 million Allies, or two and a half times their numbers. With the Allies also controlling two-thirds of the global deposits and production of iron, steel, oil and coal from 1941 onwards, victory should have been assured. Yet it was not until May 1945 that Germany bowed to her conquerors, and it took two nuclear bombs to force the Japanese into the same posture three months later. The sheer, bloody-minded determination of both Axis nations was one reason for the length of time they were able to hold out against the Allies, but the high quality of their troops, especially the Germans, was the other. The statistics are unequivocal: up until the end of 1944, on a man-for-man basis, the Germans inflicted between 20 and 50 per cent higher casualties on the British and Americans than they suffered, and far higher than that on the Russians, under almost all military conditions.[27] Although they lost because of their Führer's domination of grand strategy as well as the sheer size of the populations and economies ranged against them, it is indisputable that the Germans were the best fighting men of the Second World War for all but the last few months of the struggle, when they suffered a massive dearth of equipment, petrol, reinforcements and air cover.

The problem with invading Russia was always going to be as much logistical as military. In the early stages of Barbarossa, the Germans defeated the Russians virtually wherever they engaged them, almost regardless of the numbers involved. Yet the problem of bringing up infantry fast enough behind the Panzer spearheads, especially with the 1941 muddy season coming in the autumn, was daunting. A two-season war, on the other hand, in which Leningrad and Moscow were captured in 1942, risked facing full Russian mobilization, of ultimately 500 divisions. The bold thrust against Moscow – the political, logistical and communications hub of European Russia – was thus still the best option for Hitler. If an entire Panzer group had gone around behind (that is, to the east of) Moscow in September 1941, the city just might have fallen, although of course it would have been defended street by street as Stalingrad was and Leningrad very nearly had to be. The key difference was that the Russians were able constantly to resupply Stalingrad across the Volga, which would not have been the case had Guderian and Hoth encircled Moscow.

As well as its dire implications for Russian morale, the fall of Moscow would have hampered the Soviets' ability to concentrate their reserves and to supply other cities in the region. Distance, transportation (plagued by partisans), logistics, mud and snow, and the marshalling – if with monstrous wastage – of overwhelming Russian manpower were the reasons why the Germans failed, yet had Fedor von Bock been allowed to continue Army Group Centre's advance on Moscow with his full force in early August 1941 even these might have been overcome. There was always the chance of a political collapse, especially had Stalin been forced to flee Moscow on the special train he had made ready for himself on 16 October 1941, to seek safety beyond the Urals. Beria privately suggested the move at the time, but did not propose it at the Stavka. In the absence of a Japanese invasion from the east, Hitler would probably have offered a post-Stalin regime peace terms that allowed it to rule everywhere east of the Urals, a far harsher version of the peace of Brest-Litovsk which the Bolsheviks signed with the Kaiser in 1918. In reality, of course, the Russians' ability – despite losing around half their heavy industry – to churn out vast numbers of T-34 tanks and mobilize almost 25 million troops, which were better led and equipped by the month, was decisive, especially considering that 70 per cent of the Luftwaffe had to be detailed to deal with the RAF and USAAF Combined Bomber Offensive from the west.

If different counsels had prevailed at Führer-conferences, such as Brauchitsch's at Dunkirk, Galland's during the battle of Britain, Manstein's at Stalingrad, Rommel's before El Alamein, Guderian's before Kursk and any number of other generals' on any number of other occasions, the Reich would have been in a better position to prosecute the war. But Hitler could not have left soldiering to the soldiers. A Führer had to be a superman, equal to any calling, and for such a spectacular know-all as Hitler – with views on everything, a love of military history and an impressive recall of military facts – the prospect of taking a back seat in a world war, like Kings George VI and Victor Emmanuel III, was an emotional and psychological impossibility. Fortunately, Nazi philosophy contained within it, once translated on to the military plane, the seeds of its own destruction. An expansionist nationalist German without a Nazi worldview – another Bismarck, say, or a Moltke – would probably not have defeated the USSR either, but he would have made the war go on even longer and claim even more lives.

Of course, in considering many of the errors made by Hitler, it is important to remember that there were usually generals, and not just Keitel and Jodl, who fully supported him, and provided telling arguments for him. There was no simple nexus of Hitler versus the High Command that post-war soldier–authors such as Manstein, Guderian and Blumentritt all too often posed. There was no German general who was always right, any more than the Führer was always wrong, and the campaigns that defeated Poland, Norway, France,

Yugoslavia, Greece and Crete were all pored over and approved by Hitler, after all. (Apart from their timing in the greater scheme of conquest, all those campaigns were very successful.) It is also worth recalling that no general opposed the concept of Operation Barbarossa, about which Halder and Brauchitsch accepted the over-optimistic intelligence assessments as much as everyone else, and that Führer Directive No. 21 – 'The armed forces of Germany must be prepared, even before the conclusion of the war with England, to defeat Soviet Russia in one rapid campaign' – set out a two-front war as early as 18 December 1940, a full six months before the blow fell. Similarly, Manstein was initially in favour of Paulus trying to hold out in Stalingrad, Kluge opposed the central thrust on Moscow, and Bock generally supported Hitler's strategy in Russia. The fact that they rarely spoke up simply shows that when dealing with Hitler the generals, for all their Iron Crosses and Knight's Crosses, were generally as cowardly as so many others in Nazi Germany. They were also aspirational professionals who knew that gainsaying the Führer was not a good way to secure promotion.

Of course the fact that the German generals often despised each other does not mean they could not have fought a more rational war than they did under Hitler, given a chief of staff more respected – or less lickspittle – than Wilhelm Keitel. As with any army, ambition played a part, as did sheer personality clashes. The personal anti-pathies described before the battle of Kursk between Zeitzler, Manstein, Kluge and Guderian – the last two having to be dissuaded from fighting a duel – were just one example of a phenomenon that was to dog the German High Command. The generals cannot be seen as a unified voice, and just as Zhukov, Konev and Rokossovsky were rivals, as more obviously were Patton, Montgomery and Bradley, so the dismissal of one German general was usually seen by the rest as an opportunity.

As Alan Clark pointed out, 'There is no evidence that Hitler ever changed his mind on questions of strategy either at the persuasion of his intimates in the Party or the senior officers of the Army.'[28] If Hitler and certain generals agreed on something it was almost always because they agreed with him rather than vice versa. With the war effectively lost after Kursk, it was indeed fortunate that Hitler listened to so few of his good generals, and tended to dismiss the very best of them, otherwise the war could have dragged on into 1946 or later. Churchill's dismissive remarks about the military genius and 'master hand' of Corporal Hitler were therefore entirely justified. By contrast, the Western Allies fought the war substantially by committee, with the American Joint Chiefs of Staff and the British Chiefs of Staff Committee creating grand strategy in conjunction with input from the politicians. This system produced fierce rows between politicians and Staff officers, and between Britons and Americans, but the traditions of gentlemanly interaction, open debate (within the obvious security parameters), freedom from fear, and an assumption that the synthesis of views was more likely to produce better results meant that the tensions that undoubtedly arose were generally creative ones.[29] Even in the Stavka, where none of those assumptions applied, Stalin permitted a reasonable degree of free discussion on military affairs, so long as it did not stray into the political sphere, which was exclusively his. The catastrophe of 1941 undoubtedly sobered him, and showed him that men like Zhukov, Konev and Rokossovsky should be heeded if Russia was to survive. Hitler, meanwhile, put his own omniscience before the need to pay attention to his advisers, however high the stakes.

The strengths of the three main Allied nations were very different, but they each contributed something vitally necessary for overall victory. Without all three in the mix, that victory might not have arrived until much later in the 1940s, if at all. Britain, by refusing Hitler's peace overtures in 1940, winning the battle of Britain, cracking the Enigma code, keeping open the sea-lanes during the battle of the Atlantic, bombing German industry enough to blunt Speer's economic miracle and providing an unsinkable aircraft carrier (a giant version of Midway or Malta) from which the liberation of western Europe could be effected after D-Day, forced Germany into a two-front war, even if the western one was to be found along the shores of the Mediterranean for much of the war, rather than in the Low Countries. The British Army had a less happy war than the Royal Navy and the RAF, especially in the early stages, with bad tactics during the fall of France and Malaya, bad strategy during the Greek and Cretan débâcles, bad equipment in the early North African campaigns, bad intelligence at Dieppe and Arnhem, and bad weather in Italy. It only really hit its stride – ably supported by excellent Commonwealth contingents – at the battle of El Alamein, which, as well as being the British Empire's first major land victory over Germans of the war, was also its last. From D-Day onwards in Europe, and certainly in Slim's campaigns in Burma in 1944–5, the British Army did well, but by then its troops had been fighting for five years. It is hard not to escape Sir Alan Brooke's conclusion that the brightest and the best British soldiers had been killed in the First World War (although that fails to explain why the Germans were so good in the Second). In all, the United Kingdom lost 379,762 military killed and 475,000 military wounded in the war, with around 65,000 civilians killed.[30] 'For every American who died, the Japanese lost 6 people, the Germans 11, and the Russians 92.' The figures for every Briton killed are four Japanese, seven Germans and sixty Russians.[31] Far from being a cause of embarrassment, of course, it should be a cause of congratulation to Roosevelt, Churchill, Marshall and Brooke that they ended the war with such little (relatively speaking) carnage among their countrymen.

It was the Russians who provided the oceans of blood necessary to defeat Germany, and it cannot be reiterated enough that out of every five Germans killed in combat – that is, on the battlefield rather than in aerial bombing or through other means – four died on the Eastern Front. It is the central statistic of the Second World War. The full cost to the Russians amounted to the truly obscene figure of around twenty-seven million dead soldiers and civilians, though it needs to be borne in mind that much of the responsibility for the catastrophe lay with Stalin himself. If he had not signed the Nazi–Soviet Pact; if he had not trusted Hitler so totally; if he had not wiped out much of the Red Army officer corps in the purges of 1937–8; if he had not gone to war with Finland; if he had not sent his troops so far forward after his hyena-like pounce on eastern Poland; if he had not refused to allow strategic withdrawals after Barbarossa: the list of his blunders is long and galling and led to the deaths of millions. Moreover, although the Russians bled the most by far, if one is to take a broader-based criterion of war effort, which includes the war at sea and the air war over Germany, the western Allies' contribution meant that the Reich was unable to concentrate as much as 60 per cent of its total armaments against the Russians, even in the make-or-break months of late 1941.[32]

It is true the American contribution was made not primarily in blood – 292,100 military dead, 571,822 wounded, and negligible numbers of civilian casualties – but in the production and distribution of armaments, the overall financing of the conflict, the size of forces mobilized and the successful campaigns fought, often in places that American strategists did not want to be. The US spent $350 billion on the war, even more than Germany and as much as the USSR and Britain combined. She also mobilized 14.9 million Americans, more than Germany's 12.9 million and twice Japan's 7.4 million. She bore the lion's share of the war in the Pacific and provided two-thirds of the forces at Overlord and the subsequent fighting in the west. The Eighth Army Air Force bombed Germany relentlessly, while the US provided many of the boots, trucks and armaments with which the Russians held back and eventually prevailed over the Germans. Much as nationalist historians like to present their own countries as central to victory, thereby belittling the contribution made by the others, the Second World War was a genuine team effort which required the full exertions of all three major partners for victory, each in their different but complementary ways.

In April 1943 Churchill ordered the War Cabinet to 'popularise' the phrase 'British Commonwealth and Empire', an inversion of the hitherto commonly used 'British Empire and Commonwealth' but a move which at least retained the word 'empire'.[33] Yet whereas Churchill was fighting for an empire in which by 1945 very many senior British decision-makers besides himself no longer believed, and Stalin for an equally doomed system, before deliberately initiating a Cold War that his country was eventually to lose, Roosevelt fought for a future which actually came to pass, that of United States 'soft' hegemony, with military bases around the world, generally unfettered access to global markets, and a *Pax Americana* that has lasted to the present day. When Churchill told the V-E Day crowds in London 'This is your victory!' and they roared back 'No, it's *yours*!' they would both be proved wrong: in fact it turned out to be the recently deceased President Roosevelt's.

The world was fortunate that it had men of the calibre of Roosevelt and Churchill, and even Stalin, for all his blunders, when it was threatened by Adolf Hitler. If Germany had managed to maintain all it had occupied by the summer of 1941, and had not invaded Russia, she would have had as large a population as the United States – even if, for the first generation at least, only around 60 per cent of them spoke German as their first language. Harnessing this vast population of hard-working, well-educated Europeans to the ambitions of the Reich, Hitler could have built the world's most formidable superpower. It was fortunate for mankind that he was too impatient and too convinced a Nazi – Operation Barbarossa stemmed primarily from ideological rather than military imperatives – to put in the years of hard work necessary to consolidate his 1940 windfall. In personal terms, although Hitler was easily able to bully and swindle fearful and naive men such as Schuschnigg, Hácha, Chamberlain and Daladier, when he came up against men of the calibre of Franklin Roosevelt, Winston Churchill and Josef Stalin he found he had more than met his match.

Allied grand strategy was forced on the three major players by circumstance as much as by choice. The Russians simply had to survive as best they could at the start of the war, and only after the German reverses at Stalingrad in January 1943 and Kursk that July could they start to impose their will upon the battlefield, which they eventually did with great vigour, especially in their *annus mirabilis* of 1944. The destruction of Army Group Centre during the Bagration offensive in the summer of that year was as decisive as anything seen in the history of warfare, and utterly dwarfed the contemporaneous Operation Overlord. Advances on the Eastern Front were still costly, however, for even by 1945 there – unlike in the west – the Germans always inflicted more losses on their opponents than they suffered themselves.

Similarly, there was no real choice for the Americans even after Japan unleashed war on them on 7 December 1941 and then Hitler declared it four days later. They theoretically could have pursued a Pacific First policy, but General George C. Marshall rightly considered that while it would be relatively easy to defeat Japan after a German surrender, the opposite was not necessarily the case. Similarly the strategy whereby American forces first engaged German forces in North Africa, then Sicily, then Italy before finally squaring up to them in north-western France was effectively forced on the Joint Chiefs of Staff by the British, who vetoed any recrossing of the Channel before 1 May 1944, which for operational reasons had to be further postponed to 6 June. The clashes between the British and the American policy-makers over the timing of Operation Overlord were titanic, but both sides knew that without British consent the Normandy landings could not have been undertaken any earlier.

Nor should they have been. After the Germans introduced an extra rotor to the Enigma machine in February 1942, the Allied navies were plunged into the dark over Kriegsmarine movements in the battle of the Atlantic for almost a year. No landings in north-west Europe could be attempted with supply lanes at the mercy of the U-boat fleet. That battle was not won until May 1943, by which time a quarter of a million Germans had surrendered in Tunisia and plans were well under way for the invasion of Sicily. Marshall might have complained about being led 'down the garden path' by Brooke and Churchill, but at the Casablanca Conference of January 1943 there was no possibility of crossing the Channel in any significant numbers that year, as he had to acknowledge, and the war could not be simply suspended until enough men had been assembled in southern England for Overlord. Sicily followed Africa logically, just as Italy followed Sicily. What were not necessary were the long and costly campaigns north of Rome once Overlord had taken place, let alone the superfluous attack on the South of France in mid-August 1944.

Without complete air superiority and massive aerial bombardment, next to impossible to achieve before the Mustang fighter came on stream in sufficient numbers in early 1944, Normandy might have been a disaster. It also needed a great deal of work done on the Mulberry Harbours and Pipeline Under The Ocean (PLUTO), which was not finished until 1944 either. The intelligence deception operations Fortitudes North and South needed to mature, which they did triumphantly that year. Above all, the Wehrmacht needed to be bled white in Russia, which was also not the case before 1944. (And no invasion was possible once the Channel weather became unpredictable in mid-September.) A defeat in the west, with the Allies being flung back into the sea – which could even have happened on 6 June 1944 with prompter Panzer action by a unified German command – might have set back the liberation of Europe, at least from the west, by years. Had the Allies not liberated western Europe in the mid-1940s, the same form of Soviet totalitarian tyranny would have been installed there as oppressed the people of eastern Europe until 1989.

The Allied armies furthermore needed to be bloodied in a series of victories before they could possibly meet the main body of the Wehrmacht in open battle, as opposed to the under-resourced Afrika Korps which had nonetheless managed to do so well at Tobruk, the Kasserine Pass and elsewhere. A supreme effort such as the Ardennes offensive, conducted against green Allied troops in 1942 or 1943, might well have succeeded, especially with the fuel and air cover available to the Germans in those years. Until quite late on in the war, therefore, the Allies had their essentially reactive grand strategies imposed on them by Hitler's *force majeure*, always responding to the Führer's iron whim. It is therefore not by chance that this book has tended to concentrate on his thoughts, his actions and his regular, colossal blunders.

Hitler's anti-Semitism, culminating in the Holocaust, was central to his Nazism but it did nothing to aid Germany's chances of winning the war, and possibly a great deal to retard them. The Reich devoted a great amount of effort, especially in terms of transportation, in its effort to render Europe *Judenfrei*. Quite apart from the sheer moral issue involved, which obviously had no bearing on Hitler, the Holocaust was a military mistake, tying up railway stock and (admittedly relatively few) SS troops, but above all denuding Germany of millions of potentially productive workers and potential soldiers. German Jews who had fought bravely for the Kaiser – Hitler's own Iron Cross First Class had come because his Jewish regimental adjutant petitioned GHQ hard for it – were not only not called up for the Volkssturm, they were gassed. Between 1939 and 1944 the German labour force shrank from thirty-nine million to twenty-nine million people, a disastrous 26 per cent fall at a time when a massive increase in production was vital for victory.[34] When production was being badly hampered by a lack of intelligent, educated, hard-working people, Hitler massacred some 5.7 million European Jews, an action that would be self-evidently self-defeating, except in the diseased mind of a Nazi fanatic. Similarly, for ideological reasons the Wehrmacht did not recruit women, while the Red Army called up between 1 million and 1.5 million of them, with the only difference in women's benefits being that they received 100 grams more soap than the men.

For all the military defeats on the European Continent to both the east and west by 1945, there was one thing that could still have won Hitler a stalemate, or even the war. In June 1942, the German physicist Werner Heisenberg reported to Hitler that an amount of uranium 'no larger than a pineapple' would be enough to destroy a city.[35] Yet the Jewish and German émigré scientists who had the knowledge and genius necessary to split the atom were by then working in New Mexico, rather than for Heisenberg in the Kaiser Wilhelm Institute in Dahlem. Hitler's Nazism had also lost him that last, albeit always slim, chance of victory. It was said of Emperor Napoleon III that his name was both his making and his undoing. Similarly, Hitler won his revolution because of his drive, willpower, impulsiveness, philosophy and policies, which seemed – however wrongly – to offer Germany hope in the 1930s. Yet it was precisely these same phenomena that led to his destruction the following decade.

On the evening of 4 February 1942 Adolf Hitler was entertaining Heinrich Himmler at the Berghof when the conversation got round to Shakespeare. It was probably *Hamlet* and *King Lear* to which the Führer was referring when he said that it was a:

misfortune that none of our great writers took his subject from German Imperial history. Our Schiller found nothing better to do than to glorify a Swiss crossbowman! The English, for their part, had a Shakespeare, but the history of his country has supplied Shakespeare, as far as heroes are concerned, only with imbeciles and madmen.[36]

Analyses of Hitler's defeat have tended to portray him as a strategic imbecile – 'Corporal Hitler' – or otherwise as a madman, but these explanations are clearly not enough. The real reason why Hitler lost the Second World War was exactly the same one that caused him to unleash it in the first place: he was a Nazi.

Notes

ABBREVIATIONS

ALAB	Papers of Field Marshal Lord Alanbrooke at the Liddell Hart Centre for Military Archives, King's College, London
BRGS	Lawrence Burgis Papers at Churchill Archives Centre Churchill College, Cambridge
Cunningham	Papers of Admiral Lord Cunningham at the British Library
Ian Sayer Archive	Private collection of Mr Ian Sayer
KENN	Papers of Major-General Sir John Kennedy at the Liddell Hart Centre for Military Archives, King's College, London
LH	Papers of Captain Basil Liddell Hart at the Liddell Hart Centre for Military Archives, King's College, London
MARS	George C. Marshall Papers at the George C. Marshall Foundation, Lexington, Virginia
MHI	US Army Military History Institute, Carlisle, Pennsylvania
NA	British National Archives at Kew, of which CAB denotes Cabinet Papers, FO Foreign Office papers and PREM premiers' papers
Portal	Papers of Sir Charles Portal at Christ Church, Oxford
TLS	*Times Literary Supplement*
Wyllie Archive	Papers of the late Mr Bruce Wyllie, in private hands

PRELUDE

1. Kershaw, *Hitler: Hubris*, p. 500
2. Ian Sayer Archive
3. Wheeler-Bennett, *Nemesis of Power*, p. 339
4. Stackelberg and Winkle, *Nazi Germany Sourcebook*, p. 176
5. Kershaw, *Hitler: Hubris*, pp. 547–8
6. Domarus, *Essential Hitler*, p. 604
7. *Ibid.*, pp. 605–14
8. Kershaw, *Hitler: Nemesis*, pp. 52–4
9. Liddell Hart, *Other Side*, p. 13
10. Goldensohn, *Nuremberg Interviews*, p. 158
11. Kershaw, *Hitler: Nemesis*, p. 58
12. ed. Self, *Neville Chamberlain Diary Letters*, p. 348
13. Cowling, *The Impact of Hitler*, p. 197
14. Hansard, vol. 339
15. Liddell Hart, *Other Side*, pp. 11–12
16. *Ibid.*, p. 14

1: FOUR INVASIONS

1. Manvell and Fraenkel, *Göring*, p. 228
2. Jablonsky, *Churchill and Hitler*, p. 131
3. Heitmann, 'Incident at Mosty', pp. 47–54; Whiting, 'Man Who Invaded Poland', pp. 2–8
4. Heitmann, 'Incident at Mosty', p. 52
5. Mellenthin, *Panzer Battles*, p. 4
6. Michel, *Second World War*, p. 32
7. Calvocoressi and Wint, *Total War*, p. 100
8. Letter from Allan Mallinson, 18/12/2008
9. Keitel's Nuremberg Papers in Ian Sayer Archive
10. Calvocoressi and Wint, *Total War*, p. 100
11. Mellenthin, *Panzer Battles*, p. 3; Michel, *Second World War*, p. 33
12. Howard, *Captain Professor*, p. 89
13. Calvocoressi and Wint, *Total War*, p. 101
14. Braithwaite, *Moscow 1941*, p. 49
15. ed. Cameron Watt, *Mein Kampf*, p. 603
16. Gilbert, *Second World War*, p. 30
17. *Ibid.*, p. 2

18. Nicholas Stargardt, *TLS*, 10/10/2008, p. 9
19. ed. Sayer, *Allgemeine SS*, p. 1
20. *Ibid.*, pp. 1–47
21. Calvocoressi and Wint, *Total War*, p. 103
22. ed. Dear, *Oxford Companion*, p. 374
23. Willmott, *Great Crusade*, p. 67
24. Edwards, *White Death*, p. 157
25. *Ibid.*, p. 161
26. *Ibid.*, p. 185
27. Clark, *Barbarossa*, p. 60; Braithwaite, *Moscow 1941*, p. 49
28. Overy, *Russia's War*, p. 49
29. Braithwaite, *Moscow 1941*, p. 43
30. ed. Dear, *Oxford Companion*, p. 375
31. ed. Nicolson, *Harold Nicolson*, p. 32
32. Spears, *Prelude to Dunkirk*, p. 32
33. Liddell Hart, *Second World War*, p. 56
34. Moulton, *Norwegian Campaign*, p. 123
35. Michel, *Second World War*, p. 76
36. Liddell Hart, *Second World War*, p. 59
37. Michel, *Second World War*, p. 75
38. *Ibid.*, p. 72
39. Ash, *Norway*, p. 133
40. Calvocoressi and Wint, *Total War*, p. 109
41. Ash, *Norway*, p. 113
42. Dahl, *Quisling, passim*
43. Adams, *Doomed Expedition*, p. 168
44. *Ibid.*, p. 171
45. Willmott, *Great Crusade*, p. 80; Adams, *Doomed Expedition*, p. 176
46. ed. Smith, *Hostage to Fortune*, p. 476
47. ed. Langworth, *Churchill by Himself*, p. 56

2: FÜHRER IMPERATOR

1. Bond, *France and Belgium*, pp. 63ff.
2. Sebag Montefiore, *Dunkirk*, p. 32
3. Goldensohn, *Nuremberg Interviews*, p. 98
4. Clark, *Barbarossa*, p. xx
5. Ryback, *Hitler's Private Library*, pp. 169–72
6. *Ibid.*, Appendix A, p. 235

7. *Ibid.*, p. 179
8. eds Heiber and Glantz, *Hitler and his Generals*, pp. 39, 86, 89–90, 109, 137–8, 151, 189, 305, 317, 320, 818 nn. 298 and 299
9. BRGS 2/21
10. Allan Mallinson, *Literary Review*, 7/2008, pp. 16–17
11. Mellenthin, *Panzer Battles*, p. 22
12. Beaufre, 1940, p. 214
13. Mellenthin, *Panzer Battles*, p. 11
14. Willmott, *Great Crusade*, p. 82
15. ed. Parrish, *Simon & Schuster*, p. 202
16. Sebag Montefiore, *Dunkirk*, p. 59
17. Kaufmann and Kaufmann, *Hitler's Blitzkrieg*, p. 173
18. Bond, *France and Belgium*, p. 97
19. Mellenthin, *Panzer Battles*, p. 24
20. Holmes, *World at War*, p. 110
21. Beaufre, 1940, p. 183
22. McCarthy and Syron, *Panzerkrieg*, p. 83
23. Liddell Hart, *Second World War*, p. 66
24. Howard, *Captain Professor*, p. 43
25. ed. Parrish, *Simon & Schuster*, p. 202
26. Beaufre, 1940, p. 215
27. Max Hastings, *Night and Day*, 18/1/2004, p. 14
28. Mellenthin, *Panzer Battles*, p. 18
29. Kershaw, *Hitler: Nemesis*, pp. 295–6
30. Liddell Hart, *Other Side*, p. 139
31. Goldensohn, *Nuremberg Interviews*, p. 342
32. Liddell Hart, *Other Side*, p. 140
33. *Finest Hour*, No. 136, Autumn 2006, p. 51
34. Holmes, *World at War*, pp. 107–8
35. ed. Barnett, *Hitler's Generals*, p. 191
36. Below, *At Hitler's Side*, p. 61
37. Ian Sayer Archive; Sayer and Botting, *Hitler's Last General*, pp. 22–3
38. Goldensohn, *Nuremberg Interviews*, p. 342
39. Atkin, *Pillar of Fire*, pp. 152–3; Sebag Montefiore, *Dunkirk*, pp. 292–302, 345–61
40. Sayer and Botting, *Hitler's Last General*, *passim*
41. Barker, *Dunkirk*, p. 108
42. Bridgeman, *Memoirs*, p. 183
43. Kaufmann and Kaufmann, *Hitler's Blitzkrieg*, p. 259
44. Lombard-Hobson, *Sailor's War*, pp. 86–7

45. Barker, *Dunkirk*, p. 108
46. Atkin, *Pillar of Fire*, p. 87
47. Levine, *Forgotten Voices*, p. 27
48. Longden, *Dunkirk*, p. 10
49. Atkinson, *Army at Dawn*, p. 376
50. KENN 4/2/4, p. 266
51. Roberts, *Holy Fox*, pp. 221–4
52. Chapman, *Why France Collapsed*, p. 237
53. Calvocoressi and Wint, *Total War*, p. 126
54. Davidson and Manning, *Chronology*, p. 38
55. David Pryce-Jones in eds Hirschfeld and Marsh, *Collaboration in France*, p. 12
56. Spears, *Fall of France*, p. 139
57. Holmes, *World at War*, p. 97
58. Willmott, *Great Crusade*, p. 102; Calvocoressi and Wint, *Total War*, p. 232
59. Looseley, 'Paradise after Hell', pp. 33–8
60. Alan Judd, *Sunday Times*, 12/10/1997, books section, p. 5
61. Holmes, *World at War*, p. 102
62. eds Hirschfeld and Marsh, *Collaboration in France*, p. 17
63. Ian Sayer Archive
64. Goldensohn, *Nuremberg Interviews*, p. 158
65. Liddell Hart, *Other Side*, p. 15
66. Holmes, *World at War*, p. 97
67. Beaufre, *1940*, p. 214; Dupuy and Dupuy, *Encyclopedia*, p. 1083
68. Holmes, *World at War*, p. 97
69. *Ibid.*, p. 98
70. KENN 4/2/4, 1/6/1942
71. Kitson, *Hunt for Nazi Spies*, *passim*
72. eds Hirschfeld and Marsh, *Collaboration in France*, p. 12
73. David Pryce-Jones, *Literary Review*, 4/2001, p. 22
74. ed. Hirschfeld and Marsh, *Collaboration in France*, p. 13
75. Alan Judd, *Sunday Times*, 12/10/1997, books section, p. 5
76. Ousby, *Occupation*, p. 109
77. *TLS*, 31/8/2001, p. 9
78. eds Hirschfeld and Marsh, *Collaboration in France*, p. 13
79. Williams, *Pétain*, pp. 441–2
80. eds Hirschfeld and Marsh, *Collaboration in France*, p. 14
81. Alan Judd, *Sunday Times*, 12/10/1997, p. 5
82. Marnham, *The Death of Jean Moulin*, *passim*

83. *Sunday Times*, 18/1/1999
84. Robert O. Paxton, *TLS*, 1/5/1998, p. 11
85. *The Economist*, 15/4/2006, p. 91
86. Conway, *Collaboration in Belgium*, p. 287
87. *Ibid.*, p. 286
88. David Cesarani, *Guardian*, 13/1/2008

3: LAST HOPE ISLAND

1. Bess, *Choices under Fire*, p. 323
2. Hudson, *Soldier, Poet, Rebel*, pp. 178–80
3. Colville, *Fringes of Power*, p. 141
4. Leighton and Coakley, *Global Logistics*, pp. 33–4
5. ed. Cameron Watt, *Mein Kampf*, p. 601
6. Liddell Hart, *Other Side*, p. 41
7. *Ibid.*, pp. 142, 160
8. Holmes, *World at War*, p. 133
9. Ray, *Battle of Britain*, p. 41
10. *Ibid.*, p. 40
11. Deighton, *Fighter*, p. xix
12. Ray, *Battle of Britain*, p. 43
13. Dupuy and Dupuy, *Encyclopedia*, p. 1166; ed. Parrish, *Simon & Schuster*, p. 81
14. Ray, *Battle of Britain*, p. 29
15. Domarus, *Speeches and Proclamations*, p. 2072
16. ed. Young, *Decisive Battles*, pp. 57–9
17. Holmes, *World at War*, p. 134
18. Ray, *Battle of Britain*, p. 29
19. Kershaw, *The Few*, p. 65
20. Bridgeman, *Memoirs*, p. 184
21. ed. Parrish, *Simon & Schuster*, p. 290
22. Richard Overy, *Literary Review*, 11/2006, p. 46; McKinstry, *Spitfire, passim*
23. Kershaw, *The Few*, pp. 67, 253 n. 57
24. Townsend, *Duel of Eagles*, pp. 361–2
25. Ray, *Battle of Britain*, p. 46
26. Price, *Spitfire Story*, pp. 192–3
27. *Ibid.*, pp. 192–3; Ray, *Battle of Britain*, p. 105
28. Ray, *Battle of Britain*, p. 82
29. McKinstry, *Spitfire*, p. 195

30. Ian Sayer Archive
31. Ray, *Battle of Britain*, p. 93
32. Nigel Jones, *Sunday Telegraph*, 23/9/2007, books section, p. 53
33. Holmes, *World at War*, pp. 133–4
34. ed. Leutze, *London Observer*, p. 51
35. eds Burdick and Jacobsen, *Halder War Diary*, p. 256
36. Ray, *Blitz*, p. 264
37. Allan Mallinson, *The Times*, 7/2/2004, books section, p. 13
38. Holmes, *World at War*, p. 132
39. Harrison, *Living through the Blitz*
40. Speer, *Inside the Third Reich*, p. 284
41. Holmes, *World at War*, p. 111
42. *Ibid.*
43. Bradford, *King George VI*, p. 320
44. Overy, *Why the Allies Won*, p. 109
45. Dupuy and Dupuy, *Encyclopedia*, p. 1166
46. ed. Young, *Decisive Battles*, p. 61
47. *London Gazette*, 15/11/1940
48. Kershaw, *The Few*, p. 76
49. *Ibid.*
50. Dupuy and Dupuy, *Encyclopedia*, p. 1167
51. Churchill, *Into Battle*, p. 259
52. Ministry of Information, *What Britain Has Done*, p. 110
53. *Ibid.*, p. 113
54. *Ibid.*, p. 110
55. Holmes, *World War II*, p. 92
56. Barnett, *Audit of War*, p. 260
57. Roberts, *Holy Fox*, pp. 296–7
58. Preston, *Franco*, p. 399
59. Schwarz, *Eye of the Hurricane*, p. 125
60. *Ibid.*, p. 127
61. ed. Trevor-Roper, *Hitler's Table Talk*, p. 260
62. BRGS 1/2
63. Monsarrat, *Cruel Sea*, pp. 160–61
64. Cookridge, *Inside SOE*, p. 3
65. Dalton, *Fateful Years*, p. 366
66. ed. Laqueur, *Second World War*, pp. 250–51
67. Foot, *SOE*, pp. 219–20
68. Dalton, *Fateful Years, passim*
69. Howard, *Captain Professor*, p. 45

4: CONTESTING THE LITTORAL

1. Ranfurly, *To War with Whittaker*, p. 91
2. Schofield, *Wavell*, p. 150
3. Holmes, *World at War*, p. 150
4. Dupuy and Dupuy, *Encyclopedia*, p. 1168
5. Carver, *Dilemmas*, p. 16
6. Dupuy and Dupuy, *Encyclopedia*, p. 1173
7. Carver, *Dilemmas*, p. 13
8. Holmes, *World at War*, p. 153
9. *Ibid.*, p. 155
10. BRGS 1/2
11. Willmott, *Great Crusade*, p. 114
12. *Ibid.*, p. 116
13. ed. Parrish, *Simon & Schuster*, p. 47
14. Atkinson, *Army at Dawn*, p. 7
15. Dupuy and Dupuy, *Encyclopedia*, p. 1176
16. Mellenthin, *Panzer Battles*, p. 28
17. Mazower, *Hitler's Greece*, passim
18. Dupuy and Dupuy, *Encyclopedia*, p. 1173
19. Michel, *Second World War*, p. 193
20. Winton, *Cunningham*, p. 211
21. Dupuy and Dupuy, *Encyclopedia*, p. 1173
22. Mazower, *Hitler's Greece*, p. xiii
23. Carver, *Dilemmas*, p. 19
24. Holmes, *World at War*, p. 162
25. Porch, *Hitler's Mediterranean Gamble*, p. 662
26. Carver, *Dilemmas*, p. 24
27. Schofield, *Wavell*, p. 152
28. Aldrich, *Intelligence*, p. 59
29. Lyman, *First Victory*, p. 2
30. Roberts, *Masters and Commanders*, p. 9
31. Carver, *Dilemmas*, p. 28
32. *Ibid.*, p. 32
33. ALAB 6/2/12/7A
34. NA CAB 69/4/38
35. Dupuy and Dupuy, *Encyclopedia*, p. 1185
36. *Daily Telegraph*, 12/6/2007, p. 23
37. Carver, *Dilemmas*, p. 132

38. *Ibid.*, p. 144
39. ed. Cameron Watt, *Mein Kampf*, p. 598

5 : KICKING IN THE DOOR

1. ed. Trevor-Roper, *Hitler's Table Talk*, p. 319
2. Kershaw, *Hitler: Nemesis*, p. 31
3. Ryback, *Hitler's Private Library*, pp. 164–5
4. *Ibid.*, p. 180
5. *Ibid.*, pp. 183–4
6. ed. Trevor-Roper, *Hitler's Table Talk*, p. 681
7. *Ibid.*, p. 68
8. *Ibid.*, p. 170
9. Kershaw, *Hitler, the Germans*, p. 90
10. ed. Gerbet, *Von Bock War Diary*, pp. 197–8
11. ed. Wright, *World at Arms*, p. 174
12. Ryback, *Hitler's Private Library*, p. 179
13. Black, *Roosevelt*, p. 645
14. Kershaw, *Hitler: Hubris*, p. 368
15. Kershaw, *Hitler: Nemesis*, p. 384
16. Clark, *Barbarossa*, p. 48
17. ed. Young, *Atlas*, p. 82
18. Ian Sayer Archive
19. Goldensohn, *Nuremberg Interviews*, p. 360
20. *Ibid.*, p. 111
21. *Ibid.*
22. *Ibid.*, p. 160
23. *Ibid.*, p. 159
24. *Ibid.*, p. 164
25. *Ibid.*, p. 165
26. Liddell Hart, *Other Side*, p. 15
27. Clark, *Barbarossa*, p. 20
28. Antony Beevor, *Literary Review*, 8/1998, p. 7
29. ed. Cameron Watt, *Mein Kampf*, p. 596
30. *Ibid.*, p. 597
31. Guderian, *Panzer Leader*, Appendix XXII, p. 513
32. Stone, *Hitler*, pp. 86–7
33. eds Burdick and Jacobsen, *Halder War Diary*, 13/7/1940
34. *Ibid.*, 31/7/1940

35. Kershaw, *Fateful Choices*, p. 70
36. *Ibid.*, p. 66
37. Domarus, *Speeches and Proclamations*, p. 2157
38. Rees, *World War Two*, pp. 66–9, 74–7
39. Kershaw, *Hitler: Nemesis*, p. 385
40. ed. Taylor, *Goebbels Diaries*, pp. 414–15
41. Domarus, *Speeches and Proclamations*, p. 2157
42. ed. Gerbet, *Von Bock War Diary*, pp. 197–8
43. Domarus, *Speeches and Proclamations*, pp. 2157–9
44. ed. Young, *Atlas*, p. 190
45. John Erickson preface to ed. Krivosheev, *Soviet Casualties*, p. ix
46. Braithwaite, *Moscow 1941*, p. 45
47. Clark, *Barbarossa*, p. 67
48. *Ibid.*, p. 57
49. Beevor, *Stalingrad*, p. 3; Murphy, *What Stalin Knew, passim*; Pleshakov, *Stalin's Folly, passim*
50. Read and Fisher, *Deadly Embrace*, pp. 608–9
51. Erickson, *Soviet High Command*, p. 587
52. Beevor, *Stalingrad*, pp. 12–13
53. Glantz and House, *Titans*, p. 51
54. Bullock, *Hitler and Stalin*, p. 797
55. Service, *Stalin*, p. 411
56. Braithwaite, *Moscow 1941*, p. 119
57. Sebag Montefiore, *Stalin*, pp. 330–34
58. Glantz, *Barbarossa*, p. 40
59. Braithwaite, *Moscow 1941*, p. 86
60. *Ibid.*
61. Service, *Stalin*, p. 417; Braithwaite, *Moscow 1941*, p. 94
62. Bellamy, *Absolute War*, p. 248
63. *Ibid.*
64. Gilbert, *Second World War*, p. 265
65. eds Heiber and Glantz, *Hitler and his Generals*, p. 280
66. Kershaw, *Hitler: Nemesis*, pp. 453, 470
67. ed. Taylor, *Goebbels Diaries*, p. 286
68. Atkinson, *Army at Dawn*, p. 8
69. John Erickson preface to ed. Krivosheev, *Soviet Casualties*, p. xii
70. Volkogonov, *Stalin*, p. 430; Overy, *Russia's War*, p. 106
71. Overy, *Russia's War*, p. 108
72. Service, *Stalin*, p. 418
73. ed. Gerbet, *Von Bock War Diary*, pp. 197–8

74. *Ibid.*, pp. 272–3
75. Mazower, *Hitler's Empire*, pp. 588–9
76. eds Heiber and Glantz, *Hitler and his Generals*, p. 158
77. Samuel J. Newland in eds Deutsch and Showalter, *What If?*, p. 64
78. Nuremberg Trial Files, Ian Sayer Archive
79. Aly and Heim, *Architects of Annihilation*, p. 242
80. Rees, *Auschwitz*, pp. 53–4
81. eds Burdick and Jacobsen, *Halder War Diary*, p. 506
82. Tooze, *Wages of Destruction*, p. 488
83. ed. Gerbet, *Von Bock War Diary*, pp. 265–6
84. *Ibid.*, p. 272
85. Liddell Hart, *Other Side*, p. 203
86. eds Howard and Paret, *Clausewitz: On War*, p. 582
87. *TLS, Essays and Reviews 1963*, p. 203
88. ed. Gerbet, *Von Bock War Diary*, pp. 289–90; ed. Young, *Atlas*, p. 83
89. ed. Gerbet, *Von Bock War Diary*, p. 289
90. *Ibid.*, p. 292
91. ed. Gorlitz, *Keitel Memoirs*, p. 165
92. ed. Gerbet, *Von Bock War Diary*, p. 293
93. Stolfi, *Hitler's Panzers*, p. 201
94. Tooze, *Wages of Destruction*, p. 490
95. ed. Young, *Atlas*, p. 90
96. Salisbury, *Unknown War*, p. 93
97. *Ibid.*, p. 94
98. Jones, *Leningrad*, p. 194
99. Liddell Hart, *Other Side*, p. 184
100. Information from Oleg Alexandrov, 10/6/2008
101. Shirer, *Rise and Fall*, p. 861
102. ed. Dear, *Oxford Companion*, p. 971
103. ed. Gorlitz, *Keitel Memoirs*, p. 166
104. *Ibid.*, p. 168
105. Atkinson, *Army at Dawn*, p. 10
106. ed. Trevor-Roper, *Hitler's Table Talk*, p. 62
107. *Ibid.*, p. 629
108. Malaparte, *Kaputt*, p. 215
109. Churchill, *End of the Beginning*, p. 102
110. Ryback, *Hitler's Private Library*, Appendix A, p. 235
111. eds Heiber and Glantz, *Hitler and his Generals*, p. 459
112. ed. Taylor, *Goebbels Diaries*, p. 207
113. ed. Trevor-Roper, *Hitler's Table Talk*, pp. 383, 402, 482, 706

114. *Ibid.*, p. 583
115. Chandler, *Campaigns of Napoleon*, p. 770
116. Le Tissier, *Zhukov at the Oder*, p. 20
117. Kershaw, *Hitler: Nemesis*, p. 453
118. Glantz and House, *Titans*, p. 60
119. Braithwaite, *Moscow 1941*, p. 53
120. Information from Oleg Alexandrov, 10/6/2008
121. Braithwaite, *Moscow 1941*, p. 151
122. Roberts, *Eminent Churchillians*, pp. 256–8
123. Colville, *Fringes of Power*, p. 344

6: TOKYO TYPHOON

1. Calvocoressi and Wint, *Total War*, pp. 738–9
2. ed. Dear, *Oxford Companion*, p. 871
3. Black, *Roosevelt*, pp. 646–7
4. Jenkins, *Roosevelt*, p. 128
5. Maney, *Roosevelt Presence*, p. 139
6. Weinberg, *World at Arms*, p. 261
7. Dupuy and Dupuy, *Encyclopedia*, p. 1232
8. Weinberg, *World at Arms*, p. 259
9. Dupuy and Dupuy, *Encyclopedia*, p. 1233
10. ed. Parrish, *Simon & Schuster*, p. 487
11. ed. Dear, *Oxford Companion*, p. 870
12. Dupuy and Dupuy, *Encyclopedia*, p. 1233
13. ed. Parrish, *Simon & Schuster*, p. 487
14. ed. Dear, *Oxford Companion*, p. 870
15. Willmott, *Great Crusade*, p. 169
16. Dupuy and Dupuy, *Encyclopedia*, p. 1233; ed Dear, *Oxford Companion*, p. 872
17. Agawa, *Reluctant Admiral*, p. 285
18. Jenkins, *Roosevelt*, p. 128
19. *Ibid.*, p. 129
20. Black, *Roosevelt*, pp. 691–2
21. Raeder testimony, Ian Sayer Archive
22. Willmott, *Great Crusade*, p. 169
23. Kershaw, *Fateful Choices*, pp. 382ff.
24. Ryback, *Hitler's Private Library*, p. 169–72
25. Dupuy and Dupuy, *Encyclopedia*, p. 1309

26. Goldensohn, *Nuremberg Interviews*, pp. 345–6
27. ed. Weinberg, *Second Book*, p. 107
28. Tooze, *Wages of Destruction*, pp. 506–8, 668–9
29. Bloch, *Ribbentrop*, p. 346
30. *Ibid.*, p. 345
31. *Ibid.*
32. Donald Cameron Watt, *Sunday Telegraph*, 11/10/1992
33. Black, *Roosevelt*, pp. 728–9
34. *Ibid.*, p. 729
35. Atkinson, *Army at Dawn*, p. 7
36. Hanson, 'In War: Resolution', *passim*
37. Lindbergh, *Wartime Journals*, p. 232
38. Churchill, *Grand Alliance*, Chapter 12
39. Michel, *Second World War*, p. 336
40. Calvocoressi and Wint, *Total War*, p. 720
41. Ministry of Information, *What Britain Has Done*, p.xv
42. Michel, *Second World War*, p. 339
43. Warren, *Singapore 1942*, p. 292
44. Calvocoressi and Wint, *Total War*, p. 723
45. Weinberg, *World at War*, p. 316
46. *Ibid.*
47. ed. Mercer, *Chronicle*, p. 252
48. Gough, '*Prince of Wales* and *Repulse*', p. 40
49. Farrell, *Defence and Fall*, p. 358
50. *Ibid.*, pp. 360–61
51. *Ibid.*, p. 356
52. Warren, *Singapore 1942*, p. 243; Farrell, *Defence and Fall*, p. 355
53. Calvocoressi and Wint, *Total War*, p. 724
54. Gary Sheffield, *TLS*, 12/4/2002, p. 27
55. Farrell, *Defence and Fall*, p. 312
56. Warren, *Singapore 1942*, p. 291
57. BRGS 2/11
58. Weinberg, *World at Arms*, p. 498
59. *Ibid.*, p. 313
60. Dupuy and Dupuy, *Encyclopedia*, p. 1237; ed. Parrish, *Simon & Schuster*, p. 129
61. Calvocoressi and Wint, *Total War*, p. 717
62. Atkinson, *Army at Dawn*, p. 10
63. Weinberg, *World at Arms*, p. 322
64. Dupuy and Dupuy, *Encyclopedia*, p. 1251

65. Weinberg, *World at Arms*, p. 317
66. Dupuy and Dupuy, *Encyclopedia*, p. 1242
67. Fraser, *Quartered Safe*, p. 106
68. *Ibid.*, p. 232
69. ed. Soames, *Speaking for Themselves*, p. 459
70. Michel, *Second World War*, p. 345
71. Harvey, *American Shogun*, p. 240
72. Royle, *Patton*, p. 75
73. Atkinson, *Army at Dawn*, p. 9
74. ed. Dear, *Oxford Companion*, pp. 1182–3

7: THE EVERLASTING SHAME OF MANKIND

1. Levi, *If This Is a Man*, p. 22
2. Kershaw, *Hitler, the Germans*, p. 104
3. ed. Cameron Watt, *Mein Kampf*, p. 620
4. Evans, *Coming of the Third Reich*, pp. 22–7
5. *Ibid.*, p. 164
6. Black, *Holocaust*, p. 24
7. *Ibid.*
8. Burleigh, *Third Reich*, p. 593
9. Rees, *Auschwitz*, p. 36
10. eds Gutman and Berenbaum, *Anatomy*, p. 302
11. Rhodes, *Masters of Death*, pp. 12–13
12. Rees, *Auschwitz*, p. 62
13. Black, *Holocaust*, p. 44
14. Braithwaite, *Moscow 1941*, p. 48
15. Peter Longerich, *BBC History*, 2/2002, p. 36
16. David Cesarani, *Literary Review*, 8/2001, p. 40
17. Browning, *Ordinary Men*, *passim*
18. *Ibid.*, p. 64
19. Black, *Holocaust*, pp. 43–4
20. *Ibid.*, p. 40
21. Ryback, *Hitler's Private Library*, p. xiv
22. Rees, *Auschwitz*, p. 22
23. *Ibid.*, p. 72
24. Manvell and Fraenkel, *Heinrich Himmler*, p. 252
25. Gilbert, *Holocaust*, p. 678
26. Levi, *If This Is a Man*, p. 35

27. Greif, *Wept without Tears*, pp. 11–16, 110, 113–17; Friedländer, *Years of Extermination*, pp. 503–4
28. Greif, *Wept without Tears*, p. 97
29. *Ibid.*
30. Hoess, *Commandant of Auschwitz*, pp. 222–3
31. Greif, *Wept without Tears*, p. 97
32. *Ibid.*, pp. 11–16
33. Overy, *Interrogations*, p. 397
34. Greif, *Wept without Tears*, pp. 60–1, 11–16
35. Steinbacher, *Auschwitz*, pp. 120–21
36. ed. Mark, *Scrolls of Auschwitz*; Greif, *Wept without Tears*, p. 341 n. 108
37. Greif, *Wept without Tears*, p. 34
38. *Ibid.*, pp. 66–8
39. *Ibid.*, p. 108
40. *Ibid.*, p. 106
41. Gilbert, *Holocaust*, p. 326
42. Greif, *Wept without Tears*, p. 109
43. *Ibid.*
44. Levi, *If This Is a Man*, p. 131
45. *Ibid.*, p. 35
46. *Ibid.*, p. 136
47. Rees, *Auschwitz*, p. 18
48. Friedländer, *Years of Extermination*, p. 500
49. Manvell and Fraenkel, *Heinrich Himmler*, p. 251
50. Friedländer, *Years of Extermination*, p. 502
51. *Ibid.*
52. *Ibid.*, p. 616
53. Gilbert, *Righteous*, for examples of, as the subtitle puts it, 'unsung heroes of the Holocaust'
54. Frankl, *Man's Search for Meaning*, p. 41
55. *Ibid.*, p. 19
56. Levi, *If This Is a Man*, p. 95
57. *Ibid.*, p. 175
58. Frankl, *Man's Search for Meaning*, p. 33
59. Greif, *Wept without Tears*, p. vii
60. Roseman, *Villa*, p. 2
61. *Ibid.*, pp. 116–17
62. Roger Moorhouse, *BBC History*, 9/2003, p. 53
63. ed. Taylor, *Goebbels Diaries*, p. 77
64. Dederichs, *Heydrich*, p. 144

65. ed. Trevor-Roper, *Hitler's Table Talk*, p. 512
66. Dederichs, *Heydrich*, p. 154
67. eds Bartoszewski and Polonsky, *Jews in Warsaw*, p. 338
68. *Ibid.*, p. 342
69. David Cesarani, *BBC History*, 2/2002, p. 38
70. Eichmann diary, 6 September 1961, *Guardian*, 6/3/2000
71. Rubinstein, *Myth of Rescue*, pp. 160–61, 163
72. *Ibid.*, p. 161
73. *Ibid.*, p. 163
74. Kitchens, 'Bombing of Auschwitz', pp. 259–61
75. Rubinstein, *Myth of Rescue*, p. 177
76. Stanley, *World War II Photo Intelligence*, p. 348
77. Gilbert, *Auschwitz and the Allies*, p. 305
78. NA FO371/42817 WR 993, 1/9/1944
79. Gilbert, *Auschwitz and the Allies*, p. 303
80. *Ibid.*, p. 308
81. Friedländer, *Years of Extermination*, p. 472
82. *Ibid.*

8: FIVE MINUTES AT MIDWAY

1. Fuchida and Okumiya, *Midway*, p. 177
2. ed. Wright, *World at Arms*, pp. 162–3
3. Prange, *Miracle at Midway*, p. 145
4. ed. Young, *Decisive Battles*, p. 152
5. *Ibid.*, p. 153
6. *Ibid.*
7. *Ibid.*, p. 156
8. Fuchida and Okumiya, *Midway*, p. 177
9. *Ibid.*, p. 181
10. ed. Young, *Decisive Battles*, p. 156
11. Dupuy and Dupuy, *Encyclopedia*, p. 1256
12. *Ibid.*, p. 1255
13. Hastings, *Nemesis*, p. 26
14. Prange, *Miracle at Midway*, p. 395
15. BRGS 2/12
16. ed. Dear, *Oxford Companion*, p. 515
17. ed. Wright, *World at Arms*, p. 346
18. ed. Parrish, *Simon & Schuster*, p. 251

19. Dupuy and Dupuy, *Encyclopedia*, p. 1250
20. ed. Wright, *World at Arms*, p. 350
21. Hastings, *Nemesis*, p. xviii
22. See the *TLS* debate following John Keegan's review of Trevor Royle's biography of Wingate, 16/6/1995 and subsequent weeks
23. KENN 4/2/5
24. Calvert, *Prisoners of Hope*, p. 12
25. Allen, *Burma*, p. 127
26. *Ibid.*, p. 138 n. 3
27. *Ibid.*, p. 143
28. Fergusson, *Beyond the Chindwin*, p. 240
29. Sykes, *Wingate*, p. 522
30. Such as Calvert, *Prisoners of Hope* and *Chindits*; Fergusson, *Beyond the Chindwin*; Masters, *Road Past Mandalay*; James, *Chindit*
31. Fraser, *Quartered Safe*, p. 130
32. Masters, *Road Past Mandalay*, p. 278
33. Hastings, *Nemesis*, p. 440
34. Allen, *Burma*, p. 662
35. Mackenzie, *All Over the Place*, p. 77
36. ed. Dear, *Oxford Companion*, p. 176
37. Allen, *Burma*, p. 228
38. The numbers vary: see Allen, *Burma*, p. 234 n. 1, and ed. Dear, *Oxford Companion*, pp. 653–4 for other estimations
39. Allen, *Burma*, p. 232
40. *Ibid.*, p. 237
41. Campbell, *Siege*, p. 81
42. Allen, *Burma*, p. 236
43. Swinson, *Kohima*, p. 151
44. ed. Prasad, *Reconquest of Burma*, p. 279
45. Allen, *Burma*, p. 238
46. Brett-James, *Ball of Fire*, p. 320
47. Swinson, *Kohima*, p. 151
48. ed. Dear, *Oxford Companion*, p. 654
49. Allen, *Burma*, p. 74
50. Dupuy and Dupuy, *Encyclopedia*, p. 1278; ed. Dear, *Oxford Companion*, p. 177
51. Allen, *Burma*, p. 74
52. ed. Cameron Watt, *Mein Kampf*, p. 601
53. Figures vary, but see Chang, *Rape of Nanking*, *passim*
54. Ferguson, *War of the World*, p. 497

55. Harvey, *American Shogun*, p. 236
56. See in particular Rees, *Horror in the East*; Williams and Wallace, *Unit 731*; MacArthur, *Surviving the Sword*; Ferguson, *War of the World*; Rawlings, *And the Dawn*
57. Felton, *Slaughter at Sea*, pp. 124–36, 145
58. *Ibid.*, p. 132
59. *Ibid.*, pp. 124–36
60. *Ibid.*, pp. 140–44
61. *Ibid.*, p. 148
62. *Ibid.*, p. 151
63. *Ibid.*, p. 172
64. *Ibid.*, pp. 173–4
65. *Ibid.*, p. 174
66. *Ibid.*, p. 176

9: MIDNIGHT IN THE DEVIL'S GARDENS

1. Richardson, *From Churchill's Secret Circle*, p. 123
2. ed. Young, *Decisive Battles*, p. 165
3. Bierman and Smith, *Alamein*, p. 223n
4. Hamilton, *Monty: The Making of a General*, p. 48
5. Hew Strachan, *TLS*, 12/10/2001, p. 26
6. Bierman and Smith, *Alamein*, p. 232
7. Ellis, *Brute Force*, p. 261
8. M. R. D. Foot, *Spectator*, 5/4/2003, p. 40
9. Ellis, *Brute Force*, p. 260
10. Mellenthin, *Panzer Battles*, pp. 139–40
11. Schulman, *Defeat in the West*, p. 115
12. John Keegan, *Sunday Telegraph*, 5/10/2002, p. A4; Bierman and Smith, *Alamein*, p. 339
13. Ellis, *Brute Force*, p. 260
14. Mellenthin, *Panzer Battles*, p. 141n
15. Bierman and Smith, *Alamein*, p. 232
16. Atkinson, *Army at Dawn*, pp. 376–7
17. Chant, *Code Names*, p. 4
18. ed. Dear, *Oxford Companion*, p. 326; ed. Young, *Decisive Battles*, p. 167
19. ed. Dear, *Oxford Companion*, p. 326; Ellis, *Brute Force*, pp. 260–64; Bierman and Smith, *Alamein*, p. 256
20. Ellis, *Brute Force*, p. 262

21. Bierman and Smith, *Alamein*, p. 265
22. Mellenthin, *Panzer Battles*, p. 142
23. Churchill, *Grand Alliance*, pp. 176–7
24. ed. Dear, *Oxford Companion*, p. 326
25. Ellis, *Brute Force*, p. 266
26. *Ibid.*, p. 267
27. ed. Liddell Hart, *Rommel Papers*, pp. 285–6
28. Carver, *El Alamein*, p. 201
29. ed. Young, *Decisive Battles*, p. 166
30. ed. Dear, *Oxford Companion*, p. 326
31. Keegan, *Second World War*, p. 336
32. Ellis, *Brute Force*, p. 264
33. Schmidt, *With Rommel*, p. 175
34. Bierman and Smith, *Alamein*, p. 282
35. *Ibid.*, p. 312
36. ed. Liddell Hart, *Rommel Papers*, p. 312
37. eds Danchev and Todman, *War Diaries*, p. 336
38. Bierman and Smith, *Alamein*, p. 311
39. Alistair Horne in ed. Roberts, *Art of War*, p. 340
40. Montgomery, *Memoirs*, pp. 138–9
41. Bierman and Smith, *Alamein*, p. 311
42. *Ibid.*, p. 325
43. ed. Tsouras, *Greenhill Dictionary*, p. 246
44. Irving, *Hitler's War*, p. 328
45. Carver, *El Alamein*, p. 204
46. ed. Liddell Hart, *Rommel Papers*, p. 315
47. Allan Mallinson, *Spectator*, 3/8/2002, p. 36
48. Carver, *El Alamein*, p. 195
49. Keegan, *Second World War*, p. 337
50. ed. Young, *Decisive Battles*, p. 182
51. Ellis, *Brute Force*, p. 264
52. Montgomery, *Memoirs*, p. 139
53. Hew Strachan, *Daily Telegraph*, 5/4/2003
54. eds Danchev and Todman, *War Diaries*, p. 250
55. Roberts, *Masters and Commanders, passim*
56. eds Danchev and Todman, *War Diaries*, p. 407
57. Royle, *Patton*, p. 95
58. Atkinson, *Army at Dawn*, p. 36
59. Royle, *Patton*, p. 34
60. Atkinson, *Army at Dawn*, pp. 33–4

61. D'Este, *Eisenhower*, p. 468
62. Atkinson, *Army at Dawn*, p. 59
63. Royle, *Patton*, p. 29
64. Atkinson, *Army at Dawn*, p. 44
65. Sainsbury, *North African Landings*, p. 149
66. *Ibid.*, p. 150
67. *Ibid.*, p. 154
68. Ian Sayer Archive
69. Max Hastings, *Sunday Telegraph*, 2/2/2003, p. 14
70. Atkinson, *Army at Dawn*, p. 57
71. ed. Kimball, *Complete Correspondence*, 1, p. 584
72. Atkinson, *Army at Dawn*, p. 28
73. Sainsbury, *North African Landings*, p. 158
74. Royle, *Patton*, p. 83
75. BRGS 2/13
76. ed. Langworth, *Churchill by Himself*, p. 347
77. Sainsbury, *North African Landings*, p. 162
78. Atkinson, *Army at Dawn*, pp. 368–9
79. *Ibid.*, p. 368
80. ed. Parrish, *Simon & Schuster*, p. 329; Max Hastings, *Sunday Telegraph*, 2/2/2003, p. 14; Atkinson, *Army at Dawn*, p. 389; Dupuy and Dupuy, *Encyclopedia*, p. 1197; Sainsbury, *North African Landings*, p. 164
81. Atkinson, *Army at Dawn*, p. 383
82. *Ibid.*, p. 384
83. *Ibid.*, p. 385
84. Butcher, *Three Years*, p. 231
85. Bradley, *Soldier's Story*, p. 43
86. Blumenson, *Patton Papers*, pp. 187–90
87. D'Este, *Genius for War*, p. 484
88. M. R. D. Foot, *Spectator*, 5/4/2003, p. 40
89. Hew Strachan, *Daily Telegraph*, 5/4/2003; Atkinson, *Army at Dawn*, p. 3
90. Churchill, *Onwards to Victory*, p. 99

10: THE MOTHERLAND OVERWHELMS THE FATHERLAND

1. Bellamy, *Absolute War*, p. 526
2. Clark, *Barbarossa*, p. 316
3. Carruthers and Erickson, *Russian Front*, p. 99

4. eds Burdick and Jacobsen, *Halder War Diary*, p. 645
5. Liddell Hart, *Other Side*, p. 51
6. eds Burdick and Jacobsen, *Halder War Diary*, p. 649
7. Paulus Museum, Volgograd
8. eds Beevor and Vinogradova, *Writer at War*, p. 123
9. Grossman, *Life and Fate*, p. 23
10. Chuikov, *Beginning of the Road*, p. 154
11. Grossman, *Life and Fate*, p. 19
12. Bellamy, *Absolute War*, p. 514
13. eds Beevor and Vinogradova, *Writer at War*, p. 145
14. Chuikov, *Beginning of the Road*, p. 173
15. eds Beevor and Vinogradova, *Writer at War*, p. 139
16. Grossman, *Life and Fate*, p. 39
17. eds Beevor and Vinogradova, *Writer at War*, p. 135
18. Bellamy, *Absolute War*, p. 515; M. R. D. Foot, *The Times*, 16/4/1998
19. Axell, *Zhukov*
20. eds Burdick and Jacobsen, *Halder War Diary*, p. 664
21. *Ibid.*, p. 667
22. ed. Dear, *Oxford Companion*, p. 1057
23. Bellamy, *Absolute War*, p. 515
24. eds Beevor and Vinogradova, *Writer at War*, p. 139
25. Bellamy, *Absolute War*, pp. 523–4
26. eds Beevor and Vinogradova, *Writer at War*, p. 141
27. Chuikov, *Beginning of the Road*, p. 175
28. eds Beevor and Vinogradova, *Writer at War*, p. 163
29. Chuikov, *Beginning of the Road*, p. 152
30. eds Burdick and Jacobsen, *Halder War Diary*, p. 670
31. *Ibid.*, p. 671
32. Goldensohn, *Nuremberg Interviews*, p. 294
33. Chuikov, *Beginning of the Road*, pp. 167–9
34. *Ibid.*, p. 165
35. eds Beevor and Vinogradova, *Writer at War*, p. 177
36. Chuikov, *Beginning of the Road*, pp. 171–2, 240
37. eds Beevor and Vinogradova, *Writer at War*, p. 175
38. John Erickson preface to ed. Krivosheev, *Soviet Casualties*, p. ix; Braithwaite, *Moscow 1941*, pp. 111–13
39. Braithwaite, *Moscow 1941*, pp. 111–13
40. Chuikov, *Beginning of the Road*, p. 159
41. Beevor, *Stalingrad*, p. 198
42. Chuikov, *Beginning of the Road*, p. 158

43. *Ibid.*
44. Bellamy, *Absolute War*, p. 517
45. *Ibid.*, pp. 511–12
46. Chuikov, *Beginning of the Road*, p. 211
47. eds Burdick and Jacobsen, *Halder War Diary*, p. 345
48. Bellamy, *Absolute War*, p. 533
49. *Ibid.*
50. Thames TV, *The World at War*, Part Two, Disc 1
51. ed. Dear, *Oxford Companion*, p. 1059
52. Clark, *Barbarossa*, p. 321
53. Bellamy, *Absolute War*, p. 536
54. Goldensohn, *Nuremberg Interviews*, p. 355
55. eds Freidin and Richardson, *Fatal Decisions*, p. 165
56. Ian Sayer Archive
57. Mellenthin, *Panzer Battles*, p. 183
58. Chuikov, *Beginning of the Road*, pp. 207, 236
59. eds Beevor and Vinogradova, *Writer at War*, p. 198
60. eds Heiber and Glantz, *Hitler and his Generals*, pp. 27–8
61. Manstein, *Lost Victories*, Appendix 1, p. 554
62. Clark, *Barbarossa*, p. 321; Dupuy and Dupuy, *Encyclopedia*, p. 1192; see Mellenthin, *Panzer Battles*, p. 184 for slightly larger estimates
63. Thames TV, *The World at War*, Part Two, Disc 1
64. Mellenthin, *Panzer Battles*, p. 185
65. Clark, *Barbarossa*, p. 321
66. *Ibid.*, pp. 321–2
67. Chuikov, *Beginning of the Road*, p. 254
68. Mellenthin, *Panzer Battles*, p. 194
69. Clark, *Barbarossa*, p. 323
70. Beevor, *Stalingrad*, p. 354
71. ed. Tsouras, *Greenhill Dictionary*, p. 464
72. eds Heiber and Glantz, *Hitler and his Generals*, p. 59
73. Historians dispute the exact figures: see Beevor, *Stalingrad*, Appendix B; Dupuy and Dupuy, *Encyclopedia*, p. 1202; Bellamy, *Absolute War*, p. 550; Mellenthin, *Panzer Battles*, p. 183; ed. Parrish, *Simon & Schuster*, p. 600
74. Bellamy, *Absolute War*, p. 550
75. Chuikov, *Beginning of the Road*, p. 359
76. John Erickson preface to ed. Krivosheev, *Soviet Casualties*, p. ix
77. Beevor, *Stalingrad*, pp. 184, 384–5
78. eds Freidin and Richardson, *Fatal Decisions*, p. 165
79. Nigel Nicolson, *Spectator*, 2/5/1998, p. 34

80. Domarus, *Essential Hitler*, pp. 767–8
81. Lacouture, *De Gaulle: The Ruler*, p. 47

11: THE WAVES OF AIR AND SEA

1. ed. Langworth, *Churchill by Himself*, p. 304
2. BBC, *Desert Island Discs*, 28/3/1988
3. Bennett, *Behind the Battle*, pp. 75, 241–2
4. *The Times*, 24/10/2008, p. 47
5. For a full explanation for how these worked, read Budiansky, *Battle of Wits* and Sebag Montefiore, *Enigma*
6. Lewin, *ULTRA Goes to War*, p. 14
7. Sebag Montefiore, *Enigma*, pp. 296–7
8. Bennett, *Behind the Battle*, p. xix n. 1
9. Budiansky, *Battle of Wits*, p. 207
10. Sebag Montefiore, *Enigma*, p. 297
11. Budiansky, *Battle of Wits*, p. 207; Hinsley, *British Intelligence*, II, p. 174
12. Sebag Montefiore, *Enigma*, p. 359
13. Bennett, *Behind the Battle*, pp. 75, 241–2
14. Ellis, *Brute Force*, p. 133
15. Churchill, *Their Finest Hour*, p. 529
16. Ellis, *Brute Force*, p. 133
17. *Ibid.*, p. 134; ed. Young, *Decisive Battles*, p. 223
18. Churchill, *Hinge of Fate*, p. 107
19. ed. Showell, *Fuehrer Conferences*, p. viii
20. Padfield, *War beneath the Sea*, p. 10
21. Kennedy, *Pursuit*, p. 22
22. ed. Dear, *Oxford Companion*, p. 905
23. Evans, *Third Reich at War*, p. 480
24. ed. Trevor-Roper, *Hitler's War Directives*, pp. 102–3
25. Ellis, *Brute Force*, p. 143
26. Kennedy, *Pursuit*, p. 54
27. Holmes, *World at War*, pp. 88–9
28. Monsarrat, *Cruel Sea*, p. 259
29. *Ibid.*, p. 277
30. ed. Young, *Decisive Battles*, p. 223
31. Evans, *Third Reich at War*, p. 481; see ed. Young, *Decisive Battles*, p. 223 for larger figures
32. Ellis, *Brute Force*, pp. 146–7

33. Bennett, *Behind the Battle*, p. 180

34. Kennedy, *Pursuit*, p. 24

35. Holmes, *World at War*, pp. 88–9

36. Monsarrat, *Cruel Sea*, pp. 139–40

37. Ministry of Information, *What Britain Has Done*, p. 51

38. Churchill, *Grand Alliance*, p. 107

39. Kennedy, *Pursuit*, pp. 24–5

40. *Ibid.*, p. 85

41. Wheal and Pope, *Dictionary*, p. 58

42. Kennedy, *Pursuit*, p. 86

43. Wheal and Pope, *Dictionary*, p. 58

44. Bennett, *Behind the Battle*, p. 66

45. ed. Trevor-Roper, *Hitler's Table Talk*, p. 708

46. Bennett, *Behind the Battle*, p. 66

47. *Ibid.*, p. 181

48. Monsarrat, *Cruel Sea*, p. 369

49. *Ibid.*

50. NA War Cabinet Minutes WM (42) 124th Meeting, p. 148

51. Bennett, *Behind the Battle*, p. 174

52. Ellis, *Brute Force*, p. 147n

53. Bennett, *Behind the Battle*, p. 184

54. Holmes, *World at War*, pp. 168, 229

55. Evans, *Third Reich at War*, p. 481

56. Budiansky, *Battle of Wits*, pp. 284–6

57. Bennett, *Behind the Battle*, p. 194

58. Budiansky, *Battle of Wits*, pp. 285–6

59. Holmes, *World at War*, pp. 168, 229

60. BRGS 2/15

61. ed. Young, *Decisive Battles*, p. 238

62. *Ibid.*, p. 239

63. ed. Showell, *Fuehrer Conferences*, p. 331; ed. Young, *Decisive Battles*, p. 224

64. ed. Showell, *Fuehrer Conferences*, p. 334

65. Evans, *Third Reich at War*, pp. 327–8

66. Bennett, *Behind the Battle*, p. 197

67. Monsarrat, *Cruel Sea*, p. 259

68. Padfield, *War beneath the Sea*, p. 374

69. Donald Michie, *Spectator*, 25/2/2006, p. 39

70. Watkins, *Cracking the Luftwaffe Codes*, p. 19

71. Holmes, *World at War*, pp. 167, 229–30; Ellis, *Brute Force*, p. 144; Bennett, *Behind the Battle*, p. 182

72. ed. Young, *Decisive Battles*, p. 224
73. Ellis, *Brute Force*, p. 157, table 6
74. *Ibid.*, p. 158

12: UP THE WASP-WAIST PENINSULA

1. Churchill, *Dawn of Liberation*, p. 86
2. Clark, *Anzio*, p. 13
3. Dupuy and Dupuy, *Encyclopedia*, p. 1199
4. Bryant, *Turn of the Tide*, p. 26
5. Clark, *Anzio*, p. 26
6. D'Este, *Genius for War*, pp. 532–5
7. MHI Hull Papers SOOHP, pp. 58–9
8. Clark, *Anzio*, p. 23
9. ed. Lochner, *Goebbels Diaries*, p. 371
10. Kesselring, *A Soldier's Record*, pp. 229–30; Porch, *Hitler's Mediterranean Gamble*, p. 507
11. Moseley, *Mussolini*, p. 131
12. Winton, *Cunningham*, pp. 328–9
13. Clark, *Anzio*, p. 24
14. *Ibid.*
15. Dupuy and Dupuy, *Encyclopedia*, p. 1200
16. Clark, *Anzio*, p. 230
17. Porch, *Hitler's Mediterranean Gamble*, p. 518
18. Holmes, *World at War*, p. 442
19. ed. Dear, *Oxford Companion*, p. 574
20. Clark, *Anzio*, p. 41
21. Harris, *Swordpoint*, p. 15
22. Porch, *Hitler's Mediterranean Gamble*, p. 507
23. Holmes, *World at War*, p. 457
24. Harris, *Swordpoint*, p. 12
25. Phillips, *Sangro to Cassino*
26. Clark, *Calculated Risk*
27. Majdalany, *Cassino*
28. ed. Young, *Decisive Battles*, p. 254
29. Holmes, *World at War*, p. 448
30. Clark, *Anzio*, p. 212
31. *Ibid.*, p. 50
32. NA FO 371/43869/21

33. Noel, *Pius* XII, *passim*
34. ed. Young, *Decisive Battles*, p. 250
35. *Ibid.*
36. *Ibid.*, pp. 261–3
37. *Ibid.*, p. 250
38. Clark, *Anzio*, p. 96
39. *Ibid.*, p. 76
40. Churchill, *Closing the Ring*, p. 426
41. Clark, *Anzio*, p. 76
42. *Ibid.*, p. 70
43. Dupuy and Dupuy, *Encyclopedia*, p. 1207; Clark, *Anzio*, pp. xxiii, 188
44. Ross, *Memoirs*, p. 209
45. BRGS 2/19
46. Clark, *Anzio*, p. 183
47. *Ibid.*, p. 219
48. Trevelyan, *Fortress*, p. 65
49. Clark, *Anzio*, p. 208
50. Churchill, *Closing the Ring*, p. 432
51. Barker, *Seven Steps Down*, p. 72
52. ed. Parrish, *Simon & Schuster*, pp. 310–11; Clark, *Anzio*, p. 274
53. Clark, *Anzio*, p. 281
54. *Ibid.*, p. 287
55. D'Este, *Fatal Decision*, p. 371
56. Truscott, *Command Missions*, p. 375
57. Trevelyan, *Rome '44*, p. 303
58. Holmes, *World at War*, p. 457
59. Clark, *Anzio*, p. 317; Trevelyan, *Rome '44*, p. 316
60. ed. Dear, *Oxford Companion*, p. 578
61. Dupuy and Dupuy, *Encyclopedia*, p. 1223
62. ed. Dear, *Oxford Companion*, pp. 579–80
63. ed. Parrish, *Simon & Schuster*, p. 313
64. Howard, *Captain Professor*, p. 155
65. ed. Lochner, *Goebbels Diaries*, p. 361
66. Stafford, *Endgame 1945*, pp. 189–91
67. *London Gazette*, 8/8/1944

13: A SALIENT REVERSAL

1. Cornish, *Images of Kursk*, p. 7
2. Dupuy and Dupuy, *Encyclopedia*, p. 1202
3. ed. Barnett, *Hitler's Generals*, p. 222
4. *Ibid.*, p. 221
5. Dupuy and Dupuy, *Encyclopedia*, p. 1202
6. Bellamy, *Absolute War*, p. 444
7. Clark, *Barbarossa*, p. 338
8. Keegan, *Second World War*, p. 458
9. Clark, *Barbarossa*, p. 362
10. Mellenthin, *Panzer Battles*, p. 212
11. Guderian, *Panzer Leader*, p. 309
12. Clark, *Barbarossa*, p. 364
13. Glantz and House, *Battle of Kursk*, p. 362
14. Chaney, *Zhukov*, p. 252
15. Clark, *Barbarossa*, p. 365
16. Carruthers and Erickson, *Russian Front*, p. 137
17. Clark, *Barbarossa*, p. 365
18. Hart, *German Soldier*, p. 138
19. Mellenthin, *Panzer Battles*, p. 226
20. *Ibid.*, p. 213
21. *Ibid.*, p. 214
22. Clark, *Barbarossa*, p. 367
23. Mellenthin, *Panzer Battles*, p. 213
24. BRGS 2/17
25. Clark, *Barbarossa*, p. 370
26. *Ibid.*, p. 367
27. Mellenthin, *Panzer Battles*, p. 226
28. ed. Parrish, *Simon & Schuster*, p. 350; eds Beevor and Vinogradova, *Writer at War*, p. 228
29. ed. Dear, *Oxford Companion*, p. 660
30. Simonov, *Days and Nights*, p. 5
31. Cross, *Citadel*, p. 193
32. Hart, *German Soldier*, p. 138
33. *Ibid.*, p. 139
34. Clark, *Barbarossa*, p. 368
35. Guderian, *Panzer Leader*, p. 311
36. ed. Dear, *Oxford Companion*, p. 660
37. Cross, *Citadel*, p. 204

38. *Ibid.*, p. 195

39. *Ibid.*, p. 205; ed. Dear, *Oxford Companion*, p. 660. See also Glantz and House, *Battle of Kursk*, Appendix D; Bellamy, *Absolute War*, p. 583

40. Keegan, *Second World War*, p. 469, quoting John Erickson

41. Carruthers and Erickson, *Russian Front*, p. 135

42. Clark, *Barbarossa*, p. 376

43. eds Beevor and Vinogradova, *Writer at War*, p. 231

44. Keegan, *Second World War*, p. 469, quoting John Erickson

45. ed. Young, *Atlas*, p. 204

46. Gilbert, *Second World War*, p. 442 for eight; Bellamy, *Absolute War*, p. 581 for nine

47. Bellamy, *Absolute War*, pp. 554–95

48. ed. Dear, *Oxford Companion*, p. 660; eds Beevor and Vinogradova, *Writer at War*, p. 231

49. Bellamy, *Absolute War*, p. 583; Keegan, *Second World War*, p. 469, quoting John Erickson; Gilbert, *Second World War*, p. 442

50. Gilbert, *Second World War*, p. 471

51. Mellenthin, *Panzer Battles*, p. 229

52. Liddell Hart, *Other Side*, p. 74

53. Mellenthin, *Panzer Battles*, p. 225

54. Keegan, *Second World War*, p. 454; eds Beevor and Vinogradova, *Writer at War*, p. 242

55. Glantz and House, *Battle of Kursk*, p. 252

56. Overy, *Russia's War*, p. 257

57. Glantz and House, *Battle of Kursk*, p. 280

58. Dupuy and Dupuy, *Encyclopedia*, p. 1203; Bellamy, *Absolute War*, p. 594

59. Mellenthin, *Panzer Battles*, p. 225

60. Bellamy, *Absolute War*, p. 587

61. Keegan, *Second World War*, p. 466

14: THE CRUEL REALITY

1. Speer, *Inside the Third Reich*, p. 288

2. For criticisms of the policy see Hastings, *Bomber Command*; Friedrich, *Fire*; Grayling, *Among the Dead Cities*. For the defence see Bishop, *Bomber Boys*; Miller, *Eighth Air Force*; Webster and Frankland, *Strategic Air Offensive*

3. Hansard, 10/11/1932

4. Lewis, *Aircrew*, p. 14

5. Overy, *Why the Allies Won*, p. 107
6. Roberts, *Holy Fox*, p. 177
7. Donald Cameron Watt, *Literary Review*, 12/2001, p. 34
8. Neil Gregor, *BBC History*, 4/2001, p. 7, and *Historical Journal*, XLIII, no. 4
9. Overy, *Why the Allies Won*, p. 133
10. Bishop, *Bomber Boys*, p. 385
11. LH 15/15/26
12. Alex Danchev, *TLS*, 28/12/2001, p. 7
13. Probert, *Bomber Harris*, p. 291
14. *History Today*, 3/2005, p. 51
15. Portal Box A File II
16. ed. Parrish, *Simon & Schuster*, p. 74
17. Bishop, *Bomber Boys*, p. 169
18. *Ibid.*, p. 167
19. Miller, *Eighth Air Force*, illustration no. 29
20. Wyllie Archive
21. BRGS 2/12
22. KENN 4/2/4
23. *History Today*, 3/2005, p. 50
24. BRGS 2/12
25. Speer, *Inside the Third Reich*, p. 279
26. Overy, *Why the Allies Won*, pp. 117–18
27. Webster and Frankland, *Strategic Air Offensive*, IV, pp. 273–83
28. Chant, *Codenames*, p. 191
29. Arthur, *Dambusters*, p. xi
30. Tooze, *Wages of Destruction*, p. 600
31. *Ibid.*, p. 671
32. Bishop, *Bomber Boys*, p. 371
33. Overy, *Why the Allies Won*, p. 131
34. *Ibid.*, p. 121
35. Lowe, *Inferno, passim*; Wheal and Pope, *Dictionary*, p. 448; ed. Parrish, *Simon & Schuster*, p. 606; Holmes, *World at War*
36. Speer, *Inside the Third Reich*, p. 284
37. ed. Lochner, *Goebbels Diaries*, p. 320
38. Miller, *Eighth Air Force*, pp. 192–208
39. Speer, *Inside the Third Reich*, p. 290
40. Gerhard L. Weinberg in eds Deutsch and Showalter, *What If?*, p. 206
41. Below, *At Hitler's Side, passim*
42. Gerhard L. Weinberg in eds Deutsch and Showalter, *What If?*, p. 207

43. Speer, *Inside the Third Reich*, pp. 288–9
44. Overy, *Why the Allies Won*, p. 5; Wheal and Pope, *Dictionary*, p. 448
45. Gregor, *Haunted City, passim*
46. Feast, *Master Bombers, passim*
47. MARS Pentagon Papers Box 81/2
48. Portal Box A File IV
49. *Ibid.*
50. Cunningham Add Mss 52577/20
51. Probert, *Bomber Harris*, p. 291
52. Cunningham Add Mss 52577/2
53. Cunningham Add Mss 52577/6
54. BRGS 2/21
55. BRGS 2/22
56. Gilbert, *Second World War*, p. 440
57. Wheal and Pope, *Dictionary*, p. 448
58. Interview with Hugh Lunghi
59. *Ibid.*, p. 14
60. Taylor, *Dresden, passim*
61. *The Times*, 7/2/2004, books section, p. 13
62. Vonnegut, *Slaughterhouse Five*, p. 109
63. *Ibid.*, p. 157
64. *Daily Telegraph*, 3/10/2008, p. 17
65. Simon Heffer, *Literary Review*, 2/2004, p. 28
66. Robin Neillands, *BBC History*, 2/2003, p. 45
67. Taylor, *Dresden*, p. 4
68. Portal File 6 Box 14
69. Probert, *Bomber Harris*, p. 322
70. ed. Parrish, *Simon & Schuster*, p. 74
71. Norman Stone, *Literary Review*, 10/2008, p. 18
72. Overy, *Why the Allies Won*, pp. 117–18
73. *Ibid.*, p. 131
74. *Ibid.*, p. 129
75. Speer, *Inside the Third Reich*, p. 278
76. *Ibid.*, p. 279

15: NORMAN CONQUEST

1. ed. Kimball, *Complete Correspondence*, II, p. 557
2. Alistair Horne, *History Today*, 1/2002, p. 57
3. eds Love and Major, *Bertram Ramsay*, p. 83
4. Below, *At Hitler's Side*, p. 184
5. eds Heiber and Glantz, *Hitler and his Generals*, p. 139
6. Liddell Hart, *Other Side*, p. 246
7. *Ibid.*
8. Hesketh, *Fortitude*, p. x
9. Overy, *How the Allies Won*, p. 151
10. Gilbert, *D-Day*, p. 81
11. Stafford, *Ten Days to D-Day*, pp. 332–3
12. Ellis, *Brute Force*, p. 360
13. ed. Parrish, *Simon & Schuster*, p. 297
14. For the gestation of the plans, see Roberts, *Masters and Commanders*, *passim*
15. eds Danchev and Todman, *War Diaries*, p. 554
16. Gilbert, *Churchill: A Life*, p. 776
17. Maggs Brothers catalogue, *Autograph Letters*, No. 1427 Item 124
18. Arthur, *Forgotten Voices*, p. 115
19. *Ibid.*, p. 116
20. Ellis, *Brute Force*, p. 360
21. Holmes, *World at War*, p. 463
22. D'Este, *Eisenhower*, p. 527
23. Hesketh, *Fortitude*, pp. 186–8
24. Nicholas Rankin, *TLS*, 23/1/2004, p. 12
25. Howard and Bates, *Pegasus Diaries*, p. 119
26. *Ibid.*, p. 136
27. ed. Penrose, *D-Day Companion*, p. 225
28. ed. Liddell Hart, *Rommel Papers*, pp. 476–7
29. MHI German Report series, Foreign Military Studies, MSS B-720
30. Kershaw, *Hitler: Nemesis*, pp. 639–40
31. Liddell Hart, *Other Side*, p. 248
32. Hastings, *Overlord*, p. 88
33. *Ibid.*, p. 89
34. ed. Penrose, *D-Day Companion*, p. 223
35. Gilbert, *D-Day*, p. 85
36. Arthur, *Forgotten Voices*, p. 117
37. Gilbert, *D-Day*, p. 145

38. Hastings, *Overlord*, p. 95
39. Gilbert, *D-Day*, pp. 146–7
40. ed. Parrish, *Simon & Schuster*, p. 303; Gilbert, *D-Day*, p. 148
41. Weinberg, *World at Arms*, p. 688
42. ed. Parrish, *Simon & Schuster*, p. 304
43. *Ibid.*
44. Dupuy and Dupuy, *Encyclopedia*, p. 1211
45. Liddell Hart, *Second World War*, p. 568
46. Ian Sayer Archive
47. Gilbert, *Second World War*, p. 536
48. Hastings, Das Reich section in *On the Offensive*, p. 247
49. ed. Trevor-Roper, *Hitler's Table Talk*, p. 639
50. *Ibid.*, pp. 451–5
51. *Ibid.*, p. 340
52. Holmes, *World at War*, pp. 167, 241
53. *TLS, Essays and Reviews 1963*, p. 197
54. Irving, *Hitler's War*, pp. 662–4
55. Ian Sayer Archive
56. The 2009 movie *Valkyrie*, starring Tom Cruise, was a classic recent manifestation of this
57. Hastings, *Armageddon*, p. 201
58. Roger Moorhouse, *History Today*, 1/2009, p. 3
59. Roberts, *Dealing with Dictators*, p. 51
60. ed. Dilks, *Cadogan Diary*, p. 129
61. For an opposing view, see Joachim Fest's *Plotting Hitler's Death*, which has taken the argument even further than the earlier works of Patricia Meehan (*The Unnecessary War*, 1992) and Klemens von Klemperer (*German Resistance against Hitler: The Search for Allies Abroad*, 1993)
62. BRGS 2/21
63. Cunningham Add Mss 52577/50
64. Royle, *Patton*, p. 136
65. Williams, *D-Day to Berlin*, p. 200
66. Royle, *Patton*, pp. 139–41; Dupuy and Dupuy, *Encyclopedia*, p. 1212
67. Gilbert, *D-Day*, p. 180
68. Tobias Gray, *History Today*, 8/2008, p. 6
69. ed. Langhorne, *Churchill by Himself*, p. 572
70. Egremont, *Under Two Flags*, p. 180
71. Lacouture, *De Gaulle: The Rebel*, p. 578

16: WESTERN APPROACHES

1. Churchill, *Dawn of Liberation*, p. 189
2. Hastings, *Armageddon*, p. 200
3. Ian Kershaw's Foreword to ed. Neitzel, *Tapping Hitler's Generals*, pp. 7–11
4. ed. Neitzel, *Tapping Hitler's Generals, passim*
5. *Ibid.*, p. 169
6. *Ibid.*, p. 205
7. *Ibid.*, p. 207
8. *Ibid.*, p. 219
9. *Ibid.*, p. 222
10. *Ibid.*, p. 228
11. Goldensohn, *Nuremberg Interviews*, p. 347
12. Royle, *Patton*, p. 151
13. Ian Sayer Archive
14. Royle, *Patton*, p. 150
15. Eisenhower, *Crusade in Europe*, pp. 225–9
16. D'Este, *Genius for War*, pp. 602–3
17. Ian Sayer Archive
18. White, *With the Jocks*, p. viii
19. BRGS 2/22
20. NA War Cabinet Meeting WM (45) 29
21. Gilbert, *Second World War*, p. 585
22. Churchill, *Dawn of Liberation*, pp. 188–9
23. Middlebrook, *Arnhem*, p. 443
24. *Ibid.*, p. 444
25. *Ibid.*, p. 439; ed. Parrish, *Simon & Schuster*, p. 680; Dupuy and Dupuy, *Encyclopedia*, p. 1215
26. Grant, *World War II: Europe*, p. 44
27. Hamilton, *Monty: The Field Marshal*, p. 181
28. General Strong's personal copy from the Ian Sayer Archive
29. eds Freidin and Richardson, *Fatal Decisions*, p. 225
30. Sayer and Botting, *Hitler's Last General*, p. 347
31. ed. Parrish, *Simon & Schuster*, pp. 88–9
32. Weintraub, *Eleven Days*, p. xiii
33. Royle, *Patton*, p. 166
34. Bradley, *General's Life*, p. 367
35. Royle, *Patton*, p. 169
36. Dupuy and Dupuy, *Encyclopedia*, p. 1218

37. Delaforce, *Battle of the Bulge*
38. Jablonsky, *Churchill and Hitler*, p. 194
39. Goldensohn, *Nuremberg Interviews*, p. 167
40. Whiting, *Field Marshal's Revenge*, p. ix
41. *Ibid.*, p. 222
42. Andrew Taylor, *TLS* 2005; Royle, *Patton*, p. 196
43. Weintraub, *Eleven Days*, p. 177; ed. Parrish, *Simon & Schuster*, p. 91; Dupuy and Dupuy, Encyclopedia, p. 1218
44. Weintraub, *Eleven Days*, p. 177; ed. Parrish, *Simon & Schuster*, p. 91; Dupuy and Dupuy, *Encyclopedia*, p. 1218
45. Hastings, *Armageddon*, p. 263
46. Davidson, *Trial of the Germans*
47. Goldensohn, *Nuremberg Interviews*, p. 131
48. Wheeler-Bennett, *Nemesis of Power*, pp. 429–30
49. Gilbert, *Second World War*, p. 386
50. Goldensohn, *Nuremberg Interviews*, p. 334
51. *Ibid.*, p. 166
52. eds Heiber and Glantz, *Hitler and his Generals*, pp. 615–16
53. Speer, *Inside the Third Reich*, p. 426
54. Ibid.
55. Hastings, *Armageddon*, p. 421
56. Weintraub, *Eleven Days*, p. 178
57. BRGS 2/23
58. eds Heiber and Glantz, *Hitler and his Generals*, p. 188
59. eds Deutsch and Showalter, *What If?*, pp. 204–6

17: EASTERN APPROACHES

1. Beevor, *Berlin*, p. 11
2. Hastings, *Armageddon*, p. 111
3. Below, *At Hitler's Side*, p. 184
4. Gerhard L. Weinberg in eds Deutsch and Showalter, *What If?*, p. 215
5. Carruthers and Erickson, *Russian Front*, p. 151
6. Beevor, *Berlin*, pp. 94–5
7. Carruthers and Erickson, *Russian Front*, p. 151
8. Dupuy and Dupuy, *Encyclopedia*, p. 1204
9. Clark, *Barbarossa*, p. 372
10. Mellenthin, *Panzer Battles*, p. 236
11. Bullock, *Hitler*, p. 657

12. Goldensohn, *Nuremberg Interviews*, pp. 345–6
13. Clark, *Barbarossa*, p. 374
14. Roberts, *Stalin's Wars*, p. 165
15. Information from Lieutenant-Colonel Alexandr Kulikov, 8/6/2008
16. eds Burdick and Jacobsen, *Halder War Diary*, p. 309
17. Information from Lieutenant-Colonel Alexandr Kulikov, 8/6/2008
18. Mellenthin, *Panzer Battles*, p. 266n
19. Dupuy and Dupuy, *Encyclopedia*, p. 1220
20. Hastings, *Armageddon*, p. 111
21. Carruthers and Erickson, *Russian Front*, p. 130
22. Goldensohn, *Nuremberg Interviews*, p. 356
23. *Ibid.*, pp. 346–7
24. *Ibid.*, p. 347
25. Carruthers and Erickson, *Russian Front*, pp. 158–9
26. Edward Harrison, *Spectator*, 29/11/2008, p. 52
27. Hastings, Das Reich section in *On the Offensive*, p. 23
28. Overy, *Russia's War*, p. 292
29. Carruthers and Erickson, *Russian Front*, p. 158
30. Hastings, Das Reich section in *On the Offensive*, p. 23
31. Dupuy and Dupuy, *Encyclopedia*, p. 1220
32. Carruthers and Erickson, *Russian Front*, p. 156
33. Churchill, *Dawn of Liberation*, pp. 155–6
34. Mellenthin, *Panzer Battles*, p. 283
35. ed. Dear, *Oxford Companion*, p. 755
36. Mellenthin, *Panzer Battles*, p. 281
37. ed. Dear, *Oxford Companion*, p. 1261
38. *Ibid.*
39. Rees, *World War Two*, pp. 295–6
40. Bor-Komorowski, *Secret Army*, pp. 316–17
41. *Ibid.*
42. ed. Dear, *Oxford Companion*, p. 1261
43. Haupt, *Army Group Center*, p. 212
44. Davies, 'Warsaw Uprising', p. 21
45. Butler, *My Dear Mr Stalin*, p. 280
46. Overy, *Why the Allies Won*, p. 3
47. Carruthers and Erickson, *Russian Front*, p. 160
48. Hastings, *Armageddon*, p. 133
49. Carruthers and Erickson, *Russian Front*, p. 171
50. Duffy, *Red Storm*, p. 252
51. *Ibid.*, p. 261

52. Guderian, *Panzer Leader*, p. 377
53. Hastings, *Armageddon*, p. 276
54. Guderian, *Panzer Leader*, pp. 277, 305–6
55. Speer, *Inside the Third Reich*, pp. 420–21
56. Le Tissier, *Zhukov at the Oder*, p. 21
57. eds Heiber and Glantz, *Hitler and his Generals*, pp. 618–67
58. *Ibid.*, p. 651
59. *Ibid.*, p. 140
60. Hastings, *Armageddon*, p. 277
61. Gilbert, *Churchill: A Life*, p. 796
62. Butler, *My Dear Mr Stalin*, p. 314
63. NA War Cabinet Meeting WM (45) 43
64. Domarus, *Essential Hitler*, p. 369
65. *Ibid.*
66. Goldensohn, *Nuremberg Interviews*, p. 98
67. Clark, *Barbarossa*, p. 359
68. Sereny, *Speer*, *passim*
69. Douglas Porch, *TLS*, 14/1/2005, p. 23
70. Toland, *Last 100 Days*, p. 5
71. Carruthers and Erickson, *Russian Front*, pp. 174–5
72. Dupuy and Dupuy, *Encyclopedia*, p. 1228
73. Eisenhower, *Crusade in Europe*, pp. 399–402; Wilmot, *Struggle for Europe*, pp. 689–95
74. Beevor, *Berlin*, p. 324; Max Egremont, *Literary Review*, 5/2002, p. 4; Alan Judd, *Sunday Telegraph*, 27/4/2002, p. A3
75. Antony Beevor, *Sunday Telegraph* Review, 10/10/2004, p. 11
76. Beevor, *Berlin*, pp. 139, 324–5
77. ed. Dear, *Oxford Companion*, p. 681
78. Le Tissier, *Zhukov at the Oder*, p. 19
79. Guderian, *Panzer Leader*, pp. 323–6
80. Carruthers and Erickson, *Russian Front*, p. 178
81. Ian Sayer Archive
82. ed. Sayer, *Allgemeine SS*, p. 43
83. Carruthers and Erickson, *Russian Front*, p. 180
84. Le Tissier, *Battle of Berlin*, p. 107
85. Alan Judd, *Sunday Telegraph*, 27/4/2002, p. A3
86. Max Egremont, *Literary Review*, 5/2002, p. 4
87. Beevor, *Berlin*, p. 410
88. Carruthers and Erickson, *Russian Front*, p. 181
89. Simon Sebag Montefiore, *Spectator*, 20/4/2002, p. 34

90. Roberts, *Stalin's Wars*, p. 264
91. Chris Bunting, letter to *TLS*, 10/2/2006, p. 17; Kuramoto, *Manchurian Legacy, passim*
92. Lilley, *Taken by Force, passim*; John Latimer, *TLS*, 18/4/2008
93. John Erickson preface to ed. Krivosheev, *Soviet Casualties*, p. vii
94. *Ibid.*, p. ix
95. *Ibid.*
96. NA War Cabinet Minutes WM (45) 43
97. *Ibid.*
98. See Kershaw, *Hitler: Nemesis*; Trevor-Roper, *Last Days of Hitler*; Beevor, *Berlin*; Stone, *Hitler*; Toland, *Last 100 Days*; Boldt, *Hitler's Last Days*; O'Donnell, *Berlin Bunker*
99. ed. Trevor-Roper, *Hitler's Table Talk*, p. 246
100. Domarus, *Speeches and Proclamations*, p. 1388
101. Norman Stone, *Literary Review*, 10/2008, p. 18
102. Kershaw, *Hitler: Nemesis*, p. 821
103. Junge, *Until the Final Hour*, p. 184
104. Norman Stone, *Literary Review*, 10/2008, p. 18
105. Colville, *Fringes of Power*, p. 596
106. Chuikov, *End of the Third Reich*, p. 217
107. *Ibid.*, p. 241
108. *Sunday Times*, 19/3/1995, p. 21
109. Tooze, *Wages of Destruction*, p. 672
110. *Ibid.*
111. eds Vinogradov and others, *Hitler's Death*, Introduction
112. Bernard Besserglick, letter to *TLS*, 28/10/2005, p. 17

18: THE LAND OF THE SETTING SUN

1. Fraser, *Quartered Safe*, p. 201
2. Dupuy and Dupuy, *Encyclopedia*, p. 1291
3. ed. Parrish, *Simon & Schuster*, p. 380
4. Dupuy and Dupuy, *Encyclopedia*, p. 1291
5. Fraser, *Quartered Safe*, pp. 283–5
6. Victor Davis Hanson's introduction to Sledge, *With the Old Breed*, p. xxiii
7. Fraser, *Quartered Safe*, pp. 52–3
8. Dupuy and Dupuy, *Encyclopedia*, p. 1303
9. Sledge, *With the Old Breed*, p. 233
10. Dupuy and Dupuy, *Encyclopedia*, p. 1305

11. ed. Parrish, *Simon & Schuster*, p. 380
12. Fraser, *Quartered Safe*, p. 141
13. Hastings, *Nemesis*, p. 11
14. Davidson and Manning, *Chronology*, p. 249
15. De Groot, *Bomb*, p. 71; Dupuy and Dupuy, *Encyclopedia*, p. 1306
16. Victor Davis Hanson's introduction to Sledge, *With the Old Breed*, p. xxi
17. Dupuy and Dupuy, *Encyclopedia*, p. 1306
18. *Ibid.*, p. 1307
19. Hastings, *Nemesis*, p. 291
20. *Ibid.*, pp. 514–19
21. ed. Dear, *Oxford Companion*, p. 531
60822. Hersey, *Hiroshima*, pp. 65–6
23. Hastings, *Nemesis*, p. 518
24. Hersey, *Hiroshima*. p. 70
25. Penney and others, 'Nuclear Explosive Yields', pp. 357–424
26. Fraser, *Quartered Safe*, p. 323
27. Hasegawa, *Racing the Enemy*, *passim*
28. De Groot, *Bomb*, p. 101; ed. Dear, *Oxford Companion*, p. 773
29. Chinnock, *Nagasaki*, pp. 9–10
30. Hastings, *Nemesis*, p. 560
31. Warren I. Cohen, *TLS*, 19/8/2005, p. 30

CONCLUSION

1. Monsarrat, *Cruel Sea*, p. 156
2. Fraser, *Quartered Safe*, p. xiii
3. ed. Tsouras, *Greenhill Dictionary*, p. 518
4. Gilbert, *Second World War*, p. 1; Dupuy and Dupuy, *Encyclopedia*, p. 1309
5. For similar figures see, Atkinson, *Army at Dawn*, p. 5
6. Nuremberg Papers in the Ian Sayer Archive
7. ed. Dear, *Oxford Companion*, pp. 189–90
8. Ian Sayer Archive
9. Goldensohn, *Nuremberg Interviews*, *passim*; Nuremberg Papers in the Ian Sayer Archive
10. Goldensohn, *Nuremberg Interviews*, p. 1
11. *Ibid.*, p. 253
12. Max Egremont, *Literary Review*, 5/2002, p. 4
13. Ian Sayer Archive

14. Hastings, *Armageddon*, p. 130
15. Nicholas Stargardt, *TLS*, 10/10/2008, p. 9; *TLS, Essays and Reviews 1963*, pp. 197–205
16. David Cesarani, *Literary Review*, 10/2000, p. 33
17. Niall Ferguson, *Financial Times*, 13/9/2008, arts section, p. 17
18. Liddell Hart, *Other Side*, p. 168
19. Nichol and Rennell, *Tail-End Charlies*, pp. 401–2
20. Norman Stone, *Literary Review*, 10/2008, p. 18
21. eds Deutsch and Showalter, *What If?*, p. 214
22. Liddell Hart, *Other Side*, pp. 228–30; Warlimont, *Inside Hitler's Headquarters*, pp. 256–7
23. Davidson and Manning, *Chronology*, p. 238
24. Nichol and Rennell, *Tail-End Charlies*, 204
25. John Keegan, *Daily Telegraph*, 18/11/2000
26. ed. Wright, *World at Arms*, p. 174
27. Dupuy, *Genius for War*, pp. 253–5
28. Clark, *Barbarossa*, p. 41
29. Roberts, *Masters and Commanders*, *passim*
30. Dupuy and Dupuy, *Encyclopedia*, p. 1309
31. *Ibid.*
32. Adam Tooze, *TLS*, 16/11/2007, p. 12
33. NA War Cabinet Minutes WM (43) 49th Meeting, p. 141
34. Jon Latimer, *Sunday Telegraph*, 21/6/2008, books section, p. 30
35. Grigg, *1943*, p. 232
36. ed. Trevor-Roper, *Hitler's Table Talk*, p. 291

Bibliography

ARCHIVES AND PRIVATE PAPERS

General Sir Ronald Adam (Liddell Hart Centre for Military Archives, King's College, London)

Field Marshal Lord Alanbrooke (Liddell Hart Centre for Military Archives, King's College, London)

General H. H. Arnold (Library of Congress, Washington DC)

Mrs Joan Bright Astley (by kind permission of the late Mrs Astley)

Lord Avon (Birmingham University Archives)

Lord Beaverbrook (Parliamentary Archives, Palace of Westminster)

General Omar N. Bradley (Military History Institute, Carlisle, Pennsylvania)

Lawrence Burgis (Churchill Archives Centre, Cambridge University)

Sir Alexander Cadogan (Churchill Archives Centre, Cambridge University)

Neville Chamberlain (Birmingham University Archives)

Sir Winston Churchill (Churchill Archives Centre, Cambridge University)

General Mark W. Clark (Military History Institute, Carlisle, Pennsylvania)

Admiral of the Fleet Lord Cunningham (British Library)

General Jacob L. Devers (Military History Institute, Carlisle, Pennsylvania)

Field Marshal Sir John Dill (Liddell Hart Centre for Military Archives, King's College, London)

Lord Halifax (Churchill Archives Centre, Cambridge University)

Harry L. Hopkins (Franklin D. Roosevelt Presidential Library, Hyde Park)

General Lord Ismay (Liddell Hart Centre for Military Archives, King's College, London)

Lieutenant-General Sir Ian Jacob (Churchill Archives Centre, Cambridge University, and private collection by kind permission of the late Sir Ian Jacob)

Major-General Sir John Kennedy (Liddell Hart Centre for Military Archives, King's College, London)

Admiral Ernest J. King (Library of Congress, Washington DC)
Admiral William D. Leahy (Library of Congress, Washington DC)
Sir Basil Liddell Hart (Liddell Hart Centre for Military Archives, King's College, London)
General George C. Marshall (George C. Marshall Foundation, Lexington, Virginia)
Henry Morgenthau (Franklin D. Roosevelt Presidential Library, Hyde Park)
Marshal of the RAF Lord Portal (Christ Church, Oxford University)
Admiral of the Fleet Sir Dudley Pound (Churchill Archives Centre, Cambridge University)
General Matthew B. Ridgway (Military History Institute, Carlisle, Pennsylvania)
Franklin D. Roosevelt (Franklin D. Roosevelt Presidential Library, Hyde Park)
Ian Sayer (private collection)
General Lucian K. Truscott (George C. Marshall Foundation, Lexington, Virginia)
General Albert C. Wedemeyer (Military History Institute, Carlisle, Pennsylvania)
R. W. W. Wilmot (Liddell Hart Centre for Military Archives, King's College, London)
Bruce Wyllie (private collection)

BOOKS

(All published in London unless otherwise stated)

Adams, Jack, *The Doomed Expedition: The Norwegian Campaign of 1940* 1989
eds Addison, Paul, and Crang, Jeremy A., *The Burning Blue: A New History of the Battle of Britain* 2000
——, *Firestorm: The Bombing of Dresden 1945* 2006
Agawa, Hiroyuki, *The Reluctant Admiral: Yamamoto and the Imperial Navy* 2000
Aldrich, Richard, *Intelligence and the War against Japan* 2000
Allen, Louis, *Burma: The Longest War* 1984
——, *Singapore 1941–42* 1993
Allen, W. E. D., *The Russian Campaigns of 1944–45* 2001
Alperovitz, Gar, *The Decision to Use the Atomic Bomb* 1995
Aly, Götz, and Heim, Susanne, *Architects of Annihilation: Auschwitz and the Logic of Destruction* 2002

Ambrose, Stephen, *D-Day* 1994

Amery, Julian, *Approach March* 1973

Anders, W., *An Army in Exile* 1949

Andrews, Allen, *The Air Marshals* 1970

Ansel, Walter, *Hitler Confronts England* 1960

Arthur, Max, *Forgotten Voices of the Second World War* 2004

——, *Lest We Forget: Forgotten Voices from 1914–1945* 2007

——, *Dambusters* 2008

Ash, Bernard, *Someone Had Blundered: The Story of the Repulse and the Prince of Wales* 1960

——, *Norway 1940* 1964

Astley, Joan Bright, *The Inner Circle* 1971

Atkin, Ronald, *Pillar of Fire: Dunkirk 1940* 1990

Atkinson, Rick, *An Army at Dawn: The War in North Africa 1942–1943* 2004

Axell, Albert, *Stalin's War through the Eyes of his Commanders* 1997

——, *Zhukov: The Man Who Beat Hitler* 2003

Axell, Albert, and Hideaki, Kase, *Kamikaze: Japan's Suicide Gods* 2002

Badoglio, Pietro, *Italy in the Second World War* 1976

Bagby, Wesley M., *The Eagle–Dragon Alliance: America's Relations with China in World War II* 1992

Bailey, Roderick, *The Wildest Province: SOE in the Land of the Eagle* 2008

Baldwin, Hanson, *Battles Lost and Won: Great Campaigns of World War II* 1966

Banham, Tony, *Not the Slightest Chance: The Defence of Hong Kong 1941* 2003

Barber, John, and Harrison, Mark, *The Soviet Home Front 1941–1945* 1991

Barber, Noel, *Sinister Twilight: The Fall and Rise Again of Singapore* 1968

——, *The Week France Fell* 1976

Barker, A. J., *The March on Delhi* 1963

——, *Eritrea 1941* 1966

——, *Dunkirk: The Great Escape* 1977

Barker, John Sears, *Seven Steps Down* 2007

Barnett, Correlli, *The Desert Generals* 1983

——, *The Audit of War* 1986

——, *Engage the Enemy More Closely: The Royal Navy in the Second World War* 1991

ed. Barnett, Correlli, *Hitler's Generals* 2003

Barr, Niall, *Pendulum of War: The Three Battles of El Alamein* 2004

eds Bartoszewski, Wladyslaw T., and Polonsky, Antony, *The Jews in Warsaw* 1991

Bartov, Omer, *The Eastern Front 1941–45: German Troops and the Barbarisation of Warfare* 1985

Bassani, Giorgio, *The Garden of the Finzi-Cortinis* 2004

Bastable, Jonathan, *Voices from Stalingrad* 2006

Bateson, Charles, *The War with Japan* 1968

Batsford, B. T., *The Battle for Normandy* 1965

Battaglia, Roberto, *The Story of the Italian Resistance* 1957

Bayly, Christopher, and Harper, Tim, *Forgotten Armies: The Fall of British Asia 1941–1945* 2004

Beaufre, André, *1940: The Fall of France* 1967

Beck, Philip, *Oradour: Village of the Dead* 1979

Beesley, P., *Very Special Intelligence* 1977

Beevor, Antony, *Crete: The Battle and the Resistance* 1991

——, *Stalingrad* 1998

——, *Berlin: The Downfall 1945* 2002

eds Beevor, Antony, and Vinogradova, Luba, *A Writer at War: Vasily Grossman with the Red Army 1941–1945* 2006

Beevor, J. G., *SOE* 1981

Behrendt, Hans-Otto, *Rommel's Intelligence in the Desert Campaign* 1985

Behrens, C. B. A., *Merchant Shipping and the Demands of War* 1955

Bekker, Cajus, *The Luftwaffe War Diaries* 1967

——, *Hitler's Naval War* 1974

Bell, P. M. H., *A Certain Eventuality: Britain and the Fall of France* 1974

Bellamy, Chris, *Absolute War: Soviet Russia in the Second World War* 2007

Below, Nicolaus von, *At Hitler's Side: The Memoirs of Hitler's Luftwaffe Adjutant 1937–1945* 2001

Bennett, C. C. T., *Pathfinder* 1958

Bennett, G. H., and Bennett, R., *Survivors: British Merchant Seamen in the Second World War* 1999

Bennett, H. Gordon, *Why Singapore Fell* 1945

Bennett, Ralph, *Ultra in the West: The Normandy Campaign* 1979

——, *ULTRA and Mediterranean Strategy 1941–45* 1989

——, *Behind the Battle: ULTRA in the War against Germany* 1994

Bergot, Erwan, *The Afrika Korps* 1976

Berkhoff, Karel C., *Life and Death in Ukraine under Nazi Rule* 2004

Bess, Michael, *Choices under Fire: Moral Dimensions of World War II* 2006

Best, Geoffrey, *Churchill and War* 2005

Bethell, Nicholas, *The War Hitler Won* 1972

Biddiscombe, Perry, *Werewolf! The History of the National Socialist Guerrilla Movement 1944–1946* 1998

Bidwell, Shelford, *The Chindit War* 1979
Bierman, John, and Smith, Colin, *Alamein* 2002
Bishop, Patrick, *Fighter Boys* 2003
——, *Bomber Boys: Fighting Back 1940–1945* 2007
Black, Conrad, *Franklin Delano Roosevelt: Champion of Freedom* 2003
Black, Jeremy, *The Holocaust* 2008
Blair, Clay, *Hitler's U-Boat War: The Hunters 1939–1942* 1997
——, *Hitler's U-Boat War: The Hunted 1942–1945* 1998
ed. Bland, Larry I., *The Papers of George Catlett Marshall* vols III, IV and V
    1996–2003
——, *George C. Marshall: Interviews and Reminiscences for Forrest C. Pogue*
    Lexington 1996
ed. Blatt, Joel, *The French Defeat of 1940* 1998
Blaxland, Gregory, *Alexander's Generals: The Italian Campaign 1944–45*
    1979
Bloch, Michael, *Ribbentrop* 1992
Blumenson, Martin, *Anzio: The Gamble that Failed* 1963
——, *Rommel's Last Victory: The Battle of Kasserine Pass* 1968
——, *The Patton Papers 1940–1945* 1974
Bodleian Library, *German Invasion Plans for the British Isles 1940* 2007
Boeselager, Philipp von, *Valkyrie: The Plot to Kill Hitler* 2009
Böhlmer, Rudolf, *Monte Cassino* 1964
Bois, Eli J., *Truth on the Tragedy of France* 1941
Boldt, Gerhard, *Hitler's Last Days* 1973
Bond, Brian, *France and Belgium 1939–1940* 1975
ed. Bond, Brian, *Chief of Staff: The Diaries of Lt-Gen. Sir Henry Pownall*
    2 vols 1972 and 1974
eds Bond, Brian, and Taylor, Michael, *The Battle of France and Flanders
    1940* 2001
Bonn, Keith E., *When the Odds Were Even: The Vosges Mountains Cam-
    paign, October 1944–January 1945* 1994
Bor-Komorowski, T., *The Secret Army* 1950
Bourke, Joanna, *The Second World War* 2001
Bowen, Wayne, *Spain during World War II* 2006
Bowlby, Alex, *The Recollections of Rifleman Bowlby* 1999
Bowyer, Chaz, *Air War over Europe 1939–1945* 1981
Boyd, Douglas, *Voices from the Dark Years: The Truth about Occupied
    France 1940–1945* 2007
Bradford, Ernle, *Siege: Malta 1940–1943* 1985
Bradford, Sarah, *King George VI* 1989

Bradley, James, *Flyboys: The Final Secret of the Air War in the Pacific* 2004
Bradley, Omar N., *A Soldier's Story of the Allied Campaigns from Tunis to the Elbe* 1951
——, *A General's Life* New York 1983
Braithwaite, Roderic, *Moscow 1941* 2006
Brendon, Piers, *Winston Churchill* 2001
Brett-James, A., *Ball of Fire: The Fifth Indian Division in the Second World War* 1951
Brickhill, Paul, *The Dambusters* 1951
——, *Reach For the Sky* 2000
Bridgeman, Robert, *Memoirs* 2007
Brooks, Thomas R., *The War North of Rome June 1944–May 1945* 1996
Broome, Jack, *Convoy Is to Scatter* 1972
Brown, David, *Tirpitz: The Floating Fortress* 1977
Brown, Louis, *A Radar History of World War II* 1999
Browning, Christopher R., *Ordinary Men: Reserve Police Battalion 101 and the Final Solution in Poland* 1998
Bruce, Colin John, *War on the Ground* 1995
——, *Invaders: British and American Experience of Seaborne Landings 1939–1945* 1999
Bruce, George, *The Warsaw Uprising* 1972
Bryant, Arthur, *The Turn of the Tide* 1957
Buckingham, William F., *Arnhem 1944: A Reappraisal* 2002
Budiansky, Stephen, *Battle of Wits: The Complete Story of Codebreaking in World War II* 2000
Bullock, Alan, *Hitler: A Study in Tyranny* 1952
——, *Hitler and Stalin: Parallel Lives* 1991
Bungay, Stephen, *The Most Dangerous Enemy: A History of the Battle of Britain* 2000
——, *Alamein* 2002
eds Burdick, Charles, and Jacobsen, Hans-Adolf, *The Halder War Diary 1939–1942* 1988
Burleigh, Michael, *Ethics and Extermination: Reflections on Nazi Genocide* 1997
——, *The Third Reich* 2000
Butcher, Harry C., *Three Years with Eisenhower* 1946
Butler, Ewan, *The Story of Dunkirk* 1955
Butler, J. R. M., *Grand Strategy* vol. II 1957
ed. Butler, Susan, *My Dear Mr Stalin: The Complete Correspondence between Franklin D. Roosevelt and Joseph V. Stalin* 2005

Calder, Angus, *The Myth of the Blitz* 1991

Calil, Carmen, *Bad Faith* 2006

Callaghan, Raymond A., *The Worst Disaster: The Fall of Singapore* 1977

——, *Burma 1942–1945* 1978

Calvert, Michael, *Prisoners of Hope* 1971

——, *The Chindits* 1973

Calvocoressi, Peter, *Top Secret Ultra* 1980

Calvocoressi, Peter, and Wint, Guy, *Total War* 1972

ed. Cameron Watt, Donald, *Hitler's Mein Kampf* 1972

Campbell, Arthur, *The Siege: A Story from Kohima* 1956

Carew, Tim, *The Longest Retreat: The Burma Campaign 1942* 1969

Carrell, Paul, *Hitler Moves East* 1977

——, *Stalingrad: The Defeat of the German Sixth Army* 1993

——, *Scorched Earth: The Russian–German War 1943–1944* 1994

Carroll, Joseph T., *Ireland in the War Years* 1975

Carruthers, Bob, and Erickson, John, *The Russian Front 1941–1945* 1999

Carver, Michael, *El Alamein* 1962

——, *Tobruk* 1964

——, *Dilemmas of the Desert War 1940–1942* 1986

——, *The War in Italy 1943–1945* 2001

Casey, Lord, *Personal Experience 1939–1946* 1962

Casey, Steven, *Cautious Crusade: Franklin D. Roosevelt, American Public Opinion, and the War against Nazi Germany* 2001

Cashman, Sean Dennis, *America, Roosevelt and World War II* 1989

Chamberlin, E. R., *Life in Wartime Britain* 1972

Chandler, David, *The Campaigns of Napoleon* 1998

Chaney, Otto Preston, *Zhukov* 1972

Chang, Iris, *The Rape of Nanking* 2007

Chant, Christopher, *The Encyclopedia of Codenames of World War II* 1986

Chapman, F. Spencer, *The Jungle Is Neutral* 1949

Chapman, Guy, *Why France Collapsed* 1968

Chinnock, Frank W., *Nagasaki: The Forgotten Bomb* 1970

Chuikov, Vasili I., *The Beginning of the Road* 1963

——, *The End of the Third Reich* 1967

Churchill, Winston S., *Into Battle* 1941

——, *The End of the Beginning* 1943

——, *Onwards to Victory* 1944

——, *The Dawn of Liberation* 1945

——, *Secret Session Speeches* 1946

——, *Victory* 1946

——, *The Second World War* vol. I: *Their Finest Hour* 1949
——, *The Second World War* vol. III: *The Grand Alliance* 1950
——, *The Second World War* vol. IV: *The Hinge of Fate* 1951
——, *The Second World War* vol. V: *Closing the Ring* 1952
——, *The Second World War* vol. VI: *Triumph and Tragedy* 1954
Ciechanowski, Jan M., *The Warsaw Rising of 1944* 1974
Clark, Alan, *Barbarossa* 1995
Clark, Lloyd, *Anzio* 2006
Clark, Mark, *Calculated Risk* 1951
Claus, H., *The Sorrow of Belgium* 1990
Coast, John, *Railroad of Death* 1946
Cobb, Richard, *French and Germans, Germans and French* 1983
Coggins, J., *The Campaign for Guadalcanal* New York 1972
Cole, Robert, *Britain and the War of Words in Neutral Europe 1939–45* 1990
Collier, Basil, *The Battle of Britain* 1962
——, *A Short History of the Second World War* 1967
——, *The Battle of the V-Weapons 1944–45* 1976
Collier, Richard, *Eagle Day: The Battle of Britain* 1966
Colville, John, *The Fringes of Power: Downing Street Diaries 1939–1955* 1985
Colvin, Ian, *Not Ordinary Men: The Battle of Kohima Reassessed* 1994
——, *Zhukov: The Conqueror of Berlin* 2004
Committee for the Compilation of Materials on Damage Caused by the Atomic Bombs in Hiroshima and Nagasaki, *The Physical, Medical, and Social Effects of the Atomic Bombs* 1981
Connelly, Mark, *Reaching for the Stars: A New History of Bomber Command in World War II* 2001
Conway, Martin, *Collaboration in Belgium* 1993
Cookridge, E. H., *Inside SOE* 1966
Cooper, Alfred Duff, *Operation Heartbreak* 1950
——, *Old Men Forget* 1954
Cooper, Artemis, *Cairo in the War 1939–1945* 1989
Cornish, Nicolas, *Images of Kursk* 2002
Cornwall, John, *Hitler's Scientists* 2003
Corrigan, Gordon, *Blood, Sweat and Arrogance and the Myth of Churchill's War* 2006
Cowling, Maurice, *The Impact of Hitler: British Politics and British Policy, 1933–1940* Cambridge 1975
Coyle, Harold, *Sword Point* 1988
Creveld, Martin van, *Hitler's Strategy: The Balkans Clue* 1973

——, *Supplying War* 1977

Crook, David, *Spitfire Pilot* 2008

Cross, Robin, *Citadel: The Battle of Kursk* 1993

Cruickshank, Charles, *The German Occupation of the Channel Islands* 1975

Cull, Nicholas, *Selling War: The British Propaganda Campaign against American 'Neutrality' in World War II* 1995

Cunningham, Viscount, *A Sailor's Odyssey* 1951

Dahl, Hans Frederick, *Quisling* 1999

D'Albas, Andrieu, *Death of a Navy: The Fleets of the Mikado in the Second World War* 1957

Dallin, A., *German Rule in Russia* New York 1957

Dalton, Hugh, *The Fateful Years: Memoirs 1931–1945* 1957

eds Danchev, Alex, and Todman, Dan, *War Diaries 1939–1945: Field Marshal Lord Alanbrooke* 2001

Davidson, Edward, and Manning, David, *Chronology of World War Two* 1999

Davidson, Eugene, *Trial of the Germans* 1966

Davies, Norman, *Rising '44: The Battle for Warsaw* 2004

——, *Europe at War* 2006

Davies, Peter, *Dangerous Liaisons: Collaboration and World War Two* 2004

Daws, Gavan, *Prisoners of the Japanese* 1994

Deakin, F. W., *The Brutal Friendship: Mussolini, Hitler and the Fall of Italian Fascism* 1962

ed. Deakin, William, and others, *British Political and Military Strategy in Central, Eastern and Southern Europe in 1944* 1988

ed. Dear, I. C. B., *The Oxford Companion to the Second World War* 1995

Dederichs, Mario R., *Heydrich: The Face of Evil* 2006

De Gaulle, Charles, *The Call to Honour 1940–1942* 1955

——, *Unity 1942–1944* 1959

——, *Salvation 1944–1946* 1960

De Groot, Gerard J., *The Bomb* 2005

De Guingand, Francis, *Operation Victory* 1947

Deichman, Paul, *Spearhead for Blitzkrieg: Luftwaffe Operations in Support of the Army 1939–1945* 1996

Deighton, Len, *Fighter* 2008

Delaforce, Patrick, *The Battle of the Bulge* 2004

Derry, T. K., *The Campaign in Norway* 1952

D'Este, Carlo, *Decision in Normandy* 1983

——, *Bitter Victory: The Battle for Sicily* 1988

——, *Fatal Decision: Anzio and the Battle for Rome* 1991

——, A Genius for War: A Life of George S. Patton 1995

——, Eisenhower 2002

——, Warlord: A Life of Winston Churchill at War 2008

eds Deutsch, Harold, and Showalter, Dennis, What If?: Strategic Alternatives of World War II 1997

Diest, Wilhelm, and others, Germany and the Second World War 7 vols 1990–2006

ed. Dilks, David, The Diaries of Sir Alexander Cadogan 1971

Dobinson, Colin, AA Command: Britain's Anti-Aircraft Defences of World War II 2001

Dobson, Alan P., US Wartime Aid to Britain 1940–46 1986

ed. Doenecke, Justus, In Danger Undaunted: The Anti-Interventionist Movement of 1940–41 1990

Domarus, Max, The Essential Hitler: Speeches and Commentary 2007

——, Hitler: Speeches and Proclamations 1932–1945 vol. III 1990

Dombrády, Lóránd, Army and Politics in Hungary 1938–1944 2005

Dorrian, James, Storming St Nazaire 1998

Douglas, Roy, New Alliances 1940–41 1982

Douglas-Hamilton, James, Motive for a Mission: The Story behind Hess's Flight to Britain 1971

Duffy, Christopher, Red Storm on the Reich: The Soviet March on Germany 1945 1991

Dugan, James, and Stewart, Carroll, Ploesti: The Great Ground–Air Battle of 1 August 1943 1963

Dupuy, R. Ernest, and Dupuy, Trevor N., The Collins Encyclopedia of Military History 4th edn 1994

Dupuy, Trevor N., A Genius for War: The German Army and General Staff 1807–1945 1977

eds Eberle, Henrik, and Uhl, Matthias, The Hitler Book 2005

Edwards, Bernard, Dönitz and the Wolf Packs 1996

Edwards, Robert, White Death: Russia's War on Finland 1939–40 2006

Egremont, Max, Under Two Flags: The Life of Major General Sir Edward Spears 1997

Ehrlich, Blake, The French Resistance 1940–1945 1966

Ehrman, John, Grand Strategy vols V and VI 1956

Eisenhower, Dwight D., Crusade in Europe 1946

——, D Day to VE Day 1944–45: General Eisenhower's Report on the Invasion of Europe 2000

Eisenhower, John, The Bitter Woods: The Dramatic Story of Hitler's Surprise Ardennes Offensive 1969

Ellis, John, *Cassino: The Hollow Victory* 1984
——, *Brute Force: Allied Strategy and Tactics in the Second World War* 1990
——, *The World War II Data Book* 2003
Elstob, Peter, *Hitler's Last Offensive* 1971
Erickson, John, *The Road to Berlin* 1983
——, *The Road to Stalingrad* 1983
——, *The Soviet High Command* 2001
Erickson, John, and Dilks, David, *Barbarossa: The Axis and the Allies* 1994
Erskine, Ralph, and Smith, Michael, *Action This Day* 2001
Eubank, Keith, *Summit at Teheran* 1985
Evans, Geoffrey, *Imphal* 1962
——, *Slim as Military Commander* 1969
Evans, Mark Llewellyn, *Great World War II Battles in the Arctic* 1999
Evans, Richard J., *The Coming of the Third Reich* 2003
——, *The Third Reich at War* 2008
Falls, Cyril, *The Second World War* 1948
Farrell, Brian, *The Basis and Making of British Grand Strategy 1940–1943: Was There a Plan?* 2 vols 1998
——, *The Defence and Fall of Singapore* 2005
Farrell, Nicholas, *Mussolini* 2003
Feast, Sean, *Master Bombers: The Experience of a Pathfinder Squadron at War 1944–1945* 2008
Felton, Mark, *Slaughter at Sea: The Story of Japan's Naval War Crimes* 2007
Fenby, Jonathan, *Alliance* 2006
Ferguson, Niall, *The War of the World* 2006
Fergusson, Bernard, *Beyond the Chindwin* 1945
——, *Trumpet in the Hall* 1970
Fest, Joachim, *Plotting Hitler's Death* 1996
——, *Speer* 2001
——, *Inside Hitler's Bunker* 2004
Fischer, Bernd J., *Albania at War 1939–1945* 1999
Fitzgibbon, Constantine, *The Blitz* 1957
Follain, John, *Mussolini's Island: The Battle for Sicily* 2005
Foot, M. R. D., *Resistance* 1976
——, *SOE: An Outline History of the Special Operations Executive* 1984
ed. Foot, M. R. D., *Holland at War against Hitler* 1990
Fort, Adrian, *Prof: The Life of Lord Lindemann* 2003
——, *Archibald Wavell* 2008
Frankl, Viktor E., *Man's Search for Meaning* 2004

Fraser, General Sir David, *Knights's Cross: A Life of Field Marshal Erwin Rommel* 1993

———, *Alanbrooke* 1997

Fraser, George MacDonald, *Quartered Safe Out Here* 1992

eds Freidin, Seymour, and Richardson, William, *The Fatal Decisions* 1956

Friedländer, Saul, *The Years of Extermination: Nazi Germany and the Jews 1939–1945* 2007

Friedrich, Jörg, *The Fire: The Bombing of Germany 1940–1945* 2006

Fuchida, Mitsuo, and Okumiya, Masatake, *Midway: The Battle that Doomed Japan* 1955

Fuller, J. F. C., *The Second World War 1939–45* 1948

Fussell, Paul, *The Boys' Crusade: American GIs in Europe* 2003

Gailey, Harry A., *The War in the Pacific* 1997

Galante, Pierre, *Operation Valkyrie: The German Generals' Plot against Hitler* 1981

Galland, Adolf, *The First and the Last: The German Fighter Force in World War II* 1955

Garfield, Simon, *Private Battles: How the War Almost Defeated Us* 2006

Garliński, Jósef, *Poland in the Second World War* 1985

Garret, Stephen A., *Ethics and Airpower* 1993

Gelb, Norman, *Scramble: A Narrative History of the Battle of Britain* 1985

ed. Gerbet, Klaus, *Generalfeldmarschall Fedor von Bock: The War Diary 1939–1945* 1996

Gilbert, Adrian, *POW: Allied Prisoners in Europe 1939–1945* 2006

Gilbert, Martin, *Auschwitz and the Allies* 1981

———, *Winston S. Churchill* vol. VI: *Finest Hour* 1983

———, *Winston S. Churchill* vol. VII: *Road to Victory* 1986

———, *The Holocaust* 1987

———, *The Second World War* 1989

———, *Churchill: A Life* 1991

———, *The Righteous: The Unsung Heroes of the Holocaust* 2002

———, *Churchill at War* 2003

———, *D-Day* 2004

———, *Churchill and America* 2005

———, *The Routledge Atlas of the Second World War* 2008

Gildea, Robert, *Marianne in Chains: In Search of the German Occupation 1940–1945* 2002

Glantz, David M., *Soviet Military Deception in the Second World War* 1989

———, *From the Don to the Dnieper: Soviet Offensive Operations December 1942– August 1943* 1991

——, *Kharkov 1942* 1998

Glantz, David M., and House, Jonathan M., *The Battle of Kursk* 1999

——, *When Titans Clashed: How the Red Army Stopped Hitler* 2000

——, *Barbarossa 1941* 2001

Goldensohn, Leon, *The Nuremberg Interviews*, ed. Robert Gellately 2004

Goldhagen, Daniel Jonah, *Hitler's Willing Executioners* 1996

Gooderson, Ian, *Air Power at the Battlefront: Allied Close Air Support in Europe 1943–45* 1998

ed. Gorlitz, Walter, *The Memoirs of Field Marshal Keitel* 1961

Gorodetsky, Gabriel, *Grand Delusion: Stalin and the German Invasion of Russia* 1999

Grant, Reg, *World War II: Europe* 2004

Graves, Charles, *The Home Guard of Britain* 1943

Grayling, A. C., *Among the Dead Cities: Was the Allied Bombing of Civilians in WWII a Necessity or a Crime?* 2006

Greenwood, Alexander, *Auchinleck* 1990

Gregor, Neil, *Haunted City: Nuremberg and the Nazi Past* 2009

Greif, G., *We Wept without Tears: Testimonies of the Jewish Sonderkommando from Auschwitz* 2005

Gretton, Vice-Admiral Sir Peter, *Convoy Escort Commander* 1964

Griffiths, Richard, *Marshal Pétain* 1970

Grigg, John, *1943: The Victory that Never Was* 1999

Gross, Jan Tomasz, *Polish Society under German Occupation* 1979

——, *Neighbours: The Destruction of the Jewish Community in Jedwabne, Poland* 2003

Grossman, Vasily, *Life and Fate* 2006

Grunberger, Richard, *A Social History of the Third Reich* 1991

Guderian, General Heinz, *Panzer Leader* 1952

eds Gutman, Israel, and Berenbaum, Michael, *Anatomy of the Auschwitz Death Camp* Bloomington 1998

Gwyer, J. M. A., *Grand Strategy* vol. III, part 1 1964

Hamilton, Nigel, *Monty: The Making of a General 1887–1941* 1981

——, *Monty: Master of the Battlefield 1942–44* 1983

——, *Monty: The Field-Marshal* 1986

Hancock, Eleanor, *The National Socialist Leadership and Total War 1941–5* 1991

Harriman, W. Averell, *Special Envoy to Churchill and Stalin 1941–1946* 1975

Harris, Arthur, *Bomber Offensive* 1947

Harris, John, *Swordpoint: A Novel of Cassino* 1980

Harrison, Tom, *Living through the Blitz* 1976

Hart, S., *The German Soldier in World War II* 2000

Hartcup, Guy, *The Challenge of War: Scientific and Engineering Contributions to World War Two* 1970

ed. Hart-Davis, Duff, *King's Counsellor: The Diaries of Sir Alan Lascelles* 2006

Harvey, Maurice, *Scandinavian Misadventure* 1990

Harvey, Robert, *American Shogun: MacArthur, Hirohito and the American Duel with Japan* 2006

Hasegawa, Tsuyoshi, *Racing the Enemy: Stalin, Truman, and the Surrender of Japan* 2005

Hastings, Max, *Bomber Command* 1979

——, *Overlord: D-Day and the Battle for Normandy* 1984

——, *On the Offensive* 1995

——, *Armageddon: The Battle for Germany 1944–45* 2004

——, *Warriors* 2005

——, *Nemesis: The Battle for Japan 1944–45* 2007

Haswell, Jock, *The Intelligence and Deception of the D-Day Landings* 1979

Haupt, Werner, *Army Group North 1941–1945* Atglen, Pa 1997

——, *Army Group Center 1941–1945* Atglen, Pa 1997

——, *Army Group South 1941–1945* Atglen, Pa 1998

Hayward, Joel S. A., *Stopped at Stalingrad: The Luftwaffe and Hitler's Defeat in the East 1942–1943* 1998

eds Heiber, Helmut, and Glantz, David M., *Hitler and his Generals: Military Conferences 1942–1945* 2002

Heller, Joseph, *Catch-22* 1994

Henderson, Michael, *See You after the Duration: The Story of British Evacuees to North America in World War II* 2004

Hersey, John, *Hiroshima* 1946

Hesketh, Roger, *Fortitude: The D-Day Deception Campaign* 1999

Hickey, Des, and Smith, Gus, *Operation Avalanche: The Salerno Landings 1943* 1983

Higham, Robin, *Diary of a Disaster: British Aid to Greece 1940–1941* 1986

Hinsley, F. H., *Hitler's Strategy* 1951

——, *British Intelligence in the Second World War* vol. II 1981

eds Hinsley, F. H., and Stripp, Alan, *Codebreakers: The Inside Story of Bletchley Park* 1993

eds Hirschfield, Gerhard, and Marsh, Patrick, *Collaboration in France* 1989

Hitchcock, William I., *Liberation: The Bitter Road to Freedom 1944–1945* 2008

HMSO, *The Battle of the Atlantic* 1946

Hoess, Rudolf, *Commandant of Auschwitz* 1961

Hogg, Ian V., *German Secret Weapons of the Second World War* 1999

Holland, James, *Fortress Malta: An Island under Siege* 2003

———, *Together We Stand: Turning the Tide in the West: North Africa 1942–1943* 2005

———, *Italy's Sorrow: A Year of War 1944–45* 2008

Holmes, Richard, *The World at War* 2007

———, *World War II: The Definitive Visual Guide* 2009

Horne, Alistair, *To Lose a Battle: France 1940* 1969

Horner, David, *High Command: Australia and Allied Strategy 1939–45* 1982

Horrocks, Sir Brian, *Corps Commander* 1978

Hough, Richard, and Richards, Denis, *The Battle of Britain* 1989

Howard, John, and Bates, Peggy, *The Pegasus Diaries: The Private Papers of Major John Howard* 2006

Howard, Michael, *The Mediterranean Strategy in the Second World War* 1968

———, *Grand Strategy* vol. IV 1972

———, *Captain Professor* 2006

eds Howard, Michael, and Paret, Peter, *Carl von Clausewitz: On War* 1989

ed. Howarth, Stephen, *Men of War: Great Naval Leaders of World War Two* 1992

ed. Howarth, Stephen, and Law, Derek, *The Battle of the Atlantic 1939–1945* 1994

Hudson, Miles, *Soldier, Poet, Rebel: The Extraordinary Life of Charles Hudson VC* 2007

Hughes, Matthew, and Mann, Chris, *Inside Hitler's Germany* 2002

Imperial War Museum, *The Black Book* 1989

Irving, David, *Hitler's War* 1977

ed. Isby, David C., *Fighting the Breakout: The German Army in Normandy from 'Cobra' to the Falaise Gap* 2004

Ismay, Lord, *The Memoirs of Lord Ismay* 1960

Jablonsky, David, *Churchill and Hitler* 1994

Jackson, Ashley, *The British Empire and the Second World War* 2006

Jackson, Julian, *France: The Dark Years 1940-1944* 2001

Jackson, Robert, *The Fall of France* 1972

eds Jacobsen, Hans-Adolf, and Rohwer, Jürgen, *Decisive Battles of World War II: The German View* 1965

James, Richard Rhodes, *Chindit* 1980

Jeffreys, Kevin, *The Churchill Coalition and Wartime Politics 1940–1945* 1991

Jenkins, Roy, *Roosevelt* 2003
Jones, Michael, *Leningrad: State of Siege* 2008
Jones, Nigel, *Countdown to Valkyrie: The July Plot to Assassinate Hitler* 2009
Jones, Robert Huhn, *The Roads to Russia: United States Lend-Lease to the Soviet Union* 1969
Jones, R. V., *Most Secret War* 1978
Junge, Traudl, *Until the Final Hour* 2003
Kakehashi, Kumiko, *Letters from Iwo Jima* 2007
Kaufmann, J. E., and Kaufmann, H. W., *Hitler's Blitzkrieg Campaign* 1993
Keegan, John, *Six Armies in Normandy* 1982
——, *The Second World War* 1989
ed. Keegan, John, *Churchill's Generals* 1991
Kennedy, John, *The Business of War* 1957
Kennedy, Ludovic, *Pursuit: The Sinking of the Bismarck* 2001
Kersaudy, François, *Churchill and De Gaulle* 1982
——, *Norway 1940* 1990
Kershaw, Alex, *The Few* 2007
Kershaw, Ian, *Hitler: 1889–1936: Hubris* 1998
——, *Hitler: 1936–1945: Nemesis* 2000
——, *Fateful Choices: Ten Decisions that Changed the World 1940–1941* 2007
——, *Hitler, the Germans, and the Final Solution* 2008
Kershaw, Robert, *Never Surrender* 2009
Kesselring, Albert, *Kesselring: A Soldier's Record* 1954
Kieser, Egbert, *Hitler on the Doorstep: Operation 'Sea Lion': The German Plan to Invade Britain* 1997
ed. Kimball, Warren, *Churchill and Roosevelt: The Complete Correspondence* 3 vols 1984
Kitchen, Martin, *British Policy towards the Soviet Union during the Second World War* 1986
Kitson, Simon, *The Hunt for Nazi Spies: Fighting Espionage in Vichy France* 2008
Kolinsky, Martin, *Britain's War in the Middle East: Strategy and Diplomacy 1936–42* 1999
Konev, I., *Year of Victory* 1969
ed. Krivosheev, G. F., *Soviet Casualties and Combat Losses in the Twentieth Century* 1993
eds Kulkov, E. N., Shukman, Harold, and Rzheshevskii, Oleg Aleksandrovich, *Stalin and the Russo-Finnish War 1939–1940* 2002

Kuramoto, Kazuho, *Manchurian Legacy* 2004

Lacouture, Jean, *De Gaulle: The Rebel 1890–1944* 1990

——, *De Gaulle: The Ruler 1945–1970* 1991

Lamb, Richard, *Churchill as War Leader* 2003

Lambourne, Nicola, *War Damage in Western Europe: The Destruction of Historic Monuments during the Second World War* 2001

Lampe, David, *The Last Ditch: Britain's Secret Resistance and the Nazi Invasion Plan* 2007

ed. Langworth, Richard M., *Churchill by Himself: The Life, Times and Opinions of Winston Churchill in his Own Words* 2008

Laqueur, Walter, *The Terrible Secret: An Investigation into the Suppression of Information about Hitler's 'Final Solution'* 1980

ed. Laqueur, Walter, *The Second World War* 1982

Latimer, Jon, *Burma: The Forgotten War* 2004

——, *Alamein* 2002

Lavery, Brian, *Churchill Goes to War* 2007

Leach, Barry A., *German Strategy against Russia 1939–1941* 1973

Leahy, William D., *I Was There* 1950

Leighton, Richard M., and Coakley, Robert W., *Global Logistics and Strategy 1940–1943* 1955

Le Tissier, Tony, *The Battle of Berlin 1945* 1988

——, *Zhukov at the Oder* 1996

ed. Leutze, James, *The London Observer: The Journal of General Raymond E. Lee 1940–1941* 1972

Levi, Primo, *If This Is a Man* 1987

Levine, Joshua, *Forgotten Voices of the Blitz and the Battle of Britain* 2006

Lewin, Ronald, *The American Magic* New York 1982

——, *ULTRA Goes to War* 1988

Lewis, Bruce, *Aircrew: The Story of the Men Who Flew the Bombers* 2000

Lewis, Norman, *Naples '44* 1983

Liddell Hart, Basil, *The Current of War* 1941

——, *The Other Side of the Hill: Germany's Generals* 1951

——, *The History of the Second World War* 1970

ed. Liddell Hart, Basil, *The Rommel Papers* 1953

Lilley, J. Robert, *Taken by Force: Rape and American GIs during World War Two* 2008

Lindbergh, Charles A., *The Wartime Journals of Charles A. Lindbergh* New York 1970

Linklater, Eric, *The Campaign in Germany* 1951

Littlejohn, David, *The Patriotic Traitors: A History of Collaboration in German-Occupied Europe 1940–45* 1972
ed. Lochner, Louis P., *The Goebbels Diaries* 1948
Lombard-Hobson, Sam, *A Sailor's War* 1983
Longden, Sean, *To the Victor the Spoils: D-Day to VE-Day* 2004
——, *Hitler's British Slaves* 2005
——, *Dunkirk: The Men They Left Behind* 2008
Longmate, Norman, *If Britain Had Fallen* 1988
Lord, Walter, *The Miracle of Dunkirk* 1982
Loringhoven, Bernd Freytag von, *In the Bunker with Hitler* 2005
eds Love, Robert W., and Major, John, *The Year of D-Day: The 1944 Diary of Admiral Sir Bertram Ramsay* 1994
Lowe, Keith, *Inferno: The Devastation of Hamburg, 1943* 2008
Lower, Wendy, *Nazi-Empire Building and the Holocaust in Ukraine* 2005
Lucas, James, *Last Days of the Reich* 1986
——, *Battle Group! German Kampfgruppen Action of World War Two* 1993
Lukacs, John, *The Last European War* 1976
——, *Five Days in London: May 1940* 1999
Lukas, Richard C., *The Forgotten Holocaust: The Poles under German Occupation 1939–1944* 1986
Lyman, Robert, *First Victory: Britain's Forgotten Struggle in the Middle East 1941* 2006
MacArthur, Brian, *Surviving the Sword: Prisoners of the Japanese 1942–1945* 2005
McCarthy, Peter, and Syron, Mike, *Panzerkrieg* 2003
MacDonald, Charles B., *The Battle of the Bulge* 1984
Macdonald, John, *Great Battles of World War II* 1986
Mackenzie, Compton, *All Over the Place* 1948
Mackenzie, S. P., *The Home Guard* 1995
Mackenzie, William, *The Secret History of SOE* 2000
Mackiewicz, Joseph, *The Katyn Wood Murders* 1951
McKinstry, Leo, *Spitfire: Portrait of a Legend* 2007
Macksey, Kenneth, *The Partisans of Europe in World War II* 1975
——, *Guderian: Panzer General* 1992
Mack Smith, Denis, *Mussolini* 1981
ed. Macleod, Colonel Roderick, *The Ironside Diaries 1937–1940* 1962
Macmillan, Harold, *The Blast of War* 1967
——, *War Diaries* 1984

Majdalany, Fred, *Cassino: Portrait of a Battle* 1959

Malaparte, Curzio, *Kaputt* 1964

Maney, Patrick J., *The Roosevelt Presence* 1992

Manstein, Erich von, *Lost Victories* 2004

Manvell, Roger, and Fraenkel, Heinrich, *Göring* 2005

——, *Heinrich Himmler* 2007

ed. Mark, Bernard, *The Scrolls of Auschwitz* 1985

Marnham, Patrick, *The Death of Jean Moulin* 2000

Masters, John, *The Road Past Mandalay* 1961

Matloff, Maurice, and Snell, E., *Strategic Planning for Coalition Warfare 1943–44* Washington DC 1959

Maugham, Barton, *Tobruk and El Alamein* 1966

Maurois, André, *Why France Fell* 1940

Mayle, Paul D., *Eureka Summit: Agreement in Principle and the Big Three at Tehran* 1943

Mazower, Mark, *Inside Hitler's Greece 1941–44* 1993

——, *Hitler's Empire: Nazi Rule in Occupied Europe* 2008

Meacham, Jon, *Franklin and Winston* 2003

Mee, Charles L., *Meeting at Potsdam* 1975

Megargee, Geoffrey P., *Inside Hitler's High Command* 2000

Mellenthin, F. W. von, *Panzer Battles 1939–1945* 1955

ed. Mercer, Derrik, *Chronicle of the Second World War* 1990

Metelmann, Henry, *Through Hell for Hitler* 1990

Michael, H., *The Shadow War* 1972

Michel, Henri, *The Second World War* 1975

Middlebrook, Martin, *Arnhem 1944* 1994

Miller, Donald L., *Eighth Air Force* 2007

Milward, Alan S., *The German Economy at War* 1965

——, *War, Economy and Society 1939–45* 1977

Ministry of Information, *What Britain Has Done* 2007

Mohammad, Fadhl Ali, *Memories of World War II in Libya* Benghazi 2005

Monsarrat, Nicholas, *HM Frigate* 1946

——, *The Cruel Sea* 2002

Montague Browne, Anthony, *Long Sunset* 1995

Montgomery, Viscount, *The Memoirs of Field-Marshal the Viscount Montgomery of El Alamein* 1958

Moorehead, Alan, *Eclipse* 2000

——, *The Desert War* 2009

Moran, Lord, *Winston Churchill: The Struggle for Survival* 1966

Mordal, Jacques, *Dieppe: Dawn of Decision* 1963

Moreman, T. R., *The Jungle, the Japanese and the British Commonwealth 1941–45* 2005

Morison, Samuel Eliot, *American Contributions* 1958

ed. Morley, James, *The Fateful Choice: Japan's Advance into Southeast Asia* 1980

Morris, Eric, *Corregidor: The Nightmare in the Philippines* 1982

Moseley, Ray, *Mussolini: The Last 600 Days of Il Duce* 2004

Mosier, John, *The Blitzkrieg Myth* 2003

Mosley, Leonard, *Backs to the Wall* 1971

Moss, W. Stanley, *Ill Met by Moonlight* 1950

Moulton, J. L., *The Norwegian Campaign of 1940* 1966

——, *Battle for Antwerp* 1978

ed. Muggeridge, Malcolm, *Ciano's Diary 1939–1943* 1947

Müllenheim-Rechberg, Burkhard von, *Battleship Bismarck* 1990

Murphy, David E., *What Stalin Knew: The Enigma of Barbarossa* 2005

Murray, Willamson, and Millett, Allan R., *A War to be Won: Fighting the Second World War* 2000

Murrow, Edward R., *This Is London* 1941

Neave, Airey, *They Have their Exits* 1953

Neillands, Robin, *The Bomber War* 2001

——, *The Dieppe Raid* 2005

ed. Neitzel, Sönke, *Tapping Hitler's Generals: Transcripts of Secret Conversations 1942–45* 2007

Newark, Tim, *The Mafia at War* 2007

Nichol, John, and Rennell, Tony, *Tail-End Charlies: The Last Battles of the Bomber War 1944–45* 2004

ed. Nicholas, H. G., *Washington Despatches 1941–45* 1981

Nicolson, Nigel, *Alex: The Life of Field Marshal Earl Alexander of Tunis* 1973

ed. Nicolson, Nigel, *Harold Nicolson: Diaries and Letters 1939–1945* 1967

Noel, Gerard, *Pius XII: The Hound of Hitler* 2008

ed. North, John, *The Alexander Memoirs 1940–1945* 1962

O'Donnell, James P., *The Berlin Bunker* 1979

Okumiya, Matasake, and Horikoshi, Jiro, *Zero! The Story of the Japanese Navy Air Force 1937–1945* 1957

Ousby, Ian, *Occupation: The Ordeal of France 1940–1944* 1997

Overy, Richard, *Why the Allies Won* 1995

——, *Russia's War* 1997

——, *The Battle* 2000

——, *Interrogations: Inside the Minds of the Nazi Elite* 2002

——, *The Dictators: Hitler's Germany and Stalin's Russia* 2005

Pabst, Helmut, *The Outermost Frontier: A German Soldier in the Russian Campaign* 1986

Pack, Stanley, *The Battle for Crete* 1973

——, *Operation Husky: The Allied Invasion of Sicily* 1977

Padfield, Peter, *Dönitz: The Last Führer* 1984

——, *War beneath the Sea: Submarine Conflict 1939–1945* 1995

Paine, Lauran, *The Abwehr: German Military Intelligence in World War Two* 1984

Panter-Downes, Mollie, *London War Notes 1939–1945* 1972

Papagos, Alexander, *The Battle of Greece 1940–1941* 1949

Paris, Edmond, *Genocide in Satellite Croatia 1941–1945* 1981

Parker, Matthew, *Monte Cassino* 2003

Parker, R. A. C., *The Second World War* 2001

Parkinson, Roger, *Blood, Toil, Tears and Sweat: The War History from Dunkirk to Alamein, Based on the War Cabinet Papers of 1940 to 1942* 1973

ed. Parrish, Michael, *Battle for Moscow: The 1942 Soviet General Staff Study* 1989

ed. Parrish, Thomas, *The Simon & Schuster Encyclopedia of World War II* New York, 1978

Patton, George S., *War as I Knew It* 1947

Paxton, Robert O., *Vichy France* 1972

Payne, Stanley G., *Franco and Hitler* 2008

ed. Penrose, Jane, *The D-Day Companion* 2004

Perret, Geoffrey, *Winged Victory: The Army Air Forces in World War II* 1993

Phillips, C. E. Lucas, *Cockleshell Heroes* 1956

Phillips, N. C. *The Sangro to Cassino*, vol. 1 of *The Official History of New Zealand in the Second World War* Wellington 1957

Pickersgill, J. W., and Forster, D. F., *The McKenzie King Record* 2 vols 1960 and 1968

Piekalkiewicz, Janus, *Cassino* 1980

Pimlott, Ben, *Hugh Dalton* 1985

ed. Pimlott, Ben, *The Second World War Diary of Hugh Dalton* 1986

Pink, M. Alderton, *The Letters of Horace Walpole* 1938

Pitt, Barrie, *The Crucible of War: Western Desert 1941* 1980

Pitt, Barrie, and Pitt, Frances, *The Chronological Atlas of World War II* 1989

Pleshakov, Constantine, *Stalin's Folly: The Secret History of the German Invasion of Russia* 2005

Pocock, Tom, *1945: The Dawn Came Up Like Thunder* 1983

Pogue, Forrest C., *The Supreme Command* Washington DC 1954

——, *George C. Marshall: Ordeal and Hope 1939–42* 1965

——, *George C. Marshall: Organizer of Victory 1943–45* 1973

Polish Cultural Foundation, *The Crime of Katyn* 1965

Ponting, Clive, *1940: Myth and Reality* 1990

Pope, Dudley, *Battle of the River Plate* 1956

Pope-Hennessy, James, *History under Fire* 1941

Porch, Douglas, *Hitler's Mediterranean Gamble* 2004

Prange, Gordon W., *Miracle at Midway* 1982

ed. Prasad, B., *Official History of the Indian Armed Forces in the Second World War: The Reconquest of Burma* vol. 1 1959

Preston, Paul, *Franco* 1994

Price, Arthur, *The Spitfire Story* 1995

Probert, Henry, *Bomber Harris: His Life and Times* 2001

Pulleston, W. D., *The Influence of Sea Power in World War II* 1947

Raczynski, Count Edward, *In Allied London* 1962

Ranfurly, Hermione, Countess of, *To War with Whitaker: The Wartime Diaries of the Countess of Ranfurly 1939–1945* 1994

Rauss, Erhard, and Natzmer, Oldwig von, *The Anvil of War: German Generalship in Defence on the Eastern Front* 1994

Rawlings, Leo, *And the Dawn Came Up Like Thunder* 1972

Ray, John, *The Battle of Britain* 1994

——, *The Night Blitz 1940–1941* 1996

Read, Anthony, *The Devil's Disciples: The Lives and Times of Hitler's Inner Circle* 2003

Read, Anthony, and Fisher, David, *The Deadly Embrace: Hitler, Stalin and the Nazi–Soviet Pact 1939–1941* 1988

Rees, Laurence, *The Nazis: A Warning from History* 1999

——, *Horror in the East* 2001

——, *Auschwitz* 2005

——, *Their Darkest Hour: People Tested to the Extreme in World War II* 2007

——, *World War Two behind Closed Doors: Stalin, the Nazis and the West* 2008

Reitlinger, G., *The Final Solution* 1953

Reynolds, David, *Rich Relations: The American Occupation of Britain 1942–1945* 1995

——, *World War to Cold War* 2006

ed. Reynolds, David, and Kimball, Warren, *Allies at War* 1994

Rhodes, Richard, *Masters of Death: The SS Einsatzgruppen and the Invention of the Holocaust* 2002

Richardson, Charles, *From Churchill's Secret Circle to the BBC: The Biography of Sir Ian Jacob* 1991

Ridley, Jasper, *Mussolini* 1997

Ritchie, Charles, *The Siren Years* 1974

Roberts, Andrew, *'The Holy Fox': A Life of Lord Halifax* 1992

——, *Eminent Churchillians* 1994

——, *Masters and Commanders: How Roosevelt, Churchill, Marshall and Alanbrooke Won the War in the West* 2008

ed. Roberts, Andrew, *The Art of War* vol. II 2009

Roberts, Frank, *Dealing with Dictators* 1991

Roberts, Geoffrey, *Stalin's Wars* 2006

Roberts, Walter E., *Tito, Mihailović and the Allies 1941–1945* 1987

Rohwer, Jurgen, *The Critical Convoy Battles of March 1943* 1977

eds ʻers, Duncan, and Williams, Sarah, *On the Bloody Road to Berlin: oline Accounts from the North-West Europe and the Eastern Fronts 1944–45* 2005

Rolf, David, *Prisoners of the Reich: Germany's Captives 1939–1945* 1988

Rollings, Charles, *Prisoner of War: Voices from Captivity during the Second World War* 2007

Rooney, David, *Stilwell the Patriot* 2005

Roseman, Mark, *The Villa, the Lake, the Meeting: Wannsee and the Final Solution* 2002

Roskill, Stephen, *The Navy at War 1939–1945* 1960

——, *Churchill and the Admirals* 1977

Ross, J. A., *Memoirs of an Army Surgeon* 1948

ed. Ross, Stephen T., *American War Plans 1938–45* 1997

ed. Rotundo, Louis C., *Battle for Stalingrad: The 1943 Soviet General Staff Study* 1989

Royle, Trevor, *Orde Wingate* 1995

——, *Patton* 2005

Rubinstein, William D., *The Myth of Rescue: Why the Democracies Could Not Save More Jews from the Nazis* 1997

Russell, Lord, *The Scourge of the Swastika: A Short History of Nazi War Crimes* 1954

——, *The Knights of Bushido: A Short History of Japanese War Crimes* 2005

Rutherford, Phillip T., *Prelude to the Final Solution: The Nazi Program for Deporting Ethnic Poles 1939–1941* 2007

Ryback, Timothy W., *Hitler's Private Library* 2009

Sainsbury, Keith, *The North African Landings 1942* 1976

——, *The Turning Point: The Moscow, Cairo and Teheran Conferences* 1986

Salisbury, Harrison O., *The Unknown War* 1978

Sanders, Paul, *The British Channel Islands under German Occupation 1940–1945* 2005

Sandys, Celia, *Chasing Churchill* 2003

Saunders, Anthony, *Hitler's Atlantic Wall* 2001

ed. Sayer, Ian, *The Allgemeine SS* 1984

Sayer, Ian, and Botting, Douglas, *Hitler's Last General: The Case against Wilhelm Mohnke* 1989

Scheiderbauer, Armin, *Adventures in my Youth: A German Soldier on the Eastern Front* 2003

Schmidt, Heinz Werner, *With Rommel in the Desert* 1951

Schmidt, Paul, *Hitler's Interpreter* 1950

Schofield, Victoria, *Wavell: Soldier and Statesman* 2006

Schroeder, Christa, *He Was my Chief: The Memoirs of Adolf Hitler's Secretary* 2009

Schulman, M., *Defeat in the West* 1973

Schulte, Theo J., *The German Army and Nazi Policies in Occupied Russia* 1989

Schwarz, Urs, *The Eye of the Hurricane: Switzerland in World War Two* 1980

Seaton, Albert, *The Russo-German War 1941–45* 1971

Sebag Montefiore, Hugh, *Enigma: The Battle for the Code* 2000

——, *Dunkirk: Fight to the Last Man* 2006

Sebag Montefiore, Simon, *Stalin: The Court of the Red Tsar* 2003

ed. Self, Robert, *The Neville Chamberlain Diary Letters* vol. IV 2005

Sereny, Gitta, *Speer: The Battle with Truth* 1995

Service, Robert, *Stalin* 2004

Sherwood, Robert E., *The White House Papers of Harry L. Hopkins* 2 vols 1949

Shirer, William L., *The Collapse of the Third Republic* 1970

——, *The Rise and Fall of the Third Reich* 1990

Short, Neil, *Hitler's Siegfried Line* 2002

ed. Showell, Jak P. Mallmann, *Fuehrer Conferences on Naval Affairs 1939–1945* 1990

Simonov, Konstantine, *Days and Nights* 1945

Simpson, A. W. Brian, *In the Highest Degree Odious: Detention without Trial in Wartime Britain* 1992

Sledge, E. B., *With the Old Breed: Peleliu and Okinawa* New York 2007

Slim, Hugo, *Killing Civilians* 2007

Slim, William, *Defeat into Victory* 1956

ed. Smith, Amanda, *Hostage to Fortune: The Letters of Joseph P. Kennedy* 2000

Smith, Colin, *Singapore Burning* 2006

Smith, Michael, *The Emperor's Codes: Bletchley Park and the Breaking of Japan's Secret Cyphers* 2000

Snell, E., *Strategic Planning for Coalition Warfare 1941–42* Washington DC 1953

Snyder, Louis L., *The War: A Concise History 1939–1945* 1962

ed. Soames, Mary, *Speaking for Themselves: The Personal Letters of Winston and Clementine Churchill* 1998

Somerville, Christopher, *Our War: How the British Commonwealth Fought the Second World War* 1998

Sorge, Martin K., *The Other Price of Hitler's War: German Military and Civilian Losses Resulting from World War II* 1986

Spears, Edward, *Prelude to Dunkirk* 1954

——, *The Fall of France* 1954

Spector, Ronald, *Eagle against the Sun* 1988

Speer, Albert, *Inside the Third Reich* 1971

Spitzy, Reinhard, *How We Squandered the Reich* 1997

Spotts, Frederic, *The Shameful Peace* 2008

Stacey, C. P., *The Canadian Army 1939–1945* 1948

Stackelberg, Roderick, and Winkle, Sally Anne, *The Nazi Germany Sourcebook* 2002

Stafford, David, *Ten Days to D-Day* 2003

——, *Endgame 1945* 2007

Stanley, Colonel Roy M., *World War II Photo Intelligence* 1981

Stansky, Peter, *The First Day of the Blitz* 2007

Steinbacher, Sybille, *Auschwitz* 2004

Stoler, Mark A., *Allies and Adversaries: The Joint Chiefs of Staff, the Grand Alliance, and US Strategy in World War II* 2000

Stolfi, R. H. S., *Hitler's Panzers* Norman, Oklahoma 1992

Stone, Norman, *Hitler* 1980

Studnitz, Hans-Georg von, *While Berlin Burns* 1964

Swinson, Arthur, *Kohima* 1966

Sykes, Christopher, *Orde Wingate* 1959

Taylor, Frederick, *Dresden: Tuesday 13 February 1945* 2004

ed. Taylor, Fred, *The Goebbels Diaries 1939–1941* 1982

Taylor, Irene, and Taylor, Alan, *The Secret Annexe: An Anthology of War Diarists* 2004

Taylor, Telford, *The Breaking Wave* 1967

Tedder, Arthur, *With Prejudice* 1966

Thompson, Laurence, *1940* 1966

Thorne, Christopher: *Allies of a Kind: The United States, Britain, and the War against Japan 1941–1945* 1978

Times Literary Supplement, Essays and Reviews 1963 1964

Toland, John, *The Last 100 Days* 1966

——, *Infamy: Pearl Harbor and its Aftermath* 1982

Tomasevich, Jozo, *The Chetniks* 1975

Tooze, *The Wages of Destruction: The Making and Breaking of the Nazi Economy* 2006

Townsend, Peter, *Duel of Eagles* 2000

Trevelyan, Raleigh, *The Fortress* 1956

——, *Rome '44* 2004

Trevor-Roper, Hugh, *The Last Days of Hitler* 1947

ed. Trevor-Roper, Hugh, *Hitler's War Directives 1939–45* 1964

——, *Hitler's Table Talk* 2000

Truman, Harry S., *Year of Decisions* 1955

Truscott, Lucian K., *Command Missions* New York 1954

ed. Tsouras, Peter G., *The Greenhill Dictionary of Military Quotations* 2000

Ungvary, Krisztian, *Battle for Budapest* 2003

Van der Vat, Dan, *The Pacific Campaign* 1992

Vassiltchikov, Marie, *The Berlin Diaries* 1985

Vaughan-Thomas, Wynford, *Anzio* 1961

Verney, Peter, *Anzio 1944: An Unexpected Fury* 1978

Vinen, Richard, *The Unfree French: Life under the Occupation* 2006

eds Vinogradov, V. K., Pogonyi, J. F., and Teptzov, N. V., *Hitler's Death* 2005

Volkogonov, Dmitri, *Stalin: Triumph and Tragedy* 1991

Vonnegut, Kurt, *Slaughterhouse Five* 2000

Warlimont, Walter, *Inside Hitler's Headquarters* 1964

Warren, Alan, *Singapore 1942* 2002

Watkins, Gwen, *Cracking the Luftwaffe Codes* 2006

Wavell, Lord, *Generals and Generalship* 1941

Webster, C., and Frankland, N., *The Strategic Air Offensive against Germany* 4 vols 1961

Webster, Donovan, *The Burma Road* 2004

Weinberg, Gerhard L., *A World at Arms: A Global History of World War Two* 1995 ed. Weinberg, Gerhard L., *Hitler's Second Book: The Unpublished Sequel to Mein Kampf by Adolf Hitler* 2003

Weintraub, Stanley, *Eleven Days in December: Christmas at the Bulge 1944* 2006

Weitz, John, *Joachim von Ribbentrop* 1992

Welchman, Gordon, *The Hut Six Story: Breaking the Enigma Codes* 1982

West, Nigel, *Secret War: The Story of SOE* 1992

Wheal, Elizabeth-Anne, and Pope, Stephen, *Dictionary of the Second World War* 2003

Wheeler-Bennett, John, *The Nemesis of Power: The German Army in Politics 1918–1945* 1964

White, Peter, *With the Jocks: A Soldier's Struggle for Europe 1944–45* 2001

Whiting, Charles, *The Field Marshal's Revenge* 2004

Williams, Andrew, *D-Day to Berlin* 2004

Williams, Charles, *The Last Great Frenchman: A Life of General de Gaulle* 1993

——, *Pétain* 2005

Williams, Peter, and Wallace, David, *Unit 731: The Japanese Army's Secret of Secrets* 1989

Willmott, H. P., *The Great Crusade: The History of the Second World War* 1989

Wilmot, Chester, *The Struggle for Europe* 1952

Wilson, Theodore, *The First Summit: Roosevelt and Churchill at Placentia Bay 1941* 1991

Winn, Godfrey, *PQ17* 1947

Winterbotham, Fred, *The ULTRA Secret* 1974

Winton, John, *Cunningham* 1998

Woodman, Richard, *The Arctic Convoys 1941–1945* 1994

Wragg, David, *Sink the French: The French Navy and the Fall of France 1940* 2007

ed. Wright, Michael, *The World at Arms* 1989

ed. Wylie, Neville, *European Neutrals and Non-Belligerents during the Second World War* 2002

Wyman, David S., *The Abandonment of the Jews: America and the Holocaust* New York 1984

Young, Donald J., *The Battle of Bataan* 1992

Young, John M., *Britain's Sea War: A Diary of Ship Losses 1941–1945* 1989

Young, Peter, *World War 1939–45* 1966

ed. Young, Peter, *Decisive Battles of the Second World War* 1967

——, *Atlas of the Second World War* 1972

Zamoyski, Adam, *The Forgotten Few: The Polish Air Force in the Second World War* 1995

Ziegler, Philip, *Mountbatten* 1985

ARTICLES

Davies, Norman, 'The Warsaw Uprising' *Everyone's War* No. 13 Spring 2008

Dilks, David, 'Great Britain, the Commonwealth and the Wider World 1939–45', University of Hull 1988

Goda, Norman J. W., 'Black Marks: Hitler's Bribery of his Senior Officials during the Second World War' *Journal of Modern History* LXXII No. 2 2000

Gough, Barry, '*Prince of Wales* and *Repulse*: Churchill's "Veiled Threat" Reconsidered' *Finest Hour* CXXXIX Summer 2008

Greene, Graham, 'The Lieutenant Died Last' in his *The Last Word* 1990

Hanson, Victor Davis, 'In War: Resolution' *Claremont Review of Books* Winter 2007

Harvey, A. D., 'The Russian Air Force versus the Luftwaffe', *Military Books Review* November 2007

Heitmann, Jan, 'Incident at Mosty', *After the Battle* No. 79

Hodgson, Charles, 'Convoy to Murmansk: The Battle of North Cape Remembered', *Nautical Magazine* CCLV No. 4 April 1996

Kitchens, Dr James H., 'The Bombing of Auschwitz Re-Examined' *Journal of Military History* LVIII No. 2 April 1994

Looseley, Rhiannon, 'Paradise after Hell' *History Today* June 2006

Overy, R. J., 'Hitler and Air Strategy' *Journal of Contemporary History* XV No. 3 1980

——, 'The Nazis and the Jews in Occupied Western Europe 1940–1944' *Journal of Modern History* LIV 1982

Penney, Lord, Samuels, D. E. J., and Scorgie, G. C., 'The Nuclear Explosive Yields at Hiroshima and Nagasaki', *Philosophical Transactions of the Royal Society of London* CCLXVI No. 1177 June 1970

Whiting, Charles, 'The Man Who Invaded Poland a Week Too Early' *World War II Investigator* I No. 1 April 1988

Index

677